MW00629359

QUEEN VICTORIA AND HER PRIME MINISTERS

BY THE SAME AUTHOR

The Life and Times of King William IV
Elizabeth I
Unnatural Murder: Poison at the Court of James I
The Affair of the Poisons
Ladies in Waiting: From the Tudors to the Present Day
Queen Anne: The Politics of Passion

QUEEN VICTORIA AND HER PRIME MINISTERS

Her Life, the Imperial Ideal, and the Politics and Turmoil That Shaped Her Extraordinary Reign

ANNE SOMERSET

Alfred A. Knopf
New York
2024

THIS IS A BORZOI BOOK PUBLISHED BY ALFRED A. KNOPF

 Published in the United States by Alfred A. Knopf, a division of PenguinRandom House LLC, New York. Originally published in hardcover in Great Britain under the title *Plagued with Politics* by William Collins, an imprint of HarperCollins Publishers, in 2024.

www.aaknopf.com

Knopf, Borzoi Books, and the colophon are registered trademarks of Penguin Random House LLC.

Names: Somerset, Anne, [date]- author.
Title: Queen Victoria and her prime ministers : her life, the imperial ideal, and the politics and turmoil that shaped her extraordinary reign / Anne Somerset.
Description: First United States edition. | New York : Alfred A. Knopf, 2024. | Includes bibliographical references and index.
Identifiers: LCCN 2023050228 | ISBN 9781101875575 (hardcover) | ISBN 9781101875582 (ebook)
Subjects: LCSH: Victoria, Queen of Great Britain, 1819–1901—Relations with prime ministers. | Prime ministers—Great Britain—Biography. | Great Britain—Politics and government—1837–1901.
Classification: LCC DA562 .S67 2024 | DDC 941.081092—dc23/eng/20240322
LC record available at https://lccn.loc.gov/2023050228

Jacket image: *Queen Victoria in Her Coronation Robes*, 1837, *The Illustrated London News*. Lebrecht History/Bridgeman Images
Jacket design by Ariel Harari

Manufactured in the United States of America
First United States Edition

In fondest remembrance of
Cristina Monet Zilkha

AUTHOR'S NOTE

In her letters, Queen Victoria was lavish in her use of underlining. When quoting, I have generally rendered the underlined word or phrase in italics; however, in the not infrequent cases where she did double underlining, I have rendered that word or phrase in underlined italics.

In her correspondence with ministers and prime ministers, convention dictated that Victoria referred to herself in the third person, as either 'she' or 'the Queen'. When replying, ministers adopted the same usage, referring to themselves, for example, as 'Mr Disraeli' or 'Mr Gladstone'.

It is notoriously difficult to compare the value of money in the past with modern monetary values. For those who are interested, The National Archives' currency converter estimates that £1 in 1850 would be worth approximately £80.19 in 2017. The Bank of England inflation calculator says £1 in 1850 would buy £110.64 worth of goods and services in May 2023. The CPI inflation calculator says £1 in 1850 would have an equivalent purchasing power in 2023 of £172.23. Readers can take their pick of these figures.

CONTENTS

1

Lord Melbourne 1837–1841

In late May 1837 the British foreign secretary, Lord Palmerston, informed Britain's ambassador to France that their seventy-one-year-old sovereign, King William IV, was in 'a very precarious state'. His asthma and respiratory problems had become so serious that it was unlikely he could live long, though Palmerston trusted the king would stave off death for a few months yet. The foreign secretary did not welcome the prospect of dealing with the king's successor, seeing 'no advantage in having a totally inexperienced girl of eighteen just out of strict guardianship to govern an Empire'.[1]

The girl in question was King William's niece, Princess Victoria. The fact that she had celebrated her eighteenth birthday on 24 May 1837 was significant because at eighteen a sovereign was deemed of age to rule without a regency. Yet, as Palmerston remarked, it was 'scarcely in the nature of things that … the nation will look with the same deference to the will of a person of eighteen as to that of one of mature age', and it was for this reason the foreign secretary had hoped that the king's life would be spared for some time to come. Palmerston's wish was not granted, for King William's health grew steadily worse. At ten past two on the morning of 20 June, he died, and his niece Victoria was 'transferred at once from the nursery to the throne'.[2]

The princess was fluent in French and German and had seen the study of English history as 'one of my first duties', but at least one observer believed she had not received 'the proper education for one who was to wear the Crown of England'. On the other hand, in her first declaration to her Privy Council, she would state: 'I have learnt from my infancy to respect and love the constitution of my native country.' Furthermore, while painfully conscious of her youth and inexperience, she felt 'sure that very few have more real good will and more real desire to do what is fit and right'.[3]

Notwithstanding his qualms about Victoria's age, Palmerston was 'inclined to think she will turn out to be a remarkable person and gifted with a great deal of strength of character'. In this he would be proved correct, in some ways rather more so than he might have wished. At just under five foot tall, the new queen was physically diminutive, but it soon became apparent she had 'a very decided will of her own'. No one – including herself – considered Victoria a beauty, and she may have had 'not a very good figure', but her appearance had much about it that was appealing. A government minister assured a friend: 'she is really in person & in face, & especially in eyes & complexion a very nice girl, & quite such as might tempt.' Another gentleman said he would have called her pretty were it not for her mouth: when she laughed – which she often did in the early stages of her reign – she opened it too wide, showing rather too much of her gums. Nonetheless, her beautiful voice and natural poise ensured 'the smallness of her stature is quite forgotten in the majesty and gracefulness of her demeanour'.[4]

Victoria's was an immense inheritance. Britain's overseas possessions included much of India, Australia, Canada, Ceylon, several West Indian islands and the southern tip of Africa. This empire had been acquired with the aid of the world's mightiest navy, which remained crucial to the maintenance of Britain's global power.

The British Isles themselves – which bore the official title the United Kingdom of Great Britain and Ireland, although often misleadingly referred to simply as 'England' – were geographically compact but populous and extremely wealthy. At the end of the Napoleonic wars in 1815 Britain was already the richest and most industrialised nation in the world. Until the mid-nineteenth-century agriculture still provided a livelihood for more people than any other occupation, but by 1837 the country's landscape and economy had been transformed by massive new towns that housed an urban proletariat. These metropolises were often grim places with virtually no sanitation, whose poorer inhabitants lived in squalor and had shockingly low life expectancy. Nevertheless, the ability to draw on a large workforce enabled capitalist entrepreneurs to harness technological change and revolutionise productivity.

Britain had a constitutional or 'limited' monarchy: the sovereign was served by ministers answerable to the legislature and who submitted advice after deliberating in Cabinet. To survive in power, ministries had to command the support of Parliament, and particularly of the House of Commons, composed of elected members rather than the hereditary peers who sat in the House of Lords. There were two main parties, known as Whigs and Tories, who espoused different political philosophies but shared many assumptions. Of the two, the Tories were the defenders of traditional values, and upheld the power of Church and Crown, while the Whigs were rather more progressive. Although many leading Whigs were immensely wealthy landed aristocrats, they saw themselves as natural guardians of the nation's civil liberties, who would work through Parliament to safeguard what they conceived to be the interests of the people. If the Whigs remained nervous of 'democracy' – a term often used in a pejorative sense at this time – the Tories (who recently had started to refer to themselves as 'Conservatives') were far more fearful that any tampering with Britain's political system and structures could unleash destructive forces.

Being himself of a conservative frame of mind, King William IV had been apprehensive when, less than a year after his accession to the throne in June 1830, a Whig government headed by Earl Grey had introduced a political Reform Bill. Repeated attempts by the House of Lords to block it had resulted in riots and fears of revolution, but it finally received the royal assent in June 1832. Yet despite the major changes effected by the bill, the British political system remained riddled with anomalies and flaws. Even after the electorate had virtually doubled so that it numbered some 800,000 voters, only about one in seven of the United Kingdom's adult male population had the franchise. Numerous so-called 'rotten boroughs', with minuscule populations, had lost the right to return Members of Parliament, and some newly populous manufacturing towns could now send men to Westminster, but many large centres of population remained unrepresented. By making it more difficult for individuals to control constituencies, the bill had reduced the power of the Crown and aristocracy, but Parliament remained largely the province of a propertied elite.

In July 1834 Earl Grey had resigned. To the amazement of many in the political world he was succeeded as prime minister by his home secretary, Viscount Melbourne, an urbane man of immense charm whom few had expected to achieve such eminence. A Whig more out of family tradition than reforming conviction, Melbourne was chosen to lead the party simply because, as one colleague recalled, he was 'the only one of whom none of us would be jealous'.[5]

The story that Melbourne had pronounced it 'a damned bore' to be offered the post of prime minister was probably apocryphal, but when William IV had dismissed him and his Whig colleagues in the autumn of 1834, he had not appeared to mind overmuch. The king had replaced the Whigs with a Tory administration headed by Sir Robert Peel, only to find himself obliged to take back his discarded ministers when Peel failed to win a majority at a general election held in January 1835. William had to promise that he would not prevent the Whigs from pursuing their legislative programme, an undertaking that illustrated how the Reform Bill had permanently undermined the influence of the Crown.

Although for the remainder of the reign William's relations with a ministry that had been imposed on him against his will were sometimes less than cordial, in May 1836 he stood by Lord Melbourne when the latter was cited in a divorce case. Eight years earlier the widowed Melbourne had managed to pay off another aggrieved husband, but George Norton tenaciously pursued a claim that Melbourne was guilty of 'criminal conversation' with Norton's wife, Caroline. When the case came to court, the prime minister robustly denied the allegations, and since Norton could not produce convincing witnesses, Melbourne emerged vindicated.

The prime minister had survived a potentially ruinous scandal, but his government was not in a strong position. Every by-election eroded Whig numbers in the House of Commons, and the Whigs lacked a majority in the House of Lords. Yet though the parliamentary arithmetic was tilting slightly in their favour, the Conservatives were still in no position to take power themselves. Having burnt his fingers trying to have a government in tune with his own sympathies rather than one reflecting the political balance in Parliament, the ailing King William did not want his niece to start her reign by making the same mistake. 'The King from his deathbed conveyed very secretly but very earnestly to her his advice not to think of changing her ministry, that Melbourne was a good man and a change … a fearful experiment.'[6] As it happened, this coincided with advice the princess had received from other quarters, and she was happy to follow it.

Accordingly on 20 June 1837, three hours after having been woken at six in the morning to be told of the king's passing, the new Queen had her first meeting with her prime minister at Kensington Palace. Until this point Victoria had been permitted only the most limited intercourse with society and a few politicians, and all such encounters had taken place under the watchful eye of her mother. Now the Queen eagerly dispensed with any kind of maternal supervision, noting in her journal she had received Melbourne '*of course quite alone*, as I shall *always* do all my Ministers'. From the first, she instinctively took to

Melbourne. Aged fifty-eight, he remained a handsome figure, but what struck the Queen most was that he was 'very kind in his manner', and this allowed the establishment of an almost instantaneous rapport. She at once informed him she had resolved to 'retain him and the rest of the present ministry at the head of affairs', believing 'it could not be in better hands than his'. By the end of the meeting she had decided, 'I like him very much and feel confidence in him. He is a very straightforward, honest, clever and good man.' Her favourable impression was confirmed when she saw him again a little later the same day and had 'a very *comfortable* conversation with him'. Five days later she recorded: 'I like to talk to him,' and within a fortnight of her accession felt sure 'there are not many like him in this world of deceit'.[7]

As this comment suggests, despite the sheltered life she had led hitherto, Victoria's existence had not been without a darker side. When she described herself as 'very young and perhaps in many, though not in all things, inexperienced',[8] she was thinking of the malign shadow cast by a sinister figure who had made her teenaged years quite miserable, and who had cherished ambitions of controlling Victoria when she came to the throne. Had William IV died just a few weeks earlier, Victoria might have found herself powerless to resist this man's plans.

Victoria's father, Edward Duke of Kent, had been the fourth son of King George III. King George had fathered fifteen children in all, but this sizeable brood had been remarkably ineffective when it came to providing the monarch with legitimate grandchildren. The king's eldest son, also named George, did sire a daughter, Charlotte, who had been expected to ascend the throne in due course, but in November 1817 the princess had died in childbirth, eighteen months after marrying Prince Leopold of Saxe-Coburg. The tragedy made it imperative that all of George III's sons who were free to marry took wives in order to carry on the royal line. In July 1818 the Duke of Kent married Princess Victoire of Saxe-Coburg, sister of Princess Charlotte's widower, Leopold. Victoire was herself a widow of thirty-one, who had had two children by her marriage to the Prince of Leiningen. Very soon after marrying the Duke of Kent she conceived again, and on 24 May 1819 gave birth to Victoria. But though the Duke of Kent had filled the dynastic void that had threatened to engulf the monarchy, he had little time to savour his triumph. On 23 January 1820 he died of pneumonia, leaving his eight-month-old daughter fatherless.

Widowed for a second time, the Duchess of Kent not only found herself friendless in a strange land, but in embarrassed circumstances because her husband had bequeathed little but debts. Feeling in urgent want of a protector, she had turned to Captain John Conroy, an Irish army officer who had served her late husband as an equerry. The duchess and Conroy both claimed that on his deathbed, the Duke of Kent had entrusted his wife and daughter to Conroy's care, urging his spouse always to follow his guidance. The duchess maintained that ever since her husband's death, Conroy had served her devotedly, although he may have actually compounded her financial difficulties by embezzling money from her. Some people came to suspect that Conroy, who was a married man with children of his own, became the duchess's lover. What is beyond dispute is that the duchess was slavishly devoted, acquiescing in the 'dreadful system of tyranny exercised' by Conroy over her Kensington Palace establishment.[9]

Once Conroy began asserting himself, Victoria's life became 'one of great misery & oppression'. Together he and her mother devised what they called the 'Kensington system', placing Victoria entirely under their own control and limiting her contacts with the royal family. Intent on promoting the princess as a future 'People's Queen', they arranged for her to make annual regional tours of England, during which she was introduced to the public and visited factories and ironworks. King William understandably disliked this parading of his niece but could not persuade his sister-in-law to discontinue it.[10]

After a particularly exhausting tour, in late September 1835 the duchess and Conroy took an ailing Victoria to Ramsgate, intent on forcing from her a pledge to make Conroy her private secretary. Conroy had cherished this ambition for some time, believing the post would afford opportunities for enrichment as well as the wielding of political power. Even after Victoria became seriously unwell, the duchess and Conroy went on subjecting her to what she later described as 'dreadful and inconceivable torments'. Although weak and debilitated Victoria would proudly recall how 'I resisted, in spite of my illness and their harshness.'[11]

Despite this setback, Conroy believed the situation was retrievable, for provided Victoria came to the throne while still a minor, he would have his 'just reward' once the Duchess of Kent was named regent. When Victoria turned eighteen on 24 May 1837, 'all his calculations' were negated. Desperate that the prize looked set to be snatched from him, he and the duchess redoubled their efforts to browbeat Victoria. The princess did not have to fight the pair completely unaided, for just before her birthday her Uncle Leopold despatched to her side Baron

Stockmar. Stockmar was a German doctor who had accompanied Leopold to England when the latter had married Princess Charlotte in 1816, and who had ever since acted as his adviser. Stockmar arrived at Kensington on 25 May and found Conroy and the duchess engaged in unremitting efforts to subjugate Victoria to their will. The princess was defiant, showing herself 'extremely jealous of … her rights and her future power'. Even so, Stockmar feared that if Conroy kept up his 'system of intimidation', Victoria could hardly withstand it. Looking back on this agonising time, Victoria herself believed she 'couldn't have borne any longer' the pressure inflicted on her, and that only the king's timely death saved her.[12]

The frustrated Conroy took the view that if Victoria would 'not listen to reason *she must be coerced*', but when William IV died, Conroy had to face the fact that he would never be given employment by the new queen. Although he continued to lurk at the Duchess of Kent's side, after being awarded a pension and baronetcy, he found himself debarred from the Queen's presence. Victoria had emerged triumphant from an ordeal so traumatic she later speculated it had stunted her growth, but which she posited, 'perhaps … did me good in another way, by forming my mind'.[13]

Conroy's ambitions had been blocked, but it seemed likely that Victoria would be amenable to the influence of another man, towards whom her feelings were far warmer. On Princess Charlotte's death, Victoria's maternal uncle, Leopold, had reverted to being a minor German prince, but in 1831 his destiny had changed again when an international conference held in London had installed him as sovereign of the newly created independent Kingdom of Belgium. Now aged thirty-six, the wily and sagacious king was keen to offer his niece the benefits of his experience, of which he assumed the novice queen would be an eager and biddable recipient.

Victoria was devoted to Leopold, whose visits to England had provided some rare highlights in her unhappy childhood. Keenly aware of what she had lost as a result of the Duke of Kent's early death, she recalled that 'from my earliest years the name of *Uncle* was the dearest I knew'. She relished his somewhat ponderous humour and Polonius-like exhortations, and at first took him at his own estimation, which was that few others were so knowledgeable and wise. She had heeded his suggestion that at her accession she should 'make no change … keep ministers and everything as it is', and Leopold looked forward to providing her

King Leopold I. (Lithograph by Charles Baugniet, 1841)

with further valuable counsel. Three days after her accession he wrote that he hoped he would 'have the *happiness of being able to be of use to you* ... Before you decide on anything important I should be glad if you would consult me.' He was tactful enough not to rush over to England at the old king's death, admitting jocularly that 'people might fancy I came to enslave you', but he sent Baron Stockmar as his representative, and urged his niece to pay close attention to all that gentleman had to say.[14]

Settling rather too expansively into his self-appointed role of royal mentor, King Leopold was lavish with advice. Even before his niece had become queen, he had urged her to 'judge questions yourself', predicting that before long this would 'become a habit and even an amusement to you'. Priding himself on his own methodical way of working, he advocated that when confronted with important questions, she should not make her mind up too quickly. He also cautioned against allowing anyone to impose on her, enjoining her '*never to permit* people' to raise matters 'without your having yourself desired them to do so'. If this did happen, she must 'change the conversation and make the individual feel that he has made a mistake'.[15] On this point Victoria would prove an apt pupil, but it was Leopold himself who found himself subjected to the treatment prescribed for the presumptuous. Fond as she was of her uncle, the Queen began to find him somewhat overbearing and intrusive.

King Leopold had taken it for granted that Victoria would defer to him, and a bossy and peremptory tone soon became discernible in his letters. 'On Foreign Politics I have no time to speak with you at any length,' he had declared self-importantly on 1 July, before issuing curt instructions. He wanted Victoria to aid the young Queens of Spain and Portugal to free themselves from the control of domineering politicians. 'The Spanish concern is for the moment the most important we have,' Leopold pronounced, although the situation in Portugal was also a priority. 'Pray have the goodness to speak to Lord Melbourne and Lord Palmerston on the subject,' he wrote imperiously on 19 August. 'Matters are pressing.'[16] Much to his surprise, the Queen declined to fall in with his wishes.

King Leopold was able to see for himself how his niece was faring in her new position when on 29 August 1837 he came to stay for three weeks, accompanied by his much younger wife, Louise, daughter of King Louis-Philippe of France. From the social point of view, the visit was an unqualified success. Victoria revelled in acting as their hostess, breakfasting with 'dearest uncle' most mornings, and riding out with him in Windsor Great Park. 'I feel so happy in being *sous sa protection*,' she rhapsodised in her journal, although this did not mean she was willing to be subject to his authority. State affairs were not permitted to cloud the idyll. Victoria now looked on Prime Minister Lord Melbourne as her oracle, and King Leopold was astute enough to realise he would be the loser if he sought to change this state of affairs. Victoria's heart was gladdened by the way the two men conversed amiably, and that 'my beloved uncle is delighted' with the prime minister. 'How I wish I had time to take minutes of the very interesting and highly important conversations I have with my Uncle and with Lord Melbourne,' she declared, feeling sure their 'sound observations … would make a most interesting book'. She was happy to think that as well as liking each other, 'Uncle and him perfectly agree in Politics too, which are the best there are.'[17]

Victoria 'cried bitterly' at Leopold and Louise's departure on 19 September, but when King Leopold wrote an interfering letter from France, where he was staying with his father-in-law, a chilly note became discernible in his niece's dealings with him. Implying that the Queen was ignorant of the way her government conducted diplomacy, Leopold suggested her ministers had rebuffed friendly overtures from France. In a reply imparting what she grandly called '*un peu de politique*', Victoria stated her ambassador in Paris had reported it was the French who were unwilling to cultivate warmer relations, and that, however much he prided himself on his omniscience, it was King Leopold who was being misled.[18]

Worse humiliations lay in store for Uncle Leopold. He had assumed his niece would take his side in an acrimonious treaty dispute between Holland and Belgium, and was affronted when it emerged he was mistaken. Having been personally briefed by her foreign secretary on 6 May 1838, Victoria was satisfied she understood what was at stake, for, 'intricate and difficult as the subject is, Lord Palmerston explained it in such a very clear, plain and agreeable manner as to put me quite *au fait* of the whole thing'. She was indignant when Leopold complained to Stockmar that whereas William IV had always been supportive, 'the moment his niece came to the throne he was abandoned'. Hotly Victoria commented: 'This is *very* wrong.'[19]

Having confided to Melbourne that she found it 'rather hard of Uncle, appealing to my feelings of affection', she wrote a kind but firm letter, stating her ministers' first priority must be Britain's own interests. Leopold remained reproachful, moaning that he felt 'put aside as one does with a piece of furniture which is no longer wanted'. His aggrieved tone merely irritated his niece further. Discussing Leopold with Melbourne on 17 June, she said that whereas his influence over her had been 'very great', it was '*now very* small'.[20]

Leopold did not help his cause by then sending a patronising letter, describing Belgian affairs as 'so complicated that I can hardly expect that you should know their nature and import'. She fired back, 'You wrong me very much, my beloved uncle … I assure you I *do* understand … & am *au courant* of all that is going on.'[21]

Months later King Leopold was still portraying himself as the wronged party, prompting his niece to suggest they avoid political subjects altogether. However, at the beginning of 1839, with the dispute with Holland still unsettled, she cautioned him: 'You might be blamed' if this state of affairs continued. Not until February did he grudgingly reach an accord with his Dutch neighbour, and then sulked for weeks. Finding his grumbles 'very unjust' Victoria chided: '(If I could) I might be even a little angry with you dear uncle.' Leopold chuckled at having 'extracted some spark of politics from your dear Majesty', but when he wrote to Lord Palmerston implying that Victoria did not condone Belgium's treatment, she was infuriated by his brazen attempt at 'separating me from my government'. On 30 April she sent Leopold a distinctly barbed letter warning, 'though you seem not to dislike my political sparks … they might finally take fire'.[22]

Gradually it dawned on King Leopold that the dynamic of his relationship with his royal niece was not going to work as he had anticipated. He remained a much-loved uncle, whose shrewdness Victoria acknowledged, but she rejected the role of docile apprentice. Because her elevation to the throne had not had the transformative effect on his own power and prestige he had expected, he had to come to terms with being still just the king of a relatively small country, whose interests were not foremost among Britain's concerns.

Ten days after her accession Victoria wrote to her first cousin, Prince Albert of Saxe-Coburg-Gotha, that while 'the business which I have to do … is not trifling either in matter or quantity', she found it exhilarating. In her journal of 1 July she recorded importantly, 'I have *so many* communications from the Ministers, and from me to them, and I get so many papers to sign every day that I have always a *very great* deal to do'; rather than thinking it too onerous, 'I delight in this work.' Her governess reported to another lady that her former charge was 'at work from morning to night, and that, even when her maid was combing out her hair, she was surrounded by official boxes and reading official papers'. The Queen assured the Duchess of Sutherland that 'far from being fatigued with signatures and business, I like the whole thing exceedingly'. Only occasionally did she ask for the flow to be paused so she could catch up. On 12 August she wrote to her foreign secretary that, 'as the Queen has got a great many foreign despatches which … she has been unable to read as yet, she requests Lord Palmerston not to send any more until she has done with those'.[23]

Palmerston had already tried to help by having the Foreign Office geographer draw up atlases that would make despatches from abroad more clearly understandable, and he sent her the latest edition of the *Almanach de Gotha*, so she could familiarise herself with the pedigrees of European royal houses. The letters sent to foreign sovereigns announcing her accession were drafted at the Foreign Office, and though the last few lines were in her own hand, 'the appropriate words of termination' had first been pencilled in and she had only to write over them in ink.[24]

Palmerston went on drafting some letters on the Queen's behalf, but within a few months she was confident enough to make insertions of her own. In October 1837, when it was deemed that 'a political letter' ought to be sent from her to King Ferdinand of Portugal, Victoria 'translated it from a sketch which Lord Palmerston had written'. Six months later, Palmerston drew up another letter destined for Ferdinand, reproving him for continued Portuguese involvement in the slave trade. This time Victoria modified it to make it appear less abrasive, showing such a natural aptitude that Lord Melbourne was 'much pleased, even touched'.[25]

At this stage Victoria liked Palmerston unreservedly. When he went over complicated matters with her, he imparted information in a succinct and easy-to-grasp manner. Within a fortnight of her becoming queen, she felt he had already improved her understanding of world affairs. 'We talked about Russia and Turkey a good deal &c,' she wrote after seeing him on 1 July 1837. 'He is very agreeable, and clear in what he says.' Palmerston (who sat in the House of Commons because his peerage was an Irish title) worked extraordinarily hard, had a formidable command of detail, and was utterly committed to upholding what he believed to be Britain's interests. In her innocence the Queen had no idea that the unmarried foreign secretary was also a womaniser and a notorious lecher, who was having a long-term affair with Prime Minister Lord Melbourne's married sister, Emily.

The home secretary, Lord John Russell, had none of Palmerston's ebullience, and was in many ways an awkward character. From an aristocratic family, he was a Whig to his fingertips, and prided himself on his libertarian principles. A man of strong convictions, he could also be impulsive and unpredictable, though always reacting furiously to accusations of inconsistency. He was physically unprepossessing, being very short, with a 'shrivelled countenance' and a voice that was simultaneously rasping and reedy. His social skills were minimal: super-sensitive to slights himself, he frequently offended others through gaucheness. As Lord Melbourne ruefully remarked to Victoria, Russell was 'apt to resent a thing', and was so protective of his dignity that he periodically threatened to leave the government over minor disagreements. When Russell talked of resigning in February 1838 if Whig backbenchers did not give him unanimous support, Melbourne told the Queen the home secretary was taking the matter much too seriously, before adding with a sigh that, of course, 'Lord John does.'[26]

Despite the fact that Russell had few endearing qualities, the Queen was ready to like him because of his association with Melbourne. The affection she felt for the prime minister himself was, however, in quite a different league. Herself fatherless, and now estranged from her mother, Victoria was perhaps unconsciously on the lookout for a surrogate parent. As well as being a quasi-paternal figure, Melbourne provided her with companionship and intimacy of a completely different kind. Whatever they discussed, there was always an ease to their discourse that delighted Victoria. When explaining things, he was authoritative but not dogmatic, seamlessly filling gaps in her knowledge without making her feel ignorant. He introduced an element of fun to her life that had hitherto been almost devoid of it, and his own evident pleasure in talking to her validated Victoria's conviction that he was worthy of her devotion. Less than a month after she inherited the throne she wrote: 'He is … my *friend*, I know it.' And in her journal, weeks later in August: 'I am so fond of him and his conversations do me much good.' With every day that passed her attachment to, 'the best-hearted, kindest and most feeling man in the world' became more fervent.[27]

Victoria had bonded with Melbourne so quickly that she had no doubt where her loyalties lay when a general election was held to mark her coming to the throne. On 17 July she dissolved Parliament, speaking in a 'soft silvery tone' that could be 'distinctly heard in every corner of the House'. A three-week election campaign ensued, in which she could take no overt part, but her sympathies were made plain enough. Whereas on the eve of her accession she had assured King Leopold 'I *do not* belong to any party', she was now an unashamed Whig, writing in her journal as the results came in, 'I trust in Heaven that we shall have a majority for us.' As a Tory indignantly noted, the Whigs were using 'the Queen's name as their war cry' to an extent that could be said 'to prostitute … the royal name of their innocent victim'. Humiliatingly, they did not reap the benefits they expected. When the results were counted, Whig numbers had been further reduced, an outcome that one Cabinet minister understood 'surprised and a little mortified our Queen'. Victoria could only hope that, notwithstanding their weakened position, 'the present government may remain firm for *long*'.[28]

Initially Victoria had been greatly taken with what she described as Melbourne's 'frank yet gentle manner', finding it appealing that 'he talks so quietly'. As they became more relaxed in each other's company, Melbourne exposed a more exuberant side. He was renowned in society as 'a *rollicking* laugher', and his guffaw was wonderfully infectious. The Queen described it as 'a very peculiar laugh; it is so joyous and truly merry and makes one laugh when one hears it'. An onlooker who saw them at dinner in October 1837 noted that Victoria was laughing just as much, 'and in quite as hearty a way'.[29]

Having formed his behavioural habits in the louche days of Regency England, Melbourne nonetheless took care to conduct himself with the decorum appropriate for the court of a young queen. The diarist and Clerk of the Privy Council, Charles Greville, noted, 'Instead of indolently sprawling ... he is always sitting bolt upright; his free and easy language interlarded with "damns" is carefully guarded and regulated with the strictest propriety.' Some people expected that after a time he would find it hardly worth the effort, but in fact Melbourne did not mind having to change his ways. He stayed with Victoria at Windsor for most of September 1837, and when she said she hoped he had not found it tedious, he exclaimed, 'Quite the contrary. I never spent a pleasanter month in my life.'[30]

Melbourne devoted an astonishing proportion of his time to Victoria, often spending six hours a day with her. They would meet every morning, alone, to discuss business for around two hours. In the afternoons Melbourne regularly accompanied her when she went out riding, going 'at full gallop' for much of the time. He would then dine with her, and though numerous other guests were generally present, he was invariably placed next to her at table. Afterwards, when the company had left the dining room, he would continue to sit by her on the drawing-room sofa, keeping up an effervescent flow of chatter.

The truth was, for all Melbourne's worldly success, there was an emotional void at the centre of his life that Victoria filled perfectly. His marriage to Lady Caroline Ponsonby had failed long before her death in 1828. Their only son, who had epilepsy and severe mental disabilities, died in 1836. Friendship – and perhaps more than friendship – with women such as Caroline Norton had played a significant part in his life, but after the 1836 court case, he saw little of her. As a result, his relationship with the young Queen fulfilled a deep need in his psyche. The acute Charles Greville commented, 'I have no doubt he is passionately fond of her as he might be of his daughter if he had one, and the more because he is a man with capacity for loving without having anything in the world to love.'[31]

Melbourne could feed the Queen's hunger for knowledge about her father and family. As a young man he had often dined with the then prince regent, a former lover of his mother. Melbourne did not disclose that his younger brother – now dead – had supposedly been fathered by the prince, but he had other recollections of huge interest to Victoria. She was pleased he declared her father the best of George III's sons, and she eagerly absorbed his vivid accounts of the 'late kings George IV and William 4th's fancies &c &c'.[32]

With Melbourne's aid Victoria acquired a much sounder understanding of the recent past. She was also highly diverted by what he told her on more trivial topics, for Melbourne gleefully shared with her his exhaustive store of gossip about members of the aristocracy. The Queen was riveted, for at this stage of her life she was very curious about such matters. After he regaled her with some particularly scintillating tales, she wrote: 'There is no end to the amusing anecdotes and stories Lord Melbourne tells and he tells them all in such an amusing and funny way.'[33]

In her turn, the Queen longed to know everything about Melbourne's life story but feared that posing direct questions would seem intrusive. It was well known that twenty-five years earlier Melbourne's wife Caroline had humiliated him by her brief but blatant affair with Lord Byron. She had publicly flaunted her passion for the poet, and after being spurned had compounded the scandal by publishing a roman à clef that exposed to the world more details about her marriage and adulterous liaison. While Victoria could hardly ask Melbourne how he felt about being cuckolded, she was titillated when, of his own accord, the prime minister made mention of Byron. He was, he said, 'quite the poet of the Devil', whose 'mind and heart were quite crooked and perverted'. Upon his adding that Byron 'behaved like a demon' to his own wife, committing 'abominations … hardly to be believed', the Queen experienced a real frisson.[34]

To find out more about Melbourne's wife, Victoria had to gather information from other sources. She was intrigued to hear that Caroline was 'the strangest person that ever lived, really half crazy, and quite so when she died'. In response to close questioning, Melbourne's widowed sister Lady Cowper revealed that Caroline was 'very clever and full of talent, but so wild and so frightfully passionate, really not quite right … and yet she had something about her which made people forgive her'. Indignant on Melbourne's behalf, Victoria was less inclined to exculpate 'that shocking wife of his'. Hotly she wrote: 'She teazed that excellent Lord Melbourne in every way, dreadfully, and quite embittered his life, which it ought to have been her pride to study to render a happy one.'[35]

Victoria soaked up all the wisdom Melbourne had to offer, finding his views on life utterly compelling. Nor was this misguided, for among the most discerning people Melbourne's 'richness of talk' was celebrated. He was an exceptionally cultivated and knowledgeable man, deeply read in classics, history, theology and literature, and wore his learning lightly. A natural teacher who loved sharing what he knew, he conveyed arcane information in the most vivid and accessible way. In wide-ranging conversations with Victoria, he touched on Shakespeare and Goethe, as well as the works of Racine, Corneille and Walter Scott. Gratified to think that they shared the same intellectual tastes, Victoria wrote effusively, 'It is *such a delight* to talk with him; he is so full of knowledge and agreeable.'[36]

By turns 'paradoxical, epigrammatic, acute, droll', Melbourne's conversation was indeed irresistible. His speculative mind and quizzical intelligence transcended conventional thinking, and much of what he said fizzed with originality and quirkiness. Endowed with an idiosyncratic turn of phrase that made his 'quaint, queer' outlook seem all the more distinctive, he eschewed the predictable, and sometimes deliberately courted controversy. 'It's a good thing to surprise,' he once told Victoria. 'It's good to give [things] a little brush.' While in some ways a cynical man, his zest and spontaneity prevented him appearing jaded. Always apt to see the funny side of things himself, he made them seem amusing to others, adding to the comical effect by putting on what Victoria called 'one of his funny faces'.[37] Irony was sometimes wasted on the literal-minded Queen, but Melbourne's humour enchanted her. She liked herself more for her ability to appreciate it, and the way they laughed together made her feel witty in her turn.

By January 1838 Melbourne was featuring in her journal simply as 'Ld M', and she started setting down their conversations in writing. She explained, 'as in *my* opinion all Lord Melbourne's remarks are clever and judicious, it is a source of great amusement to me to collect these "sayings"'.[38] Posterity has cause to be grateful, for her accounts perfectly capture the flavour of this most touching relationship.

Victoria jotted down numerous examples of Melbourne's worldly wisdom, such as his belief that 'actresses are the dullest people that ever lived'. In his opinion it was 'all humbug' to claim to be ravished by the beauty of birdsong, while 'cookery is the first art in the world'. He pronounced 'forcing flowers is questionable', even though he frequently presented her with bouquets from his own hothouses. Rather than always reproducing his words exactly, the Queen sometimes confined herself to reporting that Melbourne had been 'very funny' on topics such as bonnets, snuff, and drinking hock.[39] In her ingenuous way, she conjures him up vividly, artlessly conveying the qualities that enchanted her.

When Victoria observed it was regrettable if anyone came out of prison 'worse than he went in', Melbourne made her 'laugh very much' by pointing out 'one often comes out worse of a ballroom than one went in'. Talking of a man who had been hurt by an owl whose nest he had disturbed, Melbourne ventured cheerfully: 'I suppose he never looked into an owl's nest again!' Having regaled Victoria with the story of a woman whose face had been distorted by a muscular problem, he pronounced: 'It's a curious machine altogether' – which the Queen found hilarious. Drawings of Māori warriors in New Zealand prompted him to assert they were such incorrigible cannibals that it was 'almost impossible to break them of it'. Victoria's lady-in-waiting Lady Mulgrave protested that they only ate their enemies. 'I fancy they eat them pretty promiscuously,' Melbourne returned.[40]

Transcribing this in her journal, the Queen declared: 'It's always my delight to make him look at these sorts of things, as his remarks are always so clever and funny.' Very often her journal entries for days when Melbourne had been 'full of fun' at dinner end with the satisfied comment it had been 'a charming' or 'most delightful evening'. At times the Queen's uncritical adoration does seem excessive, and it is not always obvious why some inconsequential observation of the prime minister's sends her into ecstasies.[41] Nevertheless, by documenting these encounters, Victoria ensured that something of Melbourne's magic survived.

For the Queen, 'this excellent and truly kind man' was someone '*for* whom and *in* whom I feel a sort of *filial* affection and confidence'. Others wondered whether her obsession with Melbourne went beyond that. Charles Greville contended that her feelings for him 'are *sexual* though she does not know it'. It is probably fairer to say that Victoria was in love with Melbourne in a girlish, and essentially innocent, sort of way. She was full of praise for his physical appearance, writing soulfully of his 'beautiful noble features and the sweet expression'. In early 1839 she avowed frankly, 'The more I see him and get to know him, the more I (and everybody who knows him well, must) get quite to love him.'

Sometimes her behaviour verged on the flirtatious. In May 1838, 'I asked him if he liked my headdress which was done in plaits round my ears … He said, looking at me and making one of his funny faces: "It's pretty. Isn't it rather curious – something new?"' A few months later he complimented her on her downy arms. With false modesty Victoria objected, 'it was exceedingly ugly having such hairy arms as I have' – to which Melbourne rejoined gallantly, 'No, very pretty.'[42]

Melbourne could hardly have been more assiduous but, even so, the Queen did not like it if others momentarily claimed his attention. At dinner one night she was 'rather put out' that the Duchess of Sutherland, who had been placed on Melbourne's other side, 'took possession of him' during the meal. When the same thing happened a few months later, she confronted Melbourne about it, who brushed it off with a smile. Such was her dependence on Melbourne that if he left the drawing room once dinner was over, 'her eyes followed him' and she was visibly tense till he returned. She had become so proprietorial that if, as very occasionally happened, he accepted an invitation to dine elsewhere, or was prevented by business or ill health from joining her, she regarded it as dereliction on his part. In June 1838 she indulged in a petulant outburst on hearing Melbourne would have to absent himself for one night. Several foreign princes had been invited to dine that evening, and she thought it '*very very provoking*' that Melbourne would not be there to welcome them. 'He *ought* to be near me, it is his *place*!' she fumed. The following month she was no less displeased when gout forced Melbourne to cancel their dinner engagement. 'This is *most provoking* and *vexatious*,' Victoria brooded, although acknowledging, 'I ought not to be selfish.'[43]

Victoria believed Melbourne to be 'truly excellent and moral' – but not everyone agreed that his character ideally suited him to be a young queen's guide and mentor. Although she declared: 'I feel *so safe* when he speaks to me,' the Duke of Wellington was 'afraid he jokes too much with her, and makes her treat things too lightly which are very serious'. When the duke's remarks were reported, Victoria was indignant, but Melbourne merely said mildly: 'There may be some truth in that.' At least one other person was far severer than Wellington. The campaigning evangelical Lord Ashley asserted that Melbourne's 'society and conversation are pernicious to a young mind … His sentiments and manner blunt the moral sense.'[44]

Melbourne could hardly be faulted with regard to impressing on Victoria the need to do her duty. While finding it very natural that she disliked holding 'drawing rooms' and 'levées', he insisted: 'You must fight against that ... A Queen's life is very laborious.' He refused to countenance any reluctance to open Parliament on Victoria's part, saying earnestly, 'Oh you will do it ... That would not be right.' At one point Victoria said there were times she felt 'unfit ... for my station', but he would have none of it, begging, 'Oh! No ... Never think that.' When she complained that the lot of a constitutional monarch was a hard one, he agreed, but added: 'You must bear it ... you've drawn the ticket.'[45]

In other ways, Melbourne was – in modern parlance – astonishingly politically incorrect, expressing opinions that he knew to be widely unacceptable even in his own day. He once cheerfully told Victoria: 'You better try to do no good, and then you'll get into no scrapes.' He was sceptical too about how much could be achieved through legislation, declaring flatly that the only job of a government was 'to prevent and punish crime and ... preserve contracts'. In particular, he saw little merit in broadening access to education. At first Victoria was impressed when he was 'clever and funny' on the subject – 'his ideas are excellent about it, I think' – but by mid-1839 a note of unease was detectable when she wrote that Melbourne 'as usual gave a little sneer at the education system'. Four months earlier he had volunteered, 'I daren't say in these times that I'm against it – but I am against it.' In 1839 the government did increase the amount of public money to be spent on education from £20,000 to a still pitiful £30,000, but Melbourne had not actively supported the change. That June, after talking with a man involved in the field, the prime minister remarked to the Queen: 'It's a wrong thing to say but Mr Kay ... told me that it was shocking to see how much like brutes the children of the lower orders are,' and therefore trying to instil learning in them was futile.[46]

Melbourne's remark that it was 'almost worth while for a woman to be beat, considering the exceeding pity she excites' was greeted by the customary peals of merriment from the Queen. It acquires a different edge once one is aware that many of Melbourne's letters to female acquaintances furnish evidence of a disconcerting fixation with flagellation. To one woman he was involved with he once wrote: 'A few twigs of a birch applied to the naked skin of a young lady produces with very little effort a very considerable sensation.'[47]

Shocked to discover that a gentleman had been sent to prison on being convicted of a crime, the prime minister did not conceal his belief that 'there ought to be a law for the rich and another for the poor; I mustn't say it, but it is so; that equality is very bad'. As home secretary during the reign of William IV, he himself had been responsible for the severe application of laws that impacted harshly on the poor. In 1834 six agricultural workers from Tolpuddle, Dorset, had been taken into custody after they set up a union. Convicted of breaking a law prohibiting the unauthorised taking of oaths, they were sentenced to seven years' transportation. Widespread protests about the men's punishment had left Melbourne indifferent, and it was not until 1836 that the freed labourers returned from Australia in triumph.

At times Melbourne's attitudes appeared positively callous. He asserted that measles and whooping cough had high mortality rates among the poor because parents dosed sick children with spirits. 'They think brandy and gin a remedy for everything and the children die like flies,' he airily assured Victoria. When Victoria had earlier expressed concern about the poor suffering from the cold, he had declared part of the problem lay in their reluctance to embrace new technology such as stoves that could heat food more efficiently.[48]

Melbourne was unworried about hardship caused by the Poor Law Amendment Act of 1834, which had received the royal assent shortly after he became prime minister. The act abolished the old system whereby paupers had been given limited relief at home at the expense of parish ratepayers, replacing this with workhouses managed by boards of guardians. To discourage people from becoming a drain on the public purse, these institutions were designed to be as unpleasant as possible, with husbands being separated from their wives, and children parted from parents. Harsh regulations, inhuman discipline and poor food ensured that only the utterly desperate would seek admission, reducing the burden on local taxpayers. The new system had recently been extended to the north of England, provoking a major outcry, but Melbourne was impervious to accusations that the law was in any way defective.

In 1837 the first instalments of Charles Dickens's *Oliver Twist* had been published in serial form, and the Queen had devoured the 'accounts of starvation in workhouses and schools', finding it all '*too* interesting'. Melbourne did not share her enthusiasm, protesting that he disliked exposure to scenes of 'low life'. A few months later, workhouses and the Poor Laws again came up in conversation when one of Victoria's ladies-in-waiting was present, and 'Lord M' was 'very funny about' these subjects. Lady Barham had read of a case where a woman had starved to death because a workhouse had refused to take her in, but Melbourne insisted it had been the woman's own fault. 'But they would not take her in,' Lady Barham repeated, at which – as Victoria indulgently recorded – 'Lord Melbourne shook his head and said "I rather doubt that."' It was true that some lurid accounts published in the papers regarding the operation of the Poor Laws were exaggerated, but Melbourne's unshakeable complacency still leaves a sour taste. On the whole the Queen accepted that her prime minister's views were sound, noting in May 1838 that: 'Lord Melbourne and I both think there must be a Poor Law.'[49]

Melbourne had been home secretary when a factory act had been passed in 1833, making it compulsory for factories to submit to inspections, but he was not in favour of limiting the hours that children could work. Victoria described how in August 1838, 'We spoke of factory children for some time. Lord Melbourne thinks the accounts of them greatly exaggerated. He said "We have to work so hard to beat the others, that I don't like to meddle with it." He says it's better children should work than be idle and starve.' Instinctively opposed to 'all that intermeddling', he maintained that all would be well, 'if you'd only have the goodness to leave them alone'. Inevitably Victoria found this highly amusing.[50]

Melbourne had little sympathy for Ireland's inhabitants. 'It isn't right to say, and indeed it is a very bad thing to say, but it does not do to trust to the Irish; they are never safe,' he informed Victoria roundly in March 1839. Because of the disparities between English and Irish laws on landholding, Irish agricultural tenants had no security of tenure and could be evicted even if they had paid their rent or spent their own money improving a property. Resentment at these injustices had helped create a lawless culture, leading to the formation of vigilante bands who murdered landlords and informants. Melbourne refused to accept that these 'crimes and outrages had much to do with former misgovernment and present politics', attributing them rather to 'a natural disposition of the people'. He assured Victoria, 'they are but a poor set … quick and clever, but uncertain, false, hypocritical'. Far from objecting, the Queen thought, 'All this is very true.'[51]

On another occasion Melbourne said he had it on good authority that while many impoverished Irish were very dirty, there was little 'real destitution' on the island. He reasoned that 'if they spend nothing on clothes and soap, they may afford to spend it on other things'. Equally shocking were his comments upon the actions of particularly harsh Irish landlord. Melbourne argued that Lord Bandon was right to turn out tenants who 'eat up everything'. The prime minister twinkled to Victoria: 'They can't all live there, and you too.' When she and another lady protested 'it was cruel, and what became of these poor people?'

Melbourne merely drawled: 'They become absorbed somehow or other, which made us laugh amazingly.'[52]

Victoria might have sometimes squealed in mock horror at Melbourne's outrageousness, but she loved him no less for it. At the beginning of 1838 she had proudly stated: 'He and I (as I may say most truly *we always do*) perfectly agree.' She was so dependent on him that going without their daily meetings seemed unthinkable, and yet it was obvious that his time in power could not last for ever. None of this escaped diarist and Clerk of the Privy Council Charles Greville, who foresaw trouble, predicting that 'whenever the government, which hangs by a thread, shall be broken up, the parting will be painful'.[53]

In March 1838 the Queen had a nasty moment when the ministry only narrowly won a vote of no confidence. Over the next few months they continued to have difficulties piloting measures through Parliament. The following February, when Parliament reassembled, Greville was scathing about the government's 'wretched state of weakness, utterly ignorant whether it can scramble through the session'. To him it appeared that Melbourne wished 'to hold office for no other purpose but that of dining at Buckingham House'.[54]

The Queen was as wedded to the Whigs as ever, not liking it when Melbourne recommended that she ask 'some tiresome Tories' to dinner.[55] Her palpable distaste inevitably meant the Tories felt resentful and excluded. As a result, when a court scandal erupted, the opposition grasped eagerly at the opportunity to cause trouble.

In January 1839 the Queen and her former governess, Baroness Lehzen, noticed that the Duchess of Kent's lady-in-waiting, Lady Flora Hastings, had a distended stomach that made her look pregnant. Several of Victoria's Ladies of the Bedchamber perceived the same thing. 'With Lehzen's concurrence,' Lord John Russell's sister-in-law, the Marchioness of Tavistock, informed Lord Melbourne. He consulted the Queen's physician, Sir James Clark, who agreed that Lady Flora's appearance gave grounds for suspicion. On 2 February Victoria said to Melbourne that she believed he was aware of 'this awkward business'. The Queen was by now not only convinced that Lady Flora was, 'to use plain words – with child!!', but that the father was 'the Monster and demon incarnate', Sir John Conroy. Melbourne sensibly told the Queen that 'the only way is to be quiet and watch it', but regrettably 'did not put an extinguisher upon it as he might and ought to have done'.[56]

On 16 February Sir James Clark confronted Lady Flora, who had previously consulted him about 'bilious attacks'. In a vain attempt to be tactful, he asked if she were privately married, for – as Lady Flora would indignantly relate – he believed, 'No one could look at me and doubt' her condition. Clark averred that 'nothing but a medical examination could satisfy the ladies of the palace'. Upon being told 'it was her Majesty's pleasure I should not appear [at court] until my character was cleared by the means suggested', Lady Flora reluctantly submitted to the invasive procedure. The next day a vaginal examination was carried out in the presence of Lady Portman, another Lady of the Bedchamber who later admitted she had discussed the matter with the Queen. The examination revealed unequivocally that Lady Flora was a virgin, but unfortunately Clark and a colleague privately informed Melbourne that the 'entire and inviolate state of her hymen' did not preclude impregnation.[57] This meant that, while Lady Flora was officially exonerated, she was still regarded with suspicion. Once she grasped that she had not been fully vindicated, her sense of grievance inevitably became still more acute.

On 23 February the Queen received Lady Flora for an interview that was meant to remove any ill-feeling, but which signally failed to do so. Lady Flora's family, staunch Tories all, now became involved. At the end of February her brother, the Marquess of Hastings, met with Victoria in the hope of finding out who had first made allegations against his sister, and Lady Flora's mother, the dowager marchioness, wrote demanding Sir James Clark's dismissal. Having learned that Lady Flora's pregnancy was still being gossiped about in London clubs, in late March her uncle published a letter his niece had sent him. In this, Lady Flora declared that all fair-minded people took the view that her slanderers – among whom she numbered both Clark and several court ladies – should be dismissed, and if this 'does not ... appear to be the view of the ministers ... I doubt whether they are quite judicious as respects the general feeling'. A few days later what the Queen termed an 'abominable and shocking' article appeared in the *Spectator*, deploring Lady Flora's treatment.[58] Shortly afterwards the Dowager Lady Hastings's correspondence on the subject was printed in the press, accompanied by a letter from Lord Hastings attacking his sister's traducers.

All this coincided with a series of political crises. On 21 March the opposition carried a vote in the House of Lords alleging that the Whigs had permitted Ireland to descend into a state of utter lawlessness.

Victoria was incensed, condemning 'such wickedness, such folly' on the part of the Tories, 'the most … unpatriotic set of people ever known'. She became still more distraught when the Cabinet agreed that the government should seek a vote of confidence from the Commons, and that if one was not forthcoming, they must resign. Appalled at the prospect of losing Melbourne, the Queen wrote melodramatically in her journal, 'I am but a poor helpless girl, who clings to him for support and protection.' As soon as she saw him, she 'burst into tears and remained crying for some time … I said I couldn't bear the Tories and hated them.' Melbourne remonstrated, 'You should have no dislikes,' but failed to recall her to her constitutional duty. 'If I was obliged to have a Tory ministry,' Victoria argued, 'I didn't see even with all fairness how we could go on well.' To this Melbourne responded that she would not mind the Tories so much once she was used to them.[59]

Lord and Lady Hastings's letters were published by the *Morning Post* on 16 April, the day after the no-confidence debate began in the House of Commons. The Queen raged that she would like 'to have hanged the editor and the whole Hastings family for their infamy', and was not mollified when Melbourne said, 'It's all aimed at me.' He had no doubt it had been 'done at this moment, while this is going on in Parliament, with a view to have an effect' on the way the vote went, and that all the fuss about 'this odious Flora business' (as the Queen termed it) was 'only for political purposes'. The Cabinet minister Lord Holland was just as sure that Sir John Conroy and the Duchess of Kent had 'cooperated underhand in these manoeuvres … exasperated equally against the Queen and Lord Melbourne'.[60]

In the early hours of the morning of 20 April the government won their vote of confidence. The rapturous Queen proclaimed: 'I feel I can breathe again. Thank God!' Yet within a week her torment was renewed when problems arose in connection with the government's colonial policy. In 1833 Parliament had passed an act abolishing slavery throughout the British Empire, but since that time slaves in the Caribbean had been forced to serve their masters as 'apprentices', effectively continuing their enslavement. This was meant to be a temporary arrangement, but it was clear that plantation owners in Jamaica were resisting granting full emancipation. Slavery was one of the few subjects about which Melbourne was never flippant. In February 1838 he had lamented to Victoria the 'dreadful cruelties' still being inflicted on slaves in Britain's West Indian colonies; and in another conversation with her the following month he had castigated the way 'shockingly cruel and cheating …

masters of slaves' evaded their new obligations by flogging and remorselessly overworking labourers. The British government now decided that matters could only be remedied by suspending Jamaica's representative assembly. Although the Queen accepted legislation was necessary, she was appalled by Melbourne's warning that the measure would not have an easy passage through Parliament. 'This filled me with new horrors,' she wrote despondently.[61]

Sure enough, in the early hours of 7 May, when the Commons voted on whether the 'Jamaica Bill' should go into committee, the government's majority was only five. It was obvious there was no hope of the measure reaching the statute book, and since the government could not in honour abandon it, Melbourne wrote to the Queen that they must resign. Plunged into 'agony, grief and despair', she wailed: '*All, all* my happiness gone!' Melbourne arrived to talk things over shortly after midday. 'You will not forsake me?' Victoria sobbed. 'Oh no,' he reassured her, but how he would manage this was unclear.[62]

Melbourne knew that the Queen particularly disliked the Conservative Party leader, Sir Robert Peel, whom she deemed 'a cold, unfeeling, disagreeable man'. The prime minister had tried to overcome her antipathy, maintaining that Peel's 'very bad manner' arose from 'gaucherie' rather than unpleasantness, but had not had much success.[63] To try and spare her feelings, he recommended she send first for the Duke of Wellington – who he supposed would be more congenial to her – and ask him, rather than Peel, to form a government. If Wellington declined the commission, she would have to turn to Peel.

Lord Melbourne also thought she could reasonably request that only members of the royal household who were actively engaged in politics would have to resign their positions when the government changed. The following day he reiterated this, saying consolingly, 'They'll not touch your ladies.' The Queen fired back, 'They dared not and I never would allow it.'[64]

Melbourne should have foreseen this would prove problematic, not least because the Lady Flora imbroglio had already discredited several of the Queen's ladies. Of the Ladies of the Bedchamber, not only was Lady Tavistock Lord John Russell's sister-in-law, but Lady Lansdowne and the Marchioness of Normanby were both wives of Cabinet ministers. The Whig ladies' dominance of the Bedchamber was certainly not accidental, for at Victoria's accession Melbourne had been adamant that all those chosen should be 'favourable to her Majesty's present ministers'. He had stressed to the Queen that if her ladies were exclusively

Whig, it would have a 'great political effect … upon the stability of the government … the pending elections & consequently upon the whole course of your Majesty's reign'. The political bias of the Queen's female household had immediately attracted unfavourable comment, with the Tory *Quarterly Review* complaining in July 1837 that Victoria should remember she was 'not the sovereign of one party, but of all'.[65]

After Melbourne left her on the afternoon of 7 May, the Queen asked Wellington to come to the palace the following day. However, before that meeting took place, she wanted another conference with 'Lord M'. She wrote suggesting he pay her an after-dinner visit that night, which he declined, saying, 'I don't think it would be right … It would be observed.' Victoria promised that though she felt '*thoroughly wretched* & miserable … she' would 'try to collect herself'; but as the day wore on she only grew more frantic. In the afternoon she sent again for him, warning that unless some means was 'found for the Queen to communicate *privately* with Lord Melbourne, not about affairs alas! – but about many things which concern her personally … this dreadful change would be quite *unbearable*'. Piteously she added, 'Oh! If Lord Melbourne saw how *very very unhappy*' she was, he would want to help. That evening she did not eat dinner, and instead remained in her room, where she 'sobbed and cried convulsively'.[66]

The next day she suggested there 'could be no earthly harm' if she met with Melbourne as he rode in the park, as if by chance. She acknowledged, 'Lord Melbourne may think this childish but the Queen … would bear through all her trials so much better if she could just see a friendly face.' Should a personal encounter prove impractical, letters between them would have to be her only solace. If so, 'He *must* write *often* to her, for the Queen has *plenty* of means of keeping it *quite secret*.' Despite this willingness to resort to subterfuge, she maintained her readiness to 'do all that is right, Lord Melbourne may depend upon it, but every now & then she feels as if her heart could break'.[67]

At their interview on 8 May the Duke of Wellington disappointed Victoria by saying he was too old and deaf to be prime minister, recommending that she instead apply to Sir Robert Peel. The Queen mentioned her concerns about possible changes in the household, but Wellington would not be drawn, saying it was best 'not to begin with conditions of this sort'.[68]

Peel arrived for an audience just after two in the afternoon, looking, to the Queen's jaundiced eye, 'embarrassed and put out'. He at once said it would be difficult for the Conservatives to take office without a majority in Parliament. It was therefore essential that she demonstrate that they enjoyed her confidence, and the composition of her household 'would be one of the marks of that'. Victoria countered that she understood that only those directly engaged in politics would have to go, to which Peel gave no answer. He did not dissent when she said she wished to continue seeing Melbourne as a friend, but she was not sure how to interpret this: as she explained to Melbourne, Peel 'is such a cold, odd man she can't make out what he means'. She only knew 'the Queen don't like his manner', which was, 'Oh! How different, how dreadfully so, to that frank, open, natural and most kind, warm manner of Lord Melbourne.'[69]

That evening Peel informed colleagues that he assumed all the Queen's ladies who were related to Whig ministers would resign, but a nasty shock awaited him when he met with Victoria the following day. Perhaps without meaning to, Melbourne had encouraged her intransigence, for while he advised that it would 'not do to … put off the negotiation' on the question of the ladies, he suggested she tell Peel that if he overrode her wishes he would be 'pressing your Majesty more hardly than any Minister ever pressed a Sovereign before'. As soon as Peel broached the matter, saying, 'Now, about the Ladies', the Queen interrupted: 'I could not give up any of my Ladies and never had imagined such a thing.' When a flustered Sir Robert 'asked if I meant to retain *all*?' she replied: '*All*.' In a letter to Melbourne Victoria jeered, 'I never saw a man so frightened,' concluding defiantly: 'The Queen of England will not submit to such trickery. Keep yourself in readiness, for you may soon be wanted.'[70]

After consulting Wellington and other colleagues, Peel informed the Queen that he could not take office unless she reconsidered. Victoria promised she would let him know by the morning and then, full of hopes that deliverance was at hand, she called Melbourne to her. He listened to her account and agreed to summon his Cabinet.

The prime minister found himself in a quandary. Naturally Melbourne was reluctant to relinquish power, and desired above all to maintain his cherished daily contact with the Queen. He did not want her to face criticism, but genuinely believed that Peel had behaved unreasonably, having somehow formed the impression Sir Robert was intending to deprive the Queen of every lady in her household.

At 9.30 that evening the Whig Cabinet met at Melbourne's house in South Street, Mayfair. Several ministers urged caution, but after Melbourne read aloud a letter from Victoria, almost all present 'caught fire'. One minister recounted, 'We waxed more loyal than I believe any of us had ever before been,' with even the waverers agreeing 'it was impossible to abandon such a Queen and such a woman.' They drew up a letter in the Queen's name accusing Peel of making demands 'contrary to usage and repugnant to her feelings'. Approving this formula as 'quite right', Victoria forwarded the letter to Peel first thing the next morning.[71]

It was only when Victoria triumphantly showed Lord Melbourne Peel's response, giving up any idea of forming a government, that the prime minister began to feel himself in a false position. He was startled that Peel claimed only to have asked for the resignation of some of the Queen's ladies, and was hardly reassured that Victoria argued, 'Some or all ... were all the same.'[72]

That evening, 10 May, the Queen gave a ball for a visiting Russian grand duke. All the country's leading political figures were invited, and many of these guests were 'anxious and preoccupied. The men, instead of making themselves agreeable to the ladies, were assembled in groups all over the rooms talking earnestly.' Victoria did not care in the slightest. 'She was in great spirits, and danced with more than usual gaiety,' only retiring to bed after three in the morning. 'Much pleased, as my mind felt happy,' she wrote in her journal. Next morning, in conversation with Melbourne, she mocked Wellington and Peel for looking foolish at the party.[73]

Melbourne was less free of misgivings. On 14 May he gave a somewhat embarrassed performance in the House of Lords, explaining that the Queen had been under the 'evidently erroneous' impression that Peel required the removal of all her ladies. He insisted that far from 'having intrigued', he 'did not entertain a notion' that the question of the ladies would arise. 'Most undoubtedly I never mentioned the subject to her Majesty,' he added, decidedly inaccurately, maintaining that he had rather acted out of chivalry. 'I will not abandon my sovereign in a situation of difficulty and distress, and especially when a demand is made upon her Majesty with which I think she ought not to comply.' In an implicit admission that his government now had scant legitimacy, he gave his listeners to understand that henceforth they would refrain from controversial legislation.[74]

Nearly sixty years later the aged Queen Victoria would cheerfully admit it had been 'entirely my own foolishness' that caused the so-called 'Bedchamber crisis', but at the time she was sure she had acted within her rights. On 12 May she told Melbourne she was 'so happy to have

A cartoon of the 'Bedchamber Crisis'. Queen Victoria, surrounded by her ladies, is reviving Lord Melbourne with smelling salts. (John Doyle, 1839)

escaped from these people', and when he warned it was too early to write off the Tories, 'I said I could not try them again, for that they really had behaved so ill.' She was satisfied that her people took her side, interpreting applause that marked her visit to the theatre on 11 May, and her being 'loudly cheered' as she drove to the Chapel Royal at St James's Palace, as meaning 'the country went with me'. She confidently declared as much to Melbourne, firmly dismissing all indications to the contrary.[75]

Condemnation of her conduct was more widespread than she realised. Charles Greville fulminated, 'It is a high trial of our institutions when the caprice of a girl of nineteen can overturn a great ministerial combination.' The Tories understandably believed themselves to have been cheated of power. Greville reported that, 'Peel, (reserved and prudent as he is) cannot conceal the indignation with which he is boiling over.' His followers were considerably less reticent. At Ascot races that June, two Tory ladies, the Duchess of Montrose and Lady Sarah Ingestrie, hissed the Queen. Victoria raged to Melbourne about the antics of these 'abominable women … who I said I wished I could have flogged'.[76]

* * *

The ill-feeling arose not just from the Queen's abuse of power, for the case of Lady Flora Hastings had continued to fester. Since the spring, Lady Flora's health had relentlessly declined, and her family represented her victimisation by the court as having exacerbated her sufferings. It would later emerge that her distended belly was attributable not to pregnancy but a tumour on her liver, but even before this was known, the Queen's failure to make amends was widely blamed. Articles incited by the Hastings family continued to appear in the press, and on 19 June Lord Hastings challenged Melbourne to a duel. 'Too monstrous, too atrocious, what a wretch,' Victoria cried, though relieved that Melbourne had evaded the summons. Her compassion was only awakened on 27 June, when, rather against her will, she visited Lady Flora in her palace sickroom, and was shocked by what she saw. Apart from her swollen abdomen, Lady Flora was now a skeletal figure, and not even the Queen could doubt she was terminally ill. Even so, she was not best pleased that Melbourne advised her to cancel a ball scheduled for the following evening.[77]

On 5 July 1839 Lady Flora died. Victoria defiantly told Melbourne, 'I felt no remorse. I felt I had done nothing to kill her' – but others were less willing to exonerate her. There was more hostile press coverage. Melbourne was so upset that his beloved sovereign was being vilified that on 7 July he was 'dreadfully silent at dinner'. The Queen's principal concern, however, was 'I passed really a dull evening'. On 11 July, ministers arriving at Buckingham Palace for a Privy Council meeting were hooted by a sullen crowd, but Victoria would not listen to 'those fools' who supposed this accurately reflected the state of public opinion. She seized on the fact that when she went riding with Melbourne six days later, 'there was not one hiss' to be heard. The Hastings family still sought retribution, but ultimately this worked in Victoria's favour: as Lord Hastings spewed out more letters and pamphlets, most people decided he had 'pushed matters too far'. Yet though gradually the scandal receded, this painful episode had lessened the Queen's popularity and diminished the standing of her ministers.[78]

By the autumn of 1839 the government were contending with other very serious problems. Poor harvests and the end of the railway and shipbuilding booms had caused a severe economic contraction and manufacturers were laying off workers or reducing their wages. There was widespread hardship, and the harsh provisions of the Poor Law – or 'Starvation Law' as some now called it – did little to alleviate this. This lay behind the emergence of Chartism, a mass movement of workers who believed that the only way of overcoming the injustices they faced was to secure themselves the vote. In May 1838 a Charter had been drawn up putting forward six demands, the most important of which was the grant of universal male suffrage. A Chartist petition, containing over 1.2 million signatures from men and women, was presented to Parliament in July 1839, but the House of Commons voted against considering it in committee. Already some Chartists had suggested they would never secure what they wanted through 'moral force', and the rejection by Parliament strengthened the case of those who instead favoured the use of 'physical force'.

In July 1839 there were riots in Birmingham, coupled with threats of strikes in other parts of the country. Numerous Chartists were arrested for affray or seditious speeches, and some ringleaders were sentenced to two years in prison. In November, still more alarming disturbances took place in Newport, Wales, when thousands of Chartists, some of them armed, converged on the town. Twenty-two insurgents were killed after troops returned fire. John Frost – a former mayor of Newport who had organised the rising – was tried for treason with two accomplices, and the trio were sentenced to death. On 29 January 1840 the Cabinet met to consider whether the sentences should be carried out. Seeing the Queen later that day, Melbourne stated: 'I'm for executing all three,' and Victoria concurred – despite the fact that those convicted had been promised clemency if they pleaded guilty.[79] Most of the Cabinet had favoured mercy but were prevailed on to change their minds. In the end the men's lives were saved because the Lord Chief Justice overturned the sentence on technical grounds. They were transported to Australia, supposedly for life. Following a campaign for their return, all three were pardoned in 1855.

If the mood of the country was turbulent and disaffected, the Queen herself was not in a particularly peaceable frame of mind. Her hatred of the Tories now verged on the pathological, and Lord Melbourne could not persuade her to listen to reason. From the Queen's own accounts, it appeared as though he was almost becoming scared of her, and certainly he feared she would damage herself by her wilfulness and obstinacy. She defied him on minor matters, ignoring it when he seconded her doctors' advice to take a hot bath, and insisting she 'couldn't and wouldn't' make any advances to her mother. Far more serious was the way she gloried in her political prejudices. 'You shouldn't give way too much to personal dislikes,' Melbourne reiterated, but when some Tories presented addresses at a levée, she received them with a 'stately look and pouting under-lip', whereas she had been 'all smiles and civilities to Whigs'.[80]

The Queen was puzzled that Melbourne found this regrettable. Once, when inveighing against the Tories to someone, she remarked naively, 'It is very odd but I cannot get Lord Melbourne to see it in that light.' Peel helped neither himself nor the party with his frigidity and awkwardness. Invited to a ball at Buckingham Palace, he pointedly avoided Victoria, failing to address a word to her even after Melbourne hissed, 'For God's sake, go and speak to the Queen.' While not denying that at times Peel could act like 'a stupid, underbred fellow', Melbourne sought to impress upon Victoria that she might yet have to reach an accommodation with him. If the Whigs fell, the Tories were 'the only party to look to', but the Queen refused to contemplate such a thing: '"Never" I said, "I couldn't, I hated them too much"', she proclaimed fiercely. '"If I was forced to take them I should try every possible means to get rid of them." "That's not right," said Lord M.'[81]

At times Victoria could be irritable with Melbourne himself. On 11 August, she was 'sulky and peevish' towards him. A fortnight later she sent him a sharp letter after he carried out a Cabinet reshuffle without forewarning her, writing tetchily she should not 'be the last person to hear what is settled and done in her name'. She softened the admonition by asking Melbourne to 'excuse the Queen's being a little eager', but within a month she flared up again when he suggested she invite some Tories to stay at Windsor. She reiterated that she hated them all, and considered them 'personal enemies', which Melbourne once more protested was 'very wrong'. Later she felt ashamed of having been so 'sadly cross', embarrassed that, having sensed her bad mood on arrival, Melbourne 'did not sit down of himself, as he usually does, but waited till I told him to do so'. She chided herself: 'I can't think what possessed me,' only to indulge in another bout of temper two days later. She complained she heard 'nothing else but politics, and always politics', and Melbourne at once agreed there was 'nothing so disagreeable'. A few days later a contrite queen apologised for having made such a fuss.[82]

It was partly the disagreeable repercussions of the Lady Flora affair that made Victoria so petulant and fretful, but, aside from this, something was lacking from her life that Melbourne could not supply. Now that her initial happiness on coming to the throne had faded, she sometimes found herself crying for no good reason. The life she led was so odd for a woman of her age that she told Melbourne poignantly, 'I often forgot I was young.' In the spring of 1839 she began to wonder if the answer lay in marriage, but worried it would not provide personal fulfilment. In addition, as she observed to Melbourne, she feared she was 'so accustomed to have my own way … that I shouldn't agree with anybody. Lord M said "Oh! But you would have it still" (my own way)'.[83]

Discussing candidates for her hand with Melbourne, she at once said that she knew her Uncle Leopold had always wanted her to marry her cousin Albert, second son of Duke Ernest of Saxe-Coburg-Gotha. He had come to England some years earlier, but though she had liked him and his elder brother, she was nervous of committing to him. Perhaps subconsciously aware that the acquisition of a husband would inevitably disrupt his own relationship with Victoria, Melbourne had private doubts about a Coburg marriage, but was aware all other contenders were unsuitable. She and Melbourne 'enumerated the various princes' of Europe who, as Protestants, could be considered, but 'not one', Victoria said, 'would do'. Melbourne mused, 'I don't think a foreigner would be popular, but marrying one of her subjects also had disadvantages.'[84] The upshot was that the Queen invited Albert to visit England in the autumn, while stressing to King Leopold she was in no way pledging herself.

Victoria was somewhat apprehensive that if she did marry she would suffer a loss of political power, but perhaps assumed that a young man some months her junior who had been brought up in a tiny German duchy would not be too assertive. It was nevertheless rash to presume that Albert would tolerate being a nonentity. Although his father and elder brother were both libertines, he was intensely serious, hating frivolity and late nights. At Brussels and Bonn universities his studies had included law, political economy, history, metaphysics, maths, languages and philosophy, and he had developed extraordinary powers of application. When Victoria and Albert became engaged, Lord Ashley understood he had been selected 'as a young gentleman who will not busy himself in politics or affairs of state, who will rather pursue hunting, shooting, dancing and other amiable distractions' – but Albert was never going to fit this profile.[85]

Albert arrived in England on 10 October 1839, and within twenty-four hours the Queen was passionately in love. Finding him 'charming and so excessively handsome', she was enraptured by his 'exquisite nose and … delicate moustachios'. On 14 October she told Melbourne she intended to propose, which he said was 'a very good thing, and you'll be much more comfortable; for a woman cannot stand alone for long'. He had already realised that the match was inevitable, having told Lord John Russell a day earlier, 'The mind is in fact made up ... I do not know that anything better could be done. He seems a very agreeable young man – he is certainly a very good looking one – and as to character, that we must always take our chances of.'[86]

Albert accepted Victoria's proposal on 15 October, which rendered her deliriously happy. In a letter to Melbourne she thanked providence for 'giving me such a perfect *being*', saying that 'such love, *such* happiness does really make up for all I have gone through in my life'. However much she worshipped her fiancé, it did not occur to her that he should have a significant share in political life. Signing letters and warrants one day, she was pleased that Albert was 'so kind as to dry them with blotting paper for me', but she did not envisage him progressing beyond this.[87]

On 14 November Albert returned home to Germany for nearly three months. The engagement was announced to the Privy Council later that month, and it was agreed that Parliament should be asked to settle his status when it met in the new year. King Leopold was of course overjoyed by the news, and at once urged his niece to confer a peerage on Albert so that he would be able to vote in the House of Lords. Victoria decisively rejected this on the grounds that 'the English are very jealous at the idea of Albert's ... meddling with affairs'. To Albert himself she explained, 'Now, though I know you never would, still if you were a Peer, they would all say, the Prince meant to play a political part.' A further 'ungracious letter' from Leopold only served to displease his niece. She told Albert, 'He appears to me to be nettled because I no longer ask for his advice, but dear Uncle is given to believe that he must rule the roast [sic] everywhere.'[88]

King Leopold did not give up, writing to Lord Melbourne that if Albert was to become Victoria's 'safest and best friend', she 'must take from the very beginning a correct view of her married position'. He had to content himself with Melbourne's reply that he trusted the Queen 'will find the means of doing that, which is not altogether easy, namely of reconciling the authority of a sovereign with the duty of a wife'.[89]

Almost immediately a serious clash of wills occurred between the betrothed couple. Lord Melbourne had decided that George Anson should become Albert's private secretary, despite the fact that Anson was already performing the same role for the prime minister himself. Albert demurred on the grounds that this would brand him irredeemably 'a party man', only for Victoria to insist the appointment must stand. She argued that otherwise it would be thought that Albert had Tory sympathies, although she did agree that Anson should no longer work for Melbourne. Albert replied that notwithstanding the loving tone of her letter, it pained him that, 'you wish to insist forcibly on something ... which you well know is very distasteful to me'. He was unimpressed when Melbourne wrote to him at the Queen's behest, saying that her husband must be unfailingly supportive. On 13 January 1840 Albert protested to Victoria, 'You could not respect a husband who never formed an opinion till you had formed yours,' and then concluded with ominous simplicity: 'I will not take Mr Anson nor anybody now.'[90]

Albert's communication left Victoria 'so agitated that she can hardly write'. She told Melbourne she considered the letter 'a foolish one' and hoped 'you will *not* form a bad idea of Albert's feeling or dispositions'. Later that day she still had not 'recovered from the fuss and distress ... It made her cry much,'[91] but she still insisted that Albert must take on Anson. After Baron Stockmar counselled compliance, Albert submitted.

In one way, Albert's influence over Victoria was already becoming discernible, for she no longer unthinkingly accepted that everything Melbourne did was beyond criticism. Only three weeks after becoming engaged she suddenly upbraided the prime minister for holding too few Cabinets and accused the government of having 'dawdled away their time'. She chided her prime minister too for not attending church and said she would abide by Albert's wishes to impose stricter moral standards at court: anyone whose reputation was in the slightest bit suspect would henceforth be excluded. She was not best pleased by Melbourne's curt prediction: 'You'll be liable to make every sort of mistake.' The Queen now had sneaking suspicions that his own conduct had not always been irreproachable, thinking it 'very wrong' that he boasted 'I never was sorry' about anything he had done in the past. Reflecting that he must have been guilty of 'failings ... when young', having grown up 'when Society was very vicious', she regretted this impenitent attitude. Some of his witticisms now seemed worthy of reproval – as when Melbourne announced, 'I don't like the middle classes,' Victoria recorded primly: 'I said to Lord M he so often kept one in hot water by saying such things to people.'[92]

This did not mean that her detestation of the Conservatives was any less virulent. On New Year's Day 1840 she offered up the heartfelt prayer, 'From the Tories, good Lord deliver us!' Three weeks earlier she had indulged in 'a tirade against the Tories' when writing to Albert, prompting Melbourne to tell her, 'You shouldn't do that. He'll be frightened.'[93]

Within days of the Queen opening Parliament on 16 January 1840 there were indications that the Tories would give trouble. Melbourne had not anticipated 'any real difficulty' being caused by the request that Albert be granted an annual income of £50,000, but when Lord John Russell proposed this to the Commons on 24 January it had a poor reception. Melbourne attributed it to consciousness on the part of MPs of the prevalent distress in the country, but Victoria was unimpressed. To her fury the eccentric Tory, Colonel Sibthorp, moved that the prince's allowance should be set at £30,000 and when the house divided, the proposal secured a majority of 104. Incensed that that 'nasty wretch' Peel, and the 'vile, confounded infernal Tories' had given it their support, Victoria vowed to Melbourne, 'I shall *never never* forgive the abominable Tories.' Melbourne's pointing out that a good many of his own backbenchers had voted with Sibthorp did not make the Queen any better disposed towards Peel's party.[94]

More setbacks lay in store for Victoria. On 22 December she had told Melbourne that Albert '*ought* to have the title of king', but it was clear that this was unfeasible. Melbourne quite agreed with her that 'having my husband so much lower than myself, was having the Laws of Nature quite reversed', but hoped to improve things by specifying in Albert's naturalisation bill that he would take precedence immediately behind the Queen on all occasions. Unfortunately, when the naturalisation bill was debated in the House of Lords towards the end of January, Tory peers led by the Duke of Wellington opposed the clause on the grounds it was unfair to the Queen's uncles, the royal dukes. Victoria 'grew quite frantic' when Melbourne informed her of this. '"Don't be angry" Lord M said calmly,' but, she ranted, 'it was too odious ... not to have the power even to give my husband rank.' The prime minister reminded her 'that was the law of the country' and looked 'grieved ... at [her] pertinacity' when she insisted he 'fight it out'.[95]

She alarmed him further with a proposal to punish Wellington by not inviting him to her wedding. Melbourne wrote twice, begging her not to snub the hero of Waterloo, for 'his age, station and position' required he should be there. He warned that if she went ahead with her plan it would 'greatly annoy' the duke and his party – to which Victoria fired back, 'This is what the Queen is <u>*striving*</u> to do! What does she owe them? Nothing but *hate*.' A few hours later she apologised for being 'hasty &

violent', asking him at dinner if he 'thought me grown obstinate. "Rather," he replied mildly.' Next day, her vengeful fury revived when Melbourne informed her that he had agreed with Wellington that the question of Albert's precedence would be left out of the naturalisation bill. 'Monsters!' she inscribed wrathfully in her journal. 'You Tories shall be punished. Revenge, revenge!'[96]

At once Victoria wrote what she later acknowledged was a 'hasty and ill-tempered letter to poor dear Lord Melbourne', fulminating against 'this *gross insult*'. She snarled: 'The Old Duke is grown foolish ... He *shall not* be asked now *certainly*.' Melbourne himself was not spared, for he 'ought really to have thought of all this before, & not led the Queen to expect *no* difficulties'. She was also displeased that he had written, rather than conveying the bad news in person, although she could not deny that had he done so, she was unlikely to have 'patiently listened' or kept 'sufficient control over her feelings'.[97]

In the end Albert's status was settled by letters patent which gave him precedence behind her at all times except when specified otherwise by act of Parliament. Victoria was prevailed upon to ask Wellington to her wedding, but hardly any other Tories were invited, which attracted unfavourable comment. With her resentment towards them in no way abated, Melbourne was hard put to stop her making her displeasure felt. Charles Greville congratulated him for making such an effort to restrain her, to which he replied feelingly: 'By God! I am moving noon and night at it.' At one point he was overheard imploring her, 'No for God's sake don't do that.'[98]

Victoria and Albert married on 10 February 1840 at the Chapel Royal, St James's, and then honeymooned at Windsor. Describing their first night together, she wrote: 'We both went to bed (of course in one bed); to lie by his side, and in his arms and on his dear bosom, and be called by names of tenderness ... was bliss beyond belief.' Next morning she wrote to tell Melbourne 'how *very very* happy she feels' to have 'an angel!' for her husband.[99] She was less pleased to discover almost immediately that she was pregnant.

As yet Albert was completely excluded from political power: Victoria still saw her ministers alone and did not show him any Foreign Office despatches. Albert told himself that 'all natural probability' pointed to his ultimately exercising real influence on state affairs, but found his current situation hard. In May 1840 he wrote to a German friend, 'In my home life I am very happy and contented; but the difficulty ... is that I am only the husband and not the master in the house.'[100]

Later that month he confronted his wife directly, complaining of her 'want of confidence … on all matters connected with the politics of the country'. Victoria discussed the matter with Melbourne, castigating herself for not being open enough with her husband. 'She said … she knew it was wrong, but when she was with the Prince she preferred talking upon other subjects.' Melbourne enjoined her to act differently, but Victoria was still wary of the prince imposing his views on her.[101]

On 1 June 1840 Albert publicly displayed his humanitarian ideals when he presided at a meeting of the Society for the Extinction of the Slave Trade held at Exeter Hall in London. In a brief speech that he had rehearsed with Victoria until word-perfect, he urged England's government and navy to keep up their 'benevolent and persevering exertions to abolish that atrocious traffic in human beings', whose continuance constituted 'the blackest stain upon civilised Europe'. His words were greeted with 'great applause' and the prince felt his intervention 'produced a good effect in the country'.[102] However, it was not until a little later in the summer that a crisis in the Middle East meaningfully augmented Albert's power.

Egypt and Syria formed part of the Ottoman Empire's dominions. They were governed by the Pasha Mehemet Ali, in theory a vassal of the Ottoman sultan, but one who in recent years had been threatening to throw off his allegiance. Worried by the threat Mehemet Ali posed to the Ottoman Empire, several of the European 'Great Powers' (as Britain, France, Austria, Russia and Prussia were collectively known at this time) announced they would take steps to shore up that crumbling structure. It had since become apparent that France was not prepared to join with other nations to impose a settlement disadvantageous to Mehemet Ali, whom the French considered their protégé. Palmerston suspected they wished to further their own ambitions in the area with Mehemet Ali's aid. Believing that Louis Philippe, France's 'citizen king' who had gained his throne following a revolution in 1830, was 'as ambitious as Louis XIV', Palmerston was determined to thwart his aspirations.

Palmerston had become accustomed to conducting foreign policy largely at his own discretion, exercising 'an absolute despotism at the Foreign Office' with 'scarcely any interference on the part of his colleagues'. Parliament and the country tended to be apathetic about international affairs, and Melbourne's sister Emily, who had recently married her lover Palmerston, declared her brother was not given to 'thinking much of foreign questions or understanding them well'. The

Queen too was unwilling to devote much attention to them. In January 1840, when the situation in the Middle East was looking worrying, she said to Melbourne: 'these Eastern affairs didn't interest me'. He sympathised but observed that, since it was said 'the fate of Europe depended on them', they could not be ignored altogether.[103]

Palmerston's hostility to Louis Philippe embroiled him with some of his more Francophile colleagues, whereupon on 5 July the foreign secretary threatened to resign unless the Cabinet backed his policy. The Queen was terrified that her government was on the verge of breaking up, but after Melbourne stretched the rules on collective responsibility, Palmerston was authorised to proceed as he saw fit. On 15 July a convention was signed between Britain, Prussia, Austria and Russia stating that Mehemet Ali must submit to the sultan if he wished to keep his territories. In readiness to enforce this, the British fleet was sent to the eastern Mediterranean.

For the first time, Albert was allowed to know what was going on, for as soon as the convention was drawn up, the Queen showed its text to him. In recent weeks his writing desk had been placed next to Victoria's, a sign of her growing trust in him. In August 1840 Albert informed his brother: 'These days I make myself acquainted with politics, read telegrams and study secret reports.' The prince likewise let his father know, 'Victoria allows me to take an active part in foreign affairs, and I think I have done some good. I always commit my views to paper and then communicate them to Lord Melbourne. He seldom answers me, but I have the satisfaction of seeing him act entirely in accordance with what I have said.'[104]

The Queen was readier to listen to Albert's views because 'the Eastern question' was proving so complex and intractable. King Leopold, who was married to Louis Philippe's daughter, thought it '*disastrous*' that Britain had signed a convention to which France was not party. Victoria herself was becoming concerned that Palmerston was being reckless. She complained to Melbourne that the foreign secretary's despatches 'were apt to be too harsh & bitter', but she could not moderate them because they had already gone abroad before she saw them. At times Melbourne himself seemed doubtful about Palmerston's approach, remarking, 'We all seem to have engaged in this treaty without thinking of the consequences.' When Victoria protested 'they ought to have thought of this before', he replied, 'I know it only too well.'[105]

To make matters worse, the splits within the government were deepening, with Lord John Russell now threatening to resign unless

Palmerston did something to conciliate France. The Queen used her pregnancy to convince Melbourne that he must regain control, begging on 26 September, 'For God's sake do not bring on a crisis; the Queen really could not go through that *now*, and it might make her *seriously ill* if she were to be in a state of agitation and excitement if a crisis were to come on.'[106]

On 26 September Victoria asked the prime minister if it would be all right to show her husband Palmerston's draft despatches on eastern affairs. Four days later Melbourne forwarded to Palmerston a memorandum composed by Albert, suggesting ways of bringing France back within the fold of the European Great Powers. Overcoming his initial misgivings, Melbourne pushed Albert's scheme through Cabinet on 1 October.[107]

Palmerston had only grudgingly agreed that his colleagues could consider the scheme, and now he tried to delay its implementation. The Turks had recently unilaterally announced a plan to depose Mehemet Ali altogether. Palmerston liked the idea, caring little that the French would see it as inflammatory.

Meanwhile, Uncle Leopold kept nagging his niece to be more considerate to the French. He deplored the way 'Palmerston *likes to put his foot on their necks*,' and warned the consequence could be war between Britain and France. Now in the late stages of pregnancy, the harassed Victoria lost her temper. She wrote to Melbourne, 'The Queen is really quite sick of these Eastern affairs, & this perpetual writing about them, backwards & forwards; *she* won't write any more for some time to come.' Melbourne's reply was uncharacteristically grave. He agreed 'these affairs are very troublesome and vexatious, but they are unfortunately, more than troublesome, they are pregnant with danger'.[108]

On 6 October, after being pressed by both the Queen and Melbourne, Palmerston did write to the British ambassador in Paris, Lord Granville, instructing him to make the overtures to France that the Cabinet had authorised. Underhand, he enclosed a private letter for Granville, making clear he did not want the approach to be successful. Fortunately, the French ambassador to Britain broke the impasse by conveying his government's relief that the British were not irrevocably committed to deposing Mehemet Ali, whereupon the Cabinet insisted Palmerston assured the French the sultan would be pressed to show leniency to his unruly vassal. Heartened by this decision, Victoria wrote on 10 October, 'Lord Melbourne's letter has greatly quieted & relieved the Prince & Queen & she trusts all will do well today.'[109]

Still hoping to frustrate the will of queen and Cabinet, Palmerston stalled. Realising that he had made no effort to communicate with the French, an incredulous Victoria wrote to Melbourne on 12 October, 'Palmerston's delaying *now* would be unpardonable, for if we didn't mark France's proposition *now* war would come; & I think Mehemet Ali ought to keep Egypt; even Palmerston wrote that to us; & the Queen took the opportunity in her letter to Palmerston this afternoon to press him very strongly to be very amiable ... Palmerston really can never delay *now*; it would be too bad.'[110]

Coincidentally both Palmerston and Russell were coming to stay at Windsor that day, so the Queen was able to appeal to them personally. Having 'preached amity to France' on Palmerston's arrival, Victoria had separate talks with the two men on 14 October. The foreign secretary listened reluctantly, but the Queen was pleased that 'I made Palmerston admit various things, though unwillingly.' That evening Palmerston finally told French ambassador Guizot of the decision reached by the Cabinet, and the following day the foreign secretary promised his sovereign he would send a friendly despatch to Paris. Victoria reported that Palmerston had been 'really very obstinate' about this but had ultimately agreed.[111]

On 16 October Palmerston had belatedly instructed the British ambassador at Constantinople to tell the Turks that Mehemet Ali must not be evicted from Egypt. The Queen was justifiably proud of what she had achieved. Two days later she wrote to King Leopold, 'Dearest Uncle, I have worked hard this last week to bring about something conciliatory, and I hope and trust I have succeeded.' She was even able to joke, 'I think our child ought to have besides its other names those of *Turco-Egypto* as we think of nothing else.'[112]

The crisis went on for a few days longer, but on 29 October Louis Philippe dismissed his hawkish foreign minister. Less than a fortnight later, the 'brilliant news' arrived that Mehemet Ali had been forced to evacuate Syria. On 25 November a settlement was signed, allowing him to retain Egypt if he abided by certain conditions. The Queen wrote to Leopold, 'the *denouement* of the Oriental affair is most fortunate, is it not?'[113]

During the crisis Palmerston's standing in the country had been enhanced by his belligerent stance, but he had damaged himself in the eyes of Victoria and Albert. Victoria thought it 'absurd' that he had maintained throughout that there was little danger France would dare fight Britain and reminded him 'how very warlike the French are'. She stressed she now felt it '*highly* and *exceedingly* important' to conciliate them in some way and was annoyed by Palmerston's evident satisfaction at having humiliated Louis Philippe. This gave King Leopold opportunity to make trouble. In November Victoria was shocked to hear that Palmerston had sent her uncle a letter 'I did not at all like the tone of', which would have made her 'excessively angry' had it been directed to her. To Albert, Leopold described Palmerston as '*rex* and autocrat … far *too irritable and violent*'. While Palmerston's brother-in-law was wrong to fear that King Leopold would prevail on Victoria to dismiss the foreign secretary, she certainly no longer trusted him as before.[114]

On 21 November 1840 the Queen gave birth to a daughter, named Victoria after her, but known to her family as Vicky. The event resulted in a further 'important advance in the Prince's position'. While his wife recuperated, Albert deputised for her. Three days after the birth Albert wrote to his brother: 'You can imagine that I have my hands very full, as I also look after V's political affairs.' He 'received and made notes of all the ministerial business', demonstrating to his wife 'his capacity for business & power to assist in … explanations'. For three weeks after the birth Victoria did not write to Melbourne at all, and when she resumed the correspondence on 14 December it was to request that Albert be given his own keys to the official boxes. As a result, Albert became 'in fact, though not by name, her Majesty's private secretary'.[115]

The change went down very badly with Victoria's former governess, the German Baroness Lehzen, who saw herself as the Queen's closest confidante. Resenting the prince's growing influence, 'she meddled and made mischief'. For some time, Albert had been irked by the baroness's possessiveness, and now he resolved on confrontation. At his request Baron Stockmar informed Melbourne that if the Queen could not see her chief ministers in person, they should communicate with her via Albert, rather than – as in the past – through Lehzen. Stockmar wanted to know whether Melbourne would take the prince's side in the event of 'open rupture' between the baroness and Albert. Melbourne replied that he would align himself with Lehzen, a stance that meant the prince now had less reason to wish for the prime minister's continuance in office.[116]

Albert had undeniably made great strides, and the fact that Victoria was very soon pregnant again boded well for his chances of further extending his influence. In April 1841 he wrote to his father, 'All I can say about my political position is, that I ... speak quite openly with the ministers on all subjects ... and ... endeavour quietly to be of as much use to Victoria in her position as I can.'[117]

If Albert did not feel beholden to the Whigs, Victoria was still their ardent partisan, and 'dreaded the idea of any change, dreadfully'.[118] Despite being weaker than ever, in the spring of 1841 the ministry planned to present an ambitious budget, including controversial changes to the sugar duties. Lord John Russell was also pressing Melbourne to amend the Corn Laws. At the end of the Napoleonic wars, the government had sought to protect British farmers by imposing duties on corn imported from abroad, and in recent years there had been growing demands for these to be reduced or even removed. At a time of rising population, restricting the supply of corn was morally questionable, and manufacturers argued it was unfair that agriculture in Britain was protected, while they had no such privileges. In March 1839 a national pressure group, the Anti-Corn Law League, had been founded to agitate for change, but they did not lack opponents.

Being strongly associated with the agricultural interest, the Tories were the Corn Laws' most ardent defenders. The Whigs were more ambivalent, and Melbourne personally was never enthusiastic for reform. Nevertheless, he now proved willing to adopt Russell's suggestion that the current sliding scale of tariffs on corn should be replaced by a low fixed duty.

In early May the Tories challenged the government by putting forward an amendment to the sugar duties. The prospect that the Whigs might be defeated put Victoria 'in a sad state of fidget', but Albert at once asked Melbourne to start planning for this eventuality. On 4 May Melbourne discussed the position with George Anson, saying that, if the government lost the vote, he would favour resigning rather than dissolving Parliament and fighting an election. He added that he would tell the Queen 'she must carefully abstain from playing the same part' with Peel as in 1839, 'for that nothing but the forbearance of the Tories had enabled himself and his colleagues to support HM at that time'. It seemed Victoria was 'quite prepared' to be reasonable. Realising that the question of her ladies was likely to arise again, she appeared amenable when Albert suggested the matter should be negotiated in advance. On 6 May she wrote to Melbourne that while the prospect of losing him made 'her feel low & sad ... she will not give up *all* hope & hopes against hope'. She knew he would 'do *what* can be done to save the Queen from having to have recourse to those hated

Tories', and 'you will not desert me' unless there was no alternative. 'I will not ask for what cannot be,' she promised. '*All* I ask is, try if you *can* manage it, either by a dissolution or any other way' to stay in power, but he could rest assured that 'if it cannot be, I shall not shrink from doing what is right.'[119]

The debate on the sugar duties began on 7 May and lasted eleven days. While it was in progress George Anson had a meeting on 9 May with Sir Robert Peel to discuss the question of Victoria's ladies. Assuring Anson, 'I have the feelings of a gentleman,' Peel emphasised he had no wish to humiliate the Queen. He agreed that if the Duchess of Sutherland, the Marchioness of Normanby and the Duchess of Bedford (as Lady Tavistock had become on the death of her father-in-law) resigned, as of their own volition, he would not demand other changes.[120]

With the debate going far from well for the Whigs, the ministers had to make up their minds what they would do if defeated. Melbourne himself still favoured 'going out, rather than dissolving', explaining to Victoria that if the government lost the election, despite her known support, it would undermine her prestige. 'For the first time the Crown would have an opposition returned smack against it; and that would be an affront to which I am very unwilling to expose the Crown.' Victoria acknowledged, 'This is very true,' and at this stage she was inclined to agree that dissolution would be too risky. Desperate to ensure that his wife acted correctly, Albert told Melbourne he must be placed in full possession of the facts. Hitherto Albert had been excluded when Melbourne had meetings with Victoria, but on 15 May, and again the following day, the prince was permitted to hear their discussions.[121]

The Queen began to think differently on the issue of dissolution when Melbourne observed that if the Tories took office, they would doubtless wish to hold an election themselves before long. 'That changed my opinion very much,' she told the prime minister on 17 May. 'You would like us to make the attempt?' Melbourne asked her. 'Almost,' she replied falteringly.[122]

On 18 May the government lost the vote on the sugar duties. Next day Victoria wrote to Melbourne, 'the Queen must say she is for Dissolution though she sees the reasons against it'. When the Cabinet met, Melbourne declared he thought they should resign, but a majority of his colleagues wanted dissolution. 'Almost in tears,' Melbourne said he would respect their wishes, adding: 'You may as well be told that the Queen is strongly for this step.'[123] Within days Peel proposed a motion of no confidence, and at 3 a.m. on 5 June this was carried by one vote.

Having hoped that the government would resign as soon as it lost the vote on the Sugar Bill, Prince Albert now sought to distance Victoria from an administration that might be thrown out by the electorate. On 13 June George Anson was deputed to tell Melbourne that Albert was 'very anxious ... that HM should not dissolve Parliament in person & could not feel that Lord M would recommend such a step'. Taken aback, Melbourne said that, on the contrary, he knew his party would be very dissatisfied if the Queen failed to show her support. When Anson suggested that, if 'clear of the shackles of office or party' he would act differently, Melbourne responded testily, 'I think you don't rightly understand. The Q has committed herself too decidedly to hold back now.' Later that day he wrote to Victoria saying the Cabinet regarded it 'of great importance that your Majesty should prorogue the Parliament in person ... It should excite observation if she should not do it now.'[124] On 22 June the Queen duly dissolved Parliament.

Not only had Albert lost that round, but another issue looked set to cause fresh problems, as 'the Bedchamber question revived in full force'. Pregnant and hormonal, a distressed Victoria told Albert she felt he and Melbourne had compromised her by committing her to give up three ladies. Albert soberly responded, 'You must be very cautious & well reflect,' whereupon the Queen said if she gave in, the Tories would gloat that 'she had been vanquished and lowered before the world'. She then 'burst out into tears which could not be stopped for some time', leaving the prince for 'two whole days much depressed'.[125]

Soon afterwards Albert was scandalised to find that, with Victoria's permission, Baroness Lehzen had given £15,000 from Her Majesty's Privy Purse to aid the Whig election campaign. When challenged, Melbourne brushed this aside. As the election results came in, it became clear that all Victoria's attempts to shore up the ministry had been fruitless – for, in what *The Times* described as a 'triumph over the influence of the Court', the Tories secured a Commons majority of over eighty. The Queen had to accept that once the new Parliament met at the end of August, the Whig government would be overturned. On 3 August she wrote despondently to King Leopold that 'what is to come hangs over me like a baneful dream'. Melbourne hoped she would take it philosophically, although 'it is perhaps no consolation to be told that events of this nature are necessary and incidental to your Majesty's high station'.[126]

Melbourne was now trying to ensure the transition went smoothly. When Victoria talked of vetoing the appointment of the Tory peer Lord

Lyndhurst, he said, 'I wouldn't do that.' The Bedchamber question was resolved by all three ladies sending in their resignations as agreed. The prime minister told Anson that, provided Albert was patient, the prince's influence would doubtless increase once he himself was out of the way. However, caution was essential. It would be disastrous if Victoria ever suspected 'that the Prince was carrying on business with Peel without her cognisance'.[127]

The Queen did not open Parliament in person when it met on 24 August, using her pregnancy as an excuse. She was also suffering 'constant headaches … caused by annoyance and vexation'. On 28 August the government was defeated by a majority of ninety-one on an amendment to the speech from the throne. The following day Victoria wrote to Peel, 'with oh! what a pang' to invite him to form a government. She told Melbourne, 'the Queen … feels as if she had signed a sort of *death warrant*'. At their farewell audience on 30 August, 'he himself was much affected', but did his best to raise her spirits. 'You will find great support in the Prince,' he assured her. 'When you were going to be married, you said he was perfection, which I thought a little overrated, but I really do think now, that it is realised in some degree.' He followed this up with a letter confirming that he had 'formed the highest opinion of His Royal Highness's judgement, temper & discretion', and that he found 'great consolation & security' in the knowledge she could count on her husband's advice.[128]

Later that day Victoria had an audience with Peel for twenty minutes, and she saw him again on 1 September. 'His manner is certainly very cold and stilted,' she grumbled afterwards, besides taking against his 'very singular coat'. She at once passed on to Melbourne the list Sir Robert had submitted of proposed Cabinet appointments, commenting, 'It is not very well constituted in her opinion & the Queen thinks will not ensure popularity or durability, but that don't signify & the Queen feels she had better not object.' She dreaded her first Privy Council meeting with these men, lamenting to Melbourne, 'the thought that tomorrow a Tory set of ministers are to kiss hands, quite horrifies me'. While conceding, 'We must try to bear up against it,' within hours this was followed with another letter, letting Melbourne know, 'he is *so* missed'.[129]

Melbourne did try to help Peel establish himself on a better footing with Victoria. He gave advice about how to handle her, asking him to understand that 'the Queen is not conceited; she is aware there are many things she cannot understand, and she likes to have them explained to her elementarily, not at length and in detail, but shortly and clearly'. In other respects, he behaved less scrupulously. The fact that he emphasised in a letter to Victoria that the 'great secrecy which your Majesty has always observed respecting public affairs is more particularly necessary at the present moment' shows he knew their communications would not bear scrutiny.[130]

The trouble was that severing contact was almost as unbearable to Melbourne as it was to Victoria. In his resignation letter of 28 August, he avowed frankly that he felt 'deeply the pain of a separation from a service' that for the past four years had been 'no less his pleasure than his pride'. However much he tried to put on a brave face, insisting to Victoria 'the only person I'm sorry for is you, Ma'am', it was not very convincing. John Campbell, the outgoing Attorney General, knew 'in truth he will feel it more than any of us. He not only loses the occupation and excitement of his office, but his whole existence is changed. With him, it is as if a man were to have his wife and children … torn from him when he falls from power.' It was this that made it particularly difficult for him to act entirely correctly. While Albert had specified that in future he wished Melbourne to confine advice to Victoria to 'private … and family concerns', the former prime minister could not resist trespassing upon politics.[131]

The Queen assured King Leopold that Melbourne 'gives really the fairest and most impartial advice possible', but it inevitably reflected his prejudices. While he praised some of Peel's appointments, Melbourne questioned Sir Charles Bagot's fitness to be Governor General of Canada. The Queen had already approved it, but she at once wrote to Peel querying whether Sir Charles had the 'qualities … for this arduous and difficult position'. Melbourne also regretted Lord Haddington being put in charge of the Admiralty, and predicted Lord Lincoln would perform badly as the Commissioner of Woods and Forests, being 'unused to business and as it is reported of a bad … temper'.[132]

No less reprehensibly, Melbourne urged her to vet Peel's diplomatic appointments, as some of the men at Sir Robert's disposal were 'of moderate abilities and … doubtful integrity'. Thanking Melbourne for his 'very sound & excellent advice' on 11 September, Victoria begged him not to accuse her 'of indifference & negligence if some appointments are made which may not be the best'. Guiltily aware that he had already overstepped proper bounds, Melbourne warned her not to veto Peel's selections unless they were 'manifestly and glaringly bad'. Victoria still saw little need for restraint, asking him, quite improperly, to keep her informed of opposition strategy. 'She will be anxious to hear how J. Russell will press the government upon the Corn Laws,' she wrote on 16 September.[133]

By 21 September Baron Stockmar was worried enough to inform George Anson he was 'very apprehensive that evil will spring' out of Melbourne's correspondence with Victoria, as 'no government could stand such undermining influence'. Anson tried to defend his former boss, claiming Peel himself would not mind, but Stockmar suggested Anson 'ask Ld Melbourne whether he would object to it' in Peel's place.[134] The baron became still more perturbed when the Queen invited Melbourne to stay at Windsor for a few days. In early October Stockmar drew up a memorandum for Anson to present to Melbourne, reminding him that Peel was still unsure of his position vis-à-vis the Queen. In the circumstances, Melbourne's 'secret interchange' with Victoria constituted 'an *essential injustice* to Sir Robert's personal situation … fraught with imminent danger'.

Melbourne read this document 'with an occasional change of countenance and compression of lips', before remarking, 'This is a most decided opinion indeed.' Anson pointed out that Melbourne had recently attacked the government in the House of Lords, and hence was hardly an inactive leader of the opposition. Melbourne thereupon leapt up from the sofa 'and went up and down the room in a violent frenzy, exclaiming "God eternally damn it … Flesh and blood cannot stand this."' He said he did not think it in the Queen's interest that he gave up his position, but when Anson asked whether he was at all worried about the situation, he answered, after a long pause, '*I certainly cannot think it right.*' He tried to defend himself by alleging that he had consistently advised Victoria to 'adhere to her ministers' until the government could be brought down. When Anson relayed this to Stockmar, the baron observed this proved Melbourne was using his connection with the Queen to judge exactly when the time would be right 'to plunge in all security, the dagger into [Peel's] back'.[135]

On 25 October Stockmar visited Melbourne in person to accuse him of having instilled in the Queen 'a most pernicious bias', by pursuing an 'underhand commerce'. At this, 'Ld Melbourne became visibly nervous, perplexed and distressed.' Stockmar suggested that as soon as the Queen had her baby, Melbourne should tell her that he had only maintained contact out of solicitude for her delicate state of health, and that henceforth their confidential communications must cease. There seemed little reason to think this advice would be heeded. The very next day

Melbourne went to stay at Windsor as planned and was plainly overjoyed to be back at the Queen's side. All that worried him, when he wrote to thank her, was the fear that his high spirits had betrayed him 'into talking too much, or too heedlessly, which he is conscious that they sometimes do'.[136]

On 9 November Victoria was delivered of a baby boy, but Melbourne did not seize the opportunity to break off their correspondence. Accordingly, Stockmar wrote to protest again on 23 November. He warned that a recent conversation he had had with Peel suggested a degree of unease on the prime minister's part. Peel had said he would unfailingly indulge Victoria 'in all her wishes relating to matters of a private nature', but the 'moment I was to learn that the Queen takes advice upon public matters in another place, I shall throw up ... I would not remain an hour.' Stockmar feared the Queen's character would never recover if Peel resigned on such grounds, but Melbourne refused to see the logic.[137]

Almost imperceptibly, the situation was evolving for the better. By late December, Anson was reporting, 'the Melbourne correspondence still is carried on, but I think not in its pristine vigour by any means. He has taken no notice of the Baron's remonstrance to him,' but this was ceasing to matter. The Queen was now so absorbed by motherhood and wifely duties that politics was taking up less of her attention, and her dislike of her current ministers was slowly subsiding.[138]

Gradually the former intimacy between Victoria and Lord Melbourne faded, and his letters display a poignant consciousness that she was receding from him. In April 1842 he wistfully described to the Queen how he had looked into the windows of Buckingham Palace as he drove past to dine with his sister. 'He could see clearly into your Majesty's room, so as to be able to distinguish the pictures, tables etc, the candles being lighted and the curtains not drawn. Your Majesty was just setting off for the opera.' Apologies from Victoria for not having written more frequently began to feature in her letters, and in December 1842 Melbourne – whose health had recently undergone a serious setback – even admitted 'he had begun to be a little annoyed at being such a very long time without hearing from your Majesty'. By that time his letters dealt mainly with trivial matters, not just because he had come to realise that politics were best avoided, but also because the Queen had become such an admirer of Peel that anything resembling criticism of him was unwelcome. The correspondence still meant everything to Melbourne. He wrote in January 1843, 'every letter that he receives from your

Majesty brings back to his mind the recollection of times which, though they were clouded with much care and anxiety, were still to Lord Melbourne a period of much happiness and satisfaction'.[139]

In November 1842 Melbourne had suffered a stroke. For a time the limbs on his right side were affected, and his mind lost some of its sharpness. He had always had a streak of sentimentality, but now he could be positively lachrymose, and poor sleep and lack of appetite robbed him of his former zest for life. The following January he took the Queen's advice not to exhaust himself by coming up to London for the start of the parliamentary session, although he begged her never to 'think for a moment that you can tire him by questions, or that it can be to him anything but a great pleasure to answer them'.[140]

In June 1843 he dined at Buckingham Palace for the first time since his stroke. The Queen had been 'dreading beforehand the thought of finding him much altered', and while he was less changed than she had feared, it saddened her that he no longer had his former 'bright, joyous, youthful look & liveliness'. She noted, 'Once only, he laughed in his old way, but more weakly,' sorry to see his face had developed 'rather a vacant look'. Some months later he was delighted to be invited when Victoria and Albert stayed at Chatsworth, though attempting 'to talk in his old strain' wore him out. In late December, he appeared better when he spent a few nights at Windsor. To the Queen's pleasure, 'the first evening he was a good deal excited and talked and laughed as of old', and while sometimes he subsequently 'lapsed into broody silence', he was still 'really *quite* himself, and there was hardly any strangeness at all'. Melbourne himself could not but be conscious of his own decline. In July 1844 he wrote that he was glad the Queen thought he seemed well when he dined last at the palace, but that his health was nothing like it was when he was her prime minister. 'He tries not to repine, because he thinks it wrong, but finds it difficult,' he concluded mournfully.[141]

Victoria was pleased he was in relatively good spirits when he next came to Windsor, 'but it always makes me sad to see him'. Within six weeks Melbourne was feeling forgotten, writing querulously, 'he had begun to think your Majesty's silence rather long', though he accepted she was busy. Thanking her for the etchings she had sent him of her dogs, he said they reminded him 'of the happiest period of his life, for … he continually misses and regrets the time when he had daily confidential communication with your Majesty'. For the Queen, however, their encounters could be 'most painful'. He was 'very nervous &

agitated' when he stayed at Windsor over New Year 1845, and not entirely coherent. 'He said some rather curious things to me which I could not quite understand,' she recorded, '& it quite distressed me to see him ... so different to what he was in former times.' Unwilling to subject herself to the ordeal too often, she made excuses for avoiding him, telling him in July that she was sorry not to have seen him before she went on holiday, 'but something or other always prevented it'.[142]

Even while relegated to the side-lines, Melbourne could not quite grasp that he had become a political irrelevance. One evening in February 1844 the company at Lord Palmerston's was embarrassed when the former premier made 'a rather melancholy spectacle' of himself. Alluding to the fact that Peel's government was at slight risk of losing a vote in the House of Commons, Melbourne confided that he had been 'kept awake half the night thinking' what advice he would give the Queen if she sent for him. 'Everybody looked amazed' he could delude himself so. In December 1845 Peel did briefly resign, but it was Lord John Russell, rather than Melbourne, whom Victoria asked to form a government. She nevertheless sent Melbourne a tactful letter saying she had not applied to him because she was worried for his health, and later anxiously asked his sister whether his feelings had been hurt.[143]

Peel soon resumed office, but when he committed himself to repealing the Corn Laws, Melbourne was indignant. Since the Tories had pledged themselves in the past to retaining protection, he felt Peel could not honourably abandon it. Dining with the Queen at Buckingham Palace Melbourne burst out: 'Ma'am, it is a damned dishonest act.' Victoria merely laughed, but he continued with his tirade, leaving 'people not knowing how to look'. Afterwards she commented, 'He has become a little excitable, talking rather rashly, which makes one nervous.'[144]

Melbourne's last years were plagued by largely imaginary money worries that surfaced after his stroke. George Anson was shocked that when dining at Buckingham Palace in December 1843, 'he told the Queen that he was dreadfully poor!!' Four years later he turned down Victoria's offer of the Garter because he feared the expense of an investiture. He alleged that 'Lord Melbourne has for a long time found himself much straitened in his pecuniary circumstances ... so that he dreads ... he shall ... add another to the list of failures and bankruptcies of which there have lately been so many'. Victoria was concerned enough to loan him £10,000 at a low rate of interest, but shortly after receiving this 'great, substantial and timely benefit' he asked her to arrange a pension for him. She did approach Lord John Russell about it, but he said Melbourne was too well off to be considered, and Melbourne took the refusal gracefully.[145]

In late November 1848 Victoria informed King Leopold, 'Our poor old friend Melbourne died on the 24th. I sincerely regret him for he was truly attached to me, and though not a good or firm minister, he was a noble, kind-hearted generous being.' By then her earlier adoration for her first prime minister was nothing more than a distant memory. Even in 1842, when she had reread journal entries written during the Bedchamber crisis of 1839, she had been amazed at having invested so much emotion in him. She annotated the pages, 'I cannot forbear remarking what an artificial sort of happiness *mine* was *then*, and what a blessing it is I have now in my beloved Husband *real* and solid happiness, which no Politics, nor worldly reverses *can* change.' Talking with the prince in December 1842 about her former 'unbounded affection' for Melbourne, she said she 'hardly knew from what it arose', and did not demur when Albert suggested she had 'worked myself up to what really became at last quite foolish'. In later years she would fondly recall Melbourne's excellent qualities, but still condemned him as 'too much of a party man [who] made me a Party Queen'.[146]

2

Sir Robert Peel 1841–1846

The Queen would ultimately come to venerate Sir Robert Peel. In February 1844 Victoria enthused, 'The more I see of him, the more I am pleased & satisfied. He is a noble-minded, very fair, very liberal, straightforward & very able man.' That she thought this way, despite being initially so 'strongly prejudiced against him', provided, to her mind, 'the greatest proofs of his *real* worth & excellence'. When it looked like Peel's government might topple in the summer of 1844, she declared she would feel his loss even more deeply than she had Lord Melbourne's, having come to believe: 'The change of government in '41 was an advantage to the country.' Peel in fact survived as prime minister for another two years, but when he did resign in June 1846, the Queen was devastated at having to forego the services of this 'great and good man'. She paid him the tribute, 'We felt so safe with him,' regretting not just the downfall of an admirable politician, but that she and Albert would see much less of a man they considered a great friend. 'I used formerly to fancy that Peel was so stiff and cold,' she acknowledged, '– but oh! no, not when I got to know him well.'[1]

The transformation of her feelings for Peel, whom she had once dubbed a 'nasty wretch', could not have been more complete. It had not, however, been an instantaneous process.

When Peel took office at the end of August 1841, the contrast between him and the supremely personable Melbourne was painfully apparent. Sir Robert was immensely wealthy but came from middle-class stock. His grandfather and father had owned cotton mills in Lancashire and Staffordshire that employed 15,000 workers. Peel's income from investments and land was estimated at an enormous £40,000 a year. Born in 1788, Peel had had a distinguished career since entering Parliament at the age of twenty-one, acting as Chief Secretary for Ireland before becoming Lord Liverpool's home secretary. In 1829, while again serving as home secretary under the Duke of Wellington, he had set up a police force for London, the first of its kind in the country. That same year, he had been prevailed upon not to resign when Wellington brought in a bill for Catholic emancipation, despite Peel having long held out against such a measure. Peel piloted the bill through the Commons, leading to accusations of betrayal from the Tory diehards who furiously opposed its passage. When Peel indicated a readiness to embrace constructive change because the Whigs' 1832 Reform Bill had permanently altered the political climate, this merely rendered him more suspect in the eyes of some Tory 'Ultras'.

Peel was somewhat lacking in emotional intelligence. For someone in the difficult position of being more liberal than many of the party he led, he was too apt to rely on reason to convert his critics. He liked to say, 'There is nothing like a fact,' but his belief that logic and statistics could override prejudice and entrenched opinions made him reluctant to devote time and effort to the careful handling of men. Disraeli commented, 'For so very clever a man he was deficient in the knowledge of human nature.' He was not at all clubbable, and shyness made this tall and ungainly figure seem haughty and aloof. The diarist Charles Greville noted: 'He is so cold, so reserved, and his ways are so little winning and attractive that he cannot attach people to him personally.'[2] Although the royal couple would come to see beyond these failings and to prize instead his intellect and integrity, a sizeable section of his own party never warmed to Peel.

Doubtless their objections owed much to snobbishness: the fact that Peel came of manufacturing stock, while his speech still betrayed traces of his Lancashire origins, did not commend him to those who would have preferred more patrician leadership. Early in their acquaintance Victoria observed that Peel spoke in a 'rather pompous, slow & formal' style, but Disraeli claimed that despite his meticulous enunciation, he sometimes dropped his aitches. Although Peel 'guarded his aspirates with immense care', Disraeli gleefully recalled: 'I have known him trip.'[3]

As far as Prince Albert was concerned, Peel's lack of breeding did not count against him; in fact, as an outsider who did not feel at home in aristocratic society, he felt in sympathy with Sir Robert on this account. In 1843 he told his private secretary he was sure the reason why Peel was 'far from popular with the Conservative Party' was that 'they could not get over his plebeian origin, and they could ill brook being dictated to by such a one'. He stressed that for his part, such considerations did not lessen his esteem in the slightest.[4]

The Queen's early dealings with Peel merely confirmed her intense antipathy. Before her first audience with him on 30 August 1841, she lamented to Melbourne, 'she never could be at ease with Peel, because his manner was so embarrassed, and that conveyed embarrassment also to her'. Victoria was by no means reassured when her new ministers came to kiss hands at a Privy Council meeting held on 3 September. Afterwards she confided to Melbourne, 'The Council was very disagreeable. The greater part of them looked so cross.' She felt relieved that she did not have to meet with Peel for the next few days 'wh is *much* pleasanter for me'.[5]

The first sign that her attitude might thaw came on 15 September. She reported to Melbourne she had been encouraged by 'two very satisfactory conversations with Peel & Aberdeen', at which both showed themselves anxious to accommodate her concerns over diplomatic appointments. The new foreign secretary, Lord Aberdeen, was in almost every respect a complete contrast to his buoyant and combative predecessor, Palmerston. Lugubrious and somewhat monkish in appearance, Aberdeen was prematurely aged by tragedy, having lost two wives and four daughters through illness. In 1813, while carrying out a diplomatic mission in his twenties, the sight of wounded men and corpses littering the battlefield at Leipzig had made a terrible impression upon him. Ever after, avoiding confrontation would be the hallmark of his foreign policy. Against her expectations, Victoria rather took to him, writing to Melbourne, 'The Queen was agreeably surprised to find Ld Aberdeen so pleasing.'[6]

At the end of September she invited Peel and his wife to stay at Windsor but felt uncertain about how the visit had gone. She asked Melbourne if he had heard whether the couple had been pleased by their reception – '*Not* that the Queen *cares* the least if they are or *not* but purely because she would like to know.' Afterwards Victoria told Anson she 'thought she really had' made an effort with Peel, but his 'awkward manner' remained impenetrable.[7]

Peel himself was unaware that the Queen felt so uncomfortable in his company, telling his colonial secretary Lord Stanley in November, 'We are going on exceedingly well in our relations with the Palace.' This assessment owed much to that 'ignorance of character' which Victoria had pronounced 'most striking and unaccountable'. Peel was on stronger ground in believing 'Prince Albert is altogether with us.' In late September, the prince was delighted when Sir Robert invited him to head the commission supervising the decoration of the Houses of Parliament, which had had to be rebuilt having burnt down in 1834. Somewhat diffidently, Victoria sought Melbourne's endorsement, 'considering its being perfectly unconnected with politics'.[8]

Albert was still happier when Peel proved supportive over his feud with Baroness Lehzen. In October 1841 Anson had warned the prime minister that Lehzen remained 'a channel for intrigue & mischief' against the government and Albert himself. Peel at once said, 'what a misfortune it was that such an influence should be permitted to exist between man and wife', and wondered, 'Could no means be devised for removing her?'[9]

On 9 November 1841 the Queen gave birth to a Prince of Wales, christened Albert Edward, but known within the family as Bertie. The Queen had gone on working until very late in her pregnancy, but once she had had the baby she struggled to cope with severe post-natal 'lowness'. Albert now took over all royal business, dealing with despatch boxes officially intended for his wife. On 30 November Albert informed Peel that he could now recommence a limited correspondence with the Queen, but at her request asked, 'that in matters which require more explanation you would for the present still write to me or see me'.[10]

Baroness Lehzen was infuriated by these developments. She declared, 'when the Queen is sufficiently recovered she intends speaking seriously to HM upon the influence the P[rince] is acquiring on her mind'. Mr Anson noted disapprovingly, 'She asserts that while the Q[ueen] is in her sickroom the P[rince] is taking advantage of it & constantly sending for Sir R Peel & impudently exercising the Q's authority who by this means has no opportunity of previously consulting L[ord] M[elbourne] or others as to Sir R's policy.'[11] By overreaching herself in this way, the baroness only made Albert more determined to be rid of her. In January 1842 Victoria and Albert had a series of bloodcurdling rows over Lehzen's control of the royal nursery. Though Albert could not yet secure her dismissal, the baroness's days at court were numbered, and the prince knew that in a showdown he could count on the prime minister being his ally.

Far from wishing Albert to do less, for the present Victoria was content to delegate to him. On 26 December Anson commented, 'Her

Majesty interests herself less and less about politics,' being instead 'a good deal occupied with the little Princess Royal.' When she did direct her mind to government matters, Anson believed 'her dislike is less than it was to her present Ministers, though she would not be prepared to acknowledge it'. Sure enough, when Peel came to Windsor in late January and read to her the speech she was to deliver at the opening of Parliament, the Queen made the grudging private acknowledgment that 'considering it is [a] *Tory speech* [it] is judicious'.[12]

The forthcoming budget represented a major advance towards free trade. Highly controversially, Peel modified the Corn Laws by adjusting the sliding scale of tariffs that set duty on imported corn lower in years of dearth. Since many Tories had committed themselves during the 1841 election campaign to maintaining full agricultural protection, diehards saw this as a betrayal. The Duke of Buckingham resigned from the Cabinet, and the Tory Lord Malmesbury harrumphed that Peel had 'thrown over the landed interest, as my father always said he would'. Most Tories nevertheless – as the Whig Lord Clarendon acerbically remarked – were fully aware 'they can't do without Peel'.[13]

For free trade ideologues and members of the Anti-Corn Law League, Peel's measures did not go nearly far enough. The leading league activist and MP for Stockport, Richard Cobden, declared them 'a bitter insult to a suffering nation'.[14] Such was the anger that Peel's effigy was carried through the streets of Cobden's constituency before being publicly burned.

To make up for lost revenue arising from lower tariffs, Peel reintroduced the income tax, abolished at the end of the Napoleonic wars. In theory it was only a temporary measure, to be reconsidered after three years. Inevitably some people grumbled, but more were impressed by Peel's bold move and his evident mastery of finance.

On 16 March Peel informed Victoria he had discovered that Lord Brougham, formerly Lord Chancellor during the reign of William IV, was planning to move in Parliament that 'none, not the highest (meaning me) would be exempt from this new income tax'. To forestall Brougham, Peel asked that Victoria undertake to pay it of her own accord. If she agreed, he could announce it to the Commons that evening, 'so that it might appear as gracious act on my part, without any legislation about it. This of course I at once assented to.' Although the rate was only 3 per cent on incomes over £150, she privately thought it 'rather hard', particularly 'on my poor dear Albert who will have to pay £900'. Peel's declaration duly 'made a great sensation' and was very well received. Only Lord Melbourne was doubtful, telling Victoria that while her decision 'certainly will be very popular', he questioned the wisdom of 'giving up a principle of the Constitution which has hitherto exempted the Sovereign from all direct taxation'.[15]

Peel was touchingly upset by the assassination attempts on Victoria and Albert that took place during the summer of 1842. On 29 May Albert had noticed a 'little swarthy ill-looking rascal' aiming a pistol at him and Victoria as they rode down Constitution Hill in their carriage. As only one other member of the public had seen the same thing, it was decided that the best way of flushing out the would-be assassin was to see if he would make another attempt when they went on their usual drive the next day. This time John Francis actually fired his pistol, but missed the royal couple and was seized.

It was the second assassination attempt they had experienced, for on 10 June 1840 Edward Oxford had fired at them, also on Constitution Hill and equally unsuccessfully. On that occasion Victoria had behaved with exemplary calmness but she had been upset that when accused of treason Oxford had been declared not guilty by reason of insanity. 'The jury seems to have been very stupid,' she had commented at the time, while Albert too had been sure that Oxford was 'not mad'. Now Albert hoped that Francis's trial 'will be conducted with the greatest strictness', as 'he is not out of his mind but a thorough scamp'.[16]

On 17 June 1842 Francis was convicted of treason. His execution by hanging, drawing and quartering was set for 4 July, but the judges reviewed his case after becoming concerned it had not been proved beyond a doubt that Francis's pistol had been loaded. The matter was referred to the Cabinet, and on 1 July Peel informed the Queen that the sentence would be commuted to transportation for life. 'I of course am glad the poor wretch's life is spared,' Victoria declared, while feeling the 'law ought to be changed and more security afforded me'. Incredulous that a treason conviction was only possible if 'intent to kill!??! could be clearly … inferred', Albert feared 'the increase of democratical and republican notions … must render people more prone to crimes of that kind'.[17]

The very next day Albert's words proved prophetic when a 'hunch-backed wretch' named Bean tried to shoot the Queen as she drove down the Mall. As soon as the news reached Sir Robert Peel, he rushed back to London from Cambridge. Prince Albert was giving him an account of the incident when the Queen entered the room, whereupon Sir Robert burst into tears.[18] The royal couple inevitably found it striking that a man normally so in control of his feelings should display such raw emotion.

On 25 August Bean was sentenced to eighteen months hard labour for firing a pistol with the intent of terrifying and harassing the Queen. By that time ministers had rushed through a law providing that in future any person who discharged or attempted to discharge a firearm at the Queen would be held to have committed a high misdemeanour, rather than high treason, punishable by transportation for seven years. The aim was to discourage those motivated primarily by a 'morbid craving after notoriety'. When informed of the government's plans, Prince Albert had professed himself 'very glad', even if he questioned whether temporary transportation constituted a sufficient deterrent.[19]

In April 1842 Peel informed the Governor General of India, 'My relations with her Majesty are most satisfactory. The Queen has acted towards me not merely (as everyone who knew her Majesty's character must have anticipated) with perfect fidelity and honour, but with great kindness and consideration. There is … a scrupulous and most punctual discharge of every public duty, and an exact understanding of the relation of a constitutional sovereign to her adviser.' The Tories gave out that the Queen was now devoted to them, and though Lord Clarendon believed her merely indifferent,[20] it was indeed true that her earlier aversion had all but evaporated.

As her husband became more active politically, Victoria felt increasingly distressed at his not being allotted an official role, and in June 1842 talked with Peel about 'dear Albert's awkward & painful position'. Peel feared if he was created prince consort, some people would worry he 'might usurp the Queen's right', but Victoria brushed aside such concerns. She confided she thought Albert's position would be so 'humiliating to any man … that at times I almost felt it would have been fairer to him, for me not to have married him. But he was so good & kind & had loved me for myself.'[21]

At this point Peel decided the question was too ticklish to be tackled, but three years later the subject arose again, after an MP asked Peel to deny a rumour that Albert was to be created king consort. The intervention merely spurred Victoria onward. Having reflected in her diary, 'Oh! if I only could make him king,' she wrote to Peel reiterating that while she recognised it was problematic, some kind of action was required. As before, Peel believed the matter best left alone. When

Albert broached the subject himself Peel informed him: 'It is power and not titles which are esteemed here.' The public were 'inclined to attach ridicule to everything of the sort', and such a step would besides entail 'great constitutional difficulties'.[22]

In 1842, what Thomas Carlyle had referred to in a pamphlet as the 'Condition of England Question', was particularly pressing. In former years the Queen had been largely indifferent to such matters, but between them, Prince Albert and Sir Robert Peel awoke her social conscience.

Two years earlier a royal commission on child employment had been set up, and in May 1842 its report was published. With its illustrations depicting horrific scenes of children dragging heavy carts through mine tunnels like beasts of burden, it captured the public imagination. When the philanthropic Lord Ashley introduced a bill that June banning children under ten and women from working underground, the home secretary promised government support. Albert wrote to Ashley saying he had been 'horror-stricken' by the conditions he had highlighted and applauding him for undertaking an 'arduous but glorious task'. He declared warmly, 'I have no doubt that the whole country must be with you; at all events I can assure you that the Queen is.'[23] With government backing, the bill swiftly passed.

A series of poor harvests coupled with a trade depression was causing widespread distress throughout the country, and in May 1842 Peel informed the Queen 'the destitute condition of the labouring classes' afforded him the gravest concern. In hopes of alleviating these 'terrible privations and sufferings', he asked Victoria to spearhead a charitable appeal. He suggested £200 would be 'a suitable and liberal contribution' on her part; she actually donated £500 in the hope of relieving hardship 'which grieves the Queen deeply'.[24]

Victoria and Albert were sympathetic to those who patiently endured penury, but less understanding when the poor resorted to political agitation. The rise of Chartism particularly alarmed them. In May 1842 a vast crowd of perhaps 150,000 processed from Oxford Street to Westminster to mark the presentation to Parliament of the latest Chartist petition. Besides rehearsing their original six demands, the petition mentioned that the Queen was allocated a daily allowance of nearly £165 for her private use, in contrast to workers who subsisted on threepence and three farthings.[25] Three million people had allegedly put their name to it, and though some of the signatures were fraudulent, the petition's mass support was undeniable. Despite this, MPs voted by a large majority not to take it into consideration.

Having failed to secure a hearing in Parliament, in the summer of 1842 the Chartists embarked on violence and industrial action. Besides wanting increased pay and better working conditions, they demanded the fulfilment of their political programme. In several factories machinery was sabotaged, and some strikers armed themselves with pitchforks, bludgeons and flails. There was trouble in many northern towns, and in Staffordshire the colliers went on strike. Home Secretary Sir James Graham told the Queen on 15 August, 'The character of these riots has assumed more decidedly a political aspect. It is no longer a strike for higher wages, but the delegates ... avow that labour shall not be resumed until the people's Charter be granted.'[26]

Severe measures were taken to repress the outbreaks. At Halifax, where many Yorkshire Chartists had congregated, eighteen men were arrested. When a mob attempted to free the prisoners, troops rode down the crowd. In the melee one soldier died and the workers suffered two fatalities. At Preston three or four strikers were killed when, as Graham informed the Queen, troops 'in self defence were compelled to fire'; in Staffordshire 'a signal example was made by a handful of your Majesty's troops opposed to a riotous multitude which had burnt houses and spread devastation'. Similar scenes took place in Blackburn and Bolton, and in Newcastle-under-Lyme more lives were lost when a 'tumultuous mob' was charged by dragoons.[27]

Peel believed 'there must have been a very extensive system of organisation' among Chartist leaders to achieve such mayhem, assuring Victoria they would be taken into custody '*the very moment* that the law will warrant their apprehension'. There were numerous arrests for treasonable felonies and Sir James Graham reported that in Manchester there had been 'a very important seizure of papers ... which discloses a conspiracy, extensive in its ramifications'.[28] At their trials, several of the alleged ringleaders were sentenced to long terms of transportation, while others were sent to British prisons.

There were fears the trouble would spread to London. The Queen later recalled how at this time, 'some great and alarming assemblages of thousands of people took place' there. When Peel reported that Chartists 'had been haranguing the mob seditiously', Victoria wrote that she was sorry to hear this, while trusting 'the example made at Preston ... will have checked the rioters somewhat'. In London the authorities successfully contained events, and if the north remained

– in Victoria's words – 'sullen and sulky', unrest gradually died down elsewhere.[29]

Peel was delighted by the way Victoria had backed the government's fierce approach. He told the Duke of Wellington, 'I have been in constant personal communication with the Queen during the late events. Her whole conduct was excellent. She was very desirous that decisive measures should be adopted and very indignant with the timidity of certain magistrates.' Writing to Lord Melbourne on 17 August, the Queen had in fact shown some sympathy for those involved in the disturbances, distinguishing between the main body of protesters and their leaders. 'These riots are dreadful & very distressing; but the unfortunate misguided wretches are not to blame – but those *whose* agitation has been the cause of this outbreak ought to be punished – for it is *too* wicked to excite people to slaughter one another.'[30]

With the country so unruly, at one point it seemed that Victoria and Albert's scheduled trip to Scotland might have to be abandoned, but in the end it went ahead. The Queen and prince were to stay in the houses of several Scottish aristocrats on what was in theory a private and unofficial visit, but while there would pass through numerous Scottish towns. Peel feared that the chief inconvenience for the royal couple would come from over-enthusiastic receptions, but he could not rule out more hostile demonstrations. Joining Victoria and Albert soon after they arrived in Scotland on 1 September 1842, Sir Robert spent the next ten days worrying about security. In Edinburgh he considered the 'police arrangements ... very defective' for 'a mob ... composed of some 50 or 60 Chartists and low blackguards' was able to run alongside the Queen's carriage. There were further nasty moments in Stirling and Linlithgow, where 'clamour and excitement' made the Queen 'so nervous'. Passing through the streets in her open carriage, she had been 'at the mercy of a very well-disposed but very boisterous mob', some of whom kept trying to grab her hand. No harm was done, but when the royal couple's ship docked at Woolwich on 18 September, Peel was 'heartily relieved' that they were 'safe out of Scotland'.[31]

The following year Peel alerted Victoria and Albert that Osborne, an estate which might suit them on the Isle of Wight, was for sale. Sir Robert helped with complicated negotiations with its owner, although it was not until 1845 that the purchase was concluded. It was paid for out of economies Albert had achieved in the Queen's Privy Purse expenses. Work soon started on a palatial new house, ready to be lived in by September 1846. Ministers now had to accustom themselves to travelling regularly back and forth to the Isle of Wight, a much more time-consuming exercise than the half-hour rail journey from London to Windsor.

In September 1842 Albert finally prevailed upon Victoria to send Baroness Lehzen back to Germany. Albert's secretary George Anson declared 'everything much improved' by her departure. With Lehzen no longer there to prejudice Victoria against Peel, the 'social, domestic & political position of the Queen and the Prince' was, in Anson's view, greatly strengthened.[32]

By this time Victoria was starting to take pleasure in Peel's company. In October 1842 she noted in her journal that she had enjoyed what he had to say about her uncles, George IV and William IV, both of whom he had served. A year later, when dining at Windsor, Sir Robert 'talked most pleasantly & interestingly on all sorts of subjects'. By February 1845 she was almost as appreciative of Peel's conversational skills as she had been of Melbourne's, enthusing, 'Sir Robert was very entertaining, telling many anecdotes after dinner & talking of the French Revolution.'[33]

When Peel showed Victoria a draft of the speech that he had written for her to deliver at the opening of the 1843 parliamentary session, she had no hesitation in declaring it 'very good'. Like Albert, she now trusted Peel completely. In February 1843 she assured Uncle Leopold he was 'undoubtedly a great statesman, a man who thinks but little of party, and never of himself'.[34]

The Queen and Albert began to fear Sir Robert would make himself ill through overwork. In February 1843 Victoria said they were 'both struck by how unwell he looked. I am afraid he does not take near enough care of himself.' Peel himself was conscious that his health suffered through stress, describing his prime ministerial duties as 'above all human strength'. He told a colleague that having to write so many letters, read all foreign despatches, sit in the Commons for eight hours a day for 118 days a year, not to mention keeping up 'the constant communication with the Queen *and the Prince*', placed such strain on him he sometimes feared mental collapse.[35]

The Queen was terribly upset when on 20 January 1843 Peel's private secretary Edward Drummond was shot by Daniel McNaughton, who had mistaken him for Peel. When Drummond died five days later Victoria wrote to Peel, 'the Queen feels really that *no* one's life is safe any more'. To her horror, when McNaughton was tried for murder on

3 March, the judge ruled him mad, and thus 'free from moral responsibility'. Having demanded of Peel 'Is it possible?' she added: 'She feels terrified and thunderstruck'.[36]

Pregnant once again, the Queen now became fearful for Albert's safety. Just before the prince held a levée on her behalf, she wrote to Peel without her husband's knowledge, explaining, 'The Queen is *very* anxious that Sir Robert Peel should give orders to the police to be very watchful and on their guard … after all that has happened lately.' She confessed 'the Prince says it is quite useless fear on the Queen's part', but hoped 'Sir Robert will understand.' Peel replied that although he was sure there was 'not … the slightest grounds for apprehension', he would, without mentioning her concerns, 'make personal enquiries into the Police arrangements and see that every precaution possible shall be taken'.[37]

With the Queen already overwrought, she was shocked to hear of 'an amazing scene in the House' that took place in February 1843 during a Commons debate on a motion – subsequently thrown out – that a parliamentary committee should enquire into prevalent distress in the country. 'Twisting his black hair through his fingers,' the anti-Corn Law campaigner Richard Cobden made an impassioned speech, alleging that Peel was '*individually responsible*' for the sufferings of the poor because he would not repeal the Corn Laws.[38]

The Queen was soon facing a new worry. In 1839 the then Governor General of India, Lord Auckland, had sent an army to Afghanistan to depose its ruler, Dost Mohammed, whom he believed, on not very strong grounds, to be pro-Russian. At first everything had gone triumphantly: Dost Mohammed had been replaced by a British puppet, Shah Shuja, and in October 1839 Victoria and Lord Melbourne had exulted together about 'this brilliant affair'. However, by November 1841 the army's position in Kabul had become untenable and after the East India Company's resident envoy there was murdered, British officers negotiated terms of retreat with the Afghans. In theory the army were guaranteed safe passage, but as they retreated through the mountain passes in January 1842, almost all were annihilated. Their womenfolk were taken back to Kabul as prisoners. When accounts were published, Victoria was appalled by what she read: 'What a tale of heartrending horrors & sufferings … It makes one's blood run cold.'[39]

In late 1841 Lord Ellenborough had been chosen to succeed Auckland as Governor General. On arriving in India in February 1842

Ellenborough promptly sent an 'army of retribution' to Afghanistan. Though all thought of occupying the country was now abandoned, the army burnt the bazaar at Kabul before withdrawing. When news was relayed to England, Victoria was delighted to hear of 'glorious victories … on the very spot where our disasters had taken place, & all the prisoners, including all the Ladies, liberated'.[40]

When Parliament reassembled in early February 1843 there were allegations that the troops had been responsible for 'massacres and havoc'. Peel admitted to the Queen, 'there was no doubt excesses had been committed', and it looked likely that Ellenborough would be criticised in Parliament. The prime minister feared this would prompt the Governor General to resign, bringing down the government. In her pregnant state, the prospect especially filled Victoria with dread. 'Felt somewhat alarmed …' she wrote in her journal, '& I begged Albert to speak with [Peel] about the impossibility of there being *any* other Minister but him at present.' Much to her relief, an opposition attempt to censure Ellenborough was rebuffed.[41]

On 19 March 1843 George Anson noted, 'The Prince relieves the Queen of much of her arduous duty – both in seeing people for her, and by assisting & guiding her in the daily transaction of business. Some of the public have a notion that he is henpecked & has his own way in nothing, whereas nothing is farther removed from the truth.'[42]

The birth on 25 April of the royal couple's third child, Princess Alice, enhanced this process. Victoria suffered quite bad post-natal depression, and five weeks later was still 'very tired, & feeling stupidly weak'. On 5 May she had begun signing papers again, even if as yet Albert continued meeting Peel on his own, and then gave the Queen a summary of their discussions. At the end of the month, still only partially recovered, she started seeing Peel again, but Albert continued to immerse himself in business more enthusiastically than her.[43]

In a not altogether felicitous image, Baron Stockmar praised the prince's ability 'at a glance to seize the essential points of a question, like the vulture that pounces on his prey, and hurries off with it to his nest'. Albert now worked indefatigably, writing memoranda and sending letters to ministers covering a wide variety of topics. At every turn, Peel proved 'open towards him & such an admirable adviser upon all subjects'. Next, Albert systematically applied himself to training the Queen to suit his own requirements, 'reforming her mind & drawing out her powers'. By the autumn of 1843 Albert was congratulating himself on 'the great & gradual change which has taken place in the Queen's character ... Her views now were just & reasonable and she was most fair in her judgement of persons & things – & from the pains she had taken with herself, she now argued very clearly & soundly.'[44]

Quite often now, when the prime minister or members of the Cabinet came to the palace, they met first with Albert before being joined by the Queen. Sometimes, if the Queen was expecting a baby, she left everything to her husband. In May 1844, when Victoria was six months pregnant with Prince Alfred, she recorded: 'Albert had a long interview with Sir Robert Peel, during which time I pored over "*Ellen Middleton*" a powerfully written novel by Lady G[eorgiana] Fullerton.' Similarly, while 'Albert was much occupied with Sir Robert Peel' in October 1845, Victoria – once again in the early stages of pregnancy – 'wrote & played'.[45]

In December 1845 Lord John Russell was struck by the change that had taken place since Melbourne's time. Whereas 'formerly the Queen received her ministers alone; with her alone they communicated ... now the Queen and Prince were together ... and both of them always said "*We* ... think or wish to do so and so."' As far as the diarist Charles Greville was concerned, Albert was 'King to all intents and purposes'. Greville declared: 'As he likes and she dislikes business, it is obvious that while she has the title, he is really discharging the functions of the Sovereign.'[46]

By the summer of 1843 the government's hold on royal favour was such that Greville could pronounce: 'The Court is entirely on their side.' Peel now prided himself on his skill at handling the Queen and prince. When some Cabinet members expressed concern about the couple's plans to travel abroad, the prime minister informed his colleagues, 'it does not do to thwart them. I know how to manage them – the way is to ... show a willingness to meet their desires – then as difficulties appear, they will grow cool.'[47]

Victoria had become such a supporter of Peel that she was annoyed if he faced difficulties in Parliament. In August 1843 what she regarded as 'a very good measure' was obstructed by a group of radical MPs adopting filibustering tactics. Victoria considered this 'really indecent conduct ... How is business to go on at all if such vexatious opposition prevails?'[48]

Far from sharing fears expressed by one MP that troops had used excessive force the previous year to quell disturbances, Victoria was clear any fresh unrest within her kingdom must be dealt with equally firmly. That summer had seen some alarming outbreaks in Wales, prompting her to write to the home secretary. Having declared that she trusted 'measures of the greatest severity will be taken, as well to suppress the revolutionary spirit as to bring the culprits to immediate trial and punishment', the Queen enthusiastically approved the establishment of a special commission in Wales to mete out justice.[49]

In January 1843 George Anson remarked that the Queen could take satisfaction in the fact that 'the reins of administration are held by a government which can assert its authority & carry its measures'. Only a few months later, there came the first signs that Peel's control of his own party was not unassailable.

In the summer of 1843 a 'small party called Young England' first came to the Queen's attention.[50] It comprised a few Tory romantics, who yearned for a softer, more patrician form of Toryism that had never really existed. However unrealistic their political vision, Peel's Irish policy afforded them opportunities to skirmish with the government.

Ireland – 'that ever rankling thorn' – remained a permanent source of discord. Peel faced new challenges there from the rise of Daniel O'Connell, an inspirational nationalist leader who was campaigning for the overturning of the 1801 Act of Union. O'Connell became the focal point of a great mass movement, holding 'monster meetings' all over Ireland that were peaceable but still highly alarming for the authorities. At the end of May 1843 Victoria read Albert a newspaper account of a gathering attended by 60,000, 'at which O'Connell presided, wearing a wreath of laurels on his head!' While conceding that, 'hitherto, perfect order has invariably prevailed', she considered 'the language used by O'Connell and some of the Roman Catholic priests is perfectly atrocious, urging the people to get free – telling them they were in chains & using altogether most inflammable language'.[51]

Added to these new concerns, Ireland's perennial lawlessness remained as problematic for the British as ever. In late 1842 Victoria and Albert talked with Peel of some 'bad murders' that had recently taken place there, one of which was of a harsh Catholic landlord. To try and reduce crime, the government introduced an Irish Arms Bill, regulating the possession of lethal weapons. The passage of the bill proved turbulent. After the second reading debate in June 1843 the Queen commented, 'I must say that the Whigs behave very badly & show a want of right patriotic feeling in not rallying round the Government at such a critical moment.' Still worse, to her mind, was the fact that 'the

Tories too behave very ill by Peel & are dissatisfied with him. Oh! For a little true disinterested patriotism.'[52]

Sitting next to her at dinner a month later Peel complained that the House of Commons was becoming quite unmanageable. The Irish Arms Bill was still 'not near through', and in a debate on the state of Ireland several Tories had voted against the government, though it still won a convincing majority. During the Arms Bill's third reading debate on 9 August, one of the leaders of 'Young England', Benjamin Disraeli, declared that Ireland was currently 'governed in a manner which conduces only to the injury of both countries'. The solution lay in 'really penetrating into the mystery of this great misgovernment', a vague assertion Peel mocked when he rose to reply.[53] The prime minister could hardly have imagined that this wayward backbencher would yet prove his nemesis by showing an infinitely greater mastery of the art of sarcasm.

It was understandable that the prime minister failed to take the threat seriously. Born in London in 1804, Benjamin Disraeli was the son of a Jewish man of letters of private means. When he was twelve his family converted to Anglicanism, after his father fell out with his local synagogue. This would allow Benjamin to be eligible to take his seat if ever elected to Parliament, from which Jews were excluded due to the requirement that all MPs took an oath swearing allegiance 'on the word of a Christian gentleman'. Unlike his brothers, who were educated at Winchester, Benjamin was not sent to any of the major public schools, nor did he attend university. Largely self-taught, he read literature voraciously, travelled widely, and assiduously cultivated an air of what was known then as 'exoticism'. It seems likely that while abroad he had some homosexual experiences.

Aged only twenty-one Disraeli published *Vivian Grey*, an example of the 'silver fork' genre of fiction that purported to afford readers glimpses of life in high society. Disraeli had not moved much in such circles and his novel was ridiculed by some for its 'ludicrous affectation of good breeding'. His father was puzzled by another of his son's works, entitled *The Young Duke*: plaintively he asked, 'What does Ben know of Dukes?'[54]

Disraeli's novels sold well but sums such as £700 earned from *Vivian Grey* were not enough to extricate him from debts incurred through speculation in South American mining shares and other risky ventures. His indebtedness worsened as he pursued the life of a man-about-town, having affairs with at least two married women. He spent extravagantly and dressed flamboyantly, sporting green velvet trousers and canary-coloured waistcoats that complemented his luxuriant black ringlets. It was only later that he adopted the more sombre style of dress that enhanced his gravitas.

Despite his ostensible frivolity, Disraeli nurtured serious political ambitions. In an 1832 by-election he unsuccessfully stood in the 'high radical interest' in High Wycombe. Over the next three years he made as many attempts to enter Parliament, only to face rejection at the polls. During campaigns he was consistently exposed to raucous anti-Semitism – being heckled at hustings with cries of 'Shylock!' – but such taunts never prevented him taking a defiant pride in his Jewish heritage. He was adopted as a Conservative candidate in April 1835, but it was not until 1837 that his persistence was rewarded when he was elected one of two Tory members for Maidstone.

Disraeli's precarious financial position at times threatened to overwhelm him. Having accepted an invitation to dine with Peel and other leading Tories in July 1836, he was fearful of being arrested for debt outside the Carlton Club. As he desperately juggled the demands of his creditors, Disraeli had frequently to reschedule his debts at exorbitant rates of interest.

The situation somewhat improved when in August 1839 he married Mary Anne Lewis, the widow of Wyndham Lewis (who in 1837 had been elected alongside Disraeli at Maidstone). Lewis bequeathed his widow an annuity of £5,000 and a London house for her lifetime at Grosvenor Gate, off Park Lane. She was twelve years older than Disraeli, and not such an heiress as could solve all his financial problems, but the marriage enabled him to stave off bankruptcy. In 1841 things were still so bad that when it seemed he might be turned out of his parliamentary seat, Disraeli's principal fear was losing his immunity from arrest. Even after Mary Anne paid off £18,000 of his debts in 1842, the shadow of the debtors' prison continued to hang over him.

When Peel became prime minister in 1841, Disraeli wrote to Sir Robert asking for a job, but this yielded nothing. 'Unprincipled and disappointed' (in the words of Peel's home secretary) he had to make his mark in other ways: within two years, as Peel bitterly remarked, 'he became independent and a patriot'. His new role afforded fine opportunities for the exercise of his elastic talents. The man dismissed by the Whig Duke of Argyll as a 'young and fantastic adventurer' would prove a fearsome adversary.[55]

* * *

When Parliament was prorogued on 24 August 1843 it was hard to foretell that difficulties lay in store. The ministry had obtained the legislation it wanted, and Charles Greville believed that, while not popular, even with its own side, the government was not unstable. Above all, ministers were secure in royal favour, with the Queen making no secret of her liking, and her husband acknowledged as 'their strenuous and avowed friend'. In November 1843 Victoria told Foreign Secretary Lord Aberdeen, 'She knew that the Whigs talked confidently of coming into office soon; but that she hoped there was no danger of it, and that it would be a very long time before they did.' At the end of that month the couple went to stay with the prime minister for a few days at his country house, Drayton, in Staffordshire. Victoria much appreciated the comforts on offer, and Albert was pleased their visit had 'made the Premier very happy and is calculated to strengthen his position'.[56]

While staying at Drayton, Albert paid an official visit to Birmingham. Peel had advised against it, as not only was the mayor a Chartist, but 'all the town Council participate in the same violent & dangerous opinions'. Home Secretary Sir James Graham had likewise 'taken a timid view of it', but Albert refused to cancel. 'He thought it right to see one of the greatest towns in the Queen's dominions,' as well as 'manufacturies … which he ought not to be ignorant of'.[57]

The visit duly went ahead, and Albert described it as 'in short … one unbroken triumph'. George Anson, who accompanied his employer, reported: 'The streets were literally jammed but nothing could exceed the good humour and good feeling … which pervaded the whole multitude.' The mayor was ready to 'vouch for the devoted loyalty of the whole Chartist body', insisting, 'the Queen has not more loyal subjects in her dominions'. Victoria proudly informed Uncle Leopold, 'My beloved Angel … has had *the greatest* success.' Birmingham factory owners had been agreeably surprised when Albert spoke to them '*in their own language*', and the prince had made an equally favourable impression on 'poor people' he encountered, who 'have only been accustomed to hear demagogues and Chartists'.[58]

At court a new moral climate prevailed. As Albert's rigid standards were enforced, people deemed of suspect character had been purged from the Royal Household. Despite Lord Melbourne's glum prediction that, 'that damned morality … would be the destruction of everything', Albert believed it crucial to establishing the monarchy on a firmer foundation.[59]

The Queen too was sure 'our happy domestic life' enhanced royal standing, 'which I all owe to my beloved Albert'. She did not doubt: 'He is so beloved & respected … by the bulk of the nation' that only 'a few fashionables of doubtful character … would prefer Albert leading a … disreputable life to being a devoted & exemplary husband, pure & moral'.[60] Whereas in Melbourne's day she had enjoyed hearing about racy goings-on in high-born circles, she was now content to follow Albert's example and distance herself from a dissolute aristocracy.

In Albert's view, the 'cheering strides' the monarchy had made since their marriage owed everything to having secured 'the *moral dignity* of the Court'. As he explained to Stockmar: 'To my mind, the exaltation of royalty is possible only through the personal character of the Sovereign. When a person enjoys complete confidence we desire for him more power and influence in the conduct of affairs.' Sir Robert Peel concurred that the moral reputation of the court was vital, telling Albert in March 1845 that the fact that, 'all in all, monarchy never stood so well … despite the encroachments of democracy' was greatly due to 'the private character of the family &c'.[61]

Together the Queen and prince actively concerned themselves in foreign and colonial affairs. In January 1844 Victoria wrote to her foreign secretary, 'The Queen, taking a deep interest in all these matters … begs Lord Aberdeen to keep her always well-informed of what is on the *tapis* in his Department.' She reminded him that despatches for diplomats stationed abroad must first be submitted to her for approval. Reading these documents took up a great deal of her and the prince's time. Even when setting off on a yachting holiday in August 1843, they read the contents of three red boxes on the train ride from Farnborough to Southampton.[62]

Victoria and Albert assiduously cultivated personal relations with foreign sovereigns. Formerly she had been nervous of such contacts but now, with Albert's encouragement, she became acquainted with several monarchs. The King of Prussia came to England in January 1842, having accepted an invitation to be Bertie's godfather. Two years later the autocratic Russian tsar, Nicholas I, arrived for a visit. Initially the Queen had been 'extremely against' his coming, dreading 'the inconvenience and bustle', and certainly the exhausting round of military reviews, opera performances, Ascot races and dinners in the tsar's honour proved somewhat of a trial. Yet Victoria agreed that it was valuable to develop 'feelings of friendship & interest, which one cannot otherwise have for a complete stranger'. She approvingly quoted Albert's dictum that such visits had 'the great advantage that I not only *see* these great people but *know* them'.[63]

The Queen found Nicholas 'very easy to get on with', but still an unsettling presence. She considered, 'His mind is an uncivilised one', and it bothered her that 'He seldom smiles, and when he does the expression is *not* a happy one.' Despite the visit going so well, it was a relief when Nicholas left on 9 June, not least because whenever the Queen and prince had gone out in public with him, they had been tormented by security fears 'as there are so many bad Poles about'.[64]

By this time Victoria had formed a close personal relationship with the King of France. Her father had befriended Louis Philippe while the latter had been an exile in England during the Napoleonic wars, but he and Victoria were linked by numerous other family connections, not least King Leopold. The Belgian monarch had first tried to arrange for his father-in-law to visit Victoria in England in 1839, but at that point she had resisted the idea. Nevertheless, her uncle, abetted by Louis Philippe himself, continued to press for a meeting. As a 'King of the Barricades' who had come to the throne as a result of the 1830 July Revolution in France, Louis Philippe and his family were treated by most other European sovereigns 'as though they were lepers',[65] so a personal encounter between him and the Queen of United Kingdom of Great Britain and Ireland held many attractions.

In August 1843 Victoria and Albert 'formed a delightful project' to visit Louis Philippe and his wife and family at their holiday home, the Château d'Eu in Normandy. It was the first time Victoria had ever gone abroad, and she was enraptured by the experience. Arriving on 2 September, she and Albert passed five enchanting days with this 'dear admirable family', who made her feel 'so gay and happy'. Lord Aberdeen accompanied them, and the visit marked the start of what was soon called the 'Entente Cordiale'.[66]

A return visit to England by the French royal family was scheduled for the following year, but only weeks beforehand it looked as though England and France might go to war. Tensions had arisen after the French had dethroned Queen Pōmare of Tahiti and imprisoned and expelled the island's British consul. By August 1844 Lord Aberdeen was so alarmed at the Cabinet's 'extremely warlike attitude' that he asked Victoria and Albert to help maintain peace. Victoria told the foreign secretary: 'the idea of my country being at war with that of my dearest relations & friends would be a terrible grief to me', and Aberdeen assured her that, for him at least, war remained unthinkable. When he discussed the matter with his counterpart Guizot, the French foreign minister agreed, declaring it would be ludicrous 'to quarrel about a set of naked savages at the other end of the world'.[67]

Louis Philippe's visit accordingly took place as planned on 8 October and – thought Victoria – 'went off to perfection'. He delighted his hostess by not only wishing Tahiti 'at the bottom of the sea', but declaring, '*Le Prince Albert, c'est pour moi le roi.*' The following year there was a reunion when Victoria and Albert returned to Château d'Eu. While they were there, another troublesome question ('Which people in England are in a great fright about') was addressed, seemingly successfully. There had been concern that Louis Philippe was scheming to marry one of his sons to the teenage Queen of Spain or her even younger sister, with the ultimate aim of uniting the crowns of France and Spain. Preventing such a thing had been a cardinal tenet of British foreign policy for well over a century, so it was a relief when Louis Philippe verbally promised Victoria and Lord Aberdeen that only after Queen Isabella had assured the Spanish succession by marrying and producing children, would he allow his son, the Duke of Montpensier, to contract a union with her younger sister, the infanta. 'This is very satisfactory,' thought Victoria.[68]

Peel told Victoria in 1844 that visits to England by foreign heads of state were invaluable 'in removing prejudices, assuaging hostile feelings and improving the national relations between countries which influence for good or evil the destinies of the whole world'. Her own contribution was pivotal, and he praised her for playing her part so well that all peace lovers 'ought to be grateful to your Majesty personally'.[69]

In the summer of 1845, the Queen further widened her horizons by travelling to Belgium to see her uncle, before going with Albert to Coburg. For Victoria, seeing Albert's homeland for the first time, and visiting his birthplace, Schloss Rosenau, was an intensely emotional experience. She wrote in her journal, 'I have a feeling for our dear "little Germany" which I cannot describe. I felt it at the Rosenau so much. It is a something which touches me so, and which goes to my heart … I fear I almost like it too much.'[70] In years to come, several of her ministers would have agreed that her affection for Germany was indeed excessive.

After Louis Philippe's successful 1844 visit, Sir Robert Peel had rhapsodised to Victoria that it had showed 'the extent to which the interests and welfare of a great Empire may be promoted by the personal qualities of its ruler'.[71] There were times, however, when Peel felt uncomfortable about the direct interest Victoria took in the affairs of her most important overseas possession, India.

The government of India was structured in accordance with the India Act of 1784. By establishing a system of 'dual control', this sought to balance the rights and interests of the East India Company with those of the Crown. Originally nothing more than a trading company, since the mid-eighteenth century the East India Company had, through conquests and treaties, established itself as the ruler of more than half of India. The native princes who controlled the remainder were not truly autonomous as they were expected to conduct themselves in a manner acceptable to the occupying power. The East India Company had its own army and its three presidencies of Bengal, Madras and Calcutta were administered by company civil servants. However, since the reign of George III, the company had ceased to operate completely independently of the British government. Its Indian possessions, with a population of 90 million, were ruled by a governor general based in Calcutta, who in turn was responsible to the 'Board of Control' in London. This body was composed principally of East India Company directors, but at its head was a Cabinet minister who was answerable to Parliament.

When Lord Ellenborough was appointed Governor General of India in 1841, it did not take long for his 'tendency to precipitation and over-activity' to cause a rift between him and the Board of Control. However, having sought – 'most irregularly' in the view of a former president of the Board of Control – the Queen's permission to correspond with her directly, Ellenborough succeeded in enlisting her on his side. In March 1843 she was intrigued by a letter from him suggesting that the supreme government of India should be 'vested in her Majesty', rather than continuing the current power-sharing arrangement with the East India Company. The Queen wrote to Peel that the suggestion was 'worthy of observation', prompting Sir Robert to reply that Ellenborough had only adopted such ideas because of differences with the East India directors. Sir Robert despatched a sharp rebuke to Ellenborough, saying such 'direct communications … without the knowledge or intervention of the Sovereign's responsible advisers … are open to considerable objection in point of constitutional principle'.[72]

There was further trouble when Ellenborough decided to extend British territory in India. Speciously claiming that the Amirs of Sindh had failed to keep treaty obligations, Britain invaded and annexed the state in March 1843. When news of this arrived in London the following

August, the East India Company directors were appalled. At the end of August, a secret court of the directors condemned the Governor General's proceedings as 'unjust and impolitic'.

Once again, Ellenborough appealed directly to the Queen in a letter she felt 'completely and positively refutes the accusations brought against him'. Before sending her reply she did check with Peel whether he saw 'anything objectionable' in it, before adding: 'The Queen ... is desirous of elevating Lord Ellenborough's spirits, who seems to be much annoyed at his ... she *must* say unfair treatment.' As respectfully as possible Peel said he regretted she accepted Ellenborough arguments, and that if she wished to communicate in future with the Governor General, the correct procedure was to do it through ministers.[73]

Ellenborough was not in the least abashed by condemnation from home. He insisted to Victoria, 'the necessity of our position may often render necessary here measures wholly unsuited to European countries'. After the government at home uneasily acquiesced in his annexation of Sindh in December 1843, he went on nurturing grandiose ambitions. He not only wished to acquire further territory but, as he explained to the Queen, 'to give an Imperial character to our position'. Conferring the title of empress upon her would, he claimed, provide 'the keystone of the arch'.[74]

The Queen thought the idea had much to commend it. She was angered when, after Lord Ashley unsuccessfully moved in Parliament that the annexation of Sindh constituted a 'foul stain' on British honour, the East India directors decided in April 1844 to recall the Governor General. Upset at the treatment of a man 'who has done so much and so well', she informed Peel she considered the directors' decision 'a very ungrateful return' for Ellenborough's eminent services. She concluded, 'The Queen would not be sorry if these gentlemen knew that this is her opinion.'[75]

On 14 April Victoria and Albert had a discussion with Peel about 'the very bad system on which the whole of the Indian possessions are managed'. Prince Albert argued that the directors' recent actions 'must break the neck of the old system', and Peel, who accepted India was governed on an 'anomalous and absurd principle', did not deny they had been rash. He agreed it would probably 'end in the Crown having the management of the whole', which Victoria thought 'the only way'.[76]

A few days later the ministers formally protested to the East India directors about Ellenborough's recall. Privately, however, Peel sympathised with the directors. The prime minister had no wish to enlarge what he considered the already 'overgrown empire of India', and when he saw a letter full of wild expansionist fantasies that Ellenborough had written to his chosen successor, Lord Hardinge, he was shocked. Peel commented drily that if the Court of Directors read this, 'it would not dissatisfy them with their recent letter of recall'.[77]

Victoria's view of Ellenborough changed when she and Albert received him soon after he returned to England in October 1844. Following the audience she wrote, he 'did not impress either of us very favourably. He seems to think so very much of himself'.[78] However, she still found the possibility of becoming Empress of India beguiling.

In the view of the disgruntled Whigs, Prince Albert appeared almost as devoted to Peel's Conservatives as Victoria had been a Whig partisan in Melbourne's day. Albert would have disputed this. Instead he was proud that, under his tutelage, Victoria had embraced the constitutional doctrine that the monarch must be above party. Urging Albert to set himself up as the Queen's 'constitutional genius', in May 1841 Baron Stockmar had pronounced, 'the great axiom … is this, viz: the Crown supports, frankly, honourably and with all its might, the Ministry of the time, whatever it be, so long as it commands a majority and governs with integrity'.[79] Albert had enthusiastically adopted the philosophy.

It was an admirable resolve, but the problem was, he and Victoria went further when they began to think that politicians too should be above party. One reason they so respected Sir Robert Peel was that he came close to conforming to this ideal. In the spring of 1843 Albert conveyed to his private secretary that his confidence in Peel was all the greater because, 'Sir Robert was … not to be turned aside by the fear of making political enemies or losing support. He was determined either to stand or fall by his own opinions … In such a man's hands, the interests of the Crown were most secure.' The following October, Peel demonstrated exactly this attitude when he told the royal couple that if he embarked on reforms in Ireland, difficulties in Cabinet 'might cause the break up of the government; but that would not signify, if it was necessary for the good of the country'. To Victoria, Sir Robert's disinterested approach set him 'far above his supporters as well as his antagonists in the impulses of his actions, which are so far from anything small'. She was certain, 'All he does is from a sense of duty, because he considers it right, & not from any party motive.'[80]

Peel's high-minded approach had its drawbacks. He assumed the Tory party would follow his lead against their own convictions, preferring to swallow measures unpalatable to them rather than risk seeing another Whig government. Sir Robert's Solicitor General, Sir Fitzroy Kelly, noted, 'Peel's contempt for his party was very apparent to those who were in office with him. He seemed to take it as a matter of course, that go where he might, they would follow.' Peel communicated to Victoria and Albert his low opinion – which they came to share – of backbench Tories of limited intellect who were more interested in blood sports than good government. In his view, they were fit only to accept dictation. Ultimately Peel would go beyond the limits of their tolerance, splitting his party and making it unelectable for a generation. In doing so, he reshaped the British political scene, making stable government unattainable. Despite Victoria and Albert's conviction that they could not have 'a *safer* Minister' than Peel, in some ways his approach placed dangerous strain on the country's political system.[81]

Peel's rigidity was exposed on 23 March 1844 when Lord Ashley secured a majority in the Commons after moving an amendment to the government's Factory Bill. Whereas the ministry proposed that women and adolescents in their early teens should work for a maximum of twelve hours a day, Ashley wanted this reduced to ten hours. Many Tory backbenchers supported this, and the next day Peel had raged to the Queen and prince about 'the conduct of his friends, who not only had voted against him, but whose tone had been very offensive'. He warned that 'the pretension of the House of Commons to force, by an anomalous majority, the government to do things' would prove 'detrimental to the prerogative', insisting he would never buckle to this 'bad spirit among the Ultras'.[82]

Telling the Queen that he was 'honour-bound' to abide by his original objective, Peel contemplated resigning immediately. Appalled, Victoria 'clearly pointed out to Sir Robert the impossibility (apart from the extreme annoyance it would be to me personally)' of his doing such a thing, and Peel acknowledged the force of what she said. Yet the fact he been ready to leave office prompted Lord Aberdeen to tell Albert, 'Sir Robert took the matter too much to heart.'[83]

Peel instructed the home secretary to withdraw the original bill and introduce another very similar one. Rejecting any idea of compromise, he called the Tory party together and made it plain that if Ashley's modifications were agreed to a second time, he would resign. The amendment was subsequently thrown out by 'an immense and unexpected majority', which the Queen thought 'indeed marvellous'.[84] Only in 1847 would a Ten Hours Bill secure parliamentary approval.

Within weeks the government was rocked by an even more severe crisis over sugar duties. When the Conservative MP for Bristol put forward alterations, Whigs, radicals and many Tories supported him in such numbers that on 14 June 1844 his proposal was carried by twenty votes. Once again, no one had realised that Peel would treat this as a vital question, but the prime minister immediately indicated to the Queen he was thinking of resigning. Lamenting 'the wrecklessness and wrongheadedness of those who bring on such a crisis', a heavily pregnant and much alarmed Victoria came up to London from Windsor. 'A resignation would be dreadful in every way, for us, & the Country, & who is there to turn to?' she fretted. 'It makes one very anxious.' With the Queen 'so near her confinement', Charles Greville thought Peel's intransigence showed 'a want of gallantry'.[85]

Despite several Cabinet members urging concessions, Peel decreed the Sugar Bill must be reintroduced with only minimal changes. Nor was he mollified when 200 Conservative MPs met at the Carlton Club and stated that, while they reserved their right to exert independent judgement, Peel could count on their 'general and cordial support'. Peel dismissed this as meaningless. To Victoria and Albert he declared haughtily that, if his backbenchers 'have confidence in the government, let them vote for this measure, & if they have not, why then, they must take the consequences'.[86]

On 17 June Peel addressed the House of Commons when the Sugar Bill was introduced anew. Perhaps unwisely, the Queen had urged him 'to give it roundly to his followers' and he took her at her word. In an 'arrogant and imperious' manner he stated that concessions on this issue would only encourage future insubordination.[87]

This gave an opening to the man the Queen was now referring to as 'obnoxious Mr Disraeli'. He made a stinging attack on the prime minister, mocking Peel for bullying 'his friends and cringing to his opponents'. Outraged by Disraeli's 'dreadfully bitter' speech, Victoria attributed his assault on Peel to his having been refused office. 'He is very troublesome, & has a bad character,' she decided. Much to her relief, Lord Stanley rallied Tory loyalty with a stirring speech, securing the government a majority of twenty-two. Victoria hastened to write to Peel, 'The Queen cannot say *how* relieved she is. Last night everyone thought the government would be beat and therefore the surprise was the more unexpected and gratifying.'[88]

She was anxious that Peel should now try and overcome the 'irritation and bad feeling' the episode had stirred up. Unfortunately, as Lord

Aberdeen remarked, 'Sir Robert did not quite possess the quality of conciliation.' Peel maintained that 'people like a certain degree of obstinacy and presumption in a Minister. They abuse him for dictation and arrogance, but they like being governed.'[89] This disinclined him from being less confrontational. The following year, Conservative unity would be placed under further pressure as a result of his Irish policy.

In November 1843 Peel had remarked that, even when the outlook was generally favourable in the country, the state of Ireland remained a 'great standing evil, which counterbalances all good'.[90] Daniel O'Connell still commanded fervent popular support in Ireland, and though in autumn 1843 he obediently cancelled a scheduled 'monster meeting' after the government ruled it unlawful, the ministry decided to charge him with sedition and conspiracy.

O'Connell was tried in February 1844 by a packed jury and, to the Queen's delight, found guilty. 'This is an immense thing and I must say I hardly dared hope for it,' she declared. When the Whigs criticised the trial as 'unjust and unfair', she scoffed 'they must be desperate'. In May O'Connell was sentenced to twelve months imprisonment, and when the Corporation of Dublin petitioned Victoria for his release, 'I had to give a very snubbing answer.' Then, on 4 September, O'Connell's conviction and sentence were quashed on appeal, an outcome that Victoria assured Peel, 'filled us both with indignation. The Queen fears in *every* way it will do *very great harm*. The conduct of three of the Law Lords is *most reprehensible*.'[91]

Though Peel had reacted repressively to O'Connell's activities, the prime minister wished to do something to help Ireland. In February 1844, Victoria described how 'Sir Robert truly says that this way of governing Ireland by troops – that is, to keep it quiet by a large force – is dreadful and cannot last.' Peel did not hide from her that Irish agrarian tenants faced terrible injustices. Whereas she and Melbourne had laughed about their plight, now Victoria was hopeful that something could be done 'to avoid those dreadful evictions of numbers of poor families'. She thought it undeniably 'hard on them to have to leave their houses & be turned out on a cold winter's night, not knowing whither to go'.[92]

With Victoria and Albert's eager approval, Peel established a commission under the chairmanship of Lord Devon to enquire into the vexed question of Irish landholding. In 1845 it produced a multi-volume report which confirmed the situation was appalling, but Peel's sole remedial effort was strangled at birth in the Lords. There was one grievance, however, that the prime minister felt he could address. While Irish Catholics had to contribute through tithe payments to the Protestant Church of Ireland, the only state aid the Catholic Church there received was an annual payment of £9,000 to the priests' training college at Maynooth. By tripling the amount, Peel hoped to secure some goodwill for English rule.

Despite knowing that the measure would prove contentious Peel had not anticipated that the first objections would come from his President of the Board of Trade, William Ewart Gladstone. By the time he joined the Cabinet in 1843, aged thirty-three, Gladstone had already proved himself one of Peel's most loyal lieutenants. Two years earlier he had been disappointed when the prime minister had appointed him a mere vice-president of the Board of Trade but had at once set himself to master all aspects of the job. Showing an extraordinary aptitude for hard work (a colleague said 'Gladstone could do in four hours what took another sixteen; he worked sixteen hours a day') he overcame his initial ignorance of commerce to become an expert on statistics and fiscal matters, knowledge that proved invaluable in assisting Peel to prepare his budgets. Discussing his young subordinate with the Queen in early 1843, Sir Robert described him as 'a most superior man, of great talent, & the purest character', though of 'a rather pronounced religious turn'.[93]

Gladstone came from a wealthy family whose money derived from corn trading and West Indian slave plantations. He had been brought up as an Evangelical but had gradually adopted much more High Church views. Having obtained a double first at Oxford in classics and mathematics, he later developed an eccentric fixation with Homer, in whose supposedly divinely inspired works he found 'supplementary revelation' of a religious nature. His own faith was central to his existence: he told his then fiancée that as an undergraduate he had intended to become a clergyman but had instead dedicated himself to the supreme experiment of making political life truly Christian.

On entering politics Gladstone had been a reactionary Tory: in his 1833 maiden speech in Parliament he had maintained with more filial piety than accuracy that his father always treated his slaves humanely; furthermore, while not opposing slavery's abolition outright, he had advocated a very gradual phasing out in Britain's colonies, with generous compensation for slave owners. However, under Peel's influence Gladstone had gravitated towards the more liberal wing of the Conservative Party. Always a man of great passion, with 'brilliant flashing eyes' and a 'rapt, intense gaze', he had to guard against being 'mastered by turbulent emotions'. He was a powerful orator, but also prone to being convoluted and obscure, capable of losing his audience in 'dim clouds of abstraction'. Sir Robert Peel once complained that Gladstone could be hard to understand, whereupon Sir James Graham agreed it was 'always difficult through the haze of words to catch a distant glimpse' of his meaning.[94]

This intensely religious man, who went to church virtually every day and sometimes three times on Sundays, was subject to other conflicting impulses. He could not always resist the wares of pornographic print shops, a habit he once described as the 'chief burden of my soul'. By the late 1840s he was also deeply involved in 'rescue work' with 'fallen women'. By night he patrolled the streets of London, seeking to persuade prostitutes to abandon sex work. His wife approved of his moral crusade but, as he himself admitted, for a prominent politician his conduct was 'not within the rules of worldly prudence'. The risks would be graphically demonstrated in 1853 when an unemployed Scottish commercial traveller tried to blackmail him after spotting the then Chancellor of the Exchequer conversing with a streetwalker. Gladstone at once summoned a policeman and the young man was later sentenced to twelve months' hard labour. Charles Greville noted there was no attempt to make political capital out of the incident because it was generally accepted Gladstone had had 'no improper motive or purpose'. In his diaries Gladstone nevertheless showed an awareness that his unorthodox pursuits meant that he 'trod the path of danger' in more ways than one. Although as an old man he assured his son he had never been 'guilty ... of infidelity to the marriage bed', some of his encounters with prostitutes clearly gave him an erotic frisson, and he was apt to become obsessed with particular women. By 1849 he had taken to flagellating himself to atone for sinful feelings of sexual excitement. Periodically he would try to give up his 'night walks', but the pain this caused merely confirmed to him they were 'carnal, or the withdrawal of them would not leave such a void'.[95]

In 1838 Gladstone had written an abstruse book on Church and state in which he had condemned the small subsidy currently awarded to the Maynooth seminary. Since then he had changed his mind, but believed himself so compromised by placing his former views on record that he could not remain in a ministry that increased the Maynooth grant. Every effort was made to dissuade him, but Gladstone insisted on leaving office. Having behaved with exemplary conscientiousness,

Gladstone was naturally mortified to find himself attacked for inconsistency by Benjamin Disraeli, whom Gladstone already believed to be a slippery man lacking integrity. On learning he intended to vote for the Maynooth Bill, Disraeli declared his sorrow that Gladstone had completely abandoned the principles expounded in 1838, saying that even so 'subtle a casuist as he may be' could not justify such a reversal.[96] It marked the start of a scabrous rivalry between the two men that lasted over thirty-five years.

Victoria told Peel the Maynooth Bill was 'so great and good' she trusted 'people ... will not oppose it'. She was soon disappointed: bigoted anti-Catholic Tories denounced the proposals so savagely that the Queen confessed to King Leopold, 'I blush for Protestantism.' The outcry afforded Disraeli a fresh opportunity to undermine Peel. Having satirised Sir Robert in his two most recent novels, from the start of the 1845 session he had been on the offensive, mocking his leader with jibes that provoked 'delirious laughter' from MPs and 'nervous twitchings' from the prime minister. In the Maynooth debates, Disraeli gave full rein to his malice, taunting Peel for 'habitual perfidy'. Listening to a speech 'so contrived as to wound him in the most sensitive and assailable points of his character, Peel hung his head down, changing colour and drawing his hat over his eyes'.[97]

Discussing Disraeli with Peel, Victoria agreed he was 'unprincipled, wreckless & not respectable', but the prime minister was damaged by the onslaught. The 'Carlton Club was in a state of insurrection', with party members' hatred 'swelling every day' for a man they now condemned as 'more of a Whig than a Tory'. Peel did not help himself with his own contributions to the debate, in which he 'said nothing calculated to coax or soothe his angry people'. He made it clear he would resign if the bill was rejected and on 23 April it did pass its third reading, but only by dint of Whig support, and with 100 Tories voting against. Many Conservatives had been 'mortally offended' and feeling in the party remained 'shivered and angry'.[98] This meant that when Peel embarked on tackling the Corn Laws, his followers were already fatally divided.

In recent years, feeling against the Corn Laws had been steadily gaining momentum. As well as winning several by-elections, members of the Anti-Corn Law League had raised hundreds of thousands of pounds while holding mass meetings all over the country. At these, the campaigning duo of Richard Cobden and John Bright whipped up enthusiasm with their oratory. MP for Stockport since 1841, Cobden passionately believed that free trade would prove a panacea for all the world's evils. John Bright, a Quaker mill owner who entered Parliament in 1843, dwelt more upon his hatred of the aristocracy. Addressing a huge audience at Covent Garden Opera House in December 1845, he noted that the campaign against the Corn Law was a form of class warfare, in which the commercial and industrial classes had as antagonists 'the Lords and great proprietors of the soil'.[99]

The massive population increases of recent years made it unfeasible for Britain to remain self-sufficient in homegrown food. The most recent census showed the population had risen by 2 million in twelve years. In 1842 Peel told the Queen it was still growing 'to an average of 1,000 a day!!' which she found 'quite fearful!'[100] In the circumstances Sir Robert felt incapable of sustaining the intellectual case for the Corn Laws.

Aware of the seismic effect repeal would have on fragile Conservative unity, Peel still shrunk from acting. In September 1845 he told Victoria and Albert he believed the Corn Laws could not be retained for much longer, 'but that he is not the man to make the change'. In due course he intended to tell his party it was impossible to fight another election pledged to uphold protection, but for the moment planned to keep quiet. Unfortunately, as Albert recounted in a memorandum drawn up on Christmas Day, Sir Robert's timetable was disrupted 'by events coming too suddenly upon him'.[101]

In the autumn of 1845 reports started coming in that all over the British Isles and elsewhere in Europe, the potato crop had been struck by a mysterious blight. Since potatoes provided the only food to millions of Irish peasants, the outlook there was fearsome. At the beginning of November, Peel summoned the Cabinet to say he wanted to suspend the Corn Laws through Orders in Council, which could be retrospectively confirmed by an emergency session of Parliament. He admitted it was unlikely the Corn Laws could subsequently be reinstated. To his dismay only Lord Aberdeen, Sir James Graham and Sidney Herbert were ready to agree. Later, Sir Robert would tell Albert that he should have resigned as soon as it emerged that he was in a minority in his own Cabinet. Instead, after informing the Queen on 5 November that the Cabinet was divided, he set about obtaining further information about the seriousness of the potato crop failure.

Once again, matters spun out of Peel's control. As rumours seeped out that the Cabinet were discussing altering the Corn Laws, the league became more clamorous, and public opinion shifted in favour of repeal. *The Times* came out for it, and Lord John Russell, fearing he was about to be outflanked by the Tories, committed the Whig party to the policy without consulting his colleagues. To Albert it seemed 'the whole country cries out: the Corn Laws are doomed'.[102]

On 26 November the Cabinet met again, and Peel reiterated that the Corn Laws must be suspended. The next day he warned the Queen that 'serious differences of opinion' were to be anticipated. Expressing her regret that 'at a moment of impending calamity' the government should be disunited, Victoria made her own position plain. 'The Queen thinks the time is come when a removal of the restrictions upon the importation of food cannot be successfully resisted,' she informed the prime minister. 'Should this be Sir Robert's own opinion, the Queen very much hopes that none of his colleagues will prevent him from doing what is *right* to do.'[103]

As the Cabinet met repeatedly over the next few days, Peel remained optimistic about winning over his colleagues, but by 4 December it became clear he had failed. Both the Duke of Buccleuch and Lord Stanley had declared they would resign rather than support Corn Law repeal. The three ministers who had earlier backed Peel still did so, but the remainder offered only tentative support, clearly 'not willingly and against their feelings'. Victoria implored, 'The Queen feels certain Sir Robert Peel will *not leave her* at a moment of such difficulty,'[104] but on 6 December he went down to Osborne to tender his resignation.

Peel saw Albert first, and while they talked, Victoria sat upstairs in a 'very anxious and fidgety' state of mind. When the two men joined her after an hour, 'I could hardly control my voice for tears.' The Queen nevertheless agreed that Peel was right to resign, which meant she had no alternative but to ask Lord John Russell to form a government. She ruled out offering the premiership to Lord Stanley, fearing that if he, 'with the aristocracy as his base' forced 'the mass of the people, amidst their great poverty, to pay for their bread a high price', insurrection would result.[105]

Russell was in Scotland at the time, but when he reached Osborne on 11 December he said he must canvass colleagues before proceeding. Pointing out that he would be in a minority in both houses of Parliament, he wanted Peel to pledge support for any measure he brought in concerning the Corn Laws. Peel was only prepared to make a general commitment, without entering into specifics. On 18 December Russell finally undertook to 'hazard forming a government', whereupon fresh difficulties arose about the composition of the Cabinet. As the Queen sat eating dessert on 19 December an 'astounding letter' arrived from Russell, informing her he was incapable of putting together a ministry. In Disraeli's words, he 'handed back with courtesy the poisoned chalice to Sir Robert'.[106]

Victoria considered Russell and the Whigs guilty of 'timid & I must say very shabby conduct'. She congratulated herself – 'I have behaved with the greatest fairness' – but was thrilled she could now legitimately call back Peel, 'the only person fitted to rule the country'. He at once declared his readiness to serve, 'even if he should have to go down alone to the House of C[ommons]'. In the event only one of his colleagues abandoned him. When he summoned another Cabinet to say he was resuming office, there was a dead silence. It was broken by Colonial Secretary Lord Stanley declaring in that case he must resign, but the other ministers rallied to Sir Robert. The Duke of Wellington said the Corn Laws were now a subordinate consideration: the main priority was 'the Queen's government must be carried on'.[107]

Overjoyed that she would not have to part with 'all Albert's best friends', the Queen was uplifted by Peel's 'unbounded *loyalty, courage*, patriotism and *high-mindedness* … His conduct towards me has been *chivalrous* almost, I might say.' She 'split her sides laughing' at a cartoon in *Punch* depicting her as the mistress of a household telling Russell – in the shape of an undersized footman applying for a better domestic post – 'You're not strong enough for the place, John.'[108]

Albert believed that in Peel's hands the question of free trade would be removed 'from the dangerous ground upon which it has got – that of a war between the manufacturers, the hungry and the poor against the landed proprietors, the aristocracy, which can only end in the ruin of the latter'. Instead, Sir Robert would legislate in the interests of the whole nation. To others it seemed Victoria and Albert took an unholy satisfaction in the prospect of the nobility being humbled. When Melbourne's brother Lord Beauvale – who shared the former prime minister's reservations about abolishing the Corn Laws – stayed at Windsor for New Year, he found the royal couple 'wild about Free Trade and the whole Household talking nonsense in the same direction. With this there is a great wish to undervalue the aristocracy and (I doubt not) a great willingness to see them lowered.'[109]

On 11 January Peel gave the Queen more details of what Prince Albert characterised as his '*immense scheme*'. Protection on corn was to be gradually reduced, until after three years it would be totally abolished.

THE QUEEN, PRINCE CONSORT, LORD JOHN RUSSELL, AND SIR ROBERT PEEL. 1846.

"On June 27, 1846, Sir Robert Peel went down to Windsor to place his resignation in the hands of Her Majesty. Three days later Lord John Russell had an audience, and received commands to form his first ministry. Leech has taken the artist's liberty of making the occasions simultaneous. We see Peel leaving by the door in sullen anger, whilst little Johnnie Russell enters, prim, buttoned and confident."

The Queen was vastly amused by this cartoon. (*Punch* cartoon by John Leech, 1846)

The next day Victoria assured the prime minister she was 'certain that what was so just and wise must succeed'. At this point Peel should have summoned his party together and confided his intentions before Parliament met. Disraeli said that, had he done so, he could have avoided disaster, but Peel decided against it. Victoria trusted that all would go well in Parliament, telling Uncle Leopold that though 'Peel will have some tough work,' he was 'in *very* good heart which is everything and the Whigs are splitting and quarrelling'.[110] Neither she nor Peel took into account the harm Disraeli could inflict.

After the Queen opened Parliament on 22 January 1846, Peel rose and made a long, boring speech explaining why the removal of protection would be beneficial. It was received in 'frigid silence' on the Tory benches, but initially it did not appear that anyone would seriously contest it. Unexpectedly, Disraeli leapt up and made an electrifying speech, full – as Albert indignantly noted – of 'violent invectives', depicting Peel as 'a traitor, a hypocrite … & ridiculing his manner &c &c'. Among several effective conceits contrived to make the prime minister 'both odious and ridiculous', Disraeli conjured up the image of Peel as an ostensibly dependable nursemaid entrusted with the child 'Protection', who suddenly 'in a fit of patriotic frenzy, dashes its brains out'. These thrusts were received with loud laughter and cheers. Victoria was dreadfully upset that Sir Robert should be subjected to such 'abuse and shameful ingratitude; it quite makes one's blood boil'.[111]

Undaunted, on 27 January Albert went to the Commons to witness Peel making a financial and commercial statement lasting three and a half hours. Victoria wished she could have been present, too, but had to content herself with reading the papers before congratulating Sir Robert on a 'beautiful & indeed *unanswerable* speech'. Peel declared himself much pleased by its reception, but Albert had observed that while he was speaking, 'his own side of the House looked gloomy & cold in the extreme. The Protectionists hardly seemed to listen to any argument from a fear of being convinced.'[112]

Like the prime minister, Victoria and Albert remained optimistic. She told King Leopold that although no doubt the House of Lords would 'make an exhibition of great violence … no *real* difficulty is to be apprehended'. She praised Peel for working 'day & night … sacrificing health & happiness for his country', and though 'the return (not from the country) but his Party is *abuse*', he still 'thinks *all* will do well and that in the end the Conservative Party will be kept together'.[113]

If Peel had been contending with Disraeli alone, this might have been the case. Tory country gentleman were stimulated by this 'exotic' figure, but also wary of him. When Lord George Bentinck, son of the Duke of Portland, entered the fray, Peel became more vulnerable. Hitherto Lord George had only been interested in his racing stable and had never uttered a word in the House of Commons. Now he 'came out like a lion forced from his lair'. Having pored over statistics to master the complex detail of the Corn Laws, he established himself as a savage and implacable opponent of the man he now referred to as 'the traitor Peel'.[114]

On 9 February 1846 the prime minister moved that his tariff proposals should be considered by the house in committee. The ensuing debate went on for twelve nights, during which Peel was 'abused like the most disgraceful criminal'. When Victoria and Albert saw the prime minister on 18 February, they 'thought him rather out of spirits'. On 27 February Lord George Bentinck attacked Albert for allowing himself 'to be seduced by the first minister of the Crown' into coming to the Commons four weeks earlier, conferring 'the semblance of the personal sanction of her Majesty to a measure which … a great majority at least of the landed aristocracy … imagine fraught with deep injury, if not ruin, to them'.[115] Albert was enraged at being targeted in this way, but never subsequently attended another Commons debate.

The government had hoped to secure a majority of at least a hundred when the house divided on the committee question. In the event, they won by a margin of only ninety-seven on 28 February, with many Tories withholding their support. Albert consoled Peel that while this did 'not look like strong government … there is a *moral* strength in the government which must tell more every day'.[116]

The Corn Importation Bill now had to make its way through the Commons. At one point there was concern that Lord John Russell would oppose Peel's measure on the grounds that the Corn Laws must be immediately repealed, rather than phased out. Albert believed such conduct on Russell's part 'would not be consistent even with the private honour of a gentleman', and ultimately Russell himself decided it would be discreditable. Whig votes could thus be counted on, but many Tory backbenchers remained hostile. Victoria wrote indignantly, 'There is a host of young men who have never in their lives paid any attention to public business, whose chief employment has been hunting, & who now come down to the House as great statesmen' to hamper the bill's progress.[117]

In the third reading debate on 15 May, Disraeli again moved in for the attack. Greville described how, 'he hacked and mangled Peel with the most unsparing severity and positively tortured his victim. It was a miserable and degrading spectacle. The whole mass of the Protectionists cheered him with vociferous delight … When Peel spoke, they screamed and hooted at him in the most brutal manner.' At one point Peel seemed close to tears.[118] Despite this, at four in the morning of 16 May, the bill passed its third reading in the Commons.

It was then sent up to the Lords, where the Duke of Wellington had undertaken to shepherd it through the Upper House. Even so, the bill could hardly expect an easy passage, and while the Lords were occupying themselves with it, Peel's enemies in the Commons found new ways to harass him. What Albert described as the 'fearful increase of crime & particularly of murders in Ireland' had prompted Peel to bring in a bill designed to make it easier to bring perpetrators to book. To the prince's indignation this measure, correctly entitled 'the Life Protection Bill', was 'obstinately termed the Coercion Bill … (in order to damage the government) by the Protectionists'. The Whigs too had given it a hostile reception on civil liberties grounds, although when Victoria had first heard that Russell was thinking of opposing the bill, she had been incredulous. 'To attempt to overturn the government on this Bill would be so factious and so very awkward … Therefore *that* cannot be his intention,' she declared. Before long, it became clear the Whigs were indeed bent on what she termed this 'most senseless move'. Lord George Bentinck had supported the bill on its first reading, but once he realised it provided an opportunity to defeat Peel, he did a volte face. He warned his followers, 'If we lose this chance, the traitor will escape.'[119]

By early June it was looking likely that even if the Corn Law Bill was accepted by the Lords, the government would not survive. For Victoria, who on 25 May had been delivered of 'a plump good-sized little girl', named Helena, the 'very uncomfortable' state of politics did not aid her recovery. She nevertheless reflected, 'Really, when one is so happy & blessed in one's home life, as I am, Politics (provided my country is safe) must take only a second place.'[120]

The debates on the 'Irish Assassination Bill' were marked by more ferocious attacks on Peel by Bentinck and Disraeli. One of Lord George's tirades left Peel so angry he wanted to challenge him to a duel. He was only dissuaded after Lord Lincoln begged his leader to consider how much it would upset the Queen. On 21 June Victoria wrote to Peel, 'She cannot say with what indignation' she had read 'those infamous attacks against Sir Robert which he has so nobly refuted. The Queen thinks that the House of Commons ought to be ashamed of having such members as Lord G. Bentinck and that detestable Mr Disraeli.' They would 'ruin their cause' by such excesses, whereas Peel could 'only stand higher with his country'.[121]

On the night of 25 June, two hours after the Corn Law Bill passed the House of Lords, the Commons threw out Peel's Irish bill. 'In one breath, triumph and defeat,' Victoria commented, deploring that, from 'mere spite' 'those abominable, short-sighted, & unpatriotic Protectionists' had exposed her country to 'mismanagement & disquiet'.[122]

Peel was not prepared to dissolve Parliament and hold an election on such a divisive issue as law and order in Ireland. He preferred to resign, and on 29 June made his valedictory speech in the Commons. Having expressed the hope that his role in removing taxation on food would ensure he was remembered fondly by those who 'earn their daily bread by the sweat of their brows', he went on to praise the part played by Richard Cobden in making Corn Law repeal such a prominent question. Gladstone and others regretted that Peel should have lauded a man who had lambasted landowners as 'plunderers', 'knaves' and 'fools'. It would obviously make it more difficult to reunite the Conservative Party, which had now split into Peelite and Protectionist wings. While thinking Peel's speech 'beautiful and magnanimous', the Queen too doubted its wisdom.[123]

'What a terrible loss such a high-minded, honourable & clever man, will be to us and the country,' Victoria lamented. She told Uncle Leopold her people owed Peel an incalculable debt, because if he 'had not wisely made this change (for which the *whole* Country blesses him) a convulsion would shortly have taken place'. Peel had never acted 'for party advantage only', whereas the incoming Whig government were already showing 'much less high and pure feeling'.[124]

Parting with Peel was a real personal wrench, and the prospect of Aberdeen's leaving office made her scarcely less sad as, 'You can't think what a delightful companion he was.' For his part, Peel said his main regret about quitting was losing his treasured personal intercourse with her and Albert, and he asked if he could commission portraits of them both in the 'simple attire' he had so often seen them wearing.[125]

While accepting that the break-up of the Conservative Party was 'no doubt … very distressing', Victoria was confident it '*will* come together again, whether under Peel or someone else'.[126] In fact, the complications arising from the rupture would last many years. In some respects the state of political flux had its advantages for the Crown, for the monarch had greater opportunities to exert influence when power did not reside in the hands of a formidable executive. It was nevertheless unsettling that the disruption of the two-party system made politics so unpredictable.

3

Lord John Russell
1846–1852

When Lord John Russell had given up his attempt to form a government in December 1845, Victoria had declared he 'never can be Prime Minister, for he has not a shadow of authority'. She added, 'I am certain & must add I *hope*' that the Whigs had 'removed themselves from office for years & years.' Now, a mere six months later, they were back in power with Lord John at their head, and the Queen was finding it hard to adjust. Even in October she was telling Uncle Leopold, 'I do nothing but sigh for Aberdeen & Peel.'[1]

Lord John Russell *c.* 1852. (Portrait by G. F. Watts)

It looked unlikely the ministry would survive very long. It lacked a majority in both houses of Parliament and, considering what the Queen called his 'unfortunate talent of mismanaging personal questions', Lord John was hardly well equipped to handle the difficult situation.[2] Fortunately the Protectionists, led by Lord Stanley, proved incapable of putting up a strong opposition. This allowed Sir Robert Peel and his followers to keep the government in office by voting with the Whigs, irrespective of their measures.

The worst problem facing the government was the famine in Ireland. By the summer of 1846 the ghastly toll of deaths from starvation and 'famine fever' – typhus, dysentery and cholera – was mounting inexorably. Peel's government had set up a public works programme in Ireland. The authorities in England matched money raised by local relief committees to pay wages to those employed on these schemes, and £100,000 of maize had been sent to Ireland. With the total failure of the latest potato crop, things looked bleaker still. The change in the Corn Laws did not help, as the Irish poor could not afford to buy wheat, whatever the price. Such corn as was grown in Ireland was exported.

Russell's government made an appalling situation worse by rigid adherence to the doctrines of political economy. Above all they feared what Russell described to Victoria as 'the cry for the government to do all'. The theory was that creating a dependency culture would increase deaths from famine by stifling private enterprise. Instead, Ireland must be left to 'the operation of natural causes'. When Russell told the Queen in July 1846 that though the state of the potato crop was 'very alarming … it would be impossible to continue giving food as hitherto', she did not question it.[3]

In August 1846 the Labour Rate Act was passed. Heeding warnings from the assistant secretary to the Treasury, Charles Trevelyan, that if the Irish went on receiving grants, 'We shall have a system of mendicancy … such as the world never saw,' the government ceased providing half of the money spent on public works. Instead, an £8 million loan was raised for Ireland, in theory to be repaid by sums recovered from Irish landlords through local poor rates. To avoid paying poor rates for those living on their lands, landlords resorted to evictions, or paid for tenants to emigrate to Canada or America. Huge numbers perished on the 'coffin ships' crossing the Atlantic. By the end of the Famine years, death and emigration had caused Ireland's population to decline by an estimated 2.5 million.

Early in 1847 public works in Ireland were abandoned in favour of soup kitchens which, Victoria understood, gave 'the people rations for almost nothing'.[4] These were soon replaced by another arrangement. The Poor Law Extension Act of August 1847 authorised the provision of some outdoor relief, whereas hitherto relief had been available only to those admitted to workhouses. Yet the criteria for supplying aid of any kind remained extremely restrictive. All too often, upon assessment, starving people were deemed ineligible and sent away to die.

Victoria and Albert were slow to comprehend the severity of the crisis. In September 1846 she noted only that she understood Ireland was now in a 'really very uncomfortable state'. Albert initially was concerned that undeserving individuals were benefiting from the public works programme, being offered 'indiscriminate employment … where even the smallest want of food could be alleged'. He believed the system open to abuse, and that 'every attempt on the part of the government to relieve [the situation] is turned by the Irish themselves to bad account'.[5]

By the end of the year they had a better idea of the scale of the problem. Victoria was shaken by a report written by a Mr Wynne who declared himself 'unmanned by the extent and intensity of suffering I witnessed in County Clare'. He described seeing women and little children 'like a flock of famishing crows', scavenging for food in snowy fields. The Queen found these 'heartrending accounts … really too terrible to think of … The scenes of horror, the starving people, shivering with cold, & devouring raw turnips, they say too dreadful.' In a memorandum of 26 December Prince Albert recorded: 'In many districts the number of deaths from starvation is very great; the lower orders generally are seized with a low fever, the workhouses … are quite full & people are found dead on the road to it.'[6]

On 27 December Russell asked the Queen and prince to make a sizeable contribution to a fund being set up to relieve distress in Ireland and Scotland. The prime minister hoped their example would inspire the public to give generously, for at present 'the feeling is very cold'. He suggested they donate £1,000 to be paid from the 'Special Service Fund'. Albert replied that the Queen was 'glad to have her name put at the head of the subscription list with £1,000 in the way you propose', but they were also 'ready to contribute from our private means'.[7] In the end Albert gave £500 and Victoria £2,000.

The Queen was overcome by fatalism about Ireland's problems. Telling Russell that 'the accounts of her poor Irish subjects make the Queen's heart bleed', she asked: 'What is to be the end of all this Misery? God only knows.' In March 1847 she wrote in her journal: 'the people are starving and the landlords are ruined, & there does not seem to be a ray of hope as to matters improving.' While Victoria believed, 'God alone can bring help, for no human means seems able', Albert did try to think of solutions. In May 1847 he wrote a lengthy memorandum suggesting that rather than being ruled, as at present, by a lord lieutenant and his 'mock court', Ireland would benefit from having its own secretary of state at Westminster. Russell responded that this was hardly the time for such a change, and certainly it is hard to see what good it could have done in a land where, as Albert acknowledged elsewhere, 'famine and pestilence are making fearful progress'. Rather more practical was his 1848 proposal that Irish landlords who provided paid employment to those in need should pay a reduced poor rate, but the idea was never implemented.[8]

At times, like many English people, Victoria and Albert felt that the Irish were ungrateful for the 'superhuman efforts' made to help them. On one occasion Albert warned, 'the patience of England & Scotland will soon be at an end, seeing that all sacrifices are brought in vain & that they are only to be repaid in hatred & accusations'. The Queen could not but think that the Irish were partly to blame for their predicament. After attending a fast day service to mark the Famine, she wrote, 'I think it almost wrong & presumptuous to say that the present troubles are judgement for our sins ... No doubt the heedless & improvident way in which the poor Irish have long lived, together with the wicked agitations ... & the deeds of violence they have committed, have all conspired to bring misery & distress upon the country.'[9]

The Queen and prince's compassion was further tested when there was an upsurge in violence in Ireland. In the districts worst affected by scarcity, of those who 'had the *inclination* to commit outrage, very few have strength left to do so', but elsewhere, as Russell told Victoria in November 1847, murders of landlords 'assumed a still more atrocious character than usual'. Albert believed, 'the most distressed, when he gets relief, instead of buying provisions, buys firearms'. Informed of another 'shocking murder' Victoria exclaimed, 'really they are a terrible people'. She wrote to Russell that the crimes 'fill one with indignation. It is really quite disgraceful that such savage acts should occur in a civilised country.' When the prime minister agreed to introduce a Coercion Bill for Ireland she was pleased, not least because 'it serves the government right' to have to adopt a measure similar to that for which they turned out Sir Robert Peel.[10]

* * *

If the state of Ireland was distressing, Victoria and Albert's relations with Lord Palmerston, now reinstalled as foreign secretary, were a cause of still more acute concern. Palmerston's jaunty and arrogant approach to foreign affairs, and what the Queen characterised as his fundamental 'principle of action – viz: *bullying*', was anathema to them. Whereas Palmerston had been accustomed to conducting his department with a free hand, he now found that the Queen and prince expected to monitor his activities. In 1851 the Whig minister Lord Clarendon remarked, 'They labour under the curious mistake that the FO is their peculiar department, and that they have a right to control, if not to direct, the Foreign Policy of England.'[11] Inevitably this made for friction.

Palmerston was put out to discover that the Queen expected to be deferred to over diplomatic appointments. There were times when she successfully vetoed his choices, but on other occasions her objections were ignored. In 1850, when she protested at Lord Howden being sent as British Minister to Spain, the foreign secretary 'never answered the Queen a syllable'. Victoria had to give way, while protesting that were it 'not for the Queen's anxiety to smooth all difficulties, the government might be exposed to most awkward embarrassments'. For his part, Palmerston deeply resented any 'extraordinary attempt to interfere with the arrangements of my Department'. In 1848, after Albert suggested extensive changes to diplomatic personnel, Palmerston scribbled in the margin: 'HRH seems ... to have forgot that there is a responsible secretary of state for foreign affairs *which* however I am not likely to *forget*.'[12]

It was the Queen's right to see and approve all despatches sent out in her name to ministers and ambassadors stationed abroad. She could propose alterations, and if the foreign secretary did not accept them, she could appeal to the prime minister. When that did not resolve the matter, the next step was to ask the prime minister to put her views to the Cabinet, although if they failed to support her, she had to accept their advice. Upon his return to office, Palmerston had been startled to find that the Queen expected to take a 'serious and prominent part in business'. With Albert guiding her and drafting many of her letters, very little escaped her. Palmerston was amazed when one of his despatches to Madrid was returned with 'her own comments and objections' that 'exhibited a very correct knowledge of the state of parties in Spain'.[13]

The foreign secretary did what he could to evade royal control. Time and again, he failed to submit despatches, sometimes claiming that doing so would cause unacceptable delays. The Queen repeatedly reminded him of the correct procedure, but as she complained to

Russell, 'No remonstrance has any effect with Lord Palmerston.' Albert believed Palmerston failed to keep Victoria informed 'not from oversight or negligence, but upon principle'. When she was shown despatches, Palmerston frequently ignored her comments. The offending documents were either sent off unaltered through what Palmerston described as 'some inadvertence & mistake' or, if they were amended, this was done in a manner that took no account of her views. Once, after the wording of a despatch had caused particular difficulty, Victoria fumed that Lord Palmerston had behaved 'really like a naughty child'. He had rephrased it without removing the parts both she and Russell

Victoria and Albert grew to detest the foreign secretary, dubbing him a 'bully'. (Lithograph by John Samuelson Templeton, after Sir William Charles Ross, 1840)

had found objectionable, and then, 'the Queen cannot help suspecting', sent it off knowing full well how much it would displease her. It was 'almost a mockery … which can really not go on so'.[14]

The root of the problem was that in some respects Palmerston's political philosophy differed from hers and Albert's. They felt a natural affinity with continental sovereigns, even those whose rule was less than enlightened. Albert wrote that he welcomed it when European monarchs improved their form of government, but 'civilisation & liberal institutions must be of organic growth'. It was '*quite wrong*' that under Palmerston's direction, 'we are frequently inclined to plunge states into constitutional reforms for which they have no inclination'. The Queen, too, deplored that Palmerston 'invariably encouraged constitutional development … in such countries which from their state of civilisation were not fit for constitutional government'. In southern European countries such as Portugal and Spain, constitutions invariably proved 'an unfortunate thing'.[15]

Palmerston, in contrast, wanted the rule of law and representative assemblies to prevail throughout Europe, and had little patience with monarchs who eschewed them. To Victoria and Albert, he seemed to have 'no strong monarchical feelings', and he certainly prided himself on denying 'the Right Divine of Kings to govern ill'. He once burst out to a colleague: 'Really, such sovereigns as those who rule over Naples and Greece are enough to make men republicans.'[16]

Victoria found it particularly distasteful that in the hope of reforming illiberal foreign regimes, Palmerston pursued an 'intriguing, immoral policy', encouraging British diplomats stationed abroad to liaise with opposition groups. Besides fearing that such 'sporting with political intrigues' bore the risk of 'getting us into some scrape' if found out, the Queen feared destabilising countries, dooming them 'to eternal convulsions and reactions'.[17]

Her horror intensified when a wave of uprisings engulfed Europe in 1848 and Palmerston sided with those trying to throw off the shackles of tyrannical monarchs. When Victoria protested that he was encouraging revolutionaries, he said they were only 'revolutionists in the same sense as the men' responsible for the Glorious Revolution of 1688, to which 'the present royal family of England, happily for the nation', owed their throne. It was not an argument that held much appeal for Victoria, who did not have the same veneration for the 1688 Revolution as the Whigs did. Reading the work of the constitutional historian Henry Hallam in 1842, she had been shocked by his assertion that, thanks to the 'blessing of the "Glorious" revolution, as he is pleased to term it', British sovereigns 'held their rights from the people alone'. Victoria felt that William of Orange 'certainly did, but not his successors'.[18]

In August 1848 Victoria discussed with Lord John Russell 'the old, & in my opinion very bad notion that a Revolution might be justifiable in some cases'. She maintained 'that Revolutions are always bad for the country & the cause of untold misery to the *people*. Obedience to the laws & to the Sovereign is obedience to a higher Power, divinely instituted for the good of the people, not of the Sovereign, who has equally duties & obligations.'[19] What recourse the people might have if the ruler neglected those duties and obligations, she did not say.

The Queen had a point when she accused Palmerston of inconsistency and double standards. After he urged the Emperor of Austria to give up his Italian provinces, she reminded Russell, '*Many people* might think that *we* would be happier without Ireland or Canada.' She found it 'really ... quite immoral, with Ireland quivering in our grasp' that Palmerston should be pressuring Austria to renounce lawful possessions. Not surprisingly, aggrieved foreign powers did not fail to draw parallels. Palmerston told the British ambassador in Vienna that if the Austrians 'twit you ... with Ireland', he was to say it bore no comparison to the situation in Italy as the British and Irish were entirely 'mixed and amalgamated' and spoke the same language.[20] This would hardly have survived scrutiny.

Palmerston was also selective in the nationalist movements he supported. He warmly favoured Italian nationalism but had little desire for the German Confederation – the loose grouping of independent German states established at the end of the Napoleonic wars – to become a more cohesive entity. Victoria and Albert cherished visions of German unity under Prussian leadership and were angry that, whereas Palmerston denounced Austrian oppression elsewhere, he let Austria retard progress towards a better political arrangement for Germany.[21]

All this ensured that Victoria and Albert came to detest Palmerston. It was not just that – as they saw it – his unscrupulous and misconceived policies brought Britain into international disrepute and lowered Victoria's standing with her fellow monarchs. From a personal point of view, they considered him 'a bad man' with 'not a grain of moral feeling'.[22]

* * *

The first major disagreements arose over Portugal. Victoria and Albert felt warm affection for Queen Maria Gloria and her consort Ferdinand. The latter was a Coburg, and hence another of Victoria's first cousins, and Victoria's feelings of solidarity for a sister queen were also strengthened by fond memories of meeting her when Maria Gloria had come to England as a child. Although she acknowledged that 'poor dear Ferdinand and Maria' could be 'very obstinate, particularly *her*', she never forgot they were 'her near and dear relations'; if they were sometimes guilty of 'impolicy and shortsightedness', allowances ought to be made for their difficult circumstances. Believing that 'Portugal has perhaps never had more really good and virtuous sovereigns than the present king and queen,' she declared: 'whoever is intimate with the Queen knows how really honest, good, well meaning and courageous she is.' Far from accepting this assessment, one Whig minister described Maria Gloria as an imbecilic despot.[23]

Victoria and Albert were inclined to be understanding about Maria Gloria and Ferdinand replacing their elected government with a military dictatorship. When this provoked a popular uprising in the autumn of 1846, Victoria was filled with indignation against 'these abominable rebels'. She was furious that Mr Southern, British legation secretary at Lisbon, showed sympathy for the insurgents, conducting himself, in her view, more like 'a Portuguese demagogue than ... an English representative'. Victoria 'much rejoiced at the news' that royalist forces had won a victory against the rebels in December and was furious when Southern remonstrated after captured rebel army officers were sent off 'to die a slow death in Africa'. She wanted him officially rebuked, for though 'transportations without previous trial is to be regretted ... Mr Southern had no business to interfere'. Palmerston retorted that it would scarcely be a cause for regret if British pressure secured the rescinding of a measure viewed with 'unqualified disapprobation'.[24]

Victoria and Prince Albert urged that Maria and Ferdinand should be given naval and military help, but Palmerston was against unconditional aid for a king and queen he blamed for their own difficulties. He would only consider it if Maria made promises of amnesty to the rebels still holding out at Oporto. Victoria considered his attitude 'unkind & improper', fearing that Maria Gloria 'would prefer no assistance to such as this, which would be so lowering to her'.[25]

The Queen had thought that Lord John Russell was 'much kinder & more feeling' about Maria and Ferdinand, so she had a nasty shock when the prime minister wrote that the Portuguese government's recent conduct 'exhibited a spirit of tyranny and cruelty … without a parallel in any part of Europe'. Victoria protested this was 'rather a strong expression', but Russell was clear 'it would be impossible to support such atrocities … without bringing disgrace on the British name'.[26]

As Maria and Ferdinand's position became more hazardous, Victoria and Albert spoke of the 'absolute necessity now for action'. In late March 1847 Palmerston and Russell agreed that Britain would join with France and Spain to broker an agreement between the Portuguese king and queen and the insurgents. Soon it emerged that Maria and Ferdinand were reluctant to offer a full amnesty, arguing it would leave their 'dignity … seriously compromised'. Victoria agreed that those Maria considered '*most* obnoxious' should be banished but backed down when Palmerston remained inexorable. On 7 May she and Albert wrote '*very strong* letters' to Portugal, which they believed 'helped considerably' to change Maria's attitude.[27]

The rebels in Oporto initially refused the terms offered. After Victoria urged that '*not a moment*' should be lost, English ships and French and Spanish forces surrounded Oporto until it surrendered. Queen Maria then tried to renege on her undertakings, first trying to exempt 200 individuals from the amnesty. When this was prevented, she delayed changing the composition of her government. Victoria thought Maria 'should not be *pressed* … but should be left to her *own time* for doing it', but Palmerston warned that if the Portuguese queen did not abide by her promises, 'nobody will ever hereafter … place the slightest confidence in her word'. Accordingly in August, Victoria sent her another frank letter, imploring Maria not to give any grounds for accusations of bad faith.[28]

For months Palmerston went on complaining that Maria was being dilatory in carrying out her obligations, and Victoria continued to think him unfair. In October 1848 she remarked that his attitude to Ferdinand and Maria remained 'really abominable'. By then, there were many other reasons why she considered being saddled with Palmerston as her foreign secretary 'a calamity'.[29]

The year 1848, the 'year of revolutions', was terrifying for monarchs. The first upheaval occurred in January when risings broke out in Sicily and Naples against the King of Naples's tyrannical rule. A month later events took place in France which Victoria found truly harrowing. Anger about Louis Philippe's refusal to countenance political reform became uncontrollable after troops fired on protesters in Paris. On the morning of 24 February, having been warned that the mob was about to break into the Tuileries, the king impulsively abdicated in favour of his grandson. The royal family fled through the gardens and had scarcely clambered into their coaches, before a horde of 'bloodthirsty ruffians were in the courtyard'. Under pressure from another 'horrid infuriated mob',[30] the National Assembly refused to recognise Louis Philippe's grandson as king, and a republic under a provisional government was proclaimed.

For the past eighteen months, the Queen had been on decidedly cool terms with Louis Philippe. Contrary to his pledges, in October 1846 he had married his son, the Duke of Montpensier, to the Queen of Spain's younger sister, while Queen Isabella herself had been forced to take as her husband the Duke of Cadiz, 'a miserable creature' believed incapable of fathering children. There was thus a good chance that one of Louis Philippe's grandchildren would in due course inherit the Spanish crown. At the time Victoria had felt 'quite ill' about Louis Philippe's duplicity and had written him a 'tickler' of a letter. Now that the French king had been brought so low, her anger was forgotten. She at once sent word via her ambassador in Paris that she would put a steamer at the disposal of the king and his wife, 'assuring him of the hospitality he would meet with here'.[31]

To Uncle Leopold Victoria raged: 'The French are a nation of monsters! What base ingratitude do they not show to their Kings & P[rin]ces!!' Having separated when they took flight, members of the French royal family had to make what shift they could to cross the Channel, being 'one by one … thrown upon our shores like shipwrecked mariners'. Louis Philippe himself had gone into hiding for some days, until the British consul at Le Havre contrived to smuggle his wife and him, heavily disguised, aboard a steamer bound for England. The exiled family were installed at Claremont, which belonged to Louis Philippe's son-in-law King Leopold. When Victoria and Albert received them at Buckingham Palace on 6 March, 'humbled poor people they looked'. Victoria told Russell the family were 'really almost destitute', and though the government did subsequently discreetly supply them with some money from 'Secret Service funds', they had to live on what she called 'a very reduced scale'. Writing to Baron Stockmar of 'these poor exiles at Claremont!' Victoria declared: 'their life, their future breaks one's heart to think of. How one must pity them all!' She found it hard to comprehend 'what it must mean to lose one's position, fortune & all, in one day'.[32]

Although Louis Philippe's son, the Duke of Nemours, told Victoria his father could not have resisted his overthrow without causing serious bloodshed, she could not help wondering whether the king should have put himself at the head of the army rather than tamely submitting. She suggested to King Leopold that 'perhaps a *few shots* fired' on 24 February '*might* have prevented all this. Why was this not done?' While possibly 'the recollection of Louis XVI … is enough to justify all', their action gave 'such a *disgraceful running-away* appearance'.[33]

What Victoria called 'this lamentable Revolution in France … stirred up all the bad feelings … in existence', and the 'wild notions & wicked example' of that 'hothouse of *iniquity* from whence *all* the mischief comes', fuelled protest movements elsewhere.[34] In Vienna the arch reactionary, Chancellor Metternich, had to flee into exile after students and workers formed revolutionary committees. In response to mounting disaffection and demand for reform, the Habsburg emperor Ferdinand granted constitutions in both Austria and Hungary.

In Berlin, the King of Prussia also agreed under pressure from his people to introduce a constitution and abolish press censorship, but on the night of 18 March Prussian troops fired on crowds in the capital, killing many. Victoria understood they did so after being 'set upon by those horrid communists'. When barricades were thrown up, the king ordered his troops to withdraw. Not only was he then forced to dismiss his ministry but, 'terrible to say', he was forced to abase himself by coming out bareheaded on to the palace balcony to salute the 'ghastly dead' shot by his forces. An appalled Victoria heard 'the poor king … was received with yells & growls and clenched fists, pointing to the bodies'.[35]

There was unrest in several other German states, and Italy too saw violent upheavals. At the Vienna settlement of 1815, large areas of Italy had reverted to being under Austrian rule. In Lombardy the Milanese now rose up and drove Austrian troops from their city, while Venice, another of Austria's subject states, declared a republic. In the northern Italian states of Parma and Modena, the ruling dukes were forced to leave. King Charles Albert of Sardinia-Piedmont opted to assist his compatriots to throw off Austrian shackles, sending his army to fight for Italian independence after declaring war on Austria on 19 March 1848.

For Victoria, who had given birth to 'a large girl' named Louise on 18 March, what Charles Greville called 'the roar of revolutionary waters … deluging the whole earth', was deeply traumatic. On 2 April she wrote in her journal, 'Such hourly startling news one no longer knows what to think ... *When* will these terrible Revolutions cease?' She added, 'We feel so sad at the ruin all round, which I even dream of.' Although she tried to put on a brave face for Uncle Leopold, insisting, '*Great* events make me quiet and calm,' she admitted, 'the future is very dark.' Ten days later she wrote to the prime minister, 'Lord John will easily understand that the Queen must feel serious & sad when she hears of & sees so much misery and terror – such violent convulsions ... on all sides.' Six months after Louis Philippe's fall she wrote another reflective letter to her uncle, noting that: 'Since the 24th February I feel an uncertainty in everything existing which ... one never felt before ... *Bores* and trifles which one would have complained of bitterly a few months ago, one looks upon as ... quite a blessing – provided one can *keep one's position in quiet!*'[36]

The great worry was that the contagion would spread to Britain. In March troops opened fire in Glasgow, killing six rioters. There were also some minor disturbances in London, but having 'broken several of Mama's windows', the mob did not try to approach Buckingham Palace. They dispersed as soon as the Guards turned out, 'so that there was no danger. But after the horrors of Paris, one cannot help being more anxious.'[37]

Then came news that the Chartists were planning to hold a massive rally in London. They predicted that 500,000 would attend and announced plans to present a petition embodying their demands, signed by 5 million. It was feared that the meeting could easily escalate into a full-scale uprising, and in her post-natal state this preyed on the Queen's mind. The entry for her journal on 3 April read, 'all this & the uncertainty everywhere, as well as for the future of our children, unarmed me & I quite gave way to my grief'.[38]

The prime minister advised that the Queen, prince and their children should retreat to Osborne two days before the rally took place on 10 April. Sir Robert Peel and Sir James Graham objected this would 'look like cowardice in her personally', and after leaving for Osborne with the family, Albert asked his Keeper of the Privy Purse, Sir Charles Phipps, to sound out opinion in London on the matter. After making enquiries, Sir Charles reassured his employer that any criticisms were 'confined to aristocratic drawing rooms'.[39]

In the end the Chartist rally proved innocuous: 170,000 Special Constables had been enrolled to preserve order, and the Duke of Wellington had arranged for large contingents of troops to be on alert.

THE MEETING ON KENNINGTON-COMMON.—FROM A DAGUERREOTYPE.

The Chartist gathering on Kennington Common, south London, 10 April 1848. Although the Queen feared it might end in violence, all went off quietly.

While they were primed to move at the first sign of trouble, they were kept out of sight to avoid provocation. Many fewer persons attended the rally than expected, with a mere 20,000 assembling on Kennington Common. There were eventually 2 million signatures on the petition, but these included 'no end of fictitious names', including Mr Punch and Queen Victoria. When London's police chief prohibited those gathered at Kennington from marching to Westminster, the Chartist leader Feargus O'Connor ordered his followers to disperse. Instead of forming part of a great procession, the petition was taken to Parliament by hackney cab. Learning all this at Osborne, the Queen at once wrote to Lord John Russell 'to say how relieved & rejoiced we are at the news of the complete failure of the Chartist Meeting and Procession; we always hoped & thought it would *not* come to any thing serious; but … in such sad & alarming times as these, one could not help feeling anxious'.[40]

The danger was not entirely over. In theory new Chartist meetings were banned, but on 6 May Albert reported to Baron Stockmar: 'We have Chartist riots every night, which result in numbers of broken heads. The organisation of these people is incredible. They have secret signals, and correspond from town to town by means of carrier pigeons.' When the Queen heard that 8–12,000 people were gathering in Finsbury Park for the second night running, she asked Russell, 'Should it not be stopped?' – advocating that those responsible for 'outrageously violent & seditious' speeches should be detained. Disturbances were still occurring in June, stimulated, as Albert acknowledged, by hunger and privation. 'Disorderly meetings' held in East London were distinguished by 'coarse language and savage spirit', so on 9 June Victoria was relieved to hear from the home secretary that 'Five of the worst Chartists have been taken.'[41]

The dangers of popular uprisings were graphically illustrated by insurgency that broke out in Paris on 22 June and lasted for three days. It was savagely suppressed by General Cavaignac, with thousands losing their lives in the violence, and mass reprisals and deportations taking place once the authorities regained control. While finding reports of the '*desperate* fighting' and 'fearful carnage' in France 'too horrid', Victoria saw it as 'an awful retribution for their shameful conduct'.[42]

Similar scenes were not destined to take place in Britain. On 20 August Albert informed Stockmar: 'On the very night that a general rising of the Chartists was to have taken place, the leaders of the conspiracy, to a man, were seized and imprisoned neatly and simultaneously … Shells with nails in them had been prepared after the Parisian model.' In early September the home secretary informed the Queen that sixty-four Chartists were either already in prison or awaiting sentence.[43]

Neither Victoria nor Albert believed that police intelligence activities and prosecutions would suffice 'to keep us out of mischief'; 'work for the suffering & unemployed' was also necessary. Albert told his brother: 'Means must necessarily be found *not for diminishing riches* (as the Communists wish) but to make facilities for the poor. But there is the rub. I believe this question will be first solved here in England.' In April the Queen and prince had asked the humanitarian campaigner Lord Ashley how they could best show their concern for workers. Albert had accompanied Ashley on a tour of London slums, and after Ashley told them 'a Sanitary Bill would in five years confer more blessing and obliterate more Chartism than Universal Suffrage in half a century', Victoria wrote to Russell recommending that 'the Health of Towns Bill ought to be taken up in earnest & with energy'. On the day of the Chartist rally of 10 April, Albert had drawn Russell's attention to recent expenditure cuts which had resulted in workmen being laid off projects such as the refurbishment of Buckingham Palace. 'Surely this is not the moment for the tax-payers to economise upon the working classes?' he had asked.[44]

Despite Russell's warnings that his safety could not be guaranteed, Albert insisted on presiding at a meeting of the Society for Improving the Condition of the Labouring Classes. Stressing 'the *immense interest* which the Queen & myself feel for the welfare & comfort of the working classes', he told Russell he wished to show 'that the Royal Family are *not* merely living upon the earnings of the people'. At the meeting on 18 May he praised projects such as the Society's Model Lodging Houses, which provided cheap accommodation for working men, while cautioning those present to 'avoid any dictatorial interference with labour & employment which frightens capital away'.[45]

Albert believed that to demonstrate she was not remote from her people, Victoria must show herself to them. He still performed duties on his own, such as laying the foundation stone of the Great Grimsby Docks in 1849, but Victoria too now made public appearances. On their way back from Scotland in 1851 they visited Manchester and Liverpool. Victoria was shocked by some things they witnessed, being struck by the sight of the 'painfully unhealthy & sickly population' ranged along Manchester's streets. When they stopped at Wolverhampton in 1852, she was depressed by its industrial landscape: 'nothing but chimneys, flaming furnaces … wretched cottages, … a thick black atmosphere … It makes me sad.'[46]

Lord Palmerston's attitude to events in Italy had further poisoned his relations with Victoria and Albert. The Queen had been incensed that rather than showing monarchical solidarity with Emperor Ferdinand of Austria, King Charles Albert of Sardinia-Piedmont had combined with fellow Italians against him. On 2 May 1848 she told Uncle Leopold: 'I *heartily* wish King Charles Albert to be beaten. He has behaved shamefully.' When Palmerston complained that Austrian forces under General Radetzky were committing atrocities, she dismissed the accounts as 'sure to be much exaggerated'.[47]

Initially the Italians were so successful that the Austrians fell back to massive fortresses in northern Italy. In May 1848 the Austrians – under pressure in their lands in eastern as well as southern Europe – sent a representative to England requesting British mediation in Italy. They were prepared to make major concessions, being ready to accept that Lombardy should become independent, or, if it wished, merge with Piedmont. Venice could possibly become a free city, but the Austrians would retain towns they still held such as Mantua and Verona. In Victoria's view, the Austrians were being too generous: 'Why Charles Albert ought to get any additional territory the Queen cannot in the least see,' she grumbled. Albert thought it acceptable that both parties keep what they currently possessed, and he and the Queen were sure that a settlement on these lines would have been achieved had it not been for Palmerston holding out hopes to the King of Sardinia that he could do better. For Palmerston declared that 'nothing could satisfy the Italians but the relinquishment of the *whole* of Italy' by Austria. As a result, the Queen was ashamed to find herself 'abetting wrong' in Italy.[48]

In July the Italian situation was transformed when the Austrians burst out of their fortified positions and went on the offensive. In these new circumstances, Palmerston began to think of joining with the French Republic to achieve a mediated settlement in Italy. For the Queen, who had found it painful enough even to recognise the Republic ('I hate the name,' she had told King Leopold in March) the prospect of combining with it to help 'revolted subjects to throw off their allegiance' appeared nothing less than 'a *disgrace*'. However, once it was confirmed that Palmerston would be looking for a settlement along the lines already indicated by Austria, the Queen did authorise a joint Anglo-French diplomatic initiative.[49]

Days later, the Austrian general whom the Queen called 'gallant old Radetsky' recaptured Milan. Victoria wrote to Uncle Leopold, 'What a wonderful & just punishment for Carlo Alberto! ... It *nearly kills* Pilgerstein [their private nickname for Palmerston] which is *another great comfort* & satisfaction.' Victoria argued to Lord John Russell that it would now be 'almost ridiculous' to expect the Austrians to relinquish Lombardy to Piedmont. To her annoyance, Palmerston continued to send despatches to Vienna, couched in the same 'angry, irritating, bullying tone', telling the Austrians to give up their Italian possessions. In a fury, Victoria wrote to Russell that 'the partiality & unfairness of Lord Palmerston in this Italian question really surpasses *all conception*'.[50]

The Queen was right in thinking that Palmerston's hand had grown much weaker, for Austria was now confident of asserting full control over its Italian dominions. It is possible that Austria's unwillingness to accept the offer of Anglo-French mediation owed something to King Leopold, who may have passed on that Victoria and Albert disapproved of it. Certainly Palmerston believed the Austrians had tried to appeal to the Queen directly. He instructed the British ambassador in Vienna to make the Austrians 'understand that, in a constitutional country like

England, these things cannot answer, and that a foreign government which places its reliance upon working upon the Court against the government of this country is sure to be disappointed'.[51]

By this time the Queen had made the first of many attempts to persuade Russell to dismiss Palmerston. In September 1848 she and Albert holidayed at Balmoral, a Scottish estate they were currently leasing, and which they would buy in 1852. Once an autumn visit to Scotland became a hallowed part of their routine, one or two ministers at a time were expected to join them at Balmoral. Some much enjoyed the deer-stalking and grouse-shooting, but others dreaded their visits. Russell was the first politician to be their guest there, and on 19 September the Queen confronted him about Palmerston. She warned that she 'could hardly go on' with a man who was making her 'quite ill'. While uttering sympathetic noises, Russell explained he feared becoming an enemy of Palmerston. Before letting the matter drop, Victoria said the day might come when, 'I could not put up with Lord Palmerston any longer.'[52]

In the summer of 1848 there was a small-scale attempt in Ireland to emulate the revolutionary movements raging on the continent. On 27 July Lord John Russell told the Queen 'insurrection appears imminent', for William Smith O'Brien and Thomas Meagher, members of a group called 'Young Ireland', were trying to organise an armed uprising. Victoria almost welcomed the prospect of a fight. The Habeas Corpus Act forbidding detention without trial had recently been suspended in Ireland, and reinforcements sent there, so the authorities were well placed to meet any challenge. She wrote fiercely, 'Cruel as it may sound … it would be better for the future peace of Ireland if the present state did not pass over without a lesson given by the troops.'[53]

The 'Young Ireland' uprising proved a fiasco and ended in Smith O'Brien and Meagher being captured. Tried for treason, they were sentenced to be hanged, drawn and quartered, subsequently commuted to transportation for life. The Queen was contemptuous about the rebellion's ignominious outcome. 'S. O'Brien let himself be taken without any resistance,' she informed King Leopold. 'In short, one must know the Irish in order to appreciate the value of their threats.' She actually regretted matters had been resolved 'without any contest', as she considered the 'unruly Irish' in need of subjugation. As it was, she feared that all too soon 'they will begin again'.[54]

The following year, Victoria and Albert visited Ireland. They had put off doing so several times because the country was either too unstable or in the grip of famine. Even in 1849, the west and south-west remained ravaged by hunger, and one Anglo-Irish peer denounced the royal visit as 'a huge lie', because the itinerary did not include any distressed areas. Astonishingly, the Queen was received with huge enthusiasm in Cork, Dublin and Belfast. She herself considered this extraordinary 'when one reflects … the country was … quite lately in open revolt & under martial law'. On 4 August she wrote from Dublin to King Leopold, 'A more good-humoured crowd I never saw, but noisy and excitable beyond belief, talking, jumping and shrieking instead of cheering.' She thought the women beautiful, while also noting 'the raggedness of the people is beyond belief … for they never mend anything.'[55]

From Ireland Lord Lansdowne reported to the prime minister that by her manner the Queen had 'given universal satisfaction, omitting nothing that could please, so that the feeling in her favour has gone on crescendo'. The populace were delighted she passed through the streets in an open carriage without a military escort, so enchanting the Irish that, according to the Lord Lieutenant, Lord Clarendon, 'the thermometer of loyalty … kept continually rising'. After her departure on 12 August 1849, *The Times* declared: 'As long as Queen Victoria lives … there will be no disaffection, no disloyalty in Ireland.' In fact, her presence could not work such wonders, for the condition of Ireland remained dire. If the threat of open revolt had subsided, this owed more to the country's state being 'one of prostration' rather than the uplifting effects of Victoria's visit.[56]

The spirit of resistance, formerly so overwhelming, was soon snuffed out in places other than Ireland. Reaction set in following what Victoria called 'a horrible new Revolution in Vienna'. After Emperor Ferdinand had proclaimed his Hungarian subjects as rebels, some of his army mutinied with the support of students and workers. Street fighting forced the emperor and imperial family to flee the capital in October, and Victoria was aghast to learn 'the poor Minister for Foreign Affairs, Count Latour had been … killed in a horrible way, with axes and clubs'. She wrote to Lord John Russell, 'This is really the worst we have seen yet.'[57]

Then the loyal part of the imperial army returned and laid siege to the capital. They successfully stormed the city, and in the ensuing violence 2,000 of its defenders died. German intellectuals who had assisted the insurrection, such as Robert Blum, were shot by firing squad – in Victoria's opinion 'a fate he much deserved'. For her, the outcome at Vienna was 'satisfactory, though sad'. She considered the revolutionaries who had taken control of the city, 'a set of the worst Ruffians & monsters in the world', exclaiming: 'Really one quite rejoices to hear of those horrid Republicans being exterminated.'[58]

On 21 November 1848 Emperor Ferdinand abdicated and was succeeded by his young nephew, Francis Joseph. Henceforth there was no question of Italy being granted the sort of concessions envisaged earlier in the year. To signify his anger about Palmerston's attitude towards Italy, the new emperor did not send an archduke to announce his accession, as he did to other European powers. The Queen asked Lord Aberdeen to tell the Austrian ambassador she understood the reasons for the snub, while feeling fury that Palmerston had caused her to be so slighted.

In Prussia too, King Frederick William reasserted himself that autumn. After revolutionaries in Berlin hoisted the red flag and decreed aristocratic titles abolished, the king called in troops and regained control of the city. Having brought in new ministers, he issued a new constitution that had some liberal aspects but endowed him with great powers. The Queen was very relieved by Frederick William's firmness.[59]

Order was also re-established in France with the 10 December election of Louis-Napoleon, a nephew of the late emperor, as President of the French Republic. The new president was an adventurer who had spent years in exile, much of it in England. He had mounted two abortive coups against Louis Philippe, and after the second in 1840 had been captured and sentenced to life imprisonment. In 1846 he had escaped to England, where he served as a Special Constable on the day of the Chartist rally in April 1848. Having returned to France in September, he was elected a deputy in the National Assembly, before successfully standing for the presidency. Victoria believed his achievement, 'a sign of better times. But that one *should have to wish for him* is really wonderful'.[60]

The following year, several monarchs whose thrones had been shaken succeeded in re-establishing their authority over turbulent subjects. Sicilian insurgents were crushed after Ferdinand II pulverised Palermo, earning himself the nickname 'King Bomba' in the process. Queen Victoria hailed their unconditional surrender as 'marvellous', although two years later she was shocked by Gladstone's accounts of the 'cruel sufferings' of political prisoners in Bomba's Neapolitan prisons, which she found 'too awful!'[61]

In the rest of Italy, the cause of unification and independence from Austria was extinguished for the present. At the end of March 1849, 'foolish, wicked Carlo Alberto' had renewed the war against Austria, only to fare disastrously. Victoria confided to Uncle Leopold that news of the 'good for nothing' king's defeat 'gave us great pleasure. I longed to see that *scoundrel ... punished*'. Charles Albert abdicated and his son Victor Emmanuel took his place on the throne of Sardinia-Piedmont. At a drawing room the Queen complimented the Austrian ambassador on the triumph; Palmerston pointedly forbore from doing the same.[62]

The Habsburgs had another triumph in Hungary, where a revolutionary government under Louis Kossuth had set up a republic. With military aid from Russia, Austria attacked. In August 1849 the Hungarian army surrendered, and thirteen of its generals were summarily executed. Numerous other atrocities committed there and in Italy caused Palmerston to burst out: 'The Austrians are really the greatest brutes that ever called themselves by the undeserved names of civilised men,' but the Queen was unperturbed. Lord Aberdeen informed Charles Greville that Victoria and Albert 'had seen with great satisfaction the downfall of the Hungarian cause and chuckled not a little at the idea of its being a mortification to Palmerston'.[63]

By September 1851, when her terror at the ordeal suffered by so many rulers in 1848 had had time to subside, the Queen could express regret that authoritarianism had triumphed so completely. She reflected, 'the position of Princes is no doubt difficult in these times, but it would be much less so if they would behave honourably and straightforwardly, giving the people gradually those privileges which would satisfy all the reasonable and well intentioned, and would weaken the power of the Red Republicans; instead of that, *reaction* and a return to all the tyranny and oppression is the cry and the principle'.[64] Although the benefit of hindsight enabled her to see things in a different perspective, at the time she had been delighted by the way the forces of order had regained supremacy.

The Queen's relations with Palmerston had deteriorated steadily throughout 1849. The year had started badly when it emerged that he had permitted an officially accredited arms dealer to sell weapons from a government arsenal to rebels in Sicily. This was a violation of Britain's neutral stance, so the Queen had been forced to apologise to the odious King Ferdinand of Naples. Furious that Palmerston had exposed her to such humiliation ('And *I* have to bear it all!') in late January she once again demanded that Russell remove Palmerston from the Foreign Office. Russell merely held out a distant prospect that Palmerston could be sent to Ireland as Lord Lieutenant. When attacked in Parliament over the Sicilian affair, the foreign secretary, 'delivered a slashing impudent speech ... the whole eminently successful', and later told a Cabinet colleague, the Queen's anger 'did not signify a pin, after all'.[65]

In June 1849 the Queen was 'flaming up about P[almerston] more strongly than ever', but the most she could secure from Russell was the introduction of a new system for transmitting despatches. To guard against them being sent off without her approval, it was arranged that the foreign secretary must first submit them to the prime minister, who would forward them to Victoria. Even so, when Russell paid a second visit to Balmoral in September 1849, she again pressed him to oust Palmerston.[66]

Palmerston's iniquities had become a complete obsession with Victoria and Albert. When Lord Clarendon dined at Buckingham Palace in February 1850, 'the Queen exploded ... with the utmost vehemence and bitterness', saying she found it 'inconceivably mortifying and degrading' that her inability to control her foreign secretary incurred her the disdain of fellow sovereigns. Palmerston's behaviour to Greece soon made matters worse. Palmerston was demanding that the Greeks pay exorbitant reparations to Britons they had supposedly wronged. Among these was 'Don' David Pacifico, whose house in Athens had been sacked by a mob. Pacifico was a Portuguese Jew, but because he had been born in Gibraltar he could claim British citizenship, and Palmerston believed him entitled to lavish compensation from the Greek government. When the Greeks refused to pay, the foreign secretary ordered a squadron of ships to go to Greece to blockade Piraeus and other ports, and to seize shipping to the value of the compensation demanded. It was an archetypal example of the 'gunboat diplomacy' with which his name became associated. The Queen felt Palmerston should have been more cautious about accepting the validity of Pacifico's claims, but when she asked him to tone down a despatch to Athens he sent it off '*without* altering it!!' which she found 'really beyond words'.[67]

On 2 March 1850 Victoria and Albert had another long discussion with Russell about Palmerston. Explaining that he dared not 'hurt Lord Palmerston's feelings', Russell suggested that at the end of the current parliamentary session, Palmerston could relinquish the Foreign Office in order to become home secretary and Leader of the House of Commons. The prime minister had already sounded out Palmerston, and he had appeared amenable. Russell passed on Palmerston's observation that he did not think he had forfeited the Queen's confidence 'on *personal* grounds', but at this Victoria fired up, interrupting that 'she distrusted him on *personal* grounds also'. Albert tactfully interjected that Palmerston was right insofar that it was his 'political doings', rather than his person, that had made him 'disagreeable to the Queen', but the prince had reservations of his own about Russell's proposal. He feared that if Palmerston became Leader of the House of Commons the position would serve as a stepping stone to the premiership itself.[68]

In the next few weeks the Greek imbroglio became worse, causing the Queen considerable embarrassment. She clung to the consoling thought that Palmerston would move offices at the end of the session, but on 17 June Lord Stanley altered everything by attacking the way Palmerston had pressed Don Pacifico's claims. Russell felt he must stand by Palmerston with a Commons motion that the government's foreign policy was 'calculated to maintain the honour and dignity of this country'. On 24 June a four-day debate began, and the next evening Palmerston vindicated himself completely in a magnificent four-and-a-half-hour speech. In the early hours of 29 June 1850, the government secured a majority, and Palmerston became the 'most popular man in the country'.[69]

On 27 June Victoria had been severely shaken when an unbalanced dandy named Pate had brought his knobbed cane crashing down upon her head as she left the house of her dying uncle, the Duke of Cambridge. Fortunately, her bonnet had protected her from serious injury, but the upsetting incident did not make it any easier to accept Palmerston's triumph with equanimity. She was still reeling when, on 30 June, Sir Robert Peel dreadfully injured himself in a riding accident, dying three days later. 'Overwhelmed with grief,' the Queen wrote to Lord John Russell it was terrible 'to think that a miserable fall from a horse should take away in 3 days a man who could certainly be less spared than almost any one in the country'. Victoria wrote in her journal: 'My poor Albert feels quite *heartbroken*.' The bereavement was as painful for both of them 'as if we had lost a father'.[70] On a more mundane level, Peel's death made the political situation more uncertain now that Sir Robert was no longer there to chivvy his supporters into keeping the Russell government in power.

'As much disgusted with [Palmerston] as ever,' on 11 July Albert summoned Russell to Buckingham Palace, hoping to convince him not just of the impossibility that Palmerston should continue at the Foreign Office, but that he was equally unfit to become Leader of the Commons.

To prove Palmerston's 'worthless private character', the prince adopted the desperate ploy of dredging up a 'dark story' dating from the start of Victoria's reign. When staying at Windsor in September 1837, in the middle of the night 'the old monster' had entered the bedroom of a young Woman of the Bedchamber named Mrs Brand 'and attempted a rape'. Having gained entrance, he locked one door and piled furniture against another, telling the young woman it was useless to resist him. She 'struggled her way across the barricade in her night shift' and escaped. At the time the incident had been successfully hushed up, and until recently it had been kept from the Queen. Albert, however, had long known of this 'brutal attack', and now he asked Russell how anyone could expect Victoria to take as a chief adviser a man guilty of such a 'fiendish scheme'? Lord John agreed this 'very bad' story showed how necessary it was 'to protect the Queen from Lord P's being thrust upon her at any time as Prime Minister', but would not advance the timetable for moving Palmerston from the Foreign Office.[71]

Worse still, as the parliamentary session neared its end, Russell reneged altogether on his undertaking, for on 7 August the prime minister sheepishly informed Victoria and Albert he would not be carrying out the promised reshuffle. When he had told Palmerston during a recent interview that his 'conduct towards the Queen had been disrespectful', the foreign secretary had responded that if so, 'he was quite unconscious of it and sorry for it'. However, after his Commons triumph, there could no longer be any question of his giving up the Foreign Office. Russell told the Queen and prince that in view of the government's precarious state, he could not 'press the matter further'. As Victoria furiously noted, the upshot was that Palmerston 'remains where he is, to be a constant thorn in my side, and to the detriment of the whole country, as well as of Europe'.[72]

All that the Queen could do was to draw up a memorandum on 12 August for submission to Palmerston, specifying the standards of conduct she expected from her foreign secretary. Noting his claim that he never 'intended any disrespect to her by the various neglects' of which she had so often complained, she formally laid down that henceforth he must be scrupulous about keeping her informed about the conduct of foreign policy. Any remissness would be regarded as 'failing in sincerity towards the Crown, and justly to be visited by the exercise of her Constitutional right of dismissing that minister'.[73]

It looked like her admonishments would have the desired effect. Having returned to London from the Isle of Wight, on 14 August Albert met with a seemingly contrite Lord Palmerston. To the prince's amazement, throughout the interview, Palmerston was 'very much agitated, shook and had tears in his eyes'. He declared that though differences over foreign policy were to be expected, the suggestion that he had been disrespectful to the Queen was 'an imputation on his honour as a gentleman' that, if well founded, would mean 'he was almost no longer fit to be tolerated in society'. Albert recorded the foreign secretary's state of distress was so marked, 'as quite to move me'.[74]

Palmerston's penitent mood proved fleeting. Within a month he incensed Victoria and Albert by his handling of an unfortunate incident that occurred during the visit to London of General Haynau, who in 1848–9 had conducted operations on Austria's behalf in Italy and Hungary. His many atrocities there had earned him the nickname 'General Hyena' and feeling against him in England had risen very high. When he came to the country in September 1850, he was savagely manhandled by angry workers while visiting a brewery in Southwark. As Victoria indignantly recounted, he was 'assailed with dirt & blows, ... so that he had to run for his life'. Palmerston repudiated Austria's demand for a formal apology, confirming the Queen in the view that the foreign secretary was 'solely governed by a spirit of vindictiveness'. Only after Russell for once took a firm line was Palmerston compelled to write a decorously worded letter to the Austrian ambassador.[75]

Palmerston's attitude towards Germany further exacerbated the ill-feeling between Palace and Foreign Office. Displaying what Lord Aberdeen described as 'violent and incorrigible German unionism', Albert dreamed of seeing the disparate collection of states that made up the German Confederation bound more tightly together under Prussian leadership. Victoria had initially been less enthusiastic about promoting Prussian hegemony, noting that Prussia 'is the country of all others which the *rest* of Germany dislikes', but she too had come warmly to embrace the concept. Palmerston, in contrast, dismissed the idea of German unification as 'that phantom'. Albert believed he was really 'afraid of a strong Germany'.[76]

When the duchies of Schleswig and Holstein rose up against their Danish overlords in 1848, seeking, with military support from Prussia, full incorporation in the German Confederation, Victoria and Albert were furious that Palmerston showed no sympathy towards Schleswig-Holstein's oppressed inhabitants. Ignoring Victoria and Albert's wishes, Palmerston helped draw up a protocol ensuring the duchies were brought back under Danish control. When Victoria protested, the foreign secretary dismissed her 'misconceived' objections, telling Russell that while she evidently wished him to act as 'Minister ... for the Germanic Confederation', he saw no reason to 'take up the cudgels for Germany'. Angered by his lack of concern about alleged Danish cruelty, the Queen asked Russell sarcastically, 'Where are the "*interests of Humanity*" on other occasions so ostentatiously put forward by Lord Palmerston?'[77]

Victoria and Albert were still more displeased that Palmerston was unconcerned by the way Austria managed to stifle Prussia's attempts to reconfigure the German Confederation in a manner that would have enabled Prussia to provide dynamic leadership. On being chided by the Queen, Palmerston retorted that Prussia was not motivated by an idealistic desire to secure constitutional government in Germany but was rather engaged in 'a struggle for political ascendancy'. As Charles Greville recorded in November 1850, this meant that Victoria and Albert's aversion to Palmerston became 'greater than ever, for to his former misdeeds is now added the part he takes about German affairs, on which Albert is insane'.[78]

By early 1851 Lord John Russell's government was decidedly unsteady. It now faced more formidable opposition, for while Lord Stanley remained the Protectionists' overall chief, Disraeli led the party in the Commons, and was performing well there. Noting that Disraeli was very much 'the rising man', the Whig Cabinet member Lord Campbell remarked: 'For anything I know, the Jew boy may ... one day be Prime Minister himself.'[79]

On 20 February the government was defeated on a backbencher's motion for franchise reform, whereupon Russell surprised everyone by resigning. Victoria and Albert believed they had no option but to invite Lord Stanley to form an administration, even though they feared that if the Corn Law was reimposed, a revolution might ensue. Initially Stanley held back, asking the Queen and Albert to explore whether other configurations were possible. For the next three days the royal couple approached numerous politicians, but none felt up to taking on the premiership. To break the deadlock, on 25 February the Queen unwillingly turned back to Lord Stanley.

Initially Victoria had found the crisis stimulating, declaring on 23 February that she and Albert were having 'a most interesting & exciting time'. Only two days later her journal entry read, 'I feel the strain on my nerves – very trying'. Lord Stanley told his son that when he arrived at the palace that morning, 'he could see plainly she had been in tears'. Albert did not disguise his scepticism about Stanley's intentions, demanding to know what policies he would pursue; when Stanley indicated he would like to reintroduce a moderate duty on corn, the prince showed his displeasure. Lord Stanley was likewise irritated that Albert made plain his fears the monarchy would suffer as a result of being associated with an unpopular government. Stanley's son reported: 'My father bore this insinuation with temper, and the Queen, feeling it to be offensive' did what she could to smooth over the awkwardness.[80]

Though somewhat more emollient than her husband, Victoria did not conceal that she found the prospect of having Disraeli in the Cabinet, possibly as home secretary, distasteful. She told Stanley frankly, 'she had not a very good opinion of Mr Disraeli on account of his conduct to poor Sir Robert Peel'. Stanley told her he could not put together an administration unless his deputy was in a prominent position. The Queen grudgingly agreed, but 'her last words were, "Remember that you make yourself responsible for him."'[81]

In the end, it proved beyond Lord Stanley to assemble a viable ministerial team. On 27 February he informed Victoria he was abandoning the attempt, eliciting from her the despairing comment that 'she had tried every possible combination and still was without a government'. It left her with no alternative but to bring back Russell as prime minister, and to her intense chagrin Palmerston was reinstalled as foreign secretary. After 'so much trouble & anxiety' Victoria was 'mortified, vexed & discouraged' to find herself exactly where she was before. 'Not even the charm of novelty,' she wrote in disgust.[82]

Charles Greville heard 'the Q[ueen] and Prince think this resuscitated concern very shaky', but the ministry was strengthened by the huge success of the Great Exhibition held in the Crystal Palace in Hyde Park, which Albert had worn himself out organising. Featuring exhibits from all over the world, when it opened on 1 May 1851, it served above all as a showcase for British inventiveness and ingenuity. The Queen was ecstatically proud of her husband's achievements, but the mood of confidence and sense of national pride that the exhibition engendered also benefited the government. Victoria was thrilled when Lord Aberdeen averred: 'the Exhibition had been the cause of everything going so smoothly in Parliament'.[83]

The tranquillity did not endure for very long. In the autumn of 1851 Palmerston added to his tally of transgressions by insisting that, despite Russell's prohibition, he would entertain the exiled Hungarian revolutionary Louis Kossuth at his home. He was eventually forced to yield about that, but then received a deputation of Kossuth's admirers at the Foreign Office. When these radicals referred to the tsar and the Austrian emperor as 'odious and detestable assassins', Palmerston made no protest. An incandescent queen told Russell that in view of 'the injuries done to her' she wished the Cabinet to consider whether it was compatible with the national interest to retain Palmerston in office. To her disappointment, Russell said Palmerston's most recent offence came within that 'latitude' he allowed to ministers.[84]

Palmerston's respite proved brief. On 2 December momentous news arrived from France via 'the wonderful electric telegraph'[85] that was currently revolutionising global communications. A telegraphic link between London and Osborne had been established as soon as technically feasible, but the submarine cable connecting England and France had only been working for a matter of weeks. Now, down this line, came reports that Louis-Napoléon, who was nearing the end of his presidential term of office, had that very day carried out a successful coup d'état. The Queen immediately gave orders that Britain should neither condemn nor endorse the proceeding. Lord Normanby, Britain's ambassador to France, duly conveyed a noncommittal message, only to be told that Lord Palmerston had already expressed his approval to the French ambassador in London. Even when it emerged that at least 2,000 people had been killed in Paris during the commotion, and numerous other individuals summarily arrested, Palmerston still maintained the coup had been in France's best interests.

At this point Russell's patience snapped. On 17 December he informed Lord Palmerston that his repeated 'violations of prudence and decorum' meant the Foreign Office could no longer be left in his hands, but he offered him the lord lieutenancy of Ireland instead. For the Queen and prince, the news came as a wonderful early Christmas surprise. An overjoyed Victoria exulted to Uncle Leopold that Palmerston 'has done with the Foreign Office for ever'. She was even more pleased when Palmerston sarcastically declined the lord lieutenancy, saying presumably 'prudence and decorum' were necessary for that position too. Victoria chortled that his comments were 'really very impertinent, but at the same time it rather serves Lord John right for his weakness in offering this post'.[86]

The Queen dismissed the possibility that, now he was out of office, Palmerston could create difficulties for the government. She told King Leopold: '*I* am not of the opinion he will be quite such a formidable enemy … Standing alone by himself, I can't think he can do much which would be *worth his while*.'[87]

Victoria and Albert were determined that the new foreign secretary must be someone who would not cause trouble abroad, and who would

The Queen is depicted as the mistress of a household telling her refractory footman, 'I'm very sorry Palmerston that you cannot agree with your fellow servants … You must go of course'. (*Punch* cartoon, January 1852)

be amenable to their wishes. Having imperiously informed Russell, 'She must reserve to herself the unfettered right to approve or disapprove the choice of a Minister for this office,' the Queen was delighted when Russell put forward the name of Lord Granville, a famously polite peer who had served under Palmerston at the Foreign Office and whom Albert had taken to when they had worked together on the Great Exhibition. Russell's colleagues thought the current Lord Lieutenant of Ireland, Lord Clarendon, would be a better choice, but Victoria 'protested against the Cabinet's taking upon itself the appointment of its own members, which rested entirely with the prime minister and the Sovereign'.[88] In the end the problem was solved when Russell offered Clarendon the post, correctly anticipating he would decline it. This left him free to appoint Granville.

Palmerston was bitter about his dismissal. His wife wrote furiously: 'No doubt the Queen and Prince wanted to get Palmerston out and Granville in because they thought he would be pliable and subservient and would let Albert manage the foreign affairs, which is what he has always wanted.' She predicted that the House of Commons would be angry about the appointment of 'a young Lordling who has done nothing but dance attendance on Albert and patch up differences amongst the Crystal Palace Commissioners'.[89]

When the new session of Parliament opened on 3 February 1852, initially all seemed well. In December Lord John had expressed satisfaction that the Queen had not been personally implicated in the foreign secretary's sacking, 'which might have exposed her to the animosity of Lord Palmerston's admirers'. The Queen herself had been relieved about this, commenting that, had it been otherwise, it would have embroiled her in no 'small amount of danger, inasmuch as it would have put me too prominently forward'. Now, however, Russell made a statement to the Commons that drew attention to the fraught nature of the relationship between Palmerston and the palace. As well as detailing the immediate circumstances surrounding the foreign secretary's fall, he read out the Queen's memorandum of 12 August 1850, in which she warned Palmerston that if he failed to observe her injunctions, she would 'exercise … her constitutional right' of dismissing him. While it was, in fact, uncertain whether the sovereign did enjoy such a right, Russell alluded to 'that full liberty which the Crown must possess of no longer continuing that Minister in office' who would not heed instructions. He declared that because Palmerston habitually 'forgot and neglected that which was due' to the monarch and colleagues, he could not retain him 'without degrading the Crown'.[90]

The prime minister's 'absolutely crushing' denunciation of Palmerston 'floored him'. As Russell spoke, he sat 'hanging his head', looking – in Disraeli's phrase – like 'a beaten fox'. Charles Greville remarked that his conduct had evidently been 'intolerable to elicit such charges and rebukes'. To her delight Victoria learned 'the moment the House heard … that his conduct had been ungentlemanly towards the Queen – he was lost'.[91]

Palmerston himself thought not just that Russell had treated him monstrously, but that he had left Victoria dangerously exposed. His 'dragging her into the discussion' had been 'unconstitutional and ungentlemanlike', and the prime minister's behaviour had been 'unhandsome by me and very wrong by the Queen'.[92]

Victoria herself had no such qualms, thanking Russell for his 'most lucid definition of the constitutional position of the prime minister & foreign secretary opposite the Crown'. She was delighted at the start made by Granville at the Foreign Office, telling King Leopold he was already showing 'great judgement & discretion … making himself master of everything with an incredible facility and rapidity'.[93]

It turned out that Victoria had not seen the last of Palmerston. He rose from the political grave with astonishing rapidity, carrying an amendment to Russell's Militia Bill on 20 February 1852. The following day, Lord John formally tendered his resignation. Savouring his triumph, Palmerston informed his brother: 'I had my tit-for-tat with John Russell, and I turned him out on Friday last.'[94]

4

Lord Derby; Lord Aberdeen 1852–1855

Shortly before Lord John Russell's government fell, Victoria had confided to her Uncle Leopold that whereas 'Albert grows daily fonder and fonder of politics and business, and is so wonderfully *fit* for both … I grow daily to dislike them both more and more.' Now the mother of seven children, having produced a third son in May 1850, she returned to the subject a few days later. She explained, 'I *cannot* enjoy these things, *much* as I interest myself in *general* European politics,' being 'every day more convinced that *we women if* we *are* to be *good women, feminine* and *amiable* and *domestic*, are *not fitted to reign*.' While there were times 'which force one to take *interest* in' these 'masculine preoccupations' (and then '*I* do, of course, *intensely*'), on the whole it was only by an effort of will that she applied herself 'to the *work*' her duty required.[1]

Now domestic politics had taken a turn which rendered them still more unpalatable to her. Parting with Lord John Russell did not cause her personal distress, for he had never become 'the same friend, guide & support as dear Sir Robert was, nor was he the prime minister he ought to have been'. It was the prospect of the 14th Earl of Derby (as Lord Stanley had become following the death of his father the previous July) taking office that truly filled her with horror, for if a Protectionist government reimposed the Corn Laws, 'I feel *convinced* … there will be commotions.'[2]

Her acquaintance with Lord Derby had hitherto been limited, and what little she had heard about him had tended to prejudice her against him. In fact, Derby was a more impressive figure than might have been assumed from the image he projected of a bluff countryman. A political opponent acknowledged he possessed, 'a marvellous acuteness of intellect and consummate power in debate. There is no subject which he cannot thoroughly master and lucidly explain.' Immensely rich from inherited wealth, Derby was a devotee of rural pursuits and horseracing, and much preferred discussing these subjects to talking of politics. Charles Greville recorded that those who had been impressed by his statesmanlike performances in the Lords – where he had taken his place even before he inherited his earldom – would have been astonished to see him at the racecourse at Newmarket, 'in the midst of a crowd of ... loose characters of every description, in uproarious spirits, chaffing, rowing and shouting with laughter and joking'.[3] No one, however, should have been deceived by this into underestimating his abilities.

The Whig Duke of Argyll thought Derby 'too rollicking, too apt to treat everything as a joke', and Derby could be insensitive in the way he teased other people. His loud humour would also sometimes make the Queen uneasy: after he visited Osborne in August 1852 she wrote in her journal, 'he turns everything too much into ridicule, which I do not quite like'. A few months later she was more appreciative, as she

The 14th Earl of Derby, who became prime minister for the first of three times in February 1852. (Photographed in 1865)

described 'Lord Derby in great force, making us all laugh at the many funny stories he told.'[4]

When in good health – which became increasingly rare, for debilitating and agonising attacks of gout kept him bedridden for weeks at a time – Derby adored shooting. After one political setback, he went out after rabbits, amusing himself by pretending that each one he bagged was a political opponent. Yet he was not just a bucolic aristocrat, prone to hearty humour. While no aesthete – Disraeli noted that his huge country seat, Knowsley, in Lancashire, was the 'ugliest house in Britain', apart from his London residence in St James's Square – Derby had fine powers of literary appreciation.[5] At night he would read Shakespeare to his family in a mellifluous voice, and in 1862 produced an acclaimed translation of *The Iliad*.

Politically Derby was both a shrewd operator and a man of strong core beliefs. He had entered politics as a Whig but having served in Lord Grey's government as Chief Secretary for Ireland and then colonial secretary, he had resigned in 1834 over the proposal of appropriating the revenues of the Irish Church for lay purposes. In 1837 he had joined Peel's Conservatives, and when they had come to power in 1841, he resumed at the Colonial Office.

While profoundly disagreeing with Derby on the Corn Law question, Victoria and Albert recognised that his opposition to repeal had been principled, unlike Disraeli's. When Peel had told his Cabinet what he was contemplating, Derby had objected, 'We cannot do this as gentlemen.'[6] He resigned despite being deeply upset about splitting the Conservative Party, and always hoped for its reunification. Yet notwithstanding his integrity, he understood the need for pragmatism, and could adapt his views when necessary. He proved an adept leader of his party, partly because his reputation as a man of honour meant he could persuade them to adopt policies they found distasteful, but also because he showed great skill at sustaining morale in disheartening times.

Having been invited to an audience with Victoria and Albert on 22 February, Derby at once agreed that he would try and form a government. He warned, however, that the difficult circumstances meant he would need firm royal support, and when the Queen tried to direct him on policy, he was understandably irritated. Asking him 'to remember that since her accession she had identified herself with a liberal policy … in conformity with the wishes of the bulk of the people', she hoped he would not propose measures 'in direct opposition to a liberal policy' – by which she meant a return to protection. 'Warming up,' Derby said, 'he thought there existed different opinions as to what the real wishes of the people were.'[7]

Derby suffered from a shortage of competent and experienced men to whom he could offer ministerial office. Having failed to entice Palmerston into joining his government, he had to fall back on members of his own party. The resulting Cabinet was known as the 'Who? Who?' ministry, after the deaf Duke of Wellington was overheard repeating this question in mystification as Lord Derby tried to tell him names of individuals who had accepted office. When Derby notified Albert that Lord Malmesbury was to be foreign secretary, the alarmed prince placed an exclamation mark besides Malmesbury's name in the margin of Derby's letter. The Queen shared these reservations, telling King Leopold, 'I cannot say [Malmesbury] ... inspires me with confidence.'[8]

The greatest sensation of all was caused by the appointment of Disraeli as Chancellor of the Exchequer and Leader of the Commons. Disraeli himself feared that he scarcely possessed the requisite economic expertise, but Derby shrugged this off: 'They give you the figures,' he said airily. Others were less sanguine. One MP considered it 'degrading to an Englishman' that 'a man formerly connected with half the disreputable bill transactions in London' was now steward of the national finances. Despite his own doubts as to whether he was qualified for the job, Disraeli was thrilled to find himself in government at last. He told Lord Malmesbury he 'felt just like a young girl going to her first ball'.[9]

To the Queen, Derby was apologetic about his undistinguished Cabinet, saying he would like to have appointed men of better calibre. Victoria was indeed disgusted at the quality of her new servants. She noted on 23 February, 'I had hoped to the last that Lord Derby would not succeed,' and though she drew some consolation from reflecting that 'such a sorry Cabinet cannot last long', she could not 'be otherwise than ashamed & humiliated'.[10]

Once the government was in place the Queen wrote to her uncle, 'I shall take the trial as patiently as I can, but it *is* one, for we can have no sympathies with the present people.' At first she and Albert scarcely hid their antipathy. Derby's son said the prime minister's initial dealings with the royal couple were difficult: 'He found the Queen reserved, the Prince manifestly unfriendly.' They made it clear they thought it their right to monitor the government's activities, demanding to be briefed about '*everything* that is going on'. Derby's son recorded: 'The Prince is constantly in the habit of expressing to Lord Derby and his colleagues what he states to be the Queen's wishes on this and that point,' doing so in a 'cold and even dictatorial manner'.[11]

Gradually things thawed as the Queen came to have a better appreciation of Derby's considerable abilities. Having been 'agreeably surprised' when Derby and Malmesbury dined at Buckingham Palace on 3 March, she was 'very well satisfied' by a meeting with the premier that took place two days later. 'He is very able, & certainly quite the prime minister,' she decided. A fortnight later she acknowledged that Derby was proving 'a most talented, capable and courageous Prime Minister', who was 'always excessively fluent and clear'. By June Derby was 'better received at every visit'. Throughout the summer Albert went on relaying the Queen's wishes to the ministers, but by August these communications were no longer delivered in such a peremptory manner, having 'become friendly and confidential'.[12]

One reason was that, by this time, protection was a much less divisive issue. Derby had only avoided having the opposition combine against him by agreeing to dissolve Parliament as soon as essential measures had been passed. Derby explained to the Queen that 'he could not with honour or credit' abandon protection until the country had pronounced against it, but once that had happened, the question could be regarded 'as entirely disposed of'. Soon he predicted that though the election would give him a working majority, it would not be a conclusive enough victory to justify the reintroduction of protection. Victoria exulted to King Leopold that Derby acknowledged that the prospects for protection were 'quite gone. It is a pity they did not find this out a little sooner; it would have saved so much annoyance.'[13]

Victoria and Albert were willing to give Derby credit for modifying measures that were politically unworkable. With Disraeli it was otherwise, for they felt his lack of commitment to protection merely showed he had only ever championed it out of opportunism. Disraeli indeed would have liked to drop it before the election, believing it had now become politically toxic. As far as Prince Albert was concerned, this merely confirmed that Disraeli had a 'laxity of political consciousness' akin to Palmerston's.[14]

If the prince remained deeply sceptical, Disraeli fared rather better with the Queen, for he much intrigued her. In the spring of 1852 she enjoyed causing a sensation by inviting Disraeli and his 'very vulgar' wife to dine at Buckingham Palace. She observed that her guest was 'most singular, – thoroughly Jewish looking, a livid complexion, dark eyes, & eyebrows, & black ringlets. The expression is disagreeable, but I did not find him so, to talk to.' She was also diverted by the 'strange notes' Disraeli sent her as Leader of the Commons, containing accounts of debates there. After receiving the first of these on 16 March, she remarked, 'I certainly formed a different estimate of the Debate, from reading it.' Soon afterwards she wrote appreciatively to Uncle Leopold of the 'very curious reports' that 'Mr Disraeli (*alias* Dizzy)' had written, 'much in the style of his books'.[15]

Disraeli had the knack of enlivening dreary proceedings with a vivid turn of phrase. On one occasion he apologised for 'a somewhat crude note', not couched in polished prose, begging that 'Your Majesty will deign to remember that these bulletins are often written in tumult, and sometimes in perplexity.' He told her he had formed 'the impression that your Majesty would prefer a genuine report of the feeling of the moment ... to a more artificial and prepared statement'. This was an artful way of creating a sense of intimacy between them, implying that he knew her to be an unstuffy woman who, rather than being constrained by formality, relished spontaneity. The Queen liked the immediacy and colourfulness of his accounts, as well as enjoying their 'very flowery' language.[16]

The general election that took place in July 1852 was disappointing for the Conservatives, as the Protectionists were once again increasingly styling themselves. It did not deliver the overall majority that Derby had expected, let alone a mandate to reintroduce a duty on corn. The government was clearly unlikely to last long unless it strengthened itself by securing the support of outsiders. Prince Albert wanted to know why Derby did not jettison Disraeli so that Gladstone – 'a man of ... the purest mind' – could replace him as Leader of the House, saying that he and Victoria 'could quite understand ... that the colleagues of Sir Robert Peel could not feel inclined to serve under Mr Disraeli'. Derby responded that, 'he could not in honour sacrifice Mr Disraeli'.

This made it inevitable that the government would struggle to secure a majority for Disraeli's budget, to be presented to the Commons in early December. Disraeli faced all sorts of problems with it anyway. Now that protection was abandoned, he had to do something for the agricultural interest, and hoped that a reduction in the malt tax would do the trick. But this, coupled with a reduction of tea duty, lowered revenues, and the shortfall had to be recouped elsewhere. Furthermore, under pressure from the Queen and Albert, Derby had agreed to a sizeable increase in defence expenditure. The introduction of steam-driven screw propellers meant that Britain's battleship fleet would have to be upgraded if the country was to maintain its naval supremacy. The previous year's coup d'état by Louis-Napoléon – whom Victoria described to Uncle Leopold as 'indeed no pleasant neighbour' – had also raised concerns that he shared his late uncle's militaristic ambitions. By the autumn of 1852 it was apparent he intended to proclaim himself Emperor of the French, and though he made a speech in October assuring his people 'the Empire means peace', this did not allay Victoria's worries. Lord Malmesbury noted on 24 October, 'the Queen writes anxiously about the national defences. Universal apprehension of war if French empire is proclaimed.'[17]

In letters and meetings with Derby, Victoria stressed 'the necessity of a *large* outlay, to protect us from foreign attack', and the prime minister agreed that funds must be found for additional seamen and soldiers. When Disraeli came to Windsor on 2 November, he too was lectured on the imperative need for higher defence spending. According to Lord Malmesbury, the chancellor returned 'in very low spirits', saying 'it would destroy his budget, and ridiculed the panic', but he did not betray his feelings to the Queen. Instead Disraeli assured her there would be enough money to 'permit the fulfilment of all your Majesty's wishes … as he gathered them from your Majesty's gracious expressions, and also from the suggestion which afterwards, in greater detail, His Royal Highness the Prince deigned to make to him'. Secretly his thoughts were very different: away from the palace he lamented the way 'those *damned defences*' had wrought havoc with his spending plans.[18]

The budget was presented to the Commons by Disraeli on 3 December, and for a time he and Derby hoped it would be accepted by the house. On 16 December a final night of debate took place as a thunderstorm raged outside, and though Disraeli 'fought desperately' to salvage the ministry's fortunes, the government's chances were scuppered when Gladstone rose, his 'features livid and distorted with passion'. Until this point, he had refrained from attacking the government in Parliament because, hating Disraeli as he did, he feared he would have difficulty 'keeping within Christian bounds of moderation'. Now, believing Disraeli's proposals to change the structure of income tax and place significant extra burdens on small householders to be 'disgusting and repulsive', he mercilessly dissected the chancellor's 'dishonest and profligate scheme'. In the early hours of the morning of 17 December, the government lost the vote by a majority of nineteen. Lord Derby, who had been watching proceedings, exclaimed: 'Now we are properly smashed. I must prepare for my journey to Osborne to resign.'[19]

The Queen noticed that when Derby arrived there late that evening, he appeared 'very sore' at his fall. Victoria was less upset about events. While Charles Greville was rather harsh to claim she was 'delighted to have got rid of Derby and his crew', she certainly did not mourn their passing overmuch. In her journal she pronounced it 'inevitable', as 'the country can have no confidence in men like Mr Disraeli'.[20]

While Derby was at Osborne proffering his resignation, Albert repeatedly spoke to him 'of Disraeli, extolled his talent, his energy, but expressed a fear that he was not in his heart favourable to the existing order of things'. Lord Derby did his best to defend his deputy, but Albert still talked darkly of Disraeli's 'democratic tendencies', saying that if he indulged these he had the potential 'to become one of the most dangerous men in Europe'.[21]

Disraeli himself was blithely unconscious that he remained an object of such suspicion. On relinquishing office he wrote to the Queen, 'The gracious & indulgent kindness wh Yr Majesty has been pleased to bestow upon him ... animated and sustained him in an unequal contest.' He thanked Albert even more fulsomely for his 'condescending kindness', asserting lyrically, 'The views wh your Royal Highness has developed to me in confidential conversation have not fallen on an ungrateful soil; and I shall ever remember with interest and admiration, the princely mind in the princely person.'[22]

As Disraeli wound up the budget debate, on realising that Whigs, radicals and Peelites were combining against the government, he had commented bitterly: 'I know ... England does not love coalitions.' Yet a coalition was precisely what the Queen desired, believing that only thus could Britain secure the strong and stable government it needed. She already had some grounds to hope that Whigs and Peelites would join together in an administration much more in tune with her own sympathies than Derby's had been. In recent months, there had been soundings on the matter between the two political groupings, giving rise to hopes that Lord John Russell would not necessarily expect to be prime minister again, but rather, under the right person, would occupy a subordinate position.[23]

The morning after Lord Derby had handed in his resignation, the Queen asked the Peelite Lord Aberdeen to come to Osborne, with a view to inviting him to form a mixed government. Before setting off for the Isle of Wight, Aberdeen happened to encounter Russell in a London park, and when Lord John indicated that he was ready to serve under him as foreign secretary and Leader of the Commons, Aberdeen 'jumped at his offer'. He reached Osborne at lunchtime on 19 December, and on the basis of Russell's undertaking, agreed to try and form a coalition. Taking rather too much upon himself, Albert then handed Aberdeen 'a list of the possible distribution of offices'. Aberdeen pocketed the paper, saying merely it contained 'valuable suggestions'. He warned, however, it would be foolish to think he would face no difficulties assembling a ministry, 'for although everybody promised to forget his personal wishes and interests, yet when brought to the test, such professions were often belied'.[24] These proved prophetic words.

Lord Aberdeen, photographed in July 1860.

Returning to London that evening, Aberdeen was appalled when early next morning Russell called upon him and withdrew his offer to serve. His wife had been working on him, telling him that anything less than the premiership represented a 'degradation' for him. The news was telegraphed to the Queen at Osborne, where she continued despite the crisis, even though Sir James Graham believed her absence from London at this juncture was 'injudicious and unfortunate'. She at once wrote to Russell entreating his 'valuable and powerful assistance', for only the 'sacrifice of personal interests and feelings' would permit the establishment of a durable and efficient government.[25] Russell partially relented, suggesting that he take the leadership of the Commons without coupling it with another office, but the Queen had doubts as to whether this would be constitutional.

Having returned to Windsor on 21 December, Victoria and Albert went on trying to ensure that the ministry assumed the shape they desired. They wanted Gladstone to be appointed Chancellor of the Exchequer, but Aberdeen offered the post to Sir James Graham. To the Queen and prince's relief, Graham turned it down, whereupon Gladstone was enlisted as they wished. Victoria's prohibition meant it was out of the question for Palmerston to have the Foreign Office, and he initially declined the Home Office, saying that he and Aberdeen had 'stood so long in hostile array' that working together was unthinkable. On 23 December he thought better of this and agreed to accept the seals. Much as Victoria and Albert disliked him, they recognised he was a valuable addition to the government. The same day Russell was prevailed upon to drop his objections to becoming foreign secretary.[26]

Victoria was overjoyed at 'the success of our excellent Aberdeen's arduous task', telling King Leopold: 'It is the realisation of the country's and our *most* ardent wishes.' She rejoiced that 'I have again in the prime minister ... a personal, truly attached, & much esteemed friend, and I cannot say how pleasant the thought is to me, of having dear Lord Aberdeen at the head of the government.'[27]

After everything had apparently been sorted out, on 24 December Victoria heard that Russell was making fresh demands. He pointed out, not entirely unreasonably, that his party – now coming to be known, rather to Russell's regret, as 'Liberals' rather than 'Whigs' – had many more MPs than the Peelites. Arguably they therefore deserved a predominant role in the coalition, but the Peelites had nevertheless secured a disproportionate share of ministerial posts.[28]

Victoria was exasperated. She had agreed that some Cabinet posts should go to men who were not her first choice, even though she believed that Aberdeen's changes to the scheme Albert had submitted were 'not for the better'. After 'waiving for the public good some wishes of her own', she expected Russell to be equally accommodating, and wrote to Aberdeen of 'her hope that political parties will not fall short in patriotic spirit of the example she has ... herself set'. The crisis spoilt the Queen's pleasure in preparations for Christmas, but all was resolved after Aberdeen took a firm line. Towards evening, Russell 'yielded an unwilling consent', agreeing that the Cabinet should comprise six Liberals, six Peelites and a single radical.[29]

The coalition had cracks in it from the start. Russell's wife had only agreed to let him become foreign secretary on the understanding that Lord Clarendon would take over 'whenever she thought Lord John ought to be relieved from it'. His colleagues assumed that Russell would retain the office for some months at least, but it turned out Russell had other ideas. Still worse, Russell believed that Aberdeen had promised that his own tenure of the premiership would be extremely brief, and at the first opportunity he would step down and make way for Russell. At the time, the Queen was unaware of the pact, but when she subsequently learnt of it, she rightly commented it was a recipe for disaster.[30]

Lady John had always intended that her husband would only remain at the Foreign Office for a month, but in this short period Russell annoyed the Queen by urging that to ensure good relations with the Napoleonic regime in France, she should stop seeing the deposed Orléans royal family. Victoria was furious at the idea that Louis-Napoléon's new status required her to grovel to him. 'It seems to me that what was done while *he* was *President* will do when he is Emperor, and I don't think that *I* am obliged to do *just* what "*pleases*" him!' she noted savagely. She was even angrier when, before Parliament met on 11 February 1853, Russell caused 'a great shindy' by announcing he intended to give up the Foreign Office. There was the 'devil to pay' at Windsor, and his colleagues remonstrated he would have done better not to have accepted the post at all, but Lady John insisted that Aberdeen and Clarendon had given their words of honour on the matter. The Queen thought it 'very shabby & unpatriotic on Lord John's part. I am quite provoked at him'.[31]

She still had misgivings about letting Russell lead the Commons without holding an official post, but Russell told her it was unlikely anyone else would copy him by 'taking upon himself a vast amount of labour without any pay at all'. He was even curter when the Queen said she feared 'that a man independent of office might consider himself independent of the Crown also'. Russell retorted that, 'he did not think any minister, as it was, thought very much of the Crown as contradistinguished from the people'. He wrote angrily that having 'done all in his power to contribute to the formation of a ministry in which he himself holds a subordinate situation, from which nearly all his dearest political friends are excluded', he felt entitled to her consideration.[32]

The upshot was Lord Clarendon became foreign secretary on 21 February, while Russell remained Leader of the Commons, but the Queen thereafter bore Lord John a grudge. She made her displeasure clear by ignoring letters Russell sent with accounts of Commons proceedings, preferring to correspond exclusively with Aberdeen. This only made Russell more bitter at his loss of status, and more prone to cause trouble. 'She thinks he is neglectful and disrespectful to her,' Charles Greville observed, 'and he thinks she is wanting in graciousness and confidence to him ... Of course when he was her PM she was obliged to talk to him about everything; and now she does so to Aberdeen instead, whom she infinitely prefers ... This mortifies and offends him.'[33]

Despite this, at the outset the coalition's prospects seemed good. On 6 February 1853 Aberdeen informed the Queen he was 'much struck by the spirit of conciliation and good will which prevailed' at Cabinet meetings. As for Victoria, she felt convinced that 'such uprightness & earnestness of purpose *must* triumph'. She did not suffer from post-natal depression after giving birth to her eighth child, Prince Leopold, in April. During the delivery she had been given for the first time 'that blessed chloroform' and afterwards noted, 'I have never recovered better.' One reason for her buoyant spirits was that she was 'devoted to this government' being 'extremely attached to Aberdeen, more than to any Minister she has ever had'.[34]

Gladstone's first budget in April 1853 raised him 'to a great political elevation', marking him as 'a *man* ... fit to lead parties and direct governments'. He reduced or abolished hundreds of duties on everyday necessities, hoping this would permit wealth to 'fructify in the pockets of the people'. The chancellor also announced that income tax would be reduced in stages, until it was phased out altogether within seven years. The Queen and prince both wrote to congratulate him on his budget speech, with Albert declaring, 'I ... should certainly have cheered had I a seat in the House.'[35]

At the Home Office, Palmerston achieved much that was valuable, including a new Factory Act, sanitary legislation, the ending of transportation, and establishing reformatory schools for young offenders. There was also progress in colonial affairs, with the passage of an India Bill that provided for recruitment to the Indian Civil Service to be conducted by competitive exams. By September 1853 Aberdeen had legitimate cause for self-congratulation when he wrote, 'We have brought the session of Parliament to a triumphant close; we have carried many useful and important measures.'[36]

There were grounds to hope that the following year's session would be equally productive. After the Northcote-Trevelyan report was submitted in November 1853, Gladstone was keen that the principle of entrance by competitive examination should be extended to the British Civil Service. The Queen wondered uneasily, 'where is ... the principle of public competition to stop, if once introduced?' but in February 1854 she gave permission for legislation to be brought in when Parliament met – albeit with 'considerable misgivings'. It was intended that another controversial proposal would be introduced in the 1854 session, namely, political reform, a cause which Lord John Russell had now taken up with enthusiasm. While apprehensive, the Queen thought it better 'not to wait till there was a cry for it'. In fact, both of these measures would have to be dropped, along with Gladstone's hopes of abolishing income tax. The reason, as Gladstone lamented to his wife was, 'War, war, war', and its capacity to 'swallow up everything good and useful'.[37]

Tsar Nicholas I had long believed that the Ottoman Empire was on the verge of breakdown and when it happened he looked to maximise Russian influence in lands still controlled by the Turks. In January and February 1853, the tsar held a series of talks with the British ambassador in Moscow, Sir Hamilton Seymour. He told Seymour, 'Turkey is falling to pieces. The sick man is dying. We must come to some understanding.' Lord Aberdeen was not alarmed, but after seeing Seymour's despatches, the Queen remarked that the tsar was hardly treating Turkey like 'a sick friend for whose life there exists much solicitude'.[38]

Far from wanting to protect the Turks, Aberdeen was appalled by the possibility that Britain might have to fight a war on their behalf. He believed the Turks' 'whole system is radically vicious and abominable', whereas Russia at least had some claim to civilisation. This brought him up against Palmerston, for maintenance of the Ottoman Empire was a cornerstone of his foreign policy, and he had always been suspicious of

Russia's global ambitions. Aberdeen believed the difference between him and his home secretary to be more fundamental still, as 'Lord Palmerston loved war for war's sake, and he peace for peace's sake.'[39]

At the beginning of March 1853, the tsar sent Prince Menshikov to Constantinople to demand that the sultan recognise his rights concerning Orthodox Christians who lived under Ottoman rule, giving the impression the tsar saw himself not just as their religious protector, but their political protector too. The Queen accepted Aberdeen's assurances that though the tsar 'has treated the Sultan rather overbearingly and roughly', he did not harbour aggressive intentions towards Turkey. Palmerston thought differently, urging that the navy must be ready to act if the Russians took aggressive action. When Russia issued an ultimatum, saying it would occupy the principalities of Moldavia and Wallachia (modern-day Romania) unless their demands were met, a British fleet was sent to the eastern Mediterranean, but Palmerston now argued it should sail up to the Bosphorus, and even beyond it into the Black Sea, to show the Russians that their actions would not go uncontested. Aberdeen was by no means ready for such a step. On 18 June he told the Queen and prince he was counting on Austria to prevent a war. When Albert remarked he feared the Austrians 'would sell the Turks to the Russians', Aberdeen said 'that would not signify as long as peace was preserved. This astounded us.' Even when the Russians occupied the principalities in early July, Aberdeen was not shaken from his passive stance. He lamented to Victoria and Albert that Palmerston was continuing to be belligerent in Cabinet, but by this time they thought Aberdeen 'rather too much in the opposite extreme'.[40]

Britain and France began acting together to counter the Russian threat. On 2 December 1852 Louis-Napoléon had, as expected, been proclaimed Emperor Napoleon III, and in January 1853 a plebiscite in France had overwhelmingly endorsed his new status. Britain immediately recognised him as emperor, a decision the Queen thought 'quite right' – however 'strange it does seem and also sounds' to address him in correspondence as 'My good brother'. But she remained wary of French expansionism and would not have welcomed developing a closer relationship with the new imperial regime were it not for the fact that, as Albert commented, the tsar's treatment of Turkey 'forced us into an alliance'.[41]

In July 1853 representatives of the major European powers met in Vienna in hopes of brokering a settlement of the Eastern crisis. By the end of the month, the 'Vienna Note' had been drawn up, setting out a solution it was hoped would be acceptable to Russia and Turkey, but on 20 August the Turks announced they could not accept it without modifications. Albert commented, 'One feels tempted to abandon the Turks to their fate' – were it not that this could have such serious consequences; as for Victoria, she thought the Turkish rejection 'too provoking and annoying'.[42]

The Cabinet became seriously split, with Aberdeen desperate to remain at peace and Palmerston and Lord John Russell arguing that the Turks were victims of Russian aggression who deserved to be supported. The timing of the crisis was unfortunate, for the Queen and Albert went to Balmoral on 8 September for a prolonged stay and were hence not on hand to give guidance and advice. Victoria actually expected Aberdeen to come to Balmoral to brief her, which he said was out of the question. While Palmerston – who was not entirely welcome – did come for a few days at the start of their stay, and Sir James Graham was in attendance later on, inevitably the Queen and prince could not keep completely in touch with what was happening in the south. Victoria complained that despatches were being sent off without being submitted for her approval, but at a time when prompt responses to diplomatic initiatives were essential, it was unrealistic to expect anything else.

Aberdeen's difficulties were increased by the fact that Lord John Russell was making his life a misery. Russell felt aggrieved that Aberdeen had not yet made way for him, and since the summer of 1853 had interspersed heavy hints that it was time for the prime minister to go, with attempts to resign. When it looked like the Vienna Note was going to resolve the crisis, Aberdeen had told Victoria and Albert that he was happy for Lord John to take his place, but with war remaining on the cards, 'I could not now run away.'[43]

In mid-September 1853 hopes of a peaceful solution grew dimmer after the Russian foreign minister published an article making it plain that he believed the tsar had such strong claims to be the protector of all Orthodox Christians in Turkish territories that it amounted effectively to suzerainty over large parts of the Sultan's dominions. Victoria told Uncle Leopold, 'the Russians have *let out* at last that they *all along* wanted *something* which they ought not to have *had*!' – meaning it was now '*utterly impossible* for *us* to make the Turks accept that Vienna Note'.[44]

The worsening situation meant that when Aberdeen informed her that he and Lord Clarendon had agreed with the French to station ships off Constantinople, the Queen declared: 'She now rejoices the Fleets should be on their way.' Despite encouraging signs at the end of

September that the tsar might be ready to moderate his stance, things continued to escalate, and on 3 October Clarendon groaned, 'The beastly Turks have actually declared war.' Aberdeen at once wrote begging Victoria and Albert to cut short their holiday in Scotland; despite his urgent plea they did not leave Balmoral till 13 October. This meant they were still away when a crucial Cabinet meeting was held on 7 October, at which there was 'considerable difference of opinion' between ministerial hawks and doves. The day before, Aberdeen had written angrily to Victoria, 'No doubt it may be very agreeable to humiliate the Emperor of Russia; but Lord Aberdeen thinks that it is paying a little too dear for this pleasure ... to cover Europe with confusion, misery and blood.' At the meeting, however, he came to what he called 'a sort of compromise', resisting Palmerston's call to despatch ships immediately into the Black Sea, but promising this would be done if the Russians attacked any part of the Turkish coast in the area. 'Perhaps it was impossible to do less than this,' he told Victoria gloomily, but convinced himself that as there was little prospect of Russia doing anything so rash, the danger was minimal.[45]

Like her husband, Victoria was 'a good deal concerned at finding we were pledged to a very dangerous policy which Ld Aberdeen himself did not like, & which I ought previously to have been asked about'. They feared Aberdeen had been bounced into it merely out of fear that the government would break up, and Albert lamented that Aberdeen had 'renounced one of his chief sources of strength' by not saying he must secure royal approval for the Cabinet's decision.[46]

After their return to Windsor, Victoria and Albert saw Aberdeen on 16 October. The prime minister said sheepishly, 'had he known what the Queen's opinion was, he might have been more firm' in Cabinet, 'but he had imagined from her letters that there was more animosity against Russia and leaning to war in her mind'. He still maintained that war could be avoided, urging that new proposals be submitted to Turkey, coupled with a warning that if she 'tried to evade a peaceful settlement, the Powers would ... leave her to fight her own battle'. The Queen had high hopes of this initiative, reflecting, 'It would never have done for this country' to be 'dragged into a war, by these fanatical, half uncivilised Turks.'[47]

In the end, the diplomatic note presented to Turkey was not nearly as robust as Aberdeen had envisaged. This was largely the fault of Lord John Russell. Throughout October, he had gone on needling Aberdeen about stepping down so he could assume the premiership. The Queen commented angrily that Russell 'never stopped to consider what *my* feelings would be, which would most certainly be *against* him as *Prime Minister*!' If Russell quit the government out of pique it would be 'an act of miserable smallness of mind & of factiousness', and she condemned his conduct as 'thoroughly unworthy – hardly honourable, & most unpatriotic & selfish'. But Russell made it clear that if the note to the Turks was not worded to his liking, this would furnish him with the pretext he needed for resignation. Accordingly, the note stated only that Turkey should delay embarking on actual hostilities with the Russians for 'a reasonable time'. Although 'the Queen and Prince both wished that the expressions should be stronger', Aberdeen agreed that Russell's formula should be adopted. Victoria pronounced, 'It is really too bad, disagreeable & abominable of Lord John,'[48] and certainly the result was damaging. Given such latitude, the Turks would only delay for a fortnight before commencing military operations, crossing the Danube to engage the Russians on 28 October.

The Queen had been annoyed that Palmerston too had been causing difficulties for Aberdeen, and she became yet more enraged when the home secretary suddenly started championing a project to marry her first cousin, Princess Mary Adelaide of Cambridge, to Napoleon III's dissolute cousin, Jerome Bonaparte. The home secretary wrote to Aberdeen that although 'the prejudices of the Queen and of [the girl's mother] the Duchess of Cambridge are, perhaps, strong against it', the match would be politically advantageous. Having stated he understood 'the inclinations of the young lady are for it', he added gratuitously the proposed bridegroom would 'make a better husband than some petty member of a petty German prince's house'. Disloyally, Aberdeen forwarded this to Albert, explaining, 'I cannot resist laying before your Royal Highness the enclosed letter.'[49]

Predictably, Albert was livid. Prince Jerome was, he wrote, notable for 'a life of profligacy which has *disgusted* even the French'. The Duchess of Cambridge 'nearly fainted away' at it being thought 'she and her daughter could have stooped so low', and Albert insisted Palmerston's 'story about Princess Mary's willingness to marry Prince Jerome is a *pure fabrication*'. After warning Palmerston that the Queen 'would visit with the highest displeasure any person who should presume to interfere in a matter of this kind', Aberdeen told him flatly, 'the marriage could not be thought of'.[50]

The Queen had a much more serious reason for anger with Palmerston, for she believed he was secretly colluding with Britain's ambassador to Turkey to sabotage hopes of peace. 'There is little doubt that Lord Palmerston corresponds in a dangerous way with Lord Stratford,' Victoria asserted, going so far as to say that what Palmerston was doing verged upon 'treasonable proceedings'. In fact, there is no evidence to suggest Palmerston was encouraging the Turks to be more warlike, and it seems Victoria likewise did Stratford an injustice.[51]

Hating and fearing Palmerston as she did, the Queen was overjoyed when the home secretary informed Lord Aberdeen he was thinking of resigning. This was not on account of the Eastern crisis, but because Palmerston disapproved of the provisions of the Reform Bill that Lord John Russell was drafting. Victoria wrote eagerly to the prime minister, 'The Queen would very much advise Lord Aberdeen to let him go at once. He will be a source of mischief to the country as long as he lives,' but the trouble 'he is able to do *in office exceeds any* he can do in opposition.' She urged, 'If he is to go … let it be on the *Reform Question*' rather than 'on a popular question of his own choosing, for which he has plenty of ingenuity.'[52] To Victoria's delight, Palmerston formally resigned on 14 December, but that very day brought confirmation of news from Turkey that effectively destroyed peace hopes.

Until then, averting war had remained a realistic possibility. At the end of October the tsar had written to the Queen defending his conduct, and Victoria had welcomed the chance 'to state certain truths' in reply. Lord Clarendon thought that while such direct communications between sovereigns were 'irregular, and generally useless', in this case a response might be valuable. 'The [Russian] Emperor does not probably *realise* the difference between the Queen's position and his own,' the foreign secretary remarked to Aberdeen, but it might be helpful if the Queen told the tsar his occupation of Turkish territory had 'created the most painful impression' on her mind and could 'lead to grave eventualities'. Sardonically Clarendon added, 'It can do no harm, though it may do no good, to let his Imperial Majesty know the truth; it is an advantage he seldom enjoys.' Victoria had written to the tsar on the recommended lines, saying that no ruler who wished to preserve his independence could have granted demands of the kind Russia had put to the sultan.[53]

It was hoped her intervention might induce the tsar to listen to two new peace initiatives, one put forward by Napoleon III, and the other devised by the supposed warmonger Lord Stratford. Unfortunately the Turks had continued to inflame the situation by sending ships into the Black Sea, which the Queen commented must have been done expressly to provoke the Russians. When the Russians had duly emerged from their naval base at Sevastopol and on 30 November annihilated a Turkish fleet anchored in the Black Sea port of Sinope, war fever in England became rampant. Although the Queen, for one, was aware that the Russians had some grounds for their actions, the 'temper of the public' grew 'quite mad', holding that the treacherous 'massacre of Sinope' could not go unpunished.[54]

On 22 December the Cabinet met and agreed that French and British ships should proceed into the Black Sea to force the Russians back into Sevastopol. Aberdeen acknowledged that it was 'possible, even probable' that the Russians would declare war on Britain and France if their fleet could not operate unmolested, but believed he could do no less.[55]

It was curious that the Cabinet had taken a decision which, as Charles Greville noted, 'amounts to war', when Palmerston, its most belligerent member, was out of office. By then, it had in fact already become apparent that Palmerston wished to be readmitted to the Cabinet. On 21 December the Queen had been 'somewhat upset' to hear from Aberdeen that Palmerston 'would like to *reconsider* the step he had taken', ostensibly on the grounds that Russell's Reform Bill might yet be altered to take account of his objections. Probably the real reason was that none of his colleagues had resigned with him, as he had assumed would happen. Victoria had demanded angrily, 'Can any useful end be obtained by allowing him to return?' – predicting that Palmerston would make out that his colleagues had been 'obliged to beg him, on their knees, to come back'. Nevertheless, after a majority of the Cabinet recommended that Aberdeen accept the retraction, the prime minister told her 'it was a political *necessity*' to do so. Consequently Palmerston returned to the Cabinet table, 'as if nothing whatever has taken place'.[56]

For the Queen that December, 'the joy of the season was much spoilt by the anxiety respecting external and internal politics'. As war loomed, she was even driven to acknowledge that perhaps the situation would not have deteriorated so, had Palmerston's approach been followed, rather than Aberdeen's line of appeasement. She pointed out to Clarendon, 'Lord Palmerston's mode of proceeding always had that advantage' that Russia would have been left in no doubt that aggression on their part would not be tolerated. Aberdeen, in contrast, had acted 'on the principle of not needlessly offending Russia by threats', with the result that England was now taking 'the very steps which we refused to threaten'.[57]

* * *

Palmerston's resignation had sparked attacks in the press, suggesting that Albert had engineered it. The Queen was sure that Palmerston himself had been behind hostile pieces alleging that 'courtly distastes and Coburg influence' accounted for his departure. She naturally assumed that once the home secretary was reinstated, the hubbub would die down, but the very reverse happened. The public was in a febrile mood, wanting to apportion blame for Turkey's victimisation by Russia. As Albert bitterly noted, 'the people ... generously made me their scape-goat'.[58]

As the campaign of vilification gathered strength, more and more 'horrid attacks' appeared in papers of varied political complexion. It was alleged that Albert directed British foreign policy, had pronounced Russian sympathies, illegally corresponded with foreign courts, altered Cabinet decisions, and even that he was undermining the army to ensure that England was vulnerable to invasion. The hysteria mounted to such a degree that it was even widely believed that Albert had been arrested for treason, and a crowd gathered outside the Tower of London in the hope of seeing him conducted there.[59]

The wilder accusations against Albert were of course nonsense, but he did have a significant role that had never been legitimised. Albert remarked to Stockmar that since his marriage, 'any one who wished to pay me a compliment at a public dinner or meeting, extolled my "wise abstinence from interfering in political matters"'. Now that it emerged that he played a more active part than had been assumed, 'the public ... fancied itself betrayed', being ready to believe him guilty of 'all kinds of secret conspiracy'.[60]

For years Albert had prided himself on exercising '*silent* influence', establishing himself as Victoria's 'sole *confidential* adviser in politics'. As he conceived it, the husband of a queen regnant must 'sink his *own individual* existence in that of his wife ... aim at no power by himself or for himself ... but ... fill up every gap which, as a woman, she would naturally leave in the exercise of her regal functions'. The problem was that none of this was officially recognised by the constitution.[61]

Several ministers had been bothered by how much Albert took on himself. Derby's son, Lord Stanley, had noted in August 1852 that his father and Lord Malmesbury 'both complained of the interference of Prince Albert in matters of Foreign Policy'. Even Gladstone, who wrote an unsigned article defending the prince, felt his position was open to criticism. He confidentially told Aberdeen that it was a matter of 'regret, nay ... jealousy', that his communications with the Queen had been invariably conducted through Prince Albert, for 'the interposition of any person whatever ... between her Majesty and her sworn advisers' was constitutionally questionable.[62]

The Queen of course had repeatedly tried to regularise her husband's position. She had most recently written a memorandum for Lord John Russell in November 1850, saying since it was apparently impossible to make Albert 'a titular king', she would settle for him being created prince consort. Nothing had been done, so, as Aberdeen acknowledged, Albert's standing remained 'somewhat anomalous'. Now the situation had become urgent, and with her husband continuing to be mauled by the press in a manner 'she DEEPLY *resents*', Victoria grew desperate. On 5 January 1854 she declared to Aberdeen: 'In attacking the *Prince* who is *one and the same with herself*, the Throne is assailed, and she must say she *little* expected that *any* portion of her subjects would *thus requite* the unceasing labours of the Prince ... with the basest ingratitude.'[63]

A few days later *The Times* defended Albert by claiming he 'had nothing to do with the duties of government', but the Queen found this unhelpful, as she wished his role as her adviser to be recognised and accepted. On 18 January she wrote to Aberdeen in near hysteria, saying that if the 'infamous attacks' genuinely reflected public opinion, adopting Salic law was the only logical remedy. 'A *woman must* have a support and an adviser; and *who can* this *properly* be but her husband, *whose duty it is* to WATCH OVER *her interests, private and public*. From this *sacred* duty NO EARTHLY POWER can absolve him!' She continued that, were it not for Albert, her 'health and strength would long since have sunk under the multifarious duties of her position as a Queen and the mother of a large family'. If she believed that more than 'a wicked and despicable few' were responsible for 'these unprincipled and immoral insinuations', she 'would LEAVE a position which nothing but her domestic happiness could make her endure, and retire to private life – leaving the country to choose another ruler after their own HEARTS' CONTENT. But she does *not* think so ill of her country, though she must say that these disgraceful exhibitions will leave behind them *very bitter* feelings in her breast.'[64]

The Queen was so angry that she threatened not to open Parliament when the new session began on 31 January, as she '*could not expose* herself to *some insult*'. However, Aberdeen assured her all would be well, and though in fact there was a 'plentiful sprinkling of hissing' when she and Albert drove by coach to Westminster, it was mostly drowned out by cheers. In Parliament Russell spoke up for Albert in the Commons, while Aberdeen told the Lords it was unthinkable 'the husband should … not … give one syllable of advice or assistance' at times of political difficulty. Confirming that Albert was 'often, very often – generally – … present' when the Queen saw her ministers, he added, 'I can only say that I extremely regret his absence when it takes place.'[65]

Although Victoria had to accept that conferring the title of prince consort on Albert 'must not be done just now', she rejoiced that the 'atrocious calumnies' against 'my beloved Lord and master' had met with 'triumphant refutation'. To King Leopold she exulted: '*Now* his position is *fixed, acknowledged & determined* in a manner wh it *never was before.*' Even so, the whole experience had been deeply traumatic. At the height of the crisis Victoria had confided to Stockmar that Albert was not only 'wounded, hurt, and outraged' but 'looking very ill'. Albert himself confirmed 'our stomachs and digestions' suffered greatly from the stress.[66]

Although Aberdeen remained in denial about the way peace attempts had collapsed, on 14 February Lord Clarendon acknowledged in Parliament, 'We are *drifting towards war.*'[67] When the tsar definitively rejected Napoleon III's latest peace plan, the Cabinet met on 26 February and agreed to issue an ultimatum demanding that Russia evacuate the principalities. No reply was received, whereupon Britain and France declared war on Russia on 28 March 1854.

The Queen had not wanted to fight. In June 1853 she had shuddered, 'The responsibility of war would be *too fearful,*' and four months later 'spoke strongly for peace' when Gladstone dined at Windsor. As late as 13 February 1854 she privately admitted, 'My heart is not in this unsatisfactory war.' Once there was no escaping it, she became utterly committed. She wrote to King Leopold, 'No one can abhor war more than we, but having tried *all* we could to prevent it – it is now … *absolutely necessary* to carry it on vigorously & energetically.'[68]

She therefore deplored the attitude of Aberdeen, who did not disguise he considered it a calamitous mistake. Although Victoria knew the war was 'popular beyond *all* belief' with the public, the prime minister told one acquaintance, '*at times he felt as if every drop of blood that would be shed would rest upon his head*'. He would have liked to resign, but when he told the Queen on 25 February that having 'such a terrible repugnance for it', he was hardly fitted to be a wartime prime minister, she countered briskly, 'This would never do.' She reproved him, 'To save more bloodshed & a more dreadful war … it was necessary it should take place *now*.' In late March King Leopold displeased her by writing to Aberdeen of the tsar's peaceable instincts. She rebuked her uncle, 'This is written to the *wrong man*, for Aberdeen has to be continually kept up to the mark & reminded of the danger of any *patch-up*.' When Aberdeen gave favourable consideration to another peer's proposal that a 'day of humiliation' should be proclaimed, Victoria was profoundly irritated. She wrote crossly that at this event it would doubtless be said, 'that the *great sinfulness of the nation* has brought about this war, when it is the selfishness and ambition of *one* man [the tsar] and his servants who have brought this about'.[69]

In his budget of March 1854 Gladstone abandoned his schedule for phasing out income tax and instead doubled the rate, justifying his decision on the grounds that 'the expenses of war are a moral check which it has pleased the Almighty to impose upon … ambition and lust of conquest'. Albert noted approvingly that such was Gladstone's financial rectitude, 'We expect to carry on the war without borrowing a shilling.'[70] In fact, Gladstone could not keep this pledge. To finance the war, he issued Exchequer bonds that added to the National Debt.

If Gladstone was willing to modify policies on account of changed circumstances, Lord John Russell proved less amenable. On 1 March Victoria had stressed to him 'the *imperative importance*' of maintaining Cabinet unity in wartime, warning that if it became known that differences of opinion existed, it would cause her 'GREAT *anxiety*'. Despite this, as it began to look likely that the Reform Bill he had introduced on 13 February was too contentious to pursue while the nation was at war, Russell at once threatened resignation. Horrified at the prospect of 'the country & myself being left without an efficient [government] *at this time*', Victoria raged to King Leopold, 'that *personal* feeling *should* have *any weight* at such a moment is beyond *all* belief'. She also blamed 'that foolish, wrong-headed Lady John. It only shows what mischief a wife may do!' On 8 April it seemed that Russell had agreed that the measure should be postponed, but when Victoria wrote to praise his putting the national interest first, he sent back 'a very pettish answer', warning that his 'deep feelings of mortification' might still compel him to go. The Queen was left spluttering at such 'peevish, selfish behaviour', but after she again appealed to his better nature, Russell relented. On 12 April he announced in the Commons that the Reform Bill was abandoned for the present, then 'burst into a hysterical fit of crying'.[71]

This did not mean that Russell was reconciled to serving under Aberdeen. On 5 May he wrote to the prime minister, 'I think the time is arrived.' When Aberdeen declined to vacate his office for him, Russell demanded administrative reform of the army, and structural alterations in government. Even after agreeing to become Lord President of the Council in June, Russell did not give up hope of supplanting Aberdeen, seizing the opportunity afforded by Disraeli mounting a parliamentary attack on him to claim his position had become intolerable. Once again, the Queen wrote to him 'begging him not to mind it', with the result, as she reported in her journal, that he 'consents to remain!! For the 20th time. It is too puerile and intolerable.'[72]

Not until the autumn of 1854 did military operations against Russia begin. On 15 September an invasion force landed on the Crimean peninsula, location of the Russian naval base at Sevastopol; five days later the Battle of the Alma took place. It was a victory for the allies that cost 2,000 British Army lives, but Sevastopol did not fall. For the first time, war correspondents were there as observers, and at once *The Times* published a leading article, not only castigating ministers for being out of London for shooting parties at such a time but questioning whether it was fitting for the Queen to be at Balmoral.

Over the next four months the incompetence, ineptitude and bungling that characterised the Crimean campaign would whip up a storm of public indignation, and ultimately bring down the government. Many troops were killed by cholera, while the wounded were transported miles by sea to Scutari in Turkey, only to face appalling conditions in hospital. After orders were misinterpreted during the Battle of Balaklava on 25 October, the Charge of the Light Brigade resulted in more than 100 pointless deaths. Victoria 'trembled with emotions as well as pride in reading … of the heroism of these devoted men', who had not questioned the impossible task set them; but the episode highlighted the military inefficiency of an army officered by aristocrats. In November, as *The Times* published critical letters from serving men, Victoria received information from a cousin in the army that showed 'what sufferings from cold & what privations are already being endured'. With a 'mind so entirely taken up by the news from the Crimea', she found it 'difficult to sleep soundly'.[73]

In the midst of all this, 'that mischievous and supremely selfish little man, Lord John' made 'a crazy move to upset everything!' – leaving Victoria aghast at his 'folly & wickedness'. Having unsuccessfully

A depiction of wounded soldiers after the Battle of the Alma in the autumn of 1854. Harrowing images such as this one published in the press led to accusations that the government were guilty of incompetence and mismanagement in their handling of the Crimean War.

demanded a Cabinet reshuffle, Russell declared he could not continue much longer as Leader of the Commons because of the government's 'absence of vigour in the prosecution of the war'.[74] He said he would stay on for the brief session of Parliament that was to meet in December so reinforcements could be sent to the Crimea but resign once it was finished.

As Aberdeen struggled to satisfy his overbearing colleague, the Queen wrote to 'express her indignation and *disgust* at Lord John Russell's conduct'. Then, at a Cabinet meeting on 16 December, 'without any embarrassment', Russell airily announced that now was not the time to make the changes he had proposed. By this stage most of his colleagues were so fed up, they were sorry not to be rid of him, but Aberdeen accepted him back, despite the 'sense of self-degradation' this instilled. Victoria was less forgiving, telling Gladstone, Russell's 'retractions only lowers him the more in her opinion'.[75]

The parliamentary session that had opened on 12 December was proving fractious, as concerns mounted about conditions in the Crimea. In the autumn, Victoria had complained to her uncle that the newspapers were 'a perfect scourge', but by December she accepted that many shortcomings reported by the press were true. In her journal she lamented, 'There seems to be a terrible want of proper arrangement & system … as well as forethought in preparing for the cold & bad weather!' She wrote to the war minister, the Duke of Newcastle, expressing concern about the state of the hospital at Scutari, where Florence Nightingale and her team were nursing the sick and wounded. Victoria was further upset by a letter from her former page, George Gordon, describing the 'misery of the men from the wet, the total want of clothes & covering, the bad roads & miserable condition of the poor wretched half-starved horses … All this is heartbreaking.'[76]

On 23 December, the day Parliament adjourned for a month, *The Times* made its most excoriating attack yet, asserting that the army in the Crimea 'has been sacrificed to the grossest mismanagement'. The leading article declared: 'Incompetence, lethargy, aristocratic hauteur, official indifference … perverseness and stupidity reign, revel and riot' at the front, 'and how much nearer home we do not venture to say'. The following day the Queen wrote to Lord Aberdeen, 'She feels distressed at the sufferings of her noble troops, much of which she thinks *might* have been avoided by proper management and more foresight; and this it is which grieves her particularly.'[77]

When Parliament reassembled on 23 January 1855, the backbencher John Roebuck gave notice that he intended to demand a parliamentary committee enquire both into the condition of the army before Sevastopol, and the performance of government departments. 'Without the slightest notice and warning,' Russell informed Aberdeen that since it was impossible to resist this, he was resigning. 'Astounded & indignant' at Russell's 'bad & cowardly' behaviour, Victoria wrote to him expressing shock 'at hearing so abruptly of his intention to desert her government'. A 'much excited and very angry' Russell then threatened to cap his resignation by voting for Roebuck's motion.[78]

Aberdeen consulted his Cabinet, who said that in Russell's absence there was no hope of winning the Roebuck division, and therefore they too must resign. The prime minister went to Windsor to notify the Queen and was nonplussed when she refused to accept it. Declaring that if the government gave up office, it would be 'unjust towards herself, injurious to [their] own character and indefensible as regards the country', she insisted Aberdeen 'appeal to the Cabinet to stand by her'. If they refused, the nation would be left rudderless, for she could not conceive how to replace them. 'Lord Palmerston she could not confide the Government to, and Lord John would not be able to form one.'[79]

When Aberdeen informed his colleagues, 'this wish of the Queen's produced a remarkable effect'. One Cabinet member praised the way she had 'recalled us to considerations of duty and public policy', having 'exercised her prerogative with wisdom as well as strength'. Upon the Lord Chancellor's questioning whether it would be honourable for them 'to run away before an attack' in Parliament, the ministers agreed to 'abide the sentence of the House of Commons'.[80]

This did not lessen the challenge they faced when debate began on Roebuck's motion on 26 January. The ministers were hardly helped when Russell made what the Queen considered, a 'really shameful' statement about the 'horrible and heartrending' state of the army, saying he had resigned because he could not promise failings would be swiftly remedied. At two in the morning on 30 January the government were defeated by 305 to 148 votes, a massive margin that Gladstone said 'sent us down with such a whack that one heard one's head thump as it struck the ground'.[81]

The Queen was so upset after seeing Aberdeen at three that afternoon, she could not 'quite pull myself round for the children's pretty little German play' staged for her in the evening. She knew it would be enormously difficult to assemble a new ministry, for she could hardly take up the suggestion of Aberdeen's son that she 'should send for Miss Nightingale to come home and form a government'.[82] Reluctantly she turned first to Lord Derby, who said he would see if Palmerston, Gladstone and Sidney Herbert would consent to serve alongside men from his own party. When all three turned him down, he said he must give up for the present, but if the Queen came back to him after failing elsewhere, he would try again. Derby was counting on this happening, calculating that Victoria would never offer the premiership to Palmerston.

Victoria and Albert next consulted with the veteran Whig Lord Lansdowne, who said he was too old and gouty to lead a government himself. He agreed to sound out other contenders, and to the Queen's surprise reported Lord John Russell 'fancies he might form a Whig administration himself'. On 2 February she therefore asked Russell to proceed, but though Palmerston conditionally agreed to serve under him, Lord John soon met with several rude shocks. 'Living hitherto in a complete delusion,' he was 'much put out and disturbed' when not just former coalition colleagues, but Whigs whom he 'had not the smallest doubt ... would cordially co-operate' rebuffed him curtly. Taking a grim satisfaction in the way Russell had 'entirely ruined himself – his own friends refusing to have any thing to do with him!' – the Queen recorded she had never expected Russell to succeed, but 'it was necessary that his eyes should be opened'.[83]

With the collapse of Lord John's attempt, Victoria and Albert had to resume what she called 'our *eternal government hunting* errand'. Beginning to despair, she told Lord Clarendon, 'Lord John Russell may resign, and Lord Aberdeen may resign, but I *can't* resign. I sometimes wish I could!' Gradually it dawned on her she could not afford to ignore an obvious solution. A year before she had sworn that Palmerston could never be her prime minister, 'as I should not feel safe with him for a moment', but now she had to bow to realities. Already the Duke of Argyll had warned, 'Should the public suspect that any personal feeling against Palmerston had led to his being set aside ... a popular *storm* might arise.' Days later Lord Clarendon told Victoria directly that to 'prevent false impressions taking root in the public mind' she must give Lord Palmerston 'his fair turn'.[84]

As it became increasingly clear that Palmerston had become '*l'inevitable*', Victoria declared: 'This would be very objectionable in many respects – and personally not agreeable to me – but *I* think of *nothing* but the country.' It remained possible that Palmerston would not manage to cobble together an administration, but on 4 February she officially invited him to do so. It turned out that Whigs who had refused to join Russell were willing to serve under Palmerston, and after an initial refusal, Gladstone, Graham and Herbert agreed to take office at the 'very patriotic and handsome' urging of Lord Aberdeen. On 5 February the Queen was able to write, '*At last* the difficult business has been brought to a close.' The next day, after Palmerston kissed hands, she told King Leopold she had been left with '*no* other alternative'. She had been 'a good deal worried and knocked up by all that has passed', but consoled herself, 'Lord Palmerston, surrounded as he will be, will be sure to do *no* mischief.' She could also take comfort in the knowledge that well-informed observers believed she had shown 'admirable sense and discretion and a complete and proper sense of her constitutional obligations'.[85]

On 7 February Lord Aberdeen came for a final audience. Victoria wrote: 'It reminded me of when I parted from Lord Melbourne, & I felt great difficulty conquering myself.' As he bent to kiss her hand, Aberdeen was 'almost startled' when she clutched his own and squeezed it 'with a strong and significant pressure'. That evening at dinner, she was gratified when Russell's brother, the Duke of Bedford, told her, 'the only pleasing thing in this whole affair was the way in which *I* had behaved'.[86]

An enamel portrait by William Essex of Queen Victoria in 1839, when she was 'in person and in face ... quite such as might tempt'.

Watercolour sketch by Victoria – a talented draughtswoman – of Lord Melbourne, painted *c.*1837–9, in which she tried to capture 'his beautiful noble features and the sweet expression'.

Queen Victoria on horseback in Windsor Great Park, by Sir Francis Grant, painted in 1839–40. Lord Melbourne is on her left, wearing a grey top hat. She went out riding with her prime minister most afternoons, going 'at full gallop' for much of the time.

Prince Albert in Field Marshal's uniform, painted by Winterhalter in 1844. The portrait shows why, in 1839, Lord Melbourne considered him 'certainly a very good looking' young man.

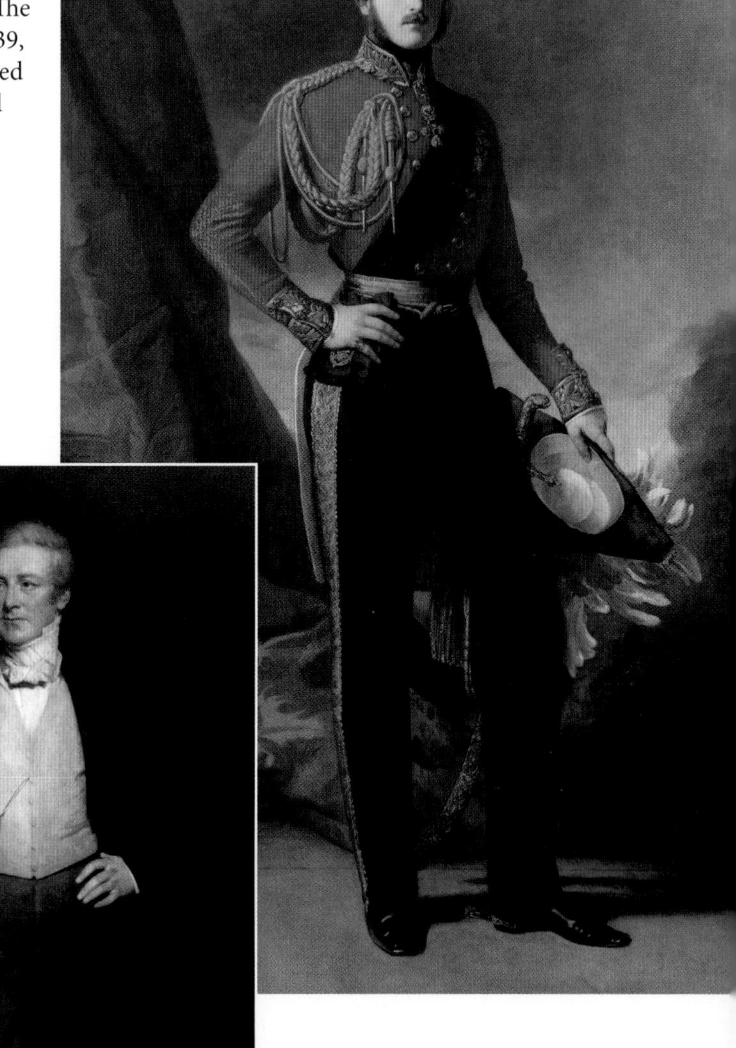

Sir Robert Peel. Portrait by Henry William Pickersgill.

An 1846 cartoon by John Doyle, illustrating the political crisis over the Corn Laws repeal. Peel is depicted as a frightened stag at bay, menaced by savage hounds with the faces of Disraeli and Lord George Bentinck.

Lord Palmerston by Frances Cruickshank in 1855 – the year Queen Victoria reluctantly took him as her prime minister.

The Coalition Ministry of 1854. An engraving after Sir John Gilbert's group portrait, painted after the government's fall. On the right, Palmerston is gesturing forcefully at a map of the Crimea. In the centre, Prime Minister Lord Aberdeen gazes out mournfully as he realises that war is looking unavoidable.

Queen Victoria and Prince Albert at Theatre Royal, Covent Garden with Napoleon and Eugenie on 19 April 1855, during the French Emperor and Empress's visit to England.

Prince Albert at his desk the year before his death in December 1861. Victoria believed that overwork was largely responsible for his death.

5

Lord Palmerston; Lord Derby; Lord Palmerston 1855–1861

The Queen had reluctantly accepted as her prime minister Palmerston, '*the man of the people*', whom the country was 'crying out for'. Only a few dissentients doubted whether, at seventy, he was up to the job. Lord Derby had told Victoria that while Lord Palmerston 'still kept up his sprightly manners of youth, it was evident that his day had gone by'. Disraeli was crueller still, informing a female friend that though the public associated Palmerston 'with energy, wisdom & eloquence', he was 'really an imposter, utterly exhausted & at the best, only ginger beer and not champagne; & now an old painted Pantaloon, very deaf, very blind & with false teeth wh would fall out of his mouth when speaking if he did not hesitate & halt so in his talk'. In recent years the Queen herself had – sometimes eagerly – observed Palmerston's physical decline, recording incidents when his hearing or eyesight had been defective, and being scornful when vanity, which caused him to dye his whiskers, precluded him from using spectacles to read documents aloud at a Privy Council meeting.[1] In general, however, there was a fervent belief that Palmerston alone could resolve the difficulties facing the nation.

As it turned out, the premiership rejuvenated Palmerston. Apart from the occasional attack of gout, he seemed to thrive on the punishing work and late nights in the Commons that came with his job. In December 1856 Charles Greville recorded that his 'wonderful constitution and superhuman vigour of mind and body make everybody forget his age'. Eighteen months later Lord Clarendon hailed Palmerston as 'really a marvel – all his colleagues were looking like old dog horses, so thin & worn, while he was like a giant refreshed by a journey to Osborne & back yesterday & not having had more than four or five hours sleep during the last month'.[2]

To their surprise, before long the Queen and prince found themselves coming round to him. While they were 'always ready to let their old rancour against him boil up', Palmerston placated them by showing consideration and respect. It helped that he proved almost as skilful a chronicler of Parliament as Disraeli. His accounts of Commons proceedings – which, the Queen said, 'No one gives so clearly as Lord Palmerston' – tended to be mockingly dismissive of opponents' speeches, whilst being informative and entertaining. In 1860 the Queen made a point of thanking him for 'some very amusing reports of the really puerile and absurd conduct of many members of the House of Commons'.[3]

More importantly she found Palmerston unexpectedly ready to take account of her wishes. In September 1855 he wanted to send ships to menace Naples, but on learning that the Queen disapproved, 'he had immediately given way ... entirely to please me'. The following year her journal contained the amazing statement, 'Albert & I agreed that of all the prime ministers we have had Lord Palmerston is the one who gives the least trouble, & is most amenable to reason.' In June 1857 relations were still so cordial that Charles Greville described her as being 'entirely reconciled' to Palmerston. 'She treats him with unreserved confidence, and he treats her with a deference and attention which have produced a very favourable change in her sentiments towards him.' She had 'become almost affectionately anxious' about his health, which, as Foreign Secretary Lord Clarendon remarked, was 'curious, considering how particularly she would have liked him to die two or three years ago'.[4]

Her relations with Palmerston would subsequently come under renewed strain as a result of foreign policy differences, but the ill-feeling never quite attained the depth of hatred that had characterised her and Albert's earlier dealings with him. The 'apprehension generally felt' among Palmerston's colleagues in 1855 that hostility between the Queen and prime minister would undermine his government, had proved groundless, with harmony being maintained far better than anyone had expected.[5]

Palmerston's first task was to address problems relating to the war. Egged on by what Victoria labelled 'a rascally press', MPs such as the archaeologist Henry Layard fulminated against all that had gone wrong in the Crimea. He and like-minded individuals suggested that mistakes and inefficiency arose from upper-class dominance of government and in the higher ranks of the army.

Victoria was already incensed with 'that infamous paper, *The Times*', thinking 'the wrecklessness with wh governments are attacked & upset is monstrous', but the 'really outrageous & degrading' behaviour of the House of Commons in some ways shocked her more. 'To cry down our troops … & expose all our sufferings & difficulties – attacking the government & the aristocracy is *indeed* wicked and unpatriotic in the highest degree,' she reflected. [6]

Palmerston knew the House of Commons was in no mood to tolerate the abandonment of the Committee of Enquiry for which they had voted, but unfortunately Gladstone, Graham and Herbert believed holding one would undermine military discipline and damage the Crown's authority. They insisted on resigning, despite the Queen begging Gladstone not to leave her in the hands of those 'least fit to govern'. Consequently Palmerston lost, in Victoria's view, his 'three best men', but managed to reconstitute his government and carry on.[7]

Tsar Nicholas died on 2 March 1855, but despite hopes his successor Alexander II would be less belligerent, the war continued. By summer Victoria could assure King Leopold 'the accounts of our troops are decidedly more cheering', but an attempt to take Sevastopol by storm ended in bloody failure. In Parliament the government was attacked on the contradictory grounds that it was both prosecuting the war with insufficient vigour and failing to pursue peace opportunities.[8]

Throughout it all, the Queen and Albert's support for the war remained unwavering, despite the 'piteous and dreadful sights' that confronted them when they visited military hospitals. The wards were full of double amputees, and men disfigured by ghastly facial wounds. Deeply affected by encountering 'some with their intellects affected … dreadful cases of frostbites', Victoria was shaken to see such large numbers brought 'home to die or lead the lives of invalids & cripples!'[9]

Victoria and Albert had shared the government's alarm when it had appeared that Napoleon III was intending to go out to the Crimea to assume personal command of the allied army. Considering the plan 'really … the height of imprudence',[10] the Queen decided that the best way of distracting him would be to invite the emperor and his wife to pay a state visit to England.

In January 1853 Victoria had been agog to learn that Napoleon was 'going to marry a beautiful young Spanish lady' named Eugénie de Montijo. The emperor had abandoned the idea of contracting a more prestigious union because he was in love with the twenty-six-year-old, although within six months he would be unfaithful to her. The Queen heard that the French were all furious and Napoleon's ministers wanted to resign for, as Lord John Russell scoffed, 'to put this *intrigante* on the throne is a lowering of the Imperial dignity with a vengeance'. One of Victoria's ladies-in-waiting wrote from court, 'I don't think it thought wise *here*', but in fact the Queen found something appealingly romantic about the emperor's choice. She felt so curious about him that, while nervous at the prospect of a personal encounter – for 'these great meetings of sovereigns … are always very agitating' – she was excited too.[11]

When the emperor and empress arrived on 16 April 1855, Victoria was enraptured. Besides admiring Eugenie's lovely profile and figure, she was delighted by her 'grace, elegance, sweetness and *nature*'. Albert was also greatly taken with the empress, which was unusual, as most women seemed to leave him indifferent. Physically, Napoleon III was far from appealing. Greville reported: 'Everybody is struck with his mean and diminutive figure and vulgar appearance.' Victoria observed that his head was disproportionately large compared to his body, but she was still captivated by his low, melodious voice and beguiling manner. The emperor's experiences as a practised seducer had given him a 'perfect knowledge of women', and without straying into suggestiveness he made her feel desirable. The Queen was flattered by the interest he showed in everything about her, and his inexplicable familiarity not just with things she had done since she was twelve years old, but even what she had been wearing. She was enthralled to think of his picaresque adventures and colourful career, marvelling that whereas only six years earlier Napoleon had been 'an exile in England, poor & not at all thought of', he had somehow turned into reality 'the deep plan which he has staked out for himself'. She gushed in her journal that he was endowed with 'a poetical & romantic turn of mind which makes him particularly attractive, without having the slightest personal outward advantages'. Having concluded, 'He is a most extraordinary, mysterious man,' she described him as being possessed of 'a *power* of *fascination* … which … is *most sensibly* felt' by all who came into close contact with him.[12]

While conceding, 'How far he is actuated by a strong *moral* sense of *right* and *wrong* is difficult to say,' she believed she could rely on Napoleon's 'behaving honestly and faithfully towards us'. As she explained to King Leopold, 'He is *very personal* and *therefore* kindness *shown* him *personally* will make a *lasting* effect on his mind, peculiarly susceptible to *kindness*.'[13] When it subsequently turned out that the emperor was not as steadfast and sincere as she had imagined, the disillusionment would be all the more bitter; but this lay in the future.

Napoleon III, Emperor of the French (1808–1873)

The idyll remained unbroken when she and Albert went on their own state visit to Paris in August 1855. Foreign Secretary Lord Clarendon, who accompanied the royal party, reported she was again 'perfectly enchanted ... with the Emperor, who she says has a charm about him that she never met with in anybody'. Despite searing heat – far in excess of temperatures the Queen generally found intolerable – she was indefatigable, going sightseeing and delighting in fêtes and balls 'worthy of the Arabian nights' thrown in her honour. Once again, the emperor took 'the surest way to ingratiate himself with her by making love to her ... As his attentions tickled her vanity without shocking or alarming her modesty ... the novelty of it ... made it very pleasant ... His success was complete.' Her smiling manner in public went down so well that Clarendon could report: 'Everybody raves of her grace and dignity, and some go so far as to think her very pretty.'[14]

On her return Victoria wrote to Baron Stockmar, 'I never enjoyed myself more, or was more delighted or more interested, *and* can *think* and talk of nothing else.' Of the emperor she declared: 'I know *no* one

Drawing of the Emperor Napoleon III by Queen Victoria. She sketched his profile while Napoleon accompanied her and Albert on the train taking them to the royal yacht on the last day of their visit to France. (27 August 1855)

who puts me more at my ease, … or in whom involuntarily I should be more inclined to confide.' There was 'something fascinating, melancholy and engaging' in his character, yet part of his appeal was that 'I felt … I do not know how to express it – safe with him.' While Albert was 'less enthusiastic than I am', he too felt warmly towards an individual 'whom certainly we were *not* over well disposed to' initially. She believed the visits to have been resoundingly successful from the political, quite as much as the personal point of view, assuring her uncle that, 'In short, the *complete* union of the two countries is stamped and sealed in the most satisfactory and solid manner.'[15]

Victoria and Albert were holidaying in their newly built house at Balmoral when a telegram arrived on the evening of 11 September to tell them that Sevastopol had fallen. Although upset that no British feat of arms had brought this about, Albert was determined to celebrate. A bonfire had been laid on a mountaintop overlooking the castle, and the prince decreed it must at once be lit. The Queen stayed indoors, watching proceedings from an upstairs window, while the Lord President of the Council, Lord Granville, current minister in residence, was required to accompany the prince over steep, rough ground. Already exhausted after a day spent tramping the moors for a disappointing bag of grouse, Granville was chagrined at having 'to rush up a precipitous hill' after Albert, in order to drink whisky with the locals.[16]

Although Sevastopol was in allied hands, the war did not end. The Queen was reluctant to seek peace until her troops had distinguished themselves further. Palmerston too was still 'snorting and pawing' on the grounds that Russia was not yet 'half beaten enough'. In contrast, the French and Napoleon III had grown weary of a conflict that was proving ruinously draining of men and money. In November 1855 it emerged that without consulting their ally, the French had entered into talks with the Austrians to devise terms that could be put to the Russians. Palmerston blustered that if the French abandoned the struggle prematurely, Britain would fight on alone. Napoleon thereupon wrote to the Queen, saying that if her country had wanted to continue the war in hopes of freeing the Poles from Russian rule, it 'would have a certain grandeur', but it was senseless to fight on for 'microscopical advantages'. Ultimately it was agreed that Austria could put a set of demands to Russia; French willingness to contemplate 'leaving us in the lurch' nevertheless sowed in Victoria and Albert the first seeds of disenchantment with Napoleon III.[17]

Rather to the Queen's regret, after a certain amount of quibbling, the Russians agreed the terms offered were an acceptable basis for negotiations. On 15 February 1856 Lord Clarendon went to Paris to represent Britain at a peace conference, where he found Napoleon III 'in a most yielding mood towards Russia'. Clarendon was firmer about standing out for disputed points, while contriving to ignore belligerent telegrams from Palmerston instructing him to make no concessions at all. Despite the fact 'that peace rather sticks in my throat', Victoria, like her husband, was more realistic than Palmerston in assessing how catastrophic it would be if England was left to fight the war on her own. Accordingly, they urged Palmerston to give Clarendon full powers to conclude a treaty without having to refer home, which led to peace being signed on 30 March.[18]

The Queen knew it to be 'very unpopular', but even if the peace was 'not tasteful to her feelings', she was philosophical. She told Palmerston that though its terms were 'not all what we could wish or what we might have obtained if France had behaved as she ought', what had been achieved was far from negligible. As 'a public token of her approval', she bestowed on Palmerston the Order of the Garter, an unexpected honour met with exuberant 'gratification and thankfulness' by its recipient.[19]

With the war over, the Queen could focus on another matter that had disturbed her for many years. The time had come, she believed, for the title of prince consort to be bestowed on Albert by act of Parliament, and she wished it laid down in law that the same title would be borne by husbands of future queens regnant. Victoria told Palmerston in May 1856, 'She cannot anticipate any real difficulty', but her optimism proved misplaced. After the Cabinet insisted on cross-party consultation, Lord Derby said he could not recommend prioritising this question when other measures were being abandoned for lack of time. The Queen was assured the matter would be dealt with in the next session of Parliament, but when she pressed Palmerston in February 1857 to name a date, she received a rude shock. He informed her the Cabinet not only still considered this an inopportune moment but had reservations about the proposal itself. In a memorandum ministers stated it was 'no accident' Albert had never been given anything approaching kingly rank. Since it did not appear that 'any practical inconvenience' had arisen from the current situation, they did not want to disturb the status quo.[20]

Victoria was mortified that the Cabinet had suddenly raised objections at 'which not one of them even hinted last year', but she now abandoned the idea of securing what she wanted through act of Parliament. Instead, on 25 June 1857 the honorary title of prince consort was given to Albert by letters patent. Charles Greville sniffed it was 'a very foolish act', which 'confers on him neither title, dignity nor privileges and I can't see the use of it.'[21] Certainly it did not raise Albert's status in foreign courts where, much to the Queen's annoyance, the prince was often outranked by archdukes or other minor royalty. Victoria nevertheless accepted it as the best settlement available.

The Cabinet's reluctance to provoke Parliament unnecessarily with contentious legislation was understandable in view of the fact that, from its opening on 3 February, the 1857 session proved fractious. After difficulties with the budget, it seemed that a foreign policy crisis would derail the government altogether. The previous December the Governor of Hong Kong (in British hands since the conclusion of the First Opium War against China in 1842) had sent a naval squadron to bombard Canton after Cantonese authorities had seized a ship flying the British flag on suspicion of piracy. The British onslaught caused considerable death and destruction, but when the Queen learned of these 'sharp attacks' she commented, 'Our Admiral … seems to have done extremely well.' Palmerston was unconcerned when the Attorney General warned the Cabinet the action had been of doubtful legality, but what Victoria termed a 'most unholy coalition' of Commons members took a different view. On 26 February Richard Cobden moved in the Commons that the violent measures resorted to had been unjustifiable. During the ensuing lengthy debates, not only Cobden and Bright, who had been vocal critics of the Crimean War, but Disraeli, Gladstone and Lord John Russell made powerful condemnatory speeches. The Queen was furious at 'the wretched cant and humbug', but what she called their 'hypocritical humanitarianism' proved so persuasive that on 3 March the government lost a division on the motion by sixteen votes.[22]

The heavily pregnant queen was appalled by this 'most wicked, unpatriotic & dishonest' act of disruption, coming 'at a moment when *all* know that I *can't* attempt to go through a ten days' crisis – that I have *not* the physical power to do so!' That such experienced politicians should expect the English 'to crouch to every other nation' was, in her view, '*quite monstrous!*' Hopefully she added: 'I think they will get well punished,' for her people would be 'shocked at the attempt to lower the tone & dignity of this great nation' by 'this most unworthy & unfit H of Commons'.[23]

Palmerston thought likewise, calculating that if he went to the country to see if they supported punishment inflicted on – as he put it – 'a set of kidnapping murdering, poisoning barbarians', he would be returned to power in a much stronger position. After the Queen gladly granted a dissolution of 'our good for nothing Parliament', the election results vindicated Palmerston's judgement, providing him with a massive personal mandate. His followers swept the board, while Cobden and other critics lost their seats. The Queen rejoiced at the ministry's securing the largest majority of any government since the Reform Bill, expecting this would bring the political stability that had been so elusive since the Tory split on the Corn Laws.[24]

On 14 April 1857 the Queen gave birth to a daughter, Princess Beatrice. She recovered well, feeling '*stronger after number 9* than I ever was before!' Beatrice would be her last baby, so never again would she have to endure a pregnancy during which, as she said, 'one feels so pinned down … only half oneself'.[25]

A month after the birth of her ninth child, the Queen requested Parliament to provide a dowry for her eldest daughter, Vicky, who was engaged to Prince Frederick of Prussia. He was the eldest son of Victoria and Albert's good friend, the Prince of Prussia – brother and heir presumptive of the current King of Prussia. Prince Frederick – known in the family as Fritz – had in fact proposed to Vicky during a visit to Balmoral in September 1855, when she was not quite fifteen. She had accepted him, but because of her extreme youth the engagement had not been made public. Victoria and Albert had been delighted at the prospect of having Fritz as a son-in-law, not simply because 'he is a dear, excellent, charming young man',[26] but because Albert believed that his highly intelligent daughter could school Fritz in enlightened political thinking. Her father envisioned that with Vicky at his side, Fritz would take Prussia in a liberal political direction, enabling the kingdom to fulfil its destiny as leader of a unified Germany.

Although for many months the betrothal remained unofficial, the Queen had at once told her ministers of it. She had stressed to Palmerston this was no arranged marriage, undertaken for dynastic reasons, for Vicky had accepted Fritz 'entirely of her own heart'. Even so, the Queen was pleased that, besides being 'charmed at it', Lords Palmerston, Granville and Clarendon all thought 'it will be of *immense political importance*'. To her uncle Victoria still maintained, 'Much as I value *that*, the *personal part* of the question *is what* pleases me the most.'[27]

On 18 May 1857 Parliament was officially informed of the forthcoming marriage and asked to make financial provision for the bride. Victoria and Albert had initially hoped that Vicky would be given an endowment of £80,000, coupled with an annuity of £10,000, but made do with £40,000 and £8,000 respectively. Since, as Victoria would subsequently point out, 'It is a most unpleasant feeling for the Queen to have continually to come, as it were as a beggar to Parliament,' she and her husband had wanted Parliament to settle money simultaneously on her other daughters, in anticipation of their eventual marriages. Reluctantly the royal parents accepted advice that it would be impolitic to press for this.[28]

The young couple married on 25 January 1858. Victoria had quashed as 'too *absurd*' the Prussian suggestion the wedding should take place in Berlin: 'It is not *every* day that one marries the eldest daughter of the Queen of England,' she remarked. Among other festivities, a splendid ball was held at Buckingham Palace, attended by 'as many princes as at the Congress of Vienna'.[29] On 2 February, Vicky left for Prussia with her husband. For Albert, parting with his daughter, whom he had been preparing with tutorials in constitutionalism and European history, was the most dreadful wrench. Victoria's bond with Vicky would, if anything, become closer, as they maintained contact through remarkably revealing letters.

In the summer of 1857 the British Empire was confronted with one of the greatest challenges of its existence. On 10 May mutinous Indian sepoys at Meerut had gone on a murderous rampage. They had been provoked by savage prison sentences imposed on some of their comrades, who had refused to use cartridges issued as ammunition for their Enfield rifles. The cartridges had reputedly been greased with beef or pork fat, and so would have defiled Hindus or Muslims who handled them. Having murdered forty-one of the Meerut garrison and freed their comrades, the mutineers proceeded forty-five miles to Delhi. There they carried out another massacre of whites and Christians and proclaimed as emperor a descendant of the Mughals. More regiments of the Bengal army came out against the British, and in station after station the soldiery rose up and murdered officers and their families. By the end of June much of northern and central India was in the grip of rebels.

The sepoys had many grievances, but disaffection with British rule was partly caused by policies pursued by the previous Governor General of India, Lord Dalhousie. Many of the sepoys came from Oudh, a territory annexed by Dalhousie in 1856 on the grounds that its rulers had abused their subjects. The annexation had not been an isolated event, for Dalhousie had boasted to the Queen that Oudh was the 'fourth kingdom in India which has passed under your Majesty's sceptre during the last eight years'. Dalhousie had been responsible for the so-called 'Doctrine of Lapse', whereby Indian territorial magnates who had no direct heirs were denied their traditional right to bequeath family members or adoptive sons their lands, which instead passed into British ownership. A land tax was levied on many native property owners previously exempt from it, and those who could not pay had their holdings confiscated. Albert might insist to a German correspondent that in India, 'Oppression is out of the question … The people bless the protectorate under which they live,' but clearly this was not the case.[30]

Albert approved of Dalhousie's attempts to bring progress to India by building roads, railways and canals, and forbidding *suttee* – or 'widow-burning' as the British called it. Some Hindus believed these advances would be followed by the suppression of their religion, not knowing that Victoria deplored attempts to interfere with her Indian subjects' faith. When told, a few months after the outbreak of the mutiny, that 'much of the mischief has been brought on by missionaries', she commented, 'How wrong!'[31]

India held great fascination for the Queen, as she had told Lady Canning in January 1856. Lord Canning had been named to succeed Dalhousie as Governor General, and his wife was accompanying him to the subcontinent. Victoria declared almost wistfully: 'If it was not for the heat & the *insects* how much I should like to see India, that most luxuriant country, full of such wealth & I am sure intended some day to become civilised.'[32]

While not questioning the Doctrine of Lapse, she did feel uneasy about 'those unfortunate Indian princes who have … been for public reasons deposed' and whose pensions from the East India Company would terminate with their lives. She had urged Dalhousie to arrange for payment to be continued to their heirs: 'It strikes the Queen that the more kindly we treat Indian Princes, whom *we* have *conquered*, and the more consideration we show for their birth and former grandeur, the more we shall attach Indian Princes and governments to us, and the more ready will they be to come under our rule.'[33]

She was particularly concerned about Maharajah Duleep Singh, the former child ruler of the Punjab. At the end of the first Sikh War, he had been confirmed as Sikh overlord by the 1846 Treaty of Lahore, but after another Sikh uprising had been defeated in 1849, the Punjab had been annexed. Aged ten, Duleep Singh had been deposed and awarded a lifetime pension. At the time, Victoria had assured Lord John Russell, 'She quite approves the annexation of the Punjab.' She had been thrilled to become the owner of the massive Koh-i-Noor diamond – originally acquired by Duleep's grandfather, Ranjit Singh – considering it 'a proud trophy'. The Queen began taking a personal interest in Duleep Singh after she met the sixteen-year-old when he visited England in 1854. Impressed by his 'striking good looks', she determined to 'befriend and protect' a young prince with 'the *strongest* claims upon our generosity and sympathy; deposed for *no* fault of his, when a little boy'. She found 'something too painful in the idea' that someone 'once so powerful' should be dependent on a pension, 'having no security that his children and descendants … should have any home or position'.[34]

When news of the Meerut massacre and capture of Delhi reached England on 26 June Lord Palmerston blithely assured the Queen, 'he has no fear of its results'. Four days later he told the minister of war that while 'distressing by reason of the individual sufferings and deaths ... it is not really alarming as to our hold upon India'. As further reports came in of the rising's spread, it became clear things were more serious than Palmerston had allowed. This was hardly surprising, considering that in India, native troops outnumbered European soldiers by more than five to one. The Queen informed Palmerston that she had 'for some time been very apprehensive of the state of affairs in the army there, and her fears are now fully realised'. Palmerston responded that about 18,000 extra troops were being sent to India, but Victoria still condemned these measures as 'not commensurate with the magnitude of the crisis'.[35]

The Queen was not the only person who thought Palmerston 'very flippant and off-hand in his views of India affairs'. After the prime minister declared that the government would proceed 'step by step', she demanded more 'vigour and determination'. She pointed out that Parliament and the press were calling for this quite as much as her, while 'the government alone takes an apologetic line, anxious to do as little as possible'.[36]

Victoria was the more exasperated because at the end of the Crimean War she and Albert had implored Palmerston not to reduce the army too much. Now she feared that as more soldiers were sent to India, England itself would be so denuded of forces that 'we may find ourselves in an awful position of helplessness!' She said that if she had been a Member of Parliament, she would have joined those calling for better arrangements for home protection, and was hardly mollified when the prime minister jocularly agreed that it was 'fortunate for those from whose opinions your Majesty differs that your Majesty is not in the House of Commons, for they would ... encounter a formidable antagonist in argument'. Unimpressed by what Albert called 'his juvenile levity', the Queen sent Palmerston a detailed memorandum her husband had compiled in her name on defence matters; thereafter she kept her promise to nag the prime minister relentlessly about it.[37]

Frightful stories kept pouring in from India. Particularly harrowing discoveries were made when Cawnpore was recaptured by the British in July 1857. It emerged that, following their surrender to the enemy the previous month, its male defenders had been ambushed and killed as they set out in boats – having been promised safe passage down the Ganges. Later, the women and children left behind as hostages had been hacked to death as Brigadier General Sir Henry Havelock approached the town to relieve it. One British officer commented that the atrocity awoke 'a fiendish craving for the blood of the cowardly brutes who had perpetrated it'. Some of those responsible were made to lick up their victims' blood prior to being executed. Elsewhere, captured mutineers were fired from a cannon, or force-fed pork or beef before being put to death. Indians who had taken no part in the uprising were hanged in indiscriminate reprisals. The vengeful bloodlust was no doubt fuelled by additional (false) reports that the rebels had indulged in mass rapes and grotesque acts of sadism, such as forcing mothers to watch their children being roasted alive before making them eat their flesh.

The Queen initially believed all such reports. In her journal she described the 'horrors committed on women, ladies & children' as 'too appalling! ... Everything that can outrage feelings, every torture that can be conceived has been perpetrated!! ... One's blood runs cold.' Having been wrongly told that the ladies left behind at Cawnpore had been subjected to 'every outrage which women must most dread', Victoria concluded that it was 'a great mercy all were *killed*'. She wrote to Lady Canning: 'My heart *bleeds* for the horrors that have been committed by people once so gentle ... on my poor countrywomen & their innocent little children ... It haunts me *day* & night.'[38]

Despite this, the Queen did not want blanket punishment imposed as her troops regained control of India. As she remarked to Lady Canning, 'the retribution will be a fearful one but I hope & trust that our officers & men will show the difference between Christian & Mussulman & Hindoo – by sparing the old men, women & children.' At the end of August, *The Times* had called for Delhi to be razed on its recapture and its inhabitants put to the sword, but in conversation with Lord Granville, Victoria and Albert showed themselves 'against any Vandal destruction of towns'. The Queen was also displeased when *The Times* provocatively labelled the Governor General 'Clemency Canning' after he issued instructions that villages should not be automatically torched and that sepoys who had merely deserted should not face the same penalties as those who had committed murder. In late September Lord Canning wrote to the Queen deploring the 'rabid and indiscriminate vindictiveness' of much of the English community in India against 'every native Indian of every class', which he found 'impossible to contemplate without something like a feeling of shame'.[39]

As the autumn wore on, Victoria grew more sceptical about some of the 'unspeakable & dreadful atrocities' that had been reported to her. At the outset of the rebellion, she had asked Lady Canning not to enter into too many ghastly details – as 'I *could not bear* to hear more' – but on 22 October she asked for exact information. She had already established that a particularly frightful incident, in which a British colonel and his wife had supposedly been 'sawn asunder', was 'sheer invention'. Now she asked Lady Canning to see if stories could be fully corroborated, rather than relying 'on *Native* intelligence & witnesses whom one cannot believe implicitly'. While '*mere* murdering – (I mean shooting or stabbing) innocent women & children' was 'very shocking', she knew such things were to be expected in wartime. Victoria was also mindful that 'ghastly deeds' had been committed when Wellington's troops had taken Spanish towns by storm during the Peninsular War (and – as she ingenuously put it – 'they were acts of British soldiers and not of *black* blood'). In the spring of 1858 the Queen felt her instincts had been sound when Lady Lawrence, wife of the Commissioner of the Punjab during the Mutiny, confirmed there had been 'dreadful exaggeration of the cruelties ... All women had been *killed, not* mutilated.'[40]

When Palmerston dined at Windsor on 1 November the Queen 'spoke to him very strongly about the bad vindictive spirit exhibited' by much of the press and public. She stressed 'the absolute necessity for showing our desire to be kind to the peaceable inhabitants; also that the death penalty should not be enforced indiscriminately on all the mutineers'. To Lord Canning she wrote that while '*no* punishment can be severe enough' for those who had genuinely committed atrocities, 'faithful and true' Indians 'should know that there is no hatred to a brown skin – none'.[41]

Delhi had been retaken on 27 September and Lucknow, whose British residents had held out against a fearsome siege that lasted months, was finally relieved in November. Palmerston had predicted that once these two places were back in British hands, the contest against the mutineers would resemble a tiger hunt. In fact, mopping up operations took a long time, and it was not until 4 July 1859 that Lord Canning could inform Victoria that India was completely pacified.

On 19 February 1858 the Queen was 'much vexed and thunderstruck' when Parlmerston's government was unexpectedly defeated in the Commons. The Tories had scented an opportunity after Palmerston bowed to French demands to introduce legislation to hamper foreign terrorists who were using England as an operational base. Victoria had been all in favour of a measure she considered 'merely an improvement of our law, and nothing to restrain the liberties of any one', but MPs were angered by Palmerston's seemingly docile acceptance of dictation from abroad.[42] As a result they voted against the government when Thomas Milner Gibson moved an amendment to the Conspiracy Bill.

Though much annoyed by the opposition's 'total want of patriotism', Victoria knew Palmerston had little alternative but to resign. When he came for a parting audience she said 'many flattering things' to him, later telling several people she much regretted losing his services. Victoria asked Lord Derby to form a government, for although he would clearly face difficulties in a Parliament where the Conservatives were heavily outnumbered, Victoria and Albert felt he 'must take the consequences of levity' for having opportunistically voted out the ministry. Derby managed to assemble a 'tolerably presentable' Cabinet, with Disraeli resuming the place of Chancellor of the Exchequer, but although the ministry was 'a more decent-looking affair than anybody expected', nobody thought it would last.[43]

Prior to his fall, Palmerston had introduced an India Bill, for as he pointed out to Victoria, the Sepoy Mutiny had highlighted 'the inconvenience of administering ... a vast country on the other side of the globe' by the current system of 'double government'.[44] Accordingly, legislation had been drawn up abolishing the role of the East India Company and placing the subcontinent under the Crown's direct control. The President of the Board of Control was to be replaced with a Secretary of State for India, while authority on the spot was to be exercised by a viceroy rather than a governor general. The bill providing for this had not gone through Parliament when Palmerston fell, meaning that the incoming government had to devise a measure of their own.

As they struggled throughout the hot summer of 1858 to get their India Bill through its final stages, the government had to contend with what became known as 'the Great Stink'. The River Thames, clogged with human waste and effluent, began emitting such a terrible stench that London's air was 'half poisoned'. The Queen wrote to Vicky on 29 June that the smell was so unbearable, 'the House of Commons can hardly sit'. Emergency measures to provide London with a better sewerage system had to be brought in, but on 2 August Parliament was prorogued and the India Bill received the royal assent. Although Prince Albert had rather fancifully suggested it would go down well with her Indian subjects if the Queen adopted a title 'such as the Great Mogul', a distinction of this sort would have to wait. Despite Disraeli's assuring her – with a flourish he perhaps later regretted – that the India Act should be looked on as 'the antechamber of an Imperial palace',[45] it would be almost twenty years before Victoria could style herself Empress of India.

A proclamation was prepared to inform the 'peoples of the subcontinent' of a new departure, whereby not only were the Doctrine of Lapse and policy of expansionism abandoned, but the British commitment to religious freedom and equality under the law was reaffirmed. The Queen was uninspired by the initial draft composed by Derby's son, Lord Stanley, who had become Secretary of State for India. She therefore asked Lord Derby to rewrite 'it himself in his excellent language, bearing in mind that it is a female sovereign who speaks to more than 100,000,000 of Eastern people on assuming the direct government over them after a bloody civil war … Such a document should breathe feelings of generosity, benevolence and religious feeling.' She was pleased when Derby produced a new text that emphasised her own Christian beliefs while disclaiming both 'the right and desire to impose our convictions on any of our subjects'. After it was proclaimed throughout India in the autumn, the Queen expressed to Lord Canning her pride at having communicated thus 'with that enormous empire which is so bright a jewel of her Crown', hoping it would mark 'the beginning of a new era, and … draw a veil over the sad and bloody past'.[46]

Despite the difficulties his weak parliamentary position had already caused him, in 1859 Derby decided to introduce a modest measure of political reform. The Queen thought this sensible, explaining to King Leopold, 'The country … in general is very indifferent to the whole subject, so that there could not be a better time to settle the *whole* affair.' She also approved when Derby assured her it would be framed so as 'to turn it to the account of the Conservative classes of society', although she was justifiably concerned this would make it unacceptable to progressives. In the end the fate of this 'dishonest measure' was sealed by Lord John Russell: much to the Queen's annoyance, on 31 March 1859 an amendment proposed by 'that good for nothing little Johnny' secured a sizeable majority.[47] When Derby requested a dissolution, Victoria made no difficulties.

Lord Derby was optimistic – and Disraeli even more so – that the Conservatives would emerge from the election with an overall majority. In the event they gained only thirty seats, which was not enough to give them one. The Queen still hoped the Tories could remain in office because the opposition was disunited. She failed to realise that the rift between Palmerston and Russell had been papered over. On 6 June 1859

– a date that arguably marks the foundation of the modern Liberal Party – their pact was sealed at a meeting in London's West End, where each publicly pledged to serve under the other if the Queen chose one of them to be prime minister. After Victoria opened the new Parliament the following day, the Whig Lord Hartington proposed an amendment to the Queen's Speech, declaring the house's want of confidence in Derby's ministry. Following several nights of debate, the amendment was carried on 11 June. 'So we are in for a crisis!' was Victoria's comment, when Derby resigned.[48]

'Nobody ... ever thought of the possibility' of anyone other than Palmerston or Lord John Russell filling Derby's place; 'the only question ... [was] which it would be'. To everyone's amazement, the Queen asked neither man to form a government. Instead, 'much to his own surprise', she opted for Lord Granville, whom she had pronounced 'the most agreeable & charming of all my ministers ... so gentle, mild & quietly good humoured' when he had served in Palmerston's first ministry. Foreign policy considerations largely accounted for her choice. Europe was currently at war over Italy, and the Queen feared that if either Palmerston or Lord John Russell were at the helm, Britain would become embroiled in the conflict. Rather than mentioning this, she justified her decision on the grounds that it would have been 'an invidious task' to choose between the Whigs' two elder statesmen, whereas it would be 'easier for the Party to act together under a third person'.[49]

Victoria wrote to the two men she had passed over, blithely asserting her hope they would serve under Granville. With 'each in his heart ... deeply mortified at not having been sent for', the prospects were never good. Palmerston did agree to take an unspecified office, 'probably foreseeing that nothing would come of G's attempt, and that he would have all the credit of his complaisance and obtain the prize after all'. Russell turned down Granville flat, telling him that whereas he would have been ready to take second place in a government headed by Palmerston, 'with you I could only occupy the third'. This was not good enough so, 'I am afraid her Majesty must encounter the difficulty of making a choice.' A disgusted Queen condemned this show of 'Dreadful personal feelings again!' Accepting that Granville could go no further, she rewarded Palmerston for his 'very proper' conduct by asking him to form a government.[50]

Palmerston did not have an easy task assembling a ministry. The Queen wanted Lord Clarendon to be made foreign secretary, but having sacrificed his pride by agreeing to serve under Palmerston, Russell claimed the Foreign Office '*as a right*'. Victoria was greatly vexed, telling Uncle Leopold: 'As usually *selfish* peevish Johnny has prevented 1st Lord Granville from forming & 2ndly Lord *Clarendon* from being *where* he ought to be!'[51]

Surprisingly, Palmerston managed to secure Gladstone's services as Chancellor of the Exchequer. Only two years earlier Gladstone had told his brother-in-law that Palmerston was 'a man who systematically panders to whatever is questionable or bad in the public mind', but now he overcame his dislike. He would later say his reasons could be summed up in one word: 'Italy'.

If 'the Italian question' was what lured Gladstone into Palmerston's Cabinet, it threatened to poison Victoria and Albert's relations with the new prime minister and foreign secretary. War had been raging in Italy since April, when Austria had invaded Piedmont, and France had gone to Piedmont's aid. The Queen and prince had been appalled that the Napoleon III had embarked on this adventure but feared that Palmerston and Russell would want to support him.

Napoleon's involvement in Italy would irrevocably change Victoria and Albert's feelings for the French leader, but their suspicions had been growing for some time. Since the end of the Crimean War it had become apparent to them that he cherished 'a number of wild projects', hoping 'to immortalise himself by a redistribution of Europe'. When Napoleon and Eugenie had visited Osborne in the summer of 1857, in many ways it had been a success. Victoria had appeared 'quite as much enchanted with the Emperor and Empress as ever', and had enthused to Uncle Leopold, 'As for *her* – we are *all* in love with her.' Meetings between lords Palmerston and Clarendon and the emperor had mostly gone well, but when Napoleon touched on 'his fixed idea, to revise the map of Europe' in a conversation with Albert, the prince 'spoiled his game'. Albert later told a Saxon diplomat, 'We parted outwardly the best of friends, but the sting of my refusal remained behind.'[52]

In August 1858 Victoria and Albert had visited Cherbourg in their yacht, but seeing the emperor there merely accelerated the cooling of relations. The Queen and prince had been alarmed by how much Napoleon was laying out on fortifying the port and building up his navy, prompting Victoria to warn Lord Derby that unless extra money was spent on the British fleet, 'this great country must ... find herself in a sad condition'. At Cherbourg the emperor had also not been nearly as agreeable as in previous encounters, being so 'reserved and taciturn' that 'a marked difference in his feelings, even towards the Queen' had been detectable.[53]

One explanation for the emperor's preoccupied manner was that, only days earlier, he had had a secret meeting with Count Cavour, principal minister of Victor Emmanuel II, King of Sardinia-Piedmont. Piedmont was the nearest thing Italy had to a constitutional monarchy, and Cavour was intent on extending the kingdom's power. At his meeting with Napoleon it had been agreed that if there were uprisings in Italy, and Austria intervened militarily, France would ally with Sardinia-Piedmont to drive the Austrians out of their Italian possessions. Once the Austrians had been expelled with French aid, Piedmont would be given Lombardy and Venetia, while France would be awarded Nice and Savoy, which currently belonged to Piedmont.

Napoleon had been sympathetic to the idea of Italian liberty since he was a young man, but Victoria would never accept that he was inspired by idealism. Her analysis was rather that the emperor calculated that turmoil in Italy would afford France opportunities to expand its own frontiers. Napoleon, she maintained, did not have 'the good of Italy in view, but his own aggrandisement, to the serous detriment of Europe'.[54]

An early indication that Napoleon intended to assist Italy to throw off Austrian domination had come at a Paris court reception held on 1 January 1859, when the emperor told the Austrian ambassador that he regretted their two countries were no longer on such friendly terms. Simultaneously a marriage had been announced between Victor Emmanuel's young daughter, Princess Clotilde, and Napoleon's notoriously louche cousin, Prince Napoleon. Victoria was upset that the king's 'poor little daughter' had been made a dynastic pawn. 'It is sacrificing a poor child to give her to such a man!' she had lamented to Uncle Leopold, expressing bewilderment that the girl's father could have allowed this. Victoria had become acquainted with Victor Emmanuel when he had visited England in 1855. She had found him rather endearing, despite his 'rough strange manner, & wild rolling eyes', while finding it regrettable 'He does not care *what* he says.' At one point the king had seriously alarmed her by bursting out at dinner: 'We must have done with Austria; she must be exterminated.' As he spoke of pursuing 'war to the death', the Queen said nervously, 'I was sure he was only joking.'[55]

For Albert recent developments showed that Napoleon, a man 'born and bred a conspirator', had reverted to type. The Queen believed that the emperor and Victor Emmanuel's 'disquieting behaviour ... produces universal indignation amongst all right-thinking people here',[56] but in fact feelings in England were mixed. Despite concerns that France would aid Italy in the hope of reaping benefits for herself, there was also widespread sympathy for the Italian cause. Whereas Victoria and Albert instinctively sided with the Austrians, many English people regarded them as oppressors.

In February 1859, when replying to a letter from Napoleon congratulating her on Vicky's having given birth to a son, the Queen had taken the opportunity to express a hope the emperor would abide by international treaties. She had also sent Lord Cowley, her ambassador to France, on a mission to Vienna to see if the Austrians could be prevailed upon to grant greater freedom to their Italian provinces. The Queen had declared to King Leopold that 'Nothing but improvement in the Italian governments *can* bring about a *better state* of things,' but admitted, 'I much fear the obstinacy of Austria.' Initially it had seemed that the Austrians might be prepared to consider reforms, but after Cowley returned to Paris, they took fright when there began to be talk of a European conference being convened upon Italy. Lord Derby's government had tried to bring Austria to reason by making it plain that if war broke out between Austria and France, Austria could not expect any assistance from Britain. Possibly, however, the Austrian court was receiving different signals from Victoria and Albert. Certainly Disraeli suspected Albert of using his German connections to this end, cautioning Derby, 'messages have been conveyed (I will not say from say from HRH) which neutralise the declarations of our ministry'. Derby had refused to believe 'that anyone in high places can have been so indiscreet'.[57]

As Britain attempted to avert war through diplomacy, 'endless telegrams' poured in from Paris, Turin and Vienna, until Victoria and Albert were almost overwhelmed. The Queen told Vicky she felt 'quite done up', as one moment a hopeful message came in, only to be contradicted minutes later. The stress made her so '*dreadfully disgusted* [with] politics and Europe', she was 'tempted to go off to Australia – *there to ignore all*'. Although the Austrians were not being at all conciliatory, the Queen blamed Napoleon for the deteriorating situation. She wrote to her uncle, 'The conduct of the Emperor grieves me. He will have a fearful responsibility upon his shoulders if he brings on war without a shadow of a reason.'[58]

Ignoring some placatory signs from Italy, on 19 April Austria had issued an ultimatum that she would invade Piedmont unless the

Sardinians unilaterally disarmed within three days. As public opinion veered strongly against the Austrians, the Queen accepted the Cabinet's decision to deliver a strong protest to Vienna. The government also announced that if war did break out, Britain would observe strict neutrality. Victoria acknowledged they could hardly have done otherwise, for 'the madness and blindness of Austria ... has put *them* in the wrong, and entirely changed the feeling here, which was all that one could desire, into the most *vehement* sympathy for *Sardinia*'. Even so, she still hoped that before long it would again be possible 'to *throw* the blame of the war on France'.[59]

On 26 April the French had informed Austria they would regard an Austrian incursion into Piedmont as tantamount to an invasion of France, and French troops had been sent south to join with Victor Emmanuel's forces. Napoleon publicly declared he would be making war 'for an idea', promising that, with his aid, Italy would be free from the Alps to the Adriatic. Victoria hoped that the presence of French soldiers in Italy would ensure sentiment in England reverted to what it was before Austria's 'great mistake' had 'temporarily turned it'. When Austria triggered war with France by crossing the Piedmontese frontier on 29 May, there was no question where the Queen's own sympathies lay. She assured King Leopold, 'I feel very confident that the Austrians will be successful & this I do most cordially pray for.'[60]

Things did not turn out as she wanted. In an unanticipated development, the rulers of Parma, Modena and Tuscany were driven out by popular uprisings, and provisional governments were set up in those duchies and the Romagna. Meanwhile the Austrian forces were soon faring so badly that Albert and Victoria believed Britain should abandon its policy of neutrality and intervene in Austria's favour. On 29 May, Derby's foreign secretary Lord Malmesbury had recorded: 'The Queen and Prince feel very strongly the defeat of the Austrians, and are anxious to take their part, but I told her Majesty that was quite impossible.' Malmesbury had pointed out to them that public sympathy lay with the cause of Italian independence, and 'there would not be ten men in the House of Commons', who would vote to aid Austria. The foreign secretary was relieved to find, 'Her Majesty and His Royal Highness are quite aware of this,' although not long afterwards Albert wrote to his daughter Vicky, 'I am itching to strike a blow at the French.'[61]

During the general election campaign, Palmerston and Russell had paraded their Italian sympathies. At Tiverton, Palmerston had 'made bad and mischievous speeches' that Victoria convinced herself were '*not* at all in accordance with the feelings of the country', but which in fact chimed better with public opinion than did her own views. In Italy, meanwhile, France continued to make headway. When news arrived that on 4 June the Austrians had lost another battle, at Magenta, Victoria wrote to King Leopold 'These constant defeats of the Austrians are most distressing & inconceivable.'[62] On 8 June Napoleon and Victor Emmanuel entered Milan together.

Before Parliament convened on 7 June, Victoria had tried to persuade Lord Derby to alter the speech she would read at its opening so that it left open the possibility that in certain circumstances Britain would drop its neutral stance and intervene in Italy. Since the belief that the Conservatives secretly wanted to aid Austria had partly accounted for their poor performance in the general election, Derby had refused. Even with the speech kept in its original form, the opposition still challenged it, and Victoria was left facing the prospect that an avowedly pro-Italian ministry would soon replace Derby's.

As she awaited the outcome of the crucial debate, the Queen told her uncle, '*I trust* the government may *weather* this storm & *wicked* people not succeed, but I *fear* it is *doubtful*.' Derby's resignation and Granville's failure imposed on her the outcome she most dreaded, as Palmerston and Russell assumed responsibility for foreign policy. Before Palmerston kissed hands on 13 June, the Queen conveyed to him her concern that 'he & Lord John were credited with being very anti-Austrian,' while having little confidence this would restrain him. Only days before, Victoria had been trying to establish that, rather than remaining neutral at all costs, Britain might conceivably fight alongside Austria; now her fears that Palmerston and Russell would want to offer military support to France made her a stickler for 'perfect neutrality'. The difficulties she would have with 'those two lamentable ministers' were confirmed almost immediately when Russell sent a 'very bad!' despatch to Prussia, 'as it were, waving the tricolour Italian flag', declaring that Britain looked forward to the day when Italians would become 'free citizens of a great country'.[63]

Austria's military position had worsened still further on 24 June when the French won another victory at Solferino. Despite this, Napoleon was wary of pressing on with the war. Even though France had won every battle so far, losses on both sides had been dreadful, and Napoleon was sickened by the bloodshed. He therefore offered the Austrians an armistice on 7 July and arranged to meet the Austrian emperor Francis Joseph at Villafranca four days later.

In the interval before the emperors met, the French ambassador Persigny came to Palmerston and proposed that Britain should give its backing to an Italian settlement providing for Piedmont to absorb Lombardy, while Venetia became an independent state, free of Austrian rule. Russell at once urged that Britain should give this its 'moral support', but the Queen objected that backing the claims of one belligerent, would compromise Britain's neutral status. The Cabinet agreed it was unwise for Britain to associate itself with terms that Austria was liable to reject, which the Queen told King Leopold was 'a *great thing*. We *must* keep out of it.'[64]

When the two emperors met on 11 June, Victoria felt vindicated when Napoleon proved ready to settle for a less advantageous deal for the Italians than the package pushed by Persigny. According to a provisional agreement drawn up that day, while Lombardy was still to be amalgamated with Piedmont, Austria retained Venetia. The central Italian duchies were to be returned to their ousted rulers, although Napoleon did secure a verbal commitment from Francis Joseph that if the duchies' inhabitants resisted their reinstatement, the rulers would not be reimposed by force.

Whatever the flaws of the proposed arrangement, as far as the Queen was concerned, the news from Villafranca counted as 'a joyous intelligence'. She pointedly told Russell she felt 'doubly glad' England had not 'fallen into the trap' of asking Austria to make concessions to Napoleon, 'which he was ready to waive'. Palmerston and Russell felt very differently about the peace. They were 'deeply mortified and annoyed' that Napoleon had not secured more for his Italian allies, and hoped he would soon conclude the agreement was unworkable. Russell wanted to send a despatch to Paris saying the Villafranca terms were unacceptable because they violated Napoleon's promise to free Italy 'from the Alps to the Adriatic'. The Queen vetoed this, commenting acerbically that the emperor 'may have cheated his clients, but that does not concern *us*'.[65]

Palmerston and Russell could comfort themselves that, within days of Villafranca, Napoleon appeared to regret the bargain he had made, and began looking to Britain to help him wriggle out of it. From Paris, proposals came for an international conference on the Italian question, in which Britain would play a prominent role. If one was convened, it was unlikely that the participating powers would leave the Villafranca agreement intact, but for that very reason the Queen dubbed it 'a hazardous experiment'. To her it was transparent that Napoleon wanted to be extricated from the complications arising from his personal diplomacy, for although he had given his word to Francis Joseph, he could say it was 'not binding, if England will propose its being broken'. With heavy sarcasm, the Queen – or rather Albert, who composed almost all her letters on Italy – pronounced, 'This is a duty which honour forbids us to undertake!'[66] The Cabinet nevertheless decided not to reject outright the idea of a conference, but to wait and see how the situation evolved.

While Palmerston and Russell hoped the Villafranca agreement would prove abortive, Victoria and Albert remained set on seeing it implemented. Their best chance lay in the Cabinet's blocking attempts to derail the agreement, but the Queen and prince could not rely on this happening. The Cabinet were meant to be informed beforehand of a general line of foreign policy, but once they had sanctioned it, it was up to the foreign secretary to execute it without constant reference to them. Russell was apt to think that, having secured his colleagues' initial approval, he could proceed as he saw fit. Often he did things which went much further than they anticipated, or which had not really been made known to them in advance. When she suspected this was happening, the Queen could try and alert the Cabinet by asking the foreign secretary to show them her letters objecting to his proceedings. In 1859 this several times resulted in the Cabinet checking Russell on the grounds they were not prepared to take collective responsibility for a course of action they had never endorsed. Nevertheless, confronting Russell in this manner was not without risks for Victoria. It would be humiliating if it emerged that he enjoyed the support of his colleagues, for there could be no question of the Queen imposing her wishes against their collective will. Obviously she would be better placed to challenge Russell if she could be reasonably confident that a majority of the Cabinet were not of his way of thinking, but establishing this was no easy matter.

The Cabinet's deliberations were strictly confidential, and no minutes were kept for submission to the Queen. Walter Bagehot, the Victorian era's foremost authority on the constitution, stated that the absolute secrecy of Cabinet proceedings was crucial to the government's ability to function, but Victoria and Albert had long regretted being denied a greater insight into ministerial thinking. The prince once told Sir Robert Peel that he considered it 'a source of great weakness for the Sovereign' not to know the arguments that shaped the Cabinet's decisions. Letters survive from the Queen to Russell, Derby and Palmerston, urging them to give her details of Cabinet discussions, but Palmerston only told her what suited him, and Derby evaded her requests. Russell later recalled that while both he and Palmerston faithfully gave Victoria and Albert 'an account of all the decisions of the Cabinet, & an explanation of the advice which is tendered', the Prince wanted 'more than this'. He asked for information about 'the opinions & views which were entertained by different members of the government', but Russell felt supplying this 'would be inconsistent with the relations constitutionally held between the Sovereign and her advisers'.[67]

Now the Queen and Albert decided that if they were to outmanoeuvre Palmerston and Russell over Italy, they must resort to espionage. On 12 July Albert had written to Lord Granville, Lord President of the Council, asking him to provide reports on Cabinet deliberations. The prince explained that, given 'the gravity of the moment', Victoria was anxious 'not to be left entirely ignorant of their feelings', but Granville said this placed him in a dilemma. The Lord President pointed out that it was Palmerston and Russell's privilege to brief the Queen on foreign affairs, and they would 'resent such information being afforded through any other channel'. On the other hand, the fraught international situation, and the need for the Queen to be aware of what was going on, made him 'more than usually anxious to obey her Majesty's commands'. Because doing so could be construed as 'improper interference' on his part, 'No one should know that I make any written communications to Your Royal Highness on this subject.'[68] By dint of subterfuge that undeniably contravened the spirit of the constitution, the Queen was able to counter Palmerston and Russell.

The Queen and Albert strongly desired the central Italian duchies to be restored to their rulers, but when they pressed this on Palmerston and Russell, the 'two dreadful old men' responded with lectures. 'The real question at issue is whether a nation belongs to its ruler, or whether the ruler belongs to the nation,' Palmerston pontificated, while Russell justified Victoria's view that he was 'twaddling and theoretical' by declaring that deposing princes who subverted fundamental laws had been 'fought for, bled for, and established by the Revolution of 1688'. The Queen did not accept that the toppled rulers deserved their fate, but she could also point out that not only was it morally questionable to encourage Napoleon III to break his pledges to the Austrian emperor, but it could involve Britain in war. Should Francis Joseph decide to renew hostilities with France because Napoleon had followed British advice to renege on his undertakings, Britain could hardly remain an onlooker and would have to weigh in on the French side. The Queen observed to Russell: 'If, on finding herself cheated, Austria were to feel herself obliged to take up arms again, we should be directly answerable for this fresh war.' Britain would then have either 'to leave France in the lurch' or join it in fighting Austria, both of which were hideous to contemplate. When her letters expounding this point were read out in Cabinet, Lord Granville reported that they had been 'of immense use' in clarifying ministers' minds.[69]

Throughout the first half of August, discussion in the Cabinet centred on whether Austria should be given notice that Britain would protest if any attempt was made to restore the duchies' rulers by military means. Albert thought this misconceived, annotating a letter from Russell with, 'Protest? On what legal grounds, if it is contemplated only to return the status quo before the war, based on treaties to which we were parties?' In Cabinet Palmerston and Russell held out for the policy, and though ministers prevailed on Russell to tone down some expressions in a despatch to Paris on the subject, it was agreed that Austria should be warned that in Britain's view, it would 'not be justifiable' for the people of central Italy to be coerced into taking back their rulers. The Queen had to console herself that, as amended, the despatches sent out were sufficiently innocuously worded to amount to 'mere paper protests'.[70]

Russell saw things differently, believing the Cabinet's support entitled him to do more to undermine the Villafranca proposals. Regarding it as a foregone conclusion that the restoration of the central Italian rulers would have to be abandoned, he decided it was incumbent on him to devise alternative schemes. On 21 August he presented the Queen with 'something like a new map of Italy', 'parcelling out' the duchies and the pope's temporal possessions as though he had a universally acknowledged right to adjudicate on these matters. For good measure his despatch asserted the name of Austria was 'odious to the people of Italy'. When 'the Queen kicked', Russell abandoned this first set of proposals, only to present others Albert considered '*worse* in tendency'. At Victoria's insistence, these too were withdrawn.[71]

The Queen's refusal to let Palmerston and Russell dictate policy towards Italy brought her relations with them near to breaking point. When Lord Clarendon went to stay at Osborne in early August, he found 'her old feeling against Palmerston ... quite returned, and she spoke with great bitterness of him and Lord John'. After she confided she was 'in a state of constant nervousness ... that some trick would be played her', Clarendon told a friend, 'These two men sit upon her mind like lead and give it permanent indigestion.' In a letter to her daughter Vicky, Victoria revealed, 'Our two Italian Masters almost drive us crazy.

Really I never saw two such obdurate … I won't use any expression because I can't trust what it would be.'[72]

For his part, Russell was almost 'ready to kick over the traces'. He told Sidney Herbert, secretary of state for war, 'We might as well live under a despotism.' Herbert passed this on to Granville, who in turn relayed it to Prince Albert. On 24 August Russell came close to offering his resignation, telling Victoria, 'he would be unworthy of a seat in your Majesty's Councils if he were to give your Majesty advice which in his opinion would lead to calamity & perhaps dishonour'.[73]

Palmerston too was 'a good deal annoyed'. Early on 25 August he went to see Herbert at the War Office, 'with rather a long face on the Queen objecting to all Johnny's despatches'. The prime minister seemed to think this amounted to unconstitutional behaviour on her part, but Herbert warned him not to challenge Victoria on these grounds. While broadly supportive of Italy, the public would be averse to any course that might involve Britain in war. If Palmerston confronted Victoria, he 'would get the worst of it … The Court could ride its race its own way.'[74]

Later that day Palmerston went down to Osborne, where he encountered 'breezy weather'. When he arrived he was told the Queen 'did not feel equal to discuss the matter with him', but Albert gave him a long interview. After dinner Victoria brought herself to talk with the prime minister, and it was agreed that although many members of the Cabinet had dispersed for summer holidays, they should be recalled for a meeting. From what Victoria had been told by Lord Granville and the Secretary of State for India, Sir Charles Wood (who had been at Osborne during Palmerston's visit), she had reason to believe that the Cabinet would restrain its two leading members.[75]

So it proved when the Cabinet reassembled on Monday 29 August. Before they met, several ministers had assumed that Victoria was being unreasonable, but 'after he knew the facts', even Gladstone, who was strongly pro-Italian, declared 'the Queen had been wantonly put to much unnecessary annoyance'. As Lord Granville informed Albert, the Cabinet wanted 'to show sympathy with Italy' and hoped the Italians 'should be left free to act and decide for themselves'. At the same time, ministers were adamant 'that in no case were [the Italians] to obtain active assistance from us'. Britain should therefore 'avoid giving any advice … which might make us responsible for the evil or danger which might accrue from following such advice'.[76]

When Russell was pressed to clarify the contents of despatches to which the Queen had objected, he 'equivocated immensely', but said enough to convince his colleagues that he had wanted to commit Britain to policies they could not support. Palmerston 'spoke for Johnny, and bitterly as regarded the Court', but the other Cabinet members declared in unison that 'the Queen had not acted unconstitutionally'. Granville told the Duke of Argyll, who had been unable to attend, 'It has ended very well. Johnny has had a lesson that the Cabinet will support the Queen in preventing him and Pam acting on important occasions without the advice of their colleagues. A schism very dangerous to the Court and to the government has been postponed.' Albert was informed by Granville that Cabinet members were 'clear that the Queen had come to the assistance of the Cabinet instead of opposing them; that reason had been entirely on her side'.[77]

To try and give himself greater freedom in future, Palmerston had suggested that for the remainder of the summer recess, he and Russell should enjoy fuller powers to act without consulting the other ministers. His colleagues had met this with 'a general assurance of readiness to come up by night trains' from every corner of the country. Palmerston's next ploy was to open unofficial talks with Napoleon III's ambassador, Persigny, urging France to agree that Piedmont could annex the central Italian duchies. The prime minister hid this from the Queen, but she found out when Britain's ambassador in Paris, Lord Cowley, mentioned it in a despatch home. Appalled, she raged, 'How dishonourable of Lord Palmerston! ... We are sold! What can the country, or I, do with men who in their blindness will ruin the country?' She was even more disturbed when Russell forwarded her a letter Palmerston had sent him, airily saying that though Austria would doubtless object to Piedmont having the duchies, if France and Britain united to bring this about, he thought it unlikely Austria would fight. In her journal of 7 September the Queen noted: 'Felt quite in despair & overwhelmed at the dangers we are being dragged into, step by step, viz war with France against Austria, by urging the former to refuse all she has promised Austria! It seems dreadful.'[78]

To Russell she wrote, 'What is the use of the Queen's open and, she fears, sometimes wearisome correspondence with her Ministers, what the use of long deliberations of the Cabinet if the very policy can be carried out by indirect means, which is set aside officially?' Russell confirmed her worst fears by saying if war broke out anew, it would be very difficult for Britain to remain neutral. Victoria declared to Palmerston that the complications caused by his talks with the French ambassador illustrated, 'the great danger and inconvenience ... of such private communications'. Palmerston retorted that if he was prohibited from conducting informal diplomacy, 'such a curtailment of the proper and constitutional functions' of his office would make it 'impossible for him to serve your Majesty'.[79] In the face of this resignation threat, the Queen did not press the point, but for the moment at least she ensured that nothing came of the overture to Persigny.

For the next four months the Italian situation remained unresolved. In October, the Cabinet agreed that Britain would attend if the question of Italy's future was submitted to a congress, but the policy Britain would adopt there continued mired in confusion. In August and September plebiscites held in the central Italian duchies had confirmed that they would not voluntarily take back their sovereigns, though Albert at least believed that 'there would have been not the slightest difficulty' about this 'if they had not been told from London to stand out'. By November even Victoria acknowledged, 'I fear the *Dukes* have no chance.'[80]

The Queen's relations with Palmerston and Russell remained tense in the extreme. She complained to King Leopold, 'We have again been *shamefully* plagued & annoyed by the 2 old Italian Masters – who are *really* too insupportable.' In a memorandum penned in December, Albert wrote of Palmerston almost as bitterly as in the days of their worst enmity: 'All his old tricks … are revived again … If impeded by the Cabinet or the Queen he is violent and overbearing, and if this be of no avail, cheats and tricks.' Believing it 'quite essential that the Cabinet should be on their guard, else they will be dragged without being aware of it into a war', Albert took more ministers into his confidence, corresponding with Sir George Grey, Chancellor of the Duchy of Lancaster, and Charles Wood, Secretary of State for India. Victoria reassured Uncle Leopold that, apart from Palmerston and Russell, 'The *rest* of the Cabinet, Gladstone excepted … are as *sound as possible.*'[81]

It infuriated Albert that Palmerston failed to realise Napoleon III's real intentions. The prince was sure the emperor wanted another war with Austria, so long as Britain was an ally. Napoleon no doubt calculated that this time Prussia would come to Austria's aid, and then, 'with English consent & *assistance*!!' he could invade Germany and grab the Rhineland for France. 'A child may see,' Albert scoffed, that this was what Napoleon had in mind. 'When victorious in Germany the Emperor would be master of Europe as much as his uncle ever was & then *we* should be entirely at his mercy. To all such considerations Ld P. turns a deaf ear!'[82]

Palmerston still wanted the duchies to be amalgamated into Piedmont, and to achieve this, was ready to contract a formal alliance with France. He was astonishingly cavalier about the possibility this might result in war with Austria, believing that Britain's involvement in the fighting would be limited to naval operations.

On 3 January 1860 Palmerston and Russell explained their views at a 'most stormy meeting' of the Cabinet. When the prime minister and foreign secretary put the case for a French alliance, committing Britain to war with Austria if hostilities reopened, the 'sober-minded majority' expressed 'insuperable objections'. Granville reported that in the face of these, 'Lord John gave hints of not being able to continue to carry on the business of the Foreign Office,' while Palmerston insisted his policy was the 'only honourable course for this country'. In the end the Cabinet adjourned for a week, but there seemed a strong likelihood the government would break up on the issue. Furthermore, the Queen declared that if asked to announce such a policy in a speech from the throne when Parliament assembled, 'She would refuse point blank to do so, let the consequences be what they might.'[83]

Over the next few days, developments occurred that made Palmerston and Russell – 'the *two*' as the Queen called them – reconsider. As a result of a leak from a Cabinet member, on 5 January *The Times* reported details of the 3 January meeting and made a 'stark declaration that the Nation or Parliament would not allow the government to take the line proposed by Lord Palmerston'. Albert trusted this would 'give courage to those in the Cabinet who have resisted it'.[84]

Ambassador Persigny then put forward an alternative diplomatic solution, suggesting that both Napoleon III and Francis Joseph should undertake to abstain from using military force in Italy. On 10 January the Cabinet reassembled, 'prepared for a serious & critical' discussion. To their surprise Russell embraced this new proposal – which was speedily approved – acting as though it was not a departure from anything he had previously wanted. Granville informed Albert that as it became clear crisis had been averted, 'The relief on some of the countenances … was amusing.'[85]

The Queen was further heartened when Parliament met on 24 January 1860, and showed itself strongly opposed to a French alliance. In the Commons, Palmerston brazenly denied that an agreement with France had ever been contemplated, when, as the Queen observed in her journal, 'God knows, *we* have reasons to know [one] was, though mischief *was* prevented.'[86]

Soon, another worry loomed. It now seemed virtually inevitable that Sardinia-Piedmont would acquire the central Italian duchies, but France had concerns about a sizeable kingdom materialising on its southern borders. Napoleon felt that if he consented to Victor Emmanuel enlarging his territory, France must be rewarded by the cession of Nice and Savoy. This should hardly have taken Palmerston and Russell by surprise: in September 1859 the French had explicitly stated that 'France must look for some compensation for herself if Sardinia is to benefit so largely,' but Palmerston had discounted the warning. There was therefore consternation when, on 21 January 1860, a 'rather alarming' letter arrived from Lord Cowley, British ambassador in Paris, confirming that, as Victoria phrased it, France harboured 'a determination to rob Sardinia of Savoy'.[87]

On 5 February the Queen wrote to Russell to say that this latest development was 'all the consequence of his policy'. Victoria chided the foreign secretary, 'We have been made regular dupes', just as she had 'apprehended and warned against all along'. Dismissing Napoleon's concern for Italian liberation as merely a cover for 'a policy of spoliation', she reminded Lord John that the French foreign minister had already declared his country's acquisition of Nice and Savoy to be 'the necessary accompaniment of the annexation of all central Italy to Sardinia'. In a fury she continued, 'Sardinia is being aggrandised solely at the expense of Austria … & France is to be compensated! … What does the Cabinet propose to do?'[88]

Stung by these barbs, the foreign secretary sent back an indignant reply. 'Lord John Russell unfortunately does not partake your Majesty's opinions in regard to Italy,' he proclaimed. 'The liberation of the Italian people from a foreign yoke is, in the eyes of Lord Palmerston and Lord John Russell, an increase of freedom and happiness at which, as well-wishers of mankind, they cannot but rejoice.' The Queen forwarded the letter to Palmerston in high displeasure. Commenting it was 'not the kind of communication which the foreign secretary ought to make', she particularly objected to Russell's 'covert insinuation … that she is no well-wisher of mankind and indifferent to its freedom and happiness'. She concluded, 'the Queen must demand that respect which is due from a Minister to his Sovereign'; since Russell's letter was 'deficient in it', she expected him to reconsider. The matter was smoothed over after Palmerston and Russell both wrote mollifying letters and Victoria accepted Lord John's 'expressions of regret'.[89]

MPs reacted angrily when they learned of the prospective annexation of Savoy, manifesting 'strong English feeling' that delighted Victoria.

She told her uncle, 'Parliament & the country are, I think, *fully* alive to the danger arising from the perfidious policy of our neighbour.' The Queen would have liked to frustrate Napoleon by joining with other European countries to 'make a united declaration against the annexation', but Russell pointed out that while there was considerable indignation against France, 'No one wishes this country to go to war for Savoy.'[90] Savoy and Nice were duly annexed after plebiscites held there showed an overwhelming desire to merge with France.

The Queen could take solace in the fact that Palmerston and Russell's view of Napoleon III had completely changed. Palmerston had tried to persuade France to abandon the annexation, and Victoria chuckled that he was 'very angry at the Emperor's *not* listening to his remonstrances'. On 26 March Russell made a strong statement in the Commons, warning that in a country as warlike as France, acquisitions of this sort might encourage 'other acts of aggression'. Victoria considered it 'an excellent

A cartoon depicting Palmerston playing 'Beggar my Neighbour' with Napoleon III. This reflected the increased tension that developed between Britain and France after Napoleon annexed Nice and Savoy.
(Sir John Tenniel, 1861)

speech'. She was even happier about Palmerston's reaction when Flahault, Persigny's successor as French ambassador, said that Russell's assertions had been 'personally offensive' to the emperor and that, if matters were pushed further, 'You will have war.' As Palmerston recounted to Victoria, 'I said that I was most anxious to prevent such a war; but if it was forced upon England, England would fearlessly accept it.' The Queen told him his account of the exchange 'gives us great pleasure'. Her feelings for Palmerston and Russell promptly underwent a complete transformation, and she now became '*very much pleased*' with the 'two old boys'.[91]

If Palmerston and Russell no longer looked kindly on Napoleon, this was nothing compared to Victoria and Albert's detestation for him. Lord Clarendon thought the prince's attitude 'demented': at one point Albert had referred to Napoleon as 'a walking lie', while to his daughter he wrote of 'the French devil'. Victoria was scarcely less 'rabid' than her husband. In early 1859 she had told Vicky she was 'so sorry' that Napoleon was behaving irresponsibly, for 'he has so much to make one like him'. Now, there was not a trace of lingering affection for this '*universal disturber!*' Such was 'the duplicity & utter untrustworthiness of the Emperor in *all* his proceedings' that, unless his 'great conspiracy' was thwarted, 'bloody wars and universal misery must be the consequences'. Finding it 'monstrous to think of *one man* trying to disturb the peace of the world', she was worried when it seemed possible Napoleon might visit England in 1861. 'I am no hypocrite,' she asserted. 'I can't conceal what I think, and I know I should show him that my feelings towards him are not what they were.' That same year, Lord Clarendon told a friend that the Queen and Albert's hatred for Napoleon 'embitters their lives & their conversations'.[92]

Victoria and Albert's loathing of Napoleon meant they had been far from pleased when, in early 1860, Gladstone had asked Parliament to approve what Albert called 'a stupid treaty of commerce' with France. The prince feared that any lowering of duties on goods traded between the two countries would be 'perverted into a means of keeping down the warlike spirit of the nation'.[93] Initially the House of Commons had been suspicious too, but Gladstone won over doubters, and the treaty was ratified by Parliament on 9 March. Had the vote taken place a few days later, the outcome might have been different, for once Napoleon had annexed Nice and Savoy, feeling in the country became much more hostile to France.

This meant that revenues from import duties on French wines fell just at the moment the public began clamouring to spend more on defence. By the late spring of 1860 England was in the grip of an invasion scare, and large numbers of men enrolled in volunteer corps to fend off possible attacks by France. The Queen hoped the 'public spirit this country has shown' would check Napoleon's 'sinister designs' but wanted more to be done. In May she warned Palmerston, 'Every day tells us of new schemes of aggression of our dangerous neighbour & the country is in a most unprotected state.'[94] Finding the money to pay for the measures she and Palmerston believed necessary would cause serious tensions between the prime minister and the Chancellor of the Exchequer.

Palmerston and Gladstone had already clashed over raising a loan of £8.5 million to cover part of the cost of fortifying the south coast. Displaying what Albert scornfully called 'full trust in the Emperor & France', Gladstone had told Palmerston in February 1860 that asking Parliament to sanction borrowing on this scale would be 'a betrayal of my public duty'. In May Palmerston informed the Queen that in Cabinet, Gladstone had showed himself 'sadly deficient in good sense and statesmanlike views'. When the matter had been discussed, the other ministers had agreed the money must be spent, although the question of how to raise funds was deferred. Palmerston wrote to Victoria he hoped Gladstone would drop his opposition to the loan, but if not 'it would be better to lose Mr Gladstone than to run the risk of losing Portsmouth or Plymouth'.[95]

By this time another source of friction had arisen. Gladstone wished to abolish the paper duties that made newspapers too pricey for working people to buy, and when the Lords threw out his proposal in May 1860, he became passionately exercised about the constitutional implications of their rejecting a financial measure when convention held these to be the province of the House of Commons. 'He is very excited,' Victoria sniffed to King Leopold; she personally thought it 'absurd to pretend it is unconstitutional for it is not.' Gladstone made repeated threats to resign if the matter was not dealt with as he wished, only to back down ungraciously once he realised none of his colleagues supported him. The Queen wrote to Palmerston, 'Mr Gladstone's conduct is much to be regretted for the pernicious effect it must have both on himself and the country.'[96]

Despite having 'announced to his colleagues, nearly a dozen times, that he was firmly resolved to resign' over the fortification question,

Gladstone crumpled on that too. He succeeded only in imposing what Palmerston described to the Queen as 'a childish condition' that the loan paying for the works must be renewed annually, rather than being granted for four years. Palmerston assured Victoria it did not matter, predicting that Gladstone would repeat next year his current pattern of 'ineffectual opposition and ultimate acquiescence'. Palmerston added that Gladstone's colleagues would actually be relieved to see the back of him, and Lord Clarendon believed that the Queen too 'would accept his resignation with satisfaction'. She wrote to King Leopold of Gladstone, 'He has done himself immense harm & is so capricious & *odd* that it is very troublesome to have any thing to do with him.'[97]

In 1860 there were further developments in Italy not to the Queen's liking. That April, uprisings broke out in Sicily against its ruler, King Francisco II of Naples. Giuseppe Garibaldi, a veteran Italian patriot and freedom fighter, at once sailed with a thousand followers to assist the insurgents in the name of 'Italy and Victor Emmanuel'. After capturing Palermo, Garibaldi prepared to cross the Strait of Messina in order to wrest Naples itself from its king. Alarmed at the prospect that an already enlarged and strengthened Piedmont could be further swollen by absorbing territory in southern Italy, Napoleon III wanted the French and British Mediterranean fleets to work together to prevent Garibaldi's crossing. The Queen would not countenance anything that 'would make us again the dupes of French policy'. While assuring Uncle Leopold that she was no enthusiast for Garibaldi, she said feeling in England was so great against King Francisco's 'miserable corrupt government ... it would be impossible to go against it'.[98]

On 6 September, a fortnight after Garibaldi's forces had landed on the mainland, King Francisco fled his capital; two days later Garibaldi entered Naples and proclaimed Victor Emmanuel its king. The Queen was contemptuous of Francisco, finding it difficult to feel sorry for 'such a wretched sovereign', while simultaneously condemning Victor Emmanuel's conduct as 'iniquitous and utterly disgraceful'.[99] Victor Emmanuel's chief minister, Count Cavour, then capitalised on Garibaldi's successes by sending troops to seize the papal states. On 16 October the Piedmontese Parliament voted both to annex those provinces and the Kingdom of the Two Sicilies.

Lord John Russell had taken exception when France, Spain, Prussia and Austria had condemned Italy's headlong progress towards unification. He sent a euphoric despatch to Turin saying it was 'but an act of justice' in the Sardinians 'to assist brave men' to overthrow oppressors. Rather than censuring such developments, 'Her Majesty's government will turn their eyes rather to the gratifying prospect of a people building up the edifice of their liberties.' The Queen was 'anything but pleased' with Russell's 'dreadful doctrines'. Already embarrassed that her foreign secretary had effectively claimed it was 'right for people to dethrone & expel their sovereigns, should they be dissatisfied with them', she was still more mortified when Count Cavour published the incendiary document. Prince Albert did not doubt that henceforth any power 'who entertained an inconvenient sympathy for Canada, for Ireland, for India ... will remember that Lord John Russell approves of foreign intervention against oppressive and unpopular governments'.[100]

'Rejoicing in the idea of having been largely instrumental in the liberation of Italy,' Russell exulted to Victoria: 'Another Prussia has risen in the south of Europe which will in all probability be a new guarantee for the Balance of Power.' Palmerston too assured her that what had happened would not just benefit Italians but would enhance Europe's stability. Victoria took a cooler view. At New Year 1861 she wrote to the prime minister that, much as she would have liked to share his optimism, 'she ... fears we shall only have seen the disruption of existing things, without the certainty of the construction of the new order of things'.[101]

The Queen was devastated when her mother died on 16 March 1861, being overtaken by such excessive grief that some thought she had succumbed to her mad grandfather George III's 'hereditary malady'. Lord Clarendon claimed that Albert anyway lived 'in perpetual terror' of this manifesting itself, feeling it incumbent on him 'to watch that mind every hour and minute – to watch as a cat watches at a mouse-hole'. Now, as Victoria wept ceaselessly, Clarendon feared she would permanently descend into 'morbid melancholy'. The Queen described her depressive symptoms to King Leopold: 'A sort of cloud ... hangs over you, and seems to *oppress* everything – and a positive *weakness* in the powers of reflection and mental exertion. The doctors *tell* me I *must not* attempt to *force* this.' Albert reported to Baron Stockmar that her every attempt to read or work brought on 'such a lassitude ... she can't recover from it', adding that his wife's 'terribly nervous' state meant 'I am well-nigh overwhelmed by business, as I do my utmost to save Victoria all trouble.'[102]

The fact that Albert stated Victoria's enervation added to his workload shows that one should be cautious about assuming that he had taken over her political role so completely that nothing whatever was done by her. Victoria herself would later say that Albert took '*almost all* the labour & <u>all</u> the responsibility off my hands', but state business still demanded a good deal of her attention. It may have been true, as Lord Clarendon asserted, that the Queen was 'absolutely guided by the superior mind of her husband', but Lord Granville went too far when, after describing the Queen as 'not clever', he insisted 'everything is done by the Prince ... and [she] never writes a letter that he does not dictate every word of'. Granville believed that in twenty-odd years of marriage, she had 'given up ... every year more, the habit of ever deciding anything, either great or small, on her own judgement'. After Albert's death Victoria echoed this when she told Lord Clarendon that the prince used 'to read and arrange everything for her to save her all trouble, to bring her things she merely had to sign and explain them to her and tell her what to do about them'.[103] Yet the Queen's role was not as passive as this implied. Though Albert dealt with an enormous amount himself, Victoria was not shut out from his working life. She was privy to almost everything he did, even if she had become the less active partner in a joint enterprise.

There is no question that Victoria relied on Albert for direction, and also to articulate their thoughts in written communications to ministers, but when she copied out letters Albert had composed for her, it was not a mindless exercise. On bringing her a draft, Albert would say, 'read it; I should think this would do', and she would check what he had written. Sometimes she altered the wording, but this tended to be because she found a phrase with Germanic overtones, and not on account of the content. Although their intensely loving relationship was periodically 'embittered by "scenes"', they rowed about matters such as the children's upbringing, not politics.[104] However her willingness to accept Albert's views did not preclude her judging them intelligently, for she understood what had shaped his conclusions. The process was mutually beneficial, for expounding his ideas to her helped Albert clarify his thoughts and made him more cogent when dealing with ministers.

During crises Victoria's involvement increased as she and Albert tackled problems together. At busy times, both of them were inundated with paperwork, with Victoria complaining more than once of being 'literally overwhelmed' by despatches. Her journal contains references to business keeping her and Albert from dinner, as well as having 'never more to read and write'. When the situation in Italy was looking worrying in 1859, she mentions being 'very busy writing a long letter to the Emperor Napoleon at the desire of the Ministers'; the following year she alludes to writing 'our observations' on one of Russell's draft despatches, clearly indicating a collaborative effort by her and Albert. It is evident, too, that when the Queen and prince jointly met with ministers, she took a prominent share in the conversation rather than letting her husband do all the talking.[105]

This is not to deny that Albert worked much harder than his wife. Propelled by a powerful sense of duty and a somewhat obsessive nature, he toiled alone at his desk for hours at a time. The voluminous memoranda and countless papers in his hand testify to how much he cogitated and fretted on every aspect of government. In general Victoria was grateful for all he did, although she did have spasms of irritation at his 'over-love of business'. The prince pushed himself so hard that his health was affected. When he was particularly stressed, what Victoria called 'his poor dear stomach' suffered, and pressure and unremitting labour sometimes left him depressed. In April 1861 he wrote to his brother, 'I go on working at my treadmill, as it seems to me,' while to his daughter he compared himself to an over-burdened donkey on the Isle of Wight.[106] In his lifetime Victoria sometimes felt her husband's ailments were self-inflicted; when he died she would depict him as a martyr to the cares of state.

The Queen's mourning for her mother fortunately coincided with a lull in domestic politics, and by the summer of 1861 she was enough of her old self to feel indignation at the 'wicked report … set about that … *I* was gone out of my mind'. In July she agreed that Lord John Russell should go to the House of Lords, where he would have an easier time presenting foreign policy. Somewhat grudgingly she granted his wish to be made an earl, rather than a mere baron, but declined to award him the Garter, because it was 'useful to keep something in hand'.[107]

The Queen and prince were still apt to grumble about the prime minister, but when Lord Clarendon dined at Windsor in November 1861 he found the couple in quite a mellow mood. He wrote to a friend: 'There were some *nags* at Palmerston,' regarding his 'insolent hostility to foreigners in general and Germans in particular,' but the Queen commented resignedly: 'He is too old to learn.' Clarendon concluded: 'On the whole there were fewer complaints of the government than usual and their tone was that of satisfaction with men and things.'[108]

Clarendon had no intimation that tragedy lay just around the corner. The prince consort had already experienced serious health problems that year, having suffered agonies in February from a dental abscess. As he endured painful sleepless nights, the Queen wrote tetchily to her daughter, 'Dear Papa never allows he is any better or will try to get over it, but makes such a miserable face that people always think he's very ill. It is quite the contrary with me always.' In late November a host of other symptoms presented themselves, afflicting the prince with rheumatism, back pain, chills, neuralgia, and insomnia. To make matters worse, he was in considerable distress of mind, having learned that the Prince of Wales had been having a sexual relationship with an actress. This had begun the previous August while Bertie had been on an army training course in Ireland, and some of his fellow young officers had arranged an assignation with Nellie Clifden. In November word of this had come to Prince Albert's ears, and had caused him, as Victoria recalled, 'agony and misery … dreadful to witness'. Aggravated by stress, Albert's digestive problems, 'to which his natural weakness of stomach made him liable', became particularly severe. It is now thought he may have suffered from Crohn's disease, a potentially fatal inflammation of the gut.[109]

Albert was already unwell when on 28 November alarming news arrived. Relations with the United States had been 'very ticklish' since the outbreak of the American Civil War in April 1861.[110] The North had wanted England to accept that the Southerners who had seceded from the Union were rebels, but in May 1861 Britain had recognised both Northern and Southern states as belligerents, while declaring her own neutrality. The British government were furious on learning that on 8 November a Northern warship had waylaid a British mail steamer near Cuba and taken off two envoys from the South, who were travelling to Europe to enlist support for the Confederates. Deeming this a 'gross outrage' and violation of international law, the Cabinet were eager to retaliate. A despatch was drawn up informing the Unionist government that unless they disavowed the action of their naval captain and freed their prisoners, Lord Lyons, British minister plenipotentiary in America, would be withdrawn from Washington.

War looked likely enough for 8,000 troops to be sent to Canada to defend it against an American incursion. Sanguine at the prospect of fighting 'such ruffians', Victoria wrote to King Leopold that since 'I conclude they will *not* grant [British demands] … I suppose war will follow wh will be utter destruction to the North Americans.'[111] Albert was less bellicose and set about defusing the crisis. When the despatch to Washington was submitted for approval, he was so ill he could hardly hold his pen, but he amended the wording to make it less aggressive. By suggesting that the Northern captain had misunderstood or exceeded his instructions, he gave the Unionist government a means of conceding gracefully. After some hesitation they grasped the lifeline, and the threat of war receded.

Albert's alterations to the despatch were 'the last thing he ever wrote'. Thereafter his condition steadily worsened, although the royal physicians, doctors Jenner, Holland and Sir James Clark, kept telling Victoria there was no cause for alarm. Palmerston was fearful, believing the trio of medical men 'scarcely fit to attend a sick cat', but when the prime minister suggested another doctor should be called in, the Queen was 'dreadfully annoyed'. To both King Leopold and her eldest daughter she maintained that there was no need to worry. On 9 December she assured her uncle, the 'beloved invalid' was improving even if, as it was a slow process, 'I need not tell you *what* a trial it is to me.' Albert's 'tiresome illness' was similar to hers at Ramsgate in 1835, 'only that I was much worse'.[112]

Her journal entries are less solipsistic and show that she was really frightened, clinging to optimism out of terror. On 7 December the physicians had diagnosed – possibly wrongly – 'gastric fever', or typhoid, and Victoria admitted that when she heard this, 'I felt as if my heart would break.' After Palmerston wrote a letter of 'fierce remonstrance' to Sir Charles Phipps, Keeper of the Queen's Privy Purse, another physician, Dr Watson, was summoned on 9 December, but 'came too late to do any good'. Even then, Victoria was angry when Palmerston suggested that Watson should stay overnight at Windsor Castle, and she instructed Phipps to rebuke the prime minister for 'most improper' interference. She went on catching at every hopeful sign, but on 13 December Phipps wrote to Palmerston that, 'in spite of her determination not to contemplate any misfortune, she must be aware of the serious nature of the disorder'.[113] By that time Albert was suffering from congestion or the lungs, or pneumonia; he died at 10.50 on the night of 14 December.

Five days later a bereft Victoria wrote to Palmerston, 'the Queen feels her life ended, in a worldly point of view'. To King Leopold she cried, 'Oh! … To see our pure, happy, quiet, domestic life, which *alone* enabled me to bear my *much* disliked position CUT OFF at forty-two … is *too awful*, too cruel!' Even in her misery, the Queen knew that she would not be the only one affected by the tragedy, for Albert's death had implications for the national welfare. To her grief-stricken daughter in Prussia Victoria wrote, 'What is to become of us all? Of the unhappy country, of Europe, of all?'[114]

6

Lord Palmerston 1861–1865

On 26 December 1861 the newly widowed Queen wrote to Lord Palmerston, 'Business she can as yet hardly think of, for her whole soul, bruised and crushed as it is … lives but in that future world,' where one day she would join her husband. When the prime minister urged her not to neglect her own health, Victoria assured him: 'She … does all the physicians ask her to do, but grief like hers is beyond all physicians' skill. It gnaws into her very heart's core & the very depths of her soul.' In the coming weeks, she would uninhibitedly share her despair with every politician she dealt with, dwelling on her heartbreak to men unaccustomed to witnessing such lacerating displays of anguish. To Earl Russell she lamented that in place of her former happiness, 'there is *now utter desolation, darkness* and *loneliness*'; Lord Derby too was apprised that such was her 'utter misery', that 'every feeling seems swallowed up in that *one* of unbounded *grief*!' When Lord Clarendon visited her at Osborne ten weeks after her bereavement, he reported that the 'embarrassing emotion' she showed made it 'by far the most affecting scene I ever remember'.[1]

Initially Victoria appeared conscious that she must not neglect her responsibilities, repeating forlornly, 'They need not be afraid, I will do my duty.' Clarendon thought it a hopeful sign that she asked for papers to be sent her as normal, and Disraeli understood her to be mindful that Albert had remonstrated about her 'giving way so completely' upon her mother's death. In the first few days of widowhood she was heard to say, 'Now, you see, I am calm, I am profiting by His advice. I am doing what He would have wished.'[2]

Her only source of comfort, according to Clarendon, lay in her belief that her late husband's 'eye is *now* constantly upon her, that he watches every action of hers'. Fully aware of Albert's cherished views on domestic and foreign policy, she wrote to Palmerston: '*He* has *left all* these important subjects to *her* to watch over.' The very day after Albert died, she somewhat alarmed the prime minister by vowing, 'The Queen's *sole* future *object* will be to *follow* in everything all HIS *wishes, great and small.*' Palmerston gloomily predicted that her determination to conform to what she conceived to be Albert's opinions, 'promises no end of difficulties for those who will have to advise her'.[3]

The Queen's belief that Albert had bequeathed her a sacred trust to see his views were respected posthumously, ensured that the monarchy did not suffer a catastrophic loss of power on his demise. According to Lord Stanley, in his lifetime, 'the Prince had undoubtedly a fixed determination to increase the personal power of the Crown'; had Albert lived longer, a combination of talent, hard work and experience would have enabled him to become 'almost as powerful as the prime minister of the day'. It was a prospect Stanley had viewed 'with some jealousy', but Disraeli thought differently. He told the King of Saxony's minister in England, apparently without irony, that if Albert had not been cut off in his prime, 'he would have given us, while retaining all constitutional guarantees, the blessings of absolute government'. Disraeli assumed the prince's death would alter things irrevocably. In fact, the Queen guarded her powers as vigilantly as Albert had done. Indeed, she intervened in politics far too much for some ministers' liking. By September 1863 Lord Clarendon was complaining that Victoria had 'absurdly high notions of her prerogative, and the amount of control which she ought to exercise over public business'.[4]

The Queen insisted that she occupied herself with such matters unwillingly, for 'it is all so *hateful* to me without the interest my Angel gave to it'. A month after Albert's death she complained to Vicky, 'I who have always hated business, have now nothing but that!' She told Lord Clarendon piteously, 'She never had *thought*, for everything had been done for her, but ... now she is obliged to work and think and she didn't know how to set about either.' However unpalatable she found it, she nevertheless accepted it as her unavoidable duty, and even in the depths of despair declared herself, 'quite determined that the public business shall not suffer from her affliction'. It was the visible aspects of her monarchical functions that she felt entitled to discard, for, in Richard Cobden's phrase, her bereavement had left her 'unequal to the pageantries of her office'. The Queen assumed that everyone would understand her state of mind made it impossible for her to carry out 'acts of representation and state ceremony' such as opening Parliament, which she had anyway '*always ... dreaded for days before*'. Three years after Albert's death she declared: 'No child can feel more shrinking and nervous than the poor Queen does' when called upon to appear in public, and she believed her solitary condition excused her from doing so. Yet she distinguished between '*these mere ceremonials*' and her 'other and higher duties … which she cannot neglect without injury to the public service'.[5] Many of her ministers wished that her priorities had been reversed, thinking she should accept the obligation of showing herself in public rather than focussing on politics.

Lord Clarendon had hoped that work would be 'the best thing for her', by compelling her 'to think of something other than the all-embracing sorrow', but when King Leopold ventured that she might find solace in it, Victoria was indignant. 'You say that work does me good; but the contrary is the fact *with me*,' she chided him. 'Ordinary mechanical work may be good for people in great distress, but not *constant* anxiety, responsibility, and interruptions of every kind.' For years to come, this would be a constant refrain. 'I am overwhelmed with business (oh! so new to me),' she complained to Vicky eight weeks after Albert's death, and the following year she described herself as 'worked to death … I am *quite* worn out.' Months earlier she had written in her journal of being exhausted by having to grapple with 'so many boxes & questions! Oh! How I realise what my beloved one went through, but he was a clever man & I have all my own work besides to carry out unassisted & with all the pleasure gone out of it.' On one occasion she told Lord Clarendon, 'her mind was strained to the utmost … and … she was afraid of going mad'.[6]

However vocally Victoria bewailed her inadequacy, in some respects she adapted well to the new demands placed on her. Partly this was because she already had a fund of valuable experience, for though she sometimes made out that Albert had relieved her of all responsibility, this was never the case. She gave a truer picture when she recalled in February 1864, 'how deeply interesting it was, working together with him'. In times of political difficulty, she had not merely acceded to his ideas, but had absorbed them, and in the process of growing familiar with the workings of his mind, she had acquired some of his analytical skills. Even when he was no longer beside her, she was rarely troubled by indecision about how to resolve a tricky political situation. Instead, what tended to bother her was that the government's views diverged from hers, and so imposing her will became a challenge. Her sense of certainty was strongest when she felt sure that her approach was what Albert would have wanted, for, as Gladstone observed in 1864, 'Whenever she quotes an opinion of the Prince she looks upon the question as completely shut up by it.'[7] As she gained confidence, her faith in her own judgement developed, and, much as she claimed to hate it all, part of her was stimulated by the challenge.

Naturally this took time. Initially it seemed that for all Victoria's resolutions to do what was needful, summoning up the energy would be beyond her. She had gone to Osborne five days after Albert's death, and there descended into a blank fog of grief. A German diplomat heard, 'The Queen stares vacantly before her all day in unutterable despair. It is only with difficulty that the royal sign-manual can be obtained for the most urgent business of state.' After brief bouts when it seemed that she was ready to apply herself, she relapsed again into hopelessness. Three days after reminding Lord Russell that all Foreign Office despatches must be submitted to her for approval, she sent back papers she was meant to sign because the black band at the edges was too narrow.[8]

When she first set about working on her own, she felt bewildered and defeated. On 5 March 1862 she wrote to Lord Russell demanding he provide her with more assistance on foreign policy matters. Plaintively she informed him, 'It is very difficult for the Queen, when she is left without one word of explanation … to draw her own conclusion from the perusal of voluminous despatches from abroad … and to judge in her ignorance of the views of the government, or of the reasons which have dictated them, whether she should approve them or not.' Russell was not at all helpful, saying he had his hands full dealing himself with his department's official correspondence, of which only a portion was sent to her.[9]

Gradually the Queen started to cope better with the demands on her. This owed a lot to the assistance provided by her Keeper of the Privy Purse, Sir Charles Phipps, and Albert's former private secretary, Lieutenant General Charles Grey. Immediately after Albert's death Phipps had proposed to Palmerston that he and Grey should be appointed joint private secretaries, but because the ministers feared they would acquire too much influence, they were not given titular posts. Despite their status remaining unofficial, between them they performed all the functions of a private secretary. Phipps would go through Foreign Office papers on Victoria's behalf, marking passages that required her attention. Either he or Grey would write in her name to ministers, with the Queen merely signing the letter, a practice that was not entirely correct, but which ministers connived at. Whereas in Albert's day Victoria had copied out letters her husband had drafted for her, preserving the fiction that their content was all her own work, she no longer felt it necessary to keep up the pretence. Though on occasion she penned her own comments to ministers – and Palmerston noted, 'she writes well sometimes' – it was 'a trouble to her to do so'. Accordingly, a system evolved whereby 'she states her meaning to Grey and leaves him to expand it into sentences'.[10]

Aided by these two men, the Queen developed more efficient working methods. She emulated some of Albert's practices, while never labouring on quite the same heroic scale as him. He had had a highly organised filing system in which papers on individual subjects were kept together, so when she wanted, the Queen could retrieve and read 'those admirable memoranda which are *gospel* now'. Occasionally Victoria drew up memoranda herself. She found her first effort 'very dreadful, very trying!' and the result 'far inferior in style to his admirable Memorandums', but she did herself an injustice. After important meetings with ministers or foreign monarchs she would also 'keep records of all such, & place papers of that kind together just as dearest Albert used to do'.[11] While never ceasing to bewail the burden work imposed on her, she felt more sure of herself as her experience deepened.

The Queen made life difficult for her ministers by shutting herself away in residences far from London. She did not want to spend any time at Buckingham Palace, which she now considered a 'dreadful, dreary, desolate place', refusing to pass a night there until several years after Albert's death. Unfortunately she also took against Windsor, likening it to a '*living grave*', and was only prepared to live there for four months of the year. She divided the rest of her time between Osborne and Balmoral, and when personal interviews were required, her ministers had to travel to these remote places. It became established practice that individual ministers took turns to see the Queen at Osborne in the middle of the week, and then returned to London after staying the night.[12] Since the journey to Balmoral took so much longer, whichever minister was in attendance had to be there for several days.

Victoria could have made life easier for herself by calling on her eldest son for assistance, but she was adamantly against this. Immediately after his father had died Bertie had thrown his arms round her and promised, 'Indeed Mama I will be all I can to you,' but she would not allow him to aid her as he wished. Although his father had forgiven Bertie at their last encounter, Victoria had persuaded herself that Albert's death had been caused by distress over his son's escapade with the actress, and she told Vicky that, as a result, 'I never can or shall look at him without a shudder.' Despite claiming that 'I try to employ and use him but I am not hopeful,' in fact she never made the slightest effort to do so. She gave strict instructions that ministers should direct all enquiries to her, and that nothing should be addressed to Bertie. Palmerston's efforts to alleviate things by warning her that, 'the country was fearful we [she and Bertie] were not on good terms', bore little fruit. In time what Palmerston described as 'her unconquerable aversion' to her eldest son did soften somewhat, but she remained resolutely opposed to letting Bertie see Foreign Office papers or other documents of consequence.[13]

The Queen avoided meeting with her prime minister until six weeks after Albert's death. She had 'disliked particularly the thought of seeing Palmerston, as she imagined that he was a hard man who could not really sympathise with her', but it turned out she wronged him. When the Queen's cousin the Duke of Cambridge had notified Palmerston of the prince consort's death, the prime minister had 'wept and sobbed like a child', and he felt keenly for the Queen. As time passed and Victoria could not bring herself to let him come to her, the situation became embarrassing, but finally Palmerston was allowed to visit Osborne on 29 January. Despite his failure to wear mourning, the Queen was impressed by his manifest concern for her. 'He could in fact hardly speak for emotion,' she wrote in her journal. 'It showed me how much he felt my terrible loss.' Palmerston in his turn was shocked by her worn and thin appearance. When she saw him another time in April, she was again moved by his solicitude. 'Poor old man, he touches me, with his excessive anxiety about me,' she recorded.[14]

It was fortunate for the Queen that 1862 was a quiet year politically. Shortly before Parliament opened, a German diplomat reported: 'Everything points to a short session, devoid of any party struggles … Lord Derby preaches to his party to respect the Queen's sorrow, and not trouble her Majesty with party contests.'[15] Despite this, Disraeli inadvertently almost caused a crisis with an attempt to amend the government's Finance Bill. The amendment was withdrawn once Palmerston announced he would treat it as a vote of no confidence, but matters had gone far enough to make the Queen panic.

A near-hysterical Victoria summoned Lord Clarendon to discuss what she supposed was a deliberate attempt by the opposition to oust the government. In great agitation Victoria declared: '*that* would be what she could not stand, that she would throw everything up', because 'all that a change of Ministry would entail upon her now … would kill her, and that through *madness*'. To emphasise the point she, several times, 'tapped her forehead with her hand and said, "My reason, my reason."' At her request, Clarendon passed this on to Derby, who promised she would not be disturbed further.[16]

In other respects the Queen's state of mind showed no signs of improvement. There was no question of happy family events alleviating her gloom. When her second daughter, Princess Alice, who had got engaged to Prince Louis of Hesse-Darmstadt before the prince consort's death, married her fiancé in July 1862, Victoria noted with satisfaction it was 'more like a funeral than a wedding'.[17] Soon afterwards the Queen took steps to find a bride for her eldest son, because Albert had been anxious for Bertie to marry. Knowing that Albert had been impressed by a photograph of Princess Alexandra, daughter of the heir presumptive to the Danish throne, Christian of Glücksburg, the Queen was ready to consider her as a possible daughter-in-law. This was despite the fact that, from a worldly point of view, the match had obvious drawbacks. Christian had been declared heir-presumptive of King Frederick VII of Denmark by virtue of the 1852 Treaty of London, which in theory had settled the Schleswig-Holstein dispute, but which had failed to ease relations between Denmark and Germany. Despite Prussia's being a signatory of the agreement, ill-feeling towards the Danes arising from the war of 1848 still festered in the country.

Nevertheless, when Victoria travelled abroad to Coburg and Belgium in the autumn of 1862, she was greatly taken with Princess Alexandra, who was presented to her at King Leopold's country residence. The Prince of Wales was more or less ordered to propose, but after he was accepted Victoria emphasised to Lord Russell that the marriage must, 'in *no* sense [be] considered a *political* one'. Even so, the news fell 'like a clap of thunder' in Prussia, making Vicky's position awkward.[18]

Victoria did not want Palmerston to think the engagement had afforded her pleasure, claiming in some ways it actually worsened her pain, as the sight of 'any happy couples … plunges daggers into the Queen's widowed heart'. At the marriage itself, which took place in March 1863 at St George's Chapel, Windsor, Victoria attended clad in deep mourning, observing proceedings from a raised closet. Disraeli – who had been thrilled to be invited – had the temerity to lift his quizzing glass to scrutinise her in her 'Gothic pavilion', but 'unfortunately caught her glance'. The severe look she gave him ensured: 'I did not venture to use my glass again.'[19]

* * *

The Queen became extremely exercised about erecting a suitable memorial to her late husband. Soon after Albert's death a committee comprising Lord Clarendon, Lord Derby and two other men was set up to discuss the design and financing of a monument. Victoria was convinced there would 'not be the slightest difficulty' obtaining funds, as Parliament would supplement money raised by public subscription, but Palmerston feared her 'notions of the liberality of Parliament' were utterly unrealistic. Gladstone warned the prime minister that it would be 'unwise and unsafe' to ask for more than £30,000, and they could count themselves lucky if granted that. Victoria was contemptuous, saying everyone she had spoken to, 'except the Queen's Cabinet', agreed nothing less than £50,000 would do, while '£30,000 is a sum utterly unworthy of ... the British House of Commons.'[20]

After consulting the Chief Whip, Palmerston decided that the house was as likely to grant the larger sum as the smaller, and the matter was scheduled for debate on 23 April 1863. The Queen met with Derby and Disraeli beforehand to ensure their support, and she was delighted by the speech Disraeli made in the Commons saying that only a generous sum could provide a fitting commemoration for Albert's 'sublime life and transcendent career'. After Palmerston too spoke movingly, the House voted £50,000 without difficulty. In gratitude the Queen sent both the prime minister and Disraeli printed copies of Albert's speeches, bound in white Morocco, eliciting in return a fulsome letter from Disraeli. Solemnly he informed her, 'The Prince is the only person, whom Mr Disraeli has known, who realized the ideal ... There was in him an union of the manly grace, & sublime simplicity, of chivalry, with the intellectual splendour of the Attic Academe.' The Queen declared it: 'the most striking and beautiful letter' she had received.[21]

Just over two months later proof came that the Commons were not prepared to expend infinite sums in Albert's memory. Having already agreed to purchase the land surrounding the Great Exhibition site, they were annoyed when unexpectedly called upon to pay additional sums to set up institutions such as a National Portrait Gallery. Lord Stanley deplored the way the scheme had 'been pressed forward by the Court with an indecent eagerness, the Queen having made no scruple of canvassing leading members personally in its favour'. Disraeli claimed to General Grey that by mishandling the whole question, Gladstone was to blame for its hostile reception, but colleagues of Disraeli alleged he too misjudged the mood of the house by boasting 'he had a letter in his pocket from the Queen' on the subject. Such was the 'jealousy of court dictation' that when Disraeli rose to speak, he was howled down, and the proposal met with 'crashing defeat'.[22]

The Queen's first testing experience of European diplomacy had come in 1862 when she had assisted in the hunt for a new king for the Greek throne, after its previous occupant had been ousted by his subjects. In early 1863 the matter was settled, not entirely to her satisfaction, when Princess Alexandra's brother became King George of the Hellenes. Victoria complained the 'Greek business' had 'worried, agitated and harassed' her,[23] but soon she found herself dealing with much more troubling concerns arising from an insurrection in Poland.

At the end of the Napoleonic wars, the Vienna settlement of 1815 had partitioned Poland between the Russians, Prussians and Austrians. In January 1863 Russia's harsh treatment of suspected Polish dissidents provoked an uprising. Prussia agreed the Russians could pursue rebels who fled over the border into Prussian territory, making it easier for the Russians to crush the insurgents without mercy.

Napoleon III, who had long cherished hopes of emulating his uncle by liberating the Poles, proposed that Britain and France should jointly protest to Prussia about the assistance given to Russia. The Queen, however, was 'terribly alarmed' at the prospect. She did not see why the Russians should not be allowed 'to pacify their troublesome Poles', for while this 'attractive, talented but thoroughly immoral people' had perhaps 'been cruelly used', they were in her view 'quite unfit to govern themselves'. She was worried that if too strong a line was taken with Prussia, it might result in war, a prospect she naturally found horrific on account of Vicky. 'But don't fear,' she reassured her daughter: she would display 'the courage of a lioness if I see danger … giving my people my decided opinion and more than that!'[24]

As ever Victoria was fiercely against operating in conjunction with France, and turned to the obliging Lord Granville to ensure the Cabinet were not led astray by rash proposals from Palmerston and Russell. To her relief, Granville confidentially informed her not only that the Cabinet 'threw cold water' on any notion of combining with France, but also that communications to Prussia were couched in such mild terms they could not be construed as a threat.[25]

While not actually prepared to fight Russia on the Poles' behalf, Palmerston and Russell were loath simply to stand by while the Polish revolt was smashed. Although the Queen pointed out the folly of using 'unnecessarily offensive' language to Russia when there was 'no intention of acting on' threats, on 9 April Russell had a blustering interview with the Russian ambassador, hinting that Britain might open hostilities if the Poles were treated too badly. Russell acknowledged to the Queen, 'Your Majesty's Ministers have no wish or intention to go to war for Poland,' but he believed that talking tough afforded the only hope of checking the Russian soldiery's 'murderous habits'.[26]

When the Poles rejected a Russian offer of amnesty, the British ambassador to Russia, Lord Napier, suggested this was because they had been given false hopes England would come to their rescue. The British government pressed Russia to grant a more generous amnesty, and when Victoria queried this, Palmerston scribbled in disgust to Russell, 'Can the Queen really and on reflection wish that the atrocities ... should continue?' On being upbraided, Victoria fired back that Russell misunderstood her if he thought she did not desire 'the stoppage of the present effusion of blood'. She had merely highlighted Napier's warnings, 'that the continuance of the struggle was very much owing to the belief on the part of the Poles that they would at last receive material support from abroad'. Sure enough, the ministry's bluff was soon exposed. In July 1863 the Russians declared 'in a tone of haughty sarcasm' that the governance of Poland counted as an internal concern, and they would not offer better amnesty terms. A few days later Russell abandoned the Poles by declaring they 'could count on our sympathies but not our material aid'.[27]

Ignoring every indication to the contrary, Prince Albert had convinced himself that when Vicky's father-in-law succeeded his brother as King of Prussia, it would mark the start of a new enlightened era. It did not take long after the accession to the throne of William I on 1 January 1861 for the vision to be exposed as chimerical. Lord Clarendon, who attended William's coronation, reported to Victoria that Vicky – now Crown Princess of Prussia – was 'much alarmed at the state of things here ... for the king ... sees democracy and revolution in every symptom of opposition to his will'.[28]

In 1862 the king became stuck in deadlock with Prussia's representative chambers, who were resisting his demand that compulsory military service should be extended. When it seemed he would not have his way, he contemplated abdicating, a solution that Queen Victoria, like Vicky, thought would make things 'far better'. To their horror, instead of making way for his son, William appointed as his Minister President Count Otto von Bismarck, a former Prussian ambassador to France known for his intransigence and hatred of liberalism. Describing Bismarck as 'a wicked man', Vicky informed her mother the thought of this 'most unprincipled and unrespectable character' governing Prussia 'makes my hair stand on end'.[29]

When elections in Prussia failed to return a more tractable representative assembly, Bismarck declared that the Prussian constitution permitted state business to be carried on without the agreement of the diet. The Queen was appalled, agreeing with Uncle Leopold that 'the poor king is *really demented*'. Vicky, meanwhile, was urging Fritz to 'listen to your little wife', and to disavow what his father had done. In 1863 new censorship laws were introduced in Prussia, whereupon Victoria too insisted her son-in-law 'must not remain passive'. She urged Vicky: 'Let Fritz be firm!' He must not shrink from separating himself from all his father's unhappy acts! ... I know Papa would have said the same.' On 5 June Fritz made a speech at Danzig indicating that the press law had been brought in without his knowledge or approval. His mother-in-law was delighted. Assuring Vicky, 'You are the best and wisest adviser he could have,' she said her ministers endorsed Fritz's defiant line.[30]

King William was predictably enraged with his son, and Vicky and Fritz found themselves ostracised. Matters became worse when *The Times* published an accurate account of the correspondence that had taken place between Fritz and his father. Vicky asked her mother if the letter she had sent her with details of these exchanges had been shown to anyone who could have passed it on, but the Queen insisted the leak could not have come from her end. It hardly disposed King William to give her a favourable hearing when she wrote to him in a bid to ease the discord between father and son. After Victoria begged that Fritz's actions 'should be regarded from a human standpoint and not as a crime',[31] the king did abandon the notion of court-martialling his son, but the crown prince and princess remained in disgrace.

In August 1863 Queen Victoria briefly saw Bismarck for herself when she engaged in some personal diplomacy during a visit to Coburg. Having grown concerned because relations between Austria and Prussia had recently become very tense, the Queen had invited King William of Prussia and Emperor Francis Joseph of Austria to meet with her on different days, hoping an appeal from her could improve things. Bismarck accompanied his sovereign to Coburg, and though he was not present for the meeting that took place between Victoria and King William on 31 August, the Queen caught a glimpse of him later, when she went out for a drive with the king. He 'has a horrid expression', she observed.[32]

King William had not been very receptive to Victoria's attempts to dissipate his ill-feeling towards Austria. She did not fare much better when she made the acquaintance of Emperor Francis Joseph on 3 September, for he simply blamed Prussia for all the current difficulties. While neither encounter had produced the results Victoria had hoped for, the fact she had undertaken these discussions confirmed she had a part to play at the European level. She could count on being given the deferential attention of her fellow monarchs, even if changing their opinions was beyond her. Victoria was pleased when Lord Granville told her that, however much of a strain she found it, she could feel 'perfect self-confidence' in her ability to conduct such interviews.[33]

By this time Victoria's advisers were counting on her realising she must participate more fully in her kingdom's public life. Soon after the Prince of Wales's wedding Lord Clarendon had written, 'I hope she is beginning to perceive that another year of total seclusion won't do.' She had regained the weight she had lost in the first weeks of widowhood, for within three months of Albert's death Clarendon noticed that, notwithstanding her conviction she was 'gradually wasting away', she was eating, drinking and sleeping 'quite enough'. The Queen herself was sure that her bereavement had not only shattered her emotionally but had grievously undermined her health. In June 1863 she informed her uncle, 'I was so *unwell* on *Sunday* from *violent* nervous headache and *complete* prostration that I nearly fainted.' She claimed her doctors had warned her that in her 'extreme state of weakness … if I did faint I might *not* come back to *life*'. This debility was, '*all* the result of overwork … and *constant* SORROW … I feel like a poor hunted hare.'[34]

The Queen clung to her grief obsessively. She acknowledged to Vicky in November 1862, 'for me my very misery is now a necessity … Yes, I long for my suffering almost.' Her daughter Princess Alice told General Grey her mother had 'owned to her she was afraid of getting too well as if it was a crime!' Though in her journal Victoria had written of feeling 'so nervous & so alone' when holding the Coburg discussions, Princess Alice believed she had enjoyed herself. At the lunch party for Francis Joseph, she had 'talked a great deal, & was interested, running to the window etc to see him drive away'. Lord Russell, who had been present for the German trip, confirmed to Palmerston that she had borne up well throughout it, but when she saw the prime minister on her return she was at pains to convince him otherwise. 'I thought the Queen looking well and apparently cheerful,' he wrote to Russell, 'but she told me herself that she grows gradually weaker. What you say of her journey does not bear out such an opinion.'[35]

While in Germany General Grey had written to his colleague Charles Phipps, 'She is so nice & touching … it is difficult to find the heart to urge her to anything she does not like; but … we must all try *gently*, to get her to resume her old habits.' In October 1863 Grey made tentative steps in this direction, but Victoria reacted fiercely to his carefully worded letter. She wrote back that she was 'grieved & surprised' by his saying he '*looked forward* to the time when she is to reappear in *public*', for while 'the Queen would certainly *not* wish her loyal people *not* to *wish* to see her … it is *utterly* useless for them *ever* to *expect* she will *take her place as before*.' When an article on the same theme appeared in *The Times* on the anniversary of Albert's death, she felt even more affronted. She wrote to Grey expressing incredulity that such expectations could be raised of 'a woman, with much impaired health, shaken & shattered by her terrible sorrow & loss!' Professing shock that no account had been taken of her '*hard* slavelike labour *for* the Country', she supposed 'it will be only when she is *dead* that people will say "Oh! Why did she work so hard?" just as they said about the dear Prince.'[36]

On Victoria's orders Sir Charles Phipps wrote to Palmerston that recent press coverage had led her to fear she would be expected to appear on public occasions. Knowing herself to be unequal to it, she had consulted her doctors, who had confirmed her state of health made it impossible. Phipps amplified, 'Although there is not, I am happy to say, any discoverable organic or distinct illness,' her Majesty was 'so constantly tired and worn out' it was unthinkable she could undertake more exertion. He suggested that ministers should let it be known that in prolonging her seclusion the Queen was acting under medical advice.[37]

Victoria had been relieved that Palmerston and Russell had resisted Napoleon III's 'wily proposals' for joint action to pressure Russia over Poland and was no keener about another suggestion put forward by France in the autumn of 1863. On 4 November Napoleon proposed that a conference of European powers should discuss a multitude of questions that affected the continent, with the aim of settling affairs in Poland, Italy, Germany, Denmark and the Danubian Principalities. The Queen vehemently disagreed. 'The Congress is in fact an impertinence,' she affirmed to Uncle Leopold, expressing the hope no sovereigns would 'lower themselves' by accepting the invitation. After considering the matter, the Cabinet decided against attending, but when Lord Russell conveyed this answer to France, he did so in 'curt and offensive terms' that Napoleon much resented. The Queen was pleased that the refusal 'put an end to … [the] humbug' that an Anglo-French alliance was still in being, but Napoleon's 'rankling disappointment' meant he was disinclined to act alongside Britain when the Schleswig-Holstein question flared up.[38]

The Schleswig-Holstein question was of an almost proverbial complexity. Palmerston is supposed to have said that only three men had ever understood it: a Danish statesman, who had since gone mad; Prince Albert, who was dead; and himself – and he had forgotten all about it. Possibly the quote is apocryphal, for tracing it to its source is problematic, and certainly in Prince Albert's lifetime, Palmerston never showed much respect for his views on Schleswig-Holstein. If Palmerston did utter this aphorism, perhaps what he principally wished to convey was that he did not number Queen Victoria among those who had mastered the question's intricacies.

In theory the problem of Schleswig-Holstein had been settled by the 1852 Treaty of London, which had confirmed the arrangement whereby both duchies were ruled by Denmark without being formally integrated into that country. The treaty had settled that on the death of the childless King Frederick VII of Denmark, the Danish Crown – and the duchies with it – would go to Christian of Glücksburg, father of Victoria's daughter-in-law, Alexandra. In 1852 a rival contender, the Duke of Augustenburg, had renounced his claim to rule the duchies in return for a generous cash settlement. Since then his son, Prince Frederick of Augustenburg, had declared his father had not been entitled to forfeit the family rights in this way. The Queen had great sympathy for the pretensions of Prince Frederick, who happened to be married to her niece, Adelaide of Hohenlohe-Langenburg. She was sure that if the duchies were permitted a choice, they would want Augustenburg as their ruler.

At the time Victoria and Albert had dubbed the Treaty of London '*an iniquity*', and her resentment of it had only grown in intervening years. Now the Queen hoped that the treaty could be modified, or even jettisoned, dreaming of honouring her husband's memory by righting an historic injustice. Regarding the problem as 'a legacy from him', during the crisis she would look at '*all* his wise writings on the subject' to ensure she was acting as he would have wanted.[39]

The Danes had precipitated this new crisis by issuing a patent in March 1863 that seemed to indicate they planned to bind the duchies closer to Denmark. The German Confederation at once began making threatening noises, prompting Palmerston – who assumed the other signatories of the Treaty of London would take an equally firm line – to warn that Denmark would not be left to deal with any trouble on her own. Unfortunately, this emboldened the Danes to proceed further, and in November 1863 a new constitution was drawn up for Schleswig, effectively incorporating it into Denmark. At this point, 'the wretched king' (as the Queen termed him), Frederick VII of Denmark died, and his successor Christian IX felt obliged to confirm the new constitution. As the German Confederation muttered about occupying Holstein, Austria and Prussia (referred to throughout this crisis as 'the German Powers') forgot their recent estrangement and began contemplating a joint intervention.

With the situation becoming tenser by the day, the possibility that Britain might become involved preyed on the Queen's mind. A conflict with any state in Germany, from 'whence all I loved come', was a horrific prospect to her, but the idea of fighting Vicky's adoptive homeland was more dreadful still. In anguish she wrote to her daughter that what it would mean 'for you and me – words cannot describe!' Her situation was of course further complicated by the fact that her daughter-in-law the Princess of Wales was the daughter of King Christian, and understandably took the view 'the Duchies belong to Papa'. Palmerston and Russell hoped that because the Queen 'has now family interests in harmony with' the Treaty of London, she would be more inclined to uphold it, but this proved far from the case. When Princess Alexandra argued that the Danes were in the right, Victoria informed King Leopold, 'Dear Alix is unfortunately *very ignorant* and does not understand the question.'[40]

The divisions within the royal family had been painfully apparent when Vicky and Fritz visited England in November 1863 and became 'very excited about this luckless business', while staying at Windsor. At breakfast on 18 November Fritz told his mother-in-law she was too dependent on the will of her ministers, causing her to contradict him indignantly. She wrote to Uncle Leopold that she was 'miserable, wretched, almost frantic' at having to cope without Albert to '*put* the *others* down, and in their right place! No respect is paid to my opinion now, and this helplessness almost drives me wild.' Things became even more unpleasant when Bertie and Alix joined the party the following week and manifested strongly pro-Danish sentiments. Clarendon reported to Lord Cowley: 'the feud at Windsor between the Waleses and Crown Prince and Princess of Prussia is at its height … Hard lines for the Queen who is unable to keep the peace between them.' Victoria had to insist that no more political discussions took place in her presence.[41]

To the Queen's distress, the Prince of Wales sided with his wife throughout the entire crisis. Angry because her 'poor stupid son … is now a *Dane*,' Victoria avowed frankly, 'He is a *fool*.' After Vicky returned to Germany her mother wrote in despair, 'Our worst fears about B's marriage realised … division in the family!! … Oh! If Bertie's wife was only a good German … It is terrible to have the poor boy on the wrong side.' Lecturing her son on the need for restraint, the Queen said she was mystified he did not realise 'his connection with *Denmark* is only of one year's standing … whereas that with Germany is from *his birth*'.[42]

Victoria maintained that unlike her son, she was not at all partisan, having '*all along felt* [it] … *my duty* … *never* to mix up *personal sympathies with* the *question* at *issue*'. This was something her chief ministers would have disputed. As 1863 neared its end Palmerston warned Russell, 'The feelings & opinions & German leanings of the Prince Consort, which he had sagacity enough to keep tolerably in the background, are breaking out in her.' When the foreign secretary hinted she was biased, Victoria angrily denied it, but it was indisputable that her views now diverged from his and Palmerston's. As troops of the German Confederation occupied Holstein on 24 December, the prime minister told Russell that if Schleswig was also invaded, this 'would in my clear opinion entitle Denmark to our active military and naval support'. Russell agreed, but both men knew this could not be embarked upon 'without the concurrence of the Cabinet and the consent of the Queen'.[43]

It seemed the latter would never be forthcoming. Before the Cabinet met on 2 January 1864, Victoria reiterated her opposition 'to any course which may tend to involve England in war'. She also suggested that if the people of Schleswig-Holstein expressed a preference for the Duke of Augustenburg, it would be wrong to impose another sovereign on them. It appeared the Cabinet thought differently. When they discussed the matter, they agreed that, provided France and other major European powers did likewise, Britain should inform the German Confederation that any attempt to set up Augustenburg as the duchies' ruler would result in military assistance being offered to Denmark. Palmerston wrote to the Queen that he understood her reluctance to countenance war with Germany, 'but he is sure your Majesty will never forget that you are Sovereign of Great Britain', and that the honour of her Crown took priority over everything.[44]

Victoria was nettled by his tone, but far from disheartened. While she could not repudiate the ministers' advice entirely, she wished it 'clearly understood' she was not agreeing to 'single-handed interference by England'. As she had hoped, for the moment no European powers showed much appetite to coerce Germany.[45] This gave the Queen a breathing space, which she used to try and mould the opinion of the Cabinet.

To assist her in this task, Victoria sought the aid not only of Granville, but also of William Gladstone, who was strongly against Britain becoming involved in a conflict that would upset his budgetary projections. Later, when Gladstone became prime minister, he would maintain that the secrecy of Cabinet proceedings must be inviolate. At this point in his career he was less scrupulous and would more than once go behind colleagues' backs to keep the Queen informed. On 19 February 1864 Palmerston would tell Russell that by 'encouraging the Teutonic propensities of her Majesty', Gladstone had acted in a way that was 'unfair by you and all of us'.[46]

Victoria believed current circumstances warranted not just obtaining information about what was said in Cabinet but also influencing the way ministers thought on the matter. Five years earlier, Russell had explicitly stated that 'to transmit your Majesty's opinion to the Cabinet before their deliberations begin is contrary to the spirit of the Constitution', and that, 'if your Majesty interferes beforehand', he could no longer serve her. Now, while taking care not to reveal to Russell what she was up to, she used Lord Granville as a conduit to convey her views to receptive ministers. Having sent Granville a memorandum alluding to her fears of being sucked into 'a mad and useless combat', she suggested, 'while not mentioning this communication', Granville could 'use the Queen's name [to his colleagues] whenever he thinks it useful'.[47]

In acting in this way Victoria undoubtedly pushed her prerogative to its limits – and possibly exceeded those limits. In her defence it can be pointed out that she was not the only one testing boundaries, for Palmerston and Russell were often lax about keeping the Cabinet abreast of what they were doing. Although most of the Cabinet were more sympathetic to Denmark than Victoria was, they had no wish to fight on its behalf, and in this respect reflected public opinion. Had it not been for the Queen, they would have been unaware that Russell was engaged in controversial moves with potentially cataclysmic consequences.

The Queen first became alarmed about the lengths to which Russell would go when she learned on 8 January that the foreign secretary had privately informed the Prussian ambassador that if Schleswig was invaded, Britain would come to Denmark's aid. Victoria wrote furiously to Palmerston that she would not permit 'the infliction upon her subjects of all the horrors of war' by taking sides 'in a quarrel in which both parties are much in the wrong'. The prime minister responded that the Germans were behaving 'like a strong man who thinks he has got a weak man in a corner, and that he can bully and heat him to his heart's content', but the Cabinet too felt Russell had overreached himself. Granville reported to Victoria that when they met on 12 January, after 'a great tussle', they forced Russell to omit from despatches destined for Berlin and Vienna any mention of what he had said to Bernstorff. Despite being 'a good deal annoyed', the foreign secretary ultimately bowed to their wishes.[48]

On 16 January the crisis took a fresh and graver turn when Prussia and Austria issued an ultimatum, announcing their forces would invade Schleswig unless the Danes revoked its new constitution within forty-eight hours. Palmerston held the Queen partly to blame, telling Russell: 'She has done infinite mischief by spreading over Germany the belief that she never would consent to be a party to active measures in favour of Denmark.' Undaunted, Victoria next ensured that the speech from the throne – to be read in her absence by the Lord Chancellor as she had refused to open Parliament – was rephrased. Having stipulated it must contain 'no violent declarations' against Germany, she requested Granville to reconcile colleagues to these changes.[49]

When Prussian troops invaded Schleswig on 1 February 1864, the Queen was still not sympathetic towards the Danes, declaring they had 'brought it *all* upon themselves'. To Lord Russell she wrote of her 'deepest sorrow that such an effusion of blood should have become unavoidable', but she remarked to King Leopold that while the war was 'distressing … I am not sure if it is not after all the only way to get this awful affair settled.'[50]

Following the opening of Parliament on 4 February one MP, named Hennessy, actually praised Victoria for having shielded her people from bloodshed, asserting since 'it was perfectly well known' she had prevented England 'from getting into this war … they might thank God they had a Queen'.[51] As the debate moved on, several MPs strongly condemned Prussia and Austria's behaviour, but the house showed little appetite to take them on in war. Noting this, Palmerston too became less belligerent.

On 11 February Denmark formally requested Britain's military assistance, and Russell was keen to make a fresh approach to France about acting together on Denmark's behalf. The Queen at once begged Lord Granville to ensure the Cabinet blocked this. Fearful of what would happen if the Danes were allowed to 'imagine they will be assisted in their reckless course', she declared him 'quite at liberty to make use of her opinion ... when speaking to his colleagues'. She said she would 'make a stand upon it' even if the foreign secretary resigned. In the end, however, it was Palmerston who reined in Russell. Doubting 'whether the Cabinet or country are as yet prepared for active interference', he told his colleague it was best 'to wait a while'.[52] When the Cabinet met on 13 February, Palmerston showed himself averse to war, effectively isolating Russell.

Frustrated at being condemned to inaction, Russell allowed his irritation to show when the Queen repeated to him her implacable opposition to 'a war in which no English interest is concerned'. Sulkily he observed that while that might be so, 'If English honour were to be concerned your Majesty would no doubt feel bound to defend it.' The Queen responded sharply, 'She does not require to be reminded of the honour of England, which touches her more nearly than anyone else.'[53]

The Danes' plight became more serious when Prussian forces advanced on 18 February into Denmark itself, inflicting not just severe losses on the Danish army but significant civilian casualties. This caused Palmerston to veer round again, for he felt Britain could not stand idly by while Austria and Prussia 'pursued their career of aggression and slaughter'. As he contemplated sending a fleet to the Baltic to forestall a possible attack on Copenhagen, telegrams were sent to Russia and France, exploring whether they would consider combined naval operations. The Queen objected in the strongest possible terms, and when the Cabinet met on 25 February, a majority of ministers also opposed this course. To Russell's chagrin, his colleagues forced him to send new telegrams to Paris and St Petersburg, rescinding what he had earlier written.[54]

The Queen wrote furiously to King Leopold, 'I am wellnigh worn to nothing with vexation, distress and worry' arising from the 'truly infamous conduct of those two dreadful old men – who are *perfectly untrustworthy*'. She lamented, 'I have *no one* ... to lay my weary head on

FRIENDLY ADVICE.

A cartoon depicting the 'two dreadful old men' as Victoria now called her prime minister and foreign secretary. Palmerston himself is shown as trying to restrain Russell from pursuing too impetuous a foreign policy. (*Punch* cartoon, 1864)

… & seeing the mischief *this* Country does *itself* by its disgraceful & bad policy' had further debilitated her weak nerves. Her only succour lay in prayer, whose power she had never truly appreciated 'till *now*!' She described how, when she knelt to 'pray *earnestly* … to be guided by my darling to *do what* HE would wish ... a calm seems to come over me', but such moments of repose afforded only brief remissions from 'constant sorrow and anxiety'.[55]

As anger mounted about the sufferings the Danes were enduring, Victoria observed crossly, 'People here are most stupid & partial, most unfair & most recklessly imprudent in insulting Germany ... to make it *our* quarrel when *we* have nothing to do with it. [It] is too bad!' The newspapers fanned what she saw as 'the shameful ignorance & one sidedness *here*'. The Prussian shelling of Sønderburg, a town with a large civilian population, was particularly strongly condemned, but Vicky, whose husband was in charge of troops marching on the nearby fortifications of Düppel, insisted there was 'nothing inhuman or improper' about the bombardment. She declared roundly: 'It was necessary and we hope it has been useful,' reminding her mother that the British had recently shown no scruples about shelling the Japanese town of Kagoshima after some Royal Navy sailors had been murdered there. Incensed by the double standards, the crown princess raged at 'the continual meddling and interfering of England in other peoples' affairs'.[56]

The Queen protested that her daughter's 'tone ... was not quite the thing to your own Mama' but did not try to defend the British press. She herself had initially thought bombing Sønderburg without giving civilians a chance to evacuate was 'not right', only to persuade herself within a few days that there had been 'gross exaggeration' of the horrors. Since it was nevertheless 'sad to think of poor Alix's poor countrymen being killed in such numbers', she hoped that a conference convened in London would result in a prompt suspension of hostilities.[57]

When the conference opened on 25 April, the German powers proved reluctant to abandon their advance into Denmark. Victoria sent a personal message to the King of Prussia begging him to expedite a truce, but only on 9 May was an armistice concluded. In the meantime, Palmerston and Russell clung to the project of sending a fleet to the Baltic. When the Cabinet met on 30 April, its members still would not agree to this, so the following day Palmerston had an unofficial conversation with the Austrian ambassador. He warned that if the Austrians sent a fleet past the British coast towards Denmark, a superior British squadron would be sent in pursuit, with war the likely outcome.[58]

Victoria became distraught when Russell informed her the Cabinet had agreed that all Palmerston had said should be officially recorded in diplomatic despatches. As soon as Lord Granville arrived at Osborne for a Privy Council meeting, she accosted him, whereupon Granville said that, as far as he knew, the Cabinet had never authorised such a proceeding. After Granville wrote to challenge Russell, the foreign secretary replied that if he had misunderstood his colleagues, he regretted it, but he and Palmerston might have to resign unless their policy received ministerial support. In the end a compromise was adopted whereby British ambassadors in Berlin and Vienna were confidentially informed of Palmerston's declarations. While relieved that the ministry had not disintegrated, the Queen told Granville the episode had naturally increased 'the feeling of distrust' Russell now inspired in her.[59]

Others felt no less disquiet about Victoria's own conduct. In June an exasperated Palmerston complained to Russell, 'the Queen … is in her heart quite as much German as English, if not more so in her affections'. Six weeks earlier Lord Stanley had written in his journal, 'The Queen's intrigues with the German Powers openly talked of,' as claims swirled about that the Court divulged 'secrets in confidence to the Prussian Cabinet'. While this was unfair, Victoria did feel sufficiently uneasy to enjoin Vicky not to reveal information she had disclosed to her. In late May the Queen further cautioned her daughter against giving the impression her mother was acting independently of her government, 'for THAT beloved Papa never permitted'.[60]

By that time allegations against the Queen had entered the public domain, for on 7 May, after writing of a 'divergence between the monarch's and the nation's desires', the *London Review* suggested that Victoria had been moved 'by family feeling … to the exercise of forbidden powers'. Sending her a copy, Palmerston contrived to be dismissive of the specific claims, while nevertheless warning of the widespread perception that her opinions were inconveniencing the government. He added that, of course, 'Nothing can be further from the truth,' but still declared, 'it would be a great evil if public opinion were to divest your Majesty of that proper and essential protection which the Constitution secures for the Sovereign, by making the responsible Ministers answerable for all that is done or not done.' Tartly agreeing that the offending piece 'ought to be put into the fire', the Queen said the knowledge she had done nothing to contravene the constitution enabled her to overlook 'unjust remarks in obscure newspapers'. To King Leopold she wrote huffily, 'Pilgerstein [their private nickname for Palmerston] is gouty, and extremely impertinent in his communications of different kinds to me.'[61]

The next intervention was less easy to ignore. On 26 May the maverick peer Lord Ellenborough alleged in the Lords that when it came to German questions, ministers of the Crown experienced, 'as much difficulty carrying out a purely English policy' as in the early days of the Hanoverian monarchy. Russell countered that the Queen had never failed to follow advice submitted by her Cabinet, and Victoria at once wrote to thank him for having defended her against an attack, 'which *to a lady* she can only characterise as ungentlemanlike'. In martyred tones she added, 'With a good *conscience* one must bear calumny with patience' – but this proved too much for Russell. He responded in what the Queen described as 'his *coldest, hardest* style', making it plain he thought she had brought difficulties upon herself.[62]

General Grey told Lord Granville he had 'never seen the Queen so completely upset' as she became on reading this letter. The general was ordered to convey to Russell that she was 'a good deal hurt' that the 'utterly undeserved' accusations had not been 'more peremptorily contradicted'. Victoria was adamant she had 'given no ground whatever for a whisper against' her, having actually 'done violence to her own feelings and sympathies' when communicating with family members overseas. She had, in fact, 'almost quarrelled with the Crown Princess' by urging that Prussia show restraint. Through gritted teeth Russell returned a somewhat frigid acknowledgement that, 'nothing could be more constitutional than the course which your Majesty has pursued'. Victoria still believed herself grievously wronged. She wrote to Lord Granville on 5 June, 'Oh how fearful it is to be suspected – uncheered – unguided – and unadvised – and how alone the poor Queen feels! Her friends must defend her.'[63]

The London conference – called in the hope of achieving a settlement in Schleswig-Holstein – was not going well. The Queen blamed 'the stiff-necked Danes', but Lord Clarendon believed progress was impossible because 'Bismarck the bold and bad' was directing things from Berlin. Victoria volunteered to write to the King of Prussia, asking him to be moderate, but though King William answered her letter politely, he made it plain that after the German powers' military successes, there could be no question of upholding the terms of the 1852 treaty. Accordingly, Russell devised a new formula whereby Denmark would retain only a portion of Schleswig, but where the boundary should be drawn provoked furious disagreement. By 11 June several members of the Cabinet were losing patience with Prussia's 'extreme demands', and this emboldened Russell. To the Queen's horror he informed her that the Cabinet had agreed that if Germany rejected a British offer of mediation, while Denmark accepted it, England should offer Denmark material aid if hostilities reopened.[64]

The Queen at once wrote querying whether the Cabinet had understood the full implications of a move, whose consequences she '*shudders* to think of'. She demanded that her letter – which, as Palmerston remarked to Russell, 'breathes strongly Germanism' – should be laid before the Cabinet and also checked with Lord Granville and Sir Charles Wood to see whether Russell had represented the ministers' position correctly. To her delight, both men denied that the Cabinet had decided anything so drastic. On 15 June the Cabinet met again, and the following day Gladstone came to Windsor to give the Queen a full account of what had transpired. Russell had been rebuked for giving Denmark the wrong impression, for a majority of ministers were not ready to make such a definite commitment. Even Palmerston concurred in this. Victoria wrote to Uncle Leopold that it defied belief that Russell had again 'most dangerously' put forward proposals '*without* the slightest authorisation from the Cabinet!!! and this for the *third* time! Is it not too bad?'[65]

Perhaps it was on account of misleading signals from Russell that the Danes became ever more obstinate and intractable. While the Prussians 'trickily and evasively' indicated they would conditionally accept mediation by a third party, the Danes '*insanely and incredibly*' – as the Queen put it – refused to consider it under any circumstances. Victoria hailed this as 'the *greatest* escape possible' because 'the *total refusal* of the Danes, which puts *them entirely* in the wrong', removed all moral pressure to assist them.[66]

At this point the French 'held out a sort of bait' that they would join with England to assist Denmark. The Queen had no doubt they would exact a heavy price and were making the offer on the understanding that '*we* let them have Italy and later the Rhine'. To Victoria's relief, Palmerston was wary of this Faustian pact. The Cabinet discussed the matter on two successive days, and on the eve of their second meeting on 25 June, the Queen sent General Grey from Windsor to London to lobby ministers to reject the French proposal. This undoubted abuse of her position was actually needless: having decided against taking action at present, the ministers would only commit to reconsidering the situation if Copenhagen was threatened. After Victoria heard the news, Grey wrote to Lord Granville: 'I have not for a long while seen the Queen more happy.'[67]

Days after the deadlocked London conference broke up, fighting resumed in Denmark. The German powers swept all before them and on 12 July the Danes were once again forced to seek an armistice – 'of course' the Queen remarked grimly, 'on *any* terms they can get'. Hostilities ceased a week later, with the Danes having to accept the forfeiture of both contentious duchies. The Queen considered this satisfactory, observing to King Leopold, 'If the Danes had not been fools they might have had better terms, but it is much better for future peace they should *not* have anything to do with the Duchies.'[68]

The Queen had the sense of a job well done. Mr Gladstone wrote to his wife, 'For the first time she takes a just credit to herself for having influenced beneficially the course of policy and of affairs in the late controversy.' Exulting to her uncle that '*this* country is *safe*', Victoria confided, 'I *feel* that my darling has blessed and guided me.' She was pleased when Sir Charles Wood 'thanked me again & again … for the *great* services I *had* done' in shielding ministers from the 'folly of Lord Russell by never allowing Dispatches to *be sent* of *any importance without* the knowledge of the Cabinet'.[69]

General Grey likewise assured her that 'Your Majesty may justly take to yourself a principal share in the maintenance of peace.' Whether Lord Russell would in fact have managed to slip more aggressive steps past the Cabinet had it not been for Victoria's intervention is difficult to judge. If Britain had gone to war with Prussia, possibly the country would have fared as disastrously as Austria did two years later. On the other hand, the fact that Britain had not challenged Bismarck in any meaningful way during the Schleswig-Holstein crisis dangerously tilted the European balance of power in Prussia's favour. If Germany was now on the path to unification under the leadership of Prussia, it was not the enlightened Prussia Prince Albert had dreamed of, but an illiberal and aggressively militaristic power whose chief minister did not hesitate to trample on conventional morality to achieve his objectives. Britain's prestige had been lowered by alternating bluster with hesitancy. Afterwards Bismarck said he had 'wasted several years of his political life by the belief that England was a great nation', but he was now disabused, and he compared Palmerston to an old toothless lion whose 'snarls and grimaces' could be safely ignored.[70]

The crisis had undoubtedly been extremely stressful for the Queen. In November 1863 she had told General Grey, 'she feels as if she must sink under the weight of her anxieties & woes!' She suffered from severe headaches as she grappled with the complex issues, increasing her yearning 'to rest on that *dear* beloved *shoulder*, & on that strong arm that *encircled* me'. When all was over, she complained of being '*very* tired, *much* fagged & worn' by the 'weary, weary work'.[71]

In April 1864 the Queen had been furious when, in the midst of all her worries about Schleswig-Holstein, *The Times* published a leading article saying her subjects would like to see more of her. In response she arranged for an unsigned statement to be placed in the paper explaining that a combination of her 'ever-abiding desolation' and arduous duties made public appearances impossible. She had wanted to publish a similar announcement the previous September but had desisted after General Grey suggested it would be 'scarcely consistent with your Majesty's dignity'. Grey had flattered himself she would henceforth 'be shy of ordering future insertions', but a mere seven months later there was no stopping her.[72]

The day after her announcement appeared, the Queen informed Lord Palmerston that in May she would have to go to Balmoral for almost a month, for 'though the depression, desolation & sorrow are ... the same' wherever she was, being outdoors in Scotland did her good. Palmerston answered gallantly that he hoped 'the bracing air of the Highlands may prove beneficial'. Sympathy was waning in other quarters, however. In the spring of 1864 Lord Stanley stated the Queen's seclusion had quite destroyed the popularity so painstakingly built up during the past twenty years. Not only had it given rise to rumours that she had gone mad, but an irreverent handbill had lately been affixed to the railings of Buckingham Palace declaring that as its occupant had retired, the premises were to be let or sold. Several politicians were losing patience with their sovereign, exasperated that she used her bereavement as an excuse to act unreasonably. Before interviews with Cabinet members, Victoria had 'adopted the custom of sending word beforehand' that it was impermissible 'to enter on such and such a subject, lest it should make her nervous'. Lord Clarendon opined that she was milking her widowed state, for despite being 'recovered in health and nearly so in spirits', she was 'afraid of being thought inconsistent if she did not persist in a show of grief. It was real enough last year; now it is only acting.' The Queen herself remained convinced that the public were appreciative of what she did manage to do for them. When she went to London for the day in late June 1864, she congratulated herself for driving in an open carriage through the crowded park, for 'though *very painful* [it] pleased people more than anything'.

Complacently she recorded that her reception differed from those accorded Bertie and Alix: 'Naturally for *them* no one stops or *runs* as they ... *do*, doubly now, for me.'[73]

Those who hoped that the Queen would show herself more once Denmark was at peace faced disappointment. Observers reported she looked robust, with Gladstone writing to his wife from Balmoral in September 1864, 'She weighs I am told 11 stone eight pounds – a secret! Rather too much for her height.' Victoria insisted she was still very frail, and when Russell tentatively suggested in December that she might open the next session of Parliament, she swiftly disabused him. Such 'great exertion ... would entail a succession of *moral shocks*' that her system could not withstand, making it '*totally out of the question*'.[74]

A few days later what the Queen considered another 'vulgar and heartless' piece appeared in *The Times*, begging 'her Majesty to return to the personal exercise of her exalted functions'. It affirmed it was unthinkable 'for a recluse to occupy the British throne without a gradual weakening of [royal] authority'. Victoria was shocked that, instead of taking her side, Palmerston agreed it would be a good idea if she held drawing rooms and levées. Expressing 'pain & surprise', the Queen wrote that she had expected he would understand that her shattered nerves necessitated quiet, or rather, '*what* quiet has she *ever*, for from morning till late at night she slaves & works, without one day's relaxation'. Warning 'that *no attempt* to *dictate any* course to her will succeed', she demanded, 'Surely it is enough to have been bereft of *all* that made her life happy & yet cheerfully & indefatigably to work ... for the welfare of her people,' without being expected to participate 'in the *frivolous* amusements of the world – for which her health & strength have fatally unfitted her!' Palmerston promised colleagues he would 'have another try' in due course, but he knew it would be futile if the Queen cited the authority of Dr Jenner – 'a thorough courtier physician' on whom she depended to say her health was not up to it.[75]

In June 1865 she was still complaining to her daughter of the 'very irksome duty' that dominated her existence, but at least the international situation was much less worrying than in the previous year. In April the American Civil War had finished in Northern victory, confounding the Queen's earlier prediction that the secession of the Southern states would prove permanent. During the war, relations with the Unionist government had been severely strained because Confederate agents had commissioned warships to be illicitly built in British shipyards, and these had preyed on Northern shipping. The

Unionists had protested at this violation of British neutrality, but when Gladstone had discussed the question with Victoria in October 1863 he had noticed, 'she did not appear to lean toward over-conciliation of the Federal Government'. In February 1865 – by which time a Northern victory was looking much more likely – Russell had asked the Federal authorities to forward to their enemy a letter from him protesting at the Confederates' abuse of British neutrality. He hoped that, once the war ended, this would dissuade the victorious Unionists from invading Canada to punish Britain. The Queen thought this a craven policy that 'will certainly be ascribed in the United States to the fear created in England by the late successes of the Federal armies'. Russell agreed that 'swaggering and insolent men' would probably say this, but 'to bring on this country the calamities of war ... because we do not like to be thought afraid, would be a course hardly becoming the dignity, the power, or the humanity of the country'.[76]

The Queen was given an opportunity to promote Anglo-American goodwill following Abraham Lincoln's assassination on 14 April, five days after the Confederate surrender. She had been shocked by this 'most dreadful and awful' event, which she hoped would 'not be *catching elsewhere*'. A letter from a distinguished American urging her to send 'a *personal* expression of sympathy' to Mrs Lincoln much impressed her, for Victoria did not question this gentleman's belief that 'towards her personally the affection of the American people ... has never abated'. Noting his conviction that 'she cannot be a greater object of household love and veneration in her own dominions than she still is throughout the Northern States', she despatched a touchingly phrased message of condolence to the president's widow. She assured Mrs Lincoln, 'No one can better appreciate than I can, who am myself utterly broken-hearted by the loss of my own beloved husband' what she was suffering – a message gratefully acknowledged by its recipient, and which earned the Queen public approval when published across the Atlantic. Having been told by Lords Granville and Clarendon that her communication would do much to conciliate feeling in the United States, Victoria confided to General Grey, 'it was worth struggling on in this wretched life, if I could be of use, could preserve peace & pour balm into wounded hearts'.[77]

The Queen had assumed that once Schleswig-Holstein had been wrested from the Danes, the victorious Prussians and Austrians would make Prince Frederick Augustenburg the ruler of the duchies, which would become autonomous statelets within the German Confederation. If anyone ventured that Prussia might be motivated by a desire for her own aggrandisement, Victoria had dismissed the very idea, stating firmly, 'I would pledge my honour that the King of Prussia *will take nothing.*' In this instance it was 'poor foolish Bertie' who was vindicated – for at the outset of the crisis he had observed, 'Neither Austria nor Prussia cares one damn for Augustenburg … They are playing for absolute possession.' Now the man Victoria called 'that dreadful Bismarck' overcame the King of Prussia's scruples to convince him that Augustenburg did not deserve the duchies. Instead the duchies were occupied by Austrian and Prussian armies, and the inhabitants were obliged to pay reparations covering the cost of 'liberation' from Denmark.[78]

When it emerged that the duchies would be treated as conquered provinces, a shocked Victoria underwent a total change of sentiment. She wrote in outrage to her uncle, 'Prussia seems inclined to behave as atrociously as possible, and as she *always has done*! Odious people the Prussians are, *that* I *must* say.' Her displeasure was such that when she paid her now near-annual summer visit to Coburg, she would have preferred the King of Prussia not to pay her his usual visit. In the end, after being pressed by her daughter and the king's wife, she agreed to a brief encounter, during which a few banalities were exchanged. She still hoped that there could be a diplomatic means 'of letting the German Powers, and especially Prussia know what we think of their conduct'. She wrote to Lord Russell that Bismarck and the King of Prussia were behaving in a way that, in private life, would have meant 'no gentleman could have dealings with them thereafter', and it would pain her if 'no word of reprobation' was uttered. Lord Palmerston was not inclined to oblige her, commenting to Russell that it was 'rather late for the Queen' to have woken up to the true situation. 'As far as the Queen is concerned … so long as the injustice committed appeared calculated to benefit Germany and the Germans it was right and proper; but now … her sense of right and wrong has become wonderfully keen.'[79]

In 1865 even Victoria could hardly complain that domestic politics caused her much inconvenience. A so-called 'Truce of Parties' prevailed because the Conservatives remained wary of seeking to turn out the government, and there were no really divisive issues. In March Lord Palmerston had reported to the Queen that during the last month, 'the Leader of Opposition has not yet opened his mouth, but the Government have no reason to complain of this'.[80]

The government was at greater risk of internal rupture than opposition attacks. In particular, relations between Palmerston and Gladstone had continued to be fractious. The prime minister had been incensed when Gladstone had made a speech at Manchester in April 1862 decrying demands for increased naval and military spending. Under normal circumstances the Queen would have been equally annoyed, but she was touched that in the same speech Gladstone had spoken of how her 'heart lay bleeding' from 'crushing sorrow'. This made her prepared to overlook the speech's less palatable parts, and she wrote to thank him for his kind words.[81]

Gladstone had paid a successful visit to Balmoral in the autumn of 1863. He enjoyed himself enormously, going for a nineteen-mile walk one day, and having animated conversation with the Queen at dinner. After an evening when they had discussed wide-ranging topics, Gladstone was told the next morning that the Queen felt guilty about appearing 'too cheerful'. During his visit she noted in her journal, 'He is very agreeable, so quiet & intellectual, with such a knowledge of all subjects, & is such a *good* man.'[82]

The following May their relations suffered a setback when Gladstone made a statement in Parliament that appeared to indicate that he favoured the introduction of universal suffrage. To Lord Palmerston the Queen quavered that she was 'deeply grieved at this strange and independent act of Mr Gladstone', but things quietened down after Gladstone assured Palmerston his words had been subject to 'strange misconstructions'.[83]

The next year the Queen's faith in Gladstone was largely restored by their similarity of outlook upon the Schleswig-Holstein question. Gladstone admired the way she fought for what she believed in, assuring his wife, 'Her love of truth and wish to do right prevent all prejudices from effectually warping her.' That autumn Gladstone was again a valued guest when he stayed at Balmoral, although he did suffer one 'calamity' in the course of his visit. Dressing hurriedly in formal knee breeches for dinner, he was drawing them up violently, 'when lo! they rent frightfully'. He had to obtain permission to appear at table in the wrong trousers.[84]

While at Balmoral Gladstone wrote to the prime minister, warning that he intended to contest defence estimates for the coming year, and when Victoria learnt this, it reawakened her disapproval. To her relief, upon arguing the point with his Chancellor, 'Ld P … completely knocked the latter over.' After a series of 'rough' Cabinet meetings,

Palmerston informed the Queen in January 1865, 'Mr Gladstone has been as troublesome and wrong-headed as he often is,' before giving way.[85]

The Chancellor of the Exchequer had been quashed, but the episode foreshadowed trouble in the future between him and the Queen. Gladstone had already made considerable progress in his career trajectory from reactionary Conservative to Liberal firebrand. While not particularly popular with colleagues or party members, he was already looked upon as 'the inevitable leader' of the Liberals in days to come. It was no less preordained that at that time his progressive views would bring him into conflict with an increasingly conservative queen.

If clashes with Gladstone loomed in the distance, Victoria's relations with Palmerston were now largely harmonious. It is true that in 1863 people had expected the prime minister to be brought down by scandal after he was cited in a divorce case. A certain Mr O'Kane sought £20,000 in damages, asserting that his wife had visited Palmerston at home and there committed adultery with him. While Disraeli had urged Tories, 'for God's sake, do not let the people of England know – or he will sweep the country', Lord Derby predicted that 'the affair, however it may end, will not increase H.M.'s affection for her minister'. When Palmerston had stayed at Windsor that autumn he was noticeably shaken and subdued, appearing 'quite unlike himself' to observers. Lord Clarendon feared 'British hypocrisy will probably soon make a move to protect its widowed Sovereign from the approach of her licentious Minister' – but in fact the whole thing blew over after it emerged that O'Kane was not even married to the lady in question.[86]

In the spring of 1865 the Queen gratefully accepted Palmerston's assistance on another delicate personal matter. After discovering in April that the Prince of Wales was behaving in an unseemly manner, Sir Charles Phipps had written to inform Palmerston. The prime minister then passed this on to the Queen. It appears that infidelity was not specifically mentioned but, as Victoria confided to Uncle Leopold, 'our foolish Boy' was involved in 'gambling, smoking all night & late hours' – in short, '*every* thing that is bad'.[87]

Thanking Palmerston for alerting her, Victoria asked him 'to *write very strongly* warning the Prince of Wales of the *precipice* upon which he stands'. She suggested 'pointing out to him how shocked & alarmed the nation would be if they thought he was following the example of the old Royal Family instead of that of his great father. Lord Palmerston

A photograph of Lord Palmerston in old age.

might also say that Parliament would not be inclined to pass over in silence any tendency to extravagance & *high living*. Lastly Lord Palmerston might say that the Queen would naturally be greatly distressed & alarmed if she knew of it but he had better *not* say that he *had* mentioned the subject to the Queen.'[88] It was curious that Victoria, who had formerly concurred with Albert that Palmerston's character made him unfit for high office, should have been reduced to relying on him to provide moral guidance for her son.

Victoria was delighted when the Liberals did very well in the general election held in the summer of 1865. She had not counted on such an outcome, but the 'wonderful' increase in the governing party's majority could not bring her the long period of political stability she would have liked.[89]

Palmerston's health had not been good for much of that year. Even so, in mid-October Victoria was almost affronted when a telegram arrived at Balmoral to say that the prime minister – within a few days of his eighty-first birthday – 'was dangerously ill & dying'. Petulantly the Queen exclaimed, 'Not a word had I heard before of his being worse!' On 18 October news came that his death had taken place that morning. 'Strange, & solemn to think of that strong, determined man, with so much worldly ambition, – *gone!*' Victoria mused. She had already told her uncle, 'Regret the poor old sinner … I cannot,' but conceded that, as prime minister, 'He managed affairs at home well, and behaved to me well.' Despite that, 'I *never* liked him … He was very vindictive, and *personal* feelings influenced his political acts very much. Still, he is a loss.'[90]

However much she had deplored the foreign secretary's 'terrible unsteadiness' during the Schleswig-Holstein crisis, the Queen had already decided that if Palmerston retired or died, 'there would be nothing for it but to send for Lord Russell'. She at once wrote asking him to take over Palmerston's responsibilities, contriving to strike a note of self-pity notwithstanding her lack of genuine sadness. As she regretted the severing of another link with the past, she lamented, 'Now she stands alone … it is very hard to bear.'[91]

Palmerston's death transformed the political landscape. Lord Clarendon commented, 'He held a great bundle of sticks together; they are now unbound and there is nobody to tie them up again.' The Queen knew with him gone it would be difficult to dampen down demand for changes such as political reform, 'which might be troublesome'. Disraeli too was aware that Palmerston's passing meant 'the truce of parties is over' – and while he scented a whiff of opportunity in this for the Conservatives, he also foresaw 'tempestuous times and great vicissitudes in public life'.[92]

7

Lord Russell; Lord Derby; Mr Disraeli 1865–1868

If Victoria had not really minded about Lord Palmerston's passing, the death of 'dearly beloved Uncle Leopold' on 10 December 1865 was a 'sad, sad blow'. Since Albert's death King Leopold had regularly visited, believing his niece as much 'in want of good advice' as emotional support. Victoria had not concealed her irritation when he urged her to resume her public duties, but now, as she contemplated having to do without his wise counsel, she realised how much she would miss it. 'To think that that intercourse, that help, has also ceased and been taken from me, is truly terrible,' she reflected.[1]

The Queen had another jolt when Sir Charles Phipps died suddenly on 24 February 1866. Victoria hoped Lord Russell would now agree that General Grey could be given the official title of private secretary, pointing out that considering every minister had at least one private secretary, 'it is perfectly absurd to pretend that the Queen has *none*'. Unfortunately, mindful of 'a nasty carping spirit abroad', Russell believed it would attract 'adverse comment' in the House of Commons if a man in no way answerable to Parliament was given such a post. Consequently, and much to Victoria's fury, 'the stupid ministers' eschewed 'the natural, simple and right course'. Sir Thomas Biddulph succeeded Phipps, while Grey retained the title of Joint Keeper of the Privy Purse, a semantical fudge that did not limit his role in the slightest.[2]

When Lord Russell had kissed hands as prime minister the previous October, he admitted to the Queen that at seventy-three he felt daunted by 'the weight of the task he had undertaken'. To demonstrate that he had her support – and perhaps also because her daughter Princess Helena had just got engaged and would need to be granted an allowance from public funds – Victoria had promised she would open Parliament when the new session began. Although she knew she must honour the commitment, she made it plain she was very unhappy about it, writing to Russell on 22 January 1866 that she was dreading having 'to go through what SHE *can* only compare to an execution'. It was, she complained, '*unreasonable* and unfeeling' of the public to wish 'to *witness* the spectacle of a poor, broken-hearted widow, nervous and shrinking, dragged in *deep mourning*, ALONE *in* STATE as a *Show*'. Since she had given her word, 'She *will* do it *this time* … but she owns she resents the unfeelingness of those who have *clamoured* for it.'[3]

Sure enough, when she went to Parliament on 6 February, wearing a coronet over her widow's cap rather than the crown, she deemed it a terrible ordeal. She claimed she nearly fainted on entering the House of Lords, despite the fact that every attempt had been made to make things easier for her. Having had what Lady Clarendon described as 'all sorts of vagaries about it', Victoria had stipulated beforehand not just that the speech from the throne must be read by the Lord Chancellor, rather than herself, but also that she could not wear the traditional formal robes. Instead, these were draped over the throne and then tucked around her when she sat down, 'rather like a railway rug' according to Lady Clarendon.[4]

Afterwards the Queen insisted it had been a fearful experience, telling General Grey, 'such *violent* agitation & nervousness as she went through today must have its consequences'. She explained fretfully, 'What the Queen deprecates so strongly – is people imagining these *Pageants are her* duties – when she has never during these four years neglected the *real* duties of her hard position.' To help her recover, she decamped to Osborne, but ten days later was infuriated when Russell requested that she return to Windsor on account of the political situation. She instructed Grey to inform Lord Granville that in future she should '*not* [be] asked to leave *this* & *that* place in the way Ld Russell is inclined to do … She does *not like* this & ministers are *too* fond of wishing the Queen to come *to them* instead of *their* coming to *her* as they *ought*.'[5]

Grey begged her to comply with Russell's summons, saying that while he understood her preference for being at Osborne and Balmoral, 'it is impossible for him to shut his eyes to the possible inconvenience & even injury to the public service of their distance from London in times of difficulty & emergency'. Artfully he suggested that if she made it difficult for her ministers to remain in close touch with her, there was 'a greater danger of Y[our]M[ajesty]'s proper constitutional authority being weakened', as it gave them 'a reasonable excuse for neglecting (as has been the case on more than one occasion) to obtain Y[our] M[ajesty]'s sanction before taking some important step'. The Queen was impressed enough by this to return to Windsor somewhat earlier than planned, but did not fail to send Russell a letter asking that henceforth he should 'trust to her doing what she believes to be *necessary* for the good of the country, without her movements being dictated to her'.[6]

Lord Russell had wanted the Queen to be closer at hand because he was in difficulties over his Reform Bill. When he had told her in October that he intended to bring in a 'moderate measure of Reform', Victoria responded 'this would be a very good thing', observing that Albert had always favoured legislating on the matter 'when there was no excitement or clamour for it'. She only specified it 'must be very carefully framed', emphasising to both Russell and Gladstone – who was now Leader of the House of Commons – it must 'be carried forward to a final result, and not trifled with or dropped'.[7]

As practical difficulties became more apparent, the Queen had come to regret Russell's having 'hampered himself' with 'wretched Reform'. Despite the fact that the Liberals had won a large majority in the previous summer's election, 'many of them were Palmerstonians, and, as such, against Reform Bills'. Some, indeed, were viscerally opposed to even modest alterations to the franchise. The Cabinet too were divided, with several prominent members being far from keen to tackle reform. In discussions Russell did not always handle his colleagues tactfully, but once a bill had been drafted, he assured the Queen that 'all the Cabinet concurred in it, though some did so less cordially than others'.[8]

Gladstone introduced the bill in the House of Commons on 12 March 1866. The measure, which would have increased the electorate by approximately 400,000, was sufficiently moderate for Lord Derby to contemplate instructing his party to support it. Disraeli would not hear of this, for he was aware that many Liberals wanted the bill to fail, and if the Conservatives joined with them in voting against it, they could bring the government down. Derby soon accepted the force of this argument. The depth of feeling among some Liberals against the proposals was exemplified by the speech made on 13 March by Robert Lowe, who had already declared he would resist lowering the franchise by 'one sixpence'. Now he denounced a measure he claimed would give the vote to 'impulsive, unreflecting and violent people', renowned for their 'ignorance ... drunkenness and facility to be intimidated'. In response, Gladstone professed outrage that he could depict working men as if they were 'an invading army'.[9]

The Queen too did not approve of Lowe's approach. While nervous of 'democracy', she had considerable respect for the aspirational labouring classes. The following year she would tell her daughter Vicky, 'The higher classes – especially the aristocracy (with of course exceptions and honourable ones) – are so frivolous, pleasure-seeking, heartless, selfish, immoral and gambling that it makes one think ... of the days before the French Revolution.' In contrast, 'the lower classes are becoming so well-informed, are so intelligent and earn their bread and riches so deservedly – that they cannot and ought not to be kept back'. When Russell raised the subject of the working classes at an audience with her in March 1866, he remarked that 'HM might herself have seen enough of them to know that they were very different from what they were represented' by Lowe and others. '"Yes indeed" said the Queen, "I think they are the best people in the country."'[10]

As the Reform Bill started to make its way through Parliament, Disraeli left it to dissident Liberals to make the most vehement attacks on it, confining himself to coordinating their activities behind the scenes. Gladstone did not commend himself to waverers on his own side by being ill-tempered in debates, and it began to look quite likely the bill would be defeated at the second reading stage. If that happened, the government was unlikely to survive.

The government's perilous situation was the more troubling because the international situation was currently so alarming. War between Prussia and Austria was looking increasingly likely, for Bismarck – or 'that monster' as Victoria now habitually referred to him – needed one in order to achieve his ambitions. He used disagreements over the way Austria and Prussia were administering the Duchies of Schleswig and Holstein to bring the two nations to breaking point.

A glimmer of hope emerged when the King of Prussia asked his son Fritz to request his mother-in-law to authorise British mediation between Austria and Prussia. On 20 March Vicky wrote exultantly to her mother that Bismarck had been unaware of King William's intentions, and '"the wicked man" is *frantic*'. Unfortunately, Bismarck soon regained control of the situation. When Clarendon tried to discuss terms with the Prussian ambassador, it became apparent that the only help Bismarck would find acceptable was that Britain should press Austria to let Prussia annex both duchies. Determined not to connive in Prussia's 'iniquitous schemes of aggrandisement', the Queen accepted that mediation would be futile.[11]

Victoria nevertheless went on working to prevent a conflict that, she told her daughter, would be 'too, too wicked'. On 30 March she wrote a memorandum for her ministers, saying that since war looked 'not only inevitable but imminent … *entirely* owing to the high-handed proceedings of Prussia', would it not be a good idea for Britain to join with France, and possibly Russia, to protest 'against a course not only unjust in itself but fraught with danger to the peace of Europe?' Reluctantly Clarendon agreed to sound out his French counterpart, but told Russell, 'I know it will be useless.' He explained to the Queen that even if France proved open to a combined diplomatic effort, Britain could not threaten Prussia with war. 'The case is one in which neither English honour nor English interests are involved,' and 'the country would not tolerate any direct interference in a quarrel with which we had no concern'.[12]

The Queen was already annoyed with Clarendon, and this firm treatment did nothing to endear him to her. She fortunately was unaware that he had irreverently nicknamed her 'The Missus', but she had had enough experience of his sardonic wit to suspect, correctly, that he sometimes made jokes at her expense. Regarding him as unsound on German affairs, earlier that year she had begun to limit her dealings with him, and things became so bad that Clarendon complained to Russell that she was being unapproachable. When Russell took the matter up with her, Victoria insisted, 'Lord Clarendon is *quite wrong* in what he says,' for she consulted him as much as ever. She blamed the foreign secretary for any awkwardness that had arisen, claiming that whenever she talked with him, 'the Queen was met most frequently by a petulant irritated tone … so unpleasant, as to make the Queen shrink from seeing him … The Queen will however, take no notice of Lord Clarendon's crossness.' A few days later Clarendon wrote jocularly to a lady friend, 'the Missus and I have had a bit of a tiff', but he hoped things were now sorted out.[13]

Because her conscience would not allow her to 'remain a passive spectator of the horrible sin of shedding so much innocent blood gratuitously', Victoria now took impulsive action. Without telling Lord Russell, on 10 April she wrote a letter to her 'Beloved Brother', the King of Prussia, begging him, 'in the name of all … most holy and sacred' not to cause carnage over 'imaginary affronts and wrongs'. Without actually naming Bismarck, she warned King William that while '*one* man' had brought him to this point, if war was embarked upon, 'the responsibility … will rest on *you alone*'. Having implored him to heed her plea, she argued, 'It is in your power to avert the calamities of a war … in which thousands of innocent lives will be lost.'[14]

The letter was presented personally to the king by the British ambassador in Berlin, who stressed it must be 'viewed as the private act of her Majesty'. It thus did not represent official government policy, but when Clarendon read her appeal, he was moved by it. Abandoning his habitual cynicism, he described it as a 'most beautiful and forcible letter'.[15]

Meanwhile, the debates on the second reading of the Reform Bill were proving challenging for the government. When the Queen heard the Cabinet were discussing whether, in the event of losing the division, they would resign or, alternatively, ask for a dissolution of Parliament, she drafted a letter to be laid before ministers saying she would support them in whichever decision they reached. General Grey queried this, fearing the Queen would be blamed if she sanctioned an election campaign 'involving every topic that is likely to set class against class'. Accordingly, Victoria rewrote her letter, asking the Cabinet to bear in mind 'the inconvenience and even risk' an election might entail.[16]

In Parliament, Gladstone was making the most strenuous efforts to persuade the Commons to support the bill. In an impassioned speech of 27 April, he told those who had spoken against it, 'You cannot fight against the future ... The great social forces which move onwards in their might and majesty, and which the tumult of our debates does not for a moment impede or disturb – those great social forces ... are marshalled on our side.'[17] In the early hours of the morning of 28 April, the second reading did pass, but by a slender margin of five votes.

Some Whigs in the Cabinet, such as Clarendon and Sir George Grey, would have liked the government to abandon the bill, or even resign, but Russell and Gladstone were determined to do neither. While the Queen had no wish for the ministry to fall, she did want them to modify the Reform Bill, or at least put it off for a while. To her disappointment Russell was adamant that altering the proposed £7 borough franchise would constitute 'a mark of ignominy'. Gladstone too would not hear of delay, informing the Commons on 7 May that, if necessary, Parliament would be kept sitting until the autumn. Victoria was so upset by his 'want of conciliatoriness' that she suggested to Russell (who turned down the offer) that she write to Gladstone urging him to be less abrasive.[18]

After the government suffered defeat on another amendment in late May the Queen decided 'entirely on my own responsibility' to write confidentially to Lord Derby, begging that his party refrain from putting up 'violent or factious opposition' to the Reform Bill. She wished the

Tories 'to treat this question *not* as a mere Party one', for she was currently 'peculiarly unfit' to cope with a political crisis. Courteously but firmly Derby rebuffed her, insisting the proposed measure would 'be fatal to the constitution of the country'. Not only would it open the way 'for more extensive and more democratic changes', it would also place 'the whole power of the state in the hands of those … least able to form a … judgement in matters of high policy, and most liable to be misled by artful and ambitious demagogues'.[19]

This being so, the Queen's next step was to write to Lord Russell, observing that since it was clearly '*absolutely* hopeless to expect the Reform measure to pass during the present session', he should postpone it. Once again, she met with failure, for on 9 June Russell declared that 'premature concession' would 'expose his own character and that of Mr Gladstone'.[20]

In urging compromise on the respective party leaders the Queen was doubtless sincerely desirous of avoiding a dangerous impasse, but also had more selfish motives, being desperate to go to Balmoral. She had in fact originally intended to take her usual Scottish break in mid-May, until on 12 May Russell had written to General Grey saying that it was essential she cancel her trip. Not only did war appear imminent in Germany, but by the end of the month the Reform Bill would have reached a critical stage, and 'in case of difficulty, public comments on the Queen's absence at such a moment will not be wanting'. Grey commissioned Princess Helena, who had a knack for managing her mother, to pass on this message, and initially it appeared the Queen would respond selflessly. Then, on 18 May, only four days after announcing Victoria was abandoning her holiday, Grey had to inform Russell she would now be spending ten days at Balmoral in June. The Queen justified this to Grey on the grounds she was going not for her '*own amusement*' but because her health required it. A change of air provided her sole respite from 'the constant labour & wear & tear of her sad and lonely life', for she '*cannot* lay down her office … though she *may* be *driven to that at last*'. On 25 May she wrote to Russell herself, enclosing a letter from Dr Jenner, confirming 'from a medical point of view' that a visit to Scotland was essential.[21]

The Queen was unmoved when the Duke of Argyll told her he could not possibly accompany her to Balmoral as the minister in residence, for the 'risk of the Cabinet having to come to some *very* critical decisions during that time' meant it was unthinkable for him to leave London. Crossly she commented to Grey, 'There certainly seems to be a system of *frightening* the Queen both on Home and F[oreign] affairs ... *Wolf* is really cried *too often*.' She claimed that when she saw Lord Clarendon on 10 June, two days before her departure, he assured her 'there was no time when I could go with greater ease than now. Reform too, would be no trouble.' Clarendon certainly did not give Russell the impression he had encouraged her in this way, instead informing the prime minister that the Queen 'seemed to think that all important events were sure to wait till she returned from Balmoral'.[22]

It certainly would have been extraordinary if the foreign secretary had taken a relaxed view, for besides the uncertain state of the Reform Bill, the international situation had continued to deteriorate. On 23 April the Queen had received 'an extraordinary, most deluded answer from the King of Prussia' in which he once again rehearsed his grievances against Austria, and insisted Bismarck was not manipulating him. In early May, Victoria had been 'horribly put out' when a telegram had arrived from the British ambassador in Paris, Lord Cowley, confirming that the French would take no action to prevent war between Austria and Prussia. The Queen then asked Clarendon if Britain could 'threaten or remonstrate' on her own, but the foreign secretary insisted 'that would *not* do'. Haunted by the horrors in store, Victoria went on hoping that something could be achieved by diplomatic means. On 27 May Clarendon remarked to Russell, 'It is not unnatural that a lady writing alone in the small hours of the night should write such a letter as the Queen's, but we should simply make ourselves ridiculous by such an appeal as she recommends.'[23]

On 10 June Prussian troops occupied Holstein, and Bismarck declared that Germany's federal structure was to be reorganised, so that Austria was excluded. Four days later, as the Queen arrived at Balmoral, Prussia broke off diplomatic relations with Austria and issued ultimatums to German states, including Hanover, Hesse-Cassel and Saxony, that had refused to accept Bismarck's dispositions. At midnight on 15 June Prussian troops marched into those states, and on 18 June Prussia formally declared war on Austria.

That very night, the government lost a Commons vote on an amendment to the Reform Bill that would have enfranchised fewer new voters. When the result of the division was announced, Gladstone stated to MPs that since the government could do nothing until they had communicated with the Queen, parliamentary sittings would be adjourned until 25 June. Victoria at once telegraphed from Balmoral, stating it was the government's 'bounden duty' to remain in office; General Grey then informed Gladstone she furthermore believed the ministry should 'accept the sacrifice of the franchise'. Despite this, after discussing the situation, the Cabinet decided, 'in the teeth of the Queen', to tender their resignation.[24]

Learning this, Victoria declared indignantly – and not entirely accurately – that before she had left for Scotland, she had been led to believe 'there was no fear of a crisis'. She repeated it was imperative that the government should make concessions over reform, and again rejected their resignations. On 21 June Gladstone pronounced her solution impractical. 'There are things that can and cannot be done,' he wrote to General Grey, and accepting a more restricted extension of the franchise 'would cover us with shame'.[25]

On 19 June Lord Russell had somewhat half-heartedly offered to come to Balmoral to see the Queen, while hoping 'such a journey on his part may be dispensed with'. He was dismayed to hear the Queen would not return home till 26 June, a day after Parliament reconvened, and asked permission for Gladstone to inform the Commons that the government had tried to resign, so far without success. Victoria agreed to this, but flatly rejected his request that her train from Scotland should take her to London so that Russell need not go to Windsor for their audience. It was fortunate few people knew she was being so disobliging, for even on 21 June Lord Stanley had recorded her refusal 'to give up any part of her holiday ... is generally commented upon ... and adds to her unpopularity'. The radical MP Ralph Bernal Osborne had threatened 'to say something very nasty on the subject' in the Commons, and in London society there was 'much foul-mouthed gossip'.[26]

While they awaited the Queen's return, the Cabinet met several times to discuss what options were available to them. By the time Lord Russell had his Windsor audience with the Queen, at lunchtime on 26 June, it was already clear that a majority of the Cabinet opposed dissolution. Postponing reform until next year had also been ruled out: as Russell had reminded colleagues, he had committed himself to securing a bill this session. There still remained a chance that the current bill could be altered in some way that would make it acceptable to Parliament, and the prime minister flustered the Queen by asking her directly whether the government should adopt this course. When she asked for time to consider, he said that was impossible as ministers had to make a parliamentary statement that evening. Accordingly, Victoria told him to go back to the Cabinet and establish if they were ready to back this approach, conceding that, if they were not, she would accept the government's resignation.

Angry at a crisis that she believed had been 'recklessly and wantonly produced' by ministers, the Queen did not disguise that she blamed Russell for his own predicament. She claimed to have 'deprecated very strongly' the way the government had set about reform, asking the prime minister to recall 'how earnestly she had warned him to try and keep out of all these difficulties'.[27] This hardly made life easier for Russell. On his return to London, the Cabinet met again, and came down against persisting with an amended Reform Bill. Accordingly, Russell telegraphed Windsor to say the government would resign, and a statement to that effect was given in both houses of Parliament.

The Queen at once wrote to Lord Derby inviting him to form a government that she hoped would include some Whigs and Liberals. She was particularly keen that Lord Clarendon – her springtime 'tiff' with him forgotten for the moment – should remain foreign secretary, so he could handle any complications arising from the Austro-Prussian War. Since Derby was amenable, she wrote to Clarendon asking him to retain office, but he replied that party loyalty precluded this.[28] Other Liberals who had voted against their own party over reform were not willing to serve under Derby and Disraeli. It became clear that if he became prime minister, Derby would once more be heading an exclusively Conservative ministry that lacked a majority in Parliament. This was something he had sworn never again to inflict on himself, but he nevertheless undertook it, and by 2 July had appointed a Cabinet.

Disraeli once again was Derby's Chancellor of the Exchequer and Leader of the Commons. Victoria was not happy when she learned that Derby had appointed his son Lord Stanley as his foreign secretary, for in earlier dealings with him she had found him 'rather peculiar, shy & reserved & difficult to get on with'. Being '*greatly alarmed*', she wrote to Derby questioning, as tactfully as she could, his son's suitability. While acknowledging Stanley's 'great abilities', she queried whether he had 'sufficient knowledge of Continental affairs and foreigners for that very difficult post?' Derby replied that while he did not consider his son an ideal foreign secretary, he was the best candidate available, and promised to supervise what he did. The Queen had to content herself with this.[29]

On 3 July, the day after the new government was settled, the situation in Europe was transformed when the Prussians defeated the Austrians at the Battle of Sadowa. Bismarck then set about reconfiguring Germany.

States that had sided with Austria, such as Hesse-Cassel and Hanover, were annexed by Prussia. Victoria felt conflicted about this. She told Vicky that she still longed to see realised 'Papa's great maxim of Prussia becoming Germany and a great German Empire', but did not think Albert would have approved of the present arrangement.[30]

She also could not but be concerned about the war's ill effects on various members of her family, among them her second daughter, Alice. The latter was married to Prince Louis of Hesse-Darmstadt, one of the states that had fought against Prussia in the war. Although Alice's father-in-law's principality was not completely annexed, it was temporarily occupied by Prussian troops, and some of its lands were siphoned off by Prussia. It was likewise distressing that Victoria's cousin, the King of Hanover, had lost his throne. The Prince of Wales and the Duke of Cambridge both urged the Queen to protest about Hanover being 'swallowed up by Prussia', but Lord Derby told her that while the British ambassador at Berlin could make representations, it was not right for the Queen to risk humiliation with a personal appeal of her own.[31]

There was no question of Vicky interceding with her father-in-law on behalf of dispossessed relatives, for she had little sympathy for the losers. She wrote to her mother, 'Those who are now in such precarious positions … chose to go with Austria … and so the poor things have broken their own necks.' When the Queen showed Lord Derby another letter Vicky sent her on the subject a few weeks later, he commented, 'I cannot but regret that the letter is not written in a more generous spirit.'[32]

Those who had opposed Lord Russell's Reform Bill had justified their conduct partly on the grounds that the public was apathetic on the whole question. Yet once the bill had been abandoned, a clamour suddenly arose for the franchise to be widened. When the National Reform League announced that a pro-reform demonstration would take place in Hyde Park on 23 July 1866, there were fears it would develop into major civic unrest. Accordingly, Hyde Park's gates were locked that day, only for what the Queen called 'the worst sort of people' to tear down the railings and surge inside. There were numerous injuries when the police sought to disperse the crowd by making free with their batons, and things could have escalated into real horror after the Commander-in-Chief of the British Army, the Duke of Cambridge, ordered out troops. Fortunately, the crowd cheered the soldiers, but the Queen was sufficiently concerned to ask Sir Thomas Biddulph to remind her cousin

Cambridge that it had always been the Duke of Wellington's policy, 'when there was fear of disturbances, not to allow the troops to be *unnecessarily* shown to the people lest [an] unexpected collision should take place'.[33]

Public feeling went on strengthening in favour of reform, with mass meetings calling for it being held in large cities. By late September both the Queen and Lord Derby were coming round to the view that steps must be taken to satisfy the demand, even if Derby did not underestimate the difficulties. The fact that the Conservatives lacked a majority in Parliament made the task particularly daunting, and it was obvious that Liberals who had resisted Russell's legislation would be furious that the question had been resurrected. Furthermore, several members of Derby's Cabinet were unlikely to support any measure that could advance democracy. Disraeli believed that all these risks made reform too dangerous to contemplate, but Derby now felt 'we cannot escape doing something'.[34]

Derby was confirmed in this view when he went to stay at Balmoral towards the end of September and the Queen told him bluntly that 'if … Reform be not taken up in earnest by her Ministers … very serious consequences may ensue'. The prime minister informed Disraeli that she was not only 'very anxious to see it settled', but, furthermore, 'settled by *us*'. Convinced now that reform was 'a positive necessity', the Queen believed she could make a constructive contribution by appealing to Lord Russell's 'loyalty and patriotism & asking him to assist in coming to some terms of agreement'. On 28 October she wrote to Derby, formally offering to act as an intermediary with opposition leaders. Noting that a settlement would prove impossible without 'a spirit of mutual conciliation', she assured the prime minister, 'Nothing would gratify the Queen more than to be instrumental in bringing about such a disposition.'[35]

Disraeli did not welcome Victoria's 'sentimental schemes', dismissing 'the royal project of gracious interposition with our rivals' as 'a mere phantom'. It might please 'the vanity of a court deprived of substantial power', but, besides being wholly impractical, would 'convey to our rivals that we are at the same time feeble and perplexed'. Derby too did not feel he could accept Victoria's offer. He wrote on 1 November that while ministers were now agreed that reform 'must be resolutely grappled with', they also took the view that '*at the present moment*' any communication between her and the leaders of the opposition, 'might be more prejudicial than advantageous' to the government.[36]

On 10 January 1867 Derby informed the Queen that rather than precipitately introducing legislation, he intended to proceed slowly on reform. He envisaged first drawing up resolutions embodying general principles, and then, once Parliament had approved these, a commission would examine the whole question. By 'gradually feeling the pulse of the House of Commons', the Government would avoid committing itself to measures that had little hope of being accepted – an approach the Queen agreed was 'dictated by common sense'. Derby exulted to Disraeli that when it came to the Court, 'We are ... on velvet.'[37]

It was unclear whether Victoria would demonstrate her support by opening Parliament. Six years after losing Albert, she was still wallowing in sadness, for though there had been an 'easing of that violent grief, those paroxysms of despair' she had experienced at first, those emotions had been replaced by 'constant depression and listlessness'. When hints were dropped that her attendance would be helpful, the signs did not look auspicious. In December, General Grey reported that she 'spoke strongly of the unfair way' pressure was being applied, but Princess Helena did not despair of persuading her mother, who 'knows she ought to do it'. Sure enough, by 10 January, Helena could declare that the Queen was not only '*quite* ready to open Parliament' but was actually expressing surprise that Derby had not approached her on the subject. The prime minister hastened to correct this, telling Victoria her presence would 'produce a most powerful effect'. She answered that '*great, trying* and *painful* as the exertion will be to her', she would undertake it, while stipulating it must be '*clearly understood* that she is *not* to be expected to do it as a *matter of course*, year after year'.[38]

Unfortunately, when she was being driven through the streets to Westminster on 4 February 1867, 'there was a good deal of hissing & even groaning' from a crowd that contained 'many nasty faces'. Not only had 'that stupid Reform agitation ... excited and irritated people', but unemployment was high, provoking 'unpleasant demonstrations' from 'a very low & rough lot'. General Grey was instructed to let Lord Derby know how much it had upset the Queen, who considered it the sort of experience, 'which I – in my present forlorn condition – ought not to be exposed to'.[39]

As soon as the parliamentary session was under way, it began to look unlikely that Derby would be allowed to follow the leisurely timetable that he wanted. On 7 February he informed the Queen he dared not announce his wish to refer the matter to a commission, for that would expose the government to the 'charge of seeking to dally'. Victoria was sorry to hear this, believing that Derby's plan had 'afforded the best hope' of achieving consensus.[40]

Derby and Disraeli were also finding it troublesome to frame resolutions that would command the support of every Cabinet member. In December Derby had hit upon what he believed to be a clever formula for enlarging the franchise, telling Disraeli, 'of all possible hares to start I do not know a better than ... household suffrage *coupled with plurality of voting*'. The idea was that although the electorate would be greatly swollen by the addition of numerous householders, certain categories of individual would be allocated two votes: since they would generally be affluent people, it would prevent poorer voters from dictating the outcome of elections. Derby believed this system provided adequate safeguards, but his secretary of state for war, General Jonathan Peel, did not agree. Disraeli told Lord Derby that whenever the phrase 'household suffrage' was mentioned in front of Peel, 'his eye lights up with insanity', and the words had to be omitted from the resolutions being drawn up for Parliament's consideration.[41]

On 11 February Disraeli gave a less than assured performance when outlining the resolutions to the Commons. Gladstone at once demanded that the government should introduce reform legislation, rather than going down the resolutions route – prompting the Queen to write to Derby on 13 February, regretting that a 'party contest' was looming. Derby told her that if Gladstone's party supported him over opposing resolutions he would be prepared to bring in a bill but insisted that the notion that she could broker an agreement with the Liberals 'must be put altogether out of sight'. On the evening of 14 February, Disraeli dealt with the difficulty in his own way: without having secured Cabinet approval, he informed the Commons that once resolutions had been approved, a Reform Bill would be introduced.[42]

This discarding of the agreed programme infuriated General Peel. At the next Cabinet meeting on 16 February, he sat glowering 'like a great brown bear', according to Disraeli. After two hours 'dogged silence', he suddenly announced that he 'thought no Reform called for', and that he must resign.[43]

Disraeli was already scheduled to go to Osborne the following day to report in person to the Queen. Now that things looked so precarious, Derby decided his deputy must 'lay the matter before her ... and, as a last resort, to invite her Majesty's aid'. When Disraeli had his audience with Victoria at 7 p.m. on 17 February she regretted the prospect of Peel's departure, for Peel – who was the younger brother of the late prime minister – was 'personally very acceptable to her'. She was nevertheless clear that 'the Reform Bill … was more important than General Peel'. While still hoping to persuade Peel to stay on, she stressed that if he insisted on going, she did not want Derby to resign.[44]

Victoria now composed an intensely personal letter to Peel, appealing to his chivalry and patriotism, saying that she feared for the nation's 'quiet and well-being' if reform was not settled speedily. 'Having frequently told her that he would do anything for her,' she hoped he would abandon his objections, 'for the good of the country & … the Queen's personal comfort & well-being.' On reading the letter Disraeli declared, 'This must do it. He would not change the dot of an i.'[45]

Sure enough on 19 February Disraeli reported exultantly: 'the magical letter effected the miracle'. In Cabinet that day Derby praised Peel for having withdrawn his resignation 'in the handsomest manner'. He added that, because the Queen was 'prepared to do anything in her power to assist … believing that the security of her throne was involved in the settlement of the question', he now felt much more optimistic.[46] He and Disraeli busied themselves in drafting a Reform Bill.

On 23 February the result was presented to Cabinet. In essentials it conferred the right to vote on all male county dwellers who annually paid £15 in rates. The borough franchise was extended to householders who had lived in a property for at least two years and who paid their own poor rates, rather than having their landlord 'compound' for them by paying a lesser sum on their behalf by agreement with local authorities. Some 'fancy franchises' conferred a second vote on certain individuals. Disraeli assured the Queen that 'the franchise they propose, which makes it necessary that a man should be rated to the Poor & *himself* pay the rates is as different from Household suffrage … as the sun is from the moon'. He now felt confident of carrying 'a large, popular & thoroughly conservative measure', an achievement that would be 'greatly owing to your Majesty's energetic interposition'.[47]

In Cabinet Derby and Disraeli did not give ministers time to scrutinise their proposals in depth. Business was hurried through after Derby said he must leave early, and Disraeli batted away questions about how many voters would be added to the electoral roll.[48] Several ministers felt uneasy, the most notable being the Secretary of State for India, Lord Cranborne – son and heir of the Marquess of Salisbury. In his prolific journalistic career, Cranborne had often written disparagingly about Disraeli, and now he was not prepared to take his word on trust. Over the next twenty-four hours, Cranborne did some frenzied computations which showed that many more men would be enfranchised than ministers had been led to believe. He passed this on to Lord Carnarvon, the colonial secretary, and General Peel, who were equally outraged. Cranborne then wrote to Derby late on 24 February saying he could not remain in office if the current measure was put forward.

Derby had planned to reveal details of the bill to a meeting of the Conservative Party on the afternoon of 25 February, and then Disraeli was to present it in the House of Commons. When Cranborne dropped his bombshell, Derby was obliged hastily to convene a morning Cabinet 'of a most unpleasant character'. The three dissenting ministers insisted they must resign if the government stuck to its course, whereupon Derby felt the only way 'to prevent a discreditable break-up' was to modify their proposals. Derby told Victoria he believed the new measure – known as the 'Ten Minute Bill' on account of the haste with which it was drawn up – to be 'far less satisfactory and comprehensive' than the original, but he had no alternative.[49]

Hardly had the details been settled than Derby had to present them to his party, to palpable disappointment. That evening Disraeli unveiled them in the Commons, showing a marked lack of conviction. They were given a decidedly unfavourable reception, and it was clear that Gladstone would have little difficulty ensuring that the Liberal Party opposed it vigorously.

At his wits' end, Derby began to wonder if he would have to accept Victoria's earlier offer to intercede with Gladstone and Russell. The only alternative was to ask her to use her persuasive powers on Cranborne, but he was 'not a man to be swayed by the Queen's opinion'. According to the Queen's journal, it was she who now came up with an audacious solution. She had been 'very annoyed' to hear of the difficulties raised – 'she must think so improperly' – by Cranborne, believing (which he and the other two would have disputed) that everything had been thoroughly explained and that he should have raised any misgivings earlier. On 26 February Derby came to her 'in terribly low spirits', and she gave him a bracing talk, urging him to accept the departure of the three Cabinet members and 'reproduce the original measure'.[50]

Disraeli was already wedded to the idea of jettisoning the Ten Minute Bill. He reported to the Queen that at a meeting in the Carlton Club, all the Tories present agreed the revised measure was 'not equal to the occasion'. They wanted Derby to 'fall back on his own policy', with one MP commenting that the Ten Minute Bill would be 'mercilessly pulled to pieces by Mr Gladstone'. At a Cabinet meeting on 2 March, most of those present were 'perfectly unanimous' that it was 'hopeless to persevere' with the discredited proposals, but Cranborne would not accept this. Carnarvon and Peel stood by him, and all three tendered their resignations.[51]

The Queen did not demur with Derby's remark that Cranborne's conduct had been 'hardly that of a gentleman'. When the departing secretary of state came to Windsor to return his seals of office, she 'said little' to him. Yet General Grey knew Victoria would enjoy hearing 'a very clever repartee' allegedly made by Lady Cranborne. Upon being asked by a Tory grandee whether she had helped her husband do the sums that had justified his objections to the bill, '"Yes" she replied, "she had, and had come to the conclusion that: take 3 from 15 and *nothing* remains."'[52]

As the date neared on which Disraeli was to introduce the bill in Parliament, Victoria became nervous. She wanted to know how effective Disraeli thought the dual vote would be 'as a counterpoise', only to discover he was already thinking of dropping it. She was also apprehensive that the borough franchise was being set too low and asked for more information on 'approximately the numbers of the working classes that will be added to the constituencies'. Disraeli tried to soothe her. He promised the vote would be given only to those of settled habits and 'general trustworthiness of life', insisting, 'the measure has really no spice of democracy'.[53]

On 18 March 1867 the 'ship was launched' when Disraeli presented the Reform Bill to the Commons. Gladstone attacked it fiercely, but his vehemence was counter-productive; General Grey reported to Victoria that one Liberal had said his 'violence was such that it seemed almost as if he was out of his mind'. There was a general feeling that his visceral hostility blinded him to the bill's possible merits: Disraeli gleefully described to the Queen how, after a time 'a murmur went about the House that "Gladstone had gone too far"', and when Disraeli rose to reply to his opponent's diatribe, he was respectfully heard.[54]

Disraeli was further heartened by what happened when Gladstone addressed a meeting of the Liberal Party. Gladstone had insisted that the second reading of the bill must be opposed, but at this – so Disraeli informed Victoria – 'there was a murmur and scuffling of feet'. Disraeli believed that the measure would make its way through Parliament provided that the dual vote was abandoned but was concerned that some ministers would insist on sticking with it. He suggested the Queen exert herself to win over doubters, for 'it may be necessary that ... the thunder of Olympus should sound!' Fortunately for him, the Cabinet agreed to drop the dual vote without prodding from Victoria, which might not have been forthcoming.[55]

When the second reading debate began on 25 March 1867, the dual vote no longer featured in the bill. Gladstone inveighed against its other provisions, but Disraeli complacently told the Queen that his 'elaborate speech of detail ... wearied the House'. In debate, Disraeli delighted in goading his opponent, taunting him for acting in 'so very excited and so alarming' a manner.[56] Despite his impassioned advocacy, Gladstone had to accept he could not take his party with him. Much to his chagrin, the Reform Bill's second reading passed unopposed in the early hours of 27 March.

Gladstone swiftly repositioned himself, intending to reshape the bill in committee. Somewhat surprisingly, one of his objections to the bill was that its provisions were too extensive, for he wanted what he considered just the right amount of enfranchisement. He had been pleased that the Liberal Bill of 1866 had sought to offer the vote to the responsible 'artisans and skilled labourers of our towns', while denying it to the 'residuum' who were unworthy of it.[57] Now he sought to refine the proposed franchise so that it conformed with his requirements.

This put Gladstone at odds with his party. Opposition MPs were conscious they would have difficulty explaining to their constituents why they wanted to alter the bill so it offered 'in one way a less liberal extension of the franchise than that proposed by the government'. After being forced to drop one amendment on 8 April, Gladstone then tried to pressure his party into supporting another that would have had the same effect. In the debate of 12 April, Disraeli accused Gladstone of wanting to bring down the government rather than simply to amend the bill. Later that night the amendment was thrown out by twenty-one votes.[58]

Victoria sent a message to Disraeli that his success should make him readier to adopt concessions in the next stages of the bill. Disraeli was happy to oblige, for from now on his strategy was to secure the bill's passage by accepting almost all amendments or changes that were not inspired by Gladstone. He had more latitude to do this because Derby's gout was currently so appalling that he could only rarely attend Parliament. On 19 April the prime minister was in such pain he had to retire to Roehampton; three weeks later General Grey remarked to the Queen, 'Mr Disraeli is evidently the directing mind of the ministry.'[59]

On 2 May the government was defeated on an amendment that reduced the two-year residency qualification for the franchise to one year, but this was conceded as not a vital point. Grey passed on the Queen's approval to Disraeli, reiterating she wanted them to be flexible, rather than holding out 'as Lord Russell did, the Queen thinks, so unnecessarily, last year'.[60] Emboldened by this, the government next accepted an amendment enfranchising lodgers who paid a rent of £10 a year.

Days later the government was once again endangered when an ally of Gladstone's, named Hibbert, put forward an amendment that would have allowed householders who were not directly rated to have the vote. Not feeling able to accept this, Lord Derby warned the Queen on 5 May 'the state of the government is most critical'. However, fears that the ministry was losing the support of its own MPs proved groundless, and Hibbert's amendment was defeated by sixty-six votes. Disraeli scribbled a triumphant note to the Queen at 1.10 in the morning of 10 May: 'result overwhelming and Bill safe'.[61]

More trouble loomed when Mr Hodgkinson, an independent Liberal Member of Parliament who was not closely affiliated to Gladstone, proposed another amendment, sweeping away the system of landlords compounding rates on behalf of renters. This change was designed to add an additional half a million voters to the electoral roll, but despite its massive impact, Disraeli felt he could accept it because it did not harm the fundamental premise that the vote would only be granted to those who directly paid rates. Confident that if he agreed to it he would 'extinguish Gladstone & co', Disraeli did not consult the Cabinet before announcing that he would not oppose the amendment. It was a tremendous gamble for there was a chance that the home secretary, Gathorne Hardy, would resign in protest. Nevertheless, Disraeli pulled it off. By now, according to Lord Malmesbury, the attitude of Tory MPs was 'in for a penny, in for a pound'.[62] They not only did not demur at Hodgkinson's amendment, but soon afterwards swallowed a further widening of the county franchise.

One amendment successfully blocked was that put forward by the political economist John Stuart Mill, who had become an MP in 1865. He proposed to alter the bill's wording so that the vote would be given to any qualified 'person', rather than specifically a 'man'. The attempt to enfranchise women was heavily voted down on 20 May. The Queen would have been relieved, for she was a committed opponent of female suffrage.

Once the borough franchise clause of the Reform Bill was carried on 20 May, Disraeli believed himself through the worst. The Redistribution of Seats Bill and other subsidiary details still had to be piloted through Parliament, but he assured the Queen that despatching these was 'merely an affair of time, temper & labour'.[63] Delighted that Disraeli had kept a promise that there would no political crisis in May, Victoria at once made preparations to leave for Balmoral.

The Queen's continuing refusal to carry out the social duties expected of a monarch was a cause of acute concern to her ministers. On 22 May Lord Stanley sent word that, after attending an international exhibition in Paris, Abdul Aziz, Sultan of Turkey, intended to visit England. The foreign secretary knew the sultan would be given a magnificent welcome by the French, and if British influence was to be upheld at Constantinople it was essential he was offered hospitality on the same scale this side of the Channel. The Queen grudgingly agreed Abdul Aziz could stay at Buckingham Palace, on condition that 'the government ... defray the expense of the Sultan's entertainment'. However, she ruled out welcoming him there herself, insisting she could not change the date of her departure for Osborne on 9 July.[64]

General Grey passed this on as instructed but was far from happy about it. He was now officially designated the Queen's private secretary because Lord Derby had declared that denying him the title while he performed all the functions of the post was 'the merest pedantry'. Grey showed his gratitude by writing privately to Derby about Victoria's conduct. 'To you & *you alone* I will say that I am a little ashamed of the little self-denial the Queen shows in these matters,' he admitted. 'She cannot bring herself to put herself out in the least or even to alter, in the minutest point, the routine of each day, even for a great public object.' Possibly Grey worked on her over the next fortnight, for on 9 June the Queen relented so far as to say that a naval review should be held off Spithead in the sultan's honour, and that she would come out in her yacht from Osborne so they could watch it together.[65]

Prior to this, Victoria had agreed she would make a rare public appearance in London at a military review that was to take place in Hyde Park on 5 July. Her ministers had hailed this as a hopeful sign, but as the date neared, new concerns arose. Intelligence that reached the government led to fears that the presence at the review of John Brown, the Queen's 'Highland servant', would provoke hostile demonstrations.

Brown, who was seven years younger than Victoria, was already working as a ghillie on the Balmoral estate when she and Albert had leased it in 1848. By 1858 he had been promoted to the Queen's 'particular ghillie', who always led her pony on outings, establishing himself in her eyes as an '*invaluable ... factotum*'. On her visits to Balmoral after Albert's death, Victoria had found solace in seeing Brown, and in 1862 he had accompanied her when she travelled to Belgium and Germany. Two years later he was summoned to Osborne in the hope he could lift her spirits. In February 1865 she had told her uncle, 'that *excellent* Highland servant' now attended her 'ALWAYS and everywhere out of doors ... and it is a *real* comfort, for he is *so* devoted to me – so simple, so intelligent, *so unlike* an *ordinary* servant'.[66]

Before long their relationship was attracting attention. In late June 1865 Lord Stanley reported: 'Strange and disagreeable stories are going about London touching the Court ... The Queen has taken a fancy to a certain Scotch servant, by name Brown, ... allows him access to her such as no one else has.' At Windsor, 'HM is talked of as "Mrs Brown" and if it lasts the joke will grow into a scandal.' In October Stanley heard further that the Queen's habit of using Brown to give her instructions to people of higher rank was causing annoyance. Certainly, General Grey had been angry when Brown had delivered a message 'in an offhand manner', and the two men subsequently remained on bad terms.[67]

In March 1866 Stanley noted the 'silly gossip' was growing louder on account of the Queen taking 'long solitary rides' with Brown, and his 'constant attendance upon her in her room'. The princesses had taken to facetiously referring to Brown as 'Mamma's lover', and while Stanley did not believe the Queen guilty of any impropriety, he regretted that by flaunting this 'absurd and unbecoming' friendship, she was 'doing all in her power to create suspicions'. He believed Victoria was aware her behaviour was exciting comment, but out of 'a kind of wilfulness which is growing upon her', paid no attention.[68]

With Brown now accompanying her – as she proudly noted – 'everywhere ... on public as well as private occasions', the irreverent comments proliferated. In July 1866 *Punch* published a spoof Court Circular, solemnly itemising Brown's movements: 'Balmoral, Tuesday. Mr John Brown walked on the slopes. He subsequently partook of haggis ...' Two months later the Swiss *Gazette de Lausanne* alleged that the Queen had morganatically married Brown and was now 'in an interesting condition'. In one issue, the socialist weekly, *Reynolds's Newspaper*, referred to the Swiss piece obliquely. In May 1867 there was much mockery when Landseer's picture *Her Majesty at Osborne* was displayed at the Royal Academy. In this painting Victoria was depicted reading a despatch as she sat on a pony whose bridle was held by Brown, and visitors to the show were overheard making ribald comments.[69]

All this made the government fearful that if Brown was present when the Queen appeared at the Hyde Park review, there would be scenes of an 'unpleasant nature'. At the first intimation that 'some people' wished 'to prevent her faithful servant going with her', the Queen flared up, writing to her equerry Lord Charles Fitzroy that she 'will not be dictated to, or *made to alter* what she has found to answer for her comfort'. Next day, 27 June, Lord Derby explained the situation to General Grey, revealing that the government understood that the National Reform League were planning 'to hoot JB if he should appear on the box of the Queen's carriage at the review in Hyde Park'. Taking it for granted that 'nothing can be said to the Queen', Derby wondered if Brown could be induced to have '*some slight illness*'. It seems, however, that either Derby or Grey did confront Victoria on the matter. On 30 June, Home Secretary Gathorne Hardy 'had a long talk on the troublesome John Brown' with a bedridden Lord Derby and was relieved when Derby informed him that, as a result of 'a remonstrance', Brown would not attend the review.[70]

Subsequently the Queen regretted that she should have been 'weak *enough* to let Lord D understand she would listen to the "alarm"', as she felt sure no 'scuffle with Mr Beales and his party' would have occurred. Resentful at '*all* the worry and uneasy sensations' she had suffered, she blamed '*ill natured* gossip in the higher classes'. The whole episode had left a 'painful bitter feeling in her heart' – but by that time the question had become academic. On 4 July disastrous news from Mexico had arrived which had thrown all the arrangements for the following day's military review into disarray.[71]

In 1864 Archduke Maximilian, younger brother of the Austrian emperor Francis Joseph, had been persuaded by Napoleon III to set himself up as ruler of Mexico. Maximilian's wife Charlotte was the daughter of King Leopold I of the Belgians, and hence Queen Victoria's first cousin. For years Mexico had been convulsed by civil war, but exiles living in Europe had convinced Napoleon that Mexicans would welcome becoming the subjects of a sovereign imposed on them by a foreign power. In theory a French army had pacified Mexico in advance of Maximilian and Charlotte's arrival there, but large swathes of the country remained unsubdued.

Shortly before setting off for the New World to take up their places as Mexican emperor and empress, Maximilian and Charlotte had stayed with Victoria. From the start the Queen had had qualms about the quixotic venture, but as their departure grew imminent her reservations crystallised, and on 7 April 1864 she had sent King Leopold a passionate entreaty. 'Oh! Dearest Uncle, in my dearest Albert's name ... *do* not let *your* poor children *go* to *what will* be *destruction!*' she had implored. '... *No*, let them break off – before it be *too late*. I would *not* write as I do, if I had not *such* a conviction that *they are hastening to their ruin*.'[72]

Victoria could not prevent Maximilian and Charlotte sailing for Mexico later that month, but her forebodings proved all too prescient. Despite the continued presence of large numbers of French troops, who conducted savage war against Mexican republicans led by Benito Juárez, Maximilian never established effective control over his kingdom. Recognising that the situation was irretrievable, in 1866 Napoleon decided to withdraw his forces. From that point the monarchist cause was hopeless, but Maximilian remained in Mexico while his increasingly unstable wife travelled to Europe in August to beg for Napoleon's continued support. After her pleas were spurned, Charlotte lost her reason completely. Victoria did not doubt that Napoleon's callous treatment had 'helped to bring on her madness'.[73] In Mexico, meanwhile, Maximilian's position grew ever more beleaguered. In May 1867 he was captured by the republicans at Querétaro, and on 19 June executed there by firing squad.

The Queen thought the news, which was confirmed on 4 July, 'too horrid!' She reflected, 'Poor unhappy Charlotte bereft of her reason & her husband killed. What a shocking end to their luckless undertaking, which I did all I could to prevent.' She at once ordered General Grey to inform the prime minister there could now be no question of the military review taking place. For Lord Derby this was particularly inopportune because only the day before he had written to the Queen asking her to do more to entertain the sultan. As feared, when Abdul Aziz came to Paris, Napoleon III had been 'unremitting in his attentions'. Derby believed that if the only hospitality the Sultan received from the Queen during his English visit was a brief excursion on her yacht, it would 'throw him into the arms of France'. The prime minister had therefore requested that she postpone her journey to Osborne so she could either receive the sultan at Buckingham Palace when he arrived on 12 July or, failing that, lay on a lunch for him at Windsor the following day. Derby explained that the ministers felt so strongly about this that he could submit a Cabinet minute on the subject, but hoped his private appeal would suffice.[74]

On 4 July, in a letter marked 'Secret', Grey informed the prime minister of the Queen's reaction. On hearing what Derby wanted, she 'flew into a towering passion, swore she could *not* receive the Sultan in London. It was unheard of for a Queen Regnant to do so.' She had at least agreed that the Turkish ruler could come to Windsor on 13 July but had turned down flat another suggestion of Derby's that the Hyde Park review should be postponed, rather than cancelled, so the sultan could attend it with her. Grey added that while he was uneasy about going behind his employer's back, his sense of crisis – 'for we *are* come to a crisis as regards the Queen' – compelled him to do so. He believed that 'no one but her [Prime] Minister' could do anything with her. If her personal servants protested, they would be 'silenced … by the subject never again being touched'; ministers, however, were entitled to remonstrate about her pursuing a course 'injurious not only to her personally but to our monarchical institutions. It is not only their privilege – it is their *duty* – to speak plainly to the Queen … I am satisfied that, however angry she may be (& I will not deny that she may be *very* angry) … the [Prime] Minister [who] speaks in the name of the Cabinet would never speak in vain.'[75]

Grey claimed the Queen's doctors would now agree that she was strong and well, but this proved over-optimistic. That same day Victoria herself wrote to Derby confirming she would receive Abdul Aziz at Windsor – 'though it is very annoying to her' – but also announcing she was sending Dr Jenner to update him on her perilous state of health. Ministers who judged from outward appearances deemed her far from frail – on 30 June Lord Stanley had described her as looking 'ruddy and fat' – but she considered herself on the verge of 'a *complete breakdown*'. When Jenner saw Derby he came close to confirming this. Trying valiantly not to be sarcastic, Derby wrote to Victoria that while 'the utmost care' must be taken of her, it was difficult for those with no access to privileged information to 'distinguish between the physical strength which enables YM to take long journeys without fatigue' and nervous problems caused by 'trifling excitement'. He added that, of course, 'this distinction shall be sedulously borne in mind' by himself.[76]

On 6 July the Cabinet 'very seriously discussed' the Queen's state. Jenner had declared that 'any strong excitement (and very little excites her) produces violent fits of bilious sickness, and if Nature did not provide this relief the effect on her mind might be dangerous'. Concerned that insanity was a real possibility, the Cabinet agreed the Hyde Park review would have to be cancelled.[77]

At least the Queen honoured her promise to entertain Abdul Aziz at Windsor. On 13 July he arrived by train and was driven to the castle through streets lined with troops. Lunch for seventeen 'went off remarkably well', with the Turkish foreign minister acting as interpreter. In her journal Victoria wrote appreciatively of the sultan's 'splendid soft brown oriental eyes', and admitted lunch had not been a great hardship, considering 'the whole was over in an hour'. She preened herself when her daughter wrote from Prussia, 'nobody knows so well how to do the honours as you do'.[78]

Four days later the naval review took place in stormy weather and a heavy swell. Having joined the Queen on her yacht, the sultan kept having to retire below to be sick. He was able to see very little of the fleet that sailed past but managed to struggle into the saloon to receive the Garter from her. As she fastened his insignia on him, 'he smiled and laughed and coloured and was very much pleased'.[79]

Two days before this, on 15 July, the Reform Bill passed its third reading in the Commons. The Queen was relieved the bill had overcome every challenge so far, while not being altogether happy about how it had been reshaped. On 25 June she had written to Derby that she was watching its progress with 'deepest interest and ... not a little anxiety'. Decisions had been taken in the Commons 'so suddenly and so unexpectedly' that it had been impossible for her even to express an opinion, but she accepted that concessions already made could hardly be rescinded. Nevertheless, since it was now 'a measure which even the most advanced Liberals regard with some degree of alarm', she hoped he would consider accepting amendments from the Lords designed 'to avert the danger which many people apprehend from the great increase in democratic power'.[80]

In reply Derby had admitted that some changes to their original proposals had been 'accepted without sufficient discussion', and there were 'one or two provisions ... inserted which Lord Derby would rather have seen omitted'. Despite these reservations, when the Lords considered the bill, Derby warned Conservative peers he would resign if they sought to alter it excessively. Only minor modifications were inserted and, when referred back to the Commons, most were removed. On 6 August the bill passed its third reading in the Upper House, 'almost without debate'. Derby made the 'rather extraordinary admission' that 'we are taking a leap in the dark' but expressed confidence that the 'sound sense of my fellow countrymen' would keep the nation steady.[81]

The Reform Bill that received the royal assent on 15 August 1867 was a far more extensive measure than that which the Tories had opposed as excessive the previous year, and from which Disraeli had claimed 'the aristocratic settlement of this country will receive a fatal blow'. By adding just over a million potential new voters it virtually doubled the electorate, so that about a third of the adult male population had the franchise. Lord Dalhousie wrote bitterly to Clarendon, a fellow Whig, 'Where we lifted the sluices of democracy an inch, [Derby] and Dizzy have raised them a foot. My only hope is that they will be the first to be washed away in the flood.'[82]

The government now had to face a resurgence of Irish nationalism. It had been around 1865 that 'Fenianism' – as the movement to overthrow British rule in Ireland was dubbed – had first been identified as a serious threat. In September of that year Victoria had written to King Leopold, 'The abominable Irish are giving a good deal of trouble. They really are a dreadful people.' Palmerston had sought to assure her that 'that treasonable association … seems devoid of leaders and resources' but the Queen rightly feared 'this Fenian conspiracy will give us a good deal of trouble'. In early 1867 Fenians abortively tried to seize arms and ammunition from Chester Castle, and in Ireland itself there were several outbreaks, including an attempt to capture Dublin. In March Victoria was relieved to hear that 'extensive risings … in Ireland … have been quelled … & many prisoners have been taken. Still, it is very annoying.'[83]

That May the Queen and the home secretary discussed the Cabinet's recommendation that the death sentences imposed on rebellious Fenians should be commuted. 'It will be done,' the Queen recorded, but she considered it 'unfortunate, as it will look as if such people were always to be pardoned, which is a bad example.' Four months later the Fenian leader Thomas Kelly was captured, but as he was being conveyed to the courthouse in Manchester, he escaped when the prison van was attacked. In the mêlée a police officer was killed. 'The Queen took it calmly,' but 'did not approve of more mercy' being extended to those responsible.[84]

In October, while Kelly's accomplices were awaiting trial, reports came in that there would be a Fenian attempt to abduct the Queen from

Balmoral. Initially Victoria dismissed this as 'too foolish!' but then artfully suggested that she should prolong her stay at her Scottish home, as 'she is in fact more safe here than anywhere else in her dominions'. Derby did not agree, being particularly concerned about 'the absolutely unprotected state of her Majesty in her late drives'. Having initially promised she would 'submit to all the painful precautions necessary', she objected it was 'next to *impossible* ... with the distances here' to return from outings before nightfall. 'It is so *sad* to have to take precautions and to feel insecure!' she lamented to Grey, before concluding defiantly 'the Queen is *not* frightened'.[85]

Safely back in the south, she was pleased when Disraeli concurred that five men convicted of the Manchester attack should be executed, for, 'dreadful as it sounds, & is, to press for such a thing' an example had to be made. Two of the prisoners were in fact reprieved after witnesses were shown to have perjured themselves, but on 28 November the remaining three 'Manchester martyrs' were hanged. A fortnight later the Queen was 'dreadfully shocked' by another 'fresh & most atrocious Fenian outrage'. On 13 December comrades of Fenian Richard Burke sought to free him from Clerkenwell gaol, where he was awaiting trial for arms offences, by blowing up the prison wall. Because too much explosive was used the slum dwellings opposite the prison were destroyed, resulting in multiple deaths and injuries. Next day Victoria wrote in her journal, 'The sufferings of these poor people from the frightful explosion occupy my mind very much. Many poor little children have been severely hurt.' She sent Dr Jenner to visit the injured in hospital, and General Grey assured the home secretary that 'her heart bleeds' for the victims.[86]

The Queen had been reluctant to tighten security at Windsor. She would not let an equerry accompany her when Brown drove her round the park, and the most she would countenance was being followed at a distance by two men armed with revolvers. Yet it appeared there was good reason to fear she was being targeted by terrorists. In December 1867 Lord Monck, the Governor of Canada, telegraphed that eighty Fenians were sailing from New York with 'murderous intentions' against her and seven government ministers. They were expected to dock at a Channel port, conveniently close to Osborne, where the Queen was spending Christmas, and which General Grey believed peculiarly vulnerable to attack. He beseeched her, 'on his knees', to withdraw to Windsor, but Victoria insisted the danger would be '*far greater*' there. When the home secretary, Gathorne Hardy, arranged for troops to be sent to the Isle of Wight for her protection, she dismissed it as 'nonsense and foolish panic'. She did grudgingly agree to be shadowed on drives by two outriders, but still 'rather pooh-poohs all that is going on'.[87]

Victoria grumbled that the 'endless, useless precautions' were 'such a bore', but was in favour of much more serious restrictions on her people's civil liberties. She urged Derby to suspend habeas corpus, believing it 'the one necessary thing' to combat the Fenian threat. She argued this would provide the best means 'to punish these horrible people', but although habeas corpus had been suspended in Ireland a year earlier, the prime minister and Cabinet were wary of enforcing the same policy nationwide.[88]

In early 1868 it emerged that Lord Monck had been duped by a rogue informant, and no band of Irish assassins had set out from New York. The Queen snorted that 'the whole of this stupid scare … has proved to be a complete fabrication … and for this we have been teased & tormented'.[89]

On 5 April 1868 Victoria proclaimed confidently, 'The Fenians (at least in England) have dwindled down to nothing, have no money, & no one thinks of them.' It was therefore all the more shocking that, less than three weeks later, she received news that her second son, Prince Alfred, who was serving in the navy, had been shot in Australia on 12 March by a Fenian extremist. The assailant had been promptly hanged, and the prince was recovering from his wounds, but the Queen was naturally terribly upset. 'It is so shamefully wicked,' she commented, 'for poor dear Affie is so entirely unconnected with anything political or Irish.'[90]

Her distress perhaps explains the intemperance of her remark to Home Secretary Gathorne Hardy, on 1 May, on hearing that all but one of those accused of the Clerkenwell bombing had been acquitted. 'It seems dreadful for these people to escape …,' she observed. 'One begins to wish that these Fenians should be lynch-lawed and on the spot.'[91] The Queen had to be satisfied with the conviction of Michael Barrett from Fermanagh, who on 26 May 1868 became the last man to be publicly hanged in England.

Lord Derby's health was becoming ever worse, and on 6 February 1868 he had written to General Grey acknowledging the time was 'not far distant' when he would have to ask the Queen to relieve him of his duties. More than a fortnight earlier, Victoria had in fact intimated to Disraeli she 'intended to make him her First Minister on Lord D's resignation', but on 21 February Derby threw all into confusion by confirming to Victoria that he wished to resign, though not with immediate effect. While proposing that Disraeli should be his successor, he did not want to relinquish office until able to submit the seals in person. This was awkward, for inevitably it would become generally known Derby was giving up as prime minister, leaving the government in limbo. In reply the Queen said she was '*deeply* grieved' that he must resign, without mentioning the manner of his going. She then sent General Grey to see Disraeli in London, who in turn commissioned Lord Stanley to seek clarification from his father.[92]

At Disraeli's suggestion the Queen wrote to Derby, saying that, 'painful as it is to us both', she must ask that he let Disraeli assume the reins of government without delay. Next day, it emerged that Derby had been holding back because he wanted the Queen to mark his resignation by conferring peerages on some close allies. Matters were complicated by

Benjamin Disraeli in 1868, the year he became prime minister.

the fact Victoria had rejected a similar request from Earl Russell when he had stepped down. Grey suggested Derby could tell his friends they were to be ennobled at his request, but the actual creation should be postponed. Even so, the situation had not been handled entirely felicitously. Lord Stanley – whose relations with his father were correct and respectful, rather than deeply loving – claimed Derby had been 'at first very sore' that in her 'curt' letter the Queen 'seems to have told him he had better resign at once, in order to save her trouble'. Stanley added he was 'not surprised', as he believed Victoria saw 'no reason for wasting civility on those who can no longer be of use to her'.[93]

Once Derby had conceded, Disraeli wrote to Victoria on 26 February to thank her for 'the high honour which your Majesty has been graciously pleased to confer on him'. Claiming that as prime minister 'He can offer only devotion,' he said it would be 'his delight and duty, to render the transaction of affairs as easy to your Majesty as possible'. He nevertheless expressed a hope that, 'in the great affairs of state your Majesty will deign not to withhold from him the benefit of your Majesty's guidance', because 'your Majesty's life has been passed in constant communion with great men, and the knowledge and management of important transactions'. He argued, 'Even if your Majesty were not gifted with those great abilities, which all now acknowledge, this rare and choice experience must give your Majesty an advantage in judgement, which few living persons, and probably no living prince, can rival.'[94]

This went down very well with Victoria. As Disraeli wrote to his wife, having travelled to Osborne on 27 February for his formal acceptance of office, at 7.30 that evening, 'the Queen came into her closet, with a very radiant face … saying "You must kiss hands."' Falling to one knee, he took her hand between both his, and murmured reverently, 'In loving loyalty and faith.' In her journal for that day the Queen mused, it 'seems a dream' that 'a man risen from the people … the son of a Jew, a mere man of letters, without any position or fortune' should have attained 'the most influential & important position in the state'. Unaware of her mother's state of mind, Vicky wrote from Prussia to commiserate with her about a change she presumed 'will not be exactly what will suit you'. Characterising Disraeli as 'a Jew and an adventurer', she asked, 'Mr Disraeli … is vain and ambitious, is he not?' Her mother hastened to disabuse her. 'I think the present man will do well, and will be particularly loyal and anxious to please me in every way,' she informed her daughter. 'He is very peculiar, but very clever and sensible and very conciliatory.'[95]

It marked the beginning of a great but unlikely partnership. A week after Disraeli kissed hands, the Queen told Vicky, 'He is full of poetry, romance and chivalry.' Disraeli was able to captivate her with letters that added a spice of enjoyment to political discourse. Informing her that Ward Hunt – a man so gargantuan that when kneeling before his sovereign, 'he was even in that position taller than the Queen' – would replace him as Chancellor of the Exchequer, he assured her Hunt had 'the sagacity of the elephant as well as the form'. The Queen exclaimed: 'What a strange description!' but she found his picturesque turn of phrase rather thrilling.[96]

He was sedulous about keeping Victoria entertained. The Queen's lady-in-waiting, Lady Augusta Stanley, told Lord Clarendon, 'Dizzy writes daily letters to the Queen in his best novel style, telling her every scrap of political news dressed up to serve his own purpose, and every scrap of social gossip cooked to amuse her. She declares that she has never had such letters in her life ... and that she never before knew *everything*.' Lord Clarendon carped that 'the Jew ... has like Eve's tempter, ingratiated himself with the Missus and made her forget that, in the opinion of [Albert] the Great and Good, he "had not one single element of a gentleman in his composition."' Yet though Lord Stanley believed that Disraeli 'not seldom disgusts, where he means to please, by overdone and manifestly artificial compliments', his handling of the Queen was never less than assured.[97] In her case, he successfully applied his own maxim, 'Everyone likes flattery; and when you come to royalty you should lay it on with a trowel.'

Disraeli rarely lost an opportunity to praise the Queen's judgement. Discussing with her who should receive the Order of the Thistle, he volunteered, 'There are very few public subjects on wh, he feels, more & more every day, your Majesty is not much more competent to advise than to be advised.' He combined elaborate deference to his sovereign with making much of her femininity, an approach Victoria found delightful. After he told her he shared her passion for wild flowers (Gladstone claimed that in Disraeli's case it was feigned) Victoria took to sending him posies of primroses gathered from the woods at Osborne and Windsor. She was rewarded with effusive assurances that 'their lustre and perfume were enhanced by the condescending hand which had showered upon him all the treasures of spring'.[98]

The prime minister did not fail to pass on his appreciation of *Leaves from the Journal of our Life in the Highlands*, the memoir of Victoria and Albert's life at Balmoral that the Queen published in January 1868.

Knowing his words would be passed on, he wrote to her editor, 'There is a freshness and fragrance about the book like the heather amid which it was written.'[99] He winningly suggested their mutual literary talents provided another link between them, conspiratorially speaking to her of 'we authors, Ma'am'.

Disraeli was optimistic about his government's prospects. But Gladstone – who was acting as de facto Liberal leader, although Russell had not officially retired – was able to reunite his party by tackling the Conservatives over Irish policy. Having stated during a debate on 16 March, 'We have reached a crisis in the affairs and in the state of Ireland,' Gladstone declared stripping the Church of Ireland of its established status was the only means of addressing this.[100] A week later he gave notice that he intended to move three resolutions on the subject, and that, before the house voted on these, he would call for a Commons committee on Ireland.

For Disraeli, Gladstone's artful choice of battleground meant that trouble had come upon him 'like a thief in the night', and he acknowledged to Victoria, 'We are embarking on stormy waters.' The Irish Church was not a popular cause, being regarded even by some Cabinet members as an arrogant institution propped up by money exacted from poor Roman Catholics. Disraeli nonetheless argued that if the Irish Church was disestablished, the Church of England would soon suffer a similar fate. To Victoria he referred to Gladstone's proposals as 'a threatened revolution, for it is not less'.[101]

The Queen agreed that Gladstone was causing 'immense mischief' and that he 'might … to say the least, have well paused' before embarking on a course guaranteed 'to revive and inflame the old sectarian feuds and to render the administration of Ireland more difficult'. While she cautioned Disraeli against 'rousing … strong Protestant feeling … a firebrand not easily to be quenched', she believed it was 'all Mr Gladstone's doing, and really very wrong'.[102]

As the debate on whether the house should go into committee on Ireland neared its conclusion, the Queen visited Lord Derby at his London house on the morning of 3 April, and there 'spoke in most unreserved terms of condemnation of Gladstone's motion and conduct'. When Derby informed her he had urged Disraeli not to resign if he lost the coming division, she said with great emphasis, 'Quite right.'[103]

That night, the government was outvoted in the Commons, prompting Disraeli to adjourn Parliament until later in the month when the resolutions themselves were to be debated. Over Easter, Disraeli, Lord Chancellor Cairns and Gathorne Hardy all stayed at Windsor, and the home secretary was struck by the Queen's 'very anti-Gladstonian' views. Full of 'dread ... of Gladstone and his scheme', Victoria asked the Dean of Windsor, an old friend of Gladstone's from Eton days, 'to point out ... the danger & recklessness of the course he was pursuing & the impossibility of my taking him as my Minister, if he violently threatened to overturn the Irish Church'.[104]

The day after the first resolution on the Irish Church was carried in the Commons on 30 April, Disraeli went to Osborne without consulting the Cabinet. He told Victoria that he wanted 'to take your Majesty's pleasure personally', for 'on great political occasions ... the visible influence, as it were, of the sovereign should be felt and recognised ... and ... Parliament should practically comprehend, that the course of a Ministry depends on the will of the Queen'.[105]

At Osborne Disraeli offered his resignation for form's sake, knowing full well Victoria would not accept it. Instead, they agreed that the government would carry on, regardless of whether it suffered further defeats. Not until new electoral registers had been compiled would Disraeli dissolve Parliament and seek a new mandate from the voters.

After the prime minister returned to London and informed his colleagues what had been decided, Lord Malmesbury reported: 'The Ministers are very angry with Disraeli for going to the Queen without calling a Cabinet.' Aghast at the prospect of struggling through the remainder of the session, Home Secretary Gathorne Hardy wrote in his diary: 'I foresee nothing but troubles & wish heartily our resignation had been real & effective. A Cabinet before Osborne would have altered everything. But now ...'[106]

There was a tremendous outcry when Disraeli announced to the Commons that while the Irish Church question was 'too important to be settled without a direct appeal to the country', he would not dissolve Parliament until everyone enfranchised by the Reform Bill could exercise their vote. Gladstone 'attacked in a white heat with an almost diabolical expression of countenance', asserting that the government should have resigned forthwith, but he stopped short of moving a vote of want of confidence.[107]

After being exposed to fresh attacks on subsequent days, Disraeli told Victoria the opposition's ferocity derived from their consciousness of failure. He was confident that, provided 'his health be spared, he shall ... steer the vessel of the state into port, sustained by your Majesty's inspiring graciousness'. Lord Cranborne, who had correctly predicted the course Disraeli would pursue if defeated on Gladstone's first resolution, bitterly told a friend, 'Matters seem very critical – a woman on the throne & a Jew adventurer who [has] found out the secret of getting round her.'[108]

Throughout the next few weeks, the ministry continued to face difficulties, but the opposition's fear of an impromptu election deterred them from bringing down the government. To the Queen Disraeli likened his situation to 'steering in a Scandinavian sea, with volcanoes beneath & icebergs on each side', and things looked even worse when on 18 May the government was defeated on its Scottish Reform Bill. A distressed Victoria told Disraeli she was 'really shocked at the way the House of Commons go on; they really bring discredit on constitutional government'. Within a week Disraeli managed to retrieve matters. 'Last night he rescinded a vote of the House of Commons, which has always been considered the greatest test of power and skill in a Minister ...' he boasted to Victoria. 'It is impossible to pretend after this that the present ministry is a minority on sufferance, or that its position is ignominious or humiliating.'[109]

On 6 May Disraeli had remarked to General Grey that, in view of the government's precarious position, the Queen 'ought not to go to Scotland but she will'. In recent weeks Victoria had somewhat increased her performance of public duties – laying the foundation stone of St Thomas's Hospital and holding several drawing rooms – but this did not stop *The Globe* newspaper criticising her for not doing more. Finding this 'very cruel!' she told Disraeli that while she would be ready to return from Balmoral at short notice if necessary, she was so '*completely* done up by the fatigue of these few days' that a change of scene was imperative. As Disraeli observed to Grey, this statement 'rendered it quite impossible for me to dissuade her Majesty from going ... and I cannot conceive, under the circumstances, that any Minister could have acted otherwise than I did'.[110]

Two days after she set off for Balmoral on 18 May, *The Times* attacked her for absenting herself. It deplored that, 'At the very hour when a most important debate was proceeding – a debate on which the question of life and death to government or Parliament might turn – the first person in the state ... was hurrying at full speed ... to a remote Highland district, 600 miles from her ministry and Parliament.'[111]

On 22 May an MP actually posed the question whether, in view of the Queen's apparent frailty, she should be advised to abdicate on health grounds. He apologised after provoking cries of 'Order!' and being rebuked by the Speaker. Informed of this by telegraph, Victoria wrote to Disraeli that doubtless people 'would wish her to be always in London for *their* convenience – but the Queen *can't*. The Queen's looks belie her & *nobody* believes how she suffers.' Deploying a threat she felt sure would bring critics to order, she warned, '*If* the public will *not* take her – as she is – she must *give all up* – & give it to the Prince of Wales.'[112]

By 26 May Disraeli could assure Grey he believed the government to be out of danger, but even so, 'I shall be very glad to hear of the return of the Court.' Yet he was anything but reproachful to the Queen. Instead he apologised to her because the government's difficulties had doubtless caused her stress, declaring it made him 'truly unhappy' that he had thus 'aggravated those sufferings which under less difficult circumstances, it might have been his pride and privilege in some degree, by sedulous devotion, to have mitigated'.[113]

The government was still not having an easy time when the Queen returned south on 16 June. That very day, an act providing that all appointments to the Irish Church should be suspended, passed its final reading in the Commons. At the end of the month it was thrown out by the Lords, but in the Lower House Disraeli still faced a struggle securing the passage of other legislation. It was a profound relief to him when Parliament was prorogued on 31 July, before being dissolved, but he was not able to rest for long. On 19 September he was required to go to Balmoral as the Queen's guest, which he did not anticipate would prove a pleasurable experience.

When it had been mooted the previous year that Disraeli should spend some days at Balmoral as minister in residence, he had successfully begged General Grey to 'extricate me from this overwhelming honour', fearing that, after an exhausting parliamentary session, it 'would quite finish me'. This year there was no escaping it. Victoria much enjoyed his ten-day visit and did her best to make her guest happy. Having organised an outing to Braemar, she decreed 'all the ladies are to go, to make it amusing to Mr Disraeli'. When he took leave of her on 28 September, he gave the impression of being 'delighted with his stay', but in fact had found it wearisome, for the rich food and unaccustomed hours had upset his stomach.[114]

All this time the government had been preparing for the election, which was to take place in November. Disraeli was extremely optimistic, assuring the Queen that 'reports from trusty agents' made him confident of victory. Victoria was heartened to hear this, for she left the prime minister in no doubt that she personally wanted a Tory triumph.[115]

The election results came as a crushing disappointment to both monarch and prime minister. By late November it was apparent that Gladstone's Liberals had secured a sizeable majority. It looked like Disraeli had miscalculated in thinking that newly enfranchised members of the working class would have conservative instincts. Instead, as John Stuart Mill remarked, having received the vote from the Tories, their response had been, 'Thank you, Mr Gladstone.'[116]

When Disraeli saw the Queen on 23 November, she found him 'very low & looking ill', but he managed to put a brave face on the 'strange and most unforeseen result'. To her relief, Disraeli decided against retiring from politics altogether. On being asked whether she thought the Conservatives should look 'for other and younger hands' to lead them, she made it clear she wished him to stay on. Disraeli was quite willing. He assured her that while some might think it 'a dreary career again to lead … an opposition party … if in that post he could really serve your Majesty … he should be quite content'.[117]

This meant that Disraeli would for the moment have to forego opting for a comfortable berth in the House of Lords. His only regret about remaining in the Commons was that his wife, who was in failing health, would have enjoyed having a title. To remedy this, he took the bold step of asking Victoria to confer a viscountcy on Mrs Disraeli. His request caused some consternation at Windsor. General Grey commented that it was, 'indeed, as your Majesty says, very embarrassing' and, if granted, likely to be greeted with 'attacks and even ridicule'. Nevertheless, since he could not 'see a satisfactory way out of it', he advised her 'to follow the dictates of your Majesty's own kind heart'.[118] Accordingly Mrs Disraeli was created Viscountess Beaconsfield.

In another departure from convention, Disraeli decided that the government should resign without delay, rather than waiting until Parliament met and the Conservatives were defeated in the Commons. The Cabinet only hesitantly endorsed this, but the Queen was all in favour of an arrangement she considered 'much more convenient for me & everyone'. She told Disraeli he was taking the 'most honourable & straightforward' course, although perhaps it was the desire to avoid a February ministerial crisis disrupting her stay at Osborne that lay behind her enthusiasm.[119]

* * *

Although there were good grounds for thinking that Gladstone was 'utterly repugnant to her', the Queen recognised he was indisputably 'the elect of the people'. She therefore wrote asking him to form a government, entrusting the letter to General Grey to deliver to Gladstone's country house, Hawarden Castle. On hearing by telegram that Grey was on his way, Gladstone had announced to a friend, 'My Mission is to pacify Ireland' – but Irish policy was precisely where he and the Queen were most likely to clash. On 26 November Lord Stanley had recorded: 'Disraeli tells me that the Queen has declared to him that she would sooner abdicate than consent to the disestablishment of the Irish Church.' Fortunately, as the Queen noted in her journal, when Disraeli formally resigned on 1 December, 'he said that I ought not to prevent Mr Gladstone from bringing forward his measure of Disestablishment, for that would be driving me into a corner'. Instead, the Queen again enlisted the aid of Gladstone's old schoolfriend, the Dean of Windsor. At her request he wrote to Gladstone saying that although the Queen still differed with him over disestablishment, she would reserve her future course until matters became clearer.[120]

For the moment, therefore, Ireland was not a source of contention; problems remained, however, about Gladstone's ministerial appointments. In particular Victoria dreaded the prospect of Lord Clarendon returning to the Foreign Office, having turned violently against him since the summer of 1866, when she had wished to keep him there. She told General Grey that Clarendon's 'feelings & opinions about Germany & Prussia, … almost offensively expressed' had convinced her he was 'the most unfit person' to be in charge of foreign affairs – but there was more to it than that. She did not disguise from Gladstone that she had 'personal grounds of complaint', and that, having formed 'the idea of some indelicacy' committed by Clarendon, she did not want regular direct intercourse with him. It appears that the Queen had learned from her cousin, Princess Mary Adelaide, that Clarendon had 'used expressions about herself which she cannot forgive'. The diary of the 15th Earl of Derby gives some clue as to their nature, for in 1870 he recorded that much of the 'absurd prejudice' surrounding the Queen's relations with John Brown had been caused by Clarendon's 'delight in spreading or inventing tales'. At any rate, as soon as it became apparent there would be a change of government, Victoria had told Grey she would bear 'all the trials before her … *except* having people who are insolent and rude to her'. Knowing 'how … bitter & even impertinent L[ord]. Clarendon is,' she warned, 'the Queen *will not* have him. She *could* not stand it.'[121]

Victoria had first alerted Gladstone that Clarendon would be unacceptable to her via the Liberal grandee, Lord Halifax. 'Taken aback,' Gladstone 'spoke very strongly' about 'the injustice of condemning Clarendon' on the strength of uncorroborated reports. When she had despatched General Grey to Hawarden, she had tasked him with pursuing the matter further. Gladstone explained to Grey that he had already promised Clarendon the Foreign Office, and if he was now excluded, people were bound to say 'some *Court manoeuvre*' was responsible. 'This would fall on the Queen direct' and prove 'a serious evil.'[122]

Gladstone and Grey travelled up together to Windsor from Cheshire, and on the way 'Grey coached him up in all the Queen's notions, feelings and fears'. On 3 December Gladstone had an audience with Victoria, at which he undertook to try and persuade Clarendon to take another office but did not hold out much hope of success. He nevertheless promised to tell Clarendon 'how necessary it was that *all* the ministers should consider my feelings'. This so far reassured Victoria that she made no further objection when Clarendon made it clear that foreign secretary was the only position that he would find acceptable. He appears never to have guessed that she had tried to block his appointment.[123]

On the whole Victoria's meeting with Gladstone on 3 December had gone extremely well. He found her 'kind, cheerful, even playful', while she in turn noted he had been 'most cordial and kind in his manner'. Another audience on 5 December was just as successful, although perhaps it was a bad omen that Gladstone had to ask, 'whether I ought not to kiss hands?' At once 'she said yes, & it was done', but it betrayed a certain lack of eagerness on her part. Gladstone was by no means discouraged, being relieved that the Queen made only a fleeting allusion to the Irish Church difficulty, and flattering himself it would not prove insuperable. Earl Granville, now Gladstone's colonial secretary, wrote afterwards to General Grey, 'He came back delighted with the Queen's reception. He is completely under the charm.' According to Grey, these warm feelings were reciprocated. Writing to Earl Russell – who, much to the relief of both Victoria and the new prime minister, had agreed not to take office – the general declared her 'much pleased with Mr Gladstone, with the kindness of his manner towards her'. Grey was confident that, 'though, as you know, she always dislikes a change, [she] will soon be reconciled to this one'.[124] Unfortunately this prediction could not have been more wrong.

8

Mr Gladstone 1868–1874

As he embarked on his first premiership, Gladstone was certainly not lacking for advice on how to handle Queen Victoria. Lord Granville suggested that if he ever had to say something unpalatable to her, he should 'probably do so in a light and airy manner in conversation'. Carrying out these instructions was unfortunately alien to Gladstone's nature, but considering the complexity of the issues he faced, it would not have been easy for anyone to have pulled off the feat. Gladstone's son Herbert later acerbically observed, 'Even Mr Disraeli could not have explained Irish disestablishment in epigrams and airy description.'[1]

The Dean of Windsor, who was both an old schoolmate of Gladstone's and on very close terms with the Queen, had also sent him a detailed letter on how he should conduct himself towards her. 'Everything depends upon your manner of approaching the Queen,' he had informed Gladstone on 29 November 1868. 'Her nervous susceptibility has much increased … and you cannot show too much regard, gentleness, I might say even tenderness towards her.' He added, 'Where you differ, it will be best not at first to try and reason her over … but pass the matter lightly over with expression of respectful regret, and reserve it.' The dean later supplemented this by stressing, as Granville had done, that it was better to address her 'viva voce' rather than relying on letters; when he did write to her, he 'should do so shortly with as few arguments as were necessary. She turned the best and most logical the wrong way.'[2]

Gladstone apparently eagerly drank in all this, assuring the dean he would 'study to the best of my small power the manner of my relations with HM'. He referred warmly to her as 'a woman, a widow, a lover of truth, a Sovereign, a benefactress to her country', and said it would greatly distress him if he ever 'caused HM one moment of gratuitous pain or trouble'. He admitted to having 'plenty of besetting infirmities' – among them being too 'eager upon things' – but he was heartened by

Victoria's past kindness to him. Furthermore, he was well aware she had always cordially supported her ministers and, 'Who could suppose that HM could now change the unbroken practice of thirty years?'[3]

Despite these good intentions, Gladstone himself would later acknowledge that he sometimes transacted his dealings with the Queen in an 'unhandy manner'. This certainly was not because he lacked respect for the monarch: on the contrary, his son Herbert insisted he entered the royal presence 'with a reverence second only to his reverence in entering a church'. It was indeed his very devotion to the institution of monarchy that convinced him that he could not shirk

William Ewart Gladstone in 1869.

confrontations with the Queen if she acted in a way that might undermine it. Although he said that tackling the Queen on her seclusion was 'the most painful of the duties of my place', he believed passionately that 'want of plain speaking' could have dreadful consequences he could not square with his conscience.[4]

Victoria famously is said to have objected, 'Mr Gladstone addresses me as if I were a public meeting', but things might have gone better had it truly been the case. When speaking in Parliament or on public platforms, Gladstone had a talent that sometimes amounted to genius, and could move an audience like a true maestro. His writing style, in contrast, was deeply off-putting: prolix, convoluted and frequently unintelligible. Disraeli would comment it was 'marvellous how so consummate an orator should, the moment he takes the pen, be so involved and cumbersome and infelicitous in expression'.[5] Unfortunately, the written word was the usual medium through which he and Victoria communicated, and his interminable screeds exacerbated her dislike of him.

Observers would notice that even when relations between Victoria and Gladstone were at their worst, they often got on surprisingly well in person. Sometimes admirers of Gladstone regretted that their encounters were comparatively infrequent, yet to a certain extent the friendliness that characterised them was deceptive. What Gladstone described as 'her high good manners' masked her real feelings, and the Queen in 1880 spoke of '*never personally* liking Mr Gladstone'. Furthermore, she shrank from arguing with him face to face, frankly admitting on one occasion that she 'dreaded controversy in conversation very much'. Instead she tended to wait until he had left her, before picking up her pen to outline objections. Doubtless she was aware that in any verbal dispute she would come off worse, for Gladstone was not an easy man to debate with. The Queen's private secretary Henry Ponsonby regretted how, when conversing, Gladstone 'forces you into his groove', displaying 'a terrible earnestness' and 'scarcely listening to any remonstrance'. He would 'dash headlong down a line which he is convinced is right', always 'taking up a view with an intensity which scarcely allows him to suppose there can be any truth on the other side'. Nor could the Queen use laughter to defuse the situation: Gladstone's son Herbert blamed Victoria because she 'rarely encouraged the lighter side of intercourse', lamenting: 'If only she had known how to chaff him!' Yet the Queen was sure Gladstone was completely humourless, confiding to a Tory politician in 1879, 'he could never understand a joke'.[6]

The Queen's antipathy to Gladstone was not purely personal, for during this first administration there were many political issues on which they disagreed. Apart from his pursuit of Irish Church disestablishment, she would be alarmed in 1871 when he attacked the House of Lords for rejecting the Ballot Bill, alluding darkly to 'powerful classes' who thwarted the will of the people. His army reforms also upset her, and from the first she regarded his attitude to Ireland as misconceived. The fact that, as one minister admitted, foreign affairs were 'uncongenial to Gladstone' meant they were never his first priority: as early as November 1869 Victoria complained to Lord Granville that England was 'being reduced to the state of a second-rate power'. All this led her frequently to quote Lord Palmerston's maxim that 'Mr Gladstone is a very dangerous man.'[7]

It was unfortunate that even when Gladstone had right on his side in a tussle with the Queen, he was inept at judging how far he should push matters. Sometimes, indeed, he should never have embarked on the battle in the first place. A case in point was his dogged defence of Mr Ayrton, whom he had made First Commissioner of Public Works, with responsibilities that included upkeep of the royal palaces. The Queen had had misgivings about the appointment from the start and became more hostile when it emerged that in 1866 Ayrton had made offensive remarks about her. Soon she was calling for his removal, saying that the post should be occupied by 'a gentleman' rather than someone of Ayrton's comparatively humble origins. Since the 'cantankerous' Ayrton managed to antagonise a host of others, Gladstone should have bowed to her wishes, even if understandably reluctant act on her suggestion that 'some place in the colonies should be found for him'. The Queen was right when she remarked, 'he can surely not be worth all this annoyance', but Gladstone stubbornly undermined relations with her by championing this unpopular figure.[8]

Gladstone's son Herbert later claimed that during his father's first administration, prime minister and Queen remained on reasonably good terms. While acknowledging that in 1872 'a certain coldness' had arisen after Gladstone pressed her to give the Prince of Wales more responsibility, Herbert believed it was not until Disraeli poisoned her mind that she really turned against Gladstone. However, his assertion that 'dislike came in 1876 and not before' is unsustainable. Although the Queen's good manners and Gladstone's own failures of perception prevented him from realising the extent of her distaste for him, it is clear she harboured deeply negative feelings long before that. In

February 1872 she described him to her eldest daughter as 'a very dangerous minister – and so wonderfully unsympathetic', adding a month later: 'He has no tact.' When Gladstone lost office in February 1874 her relief was palpable. She told Vicky she had found him 'so very arrogant, tyrannical and obstinate, with no knowledge of the world or human nature', and she voiced similar complaints to her private secretary, Henry Ponsonby. In November 1874 she declared, 'she always felt in his manner an overbearing obstinacy & imperiousness (without being actually wanting in respect as to form) which she never experienced from *anyone* else, & which she found most disagreeable'. When Ponsonby protested that Gladstone was 'honest and true', she conceded, 'He was loyal & meant to be so, but he was often very harsh & ... very dictatorial & wished the Queen to do what *he* liked & would listen to *no* reasoning or argument.'[9]

Gladstone wasted no time before embarking on Irish Church disestablishment. At one point the Queen had expressed fears that she would contravene her coronation oath by assenting to such a measure, but in view of Gladstone's undeniable electoral mandate, she now accepted she could not resist it altogether. On 21 January 1869 he sent her a very lengthy written account detailing how he planned to set about it, which the Queen found so overwhelming that she asked the prince consort's biographer, Theodore Martin, to precis it for her. Presenting her with the shortened text, Martin said it was hardly surprising she had found herself 'lost in the fog of the long and far from lucid sentences'.[10]

Two days later Gladstone came down to Osborne with his wife, and when he further expounded his plans to Victoria, he flattered himself that they 'appeared to be well taken'. In fact, as the Queen explained in a letter a week later, she still understood his intentions 'but imperfectly'. She observed that Gladstone was already aware that she considered it unfortunate he felt 'compelled to raise this question ... and still more that he should have committed himself to so sweeping a measure'. Nevertheless, since 'regret ... is now useless', she hoped 'it may all end in the framing of a measure ... to which she can conscientiously assent'.[11]

Although on 3 February the Queen spoke to Lord Granville of her 'readiness to help in smoothing matters', the following day she informed Gladstone she would not be opening Parliament on 16 February. Not only was she 'more than normally suffering from severe headache', but also, 'feeling, as *she must own* she does, on the subject of the Irish Church', she did not want to take 'a *personal* part till after this question is settled'. To her daughter Vicky the Queen enlarged, 'I am quite ready to give way to what may be inevitable. But I will not give it the sanction of my presence.'[12]

The Queen's reservations about the Irish Church Bill grew apace. The Irish Church had assets worth about £16 million, and Gladstone intended approximately half should be appropriated and applied to secular purposes. Inevitably this would meet with strong opposition, and Victoria was not reassured by Gladstone's insistence that 'the difficulties were exaggerated'. Even when the bill passed its second reading on 23 March with the huge majority of 118, the Queen still viewed it with misgiving. She warned Lord Granville, 'this Irish bill would do great harm, especially ... the ... unfairness of the disendowment'. When she discussed the measure with the Dean of Westminster on 6 April, 'We both felt more & more what a mistake it was & that the House of Lords must alter the Bill as much as they can.'[13]

Gladstone, in contrast, was confident that his striking at the Protestant Ascendancy would 'soothe the general sentiment of Ireland'. To generate additional goodwill, in February 1869 some Fenians involved in risings two years earlier were released from prison. The Queen was not pleased, telling Gladstone, their 'liberation ... was a great misfortune ... universally condemned'. It was, she complained, 'a proof of weakness', and made it clear she opposed any more being set free.[14]

To her mind, a conciliatory approach of this sort was completely inappropriate. Shocked by 'the agrarian outrages and frightful murders which are constantly occurring', Victoria wrote to the prime minister on 1 May, 'For many years the state of Ireland has not been *so* alarming as it is now.' Gladstone replied that while these crimes were deplorable, they were the consequences of 'the perverseness of centuries', deriving more from 'evil tradition' than 'individual depravity'. By no means mollified, the Queen repeated 'her firm conviction' that the Irish Church Bill 'has had the very *opposite* effect of calming & conciliating Ireland'.[15]

Despite this, the Queen was concerned when, after the bill passed its third reading in the Commons on 31 May, it began to look as though the House of Lords would throw out the bill in its entirety. Realising that this would provoke an alarming clash between the two houses of Parliament, she exerted herself to avert this. The Archbishop of Canterbury was alerted about her alarm at the prospect of the Lords repudiating a measure overwhelmingly passed by 'a House of Commons chosen expressly to speak the feeling of the country on the question'. The Queen also wrote directly to her former prime minister, Lord Derby, declaring that rejecting the bill on its second reading 'would be most dangerous, if not *disastrous*'. Derby replied that as a known opponent of disestablishment, he personally could not vote for it, but he thought it likely that the second reading would pass. The Queen was relieved when this duly happened, even if she could not resist grumbling to Lord Granville that 'all this anxiety and all this *danger* to the country ... has been unnecessarily brought on'.[16]

The anxiety and danger were far from over, for when the bill went into committee in the Lords, it soon became apparent they intended to change the bill in ways the government would not accept. Among other things, it was proposed that the Irish Church should keep £3 million of assets that had been earmarked for confiscation. In Gladstone's view, this was 'utterly inadmissible'.

Once it became clear that the Lords intended 'war to the knife', Gladstone decided that the Queen must be on hand to exercise 'her great and just influence and mediating power'. She had been at Balmoral throughout the period when it looked as though the peers would throw out the second reading, and at the time Gladstone had written reproachfully that her peace-making efforts would have had 'yet greater authority' if 'they could have been made on the spot'. Although she had returned to Windsor on 16 June, the prime minister was appalled to learn that she planned to go to Osborne on 9 July and then back to Balmoral in mid-August. He accordingly informed her that she must not leave for the Isle of Wight until 20 July, for her absence would not only excite comment, but would result in 'hazard' and 'strain on ... the constitution'.[17]

Victoria was most indignant, objecting, 'the Queen has had repeated Crisises *there* in the PRINCE'S *time*'. Nevertheless, on 5 July she grudgingly agreed that despite 'so great a sacrifice of the Queen's *health* and *comfort*', she would remain at Windsor to help with this '*very uncommon* crisis in public affairs'. She stressed, however, that 'this *must* be regarded as an *entirely isolated* case, and that it must NEVER be made a *precedent*'. The Dean of Windsor confided to Lord Granville that she actually thought about breaking her promise and going to Osborne anyway.[18]

On 11 July the Queen had grumbled to Granville that it was 'impossible to coerce the House of Lords', but she wrote warning Archbishop Tait that if the bill was postponed until a later session of Parliament, it would entail 'another year of agitation', and a revised bill might prove even worse. She also tried to persuade Gladstone to accept some of the Lords' amendments, suggesting he should be more generous about disendowment. The prime minister replied grimly, 'There are limits,' for the Lords were proposing that the Irish Church retain nine-tenths of its current property, while the most he was prepared to offer was that an additional £750,000 of assets could be kept. On 16 July, a day after Gladstone urged the Commons to reject the preposterous proposals of 'men living in a balloon', its members threw out most of the Lords' amendments.[19]

The next day Gladstone went down to Windsor to discuss the situation with the Queen. He passed on to her the Cabinet's desire that she request the Archbishop of Canterbury to take steps 'in sense of peace', and she did so, using the Dean of Windsor as an intermediary. But it appeared an impasse had been reached when on 20 July the Lords again sought to alter the bill to an extent that Gladstone warned 'no power could induce the present House of Commons to accept'. The next day a 'very much annoyed' Gladstone urged the Cabinet that the bill should be abandoned for the present. He calculated that a wave of public anger would engulf the Lords before the bill was reintroduced in the autumn, and if they resisted it again an election could be held amidst agitation for the Upper House's abolition. Much to the Queen's relief, 'the Cabinet … decided otherwise', and she wrote to Gladstone rejoicing that 'moderate counsels have prevailed'.[20]

Instead of taking the course Gladstone favoured, Lord Granville undertook talks with Disraeli's former Lord Chancellor, Lord Cairns. Agreement was reached after some more money was found for the Irish Church, and the Lords accepted these terms on 22 July. 'Everything is settled!!! Such a wonderful change! … How thankful I feel,' the Queen exulted in her journal, feeling justifiable pride when Lord Granville congratulated her on having contributed to the happy outcome. Fortunately, perhaps, Gladstone had been ill while negotiations had taken place. Had he participated, he might have proved less accommodating than Granville, but once the deal had been hammered out, he rose from his sickbed to recommend it to the Commons in what the Queen acknowledged was a 'really very fine & *handsome*' speech.[21]

One constitutional crisis had been averted, but Gladstone had other major concerns, for Victoria was still performing very few public duties. While she could say truthfully that she was doing more than in recent years, it was not enough to prevent the press complaining about her continued seclusion. Victoria was adamant no more could be expected of her. When *The Times* published a 'most insolent' article stating she should entertain the Khedive of Egypt during his forthcoming visit, she wrote angrily to Gladstone from Balmoral on 31 May that not only did she object to the expense of providing hospitality to visiting heads of state, but '*all* the good which she would derive (temporary though it *will* be)' from the pure Scottish air would be undone by her being bothered about such matters. Criticism was particularly unreasonable, 'coming annoyingly *after* she *has* been *exerting* herself *so much* as she has done this spring in London & *suffering SO severely* as she did from it'. As she explained, 'Her health requires – alas! She feels daily – *more & more rest*,' and if the government would not allow her this, before long 'she may be *quite unable* to exert *herself* AT ALL'. In fact, even writing this letter had so agitated her that her hand 'shakes much'.[22]

Such protests cut little ice with the Queen's private secretary, General Grey, who by now had lost all patience with his royal employer. In June 1869 he wrote to Gladstone that it was imperative the Queen be recalled to her duty. When he had tried to remonstrate with her himself, she had taken refuge in 'dogged silence', but whereas he was 'of course shut up' by such tactics, 'the government cannot be shut up so ... It is their *duty* to give honest counsel to HM even when it is unpalatable'. Grey told Gladstone pitilessly: 'All she says of the "weight of work", "weakened health", "shattered nerves &c" has simply no effect whatever on me', and ministers must act now, to prevent 'more serious evils'.[23]

In a letter to Grey of 3 June, Gladstone agreed that the Queen's doctor, William Jenner, possibly encouraged her hypochondria, but the prime minister was nevertheless 'disposed ... to allow rather more than you do for reality in the Queen's ailments'. Showing more compassion than Victoria ever gave him credit for, he told Grey, 'I have a strong sense of the weariness and shrinking of mind which the want of interruption in her work must produce.' Grey was having none of it, firing back that Victoria's workload was not really very onerous, and 'as to health – the Queen is wonderfully well & has physical strength beyond that of any lady in her dominions'.[24]

Accordingly, Gladstone asked the Queen to open the newly completed Blackfriars Bridge over the Thames, and then inspect Holborn Viaduct and London's Metropolitan Railway – 'a series of great and interesting public works' that could not fail to engage her. Instantly Victoria responded this was 'quite *impossible* ... The fatigue and excitement would be *far too great*'. Reporting this to Grey, Gladstone fretted that he wished he had more exact information about the Queen's health, for Jenner had told him she frequently suffered from 'severe headaches & vomiting' for no apparent cause, which was undeniably worrying. 'On the other hand,' he mused, 'will lies at the root of many human and especially of many feminine complaints.'[25]

Grey replied with a devastating confidential analysis, warning Gladstone that with the Queen '*nothing* will have any effect but a strong – even a *peremptory* tone'. He went on, 'I believe that neither health nor strength are wanting, were the *inclination* what it should be.' Rather, it was 'simply the long unchecked habit of self-indulgence' that stopped Victoria from foregoing 'even for ten minutes, the gratification of a single inclination or even *whim*'.[26]

On 9 June Gladstone tackled the Queen afresh, bringing up not just her absence while Parliament was in session, but also her failure to show herself in public. Only by doing so was it possible to maintain the full influence of the monarchy, which was in danger of being 'impaired during your Majesty's general withdrawal from visible and sensible contact with the people of your realm'. While he recognised the heavy burden public appearances entailed, 'special and heavy sacrifices' were required from occupants of thrones.[27]

The Queen retorted she had never neglected her duty, which she could perform 'quite as well in one part of her dominions as in another'. She pointed out that her engagement diary was already fuller than before, 'but the more she does, the more is *expected*'. The only glimmer of hope she could offer was that, while it was still '*quite out of the question*' to open Blackfriars Bridge during the summer, she might consider doing so come autumn. Nevertheless, she remained determined to stop excessive demands being made of her. In early August, she approached Lord Granville to suggest that ministers should make a statement in Parliament, explaining why she could not be more active. Granville answered this would merely 'afford food for disagreeable discussion', for 'hardly a week passes during which Mr Gladstone and I are not reproached for not pressing the Queen on the subject'.[28]

On 20 August, the Queen went back to Balmoral, and shortly afterwards Granville came to stay. He was under orders from Gladstone to persuade her to make a sizeable creation of Liberal peers, for the party was so outnumbered in the House of Lords that the government's position was very difficult. Gladstone had ten men in mind for elevation to the peerage, including the financier Sir Lionel Rothschild. The Queen's initial reaction was that four was the maximum she could sanction, and Rothschild was not one of them. 'To make a *Jew a Peer* is a step she *could not consent to*,' she explained to Granville. 'It would be very ill-taken & would do the government great harm.' Granville worked on her to enlarge the number and begged her not to dismiss Rothschild out of hand, even if 'the notion of a Jew Peer is startling'. A few days later Granville wrote exultantly to Gladstone that she now seemed agreeable to 'everything but the Jew', and he presumed the prime minister would not press her on that.[29]

This proved far from the case. On 10 September it was Gladstone's turn to stay at Balmoral, and in his eyes the visit went extremely well. The Queen was 'exceedingly easy and gracious', and though she held out about the Rothschild peerage, she was so good humoured that Gladstone resolved not to give up on it. In reality, the Queen considered Gladstone's presence very trying. 'I cannot find him agreeable and he talks so very much,' she confided to her eldest daughter. Lord Granville was therefore right to be alarmed when Gladstone declared that as soon as she came south, he would 'gently try the Queen a little farther … about Rothschild'. Granville pointed out that if she yielded on the point, there would be enough of an outcry, 'to confirm her in her opinion that she was a better judge than her government, and make her more difficult on another occasion'. Gladstone refused to listen. He persisted with his advocacy of Rothschild, and it was not until the end of October that he finally promised not to raise the matter again. The Queen had convinced him it was hopeless by explaining she did not object to Rothschild's ennoblement simply because he was a Jew, but because he owed his wealth 'to successful speculations on the Stock Exchange'. This was 'not the less a species of gambling because it is on a gigantic scale'.[30]

At least Gladstone could take some consolation in the fact that on 6 November the Queen did honour her promise to open Blackfriars Bridge. In the days leading up to it she had repeatedly threatened to back out, but in the event she was delighted by her reception. She estimated that nearly a million people had turned out, and everyone who lined the streets was 'cheering & bowing & in the best humour'. 'Never did I see a more enthusiastic, loyal or friendly crowd & there were numbers of the very humblest & lowest. This, in the very heart of London at the time people were said to be … full of all sorts of ideas.' Convinced this disproved the notion that the public were fed up with her, she wrote sunnily to Gladstone, 'Nothing could go off better … Most fortunately the Queen *was* free from headache.'[31] Though it was all 'most successful and gratifying', it did not however make her more eager to open Parliament in February 1870. She had agreed to do so if her health permitted, but days before she cancelled, citing neuralgia.

Gladstone was now intent on following up Irish disestablishment with an Irish Land Reform Bill. He aimed to ensure that Irish tenants who were evicted should not only be reimbursed for improvements carried out at their own expense, but also in some cases compensated if they were turned off the land, with judgement being entrusted to a special land court. His proposals were immensely controversial, and he had great difficulty getting the Cabinet to agree. He had great hopes that the measure would transform the state of Ireland – although at least one member of the Cabinet thought, 'He lives in a fool's paradise, imagining that his measures will produce a speedy change.'[32]

After Gladstone provided an apprehensive Victoria with a brief summary of the bill's provisions, she expressed cautious approval, but remained concerned by an 'apparent lack of sympathy with the landlords'. Privately she was pessimistic about what would be achieved. She declared to Vicky, 'the government are busy about a land measure for Ireland, which I think they will be unsuccessful in – as in the Irish Church. Ireland never was in a worse state.'[33]

A week after Parliament opened on 8 February 1870, Gladstone introduced his Land Bill. On the whole it was well received. Despite encountering some difficulties in committee, it had passed its Commons third reading by 2 June. The House of Lords dealt with it more stringently, effectively seeking to nullify the bill. Once again Granville negotiated a settlement, and the bill was modified so that rents in Ireland had to be deemed 'extortionate' before any compensation was offered to an evicted tenant. This did not make Gladstone feel better disposed towards their lordships.

On 26 March 1870 the Queen's private secretary General Grey had a stroke, and he died five days later. Victoria had been unaware of his confidential dealings with Gladstone, but the general had been sufficiently severe and outspoken to fall somewhat out of favour. She told her daughter on 2 April, 'He had much altered of late, and it was very difficult for one to get on with him – often very irritable and excited and impatient.' The year before Lord Granville had heard, 'She complained of Grey meddling in things which did not concern him.' He had also 'latterly made a foolish stir about John Brown, talking more than was wise about that silly scandal ... This is said to have annoyed the Queen.' None of this prevented her from feeling acute self-pity at Grey's being 'taken from me'. She wrote in her journal, 'Poor dear General, I could not bear to think I should never look again on his face ... He was truly devoted and faithful and had such a kind heart.'[34]

Grey was succeeded by Colonel Henry Ponsonby, a Grenadier Guards officer who had served in the Crimea and then become an equerry to Prince Albert. After Albert's death he had become an extra equerry to the Queen, and from 1869 he had started assisting General Grey (whose niece he had married) in his work as private secretary. Ponsonby was a Liberal, so the Queen's decision to appoint him surprised and even alarmed some members of the royal family, but he was an excellent choice. Although at moments he would find himself in the Queen's 'black books' for not being supportive enough of the Conservatives, he was in fact (as Disraeli acknowledged) scrupulously fair, and never allowed political bias to interfere with his work. He proved highly adept at handling the Queen, although perhaps not always so firm with her as some would have liked. He said that as her servant, it was not his place to 'thrust unasked my views on her'; he was nevertheless ready to take an 'opportunity for gentle observation' when one presented itself. While he noted that 'any advice I give to HM must be given in a most gingerly way', he was not naturally obsequious, and once she had raised a subject, he had the courage to tell her things she did not want to hear.[35]

Ponsonby was also masterly at interpreting the Queen's instructions in a way that faithfully fulfilled them but prevented them having a harmful effect. When she suggested what he should write to ministers on her behalf, he preserved her meaning, while diplomatically softening her more aggressive phraseology. Ponsonby was quizzical and sardonic, sharing with his wife a good eye for the absurdities of court life, whilst always being respectful and protective of Victoria's interests. On appointing him, she had asked him to exercise the 'greatest watchfulness' against the 'growing assumption of her ministers'. He was as vigilant about preventing any encroachment on her powers as he was about the need to protect the Queen from her own worst instincts.[36]

General Grey was not the only significant figure to pass out of the Queen's life that year, for on 27 June the foreign secretary, Lord Clarendon, died. Although Victoria had tried to block his appointment eighteen months earlier, once he was dead she felt fondly for him, describing him as 'very satirical' but 'much attached to me'. She approved when Gladstone decided to move Lord Granville from the Colonial Office to become foreign secretary, the assumption being that, initially at least, the job would not be too challenging. On Granville's first day at the Foreign Office, his permanent under-secretary told him he had never 'known so great a lull in foreign affairs'.[37] Unfortunately, the calm was illusory.

Since 1866 the French had resented the way Prussia's power had been enormously enhanced by her victory over Austria. The Emperor Napoleon was keen to redress the balance, perhaps by acquiring Belgium or Luxembourg, or by striking a direct blow against Prussia herself. Bismarck believed the situation could be exploited, for if Prussia fought a successful war against France, it might enable him to complete the work of unifying Germany. Accordingly, when a dispute arose, he had no desire to keep the peace between the two countries.

In July 1870 Bismarck artfully misrepresented the way in which Prussian King William I had reacted to a French request regarding a candidate for the Spanish throne. Bismarck made it appear that his sovereign had curtly rejected France's concerns, and when this version of events was published, French opinion was inflamed. With the streets of Paris thronged with crowds shouting '*à Berlin*!' Napoleon succumbed to war fever. On 15 July 1870, France declared war on Prussia.

The Queen accepted that England must stay neutral but left no doubt where her sympathies lay. She wrote to Vicky, 'My whole heart and my fervent prayers are with beloved Germany.' To Gladstone she affirmed passionately on 19 July, 'It is not a question of *Prussia* against France but of *United Germany* most *unjustifiably attacked*, fighting for hearth & home.' The following day she reiterated to Vicky, 'We must be neutral *as long as* we can, but no one here conceals their opinion as to the *extreme iniquity* of the war and the unjustifiable conduct of the French! Still, *more publicly* we cannot say; but the feeling of the people and country here *is all* with you, which it was not *before*.'[38]

Unlike in 1866, this time all her German sons-in-law were ranged on the Prussian side. Her whole family was not united, however, for the Prince of Wales's sympathies were believed to be with the French. After he was reported to have said in company, 'He hopes the French will give the Prussians a good licking,' Gladstone cautioned him to be more circumspect. The Queen suspected that her son's attitude arose not just from a lingering bitterness over Schleswig-Holstein, but because of his fondness for the fleshpots of 'that horrid Paris'. As she told Lord Granville, her thoughts, in contrast, centred on 'the country she loves best next to her own ... her second home ... in peril of the gravest kind, insulted and attacked, and *she* unable to help ... She knows what her duty is and will do what must be done, but she will suffer dreadfully.' Given her strength of feeling, she was all the more distressed to hear that the Germans were alleging that Britain was not observing strict neutrality, enabling France to obtain horses, coal and even ammunition from England.[39]

The Queen was overjoyed when the French suffered repeated reverses. She exulted to Gladstone on 20 August their 'utter discomfiture' was 'marvellous! ... It is a great moral!' Two days later she wrote in wonderment to Vicky, 'Such a complete tumbling to pieces of their empire and its far-famed army has really never been seen.' While the sight of 'a great ... nation so utterly crushed is a fearful and sad thing', it was nevertheless 'a just retribution on ... a very frivolous, vainglorious people'.[40]

On 1 September 1870 the French army was utterly routed at Sedan. Napoleon III was taken prisoner, and four days later a republic was proclaimed in France. Despite herself, the Queen could not help being rather shocked at how Napoleon was treated by his subjects. She wrote in her journal of 5 September, 'Heard that the mob at Paris had rushed into the Senate & proclaimed a Republic!! ... Not one voice was raised in favour of the unfortunate Emperor! How ungrateful!'[41]

The Empress Eugenie arrived in England as a refugee on 8 September and six weeks later the Queen visited her at Chislehurst, where she had taken up residence. The following year Napoleon joined his wife after being freed from German captivity. In late March 1871 the Queen invited the couple to Windsor, where the fallen emperor cut a sad figure. Shrunken and unwell, with his formerly waxed moustache now limp and wilting, he was a shadow of his former self. With his past transgressions forgotten, the Queen was 'quite sad' when he died in January 1873. She wrote to Henry Ponsonby, 'The Queen feels the poor Emperor's death very much ... He had many faults no doubt,' but could also be 'most loveable, charming and amiable. The Queen can never forget that.'[42] She remained on close terms with the widowed Eugenie for the rest of her life.

After such devastating defeats, it seemed inevitable that the French would have to concede all that Germany demanded of them, but on 9 September 1870 an incredulous queen noted they 'seem still to think *they* can dictate terms! ... Madness!' She was alive to the danger that if France had to cede territory to the victors, the desire for revenge would make another war more likely in future, but despite this did not want Britain to mediate between the two parties. Conscious that her country was already unpopular in Germany, she wrote a memorandum warning ministers they must do nothing to 'confirm the bad feeling'. If it appeared that England wished Germany '*not* to reap the benefits of her hard won victories' while helping 'the aggressor and cause of all this bloodshed … this would *never* be forgotten'. She was confident that pursuing a different approach entailed no risks, for 'a powerful Germany can never be dangerous to England, but the very reverse', as the Germans were 'our natural allies'.[43]

She did write to King William urging him 'to be generous to the vanquished foe', but this achieved nothing. France was informed that peace was unobtainable until Alsace-Lorraine had been given up. Gladstone wished to join with other European countries to prevent the provinces' surrender without consent from their inhabitants, but to the Queen's relief the Cabinet did not support him. On 1 October she informed the foreign secretary that she was 'so glad to see how firmly and *resolutely* Lord Granville refuses to be dragged *into* mediation and interference'. For weeks Gladstone went on insisting that no handover could take place until those affected had been consulted, but in late November the Queen told him firmly it was 'not our business to object'.[44]

With France's new minister for foreign affairs, Jules Favre, insisting that the republic would not forego an inch of French soil, the war continued, and Paris came under siege. The Queen commented to Gladstone on 2 October, 'What a dreadful exhibition of falsehood & boastfulness the French continue to make! It shows a corruption which is the cause of the country's downfall!' Though she remained staunchly pro-German, opinion at home was changing. There was growing suspicion that Bismarck had inveigled France into war, while French sufferings also excited compassion. When at the end of December the bombardment of Paris began, Victoria warned her daughter, 'To my despair the feeling is becoming more and more bitter here against the Prussians … I can't tell you how it worries me, and what lances I break for them.'[45]

By that time Prussia's victory had brought about German unification. In December, King William was invited by Germany's princes and Reichstag to become leader of the German Empire, and on 18 January 1871 he was proclaimed Emperor of Germany in the Hall of Mirrors at Versailles. Victoria was not over-pleased by a development that arguably meant William now outranked her; worse still was the prospect that when her son-in-law succeeded his father, her own daughter would have a more illustrious title than hers.

On 23 January 1871 the French were finally obliged to seek an armistice and to resign themselves to the loss of Alsace and northern Lorraine. When peace was signed in February, they not only forfeited these territories but had to promise payment of a massive indemnity. In March 1871 Victoria wrote 'with a heavy heart' to Vicky that she was being criticised for favouring Germany too much, for, 'Alas! The people ... from being very German ... are now very French!'[46]

Although the Queen claimed her 'nerves have been *so much* shaken by the war ... & her sleep so impaired that she is utterly unfit for any exertion', she unexpectedly undertook to open Parliament on 9 February 1871. Her willingness owed something to the fact that in the autumn her fourth daughter Princess Louise had become engaged to the Duke of Argyll's son, the Marquess of Lorne. Victoria expected the country to provide Louise with a dowry and income, and since her third son, Prince Arthur, would also be applying for an annuity from Parliament to mark his coming of age, she realised it would be advisable to show herself in public. She nevertheless stressed that this was highly unusual. The fatigue of Princess Louise's marriage celebrations would be such a 'terrible trial' that she would be fit for very little else all year.[47]

Gladstone feared the Queen's reclusiveness was contributing to a disastrous decline in public esteem for the monarchy. The press were becoming more vocal in their criticism, which faithfully reflected sentiment among their readers. The royal family had been further damaged the previous year when the Prince of Wales had been forced to testify in the Mordaunt divorce case, although he had at least avoided being cited as a co-respondent. The Queen had accepted that his relations with Harriet Mordaunt were innocent, but found it 'a painful, lowering thing' that his name had been 'dragged in the dirt'. While the trial was in progress she had asked Gladstone 'to speak to the Prince seriously', and she regretted that her son and daughter-in-law were 'far too intimate with ... people who consider being fast the right thing!' With talk abounding of Bertie's infidelities and extravagance, Gladstone groaned to Lord Granville in December 1870, 'to speak in rude and general terms, the Queen is invisible and the Prince of Wales not respected'.[48]

It was hardly the ideal moment to ask the country to subsidise her daughter's union with a landed magnate, but on 13 February 1871

Gladstone requested that Parliament grant Princess Louise a dowry of £30,000 and an annuity of £6,000. He was understandably nervous, for already the Queen's having 'rattled her begging box' (as one radical journal described it) had given rise to what she called 'unpleasant cavilling'. In the Commons debate that followed, one MP mentioned 'manifestations' by 'large masses out of doors in disapproval of it ... There was a very bitter feeling ... on the subject'.[49] Only one MP actually voted against the grant, but two others acted as tellers for him.

In the next few weeks, anti-monarchist feeling grew stronger, with left-wing views being stimulated by events in Paris. In March 'Red Republicans' (as the Queen termed them) seized control of Paris. The official French government withdrew to Versailles, while in the capital a 'dreadful Commune' held sway. Soon an appalled queen reported: 'The Reds have it all their own way.' With 'atheism openly avowed!' priests and bishops were imprisoned, and there were accounts of shootings and violence. It was only towards the end of May that the French government regained the city, but not before much of Paris, including the Tuileries, burned down, and several distinguished hostages were murdered. The government took a fearful revenge, exacting 'endless reprisals'. The Queen had little sympathy for the 'horrid communists' who perished but did fear many innocents had been killed alongside them.[50]

While the Commune was in being, some people in England hailed it as inspirational. A gathering in Hyde Park was held in solidarity, and at an 'indignation meeting' elsewhere, there was angry mention of Princess Louise's dowry. Furthermore, republican clubs were springing up throughout the country. There was an ominous reaction when on 7 April the Prince and Princess of Wales's baby died. The Queen was sure 'everyone feels very much for dear Bertie and Alix', but the radical *Reynold's Newspaper* announced the child's demise 'with much satisfaction'. On 18 April Mr Gladstone informed his wife, 'things are certainly on the road to bad' as regards the monarchy.[51]

Resentment at economic injustice was exacerbated when the government sought to pay for increased military expenditure by imposing a match tax. While she herself had been one of the keenest advocates for higher defence spending, the Queen disapproved of this means of financing it. On 23 April she wrote to Gladstone asserting it 'would be very wrong and most impolitic' to impose a levy that would 'seriously affect the manufacture and sale of matches ... the sole means of support of a vast number of the very poorest people and little children'. After a protest march by London match girls, the government hastily withdrew the measure, but still looked foolish and uncaring.[52]

The government encountered other difficulties when secretary of state for war Edward Cardwell proposed to abolish the purchase of commissions in the army, meaning that in future officers would be promoted on merit alone. Victoria could not resist the proposals outright but had misgivings from the start. One of her main worries was the effect the changes would have on the position of the Commander-in-Chief of the Army, her cousin the Duke of Cambridge, of whom she was extremely fond and supportive. As a vehement opponent of modernisation, Cambridge predictably objected to abolition of purchase, asserting the existing system 'enabled us to officer our army with gentlemen'.[53]

When Cardwell introduced his legislation, the government had some difficulty getting it through the Commons. It was obvious that in the Lords the measure would face yet stronger opposition. After learning he was required to ease its passage through the Upper House, the Duke Cambridge appealed to the Queen, asking to be spared this. Victoria passed this on to Gladstone, who informed her that if Cambridge withheld his support, the government would find it impossible to defy calls for his dismissal.

Since the Queen refused to press the duke to act contrary to his feelings, it was ultimately agreed Cambridge would say what he could in favour of the bill without actually voting for it. In private, Cambridge continued to make plain his true views, indulging in what Gladstone described as 'extreme if not habitual indiscretion'. On 24 July the Queen had to write politely to her cousin, begging him to be more reticent.[54]

As expected, Cardwell's bill had been mauled by the Lords, who on 17 July had voted for an amendment that effectively ensured the measure would never come into operation. Losing all patience, the government announced they would not only bring in the changes regardless but would cancel arrangements to compensate holders of commissions which became valueless. The Queen noted that when asked to agree to this 'rather violent course … I rather hesitated', but soon gave way. Thereupon the peers caved in too. Gladstone would later assert that these reforms ensured the army belonged to the nation, rather than being solely 'the property of the rich'. The Queen, however, still mourned the abolition of purchase. She wrote to Cardwell in late October 1871, 'She must honestly own … that she sees with deep regret the destruction of a system which has worked so well for so long.'[55]

The delays to the Army Regulation Bill had held up the government's entire legislative programme, meaning that Parliament would have to sit much later than usual. This did not put MPs in a good mood. On 31 July Gladstone proposed to them that Prince Arthur should be granted an annuity of £15,000, but eleven MPs voted against giving him anything, and another fifty-one favoured reducing the sum to £10,000. Matters looked more serious when the debate broadened into an expression of resentment against Victoria's seclusion, with one MP wanting to know whether the government would advise the Queen to remain in the south for the Privy Council meeting necessary for Parliament's prorogation. On 8 August Gladstone warned her there was 'danger of some irritation' if ministers were required to travel up to Balmoral for a council, particularly since this might further delay the end of session. The next day he added that feeling about this was all the stronger because many MPs who had voted for Prince Arthur's annuity were conscious that their constituents would be displeased by it. If she was willing to help, she would only have to delay her departure for Scotland till 21 August, which would allow Parliament to be prorogued the following day.[56]

It looked likely Victoria would not listen. Having heard she was 'saying things you would not believe', Gladstone lamented to his wife, 'The conduct of the Queen ... weighs upon me like a nightmare.' Within days he had to field more questions in the Commons, an experience he found 'sad indeed'. The Cabinet decided they must send the Lord Chancellor Hatherley down to Osborne, and after reaching there on 10 August he had a long talk with the Queen. By ill luck, just when the government had resolved to confront her, she really was sickening for a bout of serious illness.[57]

Following their meeting she wrote at length to Hatherley. She claimed to have learned from experience that 'the more she yields to pressure & clamour ... it only encourages further demands'; should she give way now, 'she will be teazed & tormented every year'. If an important question were at stake, 'the Queen would not hesitate in sacrificing her convenience', even at some cost to her health, but she could not do so 'merely to gratify a fancy of the troublesome House of Commons'. Although she was already 'feeling extremely unwell', she would postpone her departure until 18 August, but if it turned out that the council would have to be held after that date, she would leave three days earlier, as planned. In future any attempt by MPs to interfere with her movements should be met with 'a firm high tone of reproof', for she could not remain queen if she was 'to become the servant of Parliament'. It was 'abominable' that she had been so abused by 'the infamous newspapers', for 'really ... what right has anyone to complain?' Reminding the Lord Chancellor that 'what killed her beloved husband' was 'overwork and worry', Victoria warned that if ministers would not give her the support she deserved, she 'must give her heavy burden up to younger hands'.[58]

Gladstone went on pressing her to stay at Windsor for a few more days. The Queen was positive this was impossible, and now set her departure date for 16 August. Ponsonby reported that she had 'got into such a nervous state' it was impossible to make her see reason. 'I cannot say how much I regret this matter,' he told Gladstone. 'But I also fully believe that it has agitated the Queen till she is really ill.'[59]

Gladstone found himself utterly at a loss. 'The whole business is one of the most deplorable I have ever known,' he wrote to Ponsonby. His despair turned to anger when Ponsonby confessed that Dr Jenner had assured the Queen the government were pressuring her to remain just to strengthen their position in Parliament. An incandescent Gladstone proclaimed it 'the most sickening piece of experience which I have had during near forty years of public life'. None of this could stop Victoria from setting off for Scotland on 16 August, although her selfishness was widely condemned.[60]

Ponsonby and Gladstone assumed her ill health was purely psychosomatic, but she was in fact suffering alarming symptoms. When the usually subservient Clerk of the Council Arthur Helps had begged her to stay, the Queen at first expressed amazement, and then justified herself on the grounds she was now 'extremely unwell, with a very troublesome relaxed swelled throat, great prostration, total loss of appetite, and want of sleep'. By the time she set off from Windsor she was feeling worse, suffering from headache and a painful arm, as well as being 'weak and shivery'. Once at Balmoral, she was capable only of 'lying on the sofa, and so sad continually'.[61] She experienced difficulty in swallowing and was troubled by a choking sensation. Possibly she had quinsy, a complication of tonsillitis, but at any rate was 'suffering tortures'. Her throat improved on 20 August, but she then developed an abscess on her arm, which had to be lanced on 3 September. Though this dealt with that problem, the Queen endured great discomfort from being bandaged too tightly, and then her other limbs became affected by agonising rheumatic gout.

She was slightly better by the time Gladstone came to stay at Balmoral on 26 September. The prime minister accepted she had had 'a serious bout' and that her throat infection had brought her at one time '*near* imminent danger'; he was however optimistic that 'a moderate time may bring her up to her usual high level'. He was therefore furious when Disraeli made a speech at his local harvest festival in Buckinghamshire, describing the Queen as 'physically and morally incapacitated' and suggesting overwork was to blame. Gladstone could take a certain grim satisfaction in Disraeli's embarrassment when the newspapers picked up on his unfortunate choice of words, which could be taken to mean that the Queen was mentally unhinged. In other respects, all that Disraeli had said was most unhelpful. Gladstone snorted, 'that speech of Dizzy's savours of his usual flunkeyism', while his claim about Victoria's tireless labours was 'absurdly untrue'. In conversation with a colleague, Gladstone 'laughed at the notion of the Queen doing as much business as the Head of a Department. Two hours a day at most he considered were devoted by her to business.'[62]

On arrival at Balmoral Gladstone had assured the Queen there was no need for her to see him if she did not feel up to it, and it was not until 1 October that she could face giving him an audience. The encounter did not go well. He reported to Lord Granville: 'The repellent power which she so well knows how to use,' had been deployed towards him: 'I … felt myself on a new and different footing with her.' It was fortunate that at this and a subsequent interview two days later he resisted raising the subject of her absences from London. He accepted it would have been 'cruel … at a time like this' to do so, but he did not doubt 'much will have to be said about it 'ere long'. While at the castle, he had several talks with the Queen's children, who were all worried about their mother's behaviour. Despite the general assumption that Victoria was on the mend, once Gladstone had left – somewhat regretful that she had not invited him to prolong his stay – she suffered a relapse and endured another three weeks of dreadful pain and complete prostration.

Gladstone believed that what he called the 'Royalty question' was becoming ever graver. An address by the radical atheist Charles Bradlaugh to the London Republic Club, founded some months earlier, was deemed by the prime minister 'a political fact of some significance'.[63] He was also worried by the appearance of a pamphlet entitled *What Does She Do With It?* This was written ostensibly by one 'Solomon Temple', but was really the work of G. O. Trevelyan, a junior minister in the government. After reading and annotating it, Gladstone had it circulated to the Cabinet. The pamphlet accused the Queen of hoarding savings Prince Albert had achieved through economies in the royal household. It also said she failed to use her annual civil list payment of £385,000 for the purposes for which it was intended, such as entertaining foreign dignitaries. Her expenditure had greatly reduced on account of her seclusion, enabling her to amass a vast fortune. As a result, 'in every tavern and mechanics' reading room in the country' it was being asked, 'What is done with the vast sums which are annually given to support the honour and dignity of the Crown?'[64]

It was true that savings in household expenditure had enabled the Queen to transfer £573,554 to her Privy Purse up to 1870. On the other hand, 'Solomon Temple' made some exaggerated or utterly false claims. He asserted that she did not pay income tax, that Albert had left her £1 million on his death and that she had a private fortune of £5 million. When Gladstone was at Balmoral in late September 1871, he had shown the pamphlet to Colonel Ponsonby, and after the prime minister had left, Ponsonby wrote to him highlighting these errors. 'There are other lies,' he observed. 'But he has as you say missed some arguments. And as a whole the pamphlet is disagreeable.'[65]

All this preyed greatly on the prime ministerial mind. When Lord Spencer stayed with Gladstone at Hawarden in mid-October, his host fretted about 'notices in papers and on placards' about the Queen and Prince of Wales and declared, 'Indications existed that the monarchy was going down.' This appeared still more plausible when the radical MP for Chelsea, Sir Charles Dilke, went on a rabble-rousing lecture tour. At Newcastle on 6 November, he repeated the slander that Victoria paid no income tax and said that if a republic could be free of the 'political corruption that hangs about the monarchy, I say ... let it come'. The Queen was enraged. Although Gladstone had made a measured rebuttal of Dilke's statements, Victoria told him nothing less than 'reprobating in very strong terms ... these revolutionary theories' was acceptable. Gladstone must also contradict Dilke's 'deliberate falsehoods' about her tax affairs. Gladstone found this awkward. Since the beginning of the reign, the Queen had paid £304,000 in income tax, but arguably had received generous treatment from the fiscal authorities. Gladstone informed Lord Granville, 'I cannot say the case of the income tax stands well for jealous debate ... The Queen has paid a great deal but there are holes in the case.'[66]

He was also wary of strongly censuring Dilke. As he explained to the Queen, Sir Charles's Newcastle speech had been very well received by the audience – 'a fact of extreme gravity, giving much cause for reflection'. Malcontents were doubtless still a minority, but a few years ago this minority did not exist. It was therefore imperative to address 'the causes of the distemper'. What he desired, he told Victoria on 5 December, was 'the return of the public sentiment to the state in which it has existed through most of your Majesty's reign ... namely the state in which republican opinions could nowhere show their head'.[67]

By this time the Queen had other things to worry about. On 21 November, just at the point she was 'returning to ordinary life' after her prolonged illness, a telegram had arrived at Balmoral to say that the Prince of Wales was unwell. The following day it was confirmed he had typhoid – the 'fearful fever' supposed to have killed his father. The Queen set off south at once, and as Bertie's condition worsened, she had gone to Sandringham on 27 November. She returned to Windsor after four days but was called back to Norfolk on 8 December because of a further deterioration. On 13 December the prince's life was despaired of, but the following day, the anniversary of Albert's death, saw an improvement. Soon he was pronounced out of danger.

While her son was fighting for his life, the Queen had been heartened by a nationwide surge of sympathy for the stricken prince. As letters and telegrams poured in, she noted in her diary on 10 December: 'The feeling shown by the whole nation is quite marvellous & most touching & striking, showing how really sound & truly loyal the people really are.' Republican sentiment dramatically declined, causing the virulent *Reynolds's Newspaper* to bemoan 'the great epidemic of typhoid loyalty'.[68]

On 17 December Ponsonby wrote to Gladstone at the Queen's command to ask 'whether some form of Thanksgiving should be prepared for the recovery of the Prince of Wales'. Taking this to mean a public service attended by Victoria, Gladstone believed it offered a providential chance of rehabilitating the monarchy. He wrote to Lord Granville, 'We have arrived at a great crisis of royalty ... *This* in all likelihood is the last opportunity ... of effecting what is requisite.'[69]

The prime minister had a long meeting with the Queen at Windsor on 21 December. To his consternation, he found her 'much discomposed' because the elder Whig statesman, Lord Halifax, had written to her expressing delight at her readiness to go in state to St Paul's for the thanksgiving. It seems that the Queen had merely wanted a form of service to be drawn up to be used at churches throughout the country and had not envisaged her own presence being part of it. While she agreed to write a letter for publication expressing gratitude for Bertie's deliverance, she 'delivered a very strong declaration' against the proposed cathedral service. 'Such a display' would be 'in point of religion, false and hollow', and marked by distasteful 'pomp and show'. She insisted, 'Nothing should induce her to be a party to it.'

Gladstone persevered, pointing out, 'Nothing short of a great public act of this kind' could satisfy her subjects, and this was surely a time when she and other personages concerned should 'properly cast aside all thought of themselves'. To his infinite relief, 'these considerations appeared to tell very much with the Queen'. Seizing the moment, Gladstone observed the event would be of great advantage for the future of the monarchy. Bertie's illness had already 'worked in an extraordinary manner' in 'putting down that disagreeable movement with which the name of Sir C Dilke had been connected. And what we should look to was … getting rid of it altogether.' By the end of the interview, although the Queen was still voicing quibbles, the principle of the thanksgiving was 'entertained, & not unfavourably'.[70]

Over the next few weeks the Queen would make endless difficulties. First of all Bertie suffered a relapse, so she was able to say a thanksgiving was premature. Even once 27 February 1872 was fixed on as the date, Victoria haggled about details. She had strong views about the service's length, at one point proposing it should last only half an hour, and insisted she would wear a bonnet, not a crown. She repeatedly warned she might have to cancel on health grounds ('though the Queen will do all she can to keep well') and grumbled that the government were treating the whole thing 'as though it was to be *merely a show*!' All through the planning stage the prince's attendance remained in doubt, but the Queen was alarmed when she discovered that, if he was well enough to be there, he might travel to the cathedral in a separate carriage to her. Clearly starting to be aware of the possible public relations' benefits, she telegraphed Gladstone, 'I think the public would like to see us together … What do government think?' In a separate letter Ponsonby discreetly explained what lay behind the Queen's concern: 'If they went separately there might be a risk of one receiving a greater and more enthusiastic reception than the other,' which could give rise to 'odious' comparisons.[71] In the end it was agreed that the Queen and her son would ride to St Paul's in the same carriage.

The Queen had reluctantly conceded that the government could announce the thanksgiving in the speech at the opening of Parliament, but when the text was sent to her, she had other objections. She wrote to Gladstone, 'the Queen would also wish that both he and Lord Granville should in Parliament allude to her own *severe* illness' – the effects of which 'have by *no means* disappeared'. Indeed, she was still suffering so much that the public should be warned not only that she might be unable to appear at the thanksgiving, but in future 'she may be *less able* than *before even* to go through *bodily* fatigue and exertion'. Gladstone responded firmly that while he was prepared to make a statement, reminding people of her illness in the autumn, an intimation that her subjects could expect 'a comparative contraction in Your Majesty's discharge of what may be termed visible public duties', was likely to prompt awkward questions in Parliament. 'He thinks it his duty, as a loyal servant of YM, to do nothing' to bring this about. The Queen backed down unreservedly.[72]

Even on 21 February Victoria was predicting to her daughter, 'This dreadful affair at St Paul's ... will be a great, great trial' – but in the end the thanksgiving proved a triumph, and she was delighted by it. 'The deafening cheers never ceased the whole way,' she recorded complacently in her journal, uplifted by the 'wonderful enthusiasm & astounding affectionate loyalty shown.' Showing an instinctive flair for theatrical gestures, she milked the adulation. 'At Temple Bar, amid deafening cheers, I took dear Bertie's hand and pressed it – people cried,' she informed Vicky. All in all, 'It was a most affecting day.' Naturally she could not resist some complaints: the shortened service was still 'too long' for her liking, and the 'dreary and dingy' cathedral, oddly for February, 'stiflingly hot'. Despite this, she wrote next day to Gladstone that, though she 'naturally feels tired & her head aches', the recollection of all the acclamations 'makes up for that'.[73]

Two days after the thanksgiving, a youth named Arthur O'Connor pointed an unloaded pistol at the Queen as she left Buckingham Palace in her carriage. He had intended to force her to sign at gunpoint an 'extraordinary document' calling for the release of imprisoned Fenians. The assailant was seized and disarmed by John Brown, but the Queen admitted she had been 'horribly frightened'. She wrote to Gladstone she hoped the culprit would not be treated with '*too great leniency*' and took satisfaction in the prime minister's assurance that the law permitted the 'infliction of a punishment of real severity'.[74]

In fact, when the case came to trial and O'Connor pleaded guilty to misdemeanour, the Queen was exasperated by the outcome. As she complained to Vicky, the judge showed mercy by 'giving him the lightest sentence possible! Only one flogging with merely a year's imprisonment and hard labour!' For once she could not blame

Gladstone, for he too was 'very indignant'. Victoria had to content herself with her prime minister's assurance that on his release, O'Connor would be forced to leave the country.[75]

Although the incident had been bad for her nerves, it had not been devoid of good effects. Gladstone's niece Lucy Cavendish noted on 1 March: 'If anything was wanted to send loyalty up to boiling point, this attempt has done it.' In the park a huge crowd cheered 'when the Queen pluckily drove out this morning in an open carriage with no extra precautions', and Victoria could not help being touched.[76]

The alteration in the public mood was further demonstrated on 19 March when Sir Charles Dilke moved in the Commons for an enquiry into the civil list. On learning of Dilke's intentions, the Queen had urged Gladstone to respond 'not at all in an apologetic tone' for, 'It is high time to ... [take] a stand against the impertinence of people like Sir C Dilke.' In the event, Dilke's demand was greeted by fellow MPs with a 'chorus of groans'. After Dilke had finished his dull speech, an ally of his named Auberon Herbert made a republican declaration of his own, whereupon the Commons erupted in fury.[77]

Clearly things were better than they had been, but Gladstone believed there was more work to be done. He had already spoken to the Queen on the importance of 'finding for the Prince of Wales some means of living worthily', and now he hoped to combine this project with improving Anglo-Irish relations. Nine months earlier he had proposed to her that public money could be used to purchase a royal residence in Ireland, but the idea had fallen on stony ground. This was predictable: when Disraeli's Lord Lieutenant, the Duke of Abercorn, had suggested in 1868 that the Prince of Wales might enjoy some time in Ireland, Victoria had retorted: 'No one visited Ireland for pleasure.' At the time her secretary General Grey had confided to Disraeli, 'she does not *like* Ireland – has a bad opinion of the people – a horror of the climate'. Gladstone would soon ruefully acknowledge, 'There is a manifest *twist* in the Queen's mind with respect to Ireland.'[78]

By December 1871 he was nevertheless moving towards an ambitious concept, entailing abolishing the lord lieutenancy and sending the Prince of Wales to Ireland for a few months each year to take the viceroy's place. Gladstone believed this would not only be beneficial for the prince's character but also have 'very powerful effects on the popular mind in Ireland'. He had first floated the idea before the Queen the previous June and had flattered himself that she was 'quite open' to it – particularly since she had commented that if it took the prince 'away from the London season … it would be a good thing'. He was further encouraged by Colonel Ponsonby's initially thinking the difficulties 'not … insurmountable', although from the start Ponsonby warned the prince himself might not favour it. However, by 8 March 1872 Ponsonby was sure 'that the Queen is strongly opposed to his going to Ireland as Viceroy or Deputy'. She had pointed out, quite rationally, that Gladstone envisaged that in Ireland the prince would merely carry out ceremonial duties, while political power would be vested in a minister for Ireland. Such a role 'would certainly not encourage him in habits of business'. What was more, Ponsonby had established that 'the Prince is even more opposed than the Queen to going in any official capacity to Ireland'.[79]

Gladstone nevertheless remained determined not to shirk the 'duty imperatively demanded' of 'framing a worthy and manly mode of life' for the heir to the throne. Warning it would be 'a calamity if we fail', he circulated a memorandum to Cabinet; but when his colleagues learned what he was contemplating, very few were in favour. Lord Spencer feared that in Ireland the prince would become prey to 'flatterers', while W. E. Forster conversely dreaded his becoming associated in Irish eyes 'with acts of administration which must sometimes be stern and would very often be unpopular'.[80]

None of this deterred Gladstone. He took immense trouble drawing up a 'letter to HM by which I am willing to live or die', and which cost him 'much pain as well as labour'. He sent it off on 5 July praying, 'God prosper it!' But on 12 July the Queen replied she considered his plan 'full of objections'. She argued, 'It does not seem to be desirable to introduce violent changes into the government of Ireland at a moment when that country appears to be in a state of fermentation.' On seeing this, Lord Granville urged him not to press the matter further. Gladstone (who routinely ignored Granville's advice) answered: 'for once I rather hesitate to accept your suggestion'. While insisting, 'I have no wish to irritate', he maintained he was 'bound in a peculiar and single way' to consider the interests of Queen and country.[81]

Within days he had sent off to her another interminable treatise, admitting his plan was 'in the nature of an experiment', but contending that nothing better could be devised. The Queen wearily promised to discuss it with her son, and having done so wrote on 5 August a letter that she believed resolved the matter for ever. She explained the prince was 'much opposed to a scheme … which offers him no real business occupation but compels him to reside in a second rate town where his sole duty would be to receive and to entertain a second rate society'. As for her, 'she does not think Ireland is in a fit state ... to be experimented upon'. If the project failed, 'as it inevitably must, the Prince of Wales will be exposed to grave condemnation', and while the 'plan at first sight presented some apparent advantages', Mr Gladstone must surely now agree 'the details are objectionable'. She concluded: 'the Queen therefore trusts this plan may now be considered as *definitely* abandoned'.[82]

Gladstone should really have given up but believed this the 'one thing I cannot do'. He was convinced, wrongly, that the Queen was inciting her son against the plan, whereas the reality was that Bertie genuinely did not want to go to Ireland. On 28 August the prime minister sent Victoria another multiple-page letter seeking to overcome her objections and requesting permission to meet with the prince himself. Provoked beyond measure, the Queen answered stonily that it was 'useless to prolong the discussion'. Finally accepting that this 'precludes any further effort on my part', he agreed to refrain 'from further trespass on your Majesty's patience'. He told Lord Granville on 6 September, 'Of course it is idle to attempt to force her: and I do not think it would be right for me to resign upon the matter.'[83]

The Queen had earlier volunteered, somewhat lukewarmly, that Gladstone would be a welcome guest at Balmoral. The prime minister had said to Granville that while there was any 'hope of making any progress in the great business I would gladly travel a long distance for it', but he was not particularly interested in going just to have 'an audience for chat and commonplace'. When the foreign secretary stayed at Balmoral in early September Ponsonby asked him to pass on that 'the Queen hoped when you came here you would not *talk* to her on the subject'. Having assured Granville, 'She need not be afraid of my pressing' her, Gladstone added: 'I must say it will be a *great* relief and pleasure to me if she lets me off Balmoral altogether.' He wrote as much to the Queen, who showed his letter to Granville. Granville reported: 'She was sorry that you were annoyed ... expressed real regret at differing from you, but said she had the strongest conviction on the subject, and when she had a strong conviction, she generally found that she was right.' Much to Gladstone's relief she then wrote that, 'if there is nothing very special to communicate, the Queen hardly likes to urge Mr Gladstone to put himself to the inconvenience and fatigue of coming', and he eagerly availed himself of the dispensation.[84]

The whole episode irreparably damaged Gladstone's relations with the Queen. A change was apparent when on 27 November he had a long audience with her after attending a council at Windsor and found her noticeably more '"shut up" so to speak, towards me'. This was permanent. Even at the end of 1878 she was still seething about his having subjected her to such 'pertinacious argument' about Bertie going to Ireland.[85]

It certainly did not make her any more obliging about performing duties. On 19 November the prime minister had requested her to open the next session of Parliament, as he understood she was willing 'to discharge that function in alternate years'. The Queen at once corrected the misconception. At best she would be capable of it every third or fourth year, and '*this* next year she *could not* think of venturing to do it. Her nerves require rest & quiet, having been very severely shaken.'[86]

In 1873 Gladstone decided that his legislative priority was to bring in an Irish University Bill, amalgamating Trinity College Dublin with existing Catholic universities. He trusted that his third great measure addressing Irish grievances would finally conciliate Ireland, but he was almost alone in having these high hopes. When Disraeli realised the extent of opposition to it, he was swift to capitalise, and on 12 March the bill – which Gladstone had declared a vital measure – was defeated on its second reading.

The Queen thought that Gladstone had brought this on himself. 'Good Mr G is not judicious and this "mission" to redeem Ireland – which has signally failed – has been the cause of his defeat,' she informed Vicky with satisfaction. Inevitably she added: 'It gives me of course a good deal of trouble' – but really she was happy that Disraeli looked set to return as prime minister. Even better was the prospect that she would never have to have further dealings with Gladstone. When he tendered his resignation to her on 13 March he said, 'he himself wished to retire … altogether … that he was very tired, the work & exertion for body and mind being beyond what human nature could bear'. The Queen offered him a peerage, but he declined it.[87]

That afternoon the government's resignation was announced in the Commons and at six in the evening the Queen saw Disraeli. She at once invited him to form a government, whereupon he told her that although he had an excellent ministerial team he could appoint, he was not prepared to take office in the present Parliament and did not request a dissolution. He claimed that Gladstone had been wrong to have resigned 'as it were in a fit' – and would later justify his own rejection of office by alleging (which others contested) it was impossible for him to hold an election immediately. Instead, he would have to head a minority government for two or three months – during which time the administration would flounder and be discredited.

The Queen – who had left Disraeli in no doubt of her 'repugnance for her present government' – 'appeared disappointed'. She warned Disraeli (as she recorded in her journal) that Gladstone 'would very likely object ... I felt sure he would not consent to continue in office', but she did not insist – as arguably she should have – that Disraeli attempt to form a government. Instead, she sent Ponsonby to see Gladstone at 7 p.m. By this time the latter was looking forward to a rest, but when he genially asked, 'Any news?' Ponsonby replied: 'A great deal.' He then informed an aghast Gladstone that the Queen 'considers this as sending for you anew'.[88]

Utterly nonplussed by this 'unheard of proceeding', Gladstone 'got rather angry'. On 15 March he submitted to Victoria a long, written statement citing numerous examples from the past fifty years that proved an opposition was obliged to make every effort to replace a government it had brought down. The Queen forwarded this to Disraeli, who insouciantly insisted he was taking a course 'at once advantageous to the public interests and tending to spare your Majesty unnecessary anxiety'.[89] Victoria then told Gladstone that since Disraeli had positively declined, she called on him to return to office.

Dejectedly accepting 'nothing more is to be expected in that quarter', Gladstone agreed to consult his colleagues. On 18 March the Cabinet met. Lord Kimberley reported: 'We all looked very gloomy but it was settled there was no alternative but to resume office.' Two days later Gladstone made a Commons statement, to which Disraeli replied 'in brilliant form ... almost ... playing with Mr Gladstone'. When Gladstone reiterated to the Queen that he considered Disraeli's arguments specious, she merely expressed pleasure 'all passed off well'. Far from feeling grateful to Gladstone, she told her daughter, 'He has been very tiresome and obstinate in this business and I think has done himself no good.'[90]

One minister noted that after being forcibly brought back into power, he and his colleagues felt 'like men who had been buried and dug up again'. Well aware of how difficult it was 'to repair that loss of *vital force* which we suffered from the affair', in August 1873 Gladstone decided on a reshuffle. The Queen was initially optimistic that the government would be reconstituted in a shape that suited her, but in the end the changes made were not to her liking. It was particularly injudicious of

Gladstone, already suffering from a 'half-exhausted brain', to add to his 'constant tumult of business' by taking on the chancellorship of the Exchequer. On 6 August the Queen wrote that, while unwilling to make 'unnecessary difficulties', she did not think the proposed arrangements satisfactory. 'Will not the additional office of Chancellor of the Exchequer, add greatly to Mr Gladstone's work, which is already too much for his health?' she asked pertinently.[91]

Surprisingly, when Gladstone stayed at Balmoral later that summer, his visit went rather well. He reported to his wife: 'Nothing can be better than her [the Queen's] humour' – and after his departure Lord Granville delightedly passed on her comment that 'she had never known you so remarkably agreeable'. Perhaps, however, it was because he had lost some of his fire. Although Henry Ponsonby still thought him 'rather mad' at times, he believed Gladstone 'was looking back and not forward. There was no keenness about future measures and he made little or no stand against anything the Queen insisted on. He gave way.'[92]

By the beginning of 1874 Gladstone had decided the government's only hope of re-election lay in major fiscal changes, and on 21 January the Queen was startled when he unexpectedly informed her he wished for a dissolution of Parliament. She was agreeable, although on learning that the Liberals were promising the abolition of income tax as – in her words – 'a bait to catch the elections', she noted primly, 'this I hardly think quite fair or right.' As it turned out, the 'huge bribe' held little attraction for voters. The Tories had been wooing them with visions of imperial greatness, capitalising on the government's undistinguished record on foreign affairs. Disraeli had claimed the Liberals wished to 'emancipate' the nation from the alleged 'incubus' of Empire, whereas under the Conservatives, Britain would be 'a great country, an Imperial country'. This had captured the public's imagination, although the electorate were also disenchanted with what Disraeli described as 'incessant and harassing legislation'. Gladstone's niece Lucy Cavendish detected 'a universal sense of weariness and wish for letting things alone', while the Queen claimed that even many Liberals 'looked with fear and trembling upon "What next?"' She noted that 'Everything was being altered and in many cases ruined' and, as a result, 'Mr Gladstone has contrived to alienate and frighten the country.'[93]

The election proved disastrous for the Liberals, with the Conservatives gaining a sizeable overall majority for the first time since Peel's day. The Queen was thrilled, telling her daughter: 'I thought they [the government] would lose – but not to the immense amount they have done!'

She was sure Gladstone was personally responsible, for it 'shows how little he is trusted and how unpopular he is'. Gladstone himself, who had had 'no expectation of anything like such a crash', was naturally greatly cast down. To the Queen he sorrowfully acknowledged, 'it was the greatest expression of public disapprobation of a government he ever remembered'.[94]

The Queen wanted the government to resign without meeting Parliament. This she found more convenient, not least because at St Petersburg on 23 February her second son Alfred Duke of Edinburgh had married the tsar's daughter, Grand Duchess Marie. In early March the couple were expected in England and a great banquet was to be held for them at Windsor. When it emerged Gladstone did not wish to follow the precedent set by Disraeli in December 1868, the Queen wrote him a sharp letter. She said that apart from the fact that a three-week delay before the new government took power would not be in the country's interests, Gladstone appeared to have overlooked 'the arrival of the Duke and Duchess of Edinburgh, bringing with it fetes etc just when Parliament meets – which would make it *physically impossible* for the Queen … to *go* through *all* the necessary fatigue accompanying a change of government'. What was more, the whole upheaval was attributable to Gladstone's unexpected dissolution. She concluded severely: 'People are apt to forget … that the Queen is a *woman* who has far more on her hands & far more to try mind & body than is good *for any one* of her sex & age.' The letter struck Gladstone as one of 'scant kindness', and Mrs Gladstone was indignant that Victoria could have been so harsh to her 'badgered and low' husband.[95] The Queen nevertheless had her way, for the Cabinet also wanted to resign before Parliament convened.

It seemed that all was put right between the Queen and Gladstone when he came to Windsor on 17 February to tender his resignation officially. They talked for three-quarters of an hour and he noted that 'Nothing could be more frank, natural and kind than her manner throughout.' She agreed to his requests for honours and offered him the Garter and a peerage, both of which he declined. He assured her that he intended to retire, and it was probably this that largely accounted for her sunny mood. Afterwards she congratulated herself for having resisted pointing out to him that his electoral defeat was 'greatly owing to his own unpopularity, and to the want of confidence people had in him'. As a result, nothing marred the encounter. Emerging from the interview, Gladstone confided to Ponsonby: 'I had feared … all might not go smooth, but she really was so natural about her regret at parting that I was quite touched.' Victoria would doubtless have been less gracious had she realised that Gladstone would remain at the centre of politics for another twenty years. She should have taken note that when he took leave of her, he qualified what he said about his retirement plans by stating that, while he thought himself 'entitled to rest', he 'might be ready to come forward for a particular call'. In the future more than one such 'special call' would arise, ensuring that the worst of her arguments with Mr Gladstone were yet to come.[96]

9

Mr Disraeli (Earl of Beaconsfield) 1874–1880

On 16 February 1874 the Queen's lady-in-waiting Jane, Marchioness of Ely, sent a letter to Mr Disraeli. A nervous woman whose 'absurd fear of the Queen' was heightened by Victoria's intermittent bullying, Lady Ely was sometimes employed by the Queen as an unofficial emissary. On this occasion, however, she offered her own heartfelt congratulations for Disraeli's return to power. 'My dear mistress will be very happy to see you again and I know how careful and gentle you are about all that concerns her,' she assured him. 'I think you understand her so well, besides appreciating her noble fine qualities.' When Disraeli came to kiss hands four days later, he justified her plaudits, delighting the Queen by murmuring fervently as he knelt before her, 'I plight my troth to the kindest of *Mistresses*.'[1]

Disraeli was now a widower, having lost his wife in December 1872. Although he had sincerely mourned her, his genuine grief had not stopped him from forming close friendships with two aristocratic siblings, the Countess of Bradford and her widowed sister Lady Chesterfield. For the remainder of his life they would be the recipients of entertaining and revealing letters from him, but he still managed to convince the Queen that she was the woman who mattered most to him. Attaching the highest value to their personal connection, he avowed himself 'fortunate in having a female sovereign', for he knew he could never have established a comparable affinity with a king.[2]

As before, he deployed shameless flattery to commend himself to Victoria, being always ready to beguile her with courtly tributes couched in the language of chivalric romance. When the Queen sent him primroses in April 1875, he thanked her with an effusion as flowery as the gift itself. 'They seem an offering from the fauns and dryads of the woods of Osborne,' he rhapsodised, assuring her he treasured all tokens emanating from 'Your Majesty's Faery Isle'. Offering her birthday wishes in May 1877, he hailed her as 'one whose existence has not only gladdened the life of a people, but has deigned to shed on his being the ineffable charm which springs from sympathy the most condescending, from never-failing grace, and from the pure and perfect trust which becomes an imperial heart'. The following year, in another ornamental offering, addressed as usual to: 'MADAM, AND MOST BELOVED SOVEREIGN', he described her as 'a mistress whom to serve is to love: and who can combine the highest attributes of Royalty with all those qualities which make life gracious and full of charm'. In January 1878 he would further assure her that, 'during a somewhat romantic and imaginative life, nothing has ever occurred to him so interesting as this confidential correspondence with one so exalted and so inspiring'.[3]

When writing to the Countess of Bradford, Disraeli generally referred to the Queen as 'the Faery'. It was a nickname in keeping with his frequent allusions to *A Midsummer Night's Dream* in letters to Victoria but was apt in other ways. It was certainly affectionate, and ostensibly reverential, but simultaneously contained the merest hint of mockery. While conjuring up her diminutive size and granting her the power of enchantment, it also conveyed that, as one who felt herself exempt from rules that governed ordinary mortals, she could be unreasonable and capricious.

Disraeli's letters to the Queen abounded with homage to her wisdom and political discernment. Asking her to open Parliament in March 1874, he promised this 'shall be a matter, always, for your Majesty alone to decide. Mr Disraeli has too high, and genuine, an opinion of your Majesty's judgement and too sincere an appreciation of your Majesty's vast political experience to doubt that, whatever your Majesty's decision ... it will be a correct one.' He pronounced communications from her invaluable, because, 'Your Majesty's gracious letters ... always encourage and, not infrequently, guide him.' On one occasion he apologised for troubling her with details of government policy, but said this arose from 'perhaps, a too anxious desire that your Majesty should ever take a leading, and recognised, part in the government of your Empire'. Another time he confessed: 'It may be unconstitutional for a Minister to seek advice from his Sovereign, instead of proffering it, but your Majesty has, sometimes, deigned to assist Mr Disraeli with your counsel, and he believes he may presume to say with respectful candour, that your Majesty cannot but be aware how highly Mr Disraeli appreciates your Majesty's judgement and almost unrivalled experience of public life.'[4]

There were those who suspected all this was mere flummery. In 1876 Henry Ponsonby told his wife that both he and Sir Thomas Biddulph believed Disraeli was 'humbugging' the Queen with his use of lavish phraseology such as 'her most puissant Majesty'. A year earlier Ponsonby had alleged that in his letters to her, Disraeli 'communicates nothing except boundless professions of love and loyalty, and if called upon to write more says he is ill'. Clearly, however, Sir Thomas did not invariably consider Disraeli a master manipulator of the Queen. In 1874 Ponsonby reported to his wife: 'Bids thinks that Dizzy is a perfect slave to the Queen and that she is always at him about something.'[5]

Certainly Victoria could be very demanding, and was not afraid to make his life difficult. When he began his second premiership, Disraeli was nearly seventy and his health was precarious. Besides agonising bouts of gout, he suffered from asthma and bronchial problems, complicated later by the onset of kidney disease. All of this ensured he was physically exhausted by the strain of being prime minister, and managing Victoria only added to the burden. Sometimes she 'telegraphed and wrote ... several times a day, wanting him to do sundry impossible things'. In January 1877 Disraeli's foreign secretary, the 15th Earl of Derby,* recorded that: 'To manage, flatter and keep in good humour the Queen is in itself an occupation (so Disraeli says and I quite believe him).'[6]

More than once she pushed him into measures he would rather have avoided. Faced with a demand he could not fulfil, he once reminded her he was constrained by constitutional limits: 'Were he your Majesty's Grand Vizier, instead of your Majesty's Prime Minister,' he would happily accomplish her every wish, 'but, alas! It is not so.' The Queen harassed him about minor matters as well as high policy. In May 1875 he reported to Lady Bradford: 'I have a long letter this morning from the Faery about vivisection, which she insists upon my stopping, as well as the theft of ladies' jewels.' She wrote to him, as he told Lord Derby, 'nearly every day, sometimes oftener'; when things were at their most intense the prime minister would be deluged with a veritable 'hurricane of words'.[7]

Disraeli prided himself on his managerial skills with the Queen. He once confided to a courtier, 'I never deny; I never contradict; I sometimes forget.' After his death, the Queen herself recalled fondly, 'He had a way when we differed of saying "Dear Madam" so persuasively.' He could display consummate tact, so that, for example, when sounding

* Lord Stanley had become the 15th Earl of Derby on his father's death in October 1869.

her out about opening Parliament in 1874, he said this was 'a subject on which he had made up his mind never to press your Majesty, as he knows a long and impending engagement harasses and disquiets'. It was a much more productive approach than Gladstone's hectoring, but Disraeli could not always be confident of the results. Sometimes he unburdened himself to Lord Derby, who he knew would be receptive to any disloyal comments. In March 1875 he confided: 'She was very troublesome, very wilful and whimsical, like a spoilt child.' A year later he went further, describing her as 'very mad'.[8]

Some people disapproved of the way Disraeli indulged Victoria. Lord Derby in particular thought him 'too submissive'. He complained that Disraeli 'flattered her incessantly and grossly: always letting her think that it was for her to guide the Cabinet and govern the country'. To any query, the prime minister 'said it was the only way of dealing with her'. Derby had first showed his impatience at this in May 1874, when Tsar Alexander II came to England to see his daughter, married to the Queen's second son. Victoria agreed to give him a banquet at Windsor, but to Derby's alarm said she would go to Scotland before the tsar left the country. Disraeli preened himself on persuading her to postpone her departure, boasting to Lady Bradford, 'Salisbury says I have saved an Afghan war.' According to him Derby too 'congratulates me on my unrivalled triumph', but when the foreign secretary had first raised the matter, he had hinted that Disraeli should adopt a firmer approach. 'Nobody can have managed the lady better than you have,' he had conceded, 'but is there not just a risk of encouraging her in too large ideas of her personal power, and too great indifference to what the public expects? I only ask: it is for you to judge.'[9]

Lady Bradford herself occasionally scolded Disraeli for pandering too much to Victoria. 'You say I spoil her,' he admitted, but protested he was always ready to utter 'grave truths' he knew would be unwelcome.[10] It is fair to say that when he exerted himself, he did generally succeed in reining the Queen in, but it would perhaps have been better if he could have brought himself to be stricter more often.

The Queen's interventionist tendencies first manifested themselves over the 1874 Public Worship Bill. She had been concerned for some time that the Church of England was being undermined from within by crypto-Catholic clergymen who were introducing rituals and observances alien to Protestant tradition. Convinced that 'something must be done' against 'Romanising tendencies', she instructed Disraeli to do everything possible to ensure that a bill drafted by the Archbishop of Canterbury outlawing the offensive practices became law.[11]

This was highly problematic for Disraeli. The High Church Lord Salisbury (formerly Lord Cranborne) had only reluctantly joined the Cabinet as Secretary of State for India after securing explicit assurances that the ministry would not legislate against ritualists. The Queen was 'deeply grieved' to learn that other members of the Cabinet were likewise far from enthusiastic, but in the end no minister resigned on the question. Although Gladstone denounced the bill during its second reading debate on 9 July, the general mood of the House of Commons strongly favoured the measure, so Disraeli realised that if he took it up himself he could please Victoria, humiliate Gladstone and improve his own standing with backbenchers. Until the final stages it was unclear whether he would pull off the difficult feat, but on 6 August the bill overcame its final hurdle.[12]

Disraeli had already told the Queen, 'if this blow is dealt against the Sacerdotal school, it will be entirely through the personal will of the Sovereign.' It was not something she should have prided herself on, for this divisive law merely resulted in a few fanatical clergymen being imprisoned, and in no way strengthened the Church. Victoria was very far from having any misgivings. Having gone down to see her at Osborne the day the bill passed, Disraeli reported to Lady Bradford: 'The Faery sent for me the instant I arrived … I really thought she was going to embrace me. She was wreathed with smiles and, as she talked, glided about the room like a bird. She told me it was all owing to my courage and tact, and then she said, "To think of your having the gout all the time. How you must have suffered! And you ought not to stand now, you shall have a chair!"'[13]

Disraeli did not undervalue this honour, for after Victoria married Albert, the rule had been strictly enforced that ministers must stand throughout all interviews. Disraeli remembered that when Lord Derby had been in great pain, the Queen had apologised she could not let him have a chair, 'the etiquette was so severe'. Further evidence of his favour came when he stayed at Balmoral that September and the Queen invited him to remain a second week. Unfortunately he then fell ill, which Lord Carnarvon said was caused by her having 'put him into draughts, and by open windows in icy cold rooms'. After the doctor ordered him to bed, Victoria visited him in his room. 'What do you think of that?' he asked Lady Chesterfield triumphantly.[14]

* * *

On 15 January 1875 *The Times* published a letter from Gladstone formally renouncing the leadership of the Liberal Party, although he remained on the backbenches. The Queen wrote to him politely that she knew 'his zeal and untiring energy' had always been directed to promoting his country's welfare, but she was buoyed that he would never again be prime minister. In Gladstone's place, the Liberals elected the Marquis of Hartington – nicknamed 'Harty Tarty' – to be their leader in the Commons. He was the forty-one-year-old heir to the Duke of Devonshire and a stolid and phlegmatic Whig. Despite his aristocratic breeding, he did not have polished or courtly manners. Laconic and plain-spoken, he cultivated an air of patrician detachment, sometimes giving the impression he was more interested in horse-racing than politics. Unlike Gladstone, he was not given to moods of exaltation or inspired rhetoric. Once, he was seen to yawn while giving a speech; when someone referred to this, he said, 'Yes, wasn't it damned dull?'[15]

Disraeli was delighted at no longer having to struggle 'with the malignity of Gladstone', but Hartington was not sole head of the opposition. Lord Granville remained chief Liberal spokesman in the House of Lords, and the Queen wrote to him emphasising, 'She looks on *him*, and on him *only* as the real leader of the Liberal Party.'[16]

During the 1875 session of Parliament, the Conservatives brought in a remarkable programme of domestic legislation. Public housing, sanitary improvements and industrial relations were all tackled, with Disraeli happy to take the credit for schemes which certainly showed vision, even if somewhat limited in effect. When Parliament dispersed that August, he told Victoria he could not recall another session in which 'so many important and truly popular measures' had been enacted.[17]

The Queen approved, but her imagination was stimulated rather more by a step taken by Disraeli towards the end of the year. The Suez Canal had opened in 1869, dramatically reducing voyage times to India. Having learned that the Khedive of Egypt was on the verge of selling his shares in the Suez Canal Company to a French consortium, Disraeli acted very fast to obtain them for Britain. On 17 November the Cabinet somewhat nervously agreed, and two days later the Queen telegraphed her consent from Balmoral. Disraeli then applied to Rothschild's for a loan of £4 million, to be repaid when Parliament met and voted funds. On 24 November Disraeli announced to Victoria, 'You have it Madam', and the following day the contract was signed. The Queen hailed his coup as 'indeed a great and important event', and Disraeli informed

Lady Bradford she was 'in ecstasies' when he next saw her at Windsor. On 26 November she wrote to Albert's biographer, Theodore Martin, that the acquisition would be 'a source of great satisfaction and pride to every British heart! It is *entirely* the doing of Mr Disraeli, who has *very large ideas* and *very lofty views* of the position this country should hold. His mind is so much greater, larger, and ... quicker than that of Mr Gladstone.'[18]

With the route to India better secured, the Queen now hoped that her position as ruler of a mighty eastern empire could be formalised by the title empress being conferred on her. To Disraeli she claimed that adopting the title officially 'merely would legalise the name which had been colloquially always used'. She argued it would go down well in India, as 'it suits Oriental ideas' and, anyway, nearly 'everyone thought' already she was in fact an empress. From her point of view there was the added advantage that when her daughter became Empress of Germany, she would be on a par with her.[19]

After she made clear what she expected, the prime minister informed the Secretary of State for India. Aghast, Lord Salisbury demanded, 'What *does* the Queen mean?' Disraeli knew there was no evading the issue. In January 1876 he warned the Lord Chancellor, 'The Empress-Queen demands her Imperial Crown,' and asked his advice on how to proceed. Disraeli knew – as he explained to the Queen – that the assumption of a new style for the sovereign 'must be an affair of legislation and not of prerogative'. He was confident, however, the alteration would be popular in the country. Unfortunately, in trying to slip it through Parliament without fuss and scrutiny, he found he had miscalculated.[20]

Unwisely Disraeli failed to liaise with the opposition, which might have eased the passage of his bill. Instead, after the Queen opened Parliament on 8 February 1876, the Speech from the Throne merely stated that in view of the fact the 1858 India Act had not made a formal addition to her title, steps would be taken to correct the omission. There was no mention of what her new nomenclature would be, and immediately it was apparent trouble lay ahead. Replying to the speech in the Lords, Lord Granville stated: 'No name can appeal to imagination so forcibly as that of Victoria, Queen of Great Britain and Ireland.' Even when Disraeli introduced the Royal Titles Bill on 17 February, he did not clarify what title she would assume. Robert Lowe, whom the Queen had rather taken to when he had stayed at Balmoral as Gladstone's Chancellor of the Exchequer, promptly said he hoped it was not planned to make her an empress. The title of emperor was not only 'un-English' but had been held by many 'who sank below ordinary human nature in debauchery and crime'. Henceforth the Queen invariably referred to him as 'that horrid Mr Lowe'.[21]

The Queen tried to facilitate matters by writing to Granville. She explained that as 'the measure was originated by her … she thinks she may count upon his using his influence' to prevent opposition MPs 'discussing the subject in a manner which would give her pain'. She apologised for not having raised it with him beforehand, but 'she did not expect that so simple a proposal would have elicited' such adverse language. Granville's reply astounded her. He said that consultations with colleagues had revealed unanimous hostility to her becoming empress, and if that was the title she intended to adopt, it was unlikely the proposals would pass harmoniously.[22]

On 9 March Disraeli confirmed to the Commons that 'Empress' was to be the designated title. At this point a 'brimful' Gladstone 'rushed into the fray' and made a speech of 'vituperative casuistry'. A more temperate line was taken by Hartington, who was willing to let the second reading pass so that the bill could be further examined in committee. An angry queen dismissed opposition as 'a *mere* attempt to injure Mr Disraeli … which is *most disrespectful* and indecorous'. She wrote again to Granville, who replied 'in rather a threatening tone', saying feeling against the bill remained so strong that even if she still considered the measure 'desirable in itself' – which he could hardly believe – the government should withdraw it for the present.[23]

The Queen instructed Disraeli that the bill must not be abandoned, for it would look like she had been 'rebuffed, when no such desire existed'. Disraeli himself was adamant that delay was out of the question, making it plain to doubtful Tory backbenchers that he would resign if he failed to get a majority. Like Victoria, Disraeli insisted 'there was no popular feeling against the measure', but it is unclear whether this was true. It was indicative that when the MP for Dundee pseudonymously published a pamphlet ridiculing the assumption of imperial dignity entitled *The Blot on the Queen's Head*, it sold 100,000 copies.[24]

Granville warned Ponsonby that when the bill entered committee, Hartington would propose an amendment, for otherwise the republican MP for Glasgow, Mr Anderson (who later called the bill an 'obnoxious' measure that only 'toadies, snobs and sycophants' could favour), would put forward a much 'more unpleasant motion'. On 16 March Hartington accordingly stated that while he was ready to consider some alteration to the royal style, he hoped the title of emperor would be dropped, as it inspired so much 'repugnance and distaste'. Although the amendment was rejected by a larger majority than a nervous Disraeli had expected, he had more nasty moments before the committee stage was over. 'In one of his white rages,' Gladstone 'gave ... as much trouble as he could', but on 21 March Disraeli triumphantly informed Victoria the bill had emerged without a single alteration.[25]

It still faced further 'disagreeable debate' in the Lords, despite the fact the Queen had asked her son-in-law, Lord Lorne, to warn Lord Granville that all such 'factious opposition' would be '*most personally* offensive to me'. The Duke of Somerset made 'most ungentlemanlike' remarks, but the bill nevertheless passed the Lords on 7 April, receiving the royal assent twenty days later.[26]

At times the Queen had felt guilty that what Lord Derby considered 'a royal whim indulged' had proved so hard to implement, but she was delighted Disraeli had managed it in the end. Her anger with the bill's opponents did not subside quickly. On 26 March she told Lord Lorne that men like Gladstone and Lowe had behaved so abominably, 'I don't see how I can ever look on them again.' She raged: 'They have allowed my name to be dragged about most disgracefully before the public, and have injured themselves very deeply in my estimation ... I wish that this should be known.' Lord Granville had also incurred her lasting resentment. He had known the risk, for when the MP Henry James tried to alter the wording of the proclamation announcing the change of title, Granville warned him: 'Our dear Queen never forgets and seldom forgives.' This appeared true later that summer when Granville and James attended a royal garden party. The Princess of Wales advised them to keep out of the Queen's sight: 'You are not forgiven and never will be.'[27]

That December Victoria sent Disraeli a Christmas card signed for the first time with her new official style – 'V R et I' – short for *Victoria Regina et Imperatrix*. On New Year's Day 1877, when the title was formally proclaimed, Disraeli attended a dinner party at Windsor, where he proposed the health of the Empress of India. The Queen was delighted by reports from her Indian viceroy, Lord Lytton, who held a magnificent durbar in Delhi that day to mark the occasion. Despite the famine raging in southern Indian and Bengal, it was a lavish pageant, calculated to excite 'the enthusiasm of the Asiatic mind'. A 'vast concourse' of ruling chiefs attended, accompanied by multitudinous camels, bullocks horses and elephants.[28]

* * *

On 5 May 1876 Disraeli wrote to the Queen, 'It has been one of the most exhausting and anxious sessions almost on record and unfortunately the burthen has fallen on your Majesty's chief minister who is not, physically at least, as able to bear it as in old days.' Before she left for Balmoral

EMPRESS AND EARL;

OR, ONE GOOD TURN DESERVES ANOTHER.

LORD BEACONSFIELD. "*Thanks, your Majesty. I might have had it before!* NOW *I think I have* EARNED *it!*"

'Empress and Earl' or, 'One Good Turn Deserves Another' suggested that the Queen's conferring the title of Earl of Beaconsfield on the prime minister was a fair return for his having made her Empress of India. (*Punch* cartoon, 1876)

later in the month, Disraeli told her he must retire, floating the idea that Lord Derby should take his place. The Queen would not hear of it, and when consulted Derby anyway said he did not want the position, not least because he 'could never manage HM'. A different solution was found when Victoria wrote to Disraeli on 5 June to say, 'she would be happy to call him up to the Other House, where the fatigue would be *far less* and where he would be able to *direct* everything'.[29] It was agreed that he would remain prime minister and go to the Lords as Earl of Beaconsfield. However, his ennoblement would only be announced at the end of the session, and until then he would remain at the helm in the Commons.

Disraeli doubtless hoped that his last weeks in the Lower House would not be too challenging, but the flaring up of the Eastern question ensured otherwise. Over the next two years, it would bring England to the very brink of war, as well as convulsing the nation internally. Passions rose extraordinarily high, with the Queen gripped by some of the strongest feelings of all.

After the Crimean War, the Turks had failed to improve the governance of their European provinces, so the Russians remained anxious to protect the Christian Slavs who lived in those areas. In May 1876 Disraeli refused to become involved in an international diplomatic attempt to alleviate grievances of subject Balkan peoples. This worried Victoria, for though wary that Russia's real aim was to build up its own influence in the Balkans, she did not want to give the Turks the impression that Britain was indifferent to problems caused by their misgovernment. She therefore hoped an international conference could be convened at which the powers could jointly decide how to resolve things.

On 29 May 1876 the Sultan of Turkey was deposed. The Queen was distressed, for she had warm memories of his being her guest in 1867. 'She *cannot* APPROVE these violent depositions,' she told Disraeli, becoming still more upset when Abdul Aziz was found dead a few days later. He had supposedly killed himself with a pair of nail scissors, but murder seemed more likely. For a time the Turks were left alone in hopes the new sultan would prove a better ruler than his uncle, but the Queen still feared her government's 'too Turkish' policy might push the Ottoman Empire's disaffected Christians into the arms of Russia.[30]

Alarming reports now came out of Bulgaria. In early May there had been an insurrection there which the Turks had suppressed with great brutality. On 23 June the Liberal newspaper *The Daily News* carried a fearful account of massacres conducted by Circassian irregular troops known as *bashi-bazouks*. The Queen commented to Disraeli that such stories 'would greatly injure the Turks, besides being horrible to think of'. Disraeli said the reports had not been authenticated, but Victoria still instructed Foreign Secretary Lord Derby 'to warn the Porte that these atrocities cannot be tolerated'.[31]

On 10 July Disraeli remained dismissive when questions were asked in the Commons, saying 'wars of insurrection are always atrocious'. Though the most lurid reports had proved baseless, the Queen nevertheless feared things had taken place that were 'too awful'. The prime minister told her he was trying to obtain exact information, but that the fuss was being stimulated by the opposition's desire 'to work the "atrocities" as a party question'. He continued to take a cool approach on 31 July when he referred in the Commons to 'imaginary atrocities' being 'coffee house babble'. In subsequent days, however, the opposition went on harrying the prime minister. On 7 August a preliminary report from a consul sent to investigate showed that while the *Daily News* had magnified the number of victims, dreadful things had indeed occurred. The Queen was 'horrified' to learn that 12,000 people could have been killed, telling Disraeli: 'I cannot rest quiet' until steps were taken to prevent a repetition of such ghastly events.[32]

By 11 August, which was his last day in the Commons, Disraeli was slightly on the defensive. He agreed that slaughter on such a scale was 'a horrible event', while still maintaining that press estimates of 30,000 dead, 'cartloads of heads' and 'a thousand girls sold as slaves' were unsubstantiated. He added that although the Turks should not suppose Britain would 'uphold them in any enormity they might commit', the country must be careful about abandoning its traditional policy of guarding Turkey against Russian aggression. Aware that opposition attacks had been 'very damaging', he was relieved when the session ended that day, and promptly went down to Osborne to calm the Queen. She remained anxious, judging the reports 'more and more verified', but as indignation with Turkey mounted in the country, she felt people were being 'most unreasoning' in holding her government responsible.[33]

There were hopes things might improve after the new sultan Murad V – who the Queen had heard was 'quite hopelessly stupid or mad from drink etc' – was deposed in his turn and replaced by his brother, Abdul Hamid. The latter was ultimately revealed as an appalling tyrant, but Disraeli (or Lord Beaconsfield, as he now was) was optimistic he would 'turn out trumps'.[34]

At this point Gladstone came fully on to the stage, after public meetings denouncing the government's failure to make Turkey answer for its misdeeds had alerted him to strength of feeling in the country. On 6 September he published a pamphlet entitled *Bulgarian Horrors and the Question of the East*. In this work he execrated Turkey's 'Satanic orgies', while dwelling on the 'heaps and heaps of dead' in Bulgaria, and 'the violated purity alike of matron, of maiden and of child'.[35] His pamphlet, which lambasted the government for being too supine, sold 200,000 copies.

Beaconsfield remarked that his rival's reappearance on the scene vindicated the prediction of Harty-Tarty's mistress, the Duchess of Manchester, that Gladstone's retirement had always been 'mere sham'. He told the Queen the only thing to do was to wait for the storm to abate, but in the next few weeks what she called the 'wild, senseless agitation' grew more intense. Gladstone undertook a northern tour, where he addressed excited crowds on the Eastern question. As the frenzy mounted, so Victoria's indignation with her 'reprehensible' former prime minister developed apace. On 26 September she wrote to Vicky fulminating that 'the disgraceful conduct of that mischief maker and firebrand … is very, very wrong'.[36]

Gladstone's intervention entirely changed the Queen's views on the Eastern question, for now she came to believe that it was Russia who had precipitated the crisis. She may have been influenced by information provided by Vicky and some of her other children, but her son Alfred's marriage to a Romanov princess did nothing to mitigate her hostility to Russia. When the tsar had visited England in 1874 Victoria thought him 'very kind-hearted' and had not disagreed when he said there was no reason 'why our countries should not be on the best terms'. Now she felt differently. On 28 September she wrote to Lord Beaconsfield, 'Hearing as we *do* all the undercurrent, and knowing as we do that Russia *instigated* this insurrection, which *caused* the cruelty of the Turks, it *ought* to be brought home to Russia, and the world *ought* to know that on *their* shoulders and *not* on *ours* rests the *blood* of the murdered Bulgarians.' Two days later she added she was 'indignant that we should be the dupes of unscrupulous Russia & fears that the foolish & injudicious agitation in this country has encouraged her!'[37]

As yet, the Queen did not believe that nothing could be done to restrain the Turks. In fact, as arrangements were put in place for a conference to settle problems relating to the Ottoman Empire, she devised a plan she wanted put to it whereby all Turkey's Balkan principalities should be granted independence with a Christian prince installed as ruler. This went much further than anything contemplated by Gladstone. Lord Beaconsfield had to explain to her that the Turks had only agreed a conference could be held at Constantinople after being assured that any settlement would respect the Porte's territorial integrity. The Queen thought this 'a sad look-out', that 'can only result in bolstering up a falling Empire for a time'.[38]

A bellicose speech made by Tsar Alexander in Moscow, alluding to a 'sacred mission' to protect oppressed Christians, caused her suspicions of Russia to flare up anew. As a result, when the Marquis of Salisbury was chosen by Beaconsfield to represent Britain at the Constantinople conference, the Queen wrote to him before his departure on 20 November, stressing his priority was to 'prevent Russia from having the upper hand in the East'. He must ensure Russia was not permitted to occupy Turkish territory, with Constantinople in particular being kept out of Russian hands. While 'certain people in the Opposition' were still making an outcry against the Turks, '*all really* sensible people' understood that British interests must not be 'sacrificed for the sake of Bulgarian atrocities'.[39]

Three days after Salisbury's arrival in Constantinople on 5 December, a meeting was held at St James's Hall in central London, organised by virulent critics of Turkey. Contrary to the wishes of the Liberal Party's leaders, Gladstone addressed it, and though his speech was relatively moderate compared to those uttered by other speakers, the Queen was incensed. When she heard Gladstone had escorted from the stage Mme Novikov, an alluring pan-Slav activist, she railed at his 'consorting with a Russian female spy'. In her view, the gathering was 'very mischievous and totally unconstitutional. The Sovereign is apparently a nonentity to be utterly disregarded ... Foreign affairs *never* were interfered with in this way before.' She was so scandalised by the '*disgraceful proceedings* of public men who would hand over the interests and honour of their country and sovereign to Russia!' that she hoped some of them could be prosecuted, telling Disraeli it was '*impossible* for the Queen to say what she *feels* at the *conduct* of Mr Gladstone and others'. Disraeli reported gleefully to Lady Bradford: 'She seems now really to hate Gladstone.'[40]

It all fanned the flames of Victoria's Russophobia. She made no objection when on 22 December the Cabinet agreed that Britain would not join in any coercive measures the powers might wish to impose if Turkey rejected their recommendations, leaving Salisbury with no leverage over the Turks. By this time she was disposed to overlook the

Porte's failings. On 17 January 1877 Lord Carnarvon – who, like Salisbury himself, was sympathetic to the suffering of Christians living under Ottoman rule – dined at Windsor and found the Queen 'very Turkish'. He wrote in his diary, 'I reminded her of the Bulgarian horrors. She disbelieved many – thought others exaggerated.'[41]

Hardly surprisingly, the Constantinople conference was a total failure. Although the Russians had moderated their demands, the Porte absolutely refused all proposals. Since Salisbury could only exert 'moral pressure', he had no chance of making them more reasonable. After the conference disbanded, the Russians made a fresh diplomatic initiative, hoping to form a new league of powers to pressure Turkey. When Britain was invited to sign a protocol to this effect, the Queen advised against it, cautioning Beaconsfield, 'No one can fathom Russian duplicity.' She was worried that he was too influenced by 'crusader' members of the Cabinet such as Salisbury and Carnarvon, and robustly declared that 'mawkish sentimentality' for Balkan people 'who hardly deserve the name of real Christians' should not dictate policy. Beaconsfield agreed it would be helpful if she tried 'to brace [Carnarvon's] mind a little', whereupon she 'talked pretty strongly' when Carnarvon next came to Windsor, deploring he did 'not take the proper view'.[42] This was the first of many interventions she made with members of the Cabinet during the crisis, arguably exceeding her constitutional powers in doing so. Despite her efforts, on 31 March 1877 Britain did sign the protocol with Russia. The Queen was 'rather alarmed', but need not have worried, for on 9 April the Turks rejected it.

This made it almost inevitable that Russia would declare war on Turkey, but the Queen was far from taking the view that Turkish obstinacy had left Russia little alternative. Having told Beaconsfield on 17 April she dreaded receiving 'a slap in the face from these false Russians', she wrote a memorandum for him to read in Cabinet. This declared it essential to show 'a bold and united front to the enemy in the country as well as outside it ... It is not the question of upholding Turkey; it is the question of Russian or British supremacy in the world!' She wrote an even stronger private letter to the prime minister: 'To him she will say (and he may make use of it) that, if England is to kiss Russia's feet, she will not be a party to the humiliation of England and would lay down her crown.'[43] This was the first of numerous abdication threats she would make throughout the crisis.

On 21 April Russian armies crossed the Turkish border. The Cabinet met to discuss the situation and the Queen's memorandum was read out, allegedly with 'marked effect'. Beaconsfield 'pressed strongly for action' against Russia, saying that otherwise Russian armies would take Constantinople within four months, but almost no members of the Cabinet were in favour. Victoria found this 'very painful'. She wrote to Beaconsfield: 'She wishes for no general war – God knows! For no one abhors it more than she does,' but 'to let it be thought that we shall never fight … would be to abdicate the position of Great Britain as one of the Great Powers … and another must wear the Crown if this is intended.'[44]

Throughout the following year the Queen would maintain her aim was to preserve peace by making it plain Britain could not stand by while the Turks were 'blotted out of the face of Europe and *exterminated*'. In fact, for much of that time, she was longing to fight Russia. When her daughter Vicky hoped it would not come to war, the Queen fired back, 'I am sure you would not wish Great Britain to eat humble pie to these horrible, deceitful, cruel Russians?' She discounted the idea that Russia had any noble motives, asserting, 'It is not for the Christians … but for conquest that this cruel wicked war is waged.' There could be no doubt of 'the *end* to which *all* Russians look to – namely to make Constantinople the Russian capital', and Russia was also committing 'monstrous' war crimes that 'throw the so-called "Bulgarian atrocities" in the shade'. She told Beaconsfield: 'Her very blood boils' that the Turks, 'fighting for their very existence, are … constantly blamed and lectured', when they were 'our poor allies, whom we so cruelly abandon to a shameful and detestable enemy and invader!'[45]

As well as her repeated abdication threats (which no one took very seriously), the Queen wrote memoranda for the Cabinet, breaching the convention that a monarch should accept the advice of ministers rather than seeking to shape policy. She also closeted ministers, encouraged by Beaconsfield, who thought it 'of the utmost importance that Your Majesty should … prepare the minds of those' whose attitude needed stiffening. 'Your Majesty's demeanour has a beneficial effect on a timid or hesitating minister,' he assured her. When the Chancellor of the Exchequer changed his views after seeing Victoria, Beaconsfield 'perceived that a "Faery Queen" had waved her magic wand over him'.[46]

On learning of the way royal pressure was being applied, Gladstone was appalled. In May 1878 he was told in confidence by a minister who had resigned earlier in the year that 'Cabinet ministers have been sent for to receive "wiggings" from the Queen.' To Gladstone this showed 'how little at present within the royal precinct Liberty is safe'. He claimed it 'recalled James II and the Bill of Rights' and was 'an outrage ... totally unknown in every Cabinet in which I had served'. He was also – rightly – fearful that Beaconsfield passed on to her details of Cabinet discussions, reporting to her which ministers were reluctant to take a firm stance against Russia. Gladstone believed that if Beaconsfield was betraying colleagues in this way, he 'was guilty of a great perfidy', as well being responsible for 'the corruption' of the Queen.[47]

Other observers felt that Beaconsfield himself deplored some of the Queen's interventions. Writing of the way the Queen 'in personal communications with various members of the Cabinet ... brought her influence to bear', Lord Carnarvon suggested that while the 'original impulse proceeded from Disraeli ... as the war proceeded ... he was no longer able to control the force which he had called into being for a much more limited purpose'. Carnarvon noted: 'He on more than one occasion in Cabinet described himself as unable to check or moderate the pressure exercised by the Queen upon him,' which Carnarvon thought 'at least partly true'. In December 1877 Beaconsfield spoke to Lord Derby 'of the constant pressure put upon him by the Queen, who has been in favour of war from the first, and of his resistance'.[48]

It is not easy to gauge whether Beaconsfield was skilfully using the Queen's bellicosity to push his colleagues in the direction he wanted, while always pulling back in time so war was avoided. Derby mused in March 1878, 'how far he really wishes for war, how much he leads the Queen or is led by her ... I cannot decide'.[49] He was certainly more realistic than the Queen of the need to take at least a majority of his Cabinet with him, and also perhaps of the devastating cost in both financial and human terms of fighting Russia. It is indisputable that during these months the Queen was in a highly excitable and unmanageable state, but when Beaconsfield exerted himself – using threats of resignation almost as specious as her own talk of abdication – this did have a sobering effect on her.

In late April 1877 Gladstone infuriated Victoria by announcing his intention to table parliamentary resolutions demanding that Britain take steps against Turkey, if necessary in concert with Russia. Undeterred by the fears of Lords Granville and Hartington that this would split the Liberal Party, Gladstone made a powerful speech in the Commons on 7 May. Initially the house was hostile, but gradually his rhetoric won over many sceptics. After five nights' debate, his resolutions were rejected on 14 May by a majority of 130. Gladstone was nevertheless confident 'much good has been done'. The Queen took a different view. The government's victory over the 'wild' and 'wicked' man – whom she characterised to Lord Beaconsfield as 'that great *enemy* to his country *Mr Gladstone*!!' – was 'a great thing'.[50]

On 6 May 1877 Lord Derby had confirmed that Britain would be neutral and had given a list of conditions Russia must observe if it wished this to continue. Although Beaconsfield ventured that Victoria would not be displeased by the 'spirited … though cautious' provisos, they fell far short of what the Queen had wanted. In particular, the bland statement that 'England' could not 'witness with indifference' Constantinople's 'passing into other hands' was much too weak for her liking. Over the next two months she kept trying to chivvy ministers into adopting a different stance, so much so that on 27 May Lord Salisbury grumbled to Lord Carnarvon, 'Balmoral is becoming a serious nuisance.'[51]

The Queen became more concerned on seeing the Russian reply to Britain's declaration of neutrality. Containing what she considered 'endless traps & sly dodges', it left it ambiguous whether Constantinople might be occupied for a short time. Already worried by Derby's 'extreme imperturbability', she warned him: 'We may find ourselves checkmated.' She was hardly reassured by Derby's suggesting that the best outcome would be for Turkey – which was faring badly in the war – to accept terms offered by Russia, even if they were severe. Britain's going to war with Russia 'would be unpopular even now, and far more so when once entered upon'. The Queen was so shocked that within a fortnight she was suggesting that Derby should be replaced as foreign secretary.[52]

For the next two months Beaconsfield came up with various schemes designed to show that Britain would not tolerate Russia crushing the Turks, or reaching Constantinople, though he had to accept that none of his ideas were feasible. The Queen begged him, 'Be bold!' and not to worry about ministerial resignations, as he would have the country with him. Beaconsfield explained he had to face the fact, 'there are not three men in the Cabinet' who would agree to war with Russia.[53]

On 18 May the Queen had gone to Balmoral for her usual late spring break, and from there pestered Beaconsfield relentlessly. 'The Faery writes every day and telegraphs every hour. This is almost literally the case,' Beaconsfield informed Lady Bradford. The Queen was back at Windsor on 22 June, her 'warlike ardour' all the stronger. She told her war minister, Gathorne Hardy, she 'would have liked to shake' Lord Derby, while the Russian ambassador, Shuvalov, reported to St

Petersburg that ministers lived in dread of 'some warlike extravagance' on her part. Shuvalov was being fed information about Cabinet proceedings by Derby's wife, probably without the foreign secretary's knowledge. The Queen and Lord Beaconsfield soon identified Lady Derby as the source of leaks about ministerial divisions, which featured prominently in Shuvalov's despatches home. He claimed Cabinet members feared war being imposed on them, as an 'expression of sovereign will', and that they were outraged by '*this conspiracy of a half-mad woman with a minister who once had genius but has degenerated into a political clown*'.[54]

On 12 July the Queen was delighted when Beaconsfield wrote he would soon inform the Cabinet that if the Russians occupied Constantinople, even briefly, Britain would regard this as a *casus belli*. The prime minister thought this would probably cause the resignations of Derby, Salisbury and Carnarvon, but provided he could count on her support, he would 'carry your Majesty's affairs to a happy and credible conclusion'. In fact, when the Cabinet met on 14 July, Beaconsfield encountered much greater opposition than expected. Only two members were in favour of the course proposed and the most the others were prepared to accept was that Russia should be given 'friendly warning' against a temporary occupation. The prime minister tried to persuade Victoria this amounted to 'something like an ultimatum notice to Russia', but she quoted back his own dictum that if Russia took possession of Constantinople for a short while, '*England ... would no longer exist as a Great Power*'.[55]

She was so frantic Beaconsfield had to go and see her at Windsor. On returning he told Derby: 'He thinks he has quieted the royal mind, but ... if the volcano breaks out again he does not know what he shall do.' Sure enough, the Queen was soon at him again writing, 'she always feels hopeful and encouraged when she has seen Lord Beaconsfield' but then 'somehow or other ... nothing material is done!!' She asked him to confirm he had said that if the Russians did not quit Constantinople within a given period, war would be declared. Beaconsfield had indeed given her this impression but overcame the difficulty by artfully offering to resign if he had inadvertently misled her. The prime minister added winningly: 'He errs, perhaps, in being too communicative ... but it relieves his mind ... to ... confer with your Majesty without the slightest reserve, and this necessarily leads to your Majesty sometimes assuming that steps will be taken, which are necessarily delayed, and sometimes even reversed.' Hastening to placate him, the Queen wrote that she was '*greatly grieved* that *he* thinks she meant *him* by what she said. How could he think so? She meant his colleagues!'[56]

Victoria did not cease to harangue her ministers. Lady Salisbury, who was also friendly with Shuvalov, if not quite so indiscreet as Lady Derby, told him that the Queen 'has lost control of herself, badgers her ministers and pushes them towards war'. Before the Cabinet met on 28 July Victoria telegraphed both Beaconsfield and Derby a curt instruction: 'Gallipoli must be occupied.' Derby replied, 'somewhat roughly to his royal mistress', that it was too late for that, and while this would annoy the numerically insignificant 'party which does not conceal its wish for war … the great bulk of the nation desires nothing so much … as … peace'.[57]

Derby was so averse to risking war that he was dilatory about carrying out the Cabinet's decision to tell Russia that if Constantinople appeared in danger, the British fleet would be sent there. When he eventually did as instructed, he sent what the Queen called a 'Derby-like telegram', stressing that England intended to adhere to its neutrality. An enraged Victoria demanded the tsar must be explicitly warned: 'we *will not let him have Constantinople!* Lord Derby & his wife *most likely* say the *reverse right & left & Russia goes on!* … The Queen must say she *can't* stand it!'[58]

To circumvent Derby, Victoria and Beaconsfield engaged in covert diplomacy. In August there arrived in England Colonel Frederick Wellesley, a British military attaché who had been stationed at Russian headquarters. After the Queen saw him at Osborne, she and Beaconsfield had the brainwave of asking him to return to the front and deliver a 'confidential message' to the tsar, warning that if Russia embarked on a second campaign, Britain would enter the war on the Turkish side. To Victoria's disappointment Wellesley's mission had a 'perfectly sterile' outcome. Tsar Alexander avoided a second campaign by continuing with the first, decreeing that rather than enjoying a winter respite, his troops must battle on without a break.[59]

The Russian advance had now halted before the town of Plevna (Pleven) in Bulgaria, but the Queen was sure they would not be held there long. At Balmoral she worked on visiting ministers, and on 7 September produced a memorandum passionately arguing that Britain must abandon neutrality. She wanted Beaconsfield to read it to the Cabinet, but he only circulated it 'with discretion' to colleagues who were likely to approve. On 24 September he unveiled to her a new plan, entailing Britain offering to mediate between Turkey and Russia. If

Russia refused to accept terms, Britain would cease to be neutral, offering material assistance to Turkey as soon as Constantinople was threatened.[60]

Victoria was delighted: 'His proposal is so clear that the Queen *cannot* think that any one could be so shortsighted & unpatriotic as to oppose it.' In fact, when the Cabinet met on 5 October, ministers were distinctly unenthusiastic. As an alternative, they were ready to consider remaining neutral provided Russia gave a secret promise not to occupy Constantinople. The Queen contemptuously dismissed this as 'a dangerous snare'. She warned: 'With regard to any *secret* assurance, or indeed *any* assurance from Russia ... she considers that of *no value.* They will *promise* but not keep it'. Despite her concern, Beaconsfield presented the plan in Cabinet on 5 November, and afterwards told her triumphantly opposition to it had been 'routed'. Derby's diary reveals he consented simply because he thought the scheme meaningless, and that Beaconsfield only pushed for it because the Queen was pressing him to do something and this provided a 'semblance of action'.[61]

The Queen became even more agitated when Derby delayed presenting a diplomatic note to the Russian ambassador. She demanded to know why nothing was being done to stop the 'horrible carnage', warning some days later that looking on while Turkey was crushed would fill her with 'a feeling of *disgrace*'. To calm her, Beaconsfield wrote what he described to Derby as a 'very stiff letter', and claimed she had 'taken it well'. She nevertheless worked herself up again when the note drafted by Derby for presentation for Russia was much weaker than Beaconsfield, and many of the Cabinet, had envisaged. Before going down to Windsor to reveal the text to the Queen on 5 December, Beaconsfield told Derby, 'I don't anticipate a very agreeable audience.'[62]

Maddened by Derby's stalling, the Queen tried to humiliate him by alerting ministers to his wife's dealings with Shuvalov. She sent Beaconsfield a letter about the leaks, which he decided not to read to the Cabinet. As he told her, he feared the foreign secretary would be 'seriously offended if such delicate matters ... were brought forward' in front of colleagues, but he did privately inform Derby what the Queen had written. Victoria then prevailed upon the Dean of Windsor to write to Lady Derby about her familiarity with Shuvalov. In an outraged reply, Lady Derby professed shock that the Queen had been fed stories suggesting she was guilty not just 'of imprudence & bad taste' but even 'of betraying ... my country'. The Queen was unimpressed by her denials. When Gathorne Hardy told her Derby had himself expressed concerns in Cabinet about Russia learning of their proceedings, Victoria suggested the foreign secretary 'should look at home' for the culprit.[63]

The British note to Russia was presented to Shuvalov on 13 December, but by that time Plevna had fallen, opening a path to Constantinople for the Russians. 'In despair,' the Queen trumpeted, 'We *must* ... take a strong line *now*.' On hearing of the town's capture Beaconsfield had summoned the Cabinet. He told the Queen he wanted Parliament to meet earlier than planned so that he could request a vote of credit and offer mediation services to the belligerents. Reiterating he must be '*very* firm', and not give way even if Derby resigned, Victoria instructed: 'Make what use of the Queen's name Lord Beaconsfield wishes.' She did not doubt 'Most of the country is strongly anti-Russian,' as well as feeling compassion (as the British '*always do* feel') for the plight of the underdog, Turkey. She concluded rousingly: 'England will *never* stand (not to speak of her Sovereign) to become *subservient* to Russia.'[64]

At the Cabinet held on 14 December Beaconsfield duly conveyed the Queen's views to his colleagues. Lord Carnarvon wrote to Lady Derby: 'I suppose you heard of the extraordinary, and I should think, unparalleled communication from the Queen which we received?' The ministers listened to Beaconsfield's suggestion that Parliament should be recalled in 'dead silence'; when it was discussed, Salisbury, Carnarvon and Derby were all opposed. The next day, 'to show publicly my support of Lord Beaconsfield's policy', Victoria went to luncheon at the prime minister's country home, Hughenden. The Queen enjoyed her visit immensely, driving from the station with Beaconsfield through beflagged and crowded streets, and planting a tree in Hughenden's grounds. The historian Edward Freeman, whose detestation of the Turks made him one of Beaconsfield's most venomous critics, wrote furiously of her 'going ostentatiously to eat with Disraeli in his ghetto'.[65]

On 17 December the Cabinet reconvened. When the three Lords still would not comply, Beaconsfield threatened to resign. This made the Queen 'very anxious', but after the Cabinet met again the following day the prime minister was able to tell her: 'The three recusant peers surrendered.' A delighted Queen wrote to her eldest daughter: 'Thank God ... the country at large is roused to the danger of Russian aggression and ambition.' With Beaconsfield having 'taken the reins firmly in his hands ... we are now ready to act in the right sense'.[66]

'Lord Beaconsfield adopts your Majesty's motto, "BE FIRM"', he told her on 27 December, but in fact he had not yet gained his way. On 23 December Lord Derby had asked Lord Salisbury to help him resist the prime minister, writing: 'I know what the pressure of the Court is on our chief & am convinced that the Queen has satisfied herself that she will have her way (it is not disguised that she wishes for war).'[67] They must therefore ensure that the Cabinet was consulted before military preparations were embarked upon, and also that when Parliament opened, the Speech from the Throne was innocuous.

The new year brought the Queen a nasty shock, delivered by her colonial secretary, 'Twitters' Carnarvon. Despite his stance on the Eastern question, she had a residual fondness for the man she called that 'absurd (though in some respects clever) little Lord Carnarvon'. However, on 2 January 1878 she was exceedingly provoked when he declared to a commercial deputation that no one was 'insane enough to desire' another Crimean War. By coincidence, Carnarvon was scheduled to visit Osborne the next day, and Beaconsfield commented grimly: 'I do not envy him his audience.' Sure enough, a livid Queen 'pitched into him with a vehemence and indignation inspired by the British lion'. Carnarvon 'looked like a naughty schoolboy who was being scolded', although he still maintained that Britain had no business fighting Russia. The Queen promised her daughter that her views would prevail. 'Oh! That Englishmen were now what they were!!' she wrote in a passion. 'But we shall yet assert our rights … and "Britons never will be slaves" will yet be our motto.'[68]

For the moment, the peace party in the Cabinet was still in the ascendant. On 9 January, after serious disagreements, the forthcoming Queen's Speech was transformed into something much less bellicose. Because the country was already suffering a trade depression there was a widespread feeling in the Cabinet that war would hit the economy further, although the Queen was incredulous her ministers could be guided by a 'low sordid love of gain'. She warned Beaconsfield she could not remain sovereign of a country readying itself 'to kiss the feet of the great barbarians … Oh, if the Queen were a man she would like to go and give those Russians … such a beating.' Beaconsfield replied, perhaps slightly ambiguously: 'It is something to serve such a Sovereign.'[69]

She wrote a memorandum for the Cabinet that met on 12 January, demanding whether their earlier acceptance that an advance on Constantinople would free Britain from its declaration of neutrality had been 'mere words?' That day's Cabinet was again 'most stormy'. Derby threatened to resign, as did Beaconsfield, but Lord Salisbury, who was coming round to the view that the Russians must be checked, devised a formula enabling his colleagues to stay together for the present.

Meanwhile, the Russians were making steady progress. Sultan Abdul Hamid telegraphed Victoria asking that Britain assist in procuring an armistice, but when the Queen offered to act as an intermediary, the tsar returned 'such a rude answer' that it made her 'blood boil'.[70]

Parliament met on 17 January 1878. The Queen was not only disappointed by a speech designed to 'satisfy the Opposition and Peace party more than it does me', but distressed the government did not immediately request a vote of credit. She was highly disturbed, however, when Beaconsfield sent her a despondent letter. He predicted the imminent break-up of the Cabinet, which would make fighting the 'inevitable war with Russia' a still more daunting task. The prime minister foresaw 'many other trials. But as long as your Majesty wishes it, he will struggle at his post.' The Queen was upset that he seemed 'so *much out of heart*. But he must *not be that*, and he must not give way an *inch*,' or worry about Derby and Carnarvon resigning. She offered him the Garter to cheer him up, but he said now was not the time for that.[71]

To the Queen's relief, Beaconsfield soon recovered his spirit. Despite the Turks seeking an armistice, the Russians were still advancing towards Constantinople. The prime minister could therefore argue on 23 January that action was essential, convincing a majority of the Cabinet that a vote of credit must be sought and ironclads sent through the Dardanelles. Lord Salisbury was in favour of these measures, so although Derby and Carnarvon still dissented, they found themselves isolated. Both men resigned.

Victoria was thrilled. 'Great news, feel so relieved!' she wrote in her journal. However, the resignations were not immediately announced. On 24 January the situation was changed by a telegram from the British ambassador in Constantinople, Sir Henry Layard, announcing (wrongly as it turned out) that the Turks had accepted Russian peace terms. The order to send the fleet was countermanded, despite the Queen's insisting by cypher it must not be rescinded. She could take some comfort in still being able to bid Carnarvon 'good riddance', as he did not withdraw his resignation, but Derby was prevailed upon to return to the Cabinet.[72]

On 28 January Chancellor of the Exchequer Sir Stafford Northcote announced the government would be seeking a £6 million vote of credit. While it was being debated, the Queen kept up her pressure on Beaconsfield, predicting that if the fleet was not sent at once, 'some awful catastrophe' would turn Britain into 'the laughing stock of Europe'. She was sure 'the Russians are only trifling with the Turks about the armistice' to gain 'time to get to Constantinople'. When

Layard sent a telegram via India saying that Russia had cut telegraph cables between Constantinople and Europe, Victoria felt vindicated. Raging at 'Russia's monstrous treachery!' she insisted: 'We must *at once* show what we feel at being *duped & led by the nose!* … The error, the fatal error, of recalling the fleet has no doubt encouraged the monstrous Russians … Only act quickly & firmly & show that Great Britain will *not be trampled upon*!'[73]

At one in the morning on 8 February the government secured a huge majority for the vote of credit, and a few hours later the Cabinet agreed the fleet should be sent to Constantinople. Yet the Queen remained far from happy, particularly when Beaconsfield confessed that on its own, a British naval force could not keep a Russian army out of Constantinople. Declaring herself 'utterly ashamed', she wrote: 'The Queen expects that we *shall* use force to drive them out … She *can & will not* abide it!' When she sent the prime minister another wild letter lambasting 'the cowardice' of Derby and Carnarvon and threatening 'to lay down her thorny crown', Beaconsfield felt it was time to curb her somewhat. On 10 February he said her words had caused him 'real unhappiness' and he hoped that on reflection she would not view the situation 'in so dark a light'. He continued coolly, 'The present state of affairs is not … a catastrophe' but if she felt that her ministers had let her down, 'Your Majesty has the clear constitutional right to dismiss them.' This highly dubious statement served to bring the Queen under control. She hastily assured him: 'He must not for a moment think she would wish to change her government.' While she did regret Britain's neutrality, she had 'perfect confidence in him and great confidence in all his colleagues *but one*'.[74]

On 14 February the British fleet sailed through the Dardanelles, anchoring some way off Constantinople. It still seemed possible the Russians would occupy the city, and war fever and anti-Russian feeling were consequently mounting in England. Gladstone's stance now made him unpopular. A jubilant Queen reported to Vicky: 'He is hooted and hissed in the streets and theatres, whereas Lord Beaconsfield is cheered wherever he goes!' She began to feel optimistic, for 'the country is thoroughly roused, and the monstrous perfidy, treachery and lying of the Russians … has enraged all patriotic people'. The state of public opinion was demonstrated by the popularity of a music hall song, whose chorus ran: 'We don't want to fight, but, by Jingo, if we do/We've got the ships, we've got the men, we've got the money too.' The ditty gave rise to a new word – 'jingoism' – denoting gung-ho nationalistic fervour. The

Queen was rightly reputed to be one of the greatest Jingos of all. Lord Derby recorded: 'At the most vehement war meetings, her name is introduced ... and enthusiastically applauded: so that her feelings are evidently known.' He was not surprised the public were aware of her 'passionate eagerness for war ... for she has taken every means to make it so'.[75]

On 3 March news came that the Turks had signed the Treaty of San Stefano with the Russians. 'Stormy' Cabinets took place on whether Britain should insist on assessing if the agreement was admissible. War with Russia remained a real possibility. The foreign secretary was most reluctant to press Russia in any way, prompting the Queen to demand, 'Lord Derby *must* go.'[76] On 16 March Britain formally requested that the peace terms be submitted to an international conference, for, as details had emerged, it had become clear that in its current form the treaty was unacceptable. Among other things it provided for an enlarged Bulgaria to be ruled by a Prince of Russia's choosing; it also granted Russia major territorial gains in the Asian part of Turkey.

The Russian ambassador gave a 'categorical refusal' to Britain's request on 25 March. Beaconsfield responded by stating in Cabinet that the army reserve must be called out and secret arrangements made to bring Indian troops to Europe. In addition, some island or port in the eastern Mediterranean should possibly be seized from Turkey to serve as a military base. Derby at once resigned – a development the Queen hailed as 'an unmixed blessing'.[77]

Lord Salisbury took Derby's place at the Foreign Office. The Queen assured Vicky: 'Lord Salisbury will make an excellent foreign secretary. He is very able and energetic.' She was pleased with the circular Salisbury produced for continental governments on 1 April. This stated that the Treaty of San Stefano must be submitted to the judgement of Europe, although Britain would not insist on the status quo before the Russian-Turkish War being maintained in entirety. The Queen described it to her daughter as, 'very able and clear ... universally admired by everyone'. As Salisbury took control of the situation, she noted approvingly that he 'writes very frequently, keeping me *au fait* of everything'.[78]

After Salisbury made it plain that Britain would not attend a conference if Russia remained intransigent, its ambassador, Shuvalov, entered into secret negotiations with him. Shuvalov then went briefly back to St Petersburg, returning to England on 22 May with points on which Russia would be prepared to compromise. The Queen telegraphed Beaconsfield: 'Have the greatest suspicions of Russian proposals,' but

Salisbury believed they formed the basis for accommodation. As an additional precaution, he pressured the sultan into concluding a secret convention whereby Britain was awarded Cyprus in return for offering Turkey a defensive alliance. On 30 May the Russians signed a secret memorandum, and with so much confidentially sorted out in advance, Britain felt able to accept an invitation to the Congress of Berlin. The Queen was not entirely pleased that the prospect of war had receded, telling Beaconsfield, 'She must own to disbelieving any *permanent* settlement of peace until we have fought and beaten the Russians, and that we shall have only put off the evil hour. But truly happy shall she be if she is mistaken.'[79]

Victoria was also alarmed when Beaconsfield told her he would attend the congress as one of Britain's two plenipotentiaries – with Salisbury being the other. Her first impulse was to declare 'his health … should on no account be risked. Berlin is decidedly too far,' but the prime minister said the job was too important to entrust to 'mere professionals'. She then relented, acknowledging, 'No one has such … power of conciliating men … or has a stronger sense of the honour and interests of his Sovereign and country.' Even so, before he left for Berlin on 8 June, she confided to her diary: 'Feel so afraid we may not be able to resist the Russian wiles.'[80]

The congress began on 13 June, and the Treaty of Berlin was signed a month later. Having boasted by telegraph of 'bringing about a settlement which will probably secure the peace of Europe for a long time, and will certainly not disgrace your Majesty's throne', Beaconsfield added, with a final gallant flourish, that he felt privileged at being 'the trusted servant of a sovereign whom he adores'. He arrived back in London on 16 July, driving through cheering crowds from Charing Cross station to Downing Street. There Henry Ponsonby was waiting to present him with a bouquet from the Queen, before the prime minister declaimed from the windows that he had brought back 'Peace with Honour'. He accepted the Queen's offer of the Garter, provided that Salisbury was made a member of the Order too but declined a dukedom. Victoria wrote rapturously, 'High and low are delighted' with the Treaty, 'excepting Mr Gladstone, who is frantic'.[81]

On 18 July Beaconsfield defended the treaty in the House of Lords, and then came down to Osborne to regale the Queen with accounts of behind-the-scenes intrigues at Berlin. He had already written her entertaining reports, but now, 'in excellent spirits' and with 'a great deal to tell', supplemented his earlier tales with thumbnail sketches of the principal personages at the congress. Naturally he did not minimise his own role in procuring a tough settlement that had left the Russians 'very sore'.[82]

Beaconsfield's triumph was sealed when the treaty was debated in the Commons. Hartington made measured criticisms, but on 30 July Gladstone delivered what the Queen called a 'most rabid' speech, denouncing what had been achieved. Despite his strictures, the government won the ensuing division with a majority of 143. The Queen considered this 'a great thing', although she still regretted that the Russians had not been chastened so much as she would have liked. On 5 November, the anniversary of a British victory during the Crimean War, she wrote to Vicky: 'Inkerman Day. I fear we shall have to have some of those, before these horrible, wicked, deceitful Russians are … properly humbled.'[83]

The Treaty of Berlin had the warm approval of the British public; the popularity it brought the government would not, however, last. Their standing would soon be damaged by an economic recession, poor harvests and foreign policy difficulties. Having narrowly avoided being involved in war in Eastern Europe, Britain became embroiled in conflicts in Asia and Africa that went badly.

The first problem arose in Afghanistan. After the Amir of Afghanistan, Sher Ali Khan, received a Russian diplomatic mission at his court, and then denied entry to a British one, the Queen was clear that 'this insult cannot be tolerated and we shall have to fight'. Several of her ministers felt less certain of this, but Victoria telegraphed Beaconsfield: '*if* we waver and delay, our prestige will be fatally lost in India'. She was therefore relieved that on 26 October the Cabinet decided the amir must be ordered to apologise. When the amir failed to do so, an army was sent to Afghanistan and Parliament was recalled for December. Just before it met, the Queen told Lord Salisbury, ministers must 'hold a very firm tone' and ensure that everyone was aware the Russians 'were at the bottom of it all'.[84]

It was fortunate for the government that General Frederick Roberts's field force won some victories just before Parliament convened on 5 December 1878, so ministers could announce that the amir was seeking terms. This meant that both Hartington's and Gladstone's attacks on Afghan policy were less effective.

* * *

The government soon had to cope with a worsening situation in South Africa. The Queen had been pleased when the experienced Indian administrator Sir Bartle Frere had been sent to the Cape in spring 1877. She was sure his 'knowledge of native character and wild races as well as his great prudence are calculated to do great good', but Frere's posting hardly improved matters. In September 1878 Frere began warning that war with the Zulus was imminent, although, as Colonial Secretary Hicks-Beach explained to the Queen, the government believed that if the Zulus were treated with 'forbearance and reasonable compromise', all would be well.[85] Ignoring directives that forces available to him must be used only for defensive purposes, on 11 December Frere delivered an ultimatum to the Zulu King, Cetshwayo. The news only arrived in England on 2 January 1879, nine days before the ultimatum expired, so the government could not prevent Frere despatching a force to Zululand under Lord Chelmsford.

On 22 January the British sustained terrible losses after the Zulus attacked their camp at Isandlwana, a disaster for which Chelmsford's incompetence was largely to blame. When the news arrived on 11 February, the Queen at once assured Frere and Chelmsford of her confidence, although Beaconsfield was angry with both men. The government considered recalling the pair, but ultimately decided only to issue official rebukes and to send out another officer to take overall command in South Africa. The Queen was displeased, saying while Frere might have been at 'fault ... in declaring (perhaps too hastily) war', he should not be humiliated. War with the Zulus, 'would *certainly have* come, though it may have been somewhat precipitated'. Beaconsfield had to tell her there would be ministerial resignations if the change was not implemented.[86]

Another disaster occurred in Zululand, when the prince imperial, son of the late Napoleon III and the exiled Empress Eugenie, was killed. The prince had contrived to get himself attached to the staff of the British force in Zululand, but on 1 June he was fatally speared when his scouting party was surprised by Zulu warriors. The Queen was appalled when news of his death arrived on 19 June. 'Poor dear Empress! Her only child, her all, gone!' she lamented. She was sure, he 'would have made such a good Emperor for France one day', but now was haunted by visions of 'those horrible Zulus' slashing at the 'dear young man'.[87]

Beaconsfield, who was not a Bonapartist, had not wanted 'that little abortion, the Prince Imperial' to go in the first place. He thought 'nothing could be more injudicious' than the Queen's decision to go to

Chislehurst on the day of the funeral, to watch the prince's coffin being conveyed to church in an elaborate procession. The prime minister feared the French republican government would protest at her honouring a dead pretender, but Victoria could not be deterred from showing solidarity with the prince's bereaved mother.[88]

After being sent reinforcements, Chelmsford did manage to defeat the Zulus at Ulundi on 4 July, but this did not mitigate his earlier failures in Beaconsfield's eyes. On his return to England, Chelmsford was received at Balmoral by the Queen, who found him 'singularly pleasing and gentlemanlike'. The prime minister baulked, however, when she suggested he invite the general to Hughenden. He wrote that having been responsible for a dreadful disaster, Chelmsford had required 20,000 troops 'to reduce a country not larger than Yorkshire'. Victoria protested she was 'grieved and astonished ... at his severity', eliciting from the prime minister only another 'sharp letter'. Greatly ruffled, she complained to Lord Cranbrook she 'was never so snubbed in her life'.[89]

On 19 September news came that the Zulu King, Cetshwayo, had been captured. Conscious that he was chief of the 'finest and bravest race in South Africa', the Queen did not want him demeaned by being forced to wear English dress. She felt still better disposed when he sent a message, 'that he had always looked on me as his mother'. This did not mean she considered the Zulu war unnecessary. On the contrary, she maintained that without pre-emptive measures, 'the colonies might have been attacked, people murdered and horrors committed'.[90]

Her faith in Britain's imperial destiny was not shaken by a fresh setback in Afghanistan. On 3 September the British representative at Kabul was killed with all his entourage, necessitating the despatch of another expedition to punish the Afghan tribesmen. The Queen believed the answer was to take over Afghanistan completely, arguing, 'It is *not* for *aggrandisement* but to *prevent war* and *bloodshed*.' What was more, 'We shall have the *same to do* in South Africa', for the annexation of Zululand would 'be the *safest* and least *expensive*' solution. Not only would it prevent future wars, it would 'produce the moral effect of our superiority over these people, which is all important'. She regretted that Parliament had been told 'we shall keep nothing' from either recent war and asked the war secretary, Lord Cranbrook, to ensure the next Queen's Speech did not rule out acquisitions. Cranbrook said the government was committed to 'avoid needless annexation' – but that this phrase was open to interpretation.[91]

* * *

The Queen was still highly satisfied with her prime minister and his colleagues, though she was conscious the feeling was not universal. After seven years in office, the government would have to seek re-election, and she dreaded the prospect of a Liberal victory. She therefore wrote to Lady Ely, asking her to request the newly knighted Sir Henry Ponsonby 'to *get at some* of the Opposition'. If there was a change of government after the election – as she hoped there would not be – 'the *principal* people of the Opposition should *know* there *are certain* things which I never can *consent* to'. These included, 'letting Russia have her way in the East', while 'our position in India, and in the Colonies, *must* be *upheld*'. Furthermore, it was out of the question for Gladstone to occupy a Cabinet position, 'for I never COULD have the slightest *particle* of confidence in Mr Gladstone *after* his violent, mischievous, and dangerous conduct for the last three years'. She added, 'Sir H Ponsonby has so many Whig friends that he might easily *get* these things *known*.'[92]

Ponsonby obediently sounded out Lord Granville, who said he would do his best to meet the Queen's wishes, but that he personally thought it unlikely the Liberals would gain a majority at the next election. Ponsonby relayed this to the Queen, adding that in the meantime the Liberals would of course go on attacking the government in their speeches. She at once demanded, 'But why ... ?' and when Ponsonby said it was the duty of an opposition to oppose, she fired back: 'Exactly so. They don't care whether the government is right or wrong, but they oppose it simply for party reasons.'[93]

When the rising Liberal politician Sir William Harcourt heard that the Queen had warned that Gladstone would be unacceptable to her in any ministerial capacity, he commented that if Gladstone became aware there had been an 'attempt to exclude him by the prerogative', it would be the very thing to make him determined to resume the Liberal leadership. As yet, however, although Victoria feared Gladstone might be willing to join a Liberal Cabinet, she did not conceive she might have to take him back as prime minister. At this stage there was reason to think Gladstone himself would eschew this. In late November 1879 he wrote to the veteran campaigner John Bright saying even if there was a popular call for him to become Liberal leader again, he could not act on it, partly because 'nothing could be so painful, I may almost say so odious to me, as to force myself ... upon the Queen'.[94]

Only four days before writing this letter, Gladstone had embarked upon a Scottish speech-making tour to introduce himself as the candidate for the Midlothian constituency, using all his rhetorical skills to commend himself to the masses. In resounding and compelling performances, he attacked what he would later call 'Beaconsfieldism' in all its aspects. He mocked the conferring of the title of 'Empress' on the Queen as 'theatrical bombast and folly' and deplored the government's pursuit of 'false phantoms of glory'. Beaconsfield's policy of upholding the Ottoman Empire in defiance of its atrocities was 'in contradiction to the whole spirit ... of civilised mankind', while 'by the most wanton invasion of Afghanistan', ministers had reduced that country to 'a miserable ruin' and 'driven mothers and children forth ... to perish in the snow'. In South Africa, 'a nation whom we term savages ... have been mowed down by hundreds and by thousands, having committed no offence'. At every venue, he was given a rapturous reception by ecstatic crowds, with an estimated 20,000 attending the largest gathering, held at the Waverley Market in Edinburgh.[95]

To the Queen the whole thing was an abomination. 'Mr Gladstone is going about in Scotland, like an American stumping orator, making most violent speeches,' she wrote in her diary. For Hartington and Granville, Gladstone's courting of the voters was also an embarrassment. Hartington had already several times contemplated giving up being Liberal leader in the Commons because Gladstone's insubordination undermined his own authority, and now he recognised that after doing well in an election, the party might decide that Gladstone was the only possible prime minister. If so, he thought it 'only fair to the Queen, to the country, to the party and to myself that this should be acknowledged at once'.[96] Nevertheless when prominent Liberals met on 16 December, they decided to retain the present leadership – so the Queen remained oblivious that Gladstone's return was a real possibility.

When Beaconsfield informed the Queen on 5 March 1880 that he would be seeking a dissolution, initially her only concern was that an election would interfere with her plans to attend the confirmation in Hesse-Darmstadt of her granddaughters, whose mother Princess Alice, Duchess of Hesse, had died of diphtheria in December 1878. After the prime minister promised that her travel arrangements need not be disrupted, her thoughts turned again to the possibility the Liberals might win. She drew up another memorandum for Ponsonby to show to leading Liberals, explaining that while ready to endorse prudent 'progress in a right direction', she could not support 'constant change for change's sake'. Fearing the document was bound to 'create a row', Ponsonby confined himself to dropping 'hints' about the Queen's thinking.[97]

Victoria left England for Germany on 24 March and was therefore absent for the election campaign. Back in Midlothian, Gladstone renewed his onslaught on the government, but Hartington also made speeches with uncharacteristic energy. From Hesse-Darmstadt the Queen moved on to Baden-Baden, so she was there when election results started coming in. To her horror, it soon became clear there had been a Liberal landslide. On 2 April she despairingly telegraphed Beaconsfield: 'Nothing more than trouble and trial await me.' She told Ponsonby, who was in Germany with her, 'the Queen cannot deny she ... thinks it a great calamity for the country'. Her strongly conservative son Prince Leopold shared her views, stating in a telegram: 'It shows what wretched ignorant misled idiots most of the electors must be.'[98]

On one point Victoria was clear. Writing to Lord Dufferin, British ambassador in St Petersburg, she was adamant, 'Mr Gladstone is *out* of the question.' She told Ponsonby on April 4, 'She will sooner *abdicate* than send for or have any communication with that *half-mad firebrand* who would soon ruin everything and be a *Dictator*.'[99]

Because Beaconsfield said there was no reason for her to be 'unnecessarily hurried', the Queen did not hasten to leave Germany. In the meantime Ponsonby did his best to convince her that a Gladstone premiership might be unavoidable, defending the former prime minister as 'loyal and devoted'. Annotating these words with three exclamation marks, Victoria retorted: 'He is *neither* for *no one* CAN be' who had vilified her government and shown such 'disgraceful spite & personal hatred to Lord Beaconsfield ... The *only* excuse is – that he is not quite *sane*.'[100]

Having returned to England on 17 April, the Queen saw Beaconsfield the following day. He had initially assumed she would offer Lord Granville the premiership, but Victoria had not forgiven the latter over the Royal Titles Bill. When she claimed Granville had become 'too liable to radical influence', Beaconsfield agreed, adding Hartington would be 'the right and constitutional course'.[101]

Although the Queen was almost reconciled to the possibility that Gladstone might join a Liberal government, she still did not imagine he would lead one. She told Beaconsfield she 'felt sure he would not expect or wish it', unaware that, having convinced himself that he alone had carried the election for the Liberals, Gladstone felt 'morally forced into this work as a great and high election of God'. On 13 April Gladstone's emissary Lord Wolverton had informed Granville and Hartington that Gladstone had in the election results discovered circumstances which demanded his return as prime minister, and that he would not consider serving in a subordinate position.[102]

Gladstone confidently awaited Victoria's call and was surprised not to have heard from her by 20 April. In some puzzlement he recorded: 'This blank day is I think probably due to the Queen's hesitation or reluctance.' In fact, on 22 April she invited Hartington to form a government. He at once said it was impossible because no administration would be sustainable unless Gladstone joined it, and he understood that would not happen. It was therefore 'best and wisest' to send for Gladstone at once. The Queen told him outright: 'There was one great difficulty, which was that I could not give Mr Gladstone my confidence.' After vainly trying to allay her indignation with Gladstone, Hartington agreed he and Granville would jointly sound out Gladstone about whether he would be in Hartington's Cabinet. The Queen expressly allowed Hartington to repeat to Gladstone all she had said during the audience.[103]

Hartington and Granville accordingly went to see Gladstone, who promptly confirmed he would not be a minister. He nominally offered to support a government formed by either Hartington or Granville, but hedged this with so many qualifications it was clear he would have no qualms opposing them should any differences arise. On 23 April Hartington returned and entreated Victoria not to 'think him and Lord Granville cowardly' for advising her to offer the government to Gladstone. On reflection he had decided against passing on her exact words, and (the Queen recorded) he also 'strongly advised me not to begin by saying that I had no confidence whatever' in Gladstone, 'as one did not how such a man … would take it'. Victoria reluctantly accepted he was right – and also took it well when, after requesting permission to 'speak very plainly', Hartington said, 'HM had never allowed her personal feelings to interfere with the discharge of her constitutional duties' and he trusted this would be the case now.[104]

At 6.30 that evening she saw Gladstone, receiving him, as he noted in his diary, with that 'perfect courtesy from which she never deviates'. She explained that Hartington and Granville had advised her to send for him, whereupon he 'humbly accepted' the premiership. While she refrained from saying she distrusted him, she did state it was 'very important that facts should remain unaltered', and she also expressed pain about 'strong expressions used' in recent months. Having assured her 'he considered all violence and bitterness as belonging to the past', Gladstone kissed hands. Throughout she had conducted herself in a manner he described as 'natural under effort', but when the interview ended the Queen was 'truly thankful this trying ordeal was over'. It was perhaps some solace that 'Mr Gladstone looked very ill and haggard,' which gave a plausibility to his prediction 'he should not be able to go on for long'. Even so, she felt very unhappy about the change, writing to Vicky, 'I had felt so sure he could not return.' 'To me,' she told her daughter, '"the people's William" is a most disagreeable person.'[105]

When it became clear that Beaconsfield would be leaving office, Victoria had written to him, 'The grief to her of having to part with the kindest and most devoted, as well as one of the wisest ministers the Queen has ever had, is not to be told.' He had replied that whereas the political setback 'costs him a pang ... his separation from your Majesty is almost overwhelming', as his relations with her 'were his chief, he might almost say his only, happiness and interest in this world'. Before long, the Queen persuaded herself there was no need for 'a real parting'. She wrote that she looked forward to corresponding 'on many a *private* subject and without anyone being astonished or offended, and even more without anyone knowing about it'. Beaconsfield could be very helpful, not just 'about my family and other things', but also 'about great public questions' – which of course should really have been taboo once he was in opposition. The fact that the Queen knew this is shown by her suggestion that they stay in touch through indirect channels. She told Beaconsfield, 'I have many about me who will write to you and I hope you will to them – so that we are not cut off. That would be too painful.' She tried to persuade Henry Ponsonby to collude with her, sending Lady Ely to suggest that Beaconsfield's former private secretary, Lord Rowton, could write to the Queen on Beaconsfield's behalf via Ponsonby. Sir Henry answered shortly, 'Most decidedly not.'[106] Despite this rebuff, she communicated with Beaconsfield nonetheless, sometimes using Lady Ely or Prince Leopold as conduits. On occasion she also saw Beaconsfield in person, for he went on coming to Windsor to dine and sleep.

In their surviving letters from this period, politics were certainly not avoided. For example, in summer 1880 Beaconsfield assured her the government's Irish Land Bill could lead to 'the destruction of all property' and predicted that the House of Lords would throw it out. When this duly happened, Victoria asked gleefully, 'Do *you* EVER remember *so* many voting against the government to whose party they belong? *I* do *not*.' That September she wrote that the government's treatment of

Ireland, Turkey and Afghanistan made her anxious, declaring: 'I look always to you for ultimate help … I … see as little of those I *cannot* unfortunately have *confidence* in as possible'. She added, 'This is a *very secret* letter; but I *must* hear your opinion and give vent to my feelings.'[107]

Replying on 23 September, Beaconsfield deplored that the Queen's inability to maintain confidential relations with her ministers deprived them of her wisdom. He observed, 'For more than forty years your Majesty has been acquainted with the secret springs of every important event that happened in the world, and … in constant communication with all the most eminent men of your kingdoms. There must, necessarily, have accrued to a Sovereign so placed, such a knowledge of affairs and of human character that the most gifted must profit by an intercourse with your Majesty, and the realm suffer by your Majesty's reserve.'[108]

Five weeks later she confided, 'As regards affairs they are sad indeed … so confused and so dreadful. Oh! If only I had you, my kind friend and wise councillor and strong arm to help and lean on! I have *no one*.' She informed him the government intended to bring in a Coercion Bill for Ireland, and Beaconsfield passed this on to Lord Salisbury with the comment, 'So much for intelligence.' He soon obtained more from the same source, for on 1 December, just before he came to Windsor for a visit, the Queen wrote, '*What* a state of affairs in Ireland! I shall have much to say to you.'[109]

Perhaps the most irresponsible thing Beaconsfield did during these months was to encourage the Queen in January 1881 when she refused to sanction the speech the government submitted to her just before the opening of Parliament. She complained to him that the home secretary was maintaining that the content of the speech was a matter for ministers alone, rather than embodying her own opinions. Beaconsfield mischievously assured her this was 'a principle not known to the British constitution'.[110]

The last time she saw him was on 1 March, when he attended a party at Windsor. Three weeks later Beaconsfield developed a cold, and an equerry sent to enquire after his health could not give a good account. On 28 March Beaconsfield wrote from his bed, 'I am prostrate, though devoted,' and the Queen at once sent him primroses. They were accompanied by a note explaining, 'I meant to pay you a little visit this week, but I thought it better you should be quite quiet and not speak.' Later she regretted 'very keenly not having seen him', but for Beaconsfield himself it was perhaps rather a relief to be left alone as the end drew near. When asked by a friend if he wished for a royal visit he answered, 'No, it is better not. She would only ask me to take a message to Albert.'[111]

His health continued to deteriorate as pneumonia set in. The Queen despatched her own doctor to attend, but it was impossible to save Beaconsfield. When Lord Rowton informed his former employer of Victoria's concern, the old man murmured 'the dear Queen'. On 19 April he died. A bereft Victoria wrote to Rowton: 'I can scarcely see for my fast falling tears ... The loss is so *overwhelming* ... Never had I *so* kind and devoted a Minister, and very few such devoted friends ... To England (or rather Great Britain) and to the *world* his loss is *immense.*' She had been 'full of hope he might be my minister again' and had not anticipated he would suffer such a rapid decline. As she told Lord Salisbury, 'The Queen can think of little else and the bitter tears will flow again and again.'[112]

Beaconsfield had specified he wished his funeral to be at Hughenden church rather than Westminster Abbey, so he could be interred at his wife's side. Prince Leopold represented his mother at the service on 26 April, but four days later she paid her last respects in person. The crypt at Hughenden was reopened so she could place a wreath of china flowers on his tomb. Afterwards she went back to the house where she had lunched with him, and 'seemed to hear his voice, and the impassioned eager way he described everything'.[113] However, she had to accept he was gone for ever and the Disraeli era had come to an end. Much to the Queen's sorrow, the era of Mr Gladstone was by no means finished.

10

Mr Gladstone 1880–1885

Hartington had tried to reconcile the Queen to Gladstone's return by pointing out that, whereas he himself would have had to placate the left wing of the Liberal Party by bringing many radicals into government, Gladstone's authority was such that he would be able to appoint a predominantly Whig Cabinet. Victoria had taken this in, and was all the more furious when, in her eyes at least, '*the very reverse*' happened.[1]

At first it had indeed appeared that Gladstone would appoint only moderates. Even then, the Queen found much to grumble at. She objected that Lord Ripon was not 'strong-willed' enough to be Viceroy of India, and that Lord Chancellor Selborne's 'constrained and peculiar manner' made her uncomfortable. She would have liked Lord Hartington to go to the War Office, rather than Gladstone's choice, Hugh Childers. Gladstone insisted that Hartington must be Secretary of State for India, and although Childers would have liked to become Chancellor of the Exchequer, Gladstone unwisely took that post himself. While not very pleased by all this, Victoria could hardly claim these men were firebrands. In fact, on 26 April 1881, Ponsonby told her the radicals were so disappointed, they were complaining 'this was a Tory government'.[2]

The very next day Victoria was 'astonished and somewhat put out' when Gladstone informed her that he wished to appoint Joseph Chamberlain to the Cabinet. Formerly a wealthy screw manufacturer, Chamberlain had been MP for Birmingham since 1876. Before that, he had been a progressive Mayor of Birmingham who had municipalised water and gas supplies and overseen a programme of slum clearance. He had also refined Liberal Party organisation with the aim of lessening Whig dominance, and he was known to be contemptuous of the aristocracy. Understandably nervous of having a 'Birmingham demagogue' as her President of the Board of Trade, she at once wrote to Gladstone asking for confirmation that Chamberlain had never spoken disrespectfully of the throne.[3]

The Queen had another shock when Gladstone submitted the name of Sir Charles Dilke for the post of under-secretary at the Foreign Office. Prior to the election Victoria had asked Ponsonby to let his Liberal friends know that she could not accept Dilke as even a junior minister, for if someone who had been 'personally most offensive' about her was given any position, it would be 'a sign to the whole world that England was sliding down into democracy and a republic'.[4]

By the time Gladstone had an audience with the Queen on 28 April, he had submitted 'more unexpected names' for junior appointments. When he started justifying his choice of men, Victoria 'interrupted ... saying I feared the Government was becoming very Radical'. Gladstone remained calm, pointing out it was usual to include some progressives in Liberal ministries, and 'these people generally became very moderate when they were in office'. He claimed Dilke now regretted his actions when 'young and foolish'. The Queen grudgingly agreed Sir Charles could take up his designated post, provided he expressed regret for past misdemeanours in writing.[5]

As Victoria saw it, a ministry of 'extreme Radicals' had been foisted upon her. Although Gladstone had many differences of opinion with Chamberlain, she was sure the prime minister constantly deferred to the man she characterised as '*his evil genius*'. She later complained: '*all* the *worst men* who had no respect for kings and princes ... *were put into the government in spite of me*'. Furthermore, 'instead of *stemming* ... Radicalism,' Gladstone '*heads and encourages it*'.[6]

This lay in the future. The day after her audience with the prime minister on 28 April, Ponsonby begged 'leave to observe that your Majesty is managing Mr Gladstone most perfectly and makes him listen, which he scarcely will do with others'. In her journal the Queen herself admitted, 'he was very courteous throughout ... & repeatedly asked me whether he did not weary me'. Certainly things had gone much better than might have been expected from the letter she had written to Lord Granville on 23 April, saying that taking back the man who had '*really* for the last *3 years preached a Crusade*' against Lord Beaconsfield would constitute 'the *greatest* trial she can have'. Defiantly she had stated, 'The Queen *cannot* & will not forget it. This must *prevent* any *cordiality* between *herself* & Mr Gladstone.'[7]

Granville did not pass this on to Gladstone, so although the latter was aware of what he called 'her special identification with Beaconsfieldism', he was slow to realise the depth of Victoria's aversion. Partly this was because initially she had tried to hide it, but after a visit to Windsor in July 1880, the prime minister mournfully observed, 'She is, as ever, perfect in her courtesy: but as to confidence, she holds me now at arm's length.' By that time reasons for disagreement had so multiplied that the Queen informed her daughter that things were going, 'Oh, far worse than I even thought,' adding a few days later: 'We are in a miserable condition thanks to the "People's William".'[8]

Gladstone was apt to blame 'Disraeli … the Grand Corrupter' for what he regarded as a deterioration in Victoria's character. In September 1880 he wrote to the Viceroy of India, Lord Ripon: 'There has been a serious and unhappy change. To what influence it is due, we may readily conjecture. What strikes me is the decline of practical understanding … The high manners and the love of truth remain I am sure unimpaired: and these are what we have to rely on.' The same month Gladstone's private secretary recorded that Victoria's letters were now 'all grumbling and finding fault', and ten days later she and Gladstone were at such variance over policy towards Turkey that the prime minister seriously feared, 'HM may turn round upon us and say she has no further occasion for our services.' The Queen herself occasionally felt pangs of guilt about her behaviour. On New Year's Day 1881 she regretted in her journal, 'how oversensitive & irritable & how uncontrollable my temper is … But I am so overdone, so vexed, & in such distress about my country that that must be my excuse.'[9]

Gladstone had at least given up nagging her to perform duties such as opening Parliament, even though he feared it was 'perhaps unmanly' of him not to press her to do more.[10] Such forbearance was uncharacteristic, for at other times he did not shirk confrontation. In particular, in the spring of 1881 he embarked on a long-running dispute with her that would have been better avoided.

In March of that year Gladstone first asked Victoria to confer a peerage on the army's quartermaster general, Sir Garnet Wolseley. The Queen disliked Wolseley, but Gladstone wished him to go to the Lords in order to push through army reforms devised by the secretary of state for war, Hugh Childers. The proposed changes were extremely distasteful to the Queen, who claimed they had made Childers '*hated* in the army'. Gladstone was well aware Wolseley's ennoblement would be 'a nasty pill' for Victoria but was still 'greatly annoyed' when she rejected it. Gladstone's private secretary, Edward Hamilton, thought it a 'pity to make too much' of what was just 'a woman's whim', but Gladstone and Childers remained 'very hot' on the matter. Enraged by what she called

'Mr Gladstone's ... inexplicable pertinacity', the Queen wrote to Granville complaining that he acted 'as if all she said was nothing ... She must say that *no* Prime Minister has ever treated the Queen with such want of respect for her opinions.'[11]

For his part, Gladstone started muttering about resigning. This alarmed Lord Granville, who protested it was 'not a good case on which to have an upstanding fight with the Crown. It is one on which plausible adverse arguments might easily be raised.' Threats of resignation should be reserved for more serious matters, he said.[12]

As their relations steadily worsened, Gladstone feared the Queen's wilfulness would bring most serious consequences. In March 1881 he 'spoke in a mournful way' to Ponsonby, taking a 'gloomy' view of the future. 'Formerly I saw no reason why Monarchy should not go on here for hundreds of years,' he told Sir Henry, but now 'the way Monarchy has been brought to the front by the late government in political and foreign affairs has shaken my confidence.' He feared a crisis that 'may weaken the power of the Crown with the rising mass of politicians ... I dread this and I dread appearing in antagonism to the Queen, which I am not.' Gladstone would tell Lord Derby that by the time he started his second term as prime minister the Queen had developed 'a disposition to self-assertion which was new'. In August 1881 he completely lost patience when Victoria tried to block the appointment of the radical Leonard Courtney as under-secretary at the Colonial Office. Gladstone burst out to several colleagues: 'I think this intolerable. It is by courtesy only that these appointments are made known to HM.' Soon afterwards he confided to John Bright that his 'position relatively to the Queen ... has certainly been upon the whole worse, and now greatly worse, than I had anticipated', and that November he talked of resignation with Hartington's brother, Lord Frederick Cavendish. One reason he gave was, 'his position towards the Queen was intolerable in one who throughout life had reverenced her as a constitutional sovereign, inasmuch as he now had to strive daily with her on the side of Liberty as opposed to Jingoism'. The problem was clearly weighing on his mind a great deal, for he told the Dean of Windsor: 'Whereas she used to be the most constitutional of sovereigns, she has now grown an imperious despot.'[13]

Certainly it was true the Queen did not always support her government as was her duty. She sometimes tried to sow division in ministerial ranks by writing to Cabinet members urging them to defy Gladstone. During their row over Wolseley's appointment, the prime minister realised she would inevitably 'feel for a soft place in the heart of the successive Ministers who may appear at Balmoral'. As yet she did not actively intrigue with opposition leaders, but she could hardly claim to be above party. In July 1883 Gladstone would tell his private secretary there was 'no greater Tory in the land'; two years later he went so far as to say the Prince of Wales was 'far more fitted for that high place [sovereign] than her present Majesty'.[14]

Bizarrely, throughout it all, their meetings in person were frequently amicable. Edward Hamilton noted in 1882: 'Audiences are good things as her graciousness and friendliness come out much more when face-to-face' and 'they seem to understand each other so much better at the end of them.' Unfortunately the effects were rarely lasting. In August 1883 Gladstone's visit to Osborne was deemed a great success, but soon afterwards she wrote him a vitriolic letter, savaging him for going on holiday abroad without permission. The following February Gladstone was again 'much pleased' by his reception at Osborne, yet the presentation copy he took away of her book, *More Leaves from our Highland Journals*, merely bore the cold inscription: 'To Mr Gladstone from the Queen.' As before, their real tussles took place on paper, for Hamilton noted, she never held back 'when she has the pen in her hand'.[15]

For a time the Queen hoped, unrealistically, that once back at the Foreign Office Lord Granville would prove an ally in her fights with Gladstone. In her journal of 23 April 1880 she had noted that when she saw Granville, he 'said he feared he had lost some of my confidence, but hoped to be able to regain it. I replied he certainly had done so, but that I should be only too glad if he could regain it.' The exchange had given the Queen false ideas about Granville's willingness to assist her. The following September she told Beaconsfield she was keeping communications with Gladstone to a minimum, preferring to 'write and telegraph very strongly' to Granville. She flattered herself that he 'takes all my remarks in good part', but in fact Granville's courtly manner had misled her: his loyalty to Gladstone was absolute, and he found himself in an awkward position when she wrote pouring out her wrath against the prime minister. Once, after passing on a particularly violent letter of 30 May 1881, he asked Gladstone whether it would be wisest to pretend he had withheld it. Gladstone said no, but Granville did screen him from some of her letters.[16]

It did not take long for the Queen to become disillusioned with the 'weak as water' foreign secretary. In September 1880 she informed Vicky she considered 'poor Lord Granville no longer up to his work'. By May

1882 her indignation had grown. She angrily informed Ponsonby that, like the rest of the government, Granville was guilty of 'want of respect & consideration' and 'lately *ignores* all her remarks! She feels *hurt & indignant* as he is the *only* friend (though he has never *really* proved to be that) or at least the only *person* she has been in the habit of speaking out to in the Cabinet.' Victoria alleged that Granville did not really support government policies, but 'has not the courage of his opinions & therefore is not of the slightest use to the Queen'.[17]

With Granville disappointing her, Victoria hoped Lord Hartington would prove more amenable. Hartington did in fact disagree with Gladstone on a number of issues, although details of Cabinet dissensions were kept from the Queen. In October 1880 she was pleased by his visit to Balmoral, recording: 'Lord Hartington is certainly wonderfully fair & impartial & listens to all my arguments.' Having divined that he desired a severe policy in Ireland, she tried to enlist him actively to press for this, and in June 1882 told him outright that she wished 'he were at the head of the government instead of Mr Gladstone'.[18]

The Queen thought she had guarded against the Conservative government's achievements being reversed, for when she had invited Gladstone to form a ministry she had stressed 'it was very important that facts should remain unaltered'. Rather surprisingly Gladstone had 'entirely agreed', citing precedents when incoming governments had abided by what their predecessors had done. In his case, this was always going to be problematic. As early as June 1880 Victoria bewailed that the Liberals were 'step by step undoing all Lord Beaconsfield's great work'.[19]

Policy towards Afghanistan was one major source of discord. After the war there, Beaconsfield's viceroy, Lord Lytton, had proposed that Kandahar should be permanently garrisoned with British troops, but Gladstone and Hartington agreed the place would be just a liability. The Queen insisted that the 'honour and name of the Empire' made it imperative the city was retained, but on 6 September 1880 Hartington told her the Cabinet had decided against this. 'Much annoyed. It quite upset me,' she wrote in her journal. She kept trying to delay the decision being implemented, demanding that opinions of military men on the spot should first be sought. Gladstone exploded to Childers: 'I do not think it to be any part of her Majesty's duty to point out to us whom we should consult.'[20]

Partly because Hartington was not explicit enough with her, the Queen failed to realise the government remained committed to

Kandahar's abandonment. As a result, there was a dreadful furore when on 5 January 1881 Earl Spencer and the ebullient home secretary, Sir William Harcourt, appeared at Osborne with a copy of the speech due to be delivered at the opening of Parliament the following day. The Queen was supposed to approve it in council, but when she saw it contained an announcement that Kandahar was to be evacuated, she demanded that paragraph be omitted. Ponsonby telegraphed Gladstone, but no reply came for some hours, and the ministers said they could not alter the text on their own responsibility. Deadlock ensued, as positions became more entrenched. While genial enough when in good humour, Harcourt was a combative man who was quite ready to stand up to the Queen. 'The Speech from the Throne,' he said, 'was in no sense an expression of HM's individual sentiments but a declaration of policy made on the responsibility of her ministers' – a correct constitutional doctrine that astounded Victoria. To Ponsonby she spluttered, she had been 'treated as a child by being kept in ignorance and then forced at the last moment to assent'. Ponsonby suggested she gave a qualified approval to the speech, but Harcourt said that amounted to rejecting it; in doing so she would 'eject the ministry' and that, 'on the eve of the opening of Parliament, was revolution'.[21]

In the end the Queen agreed to approve the speech but instructed Ponsonby to let those present know she was 'highly displeased'. At the Privy Council meeting, 'I spoke to no one & the Ministers nearly tumbled over each other going out.' She told Ponsonby she had started the day with a headache, 'and this incredible behaviour of Ministers did *not* make it better. The Queen has never before been treated with such want of respect and consideration in the forty-three and a half years she has worn her thorny crown.' Next day she sent him to London to tell Gladstone, Granville and Hartington 'she will not *stand* such treatment', adding that Gladstone should not think he could boss her about as Bismarck did Emperor William.[22]

The government's handling of southern Africa caused the Queen still deeper vexation. In his Midlothian campaigns, Gladstone had repeatedly condemned the Tory government's 1877 annexation of the Transvaal, the area north of the Vaal River that had been taken over by Boer descendants of Dutch colonists who had settled at the Cape before the British arrived there. Despite his disapproval of the Transvaal's appropriation, when the Liberals came to power Gladstone said it could not be reversed but promised in due course to confer free institutions on the Boers who lived there. In December 1880 the impatient Boers had risen up and proclaimed a republic. Over 150 British troops sent to deal with the insurrection were killed or wounded in clashes. The Queen did not doubt this called for energetic reprisals, but in the belief the Boers had genuine grievances, the government offered to negotiate if the Boers disarmed.

Victoria wrote indignantly that, while she was anxious for peace, such a 'confession of weakness' would have 'disastrous results'. The government persisted with their policy, but unfortunately poor communications resulted in the Boers failing to respond to the offer until the deadline set for their answer had expired. As a result the British commander, Major General Colley, took up a position at Majuba Hill with a view to resuming hostilities. On 27 February 1881 the Boers attacked and wiped out his force, with Colley himself among the dead. A guilty Gladstone asked himself, 'Is it the hand of judgement?' The Queen's response was more robust. She was appalled when the Cabinet agreed with Gladstone that an armistice should be concluded. Horrified that the Transvaal would be converted into a British protectorate, rather than a full possession, Victoria argued that 'even the semblance of any concessions after our recent defeats would have a deplorable effect'. On 22 March a 'tumultuary' Cabinet considered her objections, only to override them, and when detailed terms were subsequently hammered out, the Boers were treated more generously still. In her journal Victoria wrote despondently, 'Feel utterly disgusted and disheartened.'[23]

She vented her anger in a particularly splenetic letter to Granville, deploring the Cabinet's 'fatal decision'. She lamented, 'One after the other, *everything is given up* ... *& all* to *satisfy the* Radicals whom alone Mr Gladstone ... leans upon'. What shocked her most was that Mr Gladstone's 'promise ... to *leave Established facts* & not to try & undo them – which certainly applied to the Transvaal – has been broken and *cast to the winds*'. Once 'the dreadful ... state of Ireland' was taken into account, 'Lord Granville *must* admit that the government have been eminently unsuccessful in 1881!' Her only comfort was 'that she has done her duty in warning the government again & again though – alas! – always in vain'. She instructed Granville to show her letter to Gladstone, which he reluctantly did. The prime minister's secretary, Edward Hamilton, was scandalised. 'This from a constitutional monarch!' he commented.[24]

* * *

It was Irish matters that caused the Queen the greatest anguish and fury. Ireland had suffered particularly severely from the agricultural depression that had begun in 1878, making it impossible for tenants to pay rents and a consequent rise in evictions. Discontent at this was harnessed by the Irish National Land League, who linked agrarian grievances with nationalist sentiment. Founded in 1879, the league was now led by Charles Stewart Parnell, MP for County Meath, himself an Anglo-Irish Protestant landlord who loathed the British. Even during the Beaconsfield government, Irish Home Ruler MPs had caused disruption in Parliament by obstructing proceedings. Their number had increased at the last election, so their potential to cause trouble at Westminster under Parnell's leadership was all the greater.

In Ireland itself, the league was suspected of discouraging even tenants who could afford to pay rent from doing so. It was likewise thought to connive at, if it did not actually incite, agrarian crimes. Gladstone found in the state of Ireland 'a judgement for our heavy sins as a nation ... for the rights of others trampled down, for blood wantonly and largely shed'. The Queen saw Irish discontent as disloyalty, and believed the solution lay in repression.[25]

Victoria was therefore displeased when, within three weeks of coming to office, Gladstone informed her he would not be renewing the Tories' Irish Peace Preservation Act. On 12 June 1880 she had been still more concerned to hear he intended to bring in a temporary measure to compensate Irish tenants evicted for non-payment of rent if it could be proved their failure arose from want of means. The prime minister insisted it was a 'small measure' that should not alarm anyone, but the Queen deemed it subversive of property rights. Others thought likewise, with some fearing it was the prelude to similar legislation being introduced in England. On 10 July the Queen wrote a '*very confidential*' letter to Granville. Describing the Irish Land Bill as 'a great misfortune', she begged: 'Could it not be given up?' Granville told her he would be glad if the Commons threw it out, but it was impossible to abandon it. This prompted another letter from Victoria about the bill's '*extreme* danger'. She wished Cabinet to dissuade Gladstone from proceeding, not least because 'the House of Lords will never pass it & there surely Mr Gladstone must be urged not to try & force it through.'[26]

The Queen was sure – rightly – that many Liberals in the Commons disliked the bill and voted '*against their convictions*' because they were fearful of bringing the government down. She felt vindicated when the bill passed its third reading by a majority of only sixty-six. This did not deter Gladstone from sending it to the Upper House but on 3 August the Lords overwhelmingly rejected it, with many Liberal peers voting alongside Conservatives. In her journal the Queen hailed it with a single word: 'Tremendous!'[27]

When the Lords threw out the bill, Gladstone had just gone down with pneumonia, and the Queen wrote to his wife urging 'quiet and complete rest'. Mrs Gladstone was touched by her solicitude, though what Victoria really wanted was for the prime minister to retire on health grounds. She took advantage of his absence by writing another confidential letter to Granville, implying she would have to abdicate if the government continued to align with those who 'encourage *reform* for the *sake of alteration* and *pulling down what exists* ... A *Democratic Monarchy* ... she will not *consent to belong to. Others* must be found *if* that is to be.' The Queen followed this by wondering on 1 September, 'if Mr Gladstone *will* recover his mental and physical powers *sufficiently* to continue in office?' A fortnight later she reported to Vicky he was still not fully recovered – 'and I doubt (and fervently hope) he won't be able to go through another session'. Gladstone confounded her by proving more resilient than she would have liked.[28]

Following the rejection of the Compensation for Disturbance Bill (as Gladstone's current land bill was officially known), the state of Ireland markedly deteriorated. Murders rose, along with outrages such as the maiming of livestock, 'cruel and barbarous treatment of poor dumb animals' that particularly enraged the Queen. The Land League introduced a new weapon, urging that any man who imposed high rents or condoned evictions should be isolated, 'as if he were a leper of old'. The verb 'to boycott' came into being after Lord Erne's land agent, Captain Boycott, was one of the first to be subjected to this treatment. The Queen was sure punitive legislation was needed. Gladstone, however, was instinctively averse to measures such as the suspension of habeas corpus. He argued that Irish homicide statistics did not yet warrant it, despite the escalation in property offences.[29]

The government instead decided to prosecute Parnell and some other members of the Land League for conspiring to prevent payment of rents. Legal difficulties meant the case could not begin till late December, but the Queen was pleased action was being taken against 'this monstrous Land League', for 'Mr Parnell's language, encouraging as it does *murder*' had resulted in 'a state of affairs unequalled in any civilised nation'.[30] She nevertheless thought more should be done, agreeing with W. E. Forster, the Chief Secretary for Ireland, who was not only calling for additional repressive legislation, but wanted Parliament recalled for an autumn session. Gladstone staved off the demand by conceding that Parliament could meet earlier than usual in the new year. For the last six weeks of 1880 the Cabinet debated what to do when the session opened, with Forster heading those who wanted a reimposition of Coercion Laws, and Chamberlain and John Bright threatening to resign in that event.

On 18 November the Queen telegraphed Lord Granville: 'Rumours are plentiful of Cabinet dissensions and I ought to be fully informed.' Gladstone thought, 'HM has rather odd ideas,' for he held that 'Cabinets existed for the purpose of ... enabling Ministers who differed to thrash out their differences – and that the Queen was only concerned with the results ... presented to her ... in the name of the Cabinet as a whole'. Having been summoned to Windsor, Granville reassured the prime minister, 'I told her next to nothing', but on 19 November Gladstone revealed to her he personally desired to introduce a new Irish Land Bill simultaneously with measures to restore order and protect property. The Queen was sure this would not improve matters. As she put it to Lord Cowper, Ireland's Lord Lieutenant: 'The more one does for the Irish, the more unruly and ungrateful they seem to be.'[31]

Victoria worked to enlist other ministers on her side. She wrote to Forster, deploring what she called 'the present [Nationalist] reign of terror in Ireland', and suggested to Hartington that Whigs in the Cabinet should gang up on Gladstone. 'Nothing but *boldness* and firmness will succeed ...' she declared. '*Don't yield* to satisfy Messrs Bright and Chamberlain, let them go.' She succeeded insofar as Hartington wrote to Gladstone on 19 December, saying that the ministry's current policy towards Ireland caused him 'pain and humiliation'.[32]

Despite Gladstone's conviction that a successful Land Bill would 'settle things once for all' in Ireland, the Queen was negative about its prospects. She quoted to him the words of an Irish peer, who dismissed the tenancy issue as 'a *mere pretext*' that justified 'sedition and revolution. The land has nothing to do with it.' At the end of December, Gladstone could tell her that the Cabinet had resolved to introduce special measures designed to tackle the lawless state of Ireland. A new Land Bill would also be introduced, but the repressive legislation would take priority. Victoria wrote that she was pleased to hear it, though if done earlier it 'would have checked the evil before it reached its present formidable aspect'.[33]

When Parliament opened on 7 January 1881, it was announced that Coercion Laws would be followed, once passed, by a Land Bill. At once Nationalist MPs set out to be obstructive, with Parnell in the forefront after his trial in Dublin collapsed. The main provision of the Bill for the Protection of Persons and Property introduced by Forster on 24 January was that habeas corpus would be suspended in Ireland, allowing detention without trial. Thanks to Parnellite filibustering, progress was agonisingly slow, prompting the Queen to demand: 'Surely something must be done to put down these shameless Home Rulers?' Arrangements had to be made to speed up procedure, preventing the Irish from holding up legislation indefinitely.[34]

Cabinet discussions on the Irish Land Bill drafted by Gladstone and Forster proved highly contentious, but on 7 April the prime minister presented it to the Commons in a masterly speech. The bill provided that Irish tenants could apply to a special court that could adjudicate on whether rents were fair and reduce them if excessive. It was an immensely complex piece of legislation, but Gladstone guided it through all its stages, and was rewarded by the bill passing its third Commons reading on 29 July. It still faced formidable obstacles, for it was inevitable that the Lords would give it a hostile reception, particularly as Lord Salisbury felt so strongly. Sure enough, as soon as they debated it, several damaging amendments were put forward. The Queen wrote to Gladstone on 7 August suggesting he accept as many as possible, for some merely provided '*security* to the landlords which was *much needed*'. Gladstone replied that without meaningful land reform, Ireland would remain in uproar, but 'short of the mutilation of the Bill', he would try and be conciliatory.[35]

Despite his assurances, when the bill returned to the Commons, Gladstone stood out against all significant amendments. For a time it looked as though matters would not be resolved. The Queen became irritated with both sides. She was always ready to blame Gladstone, who she thought had shown himself 'contemptuous' of peers' sensibilities, but was aware Salisbury was not being wholly reasonable. She asked Ponsonby fretfully, 'If the Lords make a stand and Mr Gladstone also, what is to happen?' She sent Sir Henry to London in the hope of sorting things out, saying Gladstone's determination to challenge the Lords had inflamed the situation, but 'Lord Salisbury should also try to meet the government.' She grumbled, 'For the sake of the country and Sovereign, this should be got over. Say so in my name. I hold both responsible.' One way out of the problem did occur to her: 'If Mr G won't submit, why does he not retire?'[36]

In the end Gladstone showed an uncharacteristic degree of tact, making some concessions that preserved the bill's essentials while enabling Salisbury to retreat. By 17 August 1881 the bill had received its third reading in the Lords, which the Queen regarded as 'a great thing for the country' – more because a collision between the two houses had been averted than because she believed in the bill's merits. She could not resist a jab at Gladstone when she congratulated Granville, writing that in future the prime minister must avoid provoking the Lords: 'That high-handed dictator style of Mr Gladstone will *not* do.'[37]

Fearing their popularity might dwindle if Irish tenants were able to use legal process to clear up grievances, Parnell and the Land League deliberately clogged the new Land Commission with vexatious cases. In the Queen's view this justified Parnell being 'taken up' and 'stopped in his wicked career' by sending him to join more than a thousand of his countrymen currently interned without trial. By the autumn of 1881 Gladstone felt likewise. On 12 October he for once delighted Victoria by informing her that Parnell and some other Home Ruler MPs were to be arrested. A week later the government went further, declaring the Land League illegal. When Sir William Harcourt set off for a stint as minister in residence he told his wife, 'I fear nothing at Balmoral but the cold, as I am sure HM will be radiant at all this coercion.'[38]

In June 1881 the Queen had been outraged that Fenians in America had been able to disseminate propaganda in the United States calling for the Prince of Wales to be assassinated. Representations were made to the US government, who refused to suppress publication of the relevant Fenian organ. The Queen considered this unwise on the politicians' part, for 'in *America generally* she is a *great favourite*, she knows'.[39]

The vulnerability of monarchs to terrorist attacks had been graphically shown when, on 13 March 1881, Tsar Alexander II had been assassinated by members of the Russian nihilist movement whilst out driving in his carriage in St Petersburg. The Queen had at once forgotten her former strident criticisms of the murdered autocrat. 'Poor, poor Emperor, in spite of his failings, he was a kind and amiable man,' she reflected. She wrote to Vicky, 'A sense of horror thrills me through and through ... No punishment is bad enough for the murderers ... That he, the mildest and best Sovereign Russia had, should be the victim of such fiends is too grievous.'[40]

One year later, on 2 March 1882, she herself became the target of another assassination bid, when Roderick Maclean shot at her coach as she was driving out of Windsor station. Maclean had earlier spent fourteen months in a lunatic asylum and since his discharge in July 1881 had lived an itinerant life. The pistol he had bought at a pawnbroker's had been loaded, and he had actually discharged a bullet, so potentially this was the most dangerous of the attacks upon her. At the time, however, the Queen had not realised she had been fired upon, and so was less shaken than by the O'Connor incident of 1872. The attempt inspired such a great outpouring of loyalty that Victoria was touched. Having been cheered wildly when she drove through Windsor and Eton the following day, she told Vicky, 'It is worth being shot at to see how much one is loved.'[41]

This did not mean she wished Maclean to be shown leniency, taking the view: 'the wretched man is strange and wicked, but not mad'. She was pleased when Gladstone too said he favoured severity and that the offender would be tried for high treason. She did not realise that by the time the case came to court, both Gladstone and the law officers had accepted that Maclean's history of mental illness meant he could not be held responsible. The Queen had assumed the attempt to prove him guilty of treason would be abandoned only once it became clear a conviction was impossible and a plea of insanity would then be accepted as second-best. In fact, at Maclean's trial on 19 April the Attorney General effectively directed the jury to acquit him.

Thinking it 'really too bad', Victoria complained to Ponsonby: 'This always happens when a Liberal government is in!' Even though Maclean was shut up in Broadmoor for the rest of his life, she sent Gladstone an admonitory telegram. The prime minister was nonplussed, as he had thought she had understood what was to happen. He did promise to investigate whether the wording of the verdict used when a mad defendant was tried could be altered, which ultimately led to the formula 'Guilty, but insane' being adopted.[42] Victoria had to be satisfied with the change, but this last of eight assassination attempts perpetrated during the reign ensured that she became still more discontented with her ministers.

By the spring of 1882 Gladstone could claim the Land Act was operating as successfully as could be hoped for at this early stage, with many tenants being satisfied with the land court's judgements. However there had not been a discernible depreciation in agrarian crime, partly because of bitterness arising from detentions without trial. This drew forth letters from the Queen 'quite in her worst style' (as Gladstone's secretary put it), demanding more arrests and stronger powers of coercion.[43] In contrast Gladstone was thinking of a new approach, being encouraged by signs that after six months imprisonment, Parnell was no longer irreconcilable.

Parnell was deeply in love with Katherine O'Shea – wife of another Irish MP, the shifty and unscrupulous Captain O'Shea. Katherine had given birth to Parnell's child in February 1882, but the baby was on the point of dying, and Parnell was desperate to comfort the infant's mother. In return for his freedom Parnell was prepared to consider cooperating with the government on certain conditions. In particular he wanted the Land Act amended so that Irish farmers who were behind with their rent could have part of their arrears settled by government grant. Furthermore, the 'Crimes Act' – as the Protection of Persons and Property (Ireland) Act was colloquially known – was coming up for renewal, and Parnell hoped to see it shorn of its most objectionable aspects.

Oddly, the first overtures exploring whether a deal might be possible came through Captain O'Shea, a shady individual who seems to have been ready to overlook his wife's infidelity if that proved to his advantage. Some members of the Cabinet were queasy about using him, believing it would add a further layer of moral ambiguity to the transaction, but Gladstone was wilfully blind about the nature of Parnell's connection with the O'Sheas and accepted the captain as a suitable agent. On 22 April the Cabinet agreed that Joseph Chamberlain could enter into negotiations with O'Shea, who would then be their intermediary with the imprisoned Parnell.

Ministers were aware the Queen would not favour this approach. On the very day the Cabinet reached their decision, Lord Granville asked Gladstone what he should say to her about Ireland at his next audience, as she was bound to ask, 'how many people are we going to hang and shoot etc etc'. Sure enough, on cue, she wrote to him one of her confidential missives about the '*simply frightful and disgraceful*' state of Ireland, calling 'upon *all* of her ministers' other than Gladstone to 'put down anarchy'.[44]

Having seen Parnell in Kilmainham gaol, O' Shea brought back a letter dated 28 April in which Parnell stated that, provided the arrears question was settled, he and his colleagues in the movement would exert themselves to stop outrage and intimidation. This obviously amounted to an implicit admission that they had condoned such activities in the past, but Gladstone believed this must be overlooked. Parnell added that once the land question was resolved, his party would be able 'to cooperate cordially for the future' with the Liberals, thus rendering further coercive measures unnecessary.[45]

On 29 April Gladstone gave the Queen a first intimation of what was afoot, saying that arguments for the release of at least some internees were now 'many and pressing'. Two days later he assured her, 'there has been nothing in the nature of a bargain or negotiation' – a dubious statement he somehow persuaded himself was true, although to the ordinary mind – not to mention Victoria herself – it would seem questionable. Next, on 2 May, a 'nervous' Lord Granville came down to Windsor by special train to inform her not just that the Cabinet had agreed to release Parnell and two of his colleagues, but also that there would only be a limited renewal of coercion. None of this was made more palatable by Granville explaining that Chief Secretary Forster was resigning because he could not agree to Parnell's release unless the latter publicly disavowed outrage and intimidation. In her journal the Queen recorded: 'I *very reluctantly* had to give my consent, but said, it was a great mistake.'[46]

Forster was replaced as chief secretary by Hartington's brother, Lord Frederick Cavendish, who was married to Gladstone's niece. He went over to Ireland at once, and on 6 May catastrophe struck when he and the under-secretary for Ireland, Thomas Burke, were stabbed in Phoenix Park by members of a Fenian terrorist group. Gladstone had looked on Cavendish almost as a son, so it was a devastating personal blow, as well as a shattering setback for his statesmanship. When he appeared in the Commons on 8 May, he almost broke down during his statement to the house, but as far as the Queen was concerned, his Irish policy 'inevitably ... led to all this'. Grimly she commented, 'Surely his eyes must be opened now.'[47]

In a letter to Granville she hammered it home that 'she considers *this* horrible event the *direct result* of ... a most fatal and hazardous step', for which her consent had been 'almost extorted'. To her mind it was indisputable that strong measures were now called for, to prevent others being 'barbarously murdered'. Lord Granville told Ponsonby her letter was so strongly worded that if he showed it to colleagues, the government would have felt compelled to resign – not necessarily an outcome Victoria would have minded.[48]

When writing to the Queen, Gladstone hypothesised that Fenian extremists may have resorted to this act of spectacular violence because they were worried that the Land League were now aligning themselves on the side of law and order. He revealed how O'Shea had opened up a channel of communication with Parnell, but Victoria merely regretted the dealing with people who 'consider pistol shots the best of arguments'. Gladstone told his wife despairingly: 'She will never be happy till she has hounded me out of office.'[49]

For the Queen, the only positive outcome of the tragedy was that Gladstone could surely not deny that the Crimes Act must now be renewed and rendered harsher. In fact, in Cabinet on 7 May Gladstone, heartened by Parnell's readiness to denounce the murders unequivocally, resisted stronger coercive measures, but was overborne by colleagues. Accordingly it was agreed that a new bill must be brought in providing for the suspension of trial by jury in certain areas of Ireland and extensive powers of search. It was sterner than previous legislation of its kind, but the Queen was positive 'no measure can be too stringent'.[50]

Seeing Gladstone on 12 May for the first time since the slaying, she found him 'greatly shaken and seemingly despondent and as if his energy was gone; very pale'. She did not handle him more gently on that account, reiterating it had been fatal to let the suspects out and asserting that the unfortunate Mr Burke had been against the step. Gladstone miserably acknowledged: 'the catastrophe had certainly followed very rapidly'.[51]

Gladstone had only been prevailed upon to agree to a new Crimes Bill on condition there was no reneging on the promise to deal with the arrears problem. To Granville, Victoria expressed incredulity that 'even after his nephew and dear friend has been murdered', Gladstone remained 'under the delusion that these dreadful Home Rulers and rebels are to be trusted'. She raged to the Prince of Wales at the way the government, composed of radicals and 'many thinly veiled *Republicans*', had 'truckled to the Home Rulers'. Their 'utter disregard of all my opinions … make me very miserable and disgust me … Patriotism is nowhere in their ranks.'[52]

Parnell had accepted some form of Crimes Bill was inevitable, but when none of his proposed alterations were adopted, he and his fellow Nationalist MPs determined to fight this one on every point. As a result its passage through Parliament was protracted and cumbersome, marked by inflammatory speeches from the Irish in what the Queen termed 'atrocious and monstrous language'. This merely confirmed her in the view that 'these Rebels – for what are these Home Rule Members of Parliament *but* Rebels?' – were beyond redemption.[53]

The Queen affected concern that terrorists might make 'some diabolical attempt' on Gladstone's life and suggested he 'be more prudent in walking about London'. Perhaps this was an oblique way of showing she had heard about his 'night walks' to rescue prostitutes. Much to the concern of his colleagues and staff, he had not relinquished these, and as he had several times been sighted late at night on the streets, there had been much gossip in London society. Oblivious to any hidden meaning, Gladstone thanked the Queen for her fears for his security but said if he could never go out for a little fresh air, life would be intolerable.[54]

By this time, despite the Queen's belief, 'Mr Gladstone cares little for and understands still less foreign affairs', a crisis in Egypt was taking up much of the government's attention. Such was the extravagance and incompetence of Egypt's Khedive Ismail that even after he sold his Suez Canal shares to Britain, his country remained at risk of bankruptcy, which would have a ruinous effect on the European bondholders who had underwritten loans to Egypt. In July 1877 the German crown princess had suggested to her mother that Britain fulfil its '*great* mission' in the world by taking over Egypt – for 'Who can it harm?' Having snubbed her by asking 'Why should we make a *wanton* aggression' of this kind? Victoria added witheringly: 'It is not *our* custom to *annex countries* (as it is in *some others*).'[55] Instead, having joined together in 1878 to depose Ismail and replace him with his son, Tewfik, France and England established a system of 'dual control', placing Egypt's finances and political system largely under their management.

By early 1882 Egyptians were chafing at this foreign domination. When popular pressure forced the khedive to appoint a nationalist army colonel named Arabi as his chief minister, there were concerns Egypt would assert its independence by defaulting on its debts. Despite himself being a major Egyptian bondholder, Gladstone was wary of intervening, even telling Granville in January 1882 he personally was sympathetic to the idea of 'Egypt for the Egyptians'. Nevertheless, following Arabi-inspired riots in which several Europeans were killed on 11 June, the French and English undertook a joint naval demonstration off Alexandria. Although neither Gladstone nor the French wished to take the matter further, the Cabinet decided otherwise, and on 11 July the British fleet bombarded Alexandria. The Queen was 'proud of the way the Navy has behaved', although critical that troops had not been landed to maintain order in the town.[56] The government now recognised that a force would have to be sent out against Arabi, and Sir Garnet Wolseley was entrusted with its command.

On 13 September Wolseley routed Arabi's forces at Tel-el-Kebir, and Arabi himself was captured. Gladstone was briefly overtaken by euphoria at the military triumph, although the Queen was not disposed to give him credit for it. At Balmoral once again, Harcourt reported to his wife: 'We had a jolly dinner last night … She is quite pleased with … everybody, except the GOM.' The three initials stood for 'Grand Old Man' – an affectionate, if semi-ironic nickname bestowed on Gladstone by admirers, and which gained such currency the Queen herself sometimes used it sarcastically. Although Victoria now granted Wolseley the barony about which there had been so much fuss earlier, she was careful to puncture Gladstone's happy mood. She let it be known she 'was a little hurt' that in his letter informing her of the victory, Gladstone had made no reference to the service of her soldier son, Prince Arthur, who had commanded the Guards Brigade in the battle. Granville hastily nudged Gladstone to make good the omission. Gladstone complied, while sighing, 'This kind of correspondence makes me sad.'[57]

Although in 1877 the Queen had been so dismissive of her daughter's idea that Britain should rule Egypt, she now envisaged something of the sort. Alarmed by the government's talk of an early withdrawal of troops, she telegraphed Lord Granville: 'We have not fought and shed precious blood and gone to great expense for nothing. Short of annexation we must obtain a firm hold and power in Egypt for the future.' Victoria's stance so infuriated the prime minister that he burst out to Hartington: 'I must own that I think the Queen's resolute attempts to disturb & impede the reduction of the army in Egypt are (to use a plain word) intolerable. It is my firm intention not to give in … to proceedings almost as unconstitutional as they are irrational.'[58]

Another source of discord arose over the treatment of the captured Colonel Arabi. The Queen assumed he would be executed by the khedive, and Gladstone too initially agreed he deserved hanging. Then a civil rights movement developed in England in Arabi's favour, and the government became uneasy at being associated with what might be viewed as judicial murder. To Victoria's stupefaction, Arabi's sympathisers arranged for a British barrister to act for him at his trial. She spluttered it was 'quite preposterous that an English counsel should defend a foreign rebel', but the government decided it would be best if Arabi plead guilty to the crime of rebellion, and then his death sentence should be commuted. It was later agreed that Arabi should be exiled to

Ceylon, a British possession. However much this maddened Victoria, she was unable to prevent it.[59]

She kept up her struggle to stop any British disengagement from Egypt. By the end of 1882, indeed, she believed it necessary to increase troop numbers there. In the Sudan, which was an Egyptian dependency, a 'false prophet' known as 'the Mahdi' was gathering a great following of tribesmen whom he was instigating to throw out their current rulers. On 2 November the Queen told Granville the government should urgently consider crushing these Sudanese rebels.[60]

In December 1882 Gladstone, who had been contemplating retirement, instead reshuffled his government. The Queen thought it 'very good' that Lord Hartington replaced Childers as secretary of state for war, and that Gladstone lessened his intolerable workload by appointing Childers Chancellor of the Exchequer. Other changes were more contentious. She was horrified when Gladstone proposed that Lord Derby – who, after his resignation from Beaconsfield's government in 1878 had started supporting the Liberals – should become Secretary of State for India. Strongly objecting to taking back 'a most disagreeable and irresolute, timid Minister', she vetoed his going to the Indian Office, saying if he had that 'the Russians would be in India' within months. She had reluctantly to accept that he would instead become Secretary of State for the Colonies, despite feeling sure Derby would 'do great harm – by letting everything go'. Having raged to Granville, 'She despises him, looks on him as a turncoat & as a man who has *no feeling* of the honour of his country,' she told Gladstone frankly that when Derby came to kiss hands, 'he cannot expect a cordial reception'.[61]

She also baulked at Sir Charles Dilke being raised to the Cabinet. His 1871 campaign still rankled, and since entering the government Dilke had compounded earlier offences by abstaining in spring 1882 on a vote for a financial grant to Prince Leopold. The Queen had picked this up at the time, telling Gladstone (questionably) that since the royal family have '*no* property – nothing of our own', such support was part of 'a *compact*' entered into when the Crown gave up its hereditary revenues in the eighteenth century, and was therefore 'the *right* of the sovereign & not the … generosity of Parliament'. Gladstone thought it better not to debate the point, confining himself to saying that Dilke's abstention was 'not unpardonable'.[62]

Now the Queen insisted that before Dilke entered the Cabinet, he must make 'some kind of public apology' for past misdemeanours. She utterly rejected Gladstone's idea that Dilke should become Chancellor of the Duchy of Lancaster, for this not only would have brought Sir Charles into regular contact with her but would have given him alarming oversight of royal finances. The Crown's civil list payments were supplemented by the revenue of the Duchy of Lancaster, which in the course of Victoria's reign had seen a twelve-fold increase. Having someone with republican leanings in charge of the department was not an inviting prospect. Victoria was no better pleased when Gladstone suggested Joe Chamberlain should become chancellor of the duchy. Ponsonby was instructed to tell Gladstone: 'The Queen will NOT have him.' In the end Dilke headed the Local Government Board, and Chamberlain remained at the Board of Trade.[63]

The whole business had been very stressful for Gladstone, and at the start of 1883 he was afflicted by a frightening bout of insomnia. Mrs Gladstone attributed this primarily to his difficulties with the 'management of *HM*'. Discussing his health problems with Lord Rosebery, Gladstone himself groaned, 'The Queen alone is enough to kill any man.' On 17 January he was sent to Cannes on doctor's orders, affording Victoria a glimmer of hope he would retire altogether. She wrote, 'he must be *really quiet* and not occupy himself at *all* with affairs,' offering him a peerage as an enticement to give up the premiership. To her regret he turned it down, and though she encouraged him to stay away till after Easter, he returned on 2 March, fully restored.[64]

On 20 January 1883 a gasworks in Glasgow was blown up, signalling the start of a bombing campaign by Irish American Fenians. In Ireland itself in 1883, the British struck a blow against Fenian terrorism by securing convictions of the men who had murdered Cavendish and Burke. The Queen had been 'most painfully interested' in the investigation's 'quite thrilling' progress. Guilty verdicts were obtained, as a result of one member of a band of assassins called 'The Invincibles' turning Queen's evidence. The man in question, Carey, was a former Dublin town councillor and his '*appalling*' testimony at the trial proved to the Queen's satisfaction – though not to everyone's – that the Land League were implicated in murders carried out by 'these frightful secret societies'. She wrote to Home Secretary Harcourt: 'Will not Mr Gladstone be dreadfully shaken by all these disclosures?' Her inevitable prescription was '*great* firmness and *strong* measures'. She was annoyed that in return for betraying his confederates, Carey was granted immunity from prosecution. He was sent overseas with his family, but his identity was uncovered by another Irish passenger, who then shot him as he voyaged from Cape Town to Durban. The Queen considered this 'well deserved but shocking'.[65]

The year 1883 brought Victoria great sadness in the form of the death of John Brown on 28 March. She told Ponsonby it had left her 'utterly crushed' and used it as an excuse not to reply to Gladstone's letters for a fortnight. Ponsonby confided to Granville she was 'very much cut up by it, though perhaps not so much as I had expected'. Possibly there was some truth in what Lord Derby heard, which was that as Brown's intake of alcohol had increased, 'he had grown imperious & rough in his manner to her, so that she was thought to be afraid of him'. Although it was sometimes alleged that Brown meddled in politics, there is little evidence for this, but he certainly had not been a fan of Gladstone and his ministers. In 1872 he had been heard to say, 'We canna have a worse lot.'[66]

Victoria's distress at Brown's passing distracted her from politics for a time. This meant she was slow to pick up on a speech made by Joseph Chamberlain two days after Brown's death, sneering that Lord Salisbury belonged to a class whose inherited wealth ensured they 'toil not, neither do they spin'. On 23 April Ponsonby issued a rebuke on the Queen's behalf to Gladstone, deploring language that 'set class against class'. Chamberlain then made matters worse by delivering a speech at Birmingham on 13 June containing what the Queen interpreted as a disparaging reference to royalty. On 27 June Victoria wrote that no one who spoke in such a 'dangerous and improper' way should be in government. Gladstone thereupon reminded Chamberlain that the 'sacred' rights of the Crown must 'be watched over ... with careful and even jealous respect'. Chamberlain merely replied he had never fallen short in this regard.[67]

Although Gladstone's visit to Osborne in August 1883 went well, soon afterwards the Queen excelled herself in unpleasantness. In September Gladstone went on a Scottish cruise as the guest of a wealthy friend, and when his host suggested they make an impromptu crossing to Scandinavia, the prime minister agreed without a qualm. Having landed at Copenhagen, they were entertained by the Danish King and Queen, whose family party included their son, the King of Greece, and son-in-law, the Tsar of Russia. On 20 September the Queen rebuked Gladstone for going abroad without her sanction, for 'the Prime Minister of Great Britain cannot move about ... as a Private Individual'. She had already written to Granville expressing astonishment at an '*escapade*' that exposed 'Mr Gladstone's want of *all knowledge*, apparently, of what is due to the Sovereign he serves', alleging that his presence at Copenhagen 'may be productive of much evil and certainly lead to misconstruction'.[68]

Gladstone admitted to Granville that her chiding 'made me rather angry'. He added, 'I should call the letter – for the first time – even somewhat unmannerly' – but 'after much care' he 'concocted a reply ... in which he carefully concealed his vexation and wrath'. His secretary Edward Hamilton believed that what lay behind the Queen's onslaught was, 'to put it bluntly, *jealousy*', and that she was irritated at seeing Gladstone's movements prominently chronicled in the newspapers. The Queen herself appears to have soon realised she had gone too far. Her next letter, Hamilton noted, was relatively friendly and chatty, 'evidently betokening a certain amount of conscience-strickenness'.[69]

Very soon her tone reverted to its usual hostile one, with many of her complaints focussing on foreign and colonial policy. She was displeased by the government's supine attitude to French colonial expansion. Ministers had acquiesced in France establishing a protectorate over Tunisia in 1881 and put up no serious resistance to France's acquisition of Madagascar two years later. In March 1883 Victoria asked Granville, 'Are we to let the French go on taking what they like with impunity?' – a comment that Gladstone believed provided 'unfortunate proof that HM's mind was becoming too warped to give judgement on public affairs'. That autumn she complained that a British missionary whom the French had briefly imprisoned during their takeover had been given inadequate compensation of £1,000. Gladstone told Granville his reply 'virtually said "I am sure you cannot be so absurd as to hold out, therefore I understand you to accept while you grumble"'.[70]

Inevitably this went down very badly. Victoria wrote to Granville that whereas she knew he had his country's honour 'strongly at heart ... she does *not* feel that Mr Gladstone has'. On 30 October she informed Gladstone himself, 'What she fears is a growing tendency to swallow insults and affronts and not taking them up in that high tone which they used formerly to be.' During the next two years what she saw as a pernicious trend developed further. Gladstone made it plain he was not bothered when Germany set about establishing itself as a colonial power. The Queen saw things differently, telling Vicky in January 1885 that the Germans' new 'colonisation mania is really too bad and foolish'.[71]

Although Victoria did not like other foreign powers extending their empires, she of course had a different attitude when it came to her own.

In her view, British administration of far-off places could only be to their benefit and so, for example, she went on vainly pressing for the annexation of Zululand. She likewise saw nothing amiss when the government of Queensland, Australia (a self-governing crown colony since 1859) announced they would be taking possession of most of New Guinea to prevent other European powers acquiring it. Gladstone privately thought the idea 'monstrous', and the British government agonised for months before finally agreeing New Guinea could become a British protectorate. Victoria had never doubted this would be a good thing, telling Lord Derby in August 1884 that establishing a British presence there would 'enable us to protect the poor natives and to advance civilisation, which she considers the mission of Great Britain'.[72]

Throughout 1883 the argument about troop reductions in Egypt had rumbled on, but at the end of the year a disaster in the Sudan proved to the Queen's satisfaction that more, rather than less, military involvement was required. After an Egyptian army sent to suppress the Sudanese uprising was annihilated by the Mahdi's forces, the Cabinet resolved on 22 November that Egyptian garrisons and personnel stationed in the Sudan must be withdrawn. The Queen reluctantly agreed, provided steps were taken to ensure not too many Egyptian lives were lost in the process. While Gladstone was at home in Cheshire, Granville and a Cabinet committee decided that General Gordon should carry out the evacuation. Known as 'Chinese Gordon' because he had put down a rebellion against the Manchus in China, Gordon was a maverick British army officer who had previously governed the Sudan on the khedive's behalf for three years. Despite his experience and his high reputation, Gordon was not an ideal choice. He was a Christian mystic, for whom divine guidance took priority over orders from secular authorities; moreover, he had already indicated he did not agree with the abandonment of the Sudan. Nevertheless Lord Granville assured Ponsonby, 'He is a genius, and of a splendid character,' even if it was 'a great pity there should be some eccentricity.'[73]

The Queen had no doubt that this 'extraordinary man, with an enormous power over uncivilised people' was the right person for the task. She merely thought it 'absolutely inexplicable' he was not despatched till 18 January 1884, and flattered herself it was only done then 'in deference to her very strong pressure'. From the outset, however, she worried for Gordon's safety, warning Gladstone on 9 February: 'If anything befalls *him* the result will be awful.'[74]

The Cabinet's concerns, on the other hand, centred more upon the general's sanity. Having arrived at Khartoum on 18 February Gordon started to make wild contradictory demands, and rather than proceeding with evacuation, opined that first 'the Mahdi must be smashed up'. After learning that telegraph lines to Khartoum had been cut by Mahdist forces, Victoria wrote to Hartington on 25 March, 'Gordon is in danger: you are bound to try and save him.' Two days later she warned Gladstone: 'If not only for humanity's sake, for the honour of the government and the nation, he must not be abandoned,' to which the prime minister answered there was as yet no evidence Gordon needed rescuing. By mid-April the minister for war, Hartington, did in fact favour sending troops with a view to aiding Gordon, but after several acrimonious Cabinets (whose disagreements were concealed from the Queen), Gladstone managed to block this. By the end of April Victoria was not alone in thinking, 'General Gordon, thanks to the deplorable conduct of the government, in considerable danger!' Early the next month several public meetings were held calling for help to be sent to him,[75] but Hartington's loyal defence of the government in a Commons vote of censure debate allowed Gladstone to resist the clamour.

Already angry enough about Gordon's treatment, the Queen became yet more wrathful when the government embarked on talks with their French former partners in the dual control of Egypt. Denying that Britain wanted permanent possession, Lord Granville proposed withdrawing troops after five years. Having given Gladstone a 'wigging', Victoria barked at Sir Henry Ponsonby: 'Why are we to be bullied and frightened by other Powers?' Branding the government's Egyptian policy 'perfectly miserable', she fulminated, 'She was never listened to, or her advice followed, and *all* she foretold *invariably* happened ... It is dreadful for her to see how we are going downhill.'[76]

She was incredulous when the French spurned the British offer, demanding a term of occupation in Egypt of no more than two years. The Cabinet were willing to make a counter-offer of three and a half years, although the Queen was adamant that 'truckling to insolent France' would 'have the very worst effect'. Gladstone said to Granville he found it 'scarcely conceivable that any one could treat the difference between 5 and 3½ years as a matter of life and death'. In the end three and a half years was the period agreed upon.[77]

'What is going to be done about General Gordon?' the Queen probed Gladstone on 30 May, but the prime minister still saw 'little occasion for present anxiety'. He clung to this view throughout the summer. His private belief was that as Gordon had disobeyed his instructions, it would be wrong to waste British lives and money extricating him from his predicament – though he justified this to himself by denying that Gordon was in danger. The Queen would later say, with some justice, the prime minister had wrapped himself up 'in his own *incomprehensible delusions & illusions*', refusing to believe what was 'in ... everyone's mouth'.[78] By mid-July most of the Cabinet were uneasy about simply abandoning Gordon to his fate, and at the end of the month a resignation ultimatum from Hartington forced Gladstone to agree that preparations for a relief force should be started. However, not until 9 October was its commander, Lord Wolseley, instructed to start up the Nile.

For the Queen, it was another example of 'what she *urged*' being '*done* when *too late*!' She was still mourning her son Prince Leopold, who had died at the end of March from complications arising from haemophilia, and who had been almost as critical of the government as she was herself. Telling her daughter that Gladstone now 'openly avowed to me that he wanted to get out of Egypt', she exclaimed, 'Oh! What would my darling Leopold have felt?'[79]

One reason why Gladstone had been unwilling to concentrate too much on the Sudan was that the prime minister was distracted by a pressing domestic issue. On 4 January 1884 he had informed Victoria that the government planned to introduce another Reform Bill, extending the household franchise to rural dwellers. However, he explained that rather than coupling the measure with a Redistribution Bill, they would wait until the next session of Parliament to deal with that. This posed problems for the Conservatives: while maintaining they were not against franchise extension per se, they feared that having increased the number of voters, the Liberals would bring in a Redistribution Bill that disproportionately favoured their own party. This could result in the Tories being 'destroyed for generations'.[80] Accordingly they wanted a Redistribution Bill to take effect simultaneously with changes to the franchise.

On 28 February Gladstone had introduced the Franchise Bill in the Commons, and four months later it passed its third reading there. Following boasts from Lord Salisbury's nephew, Arthur Balfour, that the measure would be 'doomed' by the House of Lords, Gladstone made what the Queen described as 'a violent and injudicious speech'. He warned peers that a collision between the two houses of Parliament would be 'fraught with danger to our institutions and sure not to end in the defeat of the House of Commons' – belligerent language that greatly displeased Victoria. She at once wrote to say the Lords could not simply acquiesce in measures passed by the Commons but found him so impenitent she feared 'the throne itself may be in danger if Mr Gladstone proceeds as he intends'.[81]

On 8 July the Lords committed what Gladstone considered 'a suicidal act', passing an amendment to the Franchise Bill which declared they could only consent to its coming into operation if it formed part of an entire scheme. Gladstone advised the Queen that since it would be improper to hold an election prompted by an adverse vote of the House of Lords, he intended to bring the session to an early close and resubmit the Franchise Bill to the Upper House in the autumn. The Queen regretted this, claiming that whereas prorogation would give rise to three months of agitation against the Lords by 'noisy demagogues', an election campaign would have allowed 'the calm and proper expression of the people's opinion'.[82]

As soon as the Lords had passed their amendment, the Queen had offered to act as a mediator between the two sides. Initially Gladstone had been dismissive, but after a few days reflection he said perhaps there was room for the exercise of 'your Majesty's skilled and experienced judgement'. However, he was disheartened by the letter she sent him on 15 July, claiming that the House of Lords 'represented the true feeling of the country'. He told Granville he considered her letter 'rather a serious fact' although, had he but known it, Sir Henry Ponsonby had toned down Victoria's original draft considerably.[83]

The Queen acknowledged to Ponsonby, 'Both parties *must* give way a little.' It seems she unsuccessfully made 'representations' to Salisbury urging him to accept a compromise put forward by another peer. Most of her anger was nevertheless reserved for Gladstone, who 'in his wild vindictive passion' could sweep away '*all* that keeps the state together'. She told Ponsonby that if the prime minister was unyielding, he should 'resign to save the country', for it was 'wicked to willingly try and ruin it'. Although Gladstone had assured her that he had instructed his party to show restraint in public about the Lords, his own son, Herbert, and Joseph Chamberlain made speeches using 'violent contemptuous language'. On 25 July Victoria demanded the prime minister rein in his radical followers, who should really 'be called *Destructives*'. Days later, however, Chamberlain delivered another provocative speech. As a result, she described him to Gladstone as 'a most dangerous man', to which the prime minister responded he could not believe she meant this literally. He complained to Granville she had so seriously 'impugned his honour' he was reluctant to visit her at Osborne. To his relief Victoria herself suggested it might be more convenient for them to meet in September, when both would be in Scotland.[84]

Gladstone now prepared for the Queen a lengthy memorandum, assuring her that although the House of Lords so regularly caused difficulties for Liberal governments, he personally had little desire to reduce its privileges. Nevertheless, many in his party already hungered to tackle an institution so inimical to them, and if the Lords again rejected a Franchise Bill in the autumn, pressure for 'organic change' would become irresistible.[85]

The Queen told Ponsonby she was 'greatly struck by the fairness and impartiality' of the document. Mindful that past attempts to deal with Salisbury had yielded little, she wished to show the memorandum to the Duke of Richmond, a more moderate Tory peer than Salisbury. Initially she was wary of 'creating a rupture' within Tory ranks by bypassing the leadership, but Ponsonby remarked that as Richmond had a house near Balmoral, if would seem perfectly natural if she invited him over 'as a country neighbour in Scotland'.[86]

On 8 September Gladstone himself spent two days at Balmoral. In some ways the visit was a success. Victoria later admitted he had been 'plausible and amiable', and she listened carefully to what he had to say. Apparently impressed by his warning that feeling in the country against the Lords was increasing, and that a second rejection by them of the Franchise Bill 'might cause many disorders', she offered again to try and broker a compromise. However, she was enraged when, after his departure he travelled about Scotland, making speeches 'almost under her very nose', which she felt whipped up further hostility against the peers. She fumed to Granville, 'Really, "stumping" about the country & speaking out of the window at every station and accepting great receptions – like Royalty – ... is quite indecorous.' She instructed Granville to make her feelings known to the prime minister, and Granville reluctantly obeyed. Unmoved, Gladstone declared he would 'take no notice of the Queen's displeasure'. The prime minister's secretary Edward Hamilton was again inclined to believe that jealousy lay behind her outburst: 'She has never before had a ... Minister who was an idol of the people.'[87]

It did not appear that much would be gained from the Queen's meeting with the Duke of Richmond on 14 September. As yet the duke was still showing solidarity with Salisbury, who maintained there was no appetite for political reform, so it would not matter if the Franchise Bill was thrown out a second time. Richmond dismissed agitation against the Lords as confected, and the Queen was soon parroting the line it was 'very much encouraged and got up' by the Liberals. Despite the fact that hundreds of political meetings were being held all over the country, the vast majority calling for reform, the Queen now appeared to have lost sight of Gladstone's warnings of the dire consequences rejecting the bill would bring. Gladstone feared she had also not taken it in that if there was an election, he would campaign on the hustings for Lords reform.[88]

Over the next few weeks Gladstone rejected several compromise solutions that Sir Henry Ponsonby put forward on behalf of moderate Tory peers; but he did suggest that perhaps progress could be made if Conservatives gave a clearer idea of the sort of Redistribution Bill they would like. Ultimately this was the route that provided the answer to the conundrum. For the moment, however, 'the terrible deadlock' continued. By 14 October Victoria was so fed up that she complained to Ponsonby, 'Mr Gladstone really acts like a dictator and Queen and country will *not* stand it. Why will they behave like obstinate children and not bring in the Redistribution Bill?' Her instinct to blame the Liberals was strengthened when Parliament assembled for the autumn session on 23 October and Gladstone told the Commons it was mad the Tories still expected unconditional surrender. The Queen found it 'all very annoying, but really it is far more the government's fault'.[89]

At times, she did wonder if Salisbury was being too intransigent. She had asked Richmond to warn Salisbury of the danger 'of matters becoming much worse if the *conflict* is envenomed', but throughout October Salisbury stuck so stubbornly to his position that Victoria began to think 'the best chance of a settlement was one produced from the ranks and not from the leaders'. Salisbury was confident that if Gladstone was forced to dissolve Parliament following a second rejection by the Lords, the Conservatives would do well in an election, but the Queen was coming round to the view 'the result ... may not be what he expects'. By 30 October Edward Hamilton understood, 'She puts down most of the onus of the present deadlock to Salisbury.'[90]

In late October she again appealed to Richmond. Urging that 'pique both *personal* & *party* should be' overcome, she argued, 'they *must* put aside offended dignity & small difficulties.' Having come to believe that 'if Lord Salisbury won't do what is right then someone else must take the lead', she entrusted her letter for delivery by the duke's cousin,

Charles Peel. He was instructed to give Richmond a verbal message that the '[Conservative] party must not be led against their convictions by Salisbury'. The result was notable, for on 30 October Richmond wrote to Salisbury that since he concurred with the Queen's view that 'very serious consequences' might arise from continued blocking of the Franchise Bill, he would no longer support the policy.[91]

The Queen also wrote directly to Salisbury for the first time since the crisis began, suggesting that party leaders should meet to discuss the provisions of a Redistribution of Seats Bill. Her assistant private secretary Arthur Bigge hoped that Salisbury would realise from this that 'his idea of forcing dissolution will receive no sympathy here'. Salisbury's response appeared to be all she could wish for, for he at once wrote that although unconcerned about throwing out the Franchise Bill, he would obey her instructions 'with great pleasure'. However, Arthur Bigge suspected Salisbury was merely feigning 'submission ... to royal commands', and Ponsonby likewise doubted his sincerity. Yet Salisbury certainly seemed more amenable than Gladstone, to whom the Queen had made the same proposal. The prime minister was hoping that unofficial talks on redistribution that had started between Hartington and Colonial Secretary Hicks-Beach would produce results, and only when those petered out was he prepared to entertain her idea.[92]

It seemed there was no hope of the situation improving when on 11 November the Tory lord John Manners declared in the Commons that the opposition would not engage in public or private negotiations with the government. Though 'much worried', the Queen did not give up, but instead sent Ponsonby to meet with Richmond and Cairns at Perth station, saying they must 'compel Salisbury to make agreement'. Now convinced that an election 'would be a bad thing and very dangerous', she asked the pair to point out to their leaders that in any electoral contest, violent members pledged to undermine the Lords would inevitably be returned, as well as more Home Rulers. Unbeknown to her, two days before Ponsonby had his meeting with the two Tory peers on 15 November, Lord Cairns had in fact written to Salisbury saying that he too could no longer oppose the Franchise Bill.[93]

Thus, although Salisbury appeared determined to hold out, the situation was more hopeful than it looked. At a meeting of prominent Tories on 12 November, Salisbury still talked of throwing out the Franchise Bill and forcing dissolution. It was becoming evident, however, that relatively few diehards now supported this. A late-night private meeting between Gladstone and Sir Stafford Northcote the following day also ended in failure, but Salisbury did indicate that perhaps agreement was possible 'if the results of previous communications be satisfactory'.[94] This meant that when Gladstone adopted a new approach, it proved fruitful.

On 15 November the prime minister informed the Queen that he and Lord Granville would make a declaration in their respective houses of Parliament saying they were prepared to make the drafting of a Redistribution of Seats Bill, 'a subject of friendly communication with the Opposition'. Gladstone was privately pessimistic about what this would yield – Sir William Harcourt admitted 'it was only done to put the Lords in the wrong' – but it provided the desired breakthrough. The Queen helped by informing the Duke of Richmond that when the conciliatory declaration was made, she wished it to 'be received in friendly spirit'.[95]

On the morning of 17 November there was a meeting of leading Tories. The Duke of Richmond urged that any offer of a meeting should be accepted, and reiterated he would not vote against the Franchise Bill. Salisbury was still unenthusiastic, but Richmond then went to tell Granville that he and Cairns were 'desirous of finding a modus vivendi'. Granville reported to Gladstone that Richmond 'spoke very openly – criticised Salisbury', before asking for 'a confidential meeting without prejudice'. Ponsonby still doubted that Salisbury would agree for, 'He has never altered his note from the beginning.'[96]

That evening Gladstone and Granville made their statements. In Gladstone's case, it was 'launched as a forlorn hope'. His low expectations seemed justified when, at a Tory party meeting held later, Salisbury appeared 'very adverse to the proposals'. However, a message from Gladstone clarifying what was on offer 'set the matter right', and next morning another party meeting at the Carlton Club was 'unanimous in favour of peace'. Much as Salisbury might regret it, he realised he could not spurn the proffered olive branch. In the Lords that evening, he 'made a most conciliatory speech', accepting the government's invitation to confer about the Seats Bill. The Lords then passed the second reading of the Franchise Bill, before Salisbury announced that the committee stage would be deferred for a fortnight while discussions took place.[97]

Granville wrote to the Queen, 'Your Majesty must feel rather proud,' even if there was no guarantee negotiations would succeed. The Duke of Argyll had predicted to her that Gladstone and Salisbury 'meeting *personally*' would prove disastrous, but in the end the conferences went surprisingly well. Gladstone found it a 'pleasure to do business with so acute a man', and he later would tell the Queen: 'Nothing could have been more pleasant or able' than Salisbury's demeanour throughout. This ensured that, 'with the help of a few cups of tea', agreement was reached on the terms of the Redistribution of Seats Bill.[98] Changes to constituencies were much more extensive than Gladstone had envisaged, and some Liberals supposed Salisbury had failed to understand the implications. In fact, the latter knew very well what he was about. A great increase in single member constituencies and absorption of small boroughs into counties helped bring about the rise of 'Villa Toryism', where suburban voters would prove crucial to the Conservatives' future electoral success.

On 27 November 1884 Gladstone telegraphed Victoria: 'Points of substance all settled this afternoon ... Humbly congratulate.' She modestly replied: 'To be able to be of use is all I care to live for now.' When she saw Salisbury later that evening he clearly was less elated. She noted in her diary, 'Lord Salisbury seemed rather depressed & evidently not exactly pleased at the peaceable arrangement. I said it was a great thing, and he answered, "I think we could have made a good fight," to which I replied "but at what a price". He seemed then to agree.' Although Salisbury had indicated there might yet be a last-minute hitch, this was averted. On 6 December the Franchise Bill received the royal assent, after passing its third reading in the Lords a day earlier. By that time the Redistribution of Seats Bill had already been introduced in the Commons, although it would not actually reach the statute book till the summer of 1885. The Franchise Bill increased the UK electorate from 3 million to approximately 5 million, meaning that about 60 per cent of adult males now had the vote.[99]

The Queen was proud of her role in the affair and wished for it to be recognised. Ponsonby told the Duke of Richmond's cousin, 'HM does not at all object to it being generally known that she has taken an active part in bringing about the present state of things.' Some historians have dismissed this as groundless vanity, denying Victoria any credit for the successful outcome. It has been argued that the most significant breakthrough came with Gladstone's offer of friendly communication on 17 November, followed by his acceptance that the Lords need not proceed with the Franchise Bill until agreement was reached on redistribution. Furthermore, Cairns had decided to drop his opposition to the Franchise Bill even before Ponsonby delivered the Queen's message at Perth station. Salisbury's readiness to compromise may have owed less to Victoria's intervention than the realisation that 'the ice was cracking' underneath him, making further resistance unsustainable.[100]

It should however be remembered it was the Queen who first proposed that a meeting should take place between Gladstone and Salisbury, and it is also notable how many admired the part she played. Gladstone personally thanked her 'for that wise, gracious and steady exercise of influence on your Majesty's part, which has so powerfully contributed to bring about this accommodation'. In a letter to Ponsonby on 19 November, Charles Peel likewise remarked that while the Duke of Richmond and Lord Cairns had 'worked hard … I am quite certain that but for the judicious intervention of the Queen … the task they undertook would have been much more difficult, if it had not proved impossible'. Others were equally complimentary. Lord Derby, usually highly critical, noted that Victoria was 'proud of having shown her influence & the enjoyment is one which nobody need grudge her, for it has been usefully exercised', while Edward Hamilton opined: 'Much credit is certainly due to her.' In his diary Gladstone not only observed 'the Queen … has been very useful,' but in a fragment of autobiography went further. 'I will not undertake to say what had been her Majesty's leanings in the earlier stages of the conflict,' he recorded. 'But undoubtedly in later stages she shared the views of her ministers and even acted herself, perhaps with important effects, in dissuading the Opposition from prolonging an important contest.' He added that he had been 'not … very sanguine' when making his parliamentary statement on 17 November, but then to his surprise and pleasure had found that within the last two days an 'entire change' had occurred in the attitude of the Conservative front bench. 'Some day I suppose the world will know what took place …,' he mused. 'It is most probable that the Queen had to do with it.'[101]

Victoria herself was hopeful that a new era in politics had dawned. Following the successful conferences between party leaders the Queen wrote to Lord Granville, 'She goes further … in thinking that these meetings are a good precedent, and should be resorted to on occasions of great moment when all statesmen and all *true* patriots should join to prevent the mischief so ardently desired by the Radicals & republicans and destructives.' Assuming that the goodwill generated would be lasting, she cheerfully remarked to a Liberal peer, 'From the way that Gladstone and Salisbury buttered each other, she does not see how she is to have an opposition again.'[102]

* * *

It did not take long for the Queen's 'exuberant good humour' to evaporate. In January 1885 she was much annoyed when Hartington protested about her telegraphing Wolseley after a column of troops on their way to Khartoum had a successful, if bloody, clash with Mahdist forces at Abu Klea. Hartington argued that such communications should go through the War Office, which the Queen maintained was '*very officious* and *impertinent*' of him. She raged to Ponsonby, 'The Queen *has* the *right* to telegraph congratulations ... and won't stand dictation. She *won't* be a *machine*. But the Liberals always wish to make her *feel* THAT.'[103]

Soon much worse news came from the Sudan. When the relief force's steamer came in sight of Khartoum, the British flag was no longer flying. It was clear the town had fallen, although Gordon's fate was unknown. The news arrived in England on 5 February 1885, when Gladstone was out of London. Instead of using a cypher, the Queen deliberately telegraphed him *en clair* – meaning that telegraph operators and anyone else who handled the telegram could read her scathing words: 'These news from Khartoum are frightful, and to think that all this might have been prevented and many precious lives saved by earlier action is too frightful.'[104]

Having clung to the idea that Gordon would manage to hold out until relieved, Gladstone was devastated by what amounted to a public rebuke. Ponsonby was alerted that being 'rather excited about the telegram', the prime minister was considering resigning. Sir Henry asked Victoria if he should do something to soothe him. Firing up at the way '*Dear Mr Gladstone's* feelings are *much more thought* of than the Queen's suffering,' she riposted: 'She *meant* that Mr G should remember what SHE suffers when the British name is humiliated.' She continued bitterly, 'He can go away & resign but she MUST REMAIN.' When she had sent her telegram, 'she was boiling over with the indignation and horror' felt by everyone in the country, so 'how could she NOT say what she did?' To try and alleviate things, Ponsonby wrote guardedly to Gladstone's secretary that, while the Queen had never conceived that her telegram might be published, she had 'with difficulty abstained from writing more strongly than she did'.[105]

The Queen at once demanded that steps be taken to retrieve British honour. The Cabinet agreed, and Gladstone was too demoralised to prevent orders being sent to Wolseley to act as he saw fit. It was decided that military operations would at once resume in East Sudan, and in the autumn another expedition would be sent to recapture Khartoum. Still

Victoria's anger against the prime minister burned bright. Like others, she was shocked when Gladstone went to the theatre on 10 February, while it was still unknown whether Gordon was alive or dead. 'Does he feel it at all?' she asked one Liberal peer. Once it was confirmed that Gordon had been killed during the storming of Khartoum, she wrote: 'Mr Gladstone and the government *have* – the Queen *feels it dreadfully* – Gordon's innocent, noble heroic blood on their consciences ... May they *feel* it, and may they be *made to do so!*' When she contracted flu, she told Ponsonby, 'it is all this that has made the Queen ill'.[106]

Soon after Parliament opened, Gladstone made an unenthusiastic announcement of the government's military plans, confirming to the Queen that he had not really been moved by Gordon's fate. The opposition immediately announced they would seek a vote of censure. After several days debate the government had a majority of only fourteen on 28 February. The Cabinet narrowly decided against resignation, with Gladstone foremost among those who wished to remain – believing doing otherwise 'would look like running away in time of difficulty'. Victoria was scornful: 'Why cling to office when they are so discredited? ... It is so humiliating and dreadful for me.'[107]

She flared up anew when the government resisted Wolseley's request to be made Governor General of the Sudan, which he believed would help him gain support from local Arab chiefs. Gladstone responded to her protests with a sarcastic letter, saying that while it might appear obvious to her that an affirmative answer should be given, 'the wisdom of the measure ... might not appear to all so clear as it appears to your Majesty'. Most improperly, the Queen then wrote '*in strict confidence*' to Wolseley's wife that, since 'the government are *more incorrigible* than ever', Wolseley should threaten resignation unless his wish was granted. She cautioned he must never '*let out* the *hint* I give *you*. But I really think they must be frightened.' Despite her efforts, Wolseley's demand was rejected.[108]

On 11 March the Gladstones dined at Windsor. Not surprisingly it was a strained and awkward occasion. The Queen recorded in her diary that Mrs Gladstone 'began lamenting over all the trouble & anxiety I had had', whereupon Victoria told her: 'I should have been far less distressed had I felt that the right thing had been done.' Mrs Gladstone 'shook her head, saying she hoped not, whereas I told her I was sure of it'.[109]

The only shred of comfort Victoria clung to was that Gordon would be revenged by military action in the Sudan, but soon that prospect receded. A new crisis arose because the Russians were in dispute with the ruler of Afghanistan about the Afghan frontier. Britain could not allow the Russians to dictate the outcome, and on 12 March the Cabinet agreed that dealing with this problem might have to take priority over operations in the Sudan. 'Quite staggered' at this, Victoria sent the Prince of Wales to remonstrate with Hartington, prompting Gladstone to burst out that 'government through the Queen was becoming impossible'. He confided to Edward Hamilton he dreaded having to see her before she left for a spring break in Aix-les-Bains, 'because he was afraid he should be unable to say anything really civil'.[110]

By 4 April war with the Russians was looking a real possibility after they submitted 'almost insulting' proposals about the Afghan frontier. When they were informed this was unacceptable, Victoria was pleased by the firm tone, although she could not resist adding they doubtless had 'expected the government would swallow everything'. She was, however, 'aghast' when on 13 April her holiday in France was disrupted by Gladstone informing her that ministers now favoured abandoning the Sudan, as it was impossible to fight two wars at once. Furiously she telegraphed she could not consent to something that would constitute 'the *triumph* of savages over British arms', an outburst that merely confirmed to Gladstone that her judgement had become 'worthless'. She in her turn told Ponsonby that the prime minister 'is insufferable, arguing & never *listening* to anything said against his *own wise notions. It is unbearable.*'[111]

On 2 May Russia agreed that the Afghan frontier should be delineated through mutual negotiation. War was thus averted, but since plans for military operations in the Sudan were not revived, there was no question of Khartoum being retaken. Using the acronym which some people now said stood for 'Gordon's Old Murderer', the Queen demanded of Ponsonby, 'Can the GOM not be roused to some sense of honour?' It left her, she told Granville, 'quite at a loss how to go on' with her prime minister.[112]

At the beginning of May 1885 Gladstone confided to Home Secretary William Harcourt, 'My relations with the Queen have lately become so unpleasant that I shall not be sorry when they are terminated.' It did not look as if he would have to endure the purgatory for much longer, for the government was now so unstable its fall appeared imminent. Apart from the Sudan, ministers were at odds over the budget, but Ireland, as ever, was the worst source of ructions. Things became so acrimonious that on 16 May, Gladstone could write, with a rare flash of irony, 'Very fair Cabinet today: only three resignations.'[113] In fact, although several ministers had provisionally resigned, none had actually departed the Cabinet when, on 8 June, the government's budget was unexpectedly defeated by Tories and Parnellites voting against the beer and spirit duties, while many Liberals abstained. The following day ministers agreed that Gladstone should telegraph their resignation to the Queen at Balmoral, with the prime minister being the only one to express any doubts that this was the right course to follow.

For months Victoria had been saying she longed for a change of government, but she was not pleased about the timing. The annual Ascot race meeting was in progress, and she always absented herself from Windsor during this time to escape the 'noise and great crowds'. Clearly, forming a new administration was going to be problematic because the Tories would be reluctant to take office while they had a minority in Parliament. The Queen however had no wish to leave her Scottish retreat. Having told Gladstone she was surprised he considered a budget defeat necessitated his resignation, she demanded that he or another minister travel to Balmoral. To her annoyance he answered that 'he had not much more to say & wished to avoid the journey'. He needed to concentrate on moving out of Downing Street (Victoria thought his selfishness merited an exclamation mark), so her early return was 'anxiously desired'.[114]

Victoria then said Hartington should come north in Gladstone's place. When, however, it was pointed out to her that people would assume she was offering him the premiership, she abruptly cancelled his visit. Instead, at 6 p.m. on 11 June, Lord Salisbury, who had said that while he did not want to form a government, he would be ready to do so should the government not reconsider their resignation, was told to take the night mail train to Scotland. 'This is being sent for with a vengeance!' he commented.[115]

Having accepted Gladstone's resignation by telegraph, Victoria followed this up with a reproving letter. She still thought he or one of his colleagues ought to have travelled to Balmoral, which 'would have shown the public how anxious the Queen was to know anything before she acted, instead of allowing it to appear that she was wasting time in Scotland'. As regards her own return, in blithe disregard of the fact that Gladstone was ten years her senior, she reminded him, 'the Queen is a lady nearer 70 than 60 … and … quite unable to rush about as a younger person and a man could do'. Ascot was a further inconvenience, but she would nevertheless return to Windsor the following week.[116]

It was somewhat surprising that the Queen had looked to Salisbury for her next prime minister. When Lord Beaconsfield had died, instead of a single successor replacing him at the head of the Conservative Party, Sir Stafford Northcote and Lord Salisbury exercised a 'dual leadership'. The Queen had nevertheless written to Northcote in May 1881, '*She* will look on Sir Stafford Northcote as the Leader of the great Conservative Party.' Since then Salisbury had defied her more than once; she had told Lord Derby (who, as it happened, was Salisbury's stepfather) he had not been easy to deal with during the Reform Bill crisis. In recent years, however, Northcote had lost authority with unruly Tory members. He had been feeble in orchestrating the vote of censure debate on Khartoum, which the government might have lost if he had gone on the offensive, and Salisbury was indisputably 'more qualified for the pitched battle' of politics. Accordingly the Queen decided Sir Stafford 'would not do' as prime minister.[117]

Salisbury arrived at Balmoral on 12 June and saw the Queen after luncheon. They discussed possible ministerial appointments, and he told her he planned to take on the Foreign Office himself, as well as being prime minister. He indicated he would still prefer the Liberals to remain in office, but when Victoria referred back to Gladstone she was told it was too late for his resignation to be rescinded. Despite all being seemingly settled when Salisbury left Scotland on 13 June, difficulties arose as soon as he reached London. Firstly it emerged that Sir Stafford Northcote would not accept being marginalised as quietly as everyone had hoped. On 14 June an anxious Queen relayed to Salisbury that a letter from Northcote indicated, he 'has not … realised that he is not to be leader!' Once Sir Stafford did grasp the situation he became disinclined to fall in with Salisbury's proposal that he go to the House of Lords as colonial secretary. Partly this was because Victoria's treatment of him rankled. To other Tories Sir Stafford manifested 'a certain feeling that she had not behaved kindly … towards him', and in his journal he noted: 'The Queen's passing me over without a word of sympathy or regret is not pleasant.' The problem was sorted out when she wrote a 'charming letter' offering him an earldom, after which he agreed to join the government. Victoria was greatly relieved but did not regret rejecting him as prime minister: 'He is too good & gentle for these turbulent times.'[118]

Another issue proved trickier to resolve. The Redistribution Bill agreed upon by Gladstone and Salisbury had only just become law, and it emerged that until new registers had been compiled for the reorganised constituencies, it would be illegal to hold an election. This meant that if Salisbury's minority government was defeated in the Commons, he could not dissolve Parliament. Having met with colleagues on returning to London, Salisbury telegraphed the Queen on 14 June that the Liberals must pledge to support the government in the Commons, for otherwise the ministry would be in limbo – unable to appeal to the country even if it proved impossible for them to conduct business or raise essential funds. Some leading Tories were reluctant to take office anyway, and without some kind of security would not participate in government.

This was the situation the Queen had to grapple with when she arrived back at Windsor on 17 June. In her irritation at having had to shave a few days off her Balmoral sojourn, she had issued a diktat that in future 'ministerial crises must not happen again in Ascot weeks and during Balmoral times'. Once back, however, she showed commendable willingness to tackle this present difficulty. That afternoon she saw Salisbury and agreed to forward his request to Gladstone. He returned the unpromising answer that, while he believed there would be 'no disposition to embarrass' her new government on the Liberals' part, he could not compromise the liberties of the House of Commons by making firm commitments. Salisbury indicated to Victoria this was not good enough, so on 18 June she met with Gladstone to see if they could find a way forward. He reiterated that in current circumstances attacks on the new government would be 'most improper and most indecent'. When the Queen pointed out that 'some of his followers might not be so scrupulous', he said that Salisbury could take his assurances in the same spirit as had characterised their talks on the Seats Bill. Afterwards, Gladstone recorded: 'She was most gracious & I thought most reasonable,' while the Queen told Ponsonby that Gladstone had been 'particularly pleasant'.[119]

Unfortunately Salisbury was by no means satisfied by what was on offer. With agreement seemingly 'further off than ever', Victoria sent Ponsonby to sound out Gladstone as to whether he would resume office if Salisbury backed out. Gladstone said that while this posed problems he would do his best not to leave the Queen without a government, but suggested she reassured Salisbury he could be trusted. The Queen acted on this by writing to both Salisbury and Gladstone, for once showing admirable balance. While showing sympathy for Salisbury's predicament, she suggested to him that Gladstone's 'promise of general support might be accepted as a binding guarantee to uphold the government until there was a dissolution', and she offered 'to strengthen these assurances by publicly recommending them'. To Gladstone she wrote that, although 'the Queen has the most perfect faith in Mr Gladstone's words', she understood why Salisbury found it 'impossible to regard a promise of general support' as a sufficient security. She fervently hoped Gladstone could devise a more satisfactory formula, for 'if the crisis continues much longer ... it may affect the best interests of the Empire'.[120]

By 21 June Gladstone believed it likely that the Liberals would have to take power again, for though the Queen was going to make a 'decided effort to induce Salisbury to persevere ... I cannot say the *odds* lie on that side'. The memorandum he wrote that day gives the impression that by now he did not altogether dislike the prospect of resuming office. In the meantime the Queen continued with her efforts, sending Ponsonby to London to confer with both party leaders. On 22 June Ponsonby had a day of exhausting personal diplomacy, shuttling back and forth between Salisbury's London residence and 10 Downing Street. Salisbury drafted a letter he wished the Queen to send to him for publication, stating exactly why she believed he could trust Gladstone. However, when Ponsonby showed it to Gladstone, the latter thought Salisbury was implying Gladstone had committed himself to giving stronger support than was actually the case. Gladstone therefore struck out some of Salisbury's text and substituted his own wording, but when this was shown back to Salisbury, he too rejected it, and made alterations of his own. The Queen noted that Ponsonby's telegrams reporting on these exchanges 'followed each other quickly & bewilderingly'. When Ponsonby left London that evening, Salisbury was still saying he could not take office on terms acceptable to Gladstone. Having had 'a dreadful day of it', Ponsonby arrived back at Windsor at 11.30 p.m. and found that while he was on his way there Salisbury had sent Victoria another amended letter, once again trying to nudge Gladstone into giving stronger guarantees. The Queen very properly said she would stick to a text Gladstone had approved. On the morning of 23 June, Salisbury telegraphed his consent, and when Ponsonby returned to London bearing a final version, Salisbury said he could now take office.[121]

Annoyed by what he saw as 'incessant attempts by the other side' to twist his words, Gladstone telegraphed Windsor warning he would not tolerate an unreasonable interpretation being put upon them, leading Victoria to fear he was 'half backing out'. However, when informed, Salisbury said the matter was now settled, so Gladstone's pique could be ignored. 'What a relief!' the Queen declared. A few Conservatives still felt Salisbury had been unwise to accept office, but he told one sceptical backbencher that the pressure Victoria put on him had been irresistible, and Sir Michael Hicks-Beach, who had been strongly against taking power, believed she had won Salisbury over with tears.[122]

When Salisbury came to kiss hands on the afternoon of 23 June, he said he feared he had given Victoria 'a great deal of trouble'. While not denying this, she was pleased by how things had turned out. Gladstone too felt that throughout the crisis she had 'played a strictly constitutional part'. On the other hand he felt Salisbury had 'been ill to deal with, requiring incessant watching', so the new government began in an atmosphere of ill will.[123]

When she had accepted Gladstone's resignation, Victoria had written offering him an earldom. Touched, Gladstone had told Granville it 'moves and almost upsets me. It must have cost her much to write, and it is really a pearl of great price.' He declined the peerage, but gave warm thanks for 'your Majesty's generous, most generous letter. He prizes every word of it ... It will be a precious possession to him, and to his children after him.' On 24 June he came to Windsor and 'kissed hands in farewell'. According to the Queen, he was again 'most amiable', and she in return gave him 'half an hour of kindly conversation'.[124]

Doubtless her graciousness stemmed largely from the assumption that she would never again have political dealings with him. A week earlier he had told his former colleagues that he would retire when the next parliamentary session ended. Victoria had little reason to doubt this, for during the last five years he had spoken often of withdrawing from political life, and recently had 'repeatedly told her' this was what he intended.[125]

Even though for the past six months relations had rarely fallen short of mutual detestation, within three weeks of Gladstone's departure the Queen had invited him to stay at Osborne. He was able to decline because his voice had given out through overuse, and his doctor had advised him to talk as little as possible. Victoria would doubtless not have found the prospect of a mute Gladstone unbearable but affected polite disappointment. Undeniably, however, the change of government afforded her a huge sense of release. Her cousin the Duke of Cambridge even heard she was 'so rejoiced and *happy* to be rid of Gladstone and his filthy lot!!' that she compared herself to 'a young girl set free from school'.[126]

Landseer's 'Her Majesty at Osborne'. The Queen hoped the painting would show that despite being forced into seclusion by grief, she continued to work hard, supported by her faithful servant John Brown. When exhibited at the Royal Academy in May 1867, the painting provoked ribald comments.

Photograph by Cornelius Jabez Hughes of Benjamin Disraeli, 1st Earl of Beaconsfield in July 1878, following his return from the congress of Berlin. The Queen found him 'full of poetry, romance and chivalry'.

A 1879 portrait of William Ewart Gladstone by John Everett Millais. The Queen came to detest 'that *half-mad firebrand*'.

Painting by George William Joy depicting General Gordon's death at Khartoum in early 1885. Queen Victoria held Gladstone and his government responsible for the spilling of 'Gordon's innocent, noble, heroic blood'.

Above: The family of Queen Victoria gathered at Buckingham Palace for the 1887 Golden Jubilee celebration, painted by Laurits Regner Tuxen. On the right, in a white uniform, Victoria's son-in-law, Fritz can be seen, already stricken by mortal illness.

Right: The Queen shaking hands with ladies at the Golden Jubilee Garden Party in June 1887, painted by Frederick Sargent. This was the event where she tried very hard – unsuccessfully – to avoid talking to Gladstone.

The two widows, Victoria and Vicky, pictured together a few months after the death in June 1888 of Vicky's husband. They are gazing at a portrait of the late Emperor Frederick.

An 1895 chromo-lithograph portrait of the Queen's last Prime Minister, Lord Salisbury. Victoria considered him 'so very wise and calm'.

A painting by Thomas Jones Barker showing Queen Victoria presenting a bible to a grateful East African envoy. It was painted before Prince Albert's death, some twenty years before the 'Scramble for Africa' got under way. When Britain set about expanding its territory in Africa, propagation of the gospel did not provide the main motivation.

An 1891 portrait by Rudolf Wimmer of Kaiser William II in the British admiral's uniform he had been granted the right to wear two years earlier. Initially 'quite giddy' with delight, his goodwill towards Britain did not last.

A 1894 photograph of the family at a wedding in Coburg. The day before, the Queen (seated, centre) had been 'quite thunderstruck' when her granddaughter, Alicky of Hesse (in fur boa) informed her she was engaged to the Tsarevich Nicholas (in bowler hat).

Tsar Nicholas II and Alexandra (with baby Olga) pictured with the Queen and Prince of Wales during their 1896 visit to Balmoral.

Queen Victoria in the Garden Cottage at Osborne, 1894, flanked by her 'Munshi' Abdul Karim.

Watercolour of Queen Victoria writing, 1897, by Mary Helen Carlisle. Despite her failing eyesight, Victoria continued working until the end of her life.

11

Lord Salisbury; Mr Gladstone 1885–1886

At fifty-five Lord Salisbury was the first of Victoria's prime ministers to be younger than her, but with his dislike of physical exercise and outdoor pursuits, this stooping, heavily bearded and overweight man, was hardly the embodiment of youthful vigour. Despite the fact that, as the second son of the 2nd Marquess of Salisbury, he came from a privileged background, he had not had an easy early life. He had been hideously bullied and very unhappy at Eton, and perhaps this had contributed to his somewhat bleak view of humanity. In his twenties he had become estranged from his family because, rather than taking an heiress wife, he married in 1857 the middle-class Georgina Alderson. For seven years he had not been welcome at the family seat, Hatfield, and had made his living partly through journalism. Only in 1865 were his prospects transformed when he inherited the courtesy title of Lord Cranborne on the death of his elder brother and became his father's heir. He had been MP for Stamford since 1853, but when his father died in 1868 he went to the Lords as the 3rd Marquess of Salisbury.

While in the Commons Salisbury had acquired a reputation for caustic attacks on opponents, and during the debates on the Second Reform Bill in 1867, he had been vitriolic about Disraeli. Even after he joined Disraeli's Cabinet in 1874, the relationship was far from friendly, but once he became foreign secretary in 1878 he and Beaconsfield became close. Having found Beaconsfield's funeral 'inexpressibly sad', he wrote the Queen a 'beautiful' letter of condolence that left her 'deeply moved'. Victoria had taken to Salisbury some time before that, describing him after his first visit to Osborne as 'particularly agreeable and gentle, and who one could not believe could be so severe and sarcastic in debate'.[1]

Salisbury's marriage was a great success, and he was never happier than when at Hatfield, surrounded by his numerous highly intelligent if somewhat eccentric progeny. He was nevertheless a fundamentally pessimistic man, prone to depression and the stress-related condition of eczema. As a natural elitist who believed passionately in a hierarchical society, he decried what he called 'the insane passion for equality'. In daily matters he was progressive, installing electric lighting at Hatfield and experimenting in his laboratory there, but in politics it was otherwise, and he had a profound distrust of democracy. While the Conservatives were in opposition, there were several occasions when the Queen felt he had jeopardised the constitution by carrying opposition to Gladstone too far, although she had welcomed the way Salisbury tore into Liberal foreign policy. While very much a conviction politician, he could be ruthless and even somewhat unscrupulous when dealing with adversaries – and was not so highly principled that he eschewed dubious manoeuvring if it yielded results.

Salisbury respected the Queen's opinions – his wife would later claim he told Victoria everything. On at least one occasion during his first premiership he actually withheld crucial information, but he valued her judgement sufficiently to tell his children that discussing public affairs with her was like doing so 'with a man'. The Queen for her part had great faith in his ability to restore Britain's prestige abroad, which she believed had been disastrously eroded by Gladstone. After reading one of Salisbury's telegrams to a diplomat stationed overseas, she enthused, 'He is so wise,' finding dealing with him infinitely more congenial than interactions with Gladstone. She told Cranbrook, the Lord President of the Council, that after years of struggling through Gladstone's convoluted and unintelligible letters, 'it was a real comfort to receive Salisbury's simple straightforward communications'. Her letters to the German crown princess soon abounded with praise of her prime minister. In early 1886 Victoria declared Salisbury: 'one of the most intelligent and large-minded and unprejudiced statesman I ever saw', and shortly afterwards described him as 'the brightest light I think in the country'. There were times when she tried Salisbury's patience: 'Balmoral has got a telegraphing fit just now – which is a great aggravation to the trials of life,' he told a colleague in the autumn of 1885,[2] but he was always attentive to her wishes. Although not malleable or given to flattery like Disraeli, he showed sensitivity and skill in handling her, and was invariably deferential and courteous. Victoria came to trust him implicitly.

Salisbury's handling of foreign affairs was soon tested by a crisis in Bulgaria. At the Congress of Berlin in 1878, Bulgaria had been divided in two. Its southern portion, Eastern Rumelia, remained a Turkish possession, but while Bulgaria itself was still under the sultan's suzerainty, a German cousin of the tsar's, Prince Alexander of Battenberg, had been installed as prince there. Before taking up his responsibilities the prince came to England and was brought to see the Queen by his younger brother Louis, an officer in the Royal Navy. The visit was a resounding success. As well as being delighted to hear that Alexander – nicknamed 'Sandro' – 'wished on no account to be considered … a tool of Russia', Victoria found him 'good looking' and utterly charming. After the prince left she wrote to Salisbury (who was Beaconsfield's foreign secretary at the time): 'recommending Sandro, whom I feel much interested in'.[3]

With Gladstone, Prince Alexander was not such a favourite. In 1883, Sandro abrogated the constitution of Bulgaria, arguing it was necessary to prevent the Russians making him their puppet. Annoyed that the prince had refused to be their pliant tool, the Russians threatened to depose him. Gladstone was reluctant to help a man he considered 'little short of an idiot', but in September 1883 the Queen ensured that Alexander was upheld with a declaration of 'moral support'. Profoundly distrustful of 'that whippersnapper of a Prince', Gladstone alleged that 'hatred of Russia, and I fear indifference to liberty' shaped the Queen's viewpoint.[4]

Six weeks after Salisbury took over as prime minister there were new developments. In September 1885 Eastern Rumelia rose up, demanding to amalgamate with Bulgaria, and Prince Alexander responded to the call. The Russians, still sore at being thwarted two years earlier, incited the sultan to take action against Alexander. Victoria was most anxious for Sandro to be supported, but Salisbury warned it would be dishonourable for England to tear 'up the arrangement which she forced on Europe seven years ago' at Berlin.[5] However, he started to contemplate the possibility that, while the two Bulgarian provinces should not be formally united, perhaps Alexander could be established as ruler of both parts, subject to the sultan's overall suzerainty.

The Queen took this up enthusiastically, assuring Salisbury that her concern about Russian intrigues was quite independent of her 'own personal regard and friendship for Prince Alexander'. When a conference of powers was convened, Salisbury indicated that Britain would only attend on the understanding there would be no return to the *status quo ante*. Further complications arose when Serbia invaded Bulgaria at the end of the year, but to Victoria's delight Alexander routed the aggressors. Thrilled at the way his success 'baffles Russia',[6] she hoped this would clear the way for Sandro's being recognised as ruler of Bulgaria's two component parts, securing his position for ever.

When someone asked Salisbury if he found it taxing to serve as foreign secretary while also heading the government, he answered that he would cope very well if he just had two departments to deal with, but 'in fact I have four – the prime ministership, the Foreign Office, the Queen and Randolph Churchill – and the burden of them increases in that order'. Lord Randolph Churchill was the erratic second son of the Duke of Marlborough. He was impulsive and uncontrollable, prone to terrible rages that may have been caused by a brain tumour, or possibly syphilis, but he also had flashes of brilliance and could be an inspiring speaker. He had built up a great following in the Conservative Party, and Salisbury had known it would be impossible to form a government unless Churchill had a prominent place in it. When Salisbury had arrived at Balmoral on 12 June he had at once asked Victoria if she had 'any insuperable objection'. Though 'rather startled' that he intended to make Churchill Secretary of State for India, she had not vetoed the appointment.[7]

Churchill proved to be a temperamental and touchy minister, and Salisbury confided he found him 'in general ... a great difficulty'. Before long, the Queen had a particular cause for annoyance with him. She wanted her son Arthur, Duke of Connaught, to be made Commander-in-Chief of the Bombay Army, which she hoped would be a stepping stone to his becoming Commander-in-Chief of the British Army. To prepare the ground she wrote to her Indian viceroy, Lord Dufferin, and also canvassed leading army officers in India. When Churchill learnt she had been communicating with the viceroy without going through him, he tendered his resignation on 17 August. Victoria was taken aback by his 'absurd behaviour', but the prime minister was able to smooth things over as regards the resignation, and Churchill soon 'returned to reason, "having taken calomel" as Lord Salisbury amusingly words it'.[8]

However, Churchill did not drop his opposition to the Duke of Connaught's appointment. On 9 October the Cabinet, incited by Churchill, agreed that Arthur should not have the Bombay command, as it might embroil him in political questions 'not ... fitting for a Prince of the Royal Family'. The Queen protested to Salisbury that the 'principles advanced are very dangerous & very wrong', and 'these objections *never* would have been raised' had it not been for Churchill. She felt

Salisbury should have 'put his *foot down* in the Cabinet', but the prime minister did not think it worthwhile taking a stand on the matter.[9]

It was only a partial consolation to her that Churchill decided – in what the Governor of the Punjab called an 'easy-going jaunty way' – to punish King Thibaw of Burma for being insufficiently mindful of British interests. After it was alleged that Thibaw was intriguing with the French and behaving despotically, an army was sent into Burma in early November 1885. By the end of the month Mandalay had been occupied, and the next step was the country's annexation. On 29 December Lord Dufferin wrote gallantly that he was placing Burma as 'a New Year's Gift at your Majesty's feet'. It would prove troublesome, as local insurgency kept large numbers of British troops busy there, but the Queen was delighted by her new acquisition.[10]

Despite this successful foreign adventure, a dominion nearer home posed a much greater challenge to what Joseph Chamberlain – in a reference to the administration's uncertain status until an election could be held in November – dubbed 'the caretaker government'. Irish policy had split Gladstone's ministry asunder, with vitriolic arguments taking place in Cabinet over local government arrangements and the maintenance there of law and order. At the time the Tory opposition had opportunistically sought to compound the Liberals' difficulties by secretive dealings with Irish Nationalist politicians, but now that Salisbury was in power he did not favour making significant concessions to them.

This being so, his choice of the Earl of Carnarvon as Ireland's new Lord Lieutenant was an odd one. Carnarvon was known to be troubled by Ireland's status as 'an English Poland', and in February 1885 had written to Salisbury that a 'fair and reasonable arrangement of Home Rule' (by which he, like all his contemporaries, meant some form of devolved government, rather than independence) was 'our best and only hope'. At the time Salisbury had answered he was 'not hopeful' such a thing was achievable, making his appointment of Carnarvon all the stranger.[11]

On 6 July Carnarvon announced in the Lords that the government would not be renewing the Crimes Act. Speaking optimistically of attaining Anglo-Irish 'unity and amity', he said he was going to Ireland 'to hear, to question, and as far as possible to understand'.[12] Eleven days later some members of the government made another gesture of sympathy to the Irish Nationalists. During a Commons debate arising from Parnell's demand for an enquiry into the execution of a man allegedly wrongly convicted of murder, Randolph Churchill conspicuously failed to defend Gladstone's Irish viceroy, Lord Spencer, who had approved the death sentence.

This made the Queen uneasy. She worried firstly about discarding coercion, writing to Salisbury, 'She hopes Lord Carnarvon will not be too eager to give up necessary precautions, for the snake is only scotched not killed.' Churchill's undermining of Lord Spencer was also not to her liking, as it made it appear the government was 'trying to cajole the Nationalists who … *everyone but* Lord Randolph in the Cabinet *must know* are *totally unreliable*'. She explicitly cautioned that 'any attempt to have any communication with Mr Parnell and his party she would greatly deprecate', and Salisbury seemed to concur completely. Promising that he would personally endorse Spencer in the House of Lords, he assured the Queen, 'He entirely agrees with your Majesty in thinking that the Nationalists cannot be trusted.'[13]

This hardly accorded with the fact that Salisbury was on the point of sanctioning a secret meeting between Carnarvon and Parnell. In theory it was to be just a listening exercise, and Carnarvon was supposed to take with him a colleague who could monitor what was said. In fact, when the encounter took place on 1 August in London, Carnarvon was unaccompanied. Salisbury had made it clear to Carnarvon beforehand that he personally could not countenance a substantial measure of Home Rule and furthermore had warned he was not prepared to split his party as Peel had by pushing through a policy unacceptable to it. Exactly what was exchanged by the two protagonists at the time remains hazy. In a memorandum he wrote for Salisbury afterwards, Carnarvon admitted discussing setting up a central legislative chamber for Ireland, but stressed he had emerged from the meeting with 'no sort of bond or engagement'. Next day, Carnarvon went down to Hatfield to give Salisbury a verbal report and the prime minister praised him for acting with perfect discretion. However, Salisbury stipulated that the Cabinet could not be informed of what had happened, and although Carnarvon wished to bring the Queen into the secret, the prime minister vetoed this.[14]

Carnarvon still hoped to take an imaginative approach in Ireland. In Cabinet on 6 October, he declared he wished to explore the feasibility of setting up an Irish assembly. The idea met with a cold reception. Six weeks later he returned to the matter in Cabinet on the eve of the election and once again received no encouragement. Afterwards Salisbury repeated to him that his own views were unchanged, and moreover said that he himself could not remain a member of a government that adopted such a policy. Carnarvon said he thought it preferable that he resign, although at Salisbury's request he agreed to defer it for a time. Much later Salisbury would observe to Carnarvon, 'No one could suggest that I coquetted with Home Rule,' and Carnarvon confirmed that he had consistently repudiated it.[15] At the time this was not how Gladstone interpreted the situation. Almost certainly he had learned of Carnarvon's meeting with Parnell and assumed that Carnarvon was embracing Home Rule with Salisbury's encouragement.

Gladstone's own ideas had been evolving over the autumn. Prior to leaving office he had confided to the Queen he now thought some form of 'central local government' for Ireland was desirable, but since she understood he was about to retire she assumed he would never have a chance of implementing his ideas. This proved a miscalculation, for Gladstone soon persuaded himself it was incumbent on him to stay on as Liberal leader. One reason for this was the likelihood of more Nationalist MPs gaining seats in the forthcoming general election, which would 'shift the centre of gravity in British politics'. With the Irish question becoming ever more pressing, he believed he could make 'some special contribution' to providing the solution.[16]

Gladstone now believed limited schemes of local government for Ireland would fail to satisfy Nationalists. Information he gleaned via indirect contacts with Parnell convinced him that the Tories had already made sweeping offers of new arrangements to be put in place in Ireland. He reasoned that, as a result of these 'heightened biddings', the Irish would accept nothing less than major constitutional changes.[17]

He was well aware that embarking on a substantial programme of Home Rule – which entailed setting up an Irish legislative chamber – was fraught with difficulty and danger. Right-wingers would inevitably object, but many Liberals would also be against it. Hartington, who had remained profoundly distrustful of Irish Nationalists since the assassination of his brother, was likely to be particularly hostile, but Joseph Chamberlain would also object to any scheme that differed significantly from his own ideas on Irish governance. What was more, Home Rule would be unwelcome to a sizeable portion of voters, so if Gladstone revealed his thinking too clearly before the election, it might well cost the Liberals many seats.

Gladstone therefore proceeded cautiously, dropping hints to sound out leading Liberals, without committing himself to anything. On the whole he received very discouraging responses. Both Hartington and

Chamberlain made speeches in the autumn reaffirming that they objected to Ireland being given its own Parliament, and Hartington tried to warn Gladstone that he was unlikely to stay in the Liberal Party if such a project was pursued. Gladstone remained wary, without being deterred.

The Queen was as yet unaware of the direction Gladstone's mind was taking and as far as Liberal policies were concerned she was more bothered about Joseph Chamberlain's domestic programme. Besides tax reforms to hit the wealthy, he was advocating a general onslaught on 'the sacred rights of property', a left-wing agenda that threatened to create a schism in the Liberal Party as well as horrifying Victoria.

Once she had grasped that Gladstone would lead the Liberals into the coming election, she wrote on 2 October urging him to disassociate 'himself entirely from the extreme set of visionaries' in his party who espoused 'destructive doctrines'. Trusting 'she will not appeal in vain to Mr Gladstone's personal devotion to herself, and to his patriotism,' she indicated that 'any words of Mr Gladstone's which affirmed that Liberalism is not Socialism, and that progress does not mean revolution' would be welcome. While thinking her comments somewhat 'peculiar', Gladstone appreciated the 'very kind tone' of the letter, and his reply was intended to be soothing. Agreeing that he was in favour of 'progress without revolution', he tried to reassure her that Chamberlain's more extreme projects would not be adopted. However, his letter ended on what, with hindsight, could be construed as an ominous note, as he observed 'that the Irish Question may after the dissolution once more assume for a time a forward or even a dominant position'.[18]

Certainly Ireland was currently Gladstone's own principal preoccupation. He wanted the Liberals to secure a large overall majority at the election, as that would allow him to tackle the Irish question on his own terms. Not only would he then not have to worry about whether the entire Liberal Party supported him on it, but he could devise a Home Rule measure that did not defer entirely to the wishes of the Nationalists. For this very reason the Nationalists did not desire an overwhelming Liberal victory, calculating that it would be more advantageous for them to hold the balance in a new Parliament. They may have deluded themselves that the Tories were contemplating Home Rule, and if so, a Conservative government would be better placed to push such a measure through the House of Lords.

Regaining power at the head of a large Liberal majority was Gladstone's preferred option but, failing that, he could envisage

Ireland's problems being resolved by a Tory government. He misinterpreted campaign speeches by Salisbury, taking them to mean that the prime minister was sympathetic to Home Rule. If Salisbury undertook it, the Liberals would gain from the Tories being split on the matter, while Gladstone would avoid the ignominy of disrupting Liberal unity. As a result, Gladstone did not encourage Parnell to look to him to fulfil Irish aspirations, telling the Nationalist leader the government were better placed to take action. Parnell was so disheartened by Gladstone's aloofness that on 21 November 1885, just before voting began in the general election, he ordered all Irishmen living in England to support the Conservatives. While recent estimates have revised downwards the number of extra seats the Tories gained from this, it certainly was of use to them, and instead of the sweeping Liberal victory Gladstone had wished for, a hung Parliament was returned. Results started coming in on 23 November. The Queen had initially been hopeful about Conservative prospects, until gradually it became clear that in rural areas newly enfranchised agricultural labourers had voted Liberal, securing the party 334 seats. The Tories had 250 MPs, while the Irish Nationalists had 86; so only if the two parties voted together in the Commons could the government retain power.

The Queen was desperate for the government's survival, but to secure it she had different combinations in mind. She prided herself on being a centrist (even if nobody else saw her as one) and for some time now had cherished visions of moderate politicians melding together in coalition. She had started propounding the idea during the Reform Bill crisis of 1884, writing of her 'great wish that a Third Party could be formed of the Moderates on both sides' to prevent 'the violents' causing mischief. Now she believed it was time for the desired fusion to take place. On 3 December – by which time it was apparent the Conservatives were performing poorly at the polls – she wrote to Salisbury, 'Things must and can not return to what they were, for it would be UTTER ruin to the country and Europe. Mr Gladstone and Lord Granville are *both utterly* unfit, from age alone, to carry on the government, and to *them* the Queen will *not* resort. Whatever *apparent* majority they may have – it is *entirely divided* and *all moderate* and *intelligent* people *have no* confidence in them ... We want a strong coalition, and to this end every nerve must be strained.'[19]

Salisbury was not terribly encouraging, saying that while it might be possible in future to detach Whigs from radicals, now was not the moment to make formal overtures. The Queen clung on, insisting that 'coalition … though difficult, would probably be the best solution'. She hoped Hartington would be part of it, and also raised the possibility of 'a middle party forming under Mr Goschen'. The latter was George Goschen, a former governor of the Bank of England who had headed the Admiralty in Gladstone's first government but had been excluded from the last Liberal ministry because he opposed extending the franchise. Goschen had commended himself to the Queen by voting against that government on several occasions, and in 1884 she described him as 'eager for' the formation of a third party. After she told Salisbury she wished to enlist Goschen, the prime minister agreed the Queen should contact him.[20]

It was not fanciful of Victoria to think this might prove fruitful, for although Gladstone's views on Ireland were still shrouded in mystery, both Hartington and Goschen feared he now leaned towards Home Rule. They were sufficiently alarmed to envisage not coalition, but rather 'some promise of independent support to the government', which would keep the ministry in without the Tories having to ally with the Irish. When the Queen sent Sir Henry Ponsonby to see Goschen, he proved gratifyingly receptive, declaring he 'was working hard' to persuade Hartington and others to 'make a strong middle party' that would frustrate any attempt of Gladstone's to bring down the government. As for coalition, 'that might come, but it must not be forced'.[21]

The problem was that until Gladstone revealed where he stood, even Liberals who were nervous about what he planned for Ireland were reluctant to desert him or defy his wishes. The Queen refused to be disheartened. When Cranbrook saw her on 13 December, he found her 'sanguine', and hinting she had 'private information as to the Moderates'. She was 'emphatic' it was realistic to look to them for help. '"I know" she said, striking the table with her hand.'[22]

Meanwhile, Gladstone was deluding himself that Salisbury, Randolph Churchill and Carnarvon favoured some form of Home Rule, and were only holding back because they were 'afraid of their colleagues and their party'. He was quite wrong about Salisbury and Churchill, even if it was true that Carnarvon now desired a joint committee of both houses to consider the government of Ireland. He had put this to the Cabinet on 23 November, but his ideas met with little favour. After the Cabinet had dispersed, Carnarvon had gone down to Windsor for two days and while there discussed Ireland with Victoria. Carnarvon reported to Salisbury he found 'HM very much alive to the whole subject and desirous … of knowing my own opinion.' Feeling it 'necessary to speak with plainness', he had declared there was 'great danger' in failing to address the Irish question 'broadly and finally', and 'a measure of self government might now be given which would not have the semblance of being extorted'.[23]

An alarmed Salisbury confessed to Ponsonby, 'I did not anticipate that Lord Carnarvon would trouble the Queen with this question at this stage.' He made it clear that his own thinking did not align with the viceroy's, explaining that he personally was strongly opposed to the notion of a separate parliament for Ireland. 'Any policy of utter surrender to Mr Parnell, such as this would be, would be profoundly repugnant to public opinion in this country, and especially to the ... Tory Party,' entailing 'an entire loss of honour among public men'. The Queen defended Carnarvon, saying she had asked him to be frank, but after she had reflected for a few days, her regard for him begun to waver. On 12 December Lord Cranbrook saw her and, 'HM spoke as if she had not been satisfied with his proposals when he was at Windsor and was evidently distrustful.'[24]

She need not have worried, for on 14–15 December the Cabinet definitively rejected Carnarvon's joint committee idea. Salisbury informed the Queen ministers had agreed, 'it was not possible for the Conservative Party to tamper with the question of Home Rule'; in his diary Carnarvon wrote dejectedly his colleagues felt that 'if a great change comes, it must be done by other hands'.[25] Despite finding himself isolated, Carnarvon was prevailed upon not to resign until Parliament met in the new year.

Since Gladstone was ignorant of these developments, he still hoped the government might move in the direction he wished. On 15 December he tried to raise the matter confidentially with Salisbury's nephew, Arthur Balfour, but before he could take this further, his son Herbert torpedoed his father's efforts to keep his views about Ireland to himself. After Herbert had given several unauthorised interviews to the press, the *Pall Mall Gazette* stated on 17 December that Mr Gladstone had not only 'definitely adopted the policy of Home Rule for Ireland' but was confident his party and the English people would concur in it. The Queen was agog at the 'extraordinary announcement ... that Mr Gladstone intended proposing a sort of Parliament for Ireland! In fact Home Rule!' To Salisbury she suggested, 'Can Mr Gladstone have thrown this *apple* of discord as a *feeler*?' – adding that, if so, she hoped this '*feeler* ... respecting Home Rule will split the Liberal Party'.[26]

Gladstone tried to stick to his strategy of prodding the Tory government into taking on the job of Home Rule for him. On 20 December he wrote to Balfour that the Tories could count on his support if they took up Home Rule, although with a typical Gladstonian qualification he spoke of 'reserving necessary freedoms'. When Balfour passed on the offer to Salisbury, his uncle was contemptuous. Sure that Gladstone simply wanted to destroy the Tory party, Salisbury commented, 'His hypocrisy makes me sick.'[27] He decided not to give Gladstone an answer until the new year, and then it was in the vaguest terms.

By that time Gladstone had decided on his course, although he made only a few trusted intimates privy to it. Ignoring the advice of Liberals who suggested it would be better to leave the Tories to grapple with difficulties posed by Ireland, he resolved that if, when Parliament met, the Conservatives brought in measures for Ireland of which he approved, he would not seek to turn the government out. On the other hand, should their policies run counter to his wishes, he would topple the ministry, take office, and bring in a plan of 'duly guarded Home Rule'.[28] To most Liberal MPs, all this was opaque. Screened from the GOM's tortuous thought processes, they told themselves that he was still uncommitted regarding Ireland.

The Queen was not among those prepared to give Gladstone the benefit of the doubt. On 20 December she wrote confidentially to Goschen to 'urge and implore' him to do everything to ensure that Liberals who did not favour the 'mischievous and incomprehensible' policy of Home Rule would not be misled by party loyalty into abetting Gladstone. In the most emotive terms, she appealed 'to all moderate, loyal and *really patriotic* men, who have the safety and well-being of the Empire and the Throne at heart' to avert the destruction that would come about 'if the government again fell into the reckless hands of Mr Gladstone'. Lord Hartington must be persuaded it was '*his duty* ... to his Queen and country, which really goes before allegiance to Mr Gladstone' to prevent the latter bringing down the government. Provided that Goschen, and other men of goodwill, stood aloof from their leader, all would be well, with the added bonus (in the Queen's eyes) that 'out of this might grow a coalition in time'. Having stressed that '*No* one knows of this letter,' she concluded, in a final spasm of emotional blackmail: 'I think a Queen, and one well on in years, and who has gone through terrible anxieties and sorrows, ought not to appeal in vain to English gentlemen.'[29]

Goschen had in fact already been badgering Hartington to make his position clear, and on 21 December the latter issued a public statement reaffirming his opposition to Home Rule. But when replying to the

Queen, Goschen outlined the difficulties of marshalling widespread Liberal resistance to Gladstone. Firstly, many MPs still hoped he was not set on Home Rule, and did not want to go against him, even if they were far from eager to turn out the government. Furthermore, while few viewed Home Rule in a positive light, the difficulties of fashioning an alternative policy were so great that some were inclined to tell themselves Gladstone knew best, and that Home Rule was inevitable. Undaunted, the Queen next despatched Ponsonby to see if Sir William Harcourt could be enlisted in the fight. Harcourt's son learned she was still promoting coalition, and that she envisaged 'that "the extremes" (meaning Gladstone and Randolph Churchill!) should be got rid of'. Then, 'Hartington should be PM and Salisbury foreign secretary under him!' Despite being 'terribly alarmed' about what Gladstone had in mind for Ireland, Harcourt said these proposals were 'utterly impossible'. The Queen therefore had to fall back on keeping Goschen and Hartington 'up to the mark'. She warned Goschen, 'Mr Gladstone (in his 77th year) is *bent* on forcing himself into office'. Once there, he would wreak havoc, having doubtless '*persuaded* himself again that he has some mission to do great things for Ireland'.[30]

To demonstrate her support for the Salisbury ministry, the Queen agreed to open the new Parliament on 21 January 1886. The prime minister and Cabinet agonised over the contents of the Speech from the Throne which, even though the Queen was present, was to be read out as usual by the Lord Chancellor. The government now had to define its own Irish policy (particularly since on 13 January news had leaked of Carnarvon's retirement) and Victoria advocated playing what Gladstone called an irresponsible 'Tory game' – namely, 'working the Irish question to split the Liberal Party'.[31] It was obvious that Gladstone might seek to turn out the government by proposing an amendment to the speech, but Victoria reasoned that if Gladstone was forced to disclose that he wanted Home Rule, a significant number of Liberals would be sufficiently dismayed not to support his tactic. Furthermore, she wanted the Conservatives to reintroduce the Coercion Laws, as this would demonstrate clarity of purpose and show undecided Liberals that Gladstone was not the only man with answers.

To her distress, Salisbury could not persuade his Cabinet that coercive legislation was necessary, and in the end the Queen's Speech was something of a fudge. Having described union with Ireland as part of Great Britain's 'fundamental law', it asserted that, should the state of

Ireland warrant it, a new Coercion Law would be introduced in due course. This was not enough to flush out Gladstone, and the Queen was angered that in the debate following the Speech from the Throne, he took refuge in 'ambiguous utterances'. Greatly disappointed that Goschen and Hartington did not probe him more deeply, she chided Goschen that this failure showed '(pray forgive the expression) "want of moral courage"'.[32]

Salisbury acknowledged to the Queen that the Speech from the Throne had created 'a bad impression' of vacillation and drift, and on 24 January he prevailed upon recalcitrant members of the Cabinet to drop their opposition to a reimposition of coercion. An announcement was made to this effect on 26 January, but it was too late to retrieve the situation, for Gladstone adopted the cunning strategy of urging Liberals to vote for an amendment to the address that regretted the government were doing nothing to improve the condition of agricultural labourers. Since this had no bearing on Irish government, many Liberals who were uneasy about Gladstone's intentions on that score could vote for the amendment in good conscience. Not all took this view: when it came to the division, seventy-six Liberals abstained, and sixteen – including Hartington and Goschen – voted with the government. However, with the support of the Irish Nationalists, the amendment secured a majority of seventy-nine.

At Osborne, the news hit the Queen 'like a thunderbolt', and Harcourt's son heard 'she wept for several hours'. She at once telegraphed Salisbury begging him not to 'resign on "a triviality"', but after convening a Cabinet, the prime minister replied it was inevitable that losing such a vote be treated as fatal. A change of government was therefore unavoidable.[33]

Victoria still hoped she could choose who would head the new ministry, telling Ponsonby fiercely: 'To call upon Mr Gladstone *with his radicals* to form a government, the Queen will NOT do.' The reality was she was not a free agent – for everyone consulted agreed she could not bypass Gladstone. Two days before the amendment vote, the leading Liberal peer Lord Rosebery had told Ponsonby, 'it would be a great calamity and a blunder' if she began by sending for Hartington. Once she applied to Gladstone, he might be unable to form a government and then Hartington could legitimately take over the task; but Gladstone must be given first opportunity. Beaconsfield's former private secretary, Lord Rowton, likewise told her, 'it would be better if I could *not avoid* sending for that dreadful Mr Gladstone, to do so at once, rather than call on others who might fail.' Hartington himself confessed to the Duchess of Manchester, 'I hope the Queen won't ask me, but I am afraid she may,' despite there being not 'the slightest chance of my being able to form a government with Lord S'. Even so, when Salisbury came down to Osborne on the evening of 28 January, and he too said there was no alternative to Gladstone, the Queen countered that she wished to speak with Goschen. Salisbury agreed she could invite Goschen to Osborne, though he suggested she give out that she was doing it at his behest rather than on her own initiative. Touched by his thoughtfulness, the Queen reflected, 'What a dreadful thing to lose such a man as Lord Salisbury for the country, the world, and *me*.'[34]

She had already written to Goschen emphasising that if Gladstone was invited to form a government, Goschen, Hartington and other 'moderate Whigs should keep aloof … Pray do your utmost in this direction.' Word duly came from Goschen that he and Hartington would not join an administration headed by Gladstone, but declining to come to Osborne, as doing so would expose her 'to much misconstruction and misinterpretation'. In conclusion he wrote, 'I would earnestly entreat your Majesty to send for Mr Gladstone.' Even now Victoria was not ready for this. She had already told Ponsonby she did 'not the least care' that her evident reluctance to call upon Gladstone might excite comment, for 'the Queen … rather wishes it should be known that she has the greatest possible disinclination to take this half-crazy & really in many ways ridiculous old man'.[35] Still refusing to resign herself to the inevitable, she sent Sir Henry to London with instructions to see Lord Salisbury first, then Goschen, and only after that, as a last recourse, to go to Gladstone.

Ponsonby did as instructed, but when he saw Salisbury on the evening of 29 January the latter repeated she must apply to Gladstone. Despite this unequivocal advice, Ponsonby then went on to Goschen's house, only to find he was out to dinner. Returning near midnight, Goschen was horrified to find Ponsonby waiting for him. He begged Sir Henry 'not to lose a moment, but to see Mr Gladstone at once', as already there was 'a disagreeable cry getting up' about the delay in offering him the premiership. Accordingly, Ponsonby moved on to Gladstone's home, reaching it at 12.15 a.m., just as Gladstone was going to bed. Somewhat lamely, but as agreed with Victoria, Ponsonby explained he had not come sooner because the Queen had taken Gladstone at his word when he had said he wished to retire. Now, although he was free to decline, she wished to know if he would take on the task of government. Gladstone at once accepted. When the Queen received the news by telegram the following morning she commented, 'Alas!'[36]

Ever since the vote on the amendment Gladstone had been impatiently awaiting her summons. As early as 27 January he had sounded out Sir Henry James as to whether he was willing to become his Lord Chancellor. When James had indicated he was not, Gladstone had mused, 'I really do not know I shall be sent for at all, but I suppose eventually the Queen must ask my assistance.' He feared that when she did, the request might not be unconditional, and 'I may have terms or restraint imposed upon me I could not consent to.' James agreed the Queen might indeed insist on the maintenance of the legislative union with Ireland and, while thinking it quite likely, Gladstone added darkly: 'She must be careful.' He also 'spoke with some bitterness' of her choosing to remain at Osborne instead of coming up to Windsor, thereby 'causing great delay … and inconvenience' to the politicians involved.[37]

By 29 January, when the summons had still not come, Gladstone was growing frantic. In the evening he held a dinner party and, according to one of the guests, observed that it was starting to look as though the Queen and the government were intending to ignore the vote in the Commons. Grimly he pronounced: 'All I can say is that, if they do, the Crown will be placed in a worse position than it has ever occupied in my lifetime.'[38]

Contrary to his fears, when Ponsonby finally arrived with her message, the Queen imposed few conditions. Her first stipulation was that Lord Granville could not return to the Foreign Office. Gladstone 'clasped his hands and said "This is most painful"' but admitted the ban was not entirely unexpected. She also excluded Sir Charles Dilke from any ministerial post, which she was able to do because he had been cited in a divorce petition, due to be heard shortly. Gladstone bowed to her wishes, saying 'he very much feared' that when the case came to court, Dilke 'would not be cleared of blame'.[39]

Gladstone at once set about trying to assemble a government, a task the Queen hoped would yet prove beyond him. To try and lure in those who were alarmed by the thought of Home Rule, he wrote a memorandum saying he simply wished to examine whether it was practicable to set up a separate legislative body in Dublin that would not undermine the Empire's unity. When he showed this to Hartington, despite Victoria's fears that the latter was 'so lukewarm and without energy' that he would agree to join the government on this basis, he refused.[40]

In contrast, when approached, Chamberlain said that while he would decline office if Gladstone had made up his mind about a separate Irish Parliament, provided it was an open question, he was ready to participate. Lords Derby and Selborne were among the peers who rejected Gladstone's overtures, but Sir William Harcourt agreed to become Chancellor of the Exchequer, despite being no enthusiast for Home Rule. Gladstone was also heartened that Earl Spencer agreed to be Lord President of the Council after declaring himself a convert to Home Rule. As the new Chief Secretary for Ireland, Gladstone selected John Morley, a controversial choice in view of his advocacy of Home Rule during the election campaign. Discussing the appointment with Victoria, Gladstone would concede that Morley was a radical, but also 'a gentleman and an agreeable man'. The Queen had been momentarily reassured until, at a farewell audience on 5 February, Lord Salisbury told her Morley was 'in fact a Jacobin'.[41]

Gladstone had still not sorted out all his difficulties when, after a sleepless night, he 'went off gallantly' to Osborne early on 1 February. He was dreading what awaited him there, telling his son: 'I think the Queen will bowl me over.' On arrival, things got off to a bad start, for he was 'much put out' when Ponsonby warned that the Queen would not allow Hugh Childers to have the War Office. Realising this was just the forerunner of troubles to come, Gladstone requested that in future Sir Henry avoid sending him 'unpleasant letters at night, as it prevented his sleeping'.[42]

In some ways, the audience with the Queen went better than anticipated. She began by remarking 'he had undertaken a great deal', and Gladstone assured her 'he felt the seriousness of it'. With brutal directness, she then said she 'feared his proposal of a Central Legislative Assembly in Dublin would never succeed', as not only would he be regarded as Parnell's puppet, but 'all the loyal Irish would rise … and there would be Civil War'. Gladstone answered simply: 'He might fail, it was 49 to 1 that he would, but he intended to try.' He pointed out that the political landscape had been altered by the return of so many Nationalist MPs – only for the Queen to dismiss them as 'mostly low, disreputable men'. In her account of the interview she recorded, 'He struck me as being … intensely in earnest, almost fanatically so, in his belief that he is almost sacrificing himself for Ireland.' He assured her that his colleagues, and she herself, would be at liberty to oppose any plan for Home Rule, should he propose it. The Queen was pleased by his readiness to consider her suggestion that Lord Rosebery should become foreign secretary, despite his being 'rather young'. She noted in her journal that Gladstone looked very pale, and 'seemed dreadfully agitated and nervous'.[43]

Gladstone was 'on the whole pleased with his visit'. While he was there, a message had come from Granville saying he would join the Cabinet as colonial secretary, so that was one less thing to worry about. Having returned to London 'tired but in good heart', Gladstone told his son that in contrast to her usual stance of 'armed neutrality', the Queen had been 'very kind'. He would doubtless have been less happy had he known that 'in strict confidence' Victoria had at once sent a full report to Salisbury. The latter replied thanking her for the update and promising to heed her request to take every 'remote chance of pressing the antagonist closely'. Aware they should not really be communicating about it, he concluded: 'Lord Salisbury, for reasons which your Majesty will understand, thought it better not to telegraph on this question.'[44]

In theory the last time that the Queen should have had contact with Salisbury was when he came down to Osborne on 5 February for the formal relinquishment of office. 'Regret very much that this is Lord Salisbury's last visit as my Minister,' she recorded in her journal. A few days before she had offered him a dukedom, which he had respectfully turned down, and now she 'told him many details' about the latest developments. Salisbury was heartened when she showed him Hartington's 'very fierce and uncompromising' letter to Gladstone declining office and agreed that 'every means *must* be used to bring Mr Gladstone to book'. He told her, 'they must force the new government to *speak out at once* on the Irish policy, and that they would have to organise and encourage meetings of the loyal Irish in Ireland and England'. When she took leave of the other outgoing ministers on 6 February, she manifested a similar fighting spirit, telling Lord Cranbrook she hoped it would be 'a *very* short time before she saw me in her service again'. Then, 'with much emphasis she added, "We must agitate (I do not like agitation) but we must agitate every place small as well as large & make people understand."' She apparently said much the same to every departing minister, declaring to Sandon, Salisbury's Lord Privy Seal: 'We must agitate in every village' on the Irish question.[45]

The incoming ministers had a trickier time when, later that afternoon, they came to kiss hands. To Lord Spencer she expressed amazement at his 'inconceivable' change of heart regarding Home Rule. He said nothing had yet been decided, but he had 'for some time had a sneaking feeling that something of this kind would have to be resorted to'. Afterwards Spencer reported to Gladstone she had listened attentively, but he wished he could have put forward some stronger arguments. 'I got in some good ones,' he maintained, 'but you know it is not very easy with HM to continue a distasteful subject.' In fact, Victoria had been unimpressed by everything he said: 'Altogether I thought his explanations very unsatisfactory and weak' was her verdict.[46]

Like Salisbury, the Queen wanted Gladstone to disclose his intentions regarding Ireland as soon as possible, believing that once he did so, moderate Liberals would desert him in droves. On 4 February she therefore demanded he '*state explicitly what* his "examination" would lead to', because it was not right that the country should be led 'step by step' towards a measure 'which Mr Gladstone *knows* the Queen cannot approve'. Gladstone fobbed her off by saying it was impossible to predict what the outcome of his enquiry would be, though confessed in his diary her letter 'made me anxious'.[47]

Unable as yet to sink her teeth into Gladstone's Irish policy, the Queen still found plenty to displease her. Gladstone had failed to find a duchess who was willing to become Mistress of the Robes, as their husbands feared it would look like an endorsement of his policies if their wives took the post. Although delighted the prime minister was finding the matter so troublesome, she wrote to the Prince of Wales, 'It is atrocious of Mr Gladstone ... to expose *me* to having only half a household.'[48]

Gladstone had 'tried very hard' to persuade the Queen to withdraw her objection to Childers having the War Office, but she had been implacable. In the end the post went to the 'good honest Scotchman' Henry Campbell-Bannerman, while Childers became home secretary. In that capacity Childers soon incurred royal displeasure, for on 8 February thousands of unemployed and impoverished workers rioted in London, wreaking much destruction on West End property (including the Carlton Club). At once the Queen informed Gladstone, she 'cannot sufficiently express her *indignation* at the monstrous riot', describing it as 'a *momentary* triumph of socialism and disgrace to the capital'. She demanded 'very *strong*' steps be taken 'to put these proceedings down with a high hand', making it clear she thought it hardly a coincidence the regrettable event should have occurred '*just* when a Liberal-Radical government' had come into office. Gladstone agreed the disturbances had been 'deplorable and disgraceful', but to Victoria's fury Childers objected it would be 'a very grave step' to outlaw future 'tumultuous assemblages' in Trafalgar Square.[49]

In April he annoyed her again when he made light of her warnings that Belgian socialists might be liaising with their English counterparts, inciting them to revolution. Childers said airily, 'Englishmen as a rule dislike foreigners,' so it was unlikely there would be much collusion between different nationalities. To Ponsonby the Queen commented angrily: 'He would let everything go on, and never punish anyone! He is frightened at his shadow.'[50]

Before that, she had been displeased by reports that at a dinner given on 24 February by leading Liberals for newly elected 'working men' MPs, hissing was heard when her health was proposed. She had anyway felt disquiet that a dozen 'Labour representatives' – such as the former miner Thomas Burt and the farm worker Joseph Arch ('a bad Socialist') – had been returned at the polls, and this increased her unease. Gladstone hastened to assure Ponsonby that press accounts had 'grossly and ludicrously exaggerated' the incident, although he could not deny something of the sort had taken place.[51]

A Commons motion demanding reform of the House of Lords that was put forward on 5 March by the radical MP Henry Labouchere afforded fresh vexation. Gladstone spoke against it – but, to the Queen's mind, did so somewhat equivocally, and she upbraided him for appearing 'to support that wretched Mr Labouchere's views while opposing his outrageous resolution'. The prime minister said it was hardly surprising that all his party wished for Lords reform, and his own reluctance to call for it was indulged as the 'pardonable superstition of an old man'. This prompted the Queen to deliver an impassioned encomium on the way the Lords provided a 'wholesome check upon the great and increasing radicalism of the present day'.[52]

Gladstone knew he must not squander any last vestiges of royal goodwill by being unnecessarily provocative. In March 1886 he asked Childers to vote against a motion calling for the disestablishment of the Welsh Church put forward by the radical MP Lewis Dillwyn. 'It is very desirable to avoid multiplying causes of the Queen's mistrust at this particular moment,' he explained. 'The day is near at hand when we shall want all our strength to be used in that quarter for the great purpose of the present juncture.'[53]

Even Victoria did not see the government as uniformly bad, for she believed the Foreign Office was in good hands. She told her eldest son, 'the *only* really good appointment (and that is *my* doing, for *I* asked for him and *insisted* on having him) is Lord Rosebery.' Not yet forty,

Rosebery was debonair, charming, and sensitive – at times almost morbidly so. Rich in his own right and made wealthier by marriage to a Rothschild heiress, he had initially commended himself to Gladstone in 1879 when he had acted as his host and impresario during the first Midlothian campaign. The Queen had taken to him while he was in his early twenties, finding him 'pleasing and gentlemanlike'. Since then, Rosebery had been a welcome guest at Balmoral, making such a favourable impression that in 1884 Victoria had suggested he buy a nearby Scottish estate, as 'we should like so to have you as a neighbour'.[54]

Rosebery had not had a great deal of ministerial experience, as Gladstone had refused to appoint him to the Cabinet until he had served an apprenticeship in junior posts, and Rosebery had turned several down as beneath him. Only in February 1885, within weeks of the government's collapse, had he finally entered the Cabinet as Lord Privy Seal. Now, when Gladstone offered him the Foreign Office at the Queen's behest, Rosebery professed himself overwhelmed. At an audience with the Queen on 6 February, he was still saying 'it was too much', but Victoria was confident she had chosen wisely. She was pleased that Rosebery said he wanted continuity in foreign policy, and even happier when Salisbury reported, after briefing Rosebery, that he seemed 'fully inclined to defer to your Majesty's views'. She at once volunteered to be Rosebery's mentor, reminding him she had 'nearly fifty years experience, and has always watched particularly and personally over foreign affairs'. He winningly replied: 'Your Majesty's great experience and Lord Rosebery's absolute inexperience in foreign affairs do indeed represent the opposite extremes and he can only congratulate himself and the country ... that the one is used to correct the other.' On 28 February she delightedly wrote to Salisbury that, besides being an assiduous correspondent, Rosebery was 'very respectful & very grateful for intelligence from her'.[55]

The Queen particularly liked the fact that the foreign secretary was a convinced imperialist. In March 1886 she responded readily when he asked her to open 'with all conceivable pomp' the Colonial and Indian Exhibition to be held at the Albert Hall in May. Cheerily she promised to do it 'with all the pomp you like as long as I don't have to wear a low-cut dress', only baulking when he suggested she wore her crown. Despite Rosebery's lamenting to Ponsonby that 'the symbol that unites this vast empire is a crown and not a bonnet', he could not prevail. Nevertheless, the opening ceremony, attended by nationalities from all countries of the Empire, was a great success. Victoria was tremendously cheered and acknowledged the crowd's plaudits with curtseys.[56]

As Gladstone bent his mind to drawing up plans for Ireland, the Queen could find comfort in the fact that the opposition were not waiting passively. As early as 9 February, Goschen had called on Salisbury and suggested that if another election was held, Tory candidates should not stand against Liberal dissidents who voted down Gladstone's Irish measures.[57]

Salisbury may have updated her about this in person. Certainly on 28 February she wrote to him from Windsor that she hoped soon to 'have the pleasure of seeing Lord Salisbury'. Prior to that, Salisbury had met with Hartington, and they had agreed to work together to resist Home Rule. Randolph Churchill was also active, visiting the north of Ireland to stir up loyalist Protestants. His bellicose speech to a vast crowd in Ulster Hall, Belfast, prompted Liberal accusations of inciting insurrection.[58]

On 10 March Gladstone sent Victoria what she described as 'a sketch of his Home Rule and Land measures'. The following day, she forwarded to Salisbury some of the 'voluminous correspondence' that had recently passed between her and the prime minister. Twelve days later Gladstone produced a more detailed memorandum. In it he argued that because the Irish viewed current laws relating to land as 'impositions by foreign authority', it was essential Ireland administered its own criminal code. For this, it was necessary to set up a statutory parliament there, although its powers would be limited, so would not touch on matters such as defence and foreign policy. It was also impossible, he said, to go on ignoring the 'strong permanent instinct of a people' for autonomy, asking: 'Is Irish Nationality of necessity a thing unreasonable and intolerable?' He tried to make the idea of an Irish legislative assembly more appealing to the Queen by saying that currently, Irish MPs tended to ally with radicals in Parliament, but since it looked likely that Home Rule would 'release them altogether from attendance at Westminster', the Commons would become more moderate.[59]

He followed this up with an audience with Victoria on 24 March, at which there was 'no indication of a seeming storm', but her apparent acquiescence was deceptive. When he wrote to inform her on 26 March that he had now unveiled his ideas in Cabinet, and Chamberlain and another Cabinet minister had resigned, she said she was anxious he was committing to a measure 'which does not appear to command the approval of the majority of her subjects'. Unbeknownst to Gladstone she had already had two secret meetings with Goschen, who had filled her in on what he was doing to coordinate opposition to Home Rule. On 29 March, she updated Salisbury on all this, claiming the outlook was encouraging. She declared blithely, 'I write in the 1st person, as this is not an official letter,' apparently persuading herself that deviating from the established forms also permitted her to break constitutional rules.[60]

Victoria had mixed feelings about Chamberlain's resignation. She wrote to Goschen that if Chamberlain and some of his radical allies helped defeat Gladstone's dangerous project, this 'would be a good thing'. On the other hand, an alliance between Hartington and Chamberlain would 'rather complicate matters' when it came to the 'so much wished' union of Whigs and Conservatives. For this reason, she hoped their collaboration would not extend beyond throwing out Home Rule. Once that had been achieved, '*then* the connection should end there, for *the* object to be *obtained* for the safety of the country *is* a *union* with the *Conservatives* to put a *check* on *revolutionary* changes'.[61]

In the days before he introduced his Home Rule Bill in the Commons, Gladstone endured difficult Cabinet meetings and tense negotiations with Nationalists. On 3 April Mrs Gladstone asked the Queen if her husband could be excused from dining at Windsor, because he was so stressed. Victoria agreed, while fearing 'his absence may be misunderstood'. She meanwhile was busily fortifying Goschen's – and through him, Hartington's – resolve to fight Home Rule, insisting there must he 'no wavering' out of 'weak kindness for a former colleague'. She was still doggedly pursuing her long-term aim of coalition – assuring Goschen 'it would be very painful if old party feelings stood in the way.' When he warned 'an actual coalition government is … extremely difficult' because constituency parties would have strong objections, the Queen insisted this '*must* be got over'. Pronouncing that 'The country calls loudly for it & I *earnestly* urge it,' she asserted that while, 'I am the last person to overlook the *great* difficulties … it is the *only chance* … to resist democracy & socialism.'[62]

To the Queen's mind it was 'a sad & cannot help saying not creditable fact' that Liberals clung so obstinately to party loyalties; but Salisbury too was discouraging. While agreeing that coalition 'would be the best thing for the country', he did not think it a viable prospect for the moment. Hartington was equally pessimistic, forcing the Queen to face reality. To Salisbury she deplored the 'narrow, timid, unpatriotic feeling' among Liberals, while accepting it was '*safer* to proceed separately *at present* till these feelings wear off, as they surely will do in time'.[63]

On 8 April Gladstone demonstrated he had lost none of his rhetorical powers when he introduced his Home Rule Bill in the Commons. Hartington then spoke against it, pleasing the Queen by pointing out Gladstone had not warned voters of his intentions during the election campaign, so could not claim a popular mandate. After several days of debate, the bill passed its first reading in the early hours of 14 April.

That evening a mass meeting was held at Her Majesty's Theatre, Haymarket, to protest against Home Rule. Hartington appeared on stage alongside Salisbury and Goschen, but found it an uncomfortable experience. Gladstone's name was greeted with hisses, and when

Gladstone in combative mode at the despatch box of the Commons. (Drawing by Harry Furniss)

Hartington begged the audience to show respect for 'one whom I shall always admire and revere', it went down badly. Although such unpleasantness made it less likely that in future Liberal opponents of Home Rule would align with Tories, the Queen was delighted by how things had gone. She wrote to Salisbury, 'How admirably the meeting went off at the theatre! ... Meetings must be organised *everywhere & every* effort be strained to prevent the passing of this iniquitous Bill.'[64]

On 16 April Gladstone introduced the second part of his plan for Ireland, comprising a Land Purchase Bill, enabling Irish tenants to buy out landlords using loans from the government. It was to be financed by a £60 million bond issue, with probably as much being added later if the initial provision was insufficient. Despite its munificence, the measure was coldly received by Tories and landlords. Gladstone told the Queen they ought to grab it while they could, for such a generous offer would never be repeated. In fact, having introduced the bill, Gladstone himself seemed to lose interest in it, and thereafter focussed his energies on the second reading of the Home Rule Bill.

Probably because Gladstone now suspected that Victoria was regularly passing confidential information to Salisbury, he became much more reserved with her than previously. At the end of April she talked with Lord Rowton, and – as he informed Salisbury – she complained of knowing, '*nothing* of Mr G's mind or intentions, not having all along had any sort of communication with him on the government proposals'. Soon afterwards she grumbled to Salisbury, 'She only saw him *twice* since December!'[65]

On 6 May an 'ill and haggard' looking Gladstone did have an audience with her at Buckingham Palace, to brief her before debates started on the second reading. She suggested he completely redraw his bill, so as to give Ireland better local government, but he said this was unthinkable. Victoria recorded: 'He went on at great length' about the merits of his measure, 'I saying but little.' After he had left she wrote explaining 'her silence ... does not imply her approval', as she 'can *only* see danger to the Empire in the course he is pursuing'. She went on, 'The Queen writes this with pain, as she always *wishes to be able* to give her Prime Minister her *full support*,' before bringing herself to add: 'She fully believes that Mr Gladstone is solely actuated by the belief that he is doing what is best not only for Ireland but for the whole Empire.'[66]

In reply, Gladstone said that while opinion in Parliament was less supportive of the bill than he would like, feeling in the country was strongly in favour of it. A day later he informed her that to secure votes for the second reading, he was contemplating modifying his bill, so that, instead of being entirely excluded from Westminster, Irish MPs would be able to vote there on taxation issues affecting Ireland. In her journal, the Queen was scornful: 'What a peculiar idea! Trimming and balancing will please no one.' She wrote severely to Gladstone that it was surely mistaken to think there was widespread public support for a measure, 'which to the Queen appears to be censured and condemned almost universally'. In her view, he was embarking on 'an experiment in which the chance of disaster outweighs the likelihood of good result'. Gladstone responded humbly that he was 'deeply sensible of the considerate and gracious manner in which your Majesty treats a question necessarily painful ... He is well aware that, if he is wrong in this capital matter, all the labours and efforts of a long life cannot save his memory from disgrace.' Nevertheless, he could not see that his proposals risked 'Imperial danger', and he hoped that, as with earlier measures heralded by 'presages of ruin', the effects would be the reverse of harmful.[67]

Gladstone assured her he was aware of her desire to give 'an unvarying constitutional support' to her advisers, but perhaps he would have been less complimentary had he been fully aware of her dealings with Salisbury. On 7 May she saw Salisbury at Windsor, 'and talked over the situation with him'. Next day, clandestine arrangements were put in place to let them stay in touch. Lady Ely wrote to Salisbury that if he wished to communicate with Victoria while she was performing public engagements in Liverpool, he should direct letters to a hotel in London's Clifford Street, and she would forward them to Victoria. The Queen resorted to similar subterfuges to enable Goschen to keep her informed about the second reading debates. On 16 May she wrote to him, 'You could easily come down [to Windsor] & go to Lady Ely's room on Sunday to attract no attention.'[68] Her passing on to Salisbury copies of all Gladstone's correspondence was a still grosser violation of confidence.

On 9 May Gladstone introduced the second reading of the Government of Ireland Bill. He outlined the modifications he was incorporating, which included allowing Irish members to vote at Westminster on specified issues. When forwarding to Salisbury Gladstone's letter giving her the details, Victoria scoffed his proposals were now 'incomprehensible' – and certainly many people were surprised his concessions were not more extensive. It was not enough to win over Chamberlain, who wanted Irish MPs to stay at Westminster. Once again this made the Queen uneasy about a convergence between Chamberlain and Hartington that would scupper all chance of coalition, while conversely remaining fearful Gladstone might yet find a way of reconciling Chamberlain to the bill.[69]

In the letter he sent describing the debate that took place in the Commons on the night of 11 May, Gladstone for the first time mentioned the possibility that the second reading would not secure a majority, so it now became necessary for the bill's opponents to decide what to do in that event. Until recently, Salisbury, Goschen and the Queen herself had all been convinced an election must be avoided, thinking it probable that the Liberal Party would reunite during the campaign. Admittedly, by 25 April Victoria was starting to think that feeling in the country against the bill was becoming so pronounced that 'a majority against the Irish policy *would* be returned'. Still, an election 'had better *not* be risked at present', for it must be certain 'there will be a good majority against Home Rule before it could be conceded'.[70]

By mid-May, Salisbury had changed his mind. At the Queen's request he wrote a secret memorandum, explaining he now believed that if Gladstone asked for a dissolution after being defeated on the second reading, she should grant it. Although it was impossible to make accurate predictions, it was likely that opponents of Home Rule would make gains in an election, but if Gladstone resigned after being denied a dissolution, and a government led by Hartington took office, it was unlikely to last long. This meant that an election would soon happen anyway but would be fought under much less advantageous circumstances. Furthermore, if Victoria would not grant a dissolution, Home Rulers would blame her, and this would 'strain, and thereby possibly ... diminish your Majesty's great influence over your people'. Heartened by the knowledge that progress was being made on an electoral pact between Tories and Liberal dissidents, Victoria accepted Salisbury's advice. On 19 May she sent Ponsonby to tell Gladstone that if he requested a dissolution, she was minded to agree; there was 'not a word of truth' in reports suggesting otherwise.[71]

Another factor played a part in the Queen's thinking. She was impatient to set off for Balmoral, but if she rejected a dissolution, duty would require her to stay close to London while Hartington tried to put together an administration. Admittedly at one point she actually wondered if a change of government could be formalised at Balmoral, suggesting optimistically that ministers could travel up for a day, and return that night. 'It might be novel,' she coaxed Salisbury, 'but in these days of *railways, telegrams & changes* it could easily be managed.' Even someone so accustomed to putting her own convenience first, realised, after a little reflection, the arrangement was bound to attract criticism. Salisbury artfully exploited her desire to go to Scotland by using it to strengthen his argument for a dissolution, saying he was worried her health would suffer if she was detained in the south. This had helped Victoria make up her mind, even though she remained anxious that the decision to hold an election might backfire. So eager was she not to postpone her Scottish holiday, that although she had initially said she would not set off until the vote on the second reading had taken place, when the debate dragged on for longer than expected, she resolved not to delay her departure further. On 20 May she informed Salisbury she would soon be leaving, as she 'will not be kept here as a slave of the H. of Commons & the GOM'.[72]

All now hinged on whether Gladstone could secure a majority for the second reading of the Home Rule Bill. On 15 May Salisbury had made a particularly militant speech saying that Ireland needed twenty years of firm government before it could expect any increase in autonomy, because the Irish were no better suited to self-rule than, say, the 'Hottentots'. While few of Salisbury's countrymen objected to the idea that African tribesmen were incapable of governing themselves, many considered his equating them with the Irish to be insulting. Goschen told the Queen that Salisbury's provocative words had made several Liberal MPs less inclined to vote against Home Rule, and Gladstone too claimed the speech helped him make 'upward progress'.[73] On the other hand, Tories were working to reassure Liberals they would not risk their seats if they voted against the government, as Conservative candidates would not contest their constituencies.

As the vote neared, the ruling elite became so sharply polarised that the Earl of Carnarvon reported, 'Nothing can be more strained and disagreeable than politics and society now are.' One aristocratic lady refused to sit next to Lord Granville at dinner, telling her hostess he was 'a traitor to his country'. Gladstone became 'seriously perplexed' when planning an event on 29 May in honour of the Queen's birthday. He was uncertain whether Liberals such as Hartington would attend and feared the Prince of Wales and his son Prince Eddy – who had accepted the invitation – would be confronted by an empty dining table. In the end a full complement of Liberal luminaries were present, but Gladstone wryly noted that if Hartington had proposed a vote of want of confidence to his fellow guests, it would probably have carried.[74]

On 25 May, the day before she left for Balmoral, Victoria saw Gladstone. He told her he planned to hold a party meeting on 27 May, at which he would assure those present that a vote for the second reading would not commit them to supporting the bill in its entirety. Instead, after a prorogation, he would bring in a modified bill in an autumn session, or even start afresh with a new one. However, it soon became apparent that any changes to the bill would be very minor, prompting Chamberlain to instruct followers to vote against the second reading. His effective sealing of the bill's fate prompted the unusual acknowledgment from Victoria: 'Mr Chamberlain has behaved well.'[75]

On the evening of 7 June, Gladstone made an impassioned speech imploring parliamentarians for their support. He said that an 'expectant, hopeful, almost suppliant' Ireland was awaiting a decision that could confer 'blessed oblivion' on a 'broad and black blot' disfiguring Britain's history.[76] His eloquence fell on stony ground: when the division was taken, there was a majority of thirty against Home Rule – far larger than predicted.

While vainly seconding Gladstone's plea not to reject Home Rule, Parnell had electrified proceedings by declaring that, although the Conservatives were decrying the measure currently on offer as irresponsible, during the last Tory government a minister of the Crown had told him they intended to offer the Irish a statutory parliament. Commons Leader Sir Michael Hicks-Beach flatly contradicted this, being ignorant of the meeting between Carnarvon and Parnell. Carnarvon felt he had no alternative but to set the record partially straight, and on 10 June made a statement in the Lords. Salisbury tried to dissuade him beforehand, and when that failed, urged Carnarvon to be 'as dry as possible'. Carnarvon obliged by formally declaring that none of his colleagues had been aware of the encounter, not even revealing it had been authorised by Salisbury. He stated he had made no promises to Parnell, and that he did not agree with Gladstone's Home Rule Bill, although he would like to find some other way of satisfying 'the national aspirations of Ireland'. While he was speaking Salisbury sat in silence, offering no support.[77]

Victoria was shocked by Carnarvon's statement. 'What can she say & what does Lord Salisbury say to Lord Carnarvon & his admission that he saw or communicated with Mr Parnell?!! Is it not too bad, too outrageous?!!' she wrote. 'The Queen hopes Lord Salisbury will *never trust* him again.' Far from enlightening her, Salisbury said Carnarvon had 'acted impulsively', having failed to realise 'the shifty character of the man with whom he was dealing'.[78] If anyone was guilty of shiftiness, it was Salisbury. Even on 29 June, when he admitted to the Lords that Carnarvon had told him of the meeting with Parnell after it took place, he did not disclose he had sanctioned it in advance, and he always kept knowledge of this crucial fact from the Queen.

After his defeat, Gladstone at once requested a dissolution and Victoria promptly agreed. He wasted no time before setting off to Scotland to embark on his campaign, angering her by engaging in what she regarded as renewed demagoguery. She wrote to him regretting he was addressing crowds at railway stations, and at his going outside his constituency to visit Glasgow, 'where there are so many Irish of the worst type'. Gladstone was defiant, telling her that having entered on 'this great contest' it was 'not possible … to conduct it in a half-hearted manner'.[79]

The election was a bitter one. The Tories generally adhered to their pact with the Liberal Unionists by not standing against those who had voted against the second reading. They felt that Unionists did not fully reciprocate by encouraging their followers to vote Conservative in some constituencies, but both parties benefited from the public's hostility towards Home Rule. Gladstone nevertheless believed the electorate's mood was not unfavourable, and on 2 July, when results had only just started coming in, he predicted to the Queen that the Tories stood little chance of winning. Despite having to contend with 'anti-Irish prejudices' and 'the power of rank, station and wealth', he had never before seen such 'popular enthusiasm among the Liberal masses'.[80]

On 4 July – by which time voting patterns were becoming clearer – the Queen sent him a blistering reply. She pointed out that, far from supporting Gladstone's policy, the Liberal masses 'apparently voted in large numbers in favour of maintaining the legislative union with Ireland'. It was regrettable he had repeated his 'cry against the wealthy and educated classes of the country' and that he seemed unable to accept the 'conscientious conviction' that motivated members of his own party who opposed him. Her final barb was perhaps the most insulting thing she ever addressed to him: 'The Queen wishes that Mr Gladstone would recognise in his opponents the same honesty of purpose which she would fain believe actuates him.'[81]

On 8 July Gladstone had to acknowledge to himself 'the defeat is a smash'. While the Tories had not won an outright majority, their 316 seats made them the largest party. Gladstonian Liberals had secured 196 constituencies, and the Irish Nationalists had another 85, but provided the 74 Liberal Unionists supported the Tories, a Conservative government was viable. The only thing that afforded Gladstone any comfort was that this meant the 'cessation of my painful relations with the Queen'; he did not doubt she would 'have a like feeling' of 'great relief'.[82]

Victoria's antagonism to Gladstone had only been heightened by wild letters he had sent out from Hawarden prior to the election, and which had subsequently been published. In one typical outburst he had ranted that everyone must vote Liberal who did not want 'Dukes & Earls to overrule the nation & wreck its fortunes'. His 'monstrous and wicked' words merely confirmed to the Queen that Gladstone was 'trying to revolutionise the country'.[83]

Once the election result was known, Victoria penned a '*very confidential*' letter to Lord Rosebery, stressing that Gladstone must 'yield to this defeat' and 'not show any hopeless struggling to remain in office'. She also wrote to Goschen, urging that everything possible must be done to render Gladstone 'as *powerless* as possible'. She enlarged: 'It is clear that at his age & *after* the extraordinary letters he has written & the violence of his language & speeches he is *utterly* unfit to become Prime Minister again. His friends should therefore get him to retire, for his own good as much as for the country.' Goschen was hardly in a position to achieve this, for he had lost his own seat in the election.[84]

To Victoria's disappointment Gladstone decided to stay on as Liberal leader. He did at least agree that the government would resign at once, but this did not make the Queen better disposed to him. When Gladstone informed her in writing on 20 July the ministry would be stepping down, she replied with a letter that Edward Hamilton described as 'icy cold'.[85]

The Queen had not been idle while she waited to hear what Gladstone planned to do. Once again her thoughts tended towards a coalition. She actually thought that if she offered the premiership to the Duke of Argyll, a Whig who had resigned from Gladstone's government over the 1881 Land Bill, this 'might produce a combination of parties'. Lord Rowton had to discourage her, saying that 'a summons of the Duke at such a moment might be misinterpreted, and even twisted by the evil-minded'. She accepted she must give up that idea, but next hoped that Salisbury could head a coalition. Meeting with Goschen on 13 July, she asked him to pass on to Hartington how keen she was that he join one.[86]

Salisbury had been out of the country for the election campaign – having treatment in France for a severe bout of eczema – and received a royal summons home on 21 July. As soon as he reached England on the evening of the 23rd, Lord Rowton appeared with a message from the

Queen. Afterwards Rowton assured her: 'Lord Salisbury feels as deeply as your Majesty the paramount importance of coalition' and had promised to discuss the matter with Hartington before setting out next day for Osborne.[87]

Hartington knew he would probably be invited to enter a coalition but could see many objections. He feared that rather than follow him into a government dominated by the Conservatives, most Liberal Unionists would gravitate back towards the Gladstonians. In fact, when Salisbury made his proposition, he went further than Hartington, or the Queen herself, had expected. He suggested that Hartington should preside over a dual-party administration and that Salisbury should serve under him as foreign secretary, on condition that Joseph Chamberlain was not made a minister. Despite being seriously tempted, Hartington knew he would lose credibility by accepting.[88]

Reluctant to take his refusal as final, on 24 July the Queen wrote begging him to reconsider, but Hartington declined again. However, with Chamberlain's concurrence, he promised the Unionists would vote with the Conservatives in Commons divisions. He suggested that sustaining them from outside 'might be of as much use to them & might more completely defeat Mr Gladstone' than a formal partnership. On 6 August the Queen assured Hartington that while she understood his reasons for not joining the government, it was now '*imperative* on him and his followers' to stand by Salisbury. Three days later she wrote to Goschen: 'I, of course, regret that my dream of a coalition, which was also that of the country, could not *yet* be realised (for I *must* think it *will* come).' Nevertheless, provided the government could count on Unionist 'support on all essential points … this is the best way for the *time being*'.[89]

On 30 July Victoria had a farewell audience with Gladstone at Osborne. In his account of it, he acknowledged that her manner had been 'altogether pleasant', though he considered 'the conversation … a singular one, when regarded as the probable last word with the sovereign after … a good quarter of a century's service rendered to her in office'. She began with trivialities – talking of the weather, and his train being late, as well as suggesting that he must be in need of rest. 'Only at three points did the conversation touch upon anything even faintly related to public affairs.' The first was an allusion to the 'horrible last trial' of Sir Charles Dilke, who had sought to clear himself from the imputation of adultery that had clung to him after the divorce case heard in February, but who had only succeeded in completely destroying his reputation. When she brought up the way in which educational opportunities had been widened during her reign, Gladstone rather surprisingly agreed this had been 'carried too far & ... rendered the working classes unfitted for good servants & labourers'. Finally she displayed somewhat tasteless self-interest, asking him about a committee supposed to adjudicate on financial provision for her grandchildren. According to Gladstone, 'the rest of the conversation ... was filled up with nothings. It is rather melancholy. But on neither side, given the conditions, could it well be helped.' The Queen was better pleased by how it had gone. After Gladstone left, she told Ponsonby the 'interview ... as they avoided the Irish question, was most amicable'.[90]

Next day she wrote to Gladstone saying she had deliberately not touched on that, but now the country had 'unequivocally decided against his plan' he should accept 'the kindest and wisest thing he can do for Ireland is to abstain from encouraging agitation by public speeches'. She had originally intended to go further, by telling him not to impede any measure designed for Ireland's benefit (by which she presumably meant coercion). Furthermore, 'he should not encourage the Irish to expect they would ever get Home Rule, as that was impossible'. With some difficulty Ponsonby persuaded her to confine herself to requesting that Gladstone do nothing to encourage open defiance of the law. As it was, Gladstone was so dismayed by what he read that he exclaimed: 'Poor Ireland! It has but a small place in her heart.'[91]

12

Lord Salisbury 1886–1892

The Queen was not entirely happy with some of Salisbury's proposed ministerial appointments. When Salisbury apologetically told her he feared Lord Randolph Churchill must be Chancellor of the Exchequer and Leader of the Commons, Victoria 'did not like' the idea as 'He is so mad & odd.' Furthermore, while fond of Lord Iddesleigh (the former Sir Stafford Northcote) she questioned the wisdom of making him foreign secretary. It was not just that she feared, correctly, that his health was not up to it, but he was 'not, in my opinion, quite fitted for the post'. She was therefore 'rather sorry' he promptly accepted it. Such quibbles did not prevent her being generally overjoyed at the change of government. In August the Lord President of the Council, the Earl of Cranbrook, came to stay at Balmoral, and Lady Ely whispered to him that the Queen was 'another person' now Gladstone was no longer prime minister.[1]

Almost immediately the new government faced a major foreign policy challenge, for in the early hours of 21 August 1886 there was a coup in Bulgaria. Rebel army officers suborned, the Queen felt sure, by 'wicked, villainous, atrocious Russia', forced Prince Alexander to abdicate at pistol point. He was hustled onto his yacht and carried away to an unknown destination; for three days it was feared he had been murdered. Lord Salisbury regarded it as a 'lamentable catastrophe', but reversing the situation was highly problematic. Although Victoria's initial instinct was that 'open hostility to Russia was the best solution', she soon accepted this was unrealistic. Instead she demanded energetic diplomatic measures, writing frantically to Salisbury: 'We *must not* tamely swallow *everything*,' for Russia's behaviour was 'clearly meant as a slap in *our face*'. If Britain's ambassador to Russia could not be recalled, at the very least a conference of the powers should be held. As current minister-in-residence at Balmoral, Cranbrook was ordered to telegraph her views to Iddesleigh. After obeying, he noted unhappily, 'action is not so clear & easy as it appears to her'.[2]

Things looked slightly better when there was a counter-revolution in Bulgaria and the principal conspirators – who had been seeking aid from Russia – were arrested. The Queen 'could have jumped for joy' after Prince Alexander was located alive and well on the Russian-Romanian border, but unfortunately, before returning to Bulgaria, 'Sandro' decided to appeal to the tsar's better nature by sending him a private telegram. In what Victoria considered a much 'too humble' tone, he hoped the tsar would endorse his reinstatement. In reply, his 'barbaric, semi-Asiatic tyrannical cousin' the tsar – a 'savage' with the 'instincts of Nero or Caligula', in the Queen's view – declined to countenance Alexander's retaining power and then published their telegraphic exchange.[3]

Throughout the crisis the Queen had felt Iddesleigh's 'slowness, weakness and too great conciliatoriness' fell far short of what was needed. It shocked her still more that several other ministers showed themselves indifferent to Sandro's fate. At a 'rather disagreeable' Cabinet held on 7 September, Secretary of State for War W. H. Smith, First Lord of the Admiralty Lord George Hamilton, and Randolph Churchill were adamant nothing should be done to aid the prince. The last two even said they did not care if Russia took Constantinople – news which, when transmitted to Victoria at Balmoral, 'excited her' a great deal. To Salisbury she expressed displeasure that 'two young men, comparatively ignorant and inexperienced in these affairs' should presume to hold such views.[4]

Utterly demoralised, Prince Alexander reaffirmed his abdication and left Bulgaria. The Queen refused to believe his removal was permanent, telling Vicky: 'Somehow I always cling to the idea that he will some day come back triumphant.' It was arranged that in his absence Bulgaria would be ruled by regents, but Victoria was concerned that Russia would seek to destabilise the country and then occupy it on pretext of restoring order. When the Russians threatened to send ships to Varna, she demanded that Britain object; much to her dismay, Salisbury warned 'defiant language ... may make us ultimately ridiculous'. On being told that backing up threats by force was unfeasible, the Queen exclaimed mournfully: 'We are nothing any more and I cannot say what I feel and suffer.'[5]

Still hankering for Sandro's return, the Queen was upset when, weeks later, the Bulgarians sent a delegation to various European capitals seeking suggestions on who should replace the prince. She was thunderstruck when her own first cousin once-removed, Prince

Ferdinand of Coburg, put himself forward as a candidate. In a rage she telegraphed Salisbury: 'He is totally unfit – delicate, eccentric and effeminate … Should be stopped at once.' These protests were unavailing.[6] Prince Ferdinand duly became ruler of Bulgaria – and made a reasonable success of it.

Like the Queen, Lord Salisbury found Lord Randolph Churchill a terrible trial. Churchill regarded it as his right to try and shape British foreign policy, and domestically also pursued his own agenda – telling one colleague he was determined 'to drive Salisbury into a more democratic policy'. The Queen later observed, 'that strange unaccountable man … who has been a perpetual thorn in the side of his colleagues … expected all to bow to him'.[7]

On 22 November Churchill dined at Windsor, and the Queen was 'not much pleased' by anything he said to her. Subsequently she warned Salisbury that it 'looked as if he was likely to be disagreeable'. Lord Randolph was now querying the need for higher defence spending, but Victoria was categorical: Churchill 'must not be given way to'. Salisbury predicted things would be 'patched up for a time', even if the government was undeniably 'not a happy family'.[8]

On 20 December Churchill once again dined at Windsor. In conversation with the Queen he exhibited 'not a symptom of resigning', instead speaking 'very sanguinely' about the forthcoming parliamentary session.[9] Then, after dinner, he retired to write Salisbury a letter on Windsor Castle-headed paper. Having explained that as chancellor he could not accept the war minister's estimates for the army, he added with extraordinary effrontery that any increased outlay would have been unnecessary had foreign policy been competently conducted.

Salisbury did not offer to reduce the military estimates, so Lord Randolph informed the editor of *The Times* that he would be resigning. This meant that the Queen only learnt Churchill would be going when she read it in the paper on 23 December. Her anger at 'the want of respect shown to me' was compounded by Churchill's having had the 'audacity to write his letter of resignation from Windsor – the night he dined!'[10] It was all the more galling because the government looked unlikely to survive Churchill's departure.

Salisbury believed the government's only hope was to prevail on Hartington to take the premiership or, failing that, for the Unionists to enter into full coalition with the Tories. Surprisingly perhaps, the Queen was 'not keen' on either prospect, for though she had previously made out she desired a coalition above all else, purely Conservative governments were really what she liked best. However, recognising that her main priority must be 'prevention of WEG coming back into office',[11] she wrote at Salisbury's request to both Hartington and Goschen, inviting them to join the government. Hartington would not accept office of any kind but did help persuade Goschen to take on the chancellorship of the Exchequer.

Goschen made it a condition that Iddesleigh should not retain the Foreign Office, and Salisbury was pleased to have an excuse to resume acting as both prime minister and foreign secretary. While the Queen had often been dissatisfied with Iddesleigh's performance, she felt he had been treated shabbily, and urged Salisbury to put things right. 'Anything that looked like his management of Foreign Affairs being considered a failure, the Queen would consider as *very* wrong and most unjust as well as impolite,' she chided the prime minister. Matters took a tragic turn when Iddesleigh went to see Salisbury, only to suffer a fatal heart attack before the meeting began. Vindicated in her diagnosis of Iddesleigh's unhealthiness, the Queen felt 'it very much, losing again one of my best friends, so truly attached to me *personally*'.[12]

Henceforward both Salisbury and Victoria were absolutely implacable towards Lord Randolph, with the Queen considering his departure 'a good riddance'. Churchill soon realised he had miscalculated by resigning over defence spending, and let it be 'understood that he did not go out on finance, but that he withstood Salisbury, who in the interest of the Court was thrusting Battenbergism on the Continent and bringing about a European War'. When news of his indiscretions reached the Queen, she was '*quite* furious at anyone daring or presuming to say *she* wanted to make war on Russia to replace Prince Alexander', particularly when it emerged these falsehoods were being bandied about 'in *the Clubs* in London!!' She fumed, 'It is monstrous!!' – instructing Salisbury to arrange for someone to '*get at* this impertinent and *not* reliable or loyal ex-minister of hers'.[13]

Despite fears that unless placated Churchill might contrive to cause trouble for the government, the Queen set herself against his rehabilitation. When the Prince of Wales suggested to her in early 1888 that Churchill should be readmitted into office, his mother told him stonily: 'I cannot, I own, quite understand *your* high opinion of a man who is clever undoubtedly but who is devoid of all principle, who holds the most insular and dangerous doctrines on foreign affairs, who is very impulsive and utterly unreliable.' Bearing in mind Churchill's past behaviour, 'To have him again in the Government would be to break *it up* AT ONCE; and I shall do all I can to prevent such a catastrophe.'[14]

June 1887 marked the Queen's fiftieth year on the throne, and somewhat surprisingly she agreed her Golden Jubilee should be celebrated in style. Following discussions with Salisbury that began in October 1886, plans were put in place for 'a mob of royalties' to descend on London. Initially Victoria – who never liked paying for overseas guests – understood that the government would foot most of the bill, but by March 1887 she feared 'the expenses ... will fall most heavily' on her, and therefore requested 'some small helps' to ease the burden. Unfortunately the 'helps' were far smaller than she had anticipated. It was ultimately agreed that the Queen would put up family members at her own expense. Many were housed in Buckingham Palace, with the overflow staying at Spencer House (generously loaned by Lord Spencer) or hotels. Non-Europeans, such as representatives sent by the rulers of Japan and Siam, had their expenses borne by the Foreign Office, but Indian princely visitors had to pay for themselves. The festivities ended up costing the Queen nearly £50,000, and this still rankled with her in August 1888 when she told Salisbury she considered 'herself very shamefully used in having no real assistance for the enormous expense of entertaining that immense number of Sovereigns and Princes last year. This was originally promised and the promise not kept.'[15]

Problems also arose when it emerged that the Queen expected that her favourite son Prince Arthur, Duke of Connaught – who had taken up command of the Bombay Army only six months earlier – would be allowed home on leave. It was explained to her the law prohibited his absenting himself from India, but she insisted a bill be brought in permitting it. After the Cabinet considered the question in early March, Salisbury had to tell her that, while the ministry was struggling with other contentious legislation, 'it was idle to hope that any such measure be passed'. The Queen simply pronounced: 'If her favourite son could not come home, she would give up the Jubilee.'[16]

By this time Victoria was starting to regret the whole thing. On 22 March she wrote to Ponsonby, 'the Queen is appalled at the prospect of these endless visitors ... She owns she knows not how she ever can live through it all, especially in the summer when she dreads the heat so much and is always unable for anything.' Press criticism of projected arrangements incensed Victoria: she ordered Ponsonby to tell ministers: 'She will not be teazed and bullied about the Jubilee, which seems to be considered only for the *people* and their *convenience* & amusement, while the Queen is to do the public and newspapers' bidding. She will do *nothing* if this goes on.'[17]

As ministers had feared, when the Duke of Connaught's 'Leave Bill' had its second reading on 12 May, things did not go smoothly. The radical MP and journalist Henry Labouchere, fast becoming a particular bugbear of the Queen, said it was 'an obsequious and servile Bill brought in to suit the private convenience of a royal prince'. Some other 'very impertinent and ignorant remarks were made' but 'language ... vulgar beyond all belief', did not stop the government securing a majority.[18] On 25 May the bill passed its final reading in the House of Lords, enabling Prince Arthur to reach England in good time for the Jubilee.

There was more unpleasantness when the government applied to Parliament for £17,000 to pay for a service in Westminster Abbey. Labouchere said the public contribution should be £2,000 at most, while the MP for Camborne, Mr Conybeare, asserted the working classes did 'not care twopence-halfpenny about the whole business'. He only hoped the Jubilee would make people see the useless parasitical nature of 'some of the institutions we are told to respect and venerate'. None of this prevented the government gaining an even larger majority of 208 in the division, allowing Victoria not to 'dwell on what is most disgraceful & better to be forgotten'.[19]

Jubilee Year added to the Queen's engagements. It was now understood that she would never open Parliament, but in other respects she was doing more, appearing in public fairly regularly. Even so, 1887 was an exceptionally busy year. As she noted, it was so 'completely filled up with ceremonies, receptions, audiences etc' that for two and a half months, 'I had *hardly a day's rest*!' It was exhausting, but she told Lady Rosebery: 'I was amply repaid for my great exertion and fatigue by the unbounded enthusiastic loyalty and devotion evinced ... by high and low, rich and poor ... which has sunk deep into my heart.'[20]

She made several significant public appearances. In March 1887 she visited Birmingham, driving through the town in an open landau – and 'though the crowd was a very rough lot, they were most friendly and cheered a great deal'. On 14 May she opened the People's Palace in the East End of London, and once again 'the crowds were immense and very enthusiastic ... quite deafening'. Admittedly the effect was 'rather damped' by a sporadic discordant sound. She complained to Salisbury of encountering at times 'a horrid noise (*quite* new to the Queen's ears) "booing" she believes it is called'. A 'much grieved' prime minister pointed out that since London contained its share of 'Socialists and the worst Irish', a display of 'ill manners' was sometimes unavoidable.[21]

The twentieth of June saw the Queen embark on an exhausting round of banquets and family lunches for the 'royal mob' that went on for days. On 21 June all the royalties and dignitaries processed to Westminster Abbey, and when Victoria followed, she was acclaimed with an 'extraordinary outburst of enthusiasm as I had hardly ever seen in London before; all the people seemed in such good humour'.[22]

A week later she was back in London to attend a Buckingham Palace garden party. Going about the grounds, 'I bowed right & left, talking to as many as I could,' while doing her best to shun one of her guests, Mr Gladstone. She would in fact have preferred to exclude him altogether: in March Lord Salisbury had somewhat gingerly suggested it 'would be a gracious act, and tend to allay the bitterness of feeling which exists, if your Majesty were to include Mr Gladstone in your Majesty's invitations. He is so famous a man that many people would be shocked by any neglect of him, even where they differ from him.' Shortly afterwards she had asked the Gladstones to dinner at Windsor, but during the Jubilee festivities she hoped to avoid any kind of intercourse with him. To her annoyance, when she went to have tea in a private tent at the garden party, her former prime minister stood outside it, clearly waiting for her to emerge. Victoria hissed to the Duke of Cambridge, 'Do you see Gladstone? There he has been standing hat in hand, straight opposite me this half hour, determined to force me to speak to him! But I am as determined *not* to speak with him!' When she left, she did not use the exit where Gladstone had positioned himself and congratulated herself on successfully dodging him. 'But alas! ... The brute contrived to get ... *inside* the house and placed himself so, that when she passed through the house to go away, at the last moment she came all suddenly *upon* him, ... and was forced to give him her hand!!! Too provoking.'[23]

Irish Nationalist MPs had boycotted the Westminster Abbey thanksgiving service, with one declaring in the Commons it would have been more appropriate to mark the Jubilee with 'a day of humiliation' to commemorate desolation wrought in Ireland by famine, plague, emigration and eviction during the past half century.[24] The defeat of Gladstone's Home Rule Bill partly accounted for the bitterness, but the economic and social condition of Ireland had also worsened during recent months. The government's response was to renew laws of coercion.

In September 1886 the government had defeated an attempt by Parnell to alter the terms of Gladstone's 1881 Land Act to aid impoverished tenants. Nationalists had responded with the so-called 'Plan of Campaign'. Dubbed by the Queen a 'shameful anti-Landlord League',[25] it enabled tenants to band together and propose reduced rents to their landlords. If their offer was not accepted, they handed the money to a campaign manager. Attempts were then made to pressure the landlord into taking the lower rate; should that fail, the group's funds were distributed among evicted tenants.

While acknowledging that these proceedings were unlawful, Gladstone maintained misgovernment had driven the Irish to desperation. On 27 January 1887 the government announced in the Queen's Speech that they would be bringing in a new Crimes Bill for Ireland, whereupon Gladstone came close to condoning the Plan of Campaign. The Queen was pleased when Salisbury told her that Gladstone's 'almost advocacy … will damage him seriously'.[26]

The novel feature of the latest Crimes Bill was that, instead of having to be renewed after a set period, it was indefinite. This meant, as John Morley put it, coercion was now a standing instrument of government. Far from being dismayed by this, Victoria was glad to hear the bill 'will be a strong one'.[27] Crimes such as intimidation, boycotting, rioting, unlawful assembly, uttering or printing seditious speeches, and incitement to crime were no longer subject to trial by jury; instead, resident magistrates could impose six months hard labour. Although the Unionists were prepared to support most of the bill's provisions – if hardly enthusiastic for it – piloting it through the Commons would clearly be hard.

In March 1887 Salisbury appointed his nephew, Arthur Balfour, to be Chief Secretary of Ireland. Despite his undoubted intellect, his promotion prompted incredulous laughter. Tall and thin, with a droopy moustache, this 'elegant, fragile creature' exuded an air of 'aristocratic languor'. The scornful Irish Nationalists were confident that, having broken earlier chief secretaries, they would swiftly dispose of 'this weakling'.[28]

The Queen was pleased by the appointment of one so 'singularly charming and agreeable', who furthermore proved adept at handling her. When Balfour first stayed at Balmoral, Sir Henry Ponsonby told his wife: 'He enters into the Queen's arguments and discusses matters with her, showing that he does not agree which makes her think over it – and not opposing her slap which never fails to make her more strong in her views.' Balfour's visit the following year was also successful. Ponsonby reported: 'I think the Queen likes him, but is a little afraid of him.'[29]

Gladstone was at his most combative during the debate on the Crimes Bill that begun on 28 March. 'Exhibiting great emotion,' he described boycotting as a 'legitimate weapon' against rack rents. When, 'amid uproar', leave was given to introduce the bill, he marched out of the house alongside Irish members. The Queen was delighted that the 'shameful conduct of the Opposition – especially of Mr Gladstone!' had proved unavailing. She wrote to W. H. Smith, who had replaced Churchill as Leader of the Commons, 'It is very shocking & very sad to see a man of his position, age and reputation heading an opposition to the efforts … to restore … *tranquillity* to a poor misguided country … which *he* has done *more than anyone* to excite and encourage in its illegitimate aspirations and wild and misplaced expectations.'[30]

Because the government clearly intended to use procedural devices to cut short debate, Gladstone decided that 'now, as in Jingo times, our battle is to be fought in the country' rather than the Commons chamber. On 8 April he wrote to the *North-Eastern Daily Gazette*, encouraging public meetings against the Crimes Bill. The Queen condemned his action as 'perfectly monstrous & very wicked'. To Lord Lansdowne she would declare it 'dreadful to see a man who was three times Prime Minister fall so low'.[31]

The Times was strongly supportive of the government's Irish policy, and to aid the passage of the Crimes Bill embarked on a campaign to establish links between Parnellism and crime. On 18 April there was sensation when the paper published a letter purportedly from Parnell condoning the murder of Thomas Burke, who had been stabbed to death in a Dublin park alongside Lord Frederick Cavendish in 1882. In the Commons Parnell denied authorship but took the matter no further, leaving the Queen unimpressed. Salisbury – who in a speech to the Primrose League spoke of Gladstone being allied to someone 'tainted with the strong presumption of conniving at assassination' – told Victoria: '*The Times* is believed to have other compromising documents.' Because Gladstone and his 'unworthy coadjutor' Sir William Harcourt declined to disavow Parnell, the Queen thought 'their position is really a terrible one, linked to rebels and traitors'. Not doubting that *The Times*' articles were 'full of truth', she observed to Smith: 'She sees Mr Parnell denies the letter, but the Queen hopes the subject will not be allowed to rest there.'[32]

The government ruthlessly pushed the Crimes Bill through its various stages. When at last it came up for its third reading, Gladstone 'denounced the Bill in the strongest language', describing it as 'unnecessary, tyrannical and utterly subversive of liberty'. He could not prevent it from passing the following day, and on 18 July it received the royal assent. Henceforward political meetings were prohibited in eighteen Irish counties, with all who attended them liable to arrest and imprisonment. The government followed this by outlawing the Land League entirely, even though Chamberlain and his followers refused to vote for this. The Queen had no doubts about it, telegraphing Salisbury, 'Rejoice at decision arrived at and firm line taken.'[33]

Immediately the arrests of Irish dissidents began. On 9 September a protest meeting at Mitchelstown turned violent, causing police to panic. Having retreated to their barracks, they fired into the crowd, killing three people. The Queen was sure the protestors only had themselves to blame: the police had responded legitimately under threat, 'and now they want to call it murder!!' Although Balfour was aware the incident had been badly mishandled, in a Commons debate of 12 September he insisted the police 'had fired in self defence' after being 'brutally attacked'. Victoria considered his statement 'excellent'. Predictably it provoked more 'dreadful language' from Gladstone, who delivered 'a violent and excited harangue'.[34]

The incident gave Gladstone a potent rallying cry. At Nottingham on 18 October he urged his audience to 'Remember Mitchelstown!' – saying the government could hardly condemn the Irish for illegality when they and their agents were acting unlawfully themselves. The Queen believed Gladstone's behaviour amounted to 'direct incitement to resistance against all authority', but public opinion was starting to become concerned about the treatment of the Irish. On 13 November a meeting in Trafalgar Square protesting against Irish arrests and unemployment in Britain escalated into a serious affray, during which police and rioters were injured. The Queen wrote to the home secretary: 'When leaders of the Opposition preach disobedience to the law and resistance of the police, one cannot be surprised' by such disorders.[35]

Over the next year Gladstone continued to denounce the way the Crimes Act was being applied, having come to equate the governance of Ireland with Naples under the Bourbons. The government was not invulnerable to censure, and after a parliamentary committee was set up to enquire into gaol conditions, there was some relaxation of prison discipline. However, ministers could claim their policy was working, for agricultural outrages were in decline in Ireland and rents were better paid. They also had grounds to hope that the Nationalists would be discredited by *The Times*'s claims about Parnellism being vindicated. During a court case in July 1888, *The Times* produced more letters allegedly written by Parnell that supposedly showed he was involved in criminality. The government decided to set up a special commission to enquire further, hoping it would uncover information damaging to Parnell and the cause of Irish nationalism in general. Given very broad terms of reference, the commission started sitting in September 1888.

During the Golden Jubilee celebrations, one person who had attracted many cheers from the crowd was the 'radiant' figure of Victoria's son-in-law, 'Fritz', the Crown Prince of Germany, who had married her eldest daughter Vicky nearly thirty years earlier. Riding in front of the Queen's carriage as she drove to Westminster Abbey, he looked magnificent in his white cuirassier's uniform. In fact, he was already mortally ill. Since becoming hoarse in January, he had completely lost his voice, and a small growth on his vocal cords had regrown after being cauterised. In May 1887 an English throat specialist named Sir Morell Mackenzie had declared the growth non-malignant, and that Fritz should recover. His wife and mother-in-law were blindly optimistic about his prospects. But, as the weeks passed and Fritz's condition failed to improve, few others felt likewise.

If her husband did not recover, it would obviously be a personal tragedy for Vicky, but the political implications were no less grave. For years the couple had looked on 'as quiet as mice' while under Bismarck's domination, Emperor William I of Germany – who had just celebrated his ninetieth birthday – had ruled in a militaristic and illiberal fashion. They had told themselves that when Fritz eventually succeeded, they could put their progressive ideas into practice. If, however, Fritz only had a short time on the throne, or even predeceased his father, the outlook changed entirely. The next heir to the imperial throne was the Queen's eldest grandson, William, a very different character to his father.

William was not unintelligent, but arrogant, erratic and unpredictable. Authoritarian by instinct, he had ranged himself with his grandfather and Bismarck against his parents, with whom his relationship had long been strained. By 1883 the two parties had become completely estranged, as William espoused views utterly repugnant to Vicky and Fritz. Besides stigmatising her son's 'boundless egotism' and '*heartlessness*', Vicky claimed he was an admirer of 'despotism and the police state'. Resolving their differences through calm discussion proved beyond them. William complained his mother became 'so very outspoken' whenever he uttered an opinion that he avoided doing so; while for her part Vicky told her husband trying to reason with Willie was a 'waste of time'. She stated: 'Years have gone by since *I* have discussed politics with him. I avoid it on principle.'[36]

It was to be feared that William would reject not only his parents' liberalism, but also their pro-British sympathies – although admittedly his attitude towards his mother's homeland was complex. In some respects he gloried in that aspect of his heritage: his mother had seen to it he was steeped in British history, and the country's past exploits and achievements seemingly inspired pride in him. Simultaneously he felt jealousy and resentment at the way Britain was held up as an ideal nation state that Germany could never equal.

William's feelings towards his grandmother were also ambivalent. Revelling in being Victoria's eldest grandchild, he outwardly professed the utmost devotion. This fondness, though not unwavering, was certainly not entirely simulated. However, her bossiness riled him intensely, and the family dynamic complicated matters further. He found it degrading that his father was in awe of a wife, 'who, for her part, is dominated by the Queen of England'.[37]

He knew that one way of annoying both his grandmother and mother was to show a leaning towards Russia. Following a visit to St Petersburg in 1884 he kept up a fulsome correspondence with Tsar Alexander, and whenever possible passed on information he hoped would damage Britain. The Queen was unaware of this but heard enough from her daughter to suspect that William was not as well disposed towards Britain as she expected. As early as January 1883 she had written to him expressing herself 'much surprised that you who used to be so fond of England had not before telegraphed or written' to congratulate her on Britain's victories in Egypt the previous year. William answered he had refrained 'out of pure modesty', being fearful she would say: 'What does Willie understand about these matters?' He avowed himself 'very much grieved that – unconsciously – I incurred your displeasure', whereas, in fact he smarted at her rebuke.[38]

Another difficulty was caused by William's fury when he discovered that his mother and Queen Victoria were very keen for his younger sister, known as Moretta, to marry the dashing 'Sandro', Prince Alexander of Battenberg. Moretta had fallen in love with him when he visited Berlin in 1882, prompting the Queen to suggest they marry. Vicky had then taken up the idea obsessively. Knowing that the tsar detested Sandro, and not wanting to jeopardise relations with Russia, Bismarck would not hear of it, telling Vicky and Fritz in 1884 he would never agree. Old Emperor William was also against the match, partly because he rarely defied Bismarck, but also because he did not think Sandro – whose princely status was compromised by his parents having married morganatically – a sufficiently illustrious partner for his granddaughter.

The proposed match likewise inspired revulsion in Prince William. In May 1884 Vicky reported to her mother that William had 'said he could not imagine how such a person [Sandro] could *dare* to think of his sister'. When Victoria's youngest daughter Beatrice became engaged in early 1885 to Prince Alexander's youngest brother, William again made plain his contempt for all Battenbergs, prompting the Queen to burst out: 'As for Willie, that very foolish, undutiful and I must add, unfeeling boy ... I wish he could get a good "skelping" as the Scotch say.' She was so cross that the following autumn she instructed the Prince of Wales to cancel William's invitation to shoot at Sandringham. Informing Bismarck's son Herbert of this, Prince William said his uncle had clearly acted at the behest of 'the old hag', his grandmother.[39]

The Queen remained in such a bad mood with William that in 1887 she contemplated not inviting him to her Golden Jubilee. She wrote to Vicky: 'You know how ill he behaved, how rude to me ... how shamefully he calumniated dear excellent noble Sandro, and how shamefully he behaves to you both, his parents ... I fear he may show his dislikes and be disagreeable.' Out of motherly loyalty Vicky remonstrated, 'He *ought* to be present,' but she regretted having spoken up for him when it began to look as if Fritz's throat problems might not allow him to come to England. Without telling his parents, William informed Victoria he would be attending as the German emperor's official representative. The Queen rejoined tartly that fortunately Vicky and Fritz had not had to cancel, so there could be no question of William superseding his father.[40]

Victoria then stipulated that if William did come he could only bring a very modest suite. 'Very much hurt and offended,' the prince 'bombarded' his grandmother with telegrams demanding she reconsider. When she held firm, William was visibly sulky throughout his stay in London. Not only did he feel slighted at being put up at Spencer

House rather than Buckingham Palace, but he and his wife Dona were outraged that at several court functions, '*she* was always placed behind the black Queen of Hawaii!!' In the end, 'Both returned [to Germany] not in the best tempers.'[41]

Vicky and Fritz went to San Remo in the autumn of 1887 hoping the Italian climate would help his recovery, but there his condition deteriorated. By November even Sir Morell Mackenzie had to acknowledge that Fritz's throat condition looked like cancer, although the Queen and Vicky still grasped at every sign of remission. Vicky was understandably reluctant to let the German doctors do the very drastic operation of removing the larynx completely. Prince William was all for it, but Vicky was right to think it life-threatening.

On 16 November an agitated Vicky informed her mother that a scheme was afoot to ensure that if Fritz outlived his father, he would be bypassed on the grounds that an emperor who could not talk was unfit to rule. Instead the throne would go direct to William, whom Vicky suspected of being behind the proposal. The Queen spluttered: 'That is a monstrous idea ... This must be stopped at once,' and both she and Salisbury raised the matter with the German ambassador. At the beginning of December the Queen felt able to assure her daughter, 'No one dreams seriously of making Fritz resign his rights,' but even so Britain had to face the fact that William's accession would probably not be long delayed. Accordingly, Salisbury sounded out Bismarck in the hope that 'Prince William's prejudices against England, if they exist, may be dispelled.' Bismarck tried to allay any fears, whereupon Salisbury explained he was sure the chancellor understood, 'the succession to the German throne of a prince who was believed to be more favourable to Russia and more averse to England than the present heir to that throne was a contingency' Britain could not ignore.[42]

When Prince William learned of these diplomatic démarches he complained to Colonel Swaine, British military attaché in Berlin, of being unjustly regarded by his mother's family as 'very anti-English and most warlike'. Swaine alerted Sir Henry Ponsonby, who in turn warned the Queen. She said William should be told that she and the rest of his relations 'bore him no ill will', even if they had been 'shocked & pained at his behaviour towards his parents for some time past'. This made it 'impossible for them to be as cordial towards him as they would wish'. Ponsonby should also say, 'as regards his anti-English feeling, this comes to the Queen's ears from many quarters', but providing William began acting as 'a dutiful and affectionate son' the Queen would be 'most happy to be on friendly & affectionate terms as when he was a child'.[43]

In February 1888 Fritz had a cannula inserted in his throat, enabling him to breathe better, though he could still barely talk. On 9 March old Emperor William died and Vicky and Fritz returned to Berlin. Disconsolately Vicky wrote to her mother: 'To think of poor Fritz succeeding his father as a sick and stricken man is so hard. How much good he might have done!' Now, '*Too late* – this agonising thought haunts me.'[44]

Emperor Frederick did not feel he could destabilise his country by dismissing Bismarck. This was a relief to Salisbury, who had ordered British ambassador Sir Edward Malet to warn the new empress to be very circumspect. Victoria too urged her daughter not to do 'anything which is in direct opposition to the poor departed Emperor's wishes ... for instance the projected marriage of Moretta with Sandro. Above all do not even contemplate such a step without the perfect acquiescence of William. You must reckon with him, as he is Crown Prince.'[45]

Vicky nevertheless remained set upon the match. Having warned the emperor that he would resign unless the marriage project was dropped, Bismarck placed stories in the press about his possible retirement, hinting at the reasons behind it. Because he assumed the Queen was encouraging her daughter, he wished to prevent her coming to Berlin that spring, predicting if the planned visit went ahead she would 'bring the parson with her in her travelling bag'. Bismarck also asked ambassador Malet to warn Salisbury that if the marriage did happen, Germany would have to find some way of conciliating Russia, imperilling good relations with Britain. Salisbury said he could do nothing to halt the marriage. He remarked to Malet: Prince Bismarck 'is asking me to assist him in thwarting the wishes of his Emperor and my Queen in order to gratify the malignant feelings of the Russian Emperor ... If German cooperation can only be had at this price we must do without it.'[46]

Despite his defiant words, Salisbury was actually very concerned at the situation and did what he could to discourage the Queen from going ahead with her visit. He wrote that with Bismarck 'in one of his raging moods' and whipping up public feeling, going to Berlin could 'expose you to great misconstruction and possibly to some disrespectful demonstration'. This only made the Queen the more determined: she retorted to the prime minister, 'Bismarck's tyranny is unbearable, and I cannot abandon my intention of seeing the dear suffering Emperor.' While she did reveal she was in fact doing nothing to encourage Moretta and Sandro's marriage, she raged that Bismarck's 'sending what amounted to a *message!* to the Queen ... was too outrageous!' She suspected the chancellor was motivated by a desire to 'please that most unnatural son' of Fritz and Vicky, who 'really considers himself Emperor already'.[47]

While no longer expecting the Queen to cancel her visit, Salisbury wanted to minimise any damage that might arise from it. After talking with the German ambassador, he warned her there was 'some anxiety ... at Berlin' about the forthcoming meeting with Prince William: 'It appears that his head is turned by his position; and the hope evidently was that your Majesty might be induced' to show him 'special consideration'. In some embarrassment he went on, 'Evidently ... they are afraid that, if any thorny subject came up in conversation, the Prince might say something that would not reflect credit on him; and that if he acted so as to draw any reproof from your Majesty, he might take it ill, and a feeling would rankle in his mind which might hinder the good relations between the two nations.' While he felt awkward putting this to the Queen, 'it is nevertheless true – most unhappily – that all Prince William's impulses, however blameable or unreasonable will henceforth be political causes of enormous potency', and hence 'everything that is said to him must be very carefully weighed'.[48]

Fearing Victoria would not heed this, Salisbury also wrote to the Duke of Rutland, who was accompanying her to Berlin. The prime minister regretfully told him, the Queen 'thinks very badly of [Prince William] ... and has more than once shown her resentment very plainly. He is intensely irritated at this treatment.' If she did the same thing at Berlin, 'most disastrous' results could ensue. 'Do what you can to warn and restrain her,' he begged the duke. 'She is very unmanageable about her conduct to her relations. She will persist in considering William only as her grandson. But the matter has become political and very grave, and she must listen to advice.'[49]

The Queen arrived at Berlin on 24 April. She had several poignant meetings with the bed-bound emperor, now clearly a dying man. When she left, she 'kissed him ... and said I hoped he would come to us when he was stronger', but both of them knew that was a polite fiction.[50]

Victoria did manage to keep her temper with her grandson, simply asking him to do all he could to help his mother. The day before she left, she also gave an audience to an 'unmistakably nervous and ill at ease' Bismarck. He came out mopping his brow, exclaiming: '*Mein Gott*! That was a woman!' For her part, Victoria was 'agreeably surprised to find him so amiable & gentle', as well as being reassured by his undertaking always to stand by Vicky.[51]

In fact, when Fritz died on 15 June 1888 Vicky was appallingly treated by both Bismarck and her own son. While his father's life ebbed away, William stationed soldiers around the palace; as soon as Fritz died, they took control, mounting searches for compromising correspondence. Bismarck did not offer Vicky his condolences, claiming he was too busy to see the dowager empress. The Queen commented it just 'showed how untrue & heartless he is, after all he seemed to promise me'.[52]

Victoria was aware that Vicky's situation was worse than hers when she was widowed – for whereas the Queen had ultimately been saved by work, all Vicky's ambitions had been destroyed. In her journal she lamented: 'My poor child's whole future gone, ruined, which they had prepared themselves for, for nearly thirty years!' Vicky herself wrote it was agony seeing others take Fritz's place: 'Theirs is now the power! I disappear with him … We had a mission, we felt and we knew it … It does seem cruel.'[53] Vicky's material position was also unhappy, for Fritz had been unable to leave her much money, and she was fearful of being evicted from her home.

On 27 June William marked his accession by sending General Winterfeldt – who had been particularly obnoxious to Vicky on Fritz's death – to see the Queen. She gave him a chilly reception, which he later complained of to Sir Henry Ponsonby. Hearing this, Victoria pronounced herself 'extremely glad … that General Winterfeldt says he was received coldly, though civilly, for such was her intention'. Winterfeldt had been 'a traitor to his beloved master', for whom he had uttered 'never … a word of regret', only speaking 'of the *pleasure* which he experienced at being chosen to announce his new master's accession'.[54]

Already she and Salisbury were concerned by signs that William did not desire warm relations with Britain. When rumours reached Victoria that William – who had not written to her since his father's death – was planning to visit the tsar, the Queen decided to take this up with him. Having begun her letter by urging him to be kind to his mother, she alluded to the rumours of his forthcoming trip abroad, trusting that months would elapse before he embarked on any travels.[55]

The kaiser was irritated by his grandmother's 'uninvited tutelage', complaining to a German diplomat she 'had been tactless enough to overwhelm him with advice'. He sent her a self-important reply, squashing the idea that his mother might keep one of her former palaces and confirming that he planned to visit Russia less than a month after his father's death. 'I would have gone later if possible, but State interest goes before personal feelings,' he wrote pompously. He hoped good would come out of his encounter with the tsar, 'as I deem it necessary that monarchs should meet often and confer together to look out for dangers which threaten the monarchical principle from democratical and republican parties'.[56]

Irate, the Queen telegraphed Salisbury: 'Trust that we shall be *very cool*, though civil in our communications with my grandson and Prince Bismarck.' When the kaiser went to Copenhagen shortly after his visit to Russia, she burst out angrily to her eldest son: 'How sickening it is to see Willy not two months after his beloved and noble father's death, going to banquets and reviews! It is very indecent and very unfeeling.'[57]

The kaiser next decided to pay a visit to Emperor Francis Joseph in Vienna. He was scheduled to arrive on 10 September, and since the Prince of Wales planned to be in Austria at that time, he wrote to tell his nephew he looked forward to seeing him. To his mortification William conveyed to him he would prefer it if his uncle was not there. Having taken himself off, Bertie told his mother that unless his nephew apologised, he would never speak to him again. The Queen quite agreed the '*outrageous* behaviour of Willie the Great (& I fear bad-hearted)' merited chastisement. To Vicky she wrote: 'If I don't speak of W's shameful ... and undignified conduct it is because I feel too furious, too indignant, too savage also to trust myself.'[58]

Awkwardly, the kaiser now started talking about coming to England. Salisbury had to raise the Vienna incident with the German ambassador, who gave him a memorandum drawn up by Bismarck, explaining that while in Berlin for Fritz's funeral, the Prince of Wales had caused offence by making unfortunate references to Alsace-Lorraine. In addition the kaiser resented the way 'the Prince treated him as an uncle treats a nephew, instead of recognising that he was an Emperor.'

The Queen was incredulous. 'This is really too *vulgar* and too absurd ... To pretend that he is to be treated *in private* as well as in public as "his Imperial Majesty" is *perfect madness*.' Vowing not to 'swallow this affront' she declared to Salisbury, '*If* he has *such* notions, he [had] better *never* come *here*.' William was evidently in 'a very unhealthy and unnatural state of mind; and he *must* be made to feel that his grandmother and uncle will not stand such insolence'. While agreeing that political relations 'should not be affected (if possible) by these miserable personal quarrels ... the Queen much *fears* that, with such a hot-headed, conceited and wrongheaded young man, devoid of all feeling, this may at ANY moment become *impossible*'.[59]

Hoping to prevent the situation being further inflamed, Salisbury suggested that the Queen avoid provoking the Germans by letting Vicky visit England. Victoria wired back: 'Intention doubtless well meant, but it would be impossible, heartless and cruel to stop my poor broken-hearted daughter from coming to her mother … It would be no use, and only encourage the Emperor and the Bismarcks still more against us. You all seem frightened of them, which is not the way to make them better.'[60] Vicky duly arrived on 19 November and stayed for ten weeks, angering her mother with further harrowing details of the ill treatment she had received.

Vicky's visit left the Queen in a still more ferocious mood towards her grandson. On 7 February 1889 she wrote to the Prince of Wales, 'William must *not* come *this* year, *you* could not meet him, and I could *not* after all he has said and done.' Salisbury therefore asked Sir Edward Malet to deter the kaiser. While not excluding the possibility of the kaiser's coming briefly to Osborne in the summer, Salisbury stressed it would be 'much better if, in all friendship, the visit can be postponed'.[61]

In his perverse and contrary way, the kaiser became keener than ever on a trip to England, eagerly seizing on the Osborne idea. Having grudgingly agreed that William could spend a few days there, the Queen wrote apologetically to Vicky. The dowager empress said she understood her mother must follow Salisbury's advice, 'but you can imagine what a stab it gives me'.[62]

The Queen had only agreed to receive her grandson provided he made 'some sort of apology' to the Prince of Wales, but all attempts to extract one proved fruitless. Troubled that the Queen remained supportive of her son, Salisbury hoped nothing would be done to 'give ground to the world to think that a rupture or estrangement with so powerful & important a nation as Germany has arisen out of discussions of a personal or family character'. Victoria could not be deterred from asking William to mount an official enquiry into the Vienna incident, whereupon on 28 May the kaiser made 'matters worse than ever' with an 'incredible!' answer that blithely asserted: 'The whole affair … originated in Uncle Bertie's own imagination.' Much to the resentment of the Prince of Wales, Salisbury managed to prevent the Queen from demanding the matter be probed further.[63]

Instead, she tried a different approach. She made William an honorary admiral in the Royal Navy, causing him to exclaim: 'Fancy wearing the same uniform as St Vincent and Nelson; it is enough to make one giddy.' Then, on 18 June, Victoria wrote to Malet suggesting her grandson show gratitude by writing to say how sorry he was about the Vienna misunderstanding. William evaded this, claiming the Queen had already indicated she 'considered the whole matter as *closed* and *finished*!' He wrote jauntily to his grandmother: 'I am happy to see that you regard the Vienna affair as concluded ... and full of joy of soon meeting you at dear old Osborne.'[64]

On 2 August the kaiser arrived on the Isle of Wight. The Prince of Wales was forced to welcome him, and for the next six days all went well. When William left on 8 August, Victoria noted he had been 'all the time very amiable and seemed delighted with his visit'. Dropping for the moment all hostility to Britain, he now became (so Herbert Bismarck claimed): 'the complete Anglomaniac'.[65]

The only member of Salisbury's government who dissatisfied the Queen was Home Secretary Henry Matthews. Having 'never thought him fit for the place', she was displeased by his tendency to show leniency towards men who had murdered their wives. Then, worse still, Matthews mishandled the investigation into the Whitechapel killings, which before long were being attributed in the press to 'Jack the Ripper'. The first death occurred on 31 August 1888 and was followed in swift succession by three others. Immediately the Queen became obsessed with these 'dreadful murders of unfortunate women of a bad class', notable for 'horrible mutilations' of the victims. Having brought the matter to Salisbury's notice, on 5 September at Balmoral she engaged in 'some rather ghastly talk' to Cranbrook, asking him to telegraph Matthews. On 9 November a 'new most ghastly murder' prompted her to intervene again. Salisbury was told that street lighting in London's East End should be improved and better detectives employed as 'They are not what they should be.' She also wrote to Matthews saying that while doubtless such crimes 'were committed in circumstances which made detection very difficult', the Whitechapel area should be flooded with police. She thought single men occupying lodging houses likely suspects, showing a forensic turn of mind by pointing out 'the murderer's clothes must be saturated with blood', which would aid identification.[66]

Before long she began pressing for Matthews to lose his job, and Salisbury promised to see whether he could be made an appeal court judge. When it proved difficult to find him a place on the bench, Victoria said the home secretary should just be sacked. Salisbury had to warn that, unless it could be shown Matthews was guilty of 'an open and palpable error', 'a bare dismissal … would be looked on as very harsh'. In the end Matthews had to be kept where he was because an election would have to be held if he vacated his seat and it was unlikely the government would win it.[67]

Royal finances also proved a ticklish question. For years the Queen had been pressing for provision to be made for her grandchildren, but both Salisbury and the Leader of the Commons, W. H. Smith, believed that if she now applied to Parliament, she must be ready to supplement any funds granted with money of her own. The prime minister even contemplated financing a 'dotation scheme' by selling the royal parks to the country for £500,000, but Victoria found it scandalous 'that *she*, in her old age and with endless expenses, should be asked to contribute so largely'. She chided, 'The constant dread of the House of Commons is a bugbear – whatever is done you *will not & cannot* conciliate *a certain* set of fools & wicked people, who will attack *whatever* is done.' Smith thought differently, warning Salisbury in late 1888 that many Conservatives would not support grants for any of her grandchildren other than the Prince of Wales's children.[68]

In 1889 the Prince of Wales's eldest son came of age, and his daughter Princess Louise got engaged, meaning they needed money. On 1 July, Smith discussed this with Gladstone, who said he could only help if the matter went before a parliamentary committee. Accordingly it was agreed one should be set up to enquire into precedents for providing for the sovereign's grandchildren. When this was proposed on 4 July, Labouchere, the radical member for Northampton, at once demanded that the committee be allowed to examine the whole question of the Queen's civil list. He put forward an amendment to that effect, and when it was put to a division, several prominent Liberals abstained from voting. Gladstone privately warned Smith this proved the impossibility of providing for cadet branches of the Queen's family.[69]

The Queen was furious with Salisbury when she learned who would be on the committee, writing: 'I am quite horrified to see the name of that horrible lying Labouchere and of that rebel Parnell … I protest vehemently against both. It is quite indecent to have such people.' Salisbury explained that the committee was weighted so that trouble-makers could be outvoted, but it looked better if 'professedly violent men' sat on it.[70]

As soon as the committee met it was clear the Queen would not have things her own way. In the view of one its members, the proposals

Salisbury submitted to them via Smith were 'stupefying' in their generosity, and there was no question of their being approved. Instead the government accepted a suggestion of Gladstone's that the Prince of Wales should be given a quarterly sum to provide for his children. Initially an annual £40,000 was envisaged, but this was reduced to £36,000, which the Queen thought 'paltry and Gladstonian'.[71]

The Queen was aggrieved that Gladstone had made his support conditional on her giving up any idea that the children of her younger sons should be endowed. She made no formal renunciation, but Gladstone assured the Commons she had given what amounted to a binding pledge. Victoria thought otherwise, telling Salisbury she had only temporarily waived her claims.[72]

Gladstone really deserved her gratitude, for many in his party disliked his willingness to give any money at all. In the Commons debate of 25 July, he praised the royal family's devotion to duty – but this did not go unquestioned. Already on 4 July Mr Picton, MP for Leicester, had asserted: 'No subject whatever excites ... more repugnance ... than voting doles and dowries' to royalty. Now the MP for Glamorgan railed 'in the name of the toiling thousands' against 'criminal extravagance' at a time of much poverty and suffering. Despite such uncomfortable moments, the measure easily passed its third reading on 5 August 1889. Still smouldering at her younger sons' exclusion, the Queen was determined 'that must be set right', until Salisbury told her it would be unwise to reopen the question.[73]

More friction arose between Queen and ministers when a government-appointed commission chaired by Lord Hartington recommended in March 1890 that the post of Commander-in-Chief of the British Army be abolished. 'This cannot be allowed for one moment,' the Queen commented when she first learnt the contents of the 'really abominable report'. She objected in the strongest possible terms to Lord Salisbury, who agreed that for the moment the change would not be implemented. The prime minister was less pliant when it came to securing promotion for her soldier son Prince Arthur, Duke of Connaught, who Victoria dreamed one day would succeed the Duke of Cambridge as Commander-in-Chief. In late March Salisbury told her he did not think the position could go to a prince of the blood. Undaunted, Victoria hoped Arthur could prove his credentials by doing a stint as either Commander-in-Chief in India or becoming Adjutant General. In April she was despondent to learn the Indian appointment was impossible. Finding it 'offensive' that Salisbury regarded the idea as 'absurd', she complained to Ponsonby the prime minister appeared 'under the extraordinary delusion that the Queen wishes to *force* her son on', whereas it was universally acknowledged Arthur was the fittest man for the post. A month later the war minister, Edward Stanhope, notified her that Arthur would not be Adjutant General either. The prince had to settle for a lesser command at Portsmouth, which his mother considered beneath him.[74]

Only after the 'Parnell Commission' had sat for six months did it examine the authenticity of the letters *The Times* had earlier made public. Once the matter was investigated, it emerged the newspaper had acquired the documents from an unsavoury individual named Piggott, who turned out to have forged them. Having broken down completely under cross-examination, Piggott fled to Madrid and killed himself. Salisbury admitted to Victoria, 'it was of course unfortunate' that Piggott had proved a 'thorough rogue'; however, he claimed, 'it did not really affect the government'. In reality the ministry's prestige had been gravely damaged.[75] On 1 March 1889 the opposition acclaimed Parnell as a hero in the House of Commons, with Gladstone leading the cheering. That autumn the Liberal leader invited Parnell to Hawarden to discuss Home Rule.

There was no denying the government was now both weak and unpopular. The Tories kept losing by-elections, and Smith, in failing health, had difficulty controlling the Commons. In July 1890 the Cabinet forced Salisbury to jettison almost all significant legislation. The prime minister acknowledged to the Queen that in normal circumstances it would have been better to resign, but fighting an election so likely to bring in a Home Rule government would have been irresponsible. Victoria agreed that staying in office was 'the wisest course, though of course it is somewhat humiliating'. Her main priority was to keep out 'the Socialist Home-ruling Party, which really contains no one of respectability'.[76]

In late 1890 the situation unexpectedly transformed. A year earlier Captain O'Shea had filed a divorce petition against his wife. Parnell had assured anyone who enquired that the case would not undermine his position. In fact, when it came to court on 15 November, Parnell entered no defence against O'Shea's citation of adultery. Witnesses titillated the court with farcical tales of Parnell shimmying down rope ladders to avoid being caught in flagrante. After O'Shea was granted his decree nisi on 17 November, the Queen observed primly that Parnell had been 'shown up as not only a man of very bad character, but as a liar, & devoid of all sense of honour or of any sort of principle'. She added happily: 'Mr Gladstone is put into great difficulties by it.'[77]

Although Gladstone initially maintained it was not for him to sit in moral judgement, the nonconformist wing of the Liberal Party erupted in 'puritanical frenzy', refusing to vote Liberal at the next election unless Parnell was disavowed. Gladstone accordingly wrote asking Parnell to resign the leadership, but Parnell ensured that his colleagues were unaware of this. On 25 November they re-elected him as their chief, upon which Gladstone published his letter. In retaliation Parnell claimed he knew from their conversations that Gladstone planned to betray the cause of Home Rule by introducing a measure that fell short of Irish requirements.

The Nationalists were thrown into disarray. Parliament had reassembled for an autumn session on 25 November but instead of taking part in proceedings, Irish members were absorbed in their internal party struggle. On 29 November the Queen gave a dinner party at Windsor that Hartington attended, and naturally there was a 'great deal of talk' about recent developments. Victoria was amused when Hartington – who might perhaps have been expected to show some charity because of his own long-standing adulterous relationship with the Duchess of Manchester – 'in his curious gruff way said "I never thought anything in politics could give me as much pleasure as this does."'[78]

On 6 December the Nationalists split, with Parnell retaining twenty-two followers, and forty-five colleagues withdrawing support. Smith reported: 'the quarrel ... seems for the present to have taken the heart out of the Opposition'.[79] Not only were the Liberals left demoralised, but Gladstone could not go on working with the Irish in the old way.

The Queen was delighted by Parnell's fall from grace. She told Vicky, 'It is satisfactory to see wickedness punished even in this world. It is a just nemesis.' After lime was thrown in Parnell's eyes during a bitter by-election campaign in Kilkenny, she found this 'very brutal, but one cannot help feeling that it is retribution for all the horrible cruelties perpetrated on all sorts of people which he never checked or even blamed!' She was no more forgiving when Parnell died on 6 October 1891, having married Katherine the previous June. Victoria reflected: 'What a startling event is Mr Parnell's death! But what a contrast!' his character was to W. H. Smith's, who had died the same day. Whereas Parnell, 'was a really bad & worthless man who had to answer for many lives lost in Ireland', Smith was 'an excellent, honest, wise, reliable, conciliatory' individual, who 'can be ill spared'.[80]

Throughout the reign the Empire had been much enlarged, with ever greater areas of Africa being placed under British control. In recent years the attitude of British politicians towards that continent had undergone a transformation. In 1873 Gladstone's colonial secretary Lord Kimberley had declared, 'Talk about an African Empire … is simply "bosh"', but in barely more than a decade everything changed. In an 1891 speech in Glasgow, Salisbury observed: 'When I left the Foreign Office in 1880 nobody thought about Africa' – but by 1885 'the nations of Europe were almost quarrelling with each other' in their thirst for territory there.[81]

Politicians who remained wary that the formal acquisition of new African colonies would entail unacceptable expense, favoured allowing charter companies to supply the necessary investment. In return for using private capital to build railways, develop infrastructure and administer vast tracts, they were authorised to retain any profits that accrued. The grant of a royal charter was generally conditional on the company 'respecting native rights', which was supposed to prevent abuses. In 1889 Colonial Secretary Lord Knutsford asked Ponsonby to assure the Queen that 'a strongly constituted Company will give us the best chance of peaceably opening up and developing the resources … south of the Zambezi, and will be most beneficial to the native chiefs and people'.[82]

In southern Africa, Cecil Rhodes, a British-born tycoon who had made a vast fortune from diamonds and gold, was seeking to extend British control over Mashonaland, an area north of the Transvaal ruled by Lobengula, King of the Ndebele. In 1888 Lobengula granted mining rights to a consortium led by Rhodes, but then had second thoughts. He sent emissaries to the Queen in early 1889 asking her to protect his people against foreign encroachments. His envoys had an audience with her on 2 March, dressed in 'great coats of a sort of opossum fur'. Asked by her whether 'they minded the cold, they answered I could make the weather cold or hot'.[83] Unfortunately their faith in the Queen would prove somewhat misplaced.

After Rhodes's British South African Company was granted a royal charter in October 1889, the Colonial Office exhorted Lobengula to honour his deal with Rhodes. The chief was initially annoyed, saying, 'the Queen must not write any more letters like that one to him again'.

In June 1890 he nevertheless let Rhodes send a column of men into Mashonaland. In theory they were meant only to prospect for gold and minerals; once there, they took over the land completely. In May 1891 the area was declared under British protection, but Rhodes was not yet satisfied. He wished to penetrate deeper into Lobengula's kingdom and make further acquisitions north of the Zambezi.[84]

The Queen looked favourably on Rhodes's ambitions. During a visit to England in February 1891 Rhodes – by then Prime Minister of Cape Colony – was invited to dine at Windsor. Interested to meet this 'very remarkable, honest, loyal man', Victoria spoke to him for some time. 'He said Great Britain was the only country fit to colonise – no other country succeeded. He hoped in time to see the English rule extend from the Cape to Egypt.'[85]

Britain's African incursions created tensions with rival European powers. Salisbury wryly remarked that the French were forever 'trying to elbow us out of unpronounceable places', and the Germans were quite as competitive. By the end of the 1880s Bismarck and William II were participating so keenly in the so-called 'Scramble for Africa' that Britain felt its interests there to be jeopardised. Salisbury's solution was to offer up Heligoland, a North Sea archipelago very close to Germany which Britain had acquired during the Napoleonic wars. The Germans were keen to own it themselves, whereas, Salisbury told Victoria, the possession was 'of no use to us'. In return Germany was prepared to give up claims to vast swathes of East Africa. The Queen approved of British control over those areas being consolidated, but forfeiting Heligoland was 'a *very serious* question which I do not like'. Uneasy about handing over its inhabitants 'to an unscrupulous despotic government like the Germans', she considered it 'a very bad precedent. The next thing will be to propose to give up Gibraltar!' Salisbury stood firm, arguing than an arrangement that would make Zanzibar a British protectorate and allow the British East Africa Company to take charge of Uganda was too good a bargain to forego. Victoria reluctantly sanctioned the exchange on 12 June 1890, while still thinking that 'Giving up what one has is always a bad thing.'[86]

When it came to her Indian empire, the Queen was wary of allowing her subjects there to exercise any form of self-rule. She was deeply suspicious of plans put forward by the viceroy Lord Lansdowne to introduce elected provincial councils, being 'doubtful whether India is ripe for such an enormous change'. Victoria was nevertheless far from thinking the governance of India beyond criticism. Conversing with the Secretary of State for India Lord Cross in October 1890, she regretted that many Indian Civil Servants were 'not gentlemen'.[87] The following spring an incident occurred at Manipur – a small hill state between Assam and Burma – that she felt exposed the Raj's deficiencies.

Some months earlier, Manipur's reigning maharaja had been supplanted by his younger brother. A third brother, who bore the title 'Senapati', had engineered the coup against his eldest sibling. Initially the British had done nothing, but then decided the *senapati* must be punished. The Commissioner of Assam had gone with a force to the principality, intending to arrest the *senapati* at a durbar (council), and send him into exile. Things had gone disastrously awry when Commissioner Quinton and the British Local Resident, Grimwood, were ambushed and seized. Soon afterwards they, and several other British officers and men, were murdered.

The Queen was very upset not just at the outcome, but because she felt the plan to arrest the *senapati* at a durbar smacked of treachery. To her mind, missteps of this sort would not have occurred had a 'better class of person' been in charge. She told Cross: 'Our Commissioners are not of the right kind: bumptious and not understanding how to deal with these people.' Lansdowne was informed that in future 'people of a higher calibre socially … more conciliatory as well as firm', should be employed. While she accepted the murderers must be held to account, she would 'earnestly deprecate any wholesale punishment … or … bloody revenge'. Steps were duly taken to ensure that reprisals did not get out of hand, but Victoria still believed something was fundamentally wrong, stating: 'Our system of sending out … people who merely get appointed for passing an examination must be altered … The Queen hears from many sides that the natives (though they are very loyal to the Queen Empress and the Royal Family) have no affection for the English rule, which is one of fear not of love, and this will *not* answer for a conquered nation.'[88]

Some suspected these views had been instilled in her by Abdul Karim, one of two Muslim men who in the Golden Jubilee year of 1887 had been sent over from India to wait on her at table. The Queen had been instantly taken by the 'fine serious countenance' of this tall young man, who within months of his arrival had started to give her Urdu lessons. In September 1887 she had enthused to Sir Henry Ponsonby: 'Abdul is most handy in helping when she *signs* by drying the signatures' – the very task Prince Albert had performed before graduating to the exercise of real power. A year later she decreed he should no longer serve her meals but instead be named her 'munshi' or teacher, 'being of rather a different class to the others'. Some months earlier she had confided to Vicky he was 'in fact no servant', and 'very useful in writing and looking after my books and things'. When a boil on his neck necessitated his taking sick leave in February 1890, Victoria felt 'quite lost without him'.[89]

Thanks to the munshi, the Queen became more biased in favour of her Muslim subjects. This influence was discernible when in July 1889 she wrote to Lord Lansdowne asking that steps be taken to prevent Hindus – whose religion she said was 'idolatrous' – from disrupting the Muslim holy month of Muharram. Lansdowne replied that it was impossible to ban all Hindu feasts at that time of year, although perhaps some lesser ones could be restricted. The Queen explained, 'I have often talked a great deal on this subject with my young Mohammedan Munshi, who is very intelligent and well informed ... and have learnt a great deal from him.' During the Manipur crisis, Lord Cross was doubtless correct in thinking that her strictures on Indian administrators were inspired by the munshi.[90]

Once Manipur had been subdued and the culprits tried, the Queen still felt disquiet. In June 1891 she was startled to hear that though acquitted of murder, the *senapati* had been sentenced to death as an accessory. Victoria at once objected he should instead be imprisoned for life, as his execution would 'create very bad feeling ... in all India'. To Cross she expostulated: 'Think no Prince was ever hung. That harsh crushing policy will not do now.' Cross felt he could not comply, for Lansdowne believed the death sentence was merited, and 'by long custom all such questions rest with the Viceroy'. Although the Queen continued to regard it as wrong, the *senapati*, Prince Tikendrajit Singh, went to the gallows on 14 August.[91]

Kaiser William's 1889 visit to England had left him, Salisbury happily noted, 'a changed man', and that November the prime minister assured the Queen: 'his present mood is all that could be desired'. Unfortunately, with someone so erratic, there could be no guarantee the improvement would last. Salisbury was 'much troubled' when in March 1890 William dismissed Bismarck, for though the chancellor had never been particularly friendly to Britain, he was a towering figure who in recent years had striven to keep Germany at peace. To Salisbury's mind, his departure was 'an enormous calamity of which the sinister effects will be felt in every part of Europe'. The kaiser's mother was equally scathing. 'William fancies he can do everything himself,' she sniffed to Victoria. 'I am afraid William is a most thorough despot.'[92]

Via Sir Edward Malet, the kaiser sent his grandmother a detailed explanation, claiming he had acted for Bismarck's own good. The chancellor had wanted to bring in a very strong anti-socialist law, whereas he himself had favoured a more conciliatory approach. William claimed that Bismarck's aim was to promote unrest, necessitating a call-out of troops, who would 'sweep the streets with grape-shot'. The kaiser argued, 'for me, a young monarch ... to have allowed my people to be shot down in the streets ... would have been disastrous to me and my whole House'. He had tried reasoning with Bismarck, but 'he became so violent ... I did not know whether he would not throw the inkstand at my head'. Not only did the kaiser have 'to think of my own dignity', but 'I was assured by the doctors that his state of mental excitement was such' it might cause a fatal seizure.[93]

The Queen thought it a hopeful sign that William had recently proposed that an international labour conference should be held in Germany. She suggested to Vicky it was surely 'a move in the *right* direction, & shows a will to do something for the working & often suffering classes'. The dowager empress dismissed her son's 'playing at state socialism' as 'very dangerous', informing her mother: 'William has never troubled his head in the least about the poor or the working classes and knows absolutely nothing about them.'[94]

In August 1890 William was very cordial when he came to Osborne to take part in sailing races at Cowes – and within weeks was hinting he would like to come again next year. Salisbury suggested May would be convenient, and Malet reported the kaiser's 'face quite brightened' when this was passed on. Somewhat irritably Ponsonby told Malet it should not have been taken as a formal invitation, 'but ... if he *would* come, he had better come in May than August'. Before long it was settled that the kaiser and his wife would pay a full state visit to England the following summer. The Queen remained less than enthusiastic however, telling Vicky: 'If he even gave up coming here of his own accord ... I should not be sorry.'[95]

Victoria demanded full reimbursement for all she spent entertaining her grandson. Salisbury considered this reasonable, arguing to the Chancellor of the Exchequer: 'If it were not for State considerations of the most cogent kind, his visits would of course be discouraged. But I need not enlarge to you on the impossibility of taking that course.' As it was, the costs involved were, 'as much part of the political expense of the country as the salary of ambassadors'.[96]

The visit went ahead on 4 July and was deemed a success. William and Dona were cheered when they drove through the City of London, and though the Queen had rejected the Lord Mayor's suggestion she accompany them as 'a most absurd idea', she gave the couple several large luncheons and dinners at Windsor, as well as attending a Marlborough House garden party in their honour. After he left on 14 July, William wrote to thank his grandmother for the way her subjects had made 'me feel quite at home'. It had all vindicated his 'unswerving and honest labour … for the … development of goodwill amongst all nations'.[97]

Britain could not feel so securely aligned with Germany that it could afford to ignore other powers. To the Queen's alarm, France was now known to be 'coquetting' with Russia, and Salisbury told Victoria it was 'important to persuade the French, if we can, that England has no antipathy' to them. After the French fleet called at the Russian Baltic port of Kronstadt (where a secret Franco-Russian convention was signed), the Queen agreed that on their way home they could put in at the Isle of Wight. Having reviewed their ships, she gave a dinner for the officers, and the evening proved a happy occasion. Afterwards the French ambassador thanked the Queen for her hospitality and kindness, telling her all present had been particularly gratified that she had stood for the Marseillaise. Victoria 'did not say that I had not particularly liked doing it'.[98]

While Britain was doing its best to stay on good terms with continental neighbours, there was no guarantee Wilhelmine Germany would do likewise, not least because the kaiser had now taken a hatred to the tsar. In December he expressed delight that Russia was in dire financial straits and its peasants starving, trusting this would 'keep the Russians from making war on their unsuspecting neighbours'. At home, William made such ill-advised speeches and worrying pronouncements that some doubted his sanity. That September he infuriated the French by referring publicly to Napoleon as a 'Corsican upstart' – a 'really dreadful' blunder the Queen found 'inconceivable'. Having inscribed in Latin 'the will of the king is the highest law', in Munich town hall's address book, he told young recruits at Potsdam in November 1891 he might one day give orders 'that you must shoot down and stab to death your own relations and brothers'. His appalled mother burst out: 'I wish I could put a padlock on his mouth.'[99]

In spring 1892 the kaiser suffered some kind of 'nervous breakdown', attributed by him to overwork. On 15 March he assured his grandmother he would recover after rest, but for some time yet his mental state remained worrying. Hearing that the kaiser had cornered the British naval attaché at Berlin to rant about the dangers of the French and Russians gaining mastery of the Mediterranean, Salisbury commented sombrely to the Queen, 'He appears to be strangely excited, and it would be a very good thing if your Majesty could see him.' Were she able to she meet with the kaiser during a forthcoming visit to Europe, she could 'recommend ... calmness both in his policy and in the speeches which he too often makes'. Unable to face the encounter, Victoria told Sir Henry Ponsonby: 'No, no, I really cannot go about keeping everybody in order.'[100]

Instead it was agreed William should 'quite privately' pay a summer visit to Osborne, although the Queen stipulated he would have to sleep aboard his yacht. She would in fact have preferred it if he had not come. On 24 June Sir Edward Malet was asked to 'hint that these regular annual visits are not quite desirable'. In the event William was once again 'very amiable' during his stay, but this did not change Salisbury's view that he was 'mad enough for anything', and potentially 'the most dangerous enemy we had in Europe'.[101]

William II was not the only member of the Queen's family to cause Salisbury difficulties. During this period the Prince of Wales was caught up in several scandals, and his eldest son Albert Victor, Duke of Clarence (known as Eddy), was also a source of disquiet. Ignorant, ineffectual and effete, he was an utterly hopeless young man who had already suffered a bout of gonorrhoea. The general consensus was that he 'needed a good wife to sort him out', yet when he appeared at Balmoral 'hand in hand' with Princess Hélène of Orléans, Salisbury was appalled. Hélène was the attractive and bright daughter of the pretender to the French throne, the Comte de Paris, and if she became Prince Eddy's consort it would inevitably enrage both French republicans and chauvinistic Germans. Another complication was that she was Catholic, and the 1701 Act of Settlement debarred anyone married to a person of that faith from succeeding to the throne. Salisbury feared the marriage would 'produce great and general offence abroad' and stimulate anti-Catholic sentiment at home,[102] but Eddy gambled he could win over his grandmother with an impassioned personal appeal.

In a memorandum describing what happened, the Queen revealed how Eddy insisted 'they were devoted to each other and hoped I would help them'. He explained the princess 'was prepared to change her religion for his sake', at which point Hélène herself interjected: 'Oh! Do help, pray do!' Victoria warned, 'there might be political difficulties, to which he replied … that he thought Lord Salisbury would not object'. The Queen more realistically was 'afraid he would think it difficult' but she was nevertheless moved by her grandson's plight. 'I never saw him so eager, so earnest,' she recorded, 'and she was touchingly pathetic in her equally earnest appeal … It was difficult not to say yes at once.' The prime minister took a less sentimental view. He telegraphed his nephew Arthur Balfour, who was staying at Balmoral: 'Prevent royal consent being given.'[103]

Balfour reported that the Queen was 'evidently nervous about the whole thing' but she held that Eddy 'ought to marry', and there was no one else suitable or whom he would take. The only available German princesses were 'ugly, unhealthy and idiotic'; whereas 'here we have a charming and clever young lady against whom no legal objection can be urged'. Eddy followed up his interview by writing: 'Of course I may be wrong but I really cannot see what difficulties Lord Salisbury can put forward after he knows dear Hélène is going to become a Protestant … Forgive me Grandmama for saying that I believe in this case it is quite sufficient to have the Sovereign's concent [sic] and that the prime minister need only be told of her decision.' Passing this on to his uncle, Balfour chortled, 'So now you know your true position under the constitution.'[104]

The reality was the young lovers faced insuperable obstacles. Because Hélène was under twenty-one, her devout father had to sanction a change of religion, a most unlikely eventuality. Salisbury told the Queen that even if parental consent were secured, he must consult the Cabinet, although Victoria had hoped to avoid referring the matter to them. Salisbury wrote crisply, 'Of course as the Duke of Clarence observes the Queen is not bound by the opinion of her ministers. But they ought to have the opportunity of submitting it to her. For her consent to this marriage is a State Act of the utmost gravity.'[105]

Before long Balfour could reassure his uncle that the Comte de Paris 'quashes the whole thing', and when a desperate Hélène went to Rome to plead her cause, the Pope too would not countenance her abandoning her religion. At one point Eddy talked in an 'extremely annoying' fashion of renouncing all claim to the throne, but the Prince of Wales's private secretary Sir Francis Knollys was justly confident it was not in Prince Eddy's languid character to marry 'at all costs'. In May 1891 Princess Hélène irrevocably broke off the relationship.[106]

Soon Eddy was flirting with Lady Sybil St Clair Erskine, and was possibly embroiled in other amorous adventures. Towards the end of the year the Queen heard enough about his 'dissipations' to take the matter up with his mother, much to the vexation of Sir Francis Knollys, who wanted to know '*who* is it tells the Queen these things?' More convinced than ever that the only solution was for Eddy to marry someone appropriate, Victoria soon identified the perfect choice. Having summoned Princess May of Teck, daughter of her first cousin Mary Adelaide, to Balmoral for inspection, Victoria pronounced her 'a superior girl'.[107] It was made plain to Eddy he should propose, and he duly did so, informing his delighted grandmother on 5 December.

Tragedy intervened when May went to stay at Sandringham for New Year. On his birthday Prince Eddy went down with flu, and after a few days of delirium, during which he called repeatedly for Hélène, he died on 14 January 1892. With Princess May apparently relegated to permanent obscurity, the nation was plunged into mourning. Victoria was sorriest for 'Poor me, in my old age to see this young promising life cut short! I who loved him so dearly & to whom he was so devoted.'[108]

The Parnellite split and consequent Liberal confusion had transformed the government's prospects. At the end of 1890 Gladstone noted gloomily that, whereas he had deemed it a 'certainty' that at the next election his party would gain a large majority, Liberal fortunes had now gone into reverse. The government passed an impressive legislative programme that included free elementary education and promoting economic development in depressed areas of Ireland. Such was the Queen's faith in Arthur Balfour's abilities that when W. H. Smith died in October 1891, she was adamant Balfour must succeed him as Commons Leader. Salisbury was willing, but demurred at Victoria's assumption that Balfour could combine his new role with retaining the Irish chief secretaryship. Drily he pointed out, 'the Leader of the House must be always in the House, while the chief secretary must occasionally be in Ireland'.[109]

While the ministry's electoral defeat was no longer a foregone conclusion, Victoria was uncomfortably aware it remained a possibility, and knew she must face up to that. Politically she considered Gladstone more reprehensible than ever, not just because of his continued espousal of Home Rule, but on account of what she perceived as his steady drift leftwards. At the Liberal Party convention held at Newcastle in October 1891 Gladstone stressed that Home Rule remained his priority, while embracing a much wider programme such as land reform, 'one man, one vote', the payment of MPs, elective parish councils, and Scots and Welsh disestablishment. It made the Queen more determined than ever to keep him out of office.

In February 1892 the Queen started to prepare for the eventuality she so dreaded, asking Ponsonby to sound out Liberal friends of his as to whether they still considered Gladstone their unassailable leader. To Victoria's chagrin every man Ponsonby spoke to was positive that if the opposition came into power, no one other than Gladstone could head the new ministry. 'No doubt Mr Gladstone is getting very old,' Ponsonby acknowledged; 'but ... while he consents to be put forward' there could be no question of anyone superseding him.[110] The best the Queen could hope for was that Gladstone would voluntarily decide against seeking a fourth term as premier.

In May 1892 Victoria urged Salisbury not to hold an election too soon. Although he was sympathetic, his colleagues insisted Parliament must be dissolved at the end of June. The Queen began to wonder whether, should the Liberals be returned, she could offer Lord Rosebery the premiership, but then he disappointed her by attacking Salisbury in a speech that struck her as 'almost communistic'. With Rosebery looking an unlikely saviour, Victoria asked Ponsonby to 'try & get at him through someone so that he may know how grieved the Queen is at what he has said'.[111]

As she still could not but think 'the GOM at 82 is a *very alarming lookout*', she asked Ponsonby to convey to his Liberal friends that she would expect them to abide by various conditions: the position of Commander-in-Chief must be retained; Egypt must not be evacuated; and 'she positively refuses to take either Sir C. Dilke or that equally horrid Mr Labouchere'. The opposition should also be warned that by pursuing Home Rule, they would be 'doing what they can to bring about a civil war'. She hoped disagreements over Ireland would, in fact, make it impossible for the Liberals to form a government, but 'anyhow, the Queen foresees a great deal of trouble'.[112]

All now depended on the outcome of the election. In Victoria's eyes, 'the idea of a deluded excited man of 82 trying to govern England and her vast Empire with the miserable democratics under him is quite ludicrous. It is a bad joke' – but still the prospect loomed. Believing his party on the verge of a great victory, Gladstone campaigned energetically, resuming his attacks on the privileged and wealthy. Furiously Victoria commented: 'Mr Gladstone has brought so much personal violence into the contest, and used such insolent language that the Queen is quite shocked and ashamed.' Agreeing that Gladstone's 'revolutionary appeal to ... jealousy ... will do much harm', Salisbury opined: 'He is making wider and wider the dangerous antagonism between rich and poor ... More and more it is evident that he has entirely out-lived his judgement, though his eloquence to a great extent remains.'[113]

By mid-July 1892 the election results were in, and in some respects fell short of Liberal expectations, denying them an outright majority. However, once Irish members were factored in, Tories and Unionists would be outnumbered in Parliament by a margin of forty. Having counted on a three-figure majority, Gladstone was 'much broken and disappointed'. The Queen was almost equally downcast, writing bitterly to Ponsonby: 'She supposes she will have that dangerous old fanatic thrust down her throat.' Rather than resigning immediately, Salisbury said he would wait until Parliament convened in mid-August, and then the government would step down after losing a key vote.[114]

Still not reconciled to her fate, Victoria kept muttering about consulting Rosebery. Defiantly she scribbled to Ponsonby, 'The Queen cannot make up her mind to send at once for that dreadful old man ... She will resist taking him to the *last*.' The Prince of Wales wanted her to face the inevitable 'gracefully', and Edward Hamilton warned Ponsonby that just calling in Rosebery for an interview would at once 'give rise to all kinds of rumours that she was trying to give Mr G the "go by"'.[115]

Victoria clung to the hope that Gladstone would decide against becoming prime minister. This was not entirely delusional, for during the election campaign he had been injured by a woman throwing a rock-hard piece of gingerbread at him: he was now 'half deaf and three parts blind' and even a devoted admirer believed him 'unfit to form a government'. Several leading Liberals doubted whether he 'would accept the charge of forming of a ministry', although it never occurred to them that Victoria would not give him a chance of doing so. Nevertheless, on 25 July, Ponsonby informed the crestfallen Queen the GOM would not allow ill health to stand in his way.[116]

As she realised that she was not to be spared unpleasantness, Victoria indulged in a bitter tirade. 'Not one of these greedy place seekers who are republicans at heart care a straw for what their old Sovereign suffers,' she scrawled to Ponsonby. 'In former times when there were changes of government, though often painful to part with those one liked and esteemed, it was to have to do with gentlemen like Lord Russell, Lord Palmerston … Sir R Peel, Lord Aberdeen etc etc, but now it is with utter disgust the Queen thinks of it. To *support* them [the Liberals] is impossible for her. Her hand is forced.'[117]

In another unpalatable development it began to look as though Rosebery would turn down the Foreign Office, if offered it. Rather than being on political grounds, this was because he was suffering from insomnia and depression after losing his wife a year earlier. His former colleagues begged him to reconsider, but the Queen held back from doing the same. While she perhaps took the view it would be unconstitutional to intervene, Gladstone suspected she really hoped that he would abandon any attempt to form a government if Rosebery held aloof.[118]

On 8 August Parliament met, and as soon as the debate on the address was under way it became obvious the government would fall within days. This being so, the Queen agreed when Gladstone suggested he and Ponsonby should meet to discuss outstanding difficulties, 'before the crisis arrives'. When the interview took place on 10 August, the first thing that had to be established was whether Gladstone intended to take on the premiership. Even now Victoria may have persuaded herself he would think better of it. With that in mind she had authorised Ponsonby to offer Gladstone an earldom on the grounds that 'a quieter place' in the Lords would suit his needs best. Expressing gratitude for her 'gracious kindness', Gladstone deferentially turned it down, but when he notified Sir William Harcourt of his rejection he did so 'with a grim and contemptuous smile'. He unambiguously conveyed to Ponsonby he was eager to take power, while ruefully admitting: 'No doubt there were some who wished for his "disappearance".'[119]

Ponsonby next broached the question of preferment for Labouchere, whom the Queen considered 'not a fit and proper person' to occupy any position involving personal contact with her. It was not just that Labouchere headed the radical wing of the Liberal Party and had incensed her with his stance on royal grants and the House of Lords. His private life was also not considered respectable, for though he was now a married man, he had cohabited with his actress wife before her divorce came through. He was also the editor of *Truth*, a scurrilous magazine that had carried numerous offensive articles about the royal family. Ponsonby had already raised these matters with Gladstone's loyal lieutenant, Earl Spencer, and had indicated that the Queen would only agree to Labouchere having a junior ministerial post providing he renounced his journalistic career. Gladstone had since shown himself 'very much agitated about the royal exclusion of Labby and rather inclined to press the Queen on the subject', so clearly the matter was likely to prove awkward.[120]

Ponsonby began by raising the question of Labouchere's home life. Gladstone countered it was not his place to act as moral arbiter but gave the impression of being unaware of details the Queen deemed 'notorious'. He also seemed 'strangely ignorant' of the exact nature of *Truth* magazine, apparently assuming Labouchere could become an under-secretary of state even if he preserved his connection with the journal. Only after further enquiries did the extent of the problem become apparent. Besides regaling readers with unsavoury references to the Prince of Wales's infidelities, *Truth* had ten years earlier featured 'a gross attack on Princess Louise', implying that Royal Chaplain Canon Duckworth had seduced her while preparing her for confirmation as a teenager. When it emerged that Labouchere was not prepared to sever his links with *Truth*, Gladstone decided not to offer him any post at all.[121]

Labouchere was 'mad with rage' at Gladstone's collusion with 'royal ostracism', moaning: 'They can't prove I ever said anything personally against the Royal Family except that the heir apparent was the associate of swindlers and prostitutes.' On the whole, however, it was accepted that the Queen had a fair case. In revenge Labouchere published more 'spiteful articles' in *Truth*, but Lord Rosebery urged Victoria to pay them no heed. To her amusement, he explained that Labouchere had expected his exclusion from office would provoke '"quite a revolution" whereas nobody cared at all, which annoyed him very much'.[122]

After four nights of debate, a vote was taken on the address, and the government were defeated by a resounding margin. The Queen considered the numbers insignificant ('Only forty caused this catastrophe,' was her comment). On 12 August the ministers resolved to resign. Salisbury at once travelled to Osborne to inform his sovereign, who deplored his readiness 'to acquiesce so much in the result of the elections'. In a memorandum that showed an almost comical incomprehension of the democratic process, the Queen solemnly pronounced: 'It seems to me a defect in our much famed constitution to have to part with an admirable government like Lord Salisbury's for no question of any importance or *any reason*, merely on account of the number of votes.'[123]

The same day she wrote to Gladstone – 'rather contrary to my own feelings', as she put it with some understatement – inviting him to form a government. She had no compunction about stating that she had accepted Salisbury's resignation 'with much regret'; the same phrase featured in the Court Circular announcement put out that day.[124] Ponsonby bore the letter to London and Gladstone at once accepted her commission.

On 15 August Gladstone travelled to Osborne to move things forward. At that point it was still unclear whether Rosebery would accept the Foreign Office. Gladstone had asked the Queen to contact the depressed peer, but she told the Prince of Wales: 'I must not interfere in the formation of this iniquitous government.' In the end she did not forbid the prince from adding his own pleas to those of Rosebery's colleagues, and this had tipped the balance. On Gladstone's arrival at Osborne a telegram from Rosebery awaited him containing the laconic declaration: 'So be it.'[125]

The meeting between the Queen and Gladstone was hardly cordial. In her account of it she noted, 'I thought him greatly altered … not only much aged & walking rather bent, with a stick, but altogether; his face shrunk, deadly pale, with a weird look in his eyes.' To ease matters, 'I did not touch on politics.' Gladstone still detected in her attitude 'another lurch in the direction opposed to ours'. He observed too 'a change in the Queen for the worse – her intellect less quick and judgement less good'; he told his wife her manner had been 'carefully polite and nothing else'. She was 'in nothing helpful' and uttered 'not one sympathetic word on any question'. He later compared the encounter to the meeting 'between Marie Antoinette and her executioner'.[126]

On 18 August the Queen received the seals of the outgoing ministers. 'The audiences of leave-taking were sad.' Showing unwonted emotion, Lord Salisbury 'could hardly speak when he gave me the FO seals'. Cranbrook too was 'much affected' by her crying out: 'Oh my dear Lord Cranbrook, I cannot tell you how sorry I am to lose you,' before bursting into tears. She showed a more pugnacious spirit to Henry Matthews, who, despite her efforts to replace him, had stayed at the Home Office to the end. He predicted that having failed to get Home Rule through the House of Lords, Gladstone's next step would be to 'bring forward a very large Reform Bill with almost manhood suffrage'. Victoria said in that case 'they might *then* look for a President as *I* should certainly not put up with such things'.[127]

She told herself that her ordeal would not be long, for Gladstone's health could surely not withstand a lengthy term in office. Even so, she found the prospect hard to bear. She unburdened herself to the Viceroy of India, Lord Lansdowne, proclaiming it dreadful that, 'by an incomprehensible reckless vote, the result of most unfair and abominable misrepresentation at the elections, one of the best and most useful governments have been defeated'. Fiercely she continued, 'the Queen can hardly trust herself to say what she feels and thinks ... The danger to the country, to Europe, to her vast Empire ... in having all ... entrusted to the shaking hand of an old, wild and incomprehensible man of 82½ is very great.' Fortunately all was not lost, for while it was, without doubt, 'a terrible trial, ... thank God, the country is sound, and it cannot last'.[128]

13

Mr Gladstone; Lord Rosebery 1892–1895

On 23 July 1892, still coming to terms with having to part with 'the best government of the century', Victoria had commented savagely to Sir Henry Ponsonby: 'The Queen is glad that Mr Gladstone is determined about his Home Rule, as that is sure to bring him into great difficulties.' Gladstone himself was well aware that putting Home Rule through Parliament would pose an almost insuperable challenge. When the disappointing election results had come in, he had contemplated focussing instead on domestic measures, but only wavered briefly. By late July he was once again ardently committed, telling Lord Ripon: 'I am as fast bound to Ireland as Ulysses was to his mast.'[1]

This renewed sense of conviction was apparent when Sir Henry Ponsonby met with Gladstone on 11 August and found him 'eager and excited, talking a great deal about Home Rule'. At Osborne four days later, Gladstone was no less animated. Rather than place him next to her at dinner, Victoria had seated him by Ponsonby's daughter Betty. Throughout the meal, Gladstone talked 'loudly and eagerly, though guests usually spoke in hushed tones at the Queen's table'. After dinner, the Queen came straight up to Betty 'and asked "What did Mr Gladstone talk to you about?" "Home Rule Ma'am!" She shrugged her shoulders and said: "I know" … He always will!"'[2]

For Victoria, the prospect of Home Rule was as abhorrent as ever. She declared to Vicky: 'Ireland has recovered its quiet and prosperity so wonderfully that it is very wicked to try and upset everything again.' When Gladstone reported to her in late September that Ireland was currently tranquil, she wrote back: 'This satisfactory state of affairs is the result of six years of firm and just government; and she cannot but regret that fresh measures should be so hastily adopted which seem uncalled for and which may encourage the lawless to fresh outbursts of crime.'[3]

At the end of October Gladstone sent her a 'very curious' memorandum, which she considered 'full of self-deception'. As he explained, he felt she needed enlightening because, although the government's views on Ireland commanded majority support, they were 'hardly at all represented … in the powerful social circles with which your Majesty has ordinary personal intercourse'. He averred that Home Rule, as conceived by him, was 'a proposal eminently conservative in the highest sense of the term', whereas, if not addressed, Irish discontent would advance 'democratic opinion', as well as encouraging Scottish and Welsh separatism. Although he said he did not expect a reply, the Queen could not resist a sarcastic rejoinder. She wrote it was impossible to follow his argument as no one knew yet what he was proposing for Ireland; until that was clear, 'the expression "Home Rule" has an empty meaning'.[4]

The Queen had a point, for she was not the only one wondering about Gladstone's intentions. Not until 11 November were the Cabinet shown some 'Heads of Consideration' concerning Home Rule, and ten days later the prime minister reluctantly agreed that a Cabinet committee should be entrusted with drawing up more detailed proposals. By then the measure had so far taken shape in his own mind that he felt able to tell the Queen it would differ from the previous Home Rule Bill in that Irish MPs would be retained at Westminster.[5]

In January 1893 the Cabinet met to consider the committee's recommendations but failed to resolve many outstanding problems. On 13 January Gladstone reported to Victoria, 'They examined the difficult subject … of the retention of Irish members at Westminster … involving … serious difficulties and inconveniences.' In the end they decided that the number of Irish MPs should be reduced to approximately eighty and that these should 'be excluded from voting on questions exclusively British'. From this 'most instructive' letter, the Queen and Ponsonby at once deduced there was 'great diversity of opinion in the Cabinet'. Reminding Victoria that Gladstone had earlier said keeping the Irish at Westminster once a Dublin parliament had been established would raise questions that 'passed the wit of man', Ponsonby was sure that Gladstone's latest plan would prove unworkable.[6]

A few days later the Queen saw Lord Chancellor Herschell and tried to find out more. She asked him about 'the many Cabinets they were having about the Home Rule Bill. He said it was a difficult question … but … things could not go on in the future as they had done. I replied that I feared I did not agree.'[7]

* * *

The Queen found dealing with Gladstone as much of a trial as ever. Just after he took over the government she told Vicky, 'He listens to no one and won't hear any contradiction … He is really half crazy, half silly, and it is better not to provoke discussion. But it is awful to have such a man at the head.' Interestingly Gladstone's former private secretary Edward Hamilton (who now worked at the Treasury) agreed that Gladstone was 'much less tolerant of opinion differing from his own than he used to be', and John Morley too thought his leader 'certainly more imperious and less open to reason'.[8]

Gladstone himself noted that when they met, Victoria tended to avoid serious discussion. On 25 November 1892 he listed in his diary 'topics' raised during an audience. These included: her health; 'the fogs of London and Westminster'; the Dowager Duchess of Sutherland; and 'has Mrs Gladstone still a nephew who is a master at Eton?' From this, he noted caustically, 'may be gathered in some degree the terms of confidence between her Majesty and the prime minister'.[9]

Gladstone blamed the Queen for their lack of communication, but she came to feel he too deliberately avoided saying anything meaningful. In March 1893 she complained to Chancellor of the Exchequer Sir William Harcourt: 'Mr Gladstone never initiated any subjects of conversation.' When this was passed on to the prime minister he acknowledged 'this was certainly so', for he would have thought it presumptuous to raise weighty matters uninvited. He continued, 'if the Queen allows greater latitude, I shall be ready to regard myself as at liberty to refer to any matter of business … not likely to be otherwise than agreeable to her Majesty', a qualification that of course severely limited the subjects that could be so raised. Since Gladstone doubtless had a shrewd idea of how she had betrayed his confidence in the past, it was understandable he was so wary, but the suspicion that information was being purposely withheld from her added to Victoria's flourishing sense of grievance.[10]

The fact was their relations were now way beyond repair. In November 1893 Gladstone opened up on the subject to Edward Hamilton, correctly identifying the row about the Prince of Wales's going to Ireland as a crucial turning point. 'From that day to this she had never been the same to him. He had never since, he knew, enjoyed her confidence.' Things had grown steadily worse, until 'he had as nearly as possible been insulted' by her 'curt note' of August 1892, informing him she had received Salisbury's resignation '*with great regret*'. The prime minister added that, 'He believed he had always shown her great consideration and attention, but none was shown in return.'[11]

The Queen was on better terms with some other members of the Cabinet. Admittedly things had got off to a tricky start when 'these horrid new people' came to receive their seals of office at Osborne on 18 August. The start of the Privy Council meeting was delayed because Lord Kimberley could not be located, and for 'fully five minutes … the line of new ministers stood facing the Queen in absolute silence'. One later remarked, 'he never saw people so uncomfortable'. Eventually they 'knelt and kissed hands … without a word being spoken to any of them'.[12]

When better acquainted, Victoria took to several of them. James Bryce, Chancellor of the Duchy of Lancaster, had earned her approval following his first stay at Balmoral. Ponsonby informed his wife: 'Bryce is a success. He makes himself very agreeable and talks to HM on literary matters which highly pleases her.' War Minister Henry Campbell-Bannerman also 'made a very good impression' at Balmoral. After he left Ponsonby wrote to him: 'You listened to her and encouraged her to speak openly which she hesitates to do with those who seem convinced that what she is going to say is wrong before she says it.' Her initial assessment of Henry Asquith, a 'very clever lawyer' whom Gladstone had appointed home secretary, was that this 'intelligent, rather good-looking man' was 'pleasant, straightforward and sensible'. However, in February 1894 she was puzzled to hear that Asquith had informed Ponsonby that the next day's *Times* would carry an announcement of his engagement to the high-spirited Margot Tennant, and had jokingly asked, 'Have I to ask the Queen's consent?' Taking this quite literally, Victoria annotated Ponsonby's report: 'How curious that *he* … should ask if my consent is required for his marriage. If this was required she would not give it, as she thinks [Miss Tennant] is most unfit for a Cabinet Minister's wife'.[13]

Her relations with the large and heavy-set Chancellor of the Exchequer, Sir William Harcourt, were not so happy. In the past they had sometimes got on well. She had been quite taken with him when he first stayed at Balmoral in autumn 1881, pronouncing him 'extremely agreeable in society, full of anecdotes and information'.[14] Later, however, her view became less favourable. When with her, Harcourt successfully controlled his volcanic temper (something he signally failed to do in Cabinet); but he and Victoria disagreed on many issues, and even when he was in good humour, she found him rather exhausting company.

When this government took office, the Queen seems momentarily to have deluded herself that Harcourt would be her ally, perhaps because she knew he was no enthusiast for Home Rule. Ponsonby informed Sir William, 'She wants to know who will ... tell her what is going on, as, of course, Gladstone cannot do so, and wants to know if you will do it.' Harcourt replied, 'This was very awkward ... He could not possibly undertake this except at the wish of Gladstone.'[15] Once it was established that Harcourt would not go behind Gladstone's back, Victoria turned decisively against him.

When Harcourt stayed at Balmoral in October 1892 the Queen told her daughter it was 'a terrible trial' to have to be hostess to 'a person I particularly dislike'. She explained: 'It was said I had better see him as he was very amenable to any attention paid him. But I hate it,' not least because 'he is rather awful looking now, like an elephant, so large and big'. Harcourt was oblivious to her antipathy. On his return he reported that he had 'found the Queen extremely amiable' and was convinced his visit had been a great success. While their views on African colonisation were clearly divergent, 'When you are face-to-face with her she is always very courteous and kind, and I soon shunted the conversation on to domestic affairs and family gossip.' He flattered himself that 'his "Disraelian method" of always putting in a little "butter"' ensured he remained on the right side of her – but this was not so. In 1899 Victoria would tell Lord Rosebery, she 'could never bear Sir William'.[16]

Rosebery himself, of course, was a different matter. Seeing him after the council held at Osborne on 18 August, she told him she was delighted he had accepted office. Mournfully he said: 'They would have done better to leave him where he was,' but she insisted: 'Work would do him good.' Reminding him how she had helped him in the past, she promised to do so again, 'which made him smile'. Five days later she wrote to him confidentially, clearly hoping to open a private channel of communication. Within weeks this paid dividends. Although Rosebery was guiltily aware that it was Gladstone's prerogative to inform her what took place in Cabinet, he did pass on some interesting details. It all confirmed the Queen in her view of Rosebery's soundness. In August 1893, having bemoaned the absurdity of having an eighty-three-year-old man as prime minister, she burst out: 'You ought to be there Lord Rosebery. I wished you to be there and I hope you will be there. You are the only one of the Ministry with whom I can talk freely.'[17]

One reason why she so approved of Rosebery was they shared the same approach to Empire. The foreign secretary prided himself on being a 'Liberal Imperialist', whereas Gladstone's scepticism on such matters was so well known that when he attended a reception at the Imperial Institute in May 1893, he was booed and hissed by the crowd. The Queen pretended to be shocked: 'Really it was not quite the right thing ...,' she told Vicky, 'though the Home Rule Bill deserves any amount of "groans".'[18]

The first flare-up between Gladstone on the one hand and Rosebery and the Queen on the other occurred over Uganda. Having become part of the British 'sphere of influence' within Africa in 1890, Uganda had initially been administered by the British East Africa Chartered Company. Because years of near civil war had disrupted Ugandan trade, there were no profits for shareholders, so the company decided to withdraw from the country at the end of 1892. Gladstone was happy for it to be given up, but Rosebery was determined to prevent this. In September 1892 he circulated to the Cabinet memoranda and diplomatic reports putting the case for annexing Uganda. A telegram from Gerald Portal, the British consul general, warned in graphic terms that if colonising efforts in East Africa were abandoned, British and French missionaries stationed there would be massacred, along with their native Christian converts.[19]

The Queen was in no doubt as to what should be done: it would be 'disastrous' if Uganda was abandoned, she wrote, for it would convince 'the public at large ... we are going to pursue a policy of giving up everything and lowering our position'. She assured Rosebery she had been stirred by warnings about the possible doom awaiting Christians, declaring darkly: 'The fate of Gordon is not, and will not be forgotten.' Almost all of Rosebery's colleagues were against deeper involvement in Uganda, but they were constrained by two considerations. Firstly, Rosebery was threatening to resign if he didn't have his way. Furthermore, his stance was popular with a public currently in the grip of what Lord Kimberley called 'violent Jingo fever'.[20]

Two stormy Cabinets were held at the end of September, and ministers reluctantly agreed to postpone withdrawal for three months. Rosebery promised Victoria he would use the delay 'to elicit the real feeling of the country, which is, he is certain, against evacuation'. True to his word, he manipulated public opinion, keeping up the pressure so persistently that in June 1894 Uganda became a British protectorate.[21]

Egypt was another source of controversy. Gladstone would have liked to oblige the French by ending the British occupation, but the Queen and Rosebery were as determined not to be dislodged from there.

In early 1893 a crisis arose when the Cabinet refused to bully Egypt's young khedive into acting more submissively towards Britain.

Gladstone's 'truckling to France' over Egypt 'made HM very wrath'. When Britain's consul general in Egypt, Lord Cromer, wrote that the British garrison in Egypt must be reinforced, Victoria was determined his request should be upheld. Rosebery warned his colleagues he would resign if Cromer's demand was rejected, but Gladstone burst out: 'They might as well ask him to put a torch to Westminster Abbey as to send more troops to Egypt.' With the Cabinet plainly reluctant to heed Cromer's call for action, the Queen wanted to know, 'How can they be so shortsighted and weak!' Convinced that 'it is Khartoum and Gordon all over again!' she wrote to Gladstone spelling out the similarities. She was hardly placated when he answered: 'After reflecting during all these years upon the sad occurrence, he finds it more difficult to reply to the objection that the government of that day did too much, than to the charge of having done too little.'[22]

The Queen had ordered that her words be relayed to the Cabinet, but when Gladstone did her bidding he did not conceal his fury. As he read her letter aloud he 'constantly interrupted himself to say of a word, "underlined"', until at length, 'much enraged … [he] could read no more and handed it to Rosebery'. He was not therefore entirely truthful when he assured Victoria the letter had been 'heard, he need hardly specify, in a spirit of deep deference and respect'. Even Rosebery felt that the Queen should be more restrained in future. He wrote to Ponsonby: 'I entirely shared the Queen's views in this business but I have great doubts of the wisdom of her sending rescripts to be read at the Cabinet. Such is the jealous temper of Britons that these utterances are more likely to produce reaction than compliance!'[23]

In the end, all turned out well from Victoria's point of view. Realising that a ship carrying troops home from India was about to dock at Suez, Lord Spencer suggested the men on board could be diverted to reinforce the garrison in Egypt. This satisfied both Queen and foreign secretary, who fulsomely informed his sovereign the outcome was 'entirely due to your Majesty's pressing remonstrances'.[24]

Three days before the opening of Parliament on 31 January 1893, the Queen queried the wording of the Speech from the Throne, objecting to the statement that a bill would be introduced 'for the *better* government of Ireland'. She at once telegraphed the prime minister: 'Can you leave out "better"?' Gladstone was 'a good deal put out', but after consultation with one or two colleagues grudgingly changed it so it merely stated an intention 'to amend the provision for the government of Ireland'.[25]

As the Home Rule Bill passed its first reading on 17 February, the Queen prayed, 'Please God in committee it will be much altered.' Three days later she wrote to Gladstone reiterating that the 'provisions of this measure, which tend towards the disruption of her Empire and the establishment of an impracticable form of government' aroused in her deep feelings of anxiety. Thanking her for the 'very frank expression of your Majesty's apprehension', the prime minister hoped that as discussion proceeded, 'it may tend to soften some of those unfavourable anticipations'.[26]

The second reading debate was fierce and protracted, and the opposition caused further delay by holding up other measures to prevent the government allocating time to Home Rule. As a result, the bill only inched forward, though to the Queen's eyes it appeared the ministry was using indecent haste to 'force it through'. When Harcourt complained on 24 March of 'organised obstruction by the Opposition', the Queen retorted: 'Nothing could equal the obstructiveness of the Liberal Radical Party when *they* were out of office,' so 'they have not much right to expect similar tactics not being pursued now'. Such problems were anyway caused by the 'very strong and growing repugnance ... to Home Rule, and what a dread there is of the Bill passing'. She added, 'this feeling is increasing in Ireland' – by which she meant the island's Protestant enclaves.[27]

Already rallies were being held in those areas, prompting Victoria to note happily: 'There are no end of meetings in Ireland against the Home Rule Bill.' In early April Balfour was present at one in Belfast where the bill was publicly torn in shreds before a parade of Orangemen. In the Commons John Morley suggested Balfour had 'encouraged disorder' by addressing protesters in inflammatory language; when Edward Hamilton heard Lord Salisbury was planning to visit Ulster too, he considered it 'little short of criminal'. The Queen thought otherwise. Having read with pleasure Lady Salisbury's account of a loyalist crowd who left no doubt 'this fatal measure would be resisted by them to the death', Victoria exulted: 'Lord Salisbury's reception in Ulster has been quite marvellous. The speeches he made were excellent.'[28]

The Queen took up the matter confidentially with Rosebery, suggesting that in view of strong feeling in Ulster, the correct course was to abandon the bill. He wrote that he did not 'undervalue or disparage' the hostile demonstrations, but 'in his opinion it would not be possible for the government to withdraw the bill without withdrawing itself, at any rate until a later stage'. In early June she tried again with him. Rosebery responded that while he himself was 'not an enthusiastic Home Ruler', he believed it offered the 'least impracticable method of governing the country' and the ministry was 'pledged in honour' to it. This was not what the Queen wanted to hear. She maintained that in recent years, 'all was going on very well' across the Irish Sea – and though perhaps some advances could have been made as regards local government, change on the scale now contemplated 'would inevitably cause great misery to Ireland and most likely civil war'.[29]

After passing its second reading, the bill entered the committee stage on 8 May. The acrimony in the Commons did not lessen, however. Gladstone was forced to modify his bill by moving that Irish MPs would be unrestricted in their voting rights at Westminster, and the financial arrangements for Ireland also had to be revised. For night after night there was 'nothing but wrangling and quarrelling', as every clause was bitterly disputed. The worst night of all was 27 July when a brawl broke out in the Commons. Gladstone gave the Queen a sorrowful account of the 'painful scene', and was angered when she claimed 'unseemly violence' was only to be expected when the government was ramming through 'a measure so repugnant' to national sentiment and 'fraught with danger to the constitution'.[30]

Despite its agonisingly slow progress, it did seem likely the bill would ultimately be passed by the Commons and would then be sent up to the Lords. Since it was bound to be rejected there, the Queen started making preparations, resuming surreptitious links with leading members of the opposition. On 11 July she saw the Duke of Argyll, who agreed to liaise with Lord Salisbury and the Duke of Devonshire (the former Lord Hartington, whose father had recently died) about what she should do when the Lords threw out the 'foolish and terrible Bill'. She wanted to know whether Salisbury thought she should insist on a dissolution. A few days later he sent back word she must not act prematurely. On 8 August he followed this up with a memorandum explaining his thinking. If she demanded a dissolution, the ministry would inevitably resign. The way she had exercised her prerogative would then feature prominently in the election campaign, with a concomitant risk that Victoria would emerge from it with her authority damaged.[31]

It was not until late August that debate on the bill entered its final stages, which the government truncated by use of the 'guillotine'. On 1 September 1893 the bill passed its third Commons reading, and the

Lords then debated the measure for four days. On 8 September the peers rejected the bill by 419 to 41 – 'a crushing majority indeed!' crowed the Queen. Far from provoking indignation, 'not a dog barked' in protest: when the result was given out, the crowd outside Parliament cheered, for Home Rule had not captured the public imagination. This meant that Gladstone could not speedily make another attempt to pass it. In January 1894 Victoria asked Lord Rosebery if the measure would be revived during the coming session. 'He said "Oh! No", there had been enough of that last year.'[32]

In July 1893 a coal dispute ushered in months of industrial unrest. Extra police and troops were sent to the areas affected, and on 9 September Home Secretary Asquith informed the Queen that at least three men had been killed when soldiers fired into a crowd in Yorkshire. Strikes and riots continued, and on 14 November the Queen wrote to Gladstone from Balmoral wanting to know what the government proposed to do about the 'very serious' situation. 'Has it been brought before the Cabinet, & is *no* mediation between the employers & their men … possible?'[33]

As it happened, the Cabinet had discussed the situation the previous day and had agreed that Rosebery should oversee a meeting between the two sides. Rosebery gloomily predicted to Victoria little good would come of it, but his assistance proved invaluable. On 17 November Harcourt reported that Rosebery had brokered 'an honourable peace, putting an end to civil war', and the men would be returning to work immediately. 'Lord Rosebery says … it is the happiest day of his life,' Sir William informed his sovereign.[34]

Still demoralised by the rejection of Home Rule, Gladstone had not shown much interest in measures introduced during Parliament's autumn session, including an employers' liability bill and proposals to set up parish councils. He paid more attention to difficulties arising from the fact that Victoria's second son, Prince Alfred, Duke of Edinburgh, had become Duke of Coburg on the death of his Uncle Ernest in August 1893. Unfortunately Coburg had tiny revenues and Duke Ernest had died heavily indebted. It had not occurred to Prince Alfred (who himself had many debts) that he would now be required to renounce the £25,000 annuity he received from the British taxpayer. When this became apparent, a 'shocked' Queen got 'on her high horse'. She suggested it would be 'simplest' (Gladstone added a sarcastic exclamation mark when informing Harcourt) if the duke retained his entire allowance for a couple of years and then had it reduced to £15,000. She added she had consulted Salisbury and two former Tory lord chancellors on the question. 'Very wrong,' growled Gladstone to his private secretary.[35]

The prime minister was understandably irritated that despite having 'publicly advertised her disgust at having anything to do' with the Liberals, she now expected him to force his followers to provide a generous endowment for her son. In fact, Gladstone was much less miserly disposed than several other ministers, but it was perhaps not surprising that Victoria failed to recognise he was on her side. The letter he wrote her castigating Prince Alfred's past extravagance had been so insensitively phrased that his wife had begged him to reword it.[36]

On 2 November the Cabinet ruled that Prince Alfred would have to forfeit his annuity altogether. Gladstone thought the decision so unfair he 'acted off his own bat' to tell Victoria her son could keep £10,000 a year. On 21 December the prime minister was called upon to defend the settlement in Parliament and had to parry a fierce onslaught from Labouchere. Finally understanding Gladstone had loyally exerted himself, the Queen did at least have the grace to thank him.[37]

By that time a much more serious issue had come to the fore. Despite the fact that in 1889 Salisbury's government had provided that an extra £20 million would be spent on the navy over the next four years, the Admiralty maintained that Britain remained dangerously weak at sea. The First Lord of the Admiralty, Earl Spencer, agreed more spending was necessary – and the public too were in favour – but Gladstone dismissed this as one of those 'irrational and discreditable panics' that periodically gripped the nation. The Queen inevitably was one of those who believed the Royal Navy must be given all it wanted. On 7 December she wrote to Gladstone saying it was vital to preserve Britain's naval supremacy, adding, for good measure, that the army should be strengthened too. The arrival of her letter coincided with the government learning that the opposition were going to put forward a motion for a substantial addition to the navy. It is not unreasonable to suppose that the Queen – who had seen Salisbury on 4 December – had been informed of what was afoot. Certainly Gladstone did not doubt she maintained close links with his opponents. When another critical letter from her arrived, he snorted it had been 'written by the Leader of the Opposition'.[38]

As instructed, he read Victoria's letter to Cabinet on 14 December, 'pretending to have great difficulty deciphering it, and sniffing contemptuously all the time'. He then warned the Queen the government would take a stand against the opposition motion. When the vote was held five days later, ministers gained a comfortable majority. The question of naval spending nevertheless remained a live issue, with Gladstone becoming ever more entrenched in his conviction that the Admiralty's 'accursed project' must be resisted.[39]

As it became clear he was virtually isolated in Cabinet, the prime minister began threatening to resign. Being under the delusion he was indispensable, Gladstone assumed his colleagues would quickly come to heel, but on 9 January 1894 he had a horrible shock when he subjected them to a fifty-minute harangue on the folly of naval increases. To his amazement, they indicated that if he was going to retire, he should do it sooner rather than later. Scathingly he said, '"Of course I can go at once if you wish it" (Sensation)' – but in fact they were far from appalled. John Morley recalled that thereafter 'the view undoubtedly was that now is the accepted time for our chief's resignation'.[40]

On 13 January Gladstone went to Biarritz for a rest, counting on the Cabinet rallying to him in his absence. While abroad he was furious and excitable, sometimes behaving as though his views commanded widespread support, and at others hinting that if he did resign he would not go quietly. By this time his eyesight was so bad he found reading almost impossible, while his deafness made Cabinets challenging. Before leaving England he had said his feeble 'eyes and ears' provided 'warrant ample for going', but now he seemed ready to make it known he would be resigning on a point of principle.[41]

The news that the Lords were putting forward troublesome amendments to the government's chief pieces of legislation suddenly propelled Gladstone in a new direction. He wrote home urging the dissolution of Parliament, to be followed by an election campaign on 'who was to rule, Lords or Commons?' Ministers were horrified by his 'impossible and preposterous' proposal, which Harcourt derided as 'the act of a selfish lunatic'. Lord Kimberley promptly telegraphed Biarritz to say the Cabinet was unanimously against it.[42]

Despite this, on 10 February Gladstone returned 'in great spirits' – 'still buoying himself up with the hope of a dissolution'. Once again he had misjudged the situation, for his colleagues were now eagerly awaiting his resignation. After days of suspense, they started pressing him to inform the Queen he was going. Because he ignored this, his private secretary Algy West then suggested alerting Ponsonby. Despite Gladstone's saying he would write, over a week elapsed before he did anything. By now, he felt very bitter. When Harcourt alluded to his possible retirement, Gladstone interrupted: 'Not retirement. I have been *put out.*' Finally, in Cabinet on 23 February, he made the statement for which his colleagues had longed, but in somewhat ominous terms. He declared when Parliament was prorogued, it would be time 'to end his cooperation with members of the Cabinet'. Since this implied he would cause trouble out of office, 'the words fell like ice' on the company.[43]

Gladstone unnecessarily protracted the process of informing Victoria, asking Ponsonby on 23 February whether he could write to her in confidence about an unspecified matter. He did have some justification for wanting secrecy, because it was realistic to fear that as soon as she learned the news she would tell Salisbury. All the same, it was understandable that Victoria was wary of giving the desired undertaking. Although Edward Hamilton thought it 'dense' of her and Ponsonby not to guess what Gladstone had in mind, in view of the numerous times nothing had come of rumours he would retire it was hardly surprising she discounted them this time. She and Ponsonby suspected that Gladstone was planning to ask for a dissolution in order to campaign against the Lords. In view of the fact that Gladstone had contemplated doing exactly that, she was scarcely being fanciful.

On 24 February Ponsonby saw Gladstone and said the Queen would like 'some hint' of what he planned before she made any promises. Ponsonby also probed Algy West, explaining she 'would not bind herself to any secrecy about matters where she must consult friends. Was it dissolution?' West declined to say, though understood the Queen's fear of becoming embroiled in 'a sort of plot in which she would be the responsible actor'.[44]

That evening Ponsonby again met briefly with Gladstone without obtaining clarification. Next day Gladstone wrote, 'As the Queen has Parliament in her mind, I may say that is not the subject of my intimation.' However, Victoria was not reassured. Only on 27 February were things sorted out. Ponsonby called early on West and explained that Victoria was 'making a fuss' because she feared Gladstone intended hostile action against the Lords. West then went to Gladstone and found him 'very cross about the Queen's want of trust', though West himself 'thought the Queen might fairly resent his want of confidence' and it was 'only reasonable that HM after receiving such a message from her PM should be apprehensive and nervous'. West sought permission to reveal all to Ponsonby, but Gladstone said Sir Henry could not pass anything on to the Queen, which West felt was too much to ask. West therefore confidentially informed Ponsonby that Gladstone would be resigning. Victoria could be told the prime minister wished to relay that his eyes were getting worse, 'and she would guess the rest'.[45]

This was duly done. The Queen was derisive that the matter Gladstone had chosen to shroud in mystification was 'nothing more or less than his resignation'. After Ponsonby left her, a letter arrived from the prime minister announcing he would soon be providing 'preliminary intimation' of his intention 'to tender to your Majesty, on physical grounds, his resignation of office'. It irritated Victoria that Gladstone was still being so opaque, particularly after she heard that newspapers hoardings in London were already emblazoned with word of his retirement. She wrote crossly, 'The secret which Mr Gladstone makes so much of is constantly leaking out – in spite of all his great fuss and anxiety about secrecy.'[46]

Somewhat perversely, far from being overjoyed at the puzzle being solved in this way, she was 'much perturbed' by the news. Naturally this was not because she was sad about Gladstone's departure. She was due to leave for Europe on 13 March and was worried about any disruption to her travel plans. Her determination not to delay her holiday meant that, while delighted that Gladstone was going, she was annoyed by his timing. Querulously she wrote to Ponsonby, 'If only it could be tided over till the Queen returns, or else the little rest and benefit she has looked forward to will be ruined; and this long suffering and pain [from rheumatism in her legs] makes her very worn out. If there is a change of government it will take a fortnight or three weeks ... Can Sir Henry not do something?' If she had ever thought of sending for Salisbury, this made her reject the idea, as such a wholesale change would plainly necessitate her presence in England. The matter was clinched when Ponsonby pointed out that, if Rosebery became prime minister, all 'could be easily arranged'.[47]

On the afternoon of 28 February the Queen received Gladstone at Buckingham Palace. As he saw it, he was still not officially resigning, but rather giving verbal confirmation of the 'preliminary intimation' sent the day before. Understandably Victoria did not attach much importance to this distinction. For his part Gladstone felt aggrieved that, considering the audience was 'doubtless my last in an official capacity', she did not endow it with any sense of occasion. 'She had much difficulty in finding topics for an adequate prolongation, but fog and rain and the coming journey to Italy all did their duty and helped.' What was more, now she knew her travel plans could go ahead, she barely hid her delight that he was stepping down. 'She was at the highest point of her cheerfulness,' Gladstone recorded. 'Any fear that the intelligence ... would be a shock to her has been entirely dispelled.' Instead of expressing regret at losing his services, she just 'said she was sorry *for the cause*', but did not make searching enquiries about his failing sight and deafness.[48]

The following day Gladstone presided over Cabinet for the last time. It was an emotional occasion: the Queen was told by two of those present that 'there was hardly a dry eye'. Yet this did not mean his colleagues wanted Gladstone to stay. Two days later Lord Kimberley would tell Victoria: 'Though it was painful to part ... he was bound to say it was better so.' The Empire needed 'a Man at the head of the Government who could look into everything ... & watch over it all', and Gladstone was no longer up to that.[49]

At the 1 March Cabinet, Gladstone had had a final tussle with colleagues on a matter guaranteed to annoy the Queen. The Lords had amended the Parish Council Bill in ways displeasing to the government, and that evening, during what turned out to be his last Commons appearance, Gladstone proceeded to 'declare war on the House of Lords', alleging they aimed 'to annihilate the whole work of the House of Commons'. In Cabinet that morning, he had wanted to go further by stating in the speech of prorogation that something must be done about the 'want of conformity' between the two houses. The Cabinet had regarded this as pointlessly provocative, and there was 'much disputation' as to whether they should insist on the passage's inclusion if Victoria withstood it. In the end it was agreed, 'we should get the paragraph if we could, and not fight if we could not get it'. Predictably Victoria did object, and Gladstone had grudgingly to promise that 'the reference disliked by the Queen will not be pressed'.[50]

On 2 March the Gladstones stayed overnight at Windsor, along with several other guests. The Queen thought Gladstone 'cheerful', though Mrs Gladstone – who was having difficulty coming to terms with the end of her husband's political career – seemed 'very low'. Next morning she saw Mrs Gladstone alone after breakfast. 'She was very much upset, poor thing,' Victoria recorded in her journal. 'Through tears, she begged leave to say that whatever her husband's errors might have been, "his devotion to your Majesty and the Crown was very great". She repeated this twice and begged me to allow her to tell him that I believed it, which I did, for I am convinced it is the case, though at times his actions might have made it difficult to believe ... I kissed her when she left.'[51]

Victoria congratulated herself on having handled this impeccably and was equally satisfied with her behaviour when Gladstone came in with an official letter of resignation. As she took it, she asked if she ought to read it at once; when he said it did not require immediate attention, she put it aside. Gladstone persuaded himself she became momentarily on the verge of tears, but even if this was not just a trick of his defective vision, she swiftly recovered her composure. Another 'neither here nor there' conversation then ensued. Although this time she did ask him about his eyesight, and made a fond reference to his wife, she pointedly forbore to seek his advice about who should succeed him.[52]

While the Queen considered this the end of the matter, Gladstone weirdly believed that since she had not formally accepted his resignation, 'he was still Prime Minister'. She had to be nudged into sending an acknowledgement, and then wrote what Gladstone called a 'curt letter', containing 'not a word of regret or gratitude'. In a few brisk lines she despatched him, declaring that after 'so many years of arduous labour … he is right in wishing to be relieved at his age'. She trusted he would now enjoy 'peace and quiet with his excellent and devoted wife' and that his eyesight would improve. Almost as an afterthought she added that she 'would gladly have conferred a peerage on Mr Gladstone, but she knows that he would not accept it'. Gladstone would bitterly comment that after serving the Crown for fifty-two and a half years, his departure from public life had been handled with 'the same brevity [that] perhaps prevails in settling a tradesman's bill'.[53]

Over the next few days Gladstone brooded constantly on the Queen's behaviour, becoming agitated when his wife told him Lord Rosebery had said, when sitting next to her at dinner, 'He hates the Queen doesn't he?' He drew up several memoranda defending himself from this 'cruel imputation', insisting he admired Victoria, even if his esteem for her had declined over the years. Pondering 'the extreme dryness of the relations which she has maintained with me now through a considerable tract of years', he decided, 'there is in them something of mystery, which I have not been able to fathom'. Unable to come to terms with the Queen's straightforward dislike, he speculated that her judgement had been clouded by being told 'shameful things' – clearly relating to his work rescuing prostitutes. He found some comfort in comparing her treatment of him to his own antipathy towards a mule that many years before had carried him across Sicily: despite its having performed the work usefully, after three weeks, 'I could not get up the smallest shred of feeling for the brute.' He was pleased by the 'force of resemblance', but since Victoria would have disputed that he had performed good service, she would not have accepted the analogy.[54]

The unsatisfactory way his relations with Victoria had terminated so preyed on his mind that nearly two years after he left office, Gladstone was still being tormented by dreams in which she featured. In one, she invited him to breakfast alone with her at Windsor, but when the hour came, he could not find where they were to meet. On waking he had realised that despite striving 'to attain as nearly as I could indifference', his feelings about her clearly had 'more hold upon me, down at the root, than I was aware'.[55]

Knowing that Gladstone did not want to go to the House of Lords, the Queen offered Catherine Gladstone a peerage. Gladstone effectively instructed his wife to turn it down, and then appears to have forgotten it had ever been proposed. Certainly, when he subsequently encountered Victoria, and she was less attentive than he expected, he took umbrage on the grounds that his wife had been slighted. After he and Mrs Gladstone came to the wedding of the Prince of Wales's daughter in 1896, he felt affronted that Victoria took '*no* notice' of his wife, 'a lady of eighty-four, who had come near two hundred miles to attend the service'.[56]

His last encounter with the Queen took place in February 1897 when she and the Gladstones were all holidaying on the French Riviera. After the Prince of Wales and his sister Princess Louise had suggested they meet one afternoon, Gladstone had been wary: while able 'to conceive the Queen's desire to see my wife', he was 'most sceptical as to any corresponding wish about myself'. Despite his reluctance to do anything that looked like an 'endeavour … to force myself upon her', in the end he did come to tea. The occasion was not a great success. Although the Queen's manner was 'very decidedly kind', and she gave him her hand for the first time ever, she did not show 'the old and usual vitality'. He noted that after they exchanged a few desultory remarks, 'it appeared to me that the Queen's peculiar faculty and habit of conversation had disappeared'. He even persuaded himself she was preparing to abdicate, but the wish was clearly father to the thought.[57]

In 1896 he had issued instructions that after his death no details of his later dealings with Victoria should be released, as they would discredit her. Once thirty years had elapsed, his son Herbert Gladstone felt justified in overriding the embargo. By that time John Morley's magisterial biography of his chief had already been published. Morley had had to be somewhat circumspect when tackling the 'difficult and delicate' subject of relations with Victoria, but he declared his 'careful perusal of all her letters' to Gladstone had left him with 'no liking and not much respect for her'.[58]

Gladstone died on 19 May 1898. He was accorded the honour of a lying-in-state in Westminster Hall, where 250,000 people filed past his coffin. There was no mention of his death in the Court Circular. Despite telling Lord Salisbury this was 'entirely an oversight', the Queen became very angry when anyone suggested she write a few words praising the late prime minister. Unwilling to do anything 'in the nature of a recantation', she said: 'I am sorry for Mrs Gladstone; as for him I never liked him.' She did write his widow a condolence letter authorised for publication, but was 'displeased' that at Gladstone's public funeral in Westminster Abbey the Prince of Wales and his eldest son were among the ten pallbearers. She telegraphed Bertie wanting to know what the precedent was and who had advised him to take part. He answered there was no precedent that he knew of, and he had taken no advice.[59]

When Vicky had written it was fitting to do honour to the memory of a great Englishman, the Queen did not let this pass. 'I cannot say that I think he was "a great Englishman,"' she corrected. 'He was a clever man full of talent, but he never *tried* to keep up the *honour* and *prestige* of Great Britain ... The harm he did cannot easily be undone.' The most she was prepared to concede was that 'he was a good and very religious man', who had 'a wonderful power of speaking and carrying the masses with him'.[60]

As soon as the Queen had grasped that Gladstone was going to retire she had applied herself to the question of who should succeed him. This did not entail asking his opinion. While there was no requirement for her to do so, it was assumed she would extend him this courtesy, and Ponsonby was embarrassed by her failure to do so. On the other hand, it would obviously have been awkward if she had consulted him and then ignored his advice, and since Gladstone would in fact have urged her to send for Lord Spencer – a most impractical recommendation – it was perhaps as well she did not apply to him.[61]

Realistically Rosebery and Harcourt were the only viable alternatives. The Queen's own preference was for Rosebery, and though Harcourt would be mortally offended at being passed over, he was not the ideal choice. While a majority of Liberal MPs might have preferred him as their leader, he had behaved so intolerably in Cabinet that his ministerial colleagues would not have him at any price. Before committing herself, however, the Queen wanted to know what Lord Salisbury thought. Very bizarrely on 28 February 1894 she sent Ponsonby to Rosebery asking whether he would mind if she summoned Salisbury for an audience. Rosebery reacted to this surreal request with great tact and forbearance. He wrote that while she would be constitutionally within her rights, she should remember, 'though all things are lawful, all things are not expedient', and that she should perhaps guard against giving an 'injurious' impression that she wanted a Tory government. 'On the other hand,' he continued, 'it is easy to consult without audiences and that I presume would be unobjectionable.' He asked Ponsonby to bear in mind this was not official advice, but that he was considering the matter 'entirely from the Queen's own point of view'.[62]

Consequently she wrote confidentially to her trusted intermediary, Lord Rowton, saying she hoped Salisbury did not think her 'wanting in openness' because of her failure to consult him. Salisbury surely could not 'doubt that her wish to see him again at the head of affairs is as great as ever', but her need to get away to the continent had made her opt for this arrangement. She added defensively that, after all, the present government did have a majority in Parliament.[63]

Even once she had settled things in her own mind, it was far from certain that Rosebery would accept her commission. He made out that he was uninterested in becoming prime minister, and while it was permissible to be sceptical of this, he was certainly realistic to expect that the premiership would prove a poisoned chalice. Harcourt believed the place should rightfully be his, and no one could doubt his ability to make colleagues' life a misery when the mood took him. Others such as John Morley were not pleased by the prospect of having a peer as their leader.

Rosebery was correct to fear that because his party was in a tiny minority in the House of Lords, it would be particularly difficult for him, as a peer, to head a Liberal government. On 1 March, after the Queen unofficially sounded him out as to whether he would 'stand by her', he wrote to Ponsonby explaining why he was reluctant to take on the job. Claiming he was 'altogether unfitted for the post as regards capacity and knowledge', he pointed out that his being stranded in the Upper House would place him in a 'wholly false position'. While the House of Commons settled the country's affairs, he would be 'shut up in an enemy's prison'.[64]

The Queen would not let him off the hook so easily. She ordered her physician Dr Reid to write him an 'urgent letter', declaring it vital for her health that the change of prime minister was settled quicky. Rosebery was informed, 'If you do not help in the present crisis, she does not know what she can do, as it would worry her beyond measure to have to fall back on anyone else.'[65]

On 3 March she wrote herself, formally offering him the place. She insisted she was 'fully aware of all the difficulties, but he is the only one of the Liberal government in whom she has any real confidence'. Thus cajoled, Rosebery answered: 'Nothing can diminish his sense of these objections, but he cannot resist your Majesty's appeal.' The Queen told him she was delighted, and that she would be ready to see him at any time. 'All she hoped was that she should not be obliged to see much of Harcourt.'[66]

Rosebery had been right to dread becoming captain of a ship crewed by malcontents. Although Harcourt did agree to be Chancellor of the Exchequer and Leader of the Commons, he seethed with malevolence. Matters were made worse by a blunder that had occurred on 3 March when Harcourt went to Windsor to attend the council held to approve the prorogation speech. The Queen had asked the lord-in-waiting to bring Lord Kimberley to her, but he mistakenly ushered in Harcourt, who assumed she was going to offer him the premiership. 'Suddenly the door opened and Sir W. Harcourt stood before her. She asked him, what was the matter? He replied that he understood she wished to see him. The Queen said "No" and he retired.' Understandably Harcourt looked 'thoroughly down in the mouth' during the council that followed. Five years later Rosebery asked Victoria if the incident had really happened, and 'she laughed heartily at the recollection. "Yes, that was terrible. No one knows to this day how it happened – no one can explain it."' The mishap so envenomed Harcourt it made him a truly insufferable subordinate, and the atmosphere within the ministry became toxic.[67]

Rosebery feared it would not only be his colleagues from whom he could expect a difficult time, for he had a shrewd idea his relations with the Queen were bound to come under strain. On 4 March he wrote to her: 'One main reason for his wishing to avoid this heavy and thankless succession was that he sets the greatest value on the character of his relations with your Majesty. Anything that changed it would cause him deep pain.' He warned that if, by 'advocating a policy already laid down, to which he is bound by honour, he was likely to find himself in acute conflict with your Majesty's views' he would prefer to 'abandon the task than incur a risk which would inflict a sharper wound than is usually involved in the relations of a Sovereign and subject'. Victoria airily dismissed his fears. 'The Queen can hardly think this possible or at any rate probable,' she replied. After all, 'She does not object to Liberal measures which are not revolutionary,' and it was unlikely Rosebery would attack cherished institutions, 'for the sole purpose of flattering useless Radicals'.[68]

Lord Rosebery, photographed in the 1890s.

Within days, Rosebery's misgivings proved all too prescient. The Liberals were committed to the disestablishment of the Welsh and Scottish Churches, but the Queen had contrived to forget this inconvenient fact. The last government had taken the first steps, but Victoria had assumed the policy would be dropped now that Gladstone had gone. She was therefore horrified that the Queen's Speech to be delivered when Parliament reconvened on 12 March announced the planned 'discontinuance' of both ecclesiastical establishments. At once she said she could not sanction this, claiming she had not been forewarned. Dr Reid was again enlisted, writing to Rosebery: 'I have never seen her Majesty more upset ... I have just left her very much agitated.' For Rosebery this came as a 'thunderclap'. To Ponsonby he bleated: 'I cannot tell you how vexed I am. But it is really not my fault.' He was clear that 'if the Queen insists on her views' he would be left with 'no resource but to give up the government'. In the end the problem was resolved when the wording was altered slightly, committing the government merely to 'dealing' with the question, but the incident had been ominous.[69]

It was hardly reassuring that Victoria had already asked Rosebery to be very vague in what he said about government policy during the coming session. Rather disgracefully she had invoked the spirit of his late wife, claiming she knew Lady Rosebery had felt like her on the subject. Surprisingly Rosebery replied that 'he was deeply touched by the reference at the end of your Majesty's letter'. He went on: 'His position is of course an almost overwhelmingly difficult one, but he will try not to lose heart.'[70]

Immediately another source of contention arose. The irrepressible Labouchere succeeded in voting through an amendment to the address urging that the powers of the House of Lords should be curbed. The government soon reversed this, but the Queen was still displeased. She administered what Rosebery ruefully called 'a nice wigging', alleging the Whips must have been neglectful. Furthermore, 'the Queen is bound to say that, if the *Ministers themselves* hold language like Mr Gladstone, Sir William Harcourt and (though in a much less strong degree) even Lord Rosebery did, one cannot be surprised when a regular revolutionist like Mr Labouchere becomes very bold.' Warming to her theme, she declared the Upper Chamber 'the ONLY REALLY independent House' as it was not in awe of constituents. The peers provided a vital '*check* (and the only one there is)' on attempts by the Commons to endanger the constitution.[71]

Rosebery did not swallow this unchallenged, for he had been interested in reforming the Lords for some years. Unlike many in his party, he did not want to abolish the Upper House altogether, but he did favour changes, such as putting a limit on the length of time the Lords could hold up measures. At the end of March he sent Victoria a memorandum that disturbed her enjoyment of her holiday in Florence. He wrote that something must be done to address the 'hereditary, irresponsible and unrepresentative character' of the Upper House, for 'of the strength of the present hostility [to it] I have little doubt'. Regarding this as a matter that 'ought not to be discussed … in public by statesmen when they are Ministers of the Crown', the Queen sent him a detailed rebuttal on 9 April. Among other things she asserted it would be pointless if a second chamber existed 'only to say "yes" to … revolutionary legislation and democratic fancies' foisted on government by a few radicals. Registering horror at the prospect of a '*deliberate* and *unjustifiable* attack on the Constitution', she pronounced it 'Lord Rosebery's duty to restrain by all means such a most revolutionary proceeding'.[72]

For the moment the matter rested there, but Victoria was disillusioned by its ever having been raised. She told Vicky: 'Lord Rosebery has pleased nobody, and has gone as far as Mr Gladstone with the further disadvantage that he has not any conviction in what he says. It is a great pity and I regret he should be Prime Minister, for as foreign Minister he could restrain the others, which he cannot or will not do now. But things cannot go on so.' When Rosebery himself wrote to her wishing he could concentrate solely on international affairs, she agreed it was unfortunate he was no longer at the Foreign Office for, 'THERE, indeed he was a great support to the Queen.'[73]

Perceiving that 'your Majesty feels some disapproval if not disappointment', Rosebery sent her an anguished screed, depicting himself as a 'Prime Minister more unfortunately placed than any man who ever held that high office.' Being pledged to the policy of Gladstone's late government, he 'has no power (even had he the desire) to disassociate himself from it', and nor could he resign with honour. If he did resign, all that would happen was 'that he and not the measures would disappear'. He concluded sadly that he wrote this, 'less as a Minister to a Sovereign, than as a gentleman grateful to one who has shown him so much kindness, and whose good opinion he hopes never to forfeit. He therefore begs that his letter may be seen by your Majesty's eye alone.'[74]

Victoria responded kindly, inviting him to Balmoral if he could manage it. Rosebery's friend Edward Hamilton thought, 'he evidently manages her very well, in spite of her being more and more difficult to manage' – but the underlying tension was unresolved. The Queen was not prepared to give the prime minister much help in his difficult task or evince gratitude for the considerate way he treated her.[75]

Hacourt's budget, introducing graduated death duties with a top rate of 10 per cent on the consolidated value of landed estates, caused further problems. Rosebery himself voiced alarm, and the upper rate was slightly lowered, but the chancellor dismissed most of the premier's objections as those of 'a rich man who disliked being taxed'. On 5 June 1894 Victoria weighed in, writing to Harcourt that the 'dangerous' increases 'cannot fail to cripple all landowners' and would cause agricultural labourers to be thrown out of work. Harcourt responded the putative effects had been 'grossly exaggerated' by the landed interest, who had escaped bearing a fair share of the tax burden for much too long. In another dig, he said it was necessary to increase revenues because of rises in defence spending that the Queen had pushed for, and it was only just that those 'loudest in their demands for augmented expenditure' should underwrite it.[76]

Rebuffed, Victoria fell back on complaining to Rosebery about the 'fatal Death Rates'. She wondered whether the budget could 'still now be modified?' and accused Harcourt of being 'actuated by spite to, and a wish to *injure* the landed proprietors!' By this time the budget was almost through its committee stage, so Rosebery answered that it could not be changed. He explained he himself had 'taken a somewhat gloomy view' of it, even if he acknowledged its provisions were 'logically just'. Anyway, there was nothing he could do because as a peer he was allowed no say in financial measures.[77] Despite the Queen's disapproval, the budget passed its third reading on 17 July.

For Victoria, this was all part of a disturbing trend whereby left-wing tendencies were in the ascendant. She wrote fretting to Rosebery about monstrous foreign anarchists and assassins who were allowed to base themselves in England to 'hatch their horrible plots'. She was also shocked by comments passed when the Prince of Wales's eldest son, the Duke of York (who, to the Queen's delight, had married his late brother's fiancée, Princess May of Teck, the previous July) presented her with a great-grandson on 23 June 1894. The Independent Labour MP Keir Hardie objected to the Commons's address of congratulations, arguing that throughout life the child would be 'surrounded by sycophants' and that MPs would have done better to offer formal condolences to the 251 victims of a recent pit disaster in south Wales. Days later, when Sir

William Harcourt was at Windsor, Victoria 'talked about Keir Hardie's performance ... with great horror'. It was fortunate she was unaware of Hardie's further remarks in his newspaper, the *Labour Leader*. There he declared the 'life of one Welsh miner' to be of greater value to the nation 'than the whole royal crowd put together, from the royal great-grand-mama down to the puling royal great-grandchild'.[78]

The only consolation Rosebery could offer was that while he was prime minister he would act, as 'some other Liberal Ministers conceivably might not', to ensure 'the interests of your Majesty's Empire are maintained abroad'. The Queen was not particularly grateful, as she tended to take this for granted, and it did not stop her being unnerved by some of his public statements on domestic matters. Writing to reprove him, she speculated that perhaps the trouble arose from his desire to make an impression on his audience, causing him to engage in inappropriate levity 'hardly befitting a Prime Minister'. Having directed him in future to adopt a 'less jocular' tone, she explained, not unkindly, 'Lord Rosebery is so clever that he may be carried away by a sense of humour, which is a little dangerous.'[79]

On 24 October 1894 Rosebery jolted the Queen by writing that, much as he regretted reverting to a matter on which they differed, he wanted to move a Commons resolution stating that the Lower House could no longer allow their measures to be mutilated or thrown out by the peers. Victoria remonstrated, but also sent a '*very private*' communication to Salisbury, enclosing a copy of Rosebery's letter. She deplored that Rosebery was contemplating something 'mischievous in the highest degree, and she must add disloyal', asking whether she should warn the prime minister that, before any such resolution could be moved, the Liberals must go to the country on the issue. Furthermore, if this pushed the government into holding an immediate election, 'Is the Unionist Party fit for a dissolution *now?*' In response, Salisbury asserted questionably that Rosebery had no right to announce a new policy without obtaining her sanction, and that she could insist on a dissolution if she considered this appropriate.[80]

The Queen could not deflect Rosebery from making a speech at Bradford on 27 October in which he stated that Lords reform was the 'greatest constitutional question which has arisen in England for two centuries'. While he did not think it would come to revolution, he told his audience: 'We fling down the gauntlet.' As far as the Queen was concerned, the very mention of the word 'revolution' was tantamount to advocating one. Telling Rosebery that he had 'pained' her, she demanded the 'sense of the country should be taken' before he engaged in further agitation. Sorrowfully she declared herself 'truly grieved at having had to write all this to Lord Rosebery, whose personal devotion and loyalty to herself are well known to her'.[81]

A clash appeared imminent between Queen and prime minister, until Rosebery – who had not forewarned the Cabinet of the contents of his speech – was 'taken rather aback' when his colleagues did not take up his ideas with any enthusiasm. Had they wanted to tackle the Lords they would have favoured abolition rather than reform and felt it inadvisable to embark on something certain to divide the Liberals further. Perhaps just to be awkward, Harcourt said he thought it true that no parliamentary resolution could be moved by the government without the sovereign's concurrence. On 1 November Rosebery wrote to Victoria saying he would anyway 'never dream' of doing such a thing, although he did not think he had to secure her approval before bringing a subject before a popular audience.[82]

In the meantime Victoria had had further surreptitious contacts with the opposition, causing her to pause. She had sent Ponsonby to see the Unionist politician Sir Henry James who, as a former Attorney General, would be knowledgeable about the legal aspects of the situation. James begged the Queen: do nothing hasty, for even if Rosebery did proceed, 'Nothing practically results from a Resolution being carried.' On the other hand, if she forced Rosebery into a dissolution, or he resigned after refusing to dissolve, the incoming government would face difficulties on calling an election. Their predecessors could 'pose as the victims of an unusual exercise' of royal authority, which would inevitably win them votes. Privately James was sure it 'would be a most dangerous act of folly' for the Crown to expose itself to such a risk, and though he put it more delicately when submitting written advice, he conveyed his view successfully. After consultation with others, Salisbury too advised the Queen not to be precipitate. 'At present opinion is so sluggish on the whole question that people would be startled by the direct intervention of the Crown,' and, ironically, feeling against the Lords might actually strengthen.[83]

By the end of November Rosebery himself realised it was unfeasible to do anything at present. Able to breathe once again, Victoria wrote him a kind letter saying she understood his motives were good and that he believed the Lords would fare better if he was in charge of their reform. She nevertheless asked him 'to bear in mind that fifty-seven years ago the Constitution was delivered into her keeping, and that, right or wrong, she has her views as to the fulfilment of that trust. She cannot but think Lord Rosebery will feel that his position is not the only difficult one in these democratic days.'[84]

On 7 December Rosebery told her 'there really was no danger' for, at worst, 'there would be nothing more than a Resolution which would result in nothing'. If, after that, dissolution did take place, 'the government would most likely be beaten'. Somewhat perversely, Victoria despised him for his defeatist attitude. She would later recall to Henry James how, after she had 'scolded him ... all he said was I need not trouble as his views had fallen very flat ... I did not think that this was a right position for my Prime Minister to take up'. Much as she had hated dealing with a conviction politician like Gladstone, she was scornful that Rosebery 'never seemed really to know his own mind'.[85]

On 7 January 1895 Sir Henry Ponsonby suffered a stroke that left him semi-paralysed and unable to speak. By May it had become clear he was unlikely to recover, and his wife sent in his resignation, but by that time his place as private secretary had already been informally filled by Sir Arthur Bigge. On 21 November Ponsonby died.

When he had first fallen ill, Victoria was 'greatly shocked but hardly surprised as Sir Henry had been so failing and altered of late, and the last few days, quite strange'. There is a story that, only days before, he said musingly to the Queen: 'What a funny little woman you are' – upon which she observed: 'Sir Henry, you cannot be well,' and rang the bell. While she noted that over the past few months, 'he had become so listless and silent', others attributed his collapse to her unceasing demands on him. Gladstone, who had appreciated Ponsonby's fair-mindedness and attempts to ease things, declared himself 'grieved but not surprised' by the news, as the 'Queen had worn out her servants'.[86]

The fifth of February 1895 saw the start of a new parliamentary session. With the Cabinet riven by personal antagonisms, and a majority eroded by by-election losses, the government was in no position to embark on an ambitious legislative programme. In the Queen's Speech mention of any kind of action against the Lords was 'conspicuous by its absence', but even so the government seemed in danger of losing votes on the address. In the event, this did not happen, but Rosebery was mortified that no Cabinet minister came to his defence when Labouchere and Charles Dilke savagely attacked him in the Commons. Rosebery wrote to Victoria on 19 February that he had informed the Cabinet that unless better supported in future, he must resign.[87]

Already demoralised and harassed, Rosebery then contracted very severe influenza. His illness was worsened by his insomnia intensifying, and though the doctor prescribed morphine, it did not work for long. Reduced to a 'moral and physical wreck', Rosebery was unable to do any work, or even to write. On 11 March he was in a pitiable state when he managed to see the Queen. She was 'very kind, insisted on my sitting down', but as he rose from his knees after kissing her hand, he 'nearly toppled over from weakness'. Much alarmed, Victoria entreated, 'Take care.' At Cabinet on 30 March, he 'trembled from hand to foot like an aspen', and his continued debility gave rise to rumours of an addiction to cocaine and opiates.[88]

Other suspicions arose in connection with this illness, with some believing it originated in a dread of being destroyed by homosexual scandal. Rosebery's private secretary, Lord Drumlanrig, had died while shooting in October 1894, and though most people accepted it was a tragic accident, suicide could not be ruled out. Drumlanrig's father was the psychotic Marquess of Queensberry, and he may have decided his son had killed himself because he was in a homosexual relationship with Rosebery. Queensberry had in fact been hounding Rosebery for some time before his son's death. In August 1893 he had followed Rosebery to the German spa town of Homburg, where he went about threatening to do 'direful things ... to ... that boy pimp and boy lover Rosebery'. At the time Rosebery had written to Victoria: 'it is a material and unpleasant addition to the labours of your Majesty's service to be pursued by a pugilist of unsound mind'. This perhaps explains the gossip of 1895 that 'his insomnia was caused by terror of being in the Wilde scandal'. However, as Rosebery fell ill before Oscar Wilde embarked on the legal case against Lord Queensberry that ultimately resulted in his being prosecuted for homosexual offences, the theory was hardly viable.[89]

In the summer of 1895, Rosebery's faltering government had to tackle the ticklish question of the Duke of Cambridge's retirement as Commander-in-Chief. At seventy-six, Cambridge remained a 'boulder' in the way of army reform, and War Minister Sir Henry Campbell-Bannerman could not resist the clamour for his removal. On 7 May an angry Cambridge begged his cousin the Queen not to let him be 'kicked out' by radicals, but despite feeling the government was acting hastily, on 19 May she informed the duke 'with *much* pain' he must give up that autumn. Cambridge assured her: 'Of course I accept the inevitable' – but did not go quietly.[90]

By 10 June the Queen was losing patience, finding it 'undignified' that the duke still clung to office. Having haggled about the wording of the statement Campbell-Bannerman would make to Parliament, Cambridge next demanded a pension of £2,000, which the Queen dismissed as 'preposterous'. Rosebery had to caution him that if he continued in this 'deplorable' way, Parliament would be told he was holding out for an allowance. 'No one would treat a shoe-black so!' the duke erupted, before finally capitulating on 20 June. Victoria's hopes of mollifying him by creating him her principal aide-de-camp were not entirely successful. While he branded Rosebery a 'regular cur!' he deemed her 'worst of all' for letting him be 'sent away like a footman in disgrace!'[91]

On 21 June Campbell-Bannerman made a statement in the house announcing the Commander-in-Chief's retirement. Later that evening the war minister himself became the victim of a parliamentary ambush when, in a surprise move, the opposition passed a vote of censure against him on the specious grounds that the country possessed inadequate supplies of cordite. Victoria, who liked Campbell-Bannerman and was grateful for the 'most kind' way he had acted over Cambridge, considered him 'scandalously treated'.[92]

Because the government could have reversed the vote, Victoria initially assumed there would be no crisis, but learned otherwise on returning to Windsor from Balmoral on 22 June. That evening she saw Rosebery, who said the Cabinet had decided to resign. She asked whether she must accept this, and he answered in the affirmative, as it was pointless to struggle on when they would soon be defeated again. She said she would be sorry to take leave of him, but he replied that personally he would find going out 'an immense relief ... as the scenes in the Cabinet had been quite dreadful'.[93] This being so, she agreed to write to Salisbury immediately. On 23 June the latter accepted her invitation to form a government, letting her know the following day it would be a coalition in which the Liberal Unionists would serve under him.

Contrary as ever, despite having complained so much about Rosebery and made his life so hard, the Queen was regretful about losing him. Perhaps she felt somewhat guilty about the way she had taken advantage of his gallant instincts, but certainly she felt a pang at parting. She wrote to Vicky: 'The change of government was not a source of such satisfaction as perhaps it might have been for I lose some people I was very fond of, and who were very able. Lord Spencer, Mr Campbell-Bannerman and Mr Fowler were terrible losses ... And *personally* I am very fond of

Lord Rosebery and prefer him [in] certain [respects] to Lord Salisbury. He is so much attached to me personally.'[94]

Amazingly, Rosebery himself still had immense affection for her. Writing to thank her 'from the bottom of my heart' for her 'abundant and gracious kindness', he said he could 'say with absolute truth that my only regret in laying down my office is the cessation of my personal relations with your Majesty'. For her part, Victoria answered she would 'ever take the warmest interest in you and yours' and offered him 'a little souvenir' in the form of a marble bust of herself. On 28 June Rosebery came to Windsor to take formal leave of her and reiterated he 'was very thankful to be out of it all, as his position had been so very unpleasant. The only thing he regretted was not seeing me so often.'[95]

On coming in, Salisbury immediately dissolved Parliament. The ensuing election revealed the hopelessly divided state of the Liberal Party, for its leaders all campaigned on different issues. Rosebery pushed for Lords reform (even though the Queen had given him 'kindly advice' not to pursue that), Harcourt argued for stricter licensing laws, while John Morley pressed for Home Rule. None of these had much appeal for the electorate. While the Tories made sweeping gains, the Liberals suffered the worst defeat of any political party since 1832. In delight the Queen noted on 26 July, 'The elections are going in a wonderful way ... and the majority is much larger than expected.' To her mind, the 'quite unprecedented' outcome was 'an important sign of the good sense of the country'.[96]

14

Lord Salisbury 1895–1901

'Every day I feel the blessing of a strong government in such safe and strong hands as yours,' Victoria informed Lord Salisbury in March 1896. She was particularly relieved to have him back in control of foreign policy, for though she had queried whether being both prime minister and foreign secretary would wear him out, she had been reassured by his promise to give up the Foreign Office if it proved too taxing. She concurred with the verdict of the Liberal Unionist politician Henry James, now raised to the peerage and a regular and favoured guest at Balmoral. Praising Salisbury in February 1897 as 'so very wise & calm', Lord James declared him: 'really at the present moment, the only very great statesman in Europe'. Personal relations between Sovereign and prime minister were warm. Salisbury's daughter-in-law Violet was touched by the way they interacted when Victoria visited him at his holiday home in the south of France. 'It is easy to see that she is very fond of him. Indeed I never saw two people get on better,' she recorded.[1]

'Lord Salisbury's great strength is his calmness and energy,' Victoria declared in January 1896. Others would have disputed his possessing the latter quality, for he had never really recovered from the severe bout of Russian influenza that assailed him at the end of 1889. In October 1897 the Earl of Balcarres noted, 'the Premier is old for his years and heavy for his legs'. A year earlier the Queen's lady-in-waiting Marie Mallet had observed, 'I fear Lord Salisbury cannot have a long life before him: he is gigantic ... and the Queen says he eats enormously; his eyes are red and the pouches beneath them purple.' When he came to the 'arctic region' of Balmoral, his private secretary stressed the temperature of his room must not fall lower than sixty degrees.[2]

Salisbury's alarming physical condition necessitated his taking regular breaks abroad. During his absences, his nephew Arthur Balfour, now once again Leader of the Commons, had to deputise for him. This was not ideal. In October 1900 Balfour recalled how on three occasions in the last five years Salisbury had 'been obliged to go abroad at rather critical moments in our national affairs'. The Prince of Wales was shocked by Salisbury's frequent abdications of responsibility. When the prime minister went overseas in August 1898 for what was expected to be a prolonged period, Bertie burst out: 'This is a nice look-out for us when we are having all these troubles with Russia through China.' The prince was also scandalised by Salisbury's turning up for a Buckingham Palace drawing room 'dressed like a guy', with his Garter ribbon over the wrong shoulder. The prince exploded that it was humiliating numerous ambassadors should have witnessed the sight: 'What will they think of a Premier who can't put on his clothes?'[3]

Salisbury's absences overseas were not quite as inconvenient for the Queen as for his colleagues, for her own annual trips to the south of France frequently coincided with Salisbury's visits there. She was doubtless more understanding about Salisbury's physical decline as she herself was having to cope with the challenges of ageing. On the eve of her seventy-ninth birthday she admitted feeling 'rather sad at my rapidly advancing age and the infirmities it brings'. Because 'lameness from rheumatism … hampers me very much', she became more dependent on a wheelchair, and if no lift was available, had to be carried up stairs. In some respects, however, she still retained a zest for life. As late as November 1900 she told Marie Mallet, 'after the Prince consort's death I wished to die but *now* I wish to live and do what I can for my country and those I love'.[4]

What bothered her most was the failing eyesight that made reading and writing a serious challenge. In January 1896 she lamented, 'So much to do & my troublesome eyes make everything much more difficult.' It meant she became much more dependent on Princess Beatrice or her ladies to read papers to her. This sometimes made for 'complications' that annoyed her private secretary, Sir Arthur Bigge. The Queen's Woman of the Bedchamber Marie Mallet reported in November 1898: 'Biggie was rather cross with me yesterday because the Queen had made me read some War Office box to her and he thinks it absurd that military messages should go through the ladies!' Sir Henry Ponsonby's son Frederick (or Fritz), who became assistant private secretary in 1897, recalled 'hideous mistakes' that occurred when important papers were not read to her because Princess Beatrice was distracted. He stressed, however, that it was only Victoria's 'eyes, nothing else' that caused problems. 'Her memory is still wonderful, her shrewdness, her power of discrimination as strong as ever.'[5]

To try and overcome the difficulties, ministers and secretaries were ordered to develop enormous handwriting in 'special ink like boot varnish'. Salisbury was asked to use a 'thicker nib and blacker ink', but Fritz Ponsonby's best efforts at legibility only elicited 'pathetic messages asking me to write larger and blacker still'. Ever 'more potent ink' was specially made, yet could not solve the problem.[6]

Arthur Balfour was a particularly bad offender when it came to handwriting. In other respects, Victoria liked and admired Balfour, even though Fritz Ponsonby had the impression that 'he never seemed to treat her seriously'. Far from finding him condescending, to Victoria his languid charm was appealing. When he stayed at Balmoral in September 1897, she declared herself 'much struck ... by Mr Balfour's ... large-mindedness. He sees all sides of a question, is wonderfully generous in his feelings towards others & very gentle and sweet-tempered.'[7]

Balfour could afford to be magnanimous, as for the first few years of this government, the opposition caused him little grief. With the Irish still in disarray from the Parnell debacle and the Liberals hopelessly disunited, the ministry faced few difficulties in Parliament. Rosebery resigned as Liberal leader in October 1896 and was succeeded by Sir William Harcourt, but he too gave up just over two years later. Sir Henry Campbell-Bannerman took his place but could make little dent in the government's confidence until the failures of the Boer War made them vulnerable. Balfour then became rather less suave at handling his opponents. In August 1900, for example, he became 'completely unhinged' when taunted over the government's record on army medical care, prompting the Queen to remark that his 'curious loss of temper is really most extraordinary'.[8]

Until the Boer War changed everything, it seemed the Queen's reign was destined to end in triumph. Her popularity was never greater, and there were no more complaints about her neglecting the public. The fact that Britain's Empire was now at its zenith added to the mood of confidence and self-belief. On the fifty-ninth anniversary of her accession to the throne, Victoria might well express gratitude at having 'lived to see my ... vast Empire prosper and expand', for at that point the British Empire covered a quarter of the world's surface, and its inhabitants numbered a quarter of the world's population. The Queen believed it an entity that contributed to the happiness and well-being of those ruled and that it was a civilising and beneficial force. Yet even some who might have been expected to glory in the achievement intermittently feared Britain was becoming too complacent. In February 1898 Salisbury warned the House of Lords against thinking it 'our duty to take everything we can, to fight everybody and to make a quarrel of every dispute'. The Queen herself felt occasional unease on this score. In spring 1898 she wrote to Arthur Balfour, 'It is I think important the world at large should not have the impression that we will not let anyone but ourselves have anything.' Others were harsher. When Britain was floundering at the outset of the Boer War, Herbert Bismarck gloated that the Empire was experiencing 'its death blow' as England 'smothered in its own fat'.[9]

Victoria was so closely intertwined with continental ruling dynasties that it was scarcely an exaggeration to call her 'the Grandmother of Europe'. In her lifetime, grandchildren occupied the Russian and German imperial thrones, while the Greek crown prince, the Romanian crown prince and the heir to the Norwegian throne all married granddaughters of hers. Notwithstanding these dynastic links, foreign affairs scarcely afforded a comforting prospect. Salisbury was adamantly against contracting formal alliances which might commit England to fighting if any of its allies were invaded, or even acted as aggressor. In January 1896 he argued to the Queen, 'Isolation is a much less danger than the danger of being dragged into wars which do not concern us.' Victoria was not entirely convinced, for at a time when Germany was allied with Italy and Austria, and France and Russia were drawing ever closer, Britain seemed friendless and vulnerable to hostile combinations. She tremulously observed: 'Affairs now are so different from what they used to be, that the Queen cannot help feeling that our *isolation* is dangerous.'[10]

It was all very well for the oleaginous Bishop Davidson of Winchester to write of the Queen's being in a position to 'wield a personal and domestic influence over the thrones of Europe absolutely without precedent in the history of Christendom',[11] but these family ties did not of themselves ease international tensions. Despite the fact that her granddaughter became the tsarina, Russia was not that friendly, and it was merely a source of anguish to Victoria that she was unable to aid her granddaughter Sophie Duchess of Sparta when Greece went to war with Turkey. Above all, her grandson, the German kaiser, was mercurial and unpredictable: in between sporadic fits of friendliness he could appear consumed with jealousy or even hatred of Britain. As well as engaging in energetic colonial rivalry, by the end of his grandmother's reign, he was already threatening England's maritime supremacy by building up a great navy.

Following a Commons debate on naval estimates in March 1898, Arthur Balfour reported that many of the speeches suggested, 'we were passing through a period of national difficulty and crisis'. This sense of besetting tension was not confined to Britain. The likelihood that Europe would be engulfed by a great conflagration disturbed the tsar sufficiently for him to propose in August 1898 that an international peace and disarmament conference should convene at the Hague. It met in May 1899 and sat till the end of June. The prospects of it achieving anything meaningful were never good, however. The kaiser agreed to send representatives, but privately dismissed his cousin, Tsar Nicholas, as a 'day dreaming boy'. Having pronounced Russian proposals not just a 'swindle' but 'hypocrisy, rubbish and lies', he implied to his grandmother that, far from being inspired by idealism, the tsar merely wanted to extricate Russia from its parlous financial position by persuading other European powers to lower defence spending. Victoria was less cynical. She told Vicky that after reading the tsar's mission statement she did not doubt he was acting 'in a peaceable sense, only I don't see how it is to be carried out'. In her view, the only hope of constructive change was to establish mechanisms for dispute resolution, and also to outlaw 'the use of secret destructive missiles'.[12]

This all goes to explain why, despite the seeming strength and prosperity of Britain in the closing years of her reign, variations on the phrase 'it makes me anxious' recurred frequently in the Queen's journal.

When Rosebery's government had been unexpectedly defeated in the Commons vote of 20 June 1895, Salisbury would have preferred it if, rather than resigning, Rosebery had called an election and remained in office till the voters had returned their verdict. Since Rosebery had refused to do this, Salisbury had had to form a government before dissolving Parliament. Because he could not forecast the outcome of the election, he assumed his ministry would be dependent for its survival on Liberal Unionist support, and he therefore brought four of them into his Cabinet. One was that former figure of terror to the Queen, Joseph Chamberlain, who was offered his pick of posts.

Much to Salisbury's surprise, Chamberlain asked to be made Secretary of State for the Colonies, having now become an imperial visionary. Henceforth he dedicated himself to expanding and integrating the Empire, as well as seeing off European rivals who had colonial ambitions of their own. In 1897 Salisbury would complain to Victoria that the colonial secretary was 'a little too warlike' for his liking, but by then her view of Chamberlain, whom she had once dubbed 'a dangerous man', had completely transformed. When he dined at Windsor with his attractive young American wife and conversed 'earnestly and deferentially', she enjoyed his company, feeling, according to Fritz Ponsonby, she was 'talking to a wild man who had been tamed'. She also admired his commitment to Britain's 'imperial destiny', telling Vicky in January 1896, 'Mr Chamberlain behaves admirably, so firmly and very strong in upholding the Empire and *giving up nothing.*'[13]

Within months of the government taking office, there was a serious colonial crisis. In 1881 the Queen had been furious when, after Britain's defeat at Majuba Hill, Gladstone's government had granted Boer rebels in the Transvaal effective autonomy. Since then the situation had been changed by the discovery of massive veins of gold in the Transvaal. This had led to an influx of outsiders (known in Afrikaans as 'Uitlanders'), of whom a high proportion were British. Although the new arrivals now outnumbered Boers, they were granted no political rights. As well as being heavily taxed, they did not have the vote, and they claimed the Boers treated them oppressively.

Chamberlain had been aware that a group of Uitlanders in Johannesburg, with the encouragement of Cecil Rhodes, were preparing to rise up and seize power from the Boers. He avoided learning details, and it is unclear whether he knew that Rhodes's close associate, Dr Leander Starr Jameson, was planning to assist by invading the Transvaal from a base in Bechuanaland. In theory this was meant to coincide with the Johannesburg rising, but even after the Uitlander conspirators decided not to go ahead, Jameson did not call off his action. Instead, he rode into the Transvaal with 500 men on 29 December 1895. After being surrounded by Boer forces and losing more than a hundred of his band, he had to surrender on 2 January 1896.

Obviously it would be disastrous if it could be proved that Britain had connived in the raid, and Chamberlain had therefore immediately distanced himself from it. While Victoria acknowledged 'this affair is very unfortunate' and Jameson's action 'of course very wrong and totally unwarranted', privately she understood his motives. She wrote to Vicky: 'This Dr Jameson is an excellent and able man and great sympathy is felt for him. The Boors [sic] are horrid people, cruel and overbearing.' She was also supportive of Chamberlain, assuring him, 'I sincerely sympathise with you in this most serious and complicated question.' Having accepted his explanation that, despite hearing talk of an insurrection, he had assumed it would come to nothing, she thought it right that Salisbury did not accept the colonial secretary's offer to resign.[14]

Chamberlain successfully weathered the storm, managing to escape censure at the hands of a Commons Select Committee set up to enquire into the affair. Yet the Jameson raid had other, more damaging results. The Transvaal's president Paul Kruger became more determined than ever to deny the Uitlanders voting rights, and to safeguard the Transvaal's independence he built up a vast armoury. Within Europe, the raid had a very adverse effect on Britain's relations with Germany.

Even before this complication, keeping on good terms with the kaiser had proved no easy matter. In January 1894 he had started dropping heavy hints that he wished to be made honorary colonel of a British regiment. His grandmother had been unwilling to oblige, for having previously made him an admiral, she thought him 'far too much spoilt already'. Despite this, when Victoria was in Germany three months later for a family wedding, she relented and made William colonel-in-chief of the 1st Dragoons. 'This seemed to please him exceedingly.' He wrote rhapsodically thanking her for enabling him to wear 'the traditional British Redcoat'.[15]

This did not make him better disposed to England for long. In June, Germany was behaving in such an 'insufferable' way that Rosebery angrily told the Queen they seemed to imagine they were dealing with Monaco. Furthermore the kaiser already cherished ambitions of challenging Britain's supremacy at sea, for on 21 June Vicky wrote to her mother: 'William's one idea is to have a navy which shall be larger and stronger than the British navy.'[16] His attitude was of greater significance because, in late October 1894, he accepted the resignation of Bismarck's successor as chancellor, Count Caprivi. William effectively now became personal ruler of Germany.

William professed to be pleased about Salisbury's return to office, writing to his grandmother shortly before coming to 'dear Osborne' for his 1895 visit that he wished her 'joy most heartily to the reappearance of the Conservatives with the Marquess at their head'. Unfortunately when he had a discussion with Salisbury on 5 August, the day of his arrival, things did not go well. The following day the kaiser wanted to meet with Salisbury again, but the prime minister had an appointment with the Queen that afternoon and failed to realise that the kaiser expected him to come to him once that audience ended. Next morning, oblivious to having caused offence, Salisbury returned to London. On 8 August the Queen warned him: 'William is a little sore … having waited some hours for you.' As she suggested, Salisbury wrote apologising, but the kaiser still regarded it as a grievance.[17]

When they had met on 5 August, Salisbury and Kaiser William had disagreed about what approach to adopt towards Turkey, and this subject would bedevil Anglo-German relations for months to come. Terrible massacres of Armenians had recently taken place in Turkey, convincing Salisbury and the Queen that something must be done to avert further atrocities. In December 1895, having registered her horror at 'dreadful accounts' that 'make one's heart bleed', Victoria suggested to the prime minister two courses of action. Firstly, she could write to the sultan, saying he was surely 'unaware of all this suffering' but, knowing his 'kindly personal feeling towards herself', she hoped he could act to alleviate it. She could supplement this by writing to the tsar and kaiser, urging them to stop these ghastly acts of bloodshed which 'quite haunt me'.[18]

Salisbury did not expect much to come from this. The sultan was in fact instigating many of the cruelties, and although Victoria's letter to him was duly sent, Salisbury was not surprised it achieved nothing. As regards her trying to enlist the support of the tsar and the kaiser, Salisbury knew the Germans were suspicious of British motives, as well as being fearful of greater cooperation between Russia and Britain. Although Victoria considered their attitude 'absurd', Salisbury explained the kaiser 'has got into his head that we are intriguing against him. It is an extraordinary delusion' but it was difficult to disabuse him. Salisbury believed it would do no good if Victoria attempted to reassure the kaiser that her dealings with the tsar were inspired purely by a desire to help the Armenians, for in all probability her grandson would merely take 'umbrage'.[19]

As a result nothing was done, and in August 1896 yet more massacres took place in Constantinople itself. The kaiser was shocked by the gruesome accounts, but the Germans remained obsessed that their 'position would become very difficult in the event of even a transitory understanding between Russia and England'. This meant that when in October 1896 Salisbury issued a circular urging six European powers to act together to prevent 'the recurrence of the frightful cruelties' of the past two years, Germany was not prepared to help. Writing to his grandmother about the sultan, the kaiser declared flippantly, 'May Allah soon take him to where it is very hot!' but he eschewed practical steps.

On the contrary, in due course it became Germany's policy to pursue closer relations with the sultan.[20]

By the autumn of 1895 another cause of friction had arisen due to Germany's disapproval of Britain's attitude towards the Boers. Sir Edward Malet, the long-serving British ambassador to Germany was due to retire, and when he went for a farewell audience with the German foreign minister in October 1895, he expressed regret that the Transvaal was casting a 'dark spot' on Anglo-German relations. Learning of his 'blustering words', the kaiser erupted in fury, claiming the mild-mannered diplomat had warned that 'England would not shrink from making war upon me if we did not knock down in Africa.' He was outraged that 'England had threatened ... the German Emperor, grandson of her Majesty the Queen' in this way, although the wretched Malet denied having been offensive. Shocked by the kaiser's violent reaction, Salisbury declared: 'there is a danger of his going completely off his head'.[21]

Matters stood thus when the Jameson raid took place. The kaiser at once instructed his ambassador in London to ask whether it had been sanctioned by Britain, intending to break off diplomatic relations if the government acknowledged responsibility. Then, after Salisbury disavowed the raid, William sent a telegram to President Kruger congratulating him for having 'safeguarded the independence' of his country 'without appealing for the help of friendly powers'. The kaiser's intervention caused such fury in England that shops and premises owned by German immigrants had their windows broken. Finding the 'violent feeling ... most distressing, but natural', the Queen asked Salisbury to ensure the police 'prevent ill-usage of innocent and good German residents'. She inadvertently may have caused puzzlement by entreating him to do 'all you can to pour oil on the flames'.[22]

Victoria felt strongly her grandson's 'outrageous' behaviour merited reproof, and on 5 January 1896, 'I gave him a piece of my mind as to his dreadful telegram.' She informed him his communication was 'considered very unfriendly towards this country ... and has, I grieve to say, made a very painful impression here ... It would have been far better to have said nothing.' William responded with a disingenuous defence, saying that having been assured the raiders had acted without authority, 'I was standing up for law, order and obedience to a Sovereign whom I revere and adore.' Victoria was unimpressed by these 'lame and illogical' arguments, but Salisbury said it was better to take them at face value.

On 15 January she therefore sent the kaiser a short letter accepting he had meant no offence.[23]

The damage caused by the incident was not so easily undone. Because resentment was slow to die down, it was conveyed to the kaiser he would not be welcome in England that summer. He would in fact not visit for another four years, and during that time his prickliness became still more pronounced. In October 1896 Vicky wrote to her mother deploring that her son apparently believed he must 'strain every nerve for Germany to … *wrest* from [England] the position of supremacy she has in the world'.[24] At every opportunity he was provocative and surly, being always ready to allege he had been slighted, or his concerns ignored.

The following year more difficulties arose. In February 1897 Crete rose up against its Ottoman overlords, with Christians on the island clamouring to be absorbed into Greece. To aid the Cretans, the King of Greece sent ships under the command of his eldest son, the Duke of Sparta, husband of Vicky's daughter Sophie. Badgered by Vicky, who was passionately Hellenic, the Queen would have liked to endorse the Greek action, but Salisbury explained that this was impossible: not only would it cause chaos throughout the Balkans but the Great Powers would be angered by Britain's undermining Turkey.[25] Accordingly Salisbury devised a formula whereby Crete would be granted autonomy within the Ottoman Empire, while the Great Powers took joint responsibility for overseeing the island's stability. The Greeks would not accept this and refused to withdraw their troops.

The Kaiser might have been expected to take the Greek side, as the Duke of Sparta was his brother-in-law, but he was violently adverse, having never forgiven his sister for converting to Greek Orthodoxy. He took what the Queen described as a 'fearfully & senselessly violent' line, denouncing the Greeks in 'brutal' terms, and demanding the powers punish them for defiance. A 'quite miserable' Vicky wrote to her mother: 'what it is to me … to see my own son embarked on a course which threatens ruin & destruction to his own sister and brother-in-law and their family I cannot tell you'. Although Victoria had wanted Greece to withdraw its troops from Crete, she was so angered by William's 'shameful behaviour' she instructed her ambassador 'to tell the German Emperor from me that I was astonished and shocked at his violent language against the country where his sister lives'.[26]

The Greeks still refused to comply with the powers' directives, so the Turks declared war. Within days the Greeks were suffering disastrous reverses. In agony, the Queen wrote to Vicky, 'I cannot say ... how my heart bleeds for our darling,' but when 'poor little Sophie' appealed for British help, her grandmother reiterated: 'Greece must yield to the conditions of the Powers.' Surreptitiously she showed where her true sympathies lay: when Vicky organised a relief fund for Greeks driven from their homes, the Queen donated to it, although Vicky cautioned her daughter, 'Please dear, not a word must be said that Grandmama contributed.'[27]

Victoria next exerted herself to see that the Turks did not impose a draconian peace on the defeated Greeks. On 7 May she sent the kaiser a telegram begging him to secure honourable terms for an armistice, 'or thousands of lives will be sacrificed'. Considering 'you have always expressed great regard for my advice', she hoped he would help. The following day, however, she received a 'rude reply' saying that Greece must grovel before he assisted in any way. After the Greeks abjectly agreed to abide by all conditions the powers thought fitting, William despatched another 'grandiloquent' telegram to England, exulting at having humbled them.[28]

The kaiser had the greatest dread of Britain and Russia drawing closer together, which he feared might be facilitated by the Queen's granddaughter Alexandra (known as Alicky) of Hesse, youngest child of Victoria's late daughter Alice, being the wife of Tsar Nicholas II. The irony was that the Queen had been bitterly opposed to this match. She had found it bad enough when Alicky's older sister Ella had become betrothed in 1883 to Grand Duke Sergei, brother of Tsar Alexander III. Convinced that 'that marriage ... would be *misery* for her, as the climate, Society etc are so *pernicious*', she persuaded Ella to break off the engagement, only for the girl to change her mind and marry Sergei the following year. After that the Queen resolved that 'lovely Alicky' must be kept out of Russian clutches. Proclaiming Russia to be 'such a *corrupt* country ... where politics are so antagonistic to one's own views & feelings', she instructed Alicky's eldest sister Victoria Battenberg to 'prevent *further* Russians ... *coming* to snap her up'.[29]

Unluckily for the Queen, Tsar Alexander III's eldest son, the Tsarevitch Nicholas, had loved Alicky almost from the moment he first set eyes on her, and by 1889 was set on marrying her. Queen Victoria meanwhile had hoped Alicky would wed the Prince of Wales's heir, Prince Eddy, but when Alicky turned him down in 1890 she remained adamant there must be 'no marriage for *Alicky in Russia*'. Discovering a few months later that the Tsarevitch was pressing his suit, she raged: '*This* must *not* be *allowed to go on* ... The state of Russia is *so bad*, so rotten, that at any moment something dreadful might happen.'[30] For a time the Queen was aided by the fact that the tsarevitch's parents were not keen on the match. Once their opposition was overcome, Alicky herself refused him, because marrying him would mean changing her religion.

The Queen met Tsarevitch Nicholas when he came to England for the Duke of York's wedding in June 1893. In his diary the tsarevitch recorded: 'the Queen – a round ball on unsteady legs – was remarkably kind to me'. For her part Victoria was favourably impressed by this 'charming' young man, who was so 'very simple & unaffected', but still did not want Alicky to marry him.[31] She was therefore delighted when at the end of the year her granddaughter appeared to give Nicholas a final refusal on grounds of conscience.

In the spring of 1894 Alicky's brother Ernie married another granddaughter of the Queen's, 'Ducky' Coburg. A vast family gathering congregated at Coburg for the wedding, with the Queen, Tsarevitch Nicholas and Kaiser William all present. A tearful Alicky once again rejected Nicholas, but the kaiser, counting on earning Nicholas's eternal gratitude, overcame her reservations. As soon as Alicky had accepted the Tsarevitch's proposal, the young couple rushed to tell Victoria. Having supposed that 'at last there was *no* danger' she was 'quite thunderstruck' but had to give her blessing. When she gave the news to Sir William Harcourt – at that time Chancellor of the Exchequer – she affected cheerfulness, declaring the betrothal 'a very romantic as well as auspicious event'. She did not hide her real feelings from Victoria Battenberg, lamenting: 'the more I think of sweet Alicky's marriage the more unhappy I am! *Not* as to the personality for I like him *very much*, but on account of the country, the policy & differences with us, & the awful insecurity to which that sweet child will be exposed ... But I will *try* ... & make the best of it.'[32]

The Queen comforted herself that the engagement would be a lengthy one, and since Alexander III was not yet fifty, Nicholas would not inherit for a considerable time. However, by September 1894 it was apparent that the tsar was seriously ill. Appalled at the prospect facing Alicky, Victoria declared, 'my blood runs cold when I think of her *so* young most likely placed on that very unsafe throne, her dear life and above all her husband's constantly threatened'. When Alexander died on 1 November, the Queen bewailed the 'terrible load of responsibility

& anxiety ... laid upon the poor children!' Within the month they were married, with Victoria reflecting portentously on the eve of the wedding, 'Tomorrow morning dear Alicky's fate will be sealed.'[33]

In July 1894 Nicky had struck Victoria as 'sensible and liberal-minded' when he and his fiancée had stayed at Osborne during their engagement. Hopes soon however faded that he would inaugurate a less autocratic style of government. It remained to be seen whether his marriage to Queen Victoria's granddaughter would improve Anglo-Russian relations. 'His feelings are very English,' Victoria had declared when the betrothal was announced, but it was unclear whether this would prove of any political value.[34]

To the Queen's delight, in 1896 the tsar and tsarina agreed to visit England while on a European tour. They accepted her invitation to stay at Balmoral for a fortnight, although initially the Queen did not intend that politics should intrude on a purely family occasion. She sent a message to Nicholas promising the visit would be 'a private one to the Empress's grandmother', so no ministers would be present. In alarm, Salisbury's private secretary wrote to Sir Arthur Bigge objecting that people would deduce from the prime minister's absence that the tsar was anti-English. After checking with Nicholas, Victoria invited Salisbury to join the party for part of the time.[35]

The Queen was overjoyed to see 'Darling Alicky' 'in great beauty and very blooming' when she and her husband arrived on 22 September. Victoria believed the tsar 'enjoyed the privacy and family life of Balmoral immensely'.[36] For him personally, however, the visit was not a success. He hated having to go out shooting every day in driving rain, particularly since he failed to bag a stag. To cap it all, he then developed toothache.

Before being stricken, the tsar had talks with Salisbury on 27 and 29 September, which proved less than productive. Nicholas was far from keen on Salisbury's suggestion that the powers should deprive the murderous Sultan Abdul Hamid of his throne and install a more reliable Muslim in his stead. Salisbury understood the tsar would countenance other measures to force the sultan to moderate his behaviour but afterwards it emerged that even here Nicholas could not be depended on. When, later that autumn Salisbury sent out his circular urging the powers to take joint action against Turkey, Nicholas responded, 'as an autocrat, he cannot agree to participate in any coercive measures against a friendly autocratic sovereign'.[37]

The Queen also had some political discussions with the tsar during his stay. The courtly Bishop of Winchester, Randall Davidson, told her beforehand that 'those unlearned in political complications' held that, 'somehow or other, "the Queen will set things right when she sees the Tsar"', yet hopes that their meeting might end 'Eastern violence and wrong' proved unfounded. During their talks, Nicholas was 'most kind and affectionate, and very frank and open', but the Queen's belief that he was 'anxious to put a stop to the Sultan's iniquities' was mistaken. Not knowing how empty his undertakings were, Victoria was pleased that he concurred when she 'said it was so important that Russia and England should go well together, as they were the most powerful Empires, for then the world must be at peace'.[38]

The Queen quizzed him about his relationship with France, with whom Russia was now in acknowledged alliance. He assured her it was a purely defensive arrangement, giving the impression he 'did not ... at all ... relish the French'. He also implied he was dreading his forthcoming visit to Paris, which was to take place as soon as he left Scotland. Emboldened by this, once Nicky and Alicky were en route to France, Victoria wrote hoping he would let the French know he could not support 'their constant inimicality to England', particularly regarding Britain's continued occupation of Egypt. Once again Nicholas would disappoint her. After leaving Paris he wrote he had not had an opportunity to raise her concerns, but as to Egypt, Russia too did not approve of Britain's presence there. 'Politics alas are not the same as private or domestic affairs and they are not guided by personal or relationship feelings,' he told her.[39]

Relations with Russia were still not overly cordial. In September 1897 Salisbury remarked to the Queen, 'Unfortunately though the Emperor himself seems to be friendly ... the Russian administration, especially in the Foreign Office, clings to the old tradition.'[40] Tensions were heightened by Russian ambitions in the Far East, where Britain feared their designs on China. This too militated against the two superpowers drawing closer.

On 23 September 1896 Victoria became the longest-reigning English sovereign in history, but decided to postpone celebrations until the sixtieth anniversary of her accession on 20 June, the following year. Although she was willing for the occasion to be marked, she had no intention of paying for it, making it absolutely plain it was a case of 'No money, no Jubilee'. Awash with a surplus, the Chancellor of the Exchequer was willing to be generous, believing that if European rulers thronged the capital, it would be prestigious for Britain. However, the kaiser's not having yet been forgiven the Kruger telegram posed a problem. By January 1897, William was already hinting he was looking forward to attending, but the Queen was fully in agreement with the Prince of Wales, who believed it would a great mistake to let him be present. Bertie warned his nephew would be bound to arrive 'with an enormous suite and would try to arrange things himself and endless trouble would arise'. Victoria answered, 'There is *not* the slightest fear of the Queen's giving way about the Emperor William's coming here in June. It would *never* do for many reasons.' Consequently the kaiser found himself out in the cold, much to his annoyance. Ten days before the anniversary he wrote to his grandmother saying his enforced absence was 'deeply mortifying & I feel like a charger chained in the stables who hears the bugle sound & stamps and champs his bit because he cannot follow his regiment'.[41]

Rather than being a great concourse of crowned heads, the Diamond Jubilee 'expanded into a significant manifestation of imperial greatness'. Eleven premiers from self-governing colonies were brought over at

Queen Victoria's carriage passing the Houses of Parliament during the 1897 Diamond Jubilee procession.

public expense and made privy councillors, while troops 'from every part of the world' took part in the procession held on 22 June. They included Royal Canadian Mounted Police, Bengal Lancers, Hong Kong constabulary in long robes and conical hats, Houssas from West Africa ('fine-looking men but very black', the Queen noted) and 'handsome' Sikhs. Having seen the 'striking sight' of 'colonial troops of every colour and every description of uniform' marching past, Edward Hamilton reflected, 'If ever there was a moment at which one might feel proud of being a member of the British Empire it was now.' The Queen's munshi Abdul Karim was equally impressed, writing in his diary, 'the gorgeous spectacle of the Jubilee procession in London ... was the grandest sight the world has ever seen'.[42]

Before taking her place in the procession on the morning of 22 June, Victoria touched an electric button that transmitted by telegraph cable throughout her Empire the words: 'From my heart I thank my beloved people; may God bless them.' Then, surrounded by her sons and sons-in-law on horseback, and flanked by an escort of Indian cavalry, she drove to St Paul's. In her journal she recorded: 'No one ever I believe has met with such an ovation as was given to me ... The cheering was quite deafening & every face seemed to be filled with real joy.' Because she had specified that she would not get out of her carriage, an open-air Te Deum was performed outside the cathedral, where 'all the Colonial troops, on foot, were drawn up round the square'. She then drove over London Bridge to pass through less affluent parts of town. She was pleased that 'along the Borough road, where there is a very poor population', her reception was 'just as enthusiastic & orderly as elsewhere'.[43]

In the ensuing days Victoria took part in an exhausting programme of banquets, gatherings of schoolchildren, military reviews and garden parties. The only untoward event was a reception held on 23 June for MPs and peers at Buckingham Palace, which was chaotic and a terrible crush. Arthur Balfour said that after this 'great fiasco', 'he found nine-tenths of his party Red Republicans', but the Queen was able to undo the damage. Despite being understandably tired, on 3 July she gave 'a sort of garden party' at Windsor for MPs, their wives and daughters. It was a lavish affair, as one of the guests recalled. 'We turned up in hundreds, including two [Irish] Nationalists whom the Queen asked to be presented to her. She was looking very well, very young and very happy. She stayed a long time among her faithful Commons, scores of whom, including plenty of Radicals and not a few Labour members, were brought up to her carriage.' Among the 'ample refreshments' was a plentiful supply of champagne, chilled to a perfect temperature. After partaking liberally, one radical told others: '"If the Prince of Wales wants his civil list increased, I am ready to support his application tomorrow." And then back to the iced champagne.' Victoria was justly pleased with how it had gone, recording: 'Drove about slowly amongst my guests & spoke to some. Some of the (so-called) Labour Members were presented which I heard afterwards gratified them very much.'[44]

Vicky would later declare to her mother that during the Jubilee, 'a spirit of affection and kindliness, peace and goodwill, was abroad'. The Bishop of London assured Victoria the event 'awakened the respectful wonder of all Europe' – but this was not entirely true. Smarting at his exclusion the kaiser wrote bitterly, the 'Jubilee swindle' gave a misleading impression of Britain's eminence.[45]

Even Lord Salisbury felt there was something hubristic about the celebrations and feared 'the intoxication of the Jubilee' gave rise to arrogance and bellicosity. The grimmest commentary on proceedings came from *Reynolds's Newspaper*. According to this socialist publication, the Jubilee procession should by rights have included ghosts of the Māori race, 'any remnant of the Aboriginal Australians who survived the murder and rapine of the most Christian monarch Victoria', and 'any Kaffirs, Zulus and other African tribes surviving the "civilising" and "Christianising" process for which England has earned notoriety'.[46]

Few Indian princes attended the Jubilee, because their country was in the grip of famine and plague. The Queen believed that the presence in her household of a more humble Indian, the munshi Abdul Karim, provided her with a valuable connection to her subjects in the subcontinent. She wrote to Salisbury's Secretary of State for India, Lord George Hamilton, 'It is … useful to hear what Indians themselves feel, which she fears is rarely the case at the India Office and even at the Viceroy's court, where the Viceroy hears nothing but Anglo-Indian insults.'[47] Her household looked less favourably on the munshi, considering it an affront that the Queen expected them to associate with him on semi-equal terms. They rationalised their dislike by convincing themselves that the munshi was politically dangerous, with Fritz Ponsonby in the vanguard of those who sought to counteract him.

Rafiuddin Ahmed was a barrister and journalist who was a close friend of the munshi's, and in the autumn of 1895 Victoria startled Lord Salisbury by suggesting this man should be given a job at the British embassy in Constantinople. She believed it would show that Britain was not anti-Muslim, but the prime minister said he feared Rafiuddin's appointment would stir up 'strong racial animosity' among embassy staff. He was also uneasy about him having access to important secrets. Victoria insisted the prime minister met with Rafiuddin, and having done so, Salisbury was able to fob her off for the present. In March 1897 she raised the matter again, only for Salisbury to reiterate that race prejudice within the diplomatic service made it impossible to employ Rafiuddin.[48]

The munshi brought some trouble on himself because of a tendency to self-aggrandisement. He was apt to talk to journalists, and in December 1895 an article had appeared in *The Times* stating that he occupied a position with respect to Indian affairs 'corresponding to that held for the United Kingdom by the late Sir Henry Ponsonby'. This provided the household with ammunition, allowing Fritz Ponsonby and Sir Arthur Bigge to raise concerns with Lord George Hamilton. Although the secretary of state did 'not think the munshi is as dangerous as some suppose', he ordered that when Abdul Karim went home on leave in February 1896, he should be subjected in India to 'a very general and unobtrusive supervision'.[49]

When the munshi returned, the Queen was as devoted to him as ever, and the household no less antagonistic. In the spring of 1897 there was a major rumpus when a royal lady-in-waiting, Harriet Phipps, had to inform Victoria that if the munshi came on holiday with her to Cimiez in the south of France, her other attendants would not accompany her. In a fearsome display of temper, the Queen swept everything off her desk on to the floor. Unnerved by this, her servants capitulated, but once at Cimiez they resumed the campaign against the munshi. Her physician Dr Reid confronted Victoria directly, saying 'people in high places' now had serious doubts about her sanity. Initially she was shaken, but next day she admonished Reid, in a 'most violent passion … [saying] we had all behaved disgracefully'.[50]

Despite this, Fritz Ponsonby pursued his vendetta. On 27 April 1897 he wrote from Cimiez to the private secretary of Indian viceroy Lord Elgin, explaining his concerns. 'Although we have tried our best, we cannot get the Queen to realise how very dangerous it is for her to allow this man to see every confidential paper relating to India, in fact to all state affairs … The Munshi is even allowed to read the Viceroy's letters and any letters of importance that come from India.' If anyone protested, 'the Queen says that it is "race prejudice" and that we are all jealous of the poor Munshi!'[51]

Victoria tried to convince Salisbury that the household's fears of the munshi were wildly exaggerated. Having previously informed Lord George Hamilton that the munshi's position was 'confidential though unpolitical', on 17 July she assured the prime minister he had no access to sensitive material. 'The Queen would just wish to assert that *no* political papers of any kind are ever in the Munshi's hands *even* in her presence. He only helps her to read words which she cannot read or merely ordinary submissions on warrants for signature. He does not read English fluently enough to be able to read anything of importance.'[52]

Victoria remained staunch to the munshi till the end, and it was only after her death that her household and family had their revenge. All the letters and photographs she had sent him were burnt outside his cottage at Osborne, and then he was despatched back to India with a pension. At Agra he lived in a house built on land granted to him by Victoria, dying aged forty-six in 1909.

The munshi may have had something to do with Victoria's continued misgivings about the arrogance and high-handedness of officials and army officers in India. She feared that racist and insulting treatment was inflicted on Indians of all classes, and when Lord Curzon was chosen to replace Elgin as viceroy, the Queen hoped he would address these problems. She wrote to Salisbury: 'The future Viceroy ... must be more independent, must *hear for himself* what the *feelings* of the Natives really are ... and not be guided by the *snobbish* and vulgar, overbearing and offensive behaviour of many of our Civil and Political Agents.' This was essential, 'if we are to go on peacefully and happily in India, and to be liked and beloved by high and low, as well as respected as we ought to be, and not trying to trample on the people and continually reminding them and make them feel they are a conquered people. They must of course *feel* that we are masters, but it should be done kindly and not offensively, which alas! is so often the case.'[53]

In late 1897 – when Lord Elgin was still viceroy – a conflict had broken out on India's North West Frontier. A Pashtun tribe, the Afridi, inhabited territory 'outside the frontier of British India proper', and there had been fighting with British forces in the area. Victoria was not only distressed by the bloodshed but felt the situation ought never to have arisen. She wrote to Lord George Hamilton, 'the Queen cannot help fearing that there was a want of preparation, of watchfulness, and of knowledge of what the wild tribes were planning, which ought not to have been'. It also worried her that local 'poor people are suffering from the necessity of supplying horses and ponies and cattle to us ... which comes heavily upon them after their famine and plague'. The Afridi and their families faced severe reprisals. At the outset Hamilton reported, 'the tribes have been punished by the destruction of their fortified villages and the capture and appropriation of all stores of food'. He was confident that this, coupled with their 'heavy loss of life' during clashes with the British, would soon force them to submit, but the Queen's prediction that it would be a 'long and troublesome affair' proved correct. In November she observed 'the fighting seems of an unexampled severity', and although the 'conduct of the British and Native troops has been quite heroic ... the losses have been very sad [and the] number of officers who have fallen very distressing. The Queen is most grieved at this.'[54]

She queried the value of the entire operation, asking Elgin, 'As we do not wish to retain any part of the country, is the continuation and indefinite prolongation of these punitive expeditions really quite justifiable at the cost of many valuable lives?' Elgin was adamant it would be 'fatal ... to leave in the minds of the tribesmen a doubt of the power and determination of the government of India' to impose its will. Accordingly, the war went on for weeks. In 1898 the Queen paid several visits to the military hospital at Netley in Hampshire, where the patients were 'chiefly sick and wounded from the frontier war'.[55]

Throughout Africa, the Empire had continued to expand and – at least from the viewpoint of its British overlords – to thrive. In 1893 Cecil Rhodes had enlarged the domain carved out some years earlier in Mashonaland (already referred to in some newspapers as 'Rhodesia') by encroaching further on the territory of Lobengula, King of the Ndebele. Having been ousted from Mashonaland, Lobengula had retreated northwards to Matabeleland, and Gladstone had directed that Rhodes's British South African Company should leave him unmolested there. Although Gladstone deluded himself that 'Rhodes wants nothing', this was far from the case, and in 1893 the arch-imperialist was able to exploit a favourable opportunity. Lobengula had sought to restrain his warriors by directing their aggressive impulses against their traditional tribal enemies, the Shona, but in July his 'young fighting men ... got out of hand'. In the course of a punitive expedition, they massacred 400 Shona – including some servants of white settlers – under the walls of company-controlled Fort Victoria. This so-called 'Victoria Incident' gave Rhodes and his associates an excuse to act. Lobengula tried to avert war by writing to the Queen, putting his side of the story, but the British high commissioner at the Cape, Sir Henry Loch, ensured the missive never reached her. He also falsely reported that the Ndebele had deliberately fired on white men, and that Lobengula had mobilised his army and was preparing to invade white territory.[56]

By October the British South Africa Company had secured the mother government's blessing to engage in hostilities. Informing the Queen of this on 6 October, Gladstone's colonial secretary Lord Ripon wrote that while this was regrettable, there was 'no cause for any apprehension as to the result'. The British South Africa Company had brought in reinforcements armed with Maxim guns and other modern weaponry, whereas their opponents were 'chiefly armed with assegais [spears]'. As expected, the company gained a crushing victory over their foes, killing hundreds. Lobengula fled and took poison after telling his people, 'Here are your masters coming ... The white people are coming now.'[57]

Matabeleland was incorporated into 'Rhodesia', and in November 1893 its administration was entrusted to the British South African Company. Colonial Secretary Lord Ripon felt somewhat uneasy about this, as giving such power to 'speculative' chartered companies was 'essentially bad' but the Queen shared none of his misgivings. In December 1894 Cecil Rhodes ('such a remarkable man') dined at Windsor while visiting England, and the Queen had 'a long conversation' with her guest. 'He said that he had had many great difficulties, but that since I had seen him last, he had added 12,0000 miles of territory to my Dominions, & that he believed in time the whole world would come under my rule.'[58]

Once Joseph Chamberlain took the helm of the Colonial Office in 1895, the buccaneering (some would say piratical) imperial spirit came strongly to the fore. Soon after being installed, Chamberlain sent a punitive raid into Ashanti, whose king had allegedly interfered with British traders while he himself was engaged in slaving and had also failed to pay reparations imposed after an earlier war. This had personal implications for the Queen, for her son-in-law 'Liko' Battenberg, husband of her youngest daughter Beatrice, volunteered to join the expedition. As he advanced into the African interior, Liko had fallen ill, and on 20 January 1896 had died aboard the ship evacuating him to Madeira. It was a devastating blow not just for Beatrice but for the Queen herself. In a letter to the nation, she declared Liko's 'presence was like a bright sunbeam in my house' and his loss overshadowed her declining years.[59]

She had to take what comfort she could from the fact that the Ashanti expedition was a resounding success, with British losses being almost exclusively due to disease rather than enemy action. Following claims that evidence had been found of human sacrifice, the King of Ashanti was deposed and his country transformed into a British protectorate. Having been presented with his footstool and umbrella as trophies, Victoria wrote on 4 March, what a 'blessing it was to feel that the awful horrors that went on have been stopped for ever … & the wicked King Prempeh and his horrible mother have been removed to an island'.[60]

Very soon fresh trouble flared up in Rhodesia, as the Ndebele, dispossessed of land and forced to work as labourers on colonists' farms, rose up against their subjugators. On 27 March 1896 Victoria recorded: 'Heard of a rising in Matabele in S. Africa & of some Whites being killed! Very unpleasant.' She at once telegraphed Chamberlain that she was 'much grieved … at the terrible murders … I fear it will not be easily put down.' Her gloomy prognosis proved accurate. After the Ndebele had been dealt with, the Shona revolted, and in July 'very uncomfortable' accounts were still coming from South Africa. 'No progress seems to be made, though the Natives are always beaten,' the Queen fretted; eventually 'order' was restored.[61]

For Salisbury the overwhelming priority when it came to African policy was to secure control of the headwaters of the Nile. Doing this would ensure the security of Egypt, itself crucial to safeguarding Britain's route to India. Victoria first cousin, King Leopold II of the Belgians, was therefore chasing a hopeless dream when he suggested to Salisbury in late 1895 that Britain's real interests lay in abandoning Egypt in order to 'annex China to the Indian empire'. The vacated valley of the Nile from Khartoum upwards should then be leased to 'some person … *au courant* with the affairs of Africa'. Salisbury chuckled that Leopold was 'too modest to mention who that person was', though was clearly referring to himself.[62]

Leopold had already carved out a personal African fiefdom in the Congo Free State, which he mercilessly exploited. He had effectively enslaved its inhabitants, imposing impossible quotas for the harvest of wild rubber and ivory, with millions who failed to satisfy his demands being mutilated, tortured or killed. There were also disquieting rumours about his private life. In 1885 his name had featured in a British court case brought against a brothel that supposedly specialised in providing clients with girls aged ten to fifteen years old. Presumably out of respect for the memory of Uncle Leopold, Victoria contrived to ignore such things. King Leopold had been a principal guest of honour at the Golden Jubilee, and thereafter saw her most years. In 1897 he came all the way to Balmoral to offer birthday wishes, bearing 'an erection of orchids' from his Belgian hothouses. The Queen's lady-in-waiting Marie Mallet commented: 'He is an unctuous old monster, very wicked I believe; we imagine he thinks a visit to the Queen gives him a fresh coat of whitewash, otherwise why does he travel 500 miles in order to partake of lunch?' Watching him dine with Victoria on another occasion, Fritz Ponsonby observed: 'It was curious that she should like him, because his morals were notorious, but the Queen seemed to overlook this.'[63]

Initially Leopold had been remarkably successful at pretending that his colonising activities were a philanthropic exercise – and possibly in 1895 Salisbury was unaware that the King of the Belgians was someone who should not be entrusted with responsibility for any more African lives. Even so, he did not for a moment consider leasing him the area of the Sudan that he coveted. As for the Queen, when told of her cousin's 'quite preposterous' delusions, she thought Leopold 'had taken leave of his senses'.[64]

Salisbury in fact wanted to reclaim the Sudan – lost to the Mahdi's forces following the fall of Khartoum in 1885 – on the Khedive of Egypt's behalf. The Mahdi had died in June 1885 but his place had been taken by a 'monstrous Khalifa' who, the Queen understood, exercised a 'reign of terror', committing 'horrors ... that ... make one's hair stand on end'.[65] The region could not be reconquered until a railway had been built across the desert; once that had been done, an army under Herbert Kitchener moved south towards Khartoum. On 2 September 1898 the Battle of Omdurman took place on its outskirts. British casualties were relatively light, but for their opponents it was 'not a battle but an execution', with at least 12,000 Dervishes being mown down by modern weaponry.

Hearing that a memorial service had been held at Khartoum on the spot where Gordon had been killed, a delighted Queen exulted, 'surely he is avenged!' Even Salisbury had been somewhat unnerved by the 'ghastly' 'butcher's bill' paid by the enemy, but the Queen accepted the explanation of an officer who had been present that, 'our men did not like killing all these people but it was unavoidable'.[66]

Having conferred a peerage on Kitchener, Victoria was soon disturbed by a report that the victorious general had not only razed the Mahdi's tomb and thrown his bones in the Nile but had even used his skull as an inkstand. When she brought up the matter with Kitchener, he said that though at one time he had thought of donating the skull to the College of Surgeons, he had ultimately buried it in a Muslim cemetery. The Queen was much relieved; she pointed out to Kitchener that, while she understood that he did not want the last resting place of the Mahdi to become a shrine, 'the destruction of the poor body of a man who, whether he was very bad and cruel, after all was a *man* of a certain *importance* … savours, in the Queen's opinion, too much of the Middle Ages'.[67]

The Battle of Omdurman was followed by a bizarre episode that brought Britain to the brink of a cataclysmic war. In 1896 a small French expedition led by a Captain Marchand had set out from the coast of West Africa, and having traversed almost the entire continent, arrived nearly two years later at Fashoda, the site of an abandoned Egyptian fort some 600 miles south of Khartoum on the White Nile. The day after the battle, Kitchener was instructed to proceed by boat upriver to dislodge the interlopers. When Kitchener delivered his message, Marchand informed him he could not depart without instructions from Paris.

The focus then shifted to Europe. In London Salisbury held urgent talks with the French ambassador, while in Paris, the British ambassador to France, Sir Edward Monson, liaised with the French foreign minister. Determined not to allow British dominance of the Nile valley to be compromised, Salisbury argued that the French had no right to be in a part of Africa that belonged, by right of conquest, to England's partner, Egypt. Flatly refusing to recall their man, the French countered that the Nile was an international waterway, and that they had been entitled to occupy territory effectively abandoned by its former owner. With France currently in the throes of a political crisis caused by the Dreyfus case, there was a real risk the French might see war with England as a way of unifying their nation – however mad it seemed 'to quarrel over a place which is nothing but a swamp in central Africa'. On 2 October the Queen acknowledged, 'It seems a deadlock.'[68]

British public opinion became dangerously inflamed and set on combatting French impudence. Victoria initially mirrored these sentiments. When Salisbury told her it was impossible to make concessions she telegraphed back: 'Quite agree. We cannot give way.' As days went by, and the French refused to shift position, she began to waver. When Lord George Hamilton took leave of her at Balmoral on 25 October in order to attend a specially convened Cabinet, she instructed him to tell colleagues, 'not a stone should be left unturned to prevent war, for I felt what an awful responsibility to God & man it would be were we to go to war, & what a sacrifice of thousands of lives!'[69]

The Queen still clung to the hope that 'surely the French will not let it come to that'; but with Salisbury maintaining that Britain could not modify its stance by 'one iota', and the French demanding 'free access to the Nile from her Congo possessions', things looked ever grimmer. Growing frantic, on 30 October Victoria telegraphed from Balmoral: 'Think a war for so miserable and small an object is what I could hardly bring myself to consent to. We have had so many losses already on the Indian frontier, and to think of sacrificing any more is too horrible and wrong.'[70]

She begged Salisbury to devise a way to 'save France from *humiliation*'. The French were meanwhile coming to the conclusion that, not only was Fashoda untenable, but staying there would profit them little. They therefore backed down without Salisbury having to make explicit concessions. On 4 November the prime minister was able to announce at a City banquet that the French would soon evacuate Fashoda. The British triumph seemed complete when, in March 1899, France concluded an agreement promising to stay entirely out of the Nile valley. However, the Fashoda affair had created bitter ill-feeling in France, which would manifest itself when the Boer War broke out.[71]

Once it became clear war had been averted, Kaiser William opined to his mother: 'I fully understand Grandmama not wanting to finish her reign with fighting. But simply taken from a cool political point of view, England has missed a grand opportunity.'[72] While he professed to have British interests at heart, really he just yearned to see England and France at each other's throats.

For the past year, Britain's relations with Germany's unpredictable ruler had remained strained. Knowing how touchy he was about criticism of him in the British press, in January 1898 the Queen had tried to improve things by asking the prince consort's biographer Theodore Martin to speak to several newspaper editors, begging them to show restraint. It seemed it would take more than this to bring about an improvement. The very day that Martin reported he was making good progress, the British military attaché in Berlin went out shooting with the kaiser. The latter 'began one of the tirades' with which Colonel Grierson was already familiar, ranting that 'for eight years he had striven to be friendly with Great Britain, to gain her alliance and to work hand-in-hand, but had failed. We should never have such a chance again, for never again would a grandson of the Queen of Great Britain be on the German throne.'[73]

However much the kaiser complained of his approaches being spurned, he was not really desirous of forging closer bonds with Britain. In April 1898 he wrote to the German foreign office that keeping 'official sentiment in England … *hopeful*' might prompt England to offer 'colonial and commercial advantages', but the real value would come from Russia thinking that they too must start courting Germany. The following month the kaiser wrote privately to the tsar, claiming Britain was currently making 'enormous offers' and that Russia should trump these by forming an alliance of its own with Germany. The Queen and Salisbury were not privy to these manoeuvres but were aware that the kaiser was less than sincere. On 24 April Victoria met with Salisbury during her annual holiday in the south of France, and after discussing Germany's apparent 'anxiety now to be on good terms with us', they agreed, 'She is not to be trusted'.[74]

Heavy-handed German attempts to convince Salisbury that if England desired to draw closer to Germany, it was essential to show 'amiability in other matters', were unavailing. In the summer of 1898 the German ambassador, Hatzfeldt, tried to persuade Salisbury to meet demands relating to Southeast Africa, the South Seas, the Philippines and the Canaries, but the prime minister flatly rejected them. An enraged kaiser scrawled on Hatzfeldt's despatch that the 'shameless scoundrel' Salisbury was 'positively Jesuitical, monstrous and insolent'. He concluded bitterly: 'The noble Lord is trifling with us … simply because he is not afraid of us, because *we have no fleet*.'[75]

Having been working for months to persuade his mother the dowager empress that he was 'MOST anxious for a *rapprochement* with England', he now sent her an angry telegram, which she in turn forwarded to the Queen. Victoria passed this to Salisbury, who replied drily: 'The German Emperor takes offence very easily.' Professing himself mystified that her grandson had complained all his overtures had been received with 'something between a joke and a snub', he stated he could not grant German demands without causing a furious reaction at home.[76]

Salisbury still hoped that the kaiser's affection for his grandmother might yet place their two countries on better terms. In November 1898 the prime minister suggested that since Emperor William presently seemed relatively well disposed, it might be a good idea to invite him to England. Accordingly, the following month the British ambassador to

Germany, Sir Frank Lascelles, told the kaiser that the Queen would be delighted to see him at some point in the coming year, although she did not want him at her eightieth birthday celebrations. Responding in his cheeriest vein, in late January 1899 the kaiser expressed delight that she wished 'her queer and impetuous colleague' to come over, and would she prefer him to stay at Balmoral or Osborne?[77]

Unfortunately matters were not put right so easily. On 17 February the Queen discussed her grandson with Lord Salisbury, who 'quite agreed with me that while William appeared to wish to be on good terms with us, he did not wish that we should be so with other countries & in particular Russia, whom he was always trying to set us against. Lord Salisbury does not believe the stories he tells'.[78]

On 1 March the Queen took the extraordinary step of writing directly to the tsar. Declaring, 'I feel I must ... tell you something which you *ought* to know and perhaps do not,' she explained that William kept telling Sir Frank Lascelles that Russia was working against Britain by offering alliances to other powers and intriguing with the Amir of Afghanistan. 'I need not say that I do not believe a word of this, neither do Lord Salisbury nor Sir F. Lascelles,' but she feared William was simultaneously doing his best to turn 'Nicky' against England. 'If so, pray tell me openly and confidentially,' for 'such mischievous and unstraightforward proceedings should be put a stop to. You are so true yourself that I am sure you will be shocked at this.'[79]

The tsar had never found the kaiser a congenial companion – during his Balmoral visit he had confided to Salisbury that he particularly disliked the way William was apt to 'poke him in the ribs, and slap him on the back like a schoolboy' – but he often received letters from him which, as the Queen suspected, contained anti-British jibes. Far from defending the kaiser, Nicholas answered, 'I am so happy you told me in that open way about William. Now I fully understand what he is up to – it is a dangerous double game he is playing at.'[80]

Although the kaiser had initially appeared to welcome the prospect of visiting England, it soon emerged he remained disgruntled. Annoyed at being excluded from Victoria's eightieth birthday festivities, he now focussed on the fact that Britain was resisting his wishes about Samoa, which Germany coveted. On 1 May 1899 he made another alarming outburst to British military attaché Colonel Grierson, reverting to the theme of being Britain's 'one true friend' who had 'received nothing in return but ingratitude'. He complained: 'He had particularly desired to be in England on her Majesty's birthday,' but had he been invited, ill-usage would have made it impossible for him to be there. 'His consistent enemy throughout had been Lord Salisbury, and, while the latter remained Prime Minister, it would be impossible for him to come to England.' When she learned William was being so 'tiresome', the Queen predicted caustically to Vicky that if he stuck to his intention of staying away so long as Salisbury was in office, 'He will have to wait a long time.'[81]

After discussing the matter with Salisbury (who sighed to Lascelles he had given no ground for the kaiser's 'unexpected reproach', and it was 'a great nuisance that one of the main factors in the European calculation should be so ultra-human') she wrote a carefully phrased letter to her grandson on 18 May. She told him she was disturbed to hear that rumours were circulating in Germany about the emperor having been made to feel he would not be welcome in England during Cowes week and asked him to enquire how such misconceptions had gained currency. The kaiser was initially rattled enough to suggest to his foreign minister that Princess Beatrice had made mischief, but then switched to a more truculent mood. In late May, at a dinner in honour of the Queen's birthday, he foamed to the British ambassador – in language Victoria later described as 'impertinent & outrageous' – that Germany was being treated as a 'nonentity'. He attributed this to Germany's current weakness at sea and said that would soon change.[82]

On 27 May the kaiser backed this up with a blustering letter to his grandmother. While suggesting she had been misinformed about unfriendly press reports, he agreed German public feeling was 'stirred to its depths' by Salisbury's behaviour over Samoa. If such 'high-handed' and 'disdainful' treatment continued, 'bad blood' between their two countries was inevitable. For the past six months of 'shame and pain' he had 'gulped everything down and held my tongue'; but could no longer stay silent. While he had 'ardently hoped ... to go over for your birthday', the alternative she had offered him of 'a pleasure trip to Cowes' was 'utterly impossible now'. And all this was 'on account of a stupid island which is a hairpin to England compared to the thousands of square miles she is annexing right and left unopposed every year'.[83]

The Queen submitted William's letter to her prime minister, who vigorously defended himself against the kaiser's Samoan allegations. He concluded sombrely, 'He entirely concurs with your Majesty in thinking that it is quite new for a Sovereign to attack in a private letter the Minister of another Sovereign ... It is not a desirable innovation.'[84]

On 13 June Victoria sent her grandson a sharp reply, saying his letter had '*greatly astonished* me' and that she could only ascribe it to 'temporary irritation on your part'. She admonished him, 'I doubt whether any Sovereign ever wrote in such terms to another Sovereign, and that Sovereign his own grandmother, about their Prime Minister,' claiming it was something she herself had never done, even in Bismarck's day. She enclosed a memorandum from Salisbury exonerating himself as regards Samoa, 'which will show you that you are under a misapprehension'. She ended on a slightly softer note, saying that while she understood he would not attend Cowes regatta this year, her invitation to Osborne still stood for late July or August.[85]

A few weeks later the kaiser suggested bringing his wife on an autumn visit to England. His tone was so much milder that Salisbury told Victoria, 'Your letter has had a most salutary effect,' and it was settled that the imperial couple would come to Windsor in November. This did not mark the end of what Salisbury called 'the German Emperor's unreasoning caprice': William's wife Dona loathed England and did all she could to persuade her husband to change his plans. Samoa still remained an object of contention, and as late as 6 November the kaiser was threatening to cancel unless things were settled to his satisfaction. Fortunately agreement was reached on 11 November, dashing the kaiserin's hopes that 'the English visit was falling through'.[86]

When he arrived at Windsor on 20 November, William underwent a complete change of heart. He riled his entourage by exclaiming, as he went on morning walks round the castle, 'from this tower the world is ruled', and marvelling that: 'Here, where as a child I went along holding my mother's hand ... I am now staying as Emperor King.' His advisers were nervous he would be sufficiently carried away to forge a full alliance. Beforehand they had urged that discussions with Salisbury should not go beyond 'everyday small-talk', arguing that the kaiser should respond with 'quiet indifference' to any soundings. In the event William did not meet with Salisbury at all, as the prime minister's wife died on the very day the kaiser arrived, and he stayed at Hatfield to mourn her. The kaiser did have two political discussions with the Queen, and on both occasions said he wished 'for a better understanding with us', but never proceeded beyond generalities.[87] When he met with Balfour and Chamberlain he was again careful not to commit himself, although Chamberlain hoped for better results after talking with the German foreign minister, Bülow. In the event nothing came of this. Days after returning to Berlin, Bülow made a Reichstag speech in support of a navy bill that aimed to double the size of the German fleet. This measure, clearly directed against England, became law on 12 June 1900. The goodwill generated by the kaiser's visit had been very ephemeral.

By the time the kaiser visited, Britain was already at war with the Transvaal and its South African neighbour, the Orange Free State – and was on the way to becoming an international pariah. Staying at Balmoral during the Fashoda crisis, Arthur Balfour had noted with amused condescension the 'singular naiveté' with which the Queen showed 'the utmost horror of war, on the simple but sufficient ground that you cannot have a war without a great many people being killed'.[88] Unfortunately in the months leading up to the Boer War, Victoria lost sight of this fundamental truth. She did very little to stop her kingdom's inexorable descent into an avoidable conflict it was assumed would be a walkover, but which proved hideously costly in blood and treasure.

In the years since the Jameson raid, the grievances of the Uitlanders had not diminished, and in March 1899 they had petitioned the Queen outlining their grounds for discontent. Talks with Transvaal president Paul Kruger proved abortive, and by June there were already calls in some quarters for troops to be sent to South Africa. On 13 June the Cabinet agreed that the time had not yet come for that, but Salisbury told Victoria that, while 'war would be very much to be deprecated', continued inaction was difficult. A month later the Queen 'urged that, whatever happened, we must not be humiliated in S. Africa. We may have to send out a large force & call out the Reserves.'[89]

The Boers then made improved offers, but after initially hailing these as satisfactory, the government determined to exact more. On 25 August the Queen once again discussed the situation with Salisbury, who remained 'full of hope' there would be no war, but he and Victoria agreed that if Britain was not entirely satisfied, 'of course we shall have to be very firm & ... show that we are in earnest'.[90]

On 28 August a despatch was sent to the Transvaal without previous consultation with the Cabinet, demanding further concessions in threatening terms. The Boers responded by withdrawing their last offer. On 8 September the Cabinet decided to send 10,000 men to Natal. Salisbury knew the Queen would approve, having told the German ambassador that much as Victoria wanted peace, 'she had in no way forgotten nor got over the Majuba defeat in February 1881'. While Salisbury said he still wanted to avoid a rupture, the government had in fact resolved to despatch additional forces to South Africa. In the meantime the Cabinet drew up an ultimatum to be presented once the 10,000 men sent earlier in the month had landed.[91]

Having been alerted by press reports that further British reinforcements were heading for South Africa, on 28 September the Transvaal mobilised; four days later the Orange Free State followed suit. The Queen was not unduly disturbed. On 7 October she spoke to the Clerk of the Privy Council, Sir Almeric Fitzroy, 'with a confident conviction of the inevitableness of the struggle and exhibited a cheerful courage and serenity of temper'. Two days later the Boers pre-empted the British by delivering an ultimatum of their own, demanding the withdrawal of troops currently in South Africa and the sending back of all those on their way. Both Queen and press hailed this as an 'astounding' piece of impudence, and the demands were curtly rejected.[92] As a result, Britain and the Boer republics were officially at war from 11 October 1899.

The Queen had been heartened when Sir Redvers Buller, who had been given overall command of British forces in South Africa, took leave of her on 5 October, and said he 'hoped it would not be a long business & did not think there would be much hard fighting'. The day war was declared, Fritz Ponsonby found Victoria 'in a bellicose mood after dinner; she seemed all in favour of teaching Kruger a sharp lesson, but later she became lachrymose at the senseless waste of human lives all this might entail'.[93]

On 26 October Parliament voted by a huge majority to grant the government the funds they had requested for the war. By that time there were already indications it would not be the painless affair many had imagined. Although the British won their initial engagements with the enemy, it was at a cost of numerous fallen. On 22 October the Queen telegraphed Lord Lansdowne, secretary of state for war: 'My heart bleeds for these dreadful losses.' The death toll increased steadily as the war continued and Fritz Ponsonby later recalled, 'the Queen would often break down and cry at the long lists of casualties'. At the outset British forces had been shut up by besieging Boers in Kimberley, Ladysmith and Mafeking, and attempts to break out of these towns all failed. The Queen told Ponsonby: 'I suppose we could not expect to have no reverses, but we must win, if the whole army has to go out.'[94]

Soon Britain was faring badly in the war. The government laid much of the fault on military incompetence, singling out individual generals for blame. The Queen was inclined to think responsibility was also attributable to the deficiencies of the War Office, the department headed by Lord Lansdowne. Having complained for years of its inefficiency, she put the failure to send out adequate supplies or organise good transport at its door. In January 1900 she talked with Lord Rowton of 'our want of preparedness which has existed for a long time and is very culpable'.[95]

The tenth of December 1899 saw the beginning of 'Black Week'. On that day, a reverse at Stormberg was followed quickly by defeats at Magersfontein and Colenso, where Buller was repulsed attempting to relieve Ladysmith. Lord Lansdowne blamed generals for having 'attacked difficult & inaccessible positions', but Victoria did not want to dishearten those in command. Earlier she had worried about Buller's dithering, but on 15 December wrote assuring him, 'the Queen Empress has great confidence in Sir R Buller, and she feels sure that he will retrieve the sad failures of brave men … who seem, alas! not to have been [as] wise and prudent as they ought.'[96]

Even before the start of Black Week the Queen had confided to the courtier Lord Esher, 'It made her ill to open telegrams about the war,' but she maintained the bravest of faces to her ministers. On 18 December, when Balfour alluded glumly to recent disasters, she told him superbly: 'Please understand that there is no one depressed in *this* house; we are not interested in the possibilities of defeat; they do not exist.' Privately, she was often downcast, as evidenced by entries in her journal such as that of 14 December: 'feel very low & anxious about the war'.[97]

Sentiment at home was intensely patriotic, and the Queen threw herself into upholding morale. She visited military hospitals on numerous occasions, being wheeled along rows of beds containing hideously wounded and maimed men. With her ladies she knitted mufflers to be sent to the troops, and on 26 December held a Christmas party at Windsor for wives and children of soldiers serving in South Africa. She also organised the distribution of chocolate bars in tins emblazoned with the royal crest as a seasonal treat for troops; she was delighted to learn later that one soldier's life had been saved when his tin stopped a Boer bullet.

In her letter to Sir Redvers Buller of 15 December, Victoria had assured him of her full confidence, but was seriously shaken when Buller suggested next day he might have to abandon all idea of relieving Ladysmith. Even so, she was disconcerted that the Cabinet decided, without consulting her, to relieve Buller of overall command. Lord Roberts became Commander-in-Chief in South Africa, with Lord Kitchener as his chief of staff; Buller remained in charge of field operations in Natal. While accepting the decision, she considered it 'very wrong' the government 'had not told me first'. She sent for Balfour to remonstrate, and he 'expressed very great regret and astonishment'. To Salisbury Balfour reported there had been 'no great difficulty in smoothing things down', but in the coming weeks ministers afforded her more grounds for misgiving.[98]

It was scarcely reassuring that on 22 December Salisbury confided to her he thought 'Lord Lansdowne quite overdone and the work beyond him', but Salisbury and Balfour themselves seemed incapable of meeting the challenges confronting them. After Buller suffered another bad reverse at Spion Kop on 25 January, Victoria became convinced ministers were being lackadaisical. She telegraphed Salisbury: 'Am much surprised ... that the very serious state of the war was not considered by the Cabinet yesterday.' On February 15 the Queen complained to Marie Mallet, 'They do not take my advice ... and civilians *cannot* understand military matters.' She believed the disaster at Spion Kop was partly caused by lack of fighting men, and though Salisbury disputed this, she wrote to Lansdowne: 'We must hurry out more troops ... we have never had enough ... and we have always underrated the number of the enemy.'[99]

The high rate of casualties among officers 'horrified' her. Lord Wolseley had told her their bearing the brunt of attacks was 'as it should be', but she wanted to protect them. On 30 January she asked Lord Lansdowne to arrange for young officers to be warned 'not to expose themselves more than is absolutely necessary'. Lansdowne quite properly replied this would be 'inadvisable'.[100]

Before Parliament reassembled on 30 January, the Queen said she was sure Salisbury would 'hold firm language and not in a depressed tone', but in fact the line he took left much to be desired. He unhelpfully suggested in the Lords that the British constitution was far from ideal as an 'instrument of war', causing Lord Rosebery to protest that the times required a 'loftier tone and ... truer patriotism'. The Prince of Wales condemned the prime minister's speech as 'simply deplorable', while Lord Esher thought it showed an 'entire misunderstanding of the people's mood'.[101]

The Queen was also worried that the government would give way to demands that a parliamentary enquiry into the war take place as soon as possible. Rightly suspecting that the government would see it as an opportunity to divert blame on to military men, on 11 January she cautioned Salisbury against holding it before the war was over. To Balfour she pointed out an early enquiry would achieve nothing: 'No doubt the War Office is greatly at fault, but it is the whole system which must be changed and that cannot be just now.' She also dreaded what would be said in the debate due to be held on 4 February, urging on Balfour 'very strongly the necessity of resisting these unpatriotic and unjust criticisms of our Generals and the conduct of the war'.[102] In the event the government came out of the debate unscathed, winning the division on it by a huge majority.

Though 'delighted' by this, the Queen was now somewhat disenchanted with her chief ministers. Marie Mallet, a lady-in-waiting who privately considered Salisbury a 'fat old cynic', reported in early February: 'Even the Queen is rather disgusted with Lord Salisbury and AJB [Balfour], and the tone is quite changed.' Marie assured her husband: 'She was not angry when I hinted that public opinion censured the government, only sighed.' Lord Esher too thought 'she has lost confidence in her ministers'.[103]

Victoria could at least console herself that more soldiers were being sent out to fight. In November 1900 her Minister of War would inform her there were currently 'over 230,000 of your Majesty's troops in South Africa'. Besides volunteer forces raised at home in the City of London and elsewhere, large bodies of men were sent out from self-governing colonies such as Canada and the various Australian territories. To her vexation, however, she could not prevail on the government to send out Indian troops. The government feared heightening the resistance of Boers who characterised the conflict as 'a white man's war', while South Africans fighting on the British side would likewise have objected. Even if Salisbury thought it a 'grave error' on the part of his Cabinet, he told the Queen that much as he deplored 'this ineradicable race prejudice', ministers would resign if their views were ignored. Victoria had to accept this but telegraphed: 'Cannot help feeling disappointed at my repeated recommendations being disregarded.'[104]

Although public opinion at home remained surprisingly supportive of the war, on the European continent attitudes were very different. Even before war had broken out, Britain's ambassador in Paris, Sir Edward Monson, had reported the French were highly critical of England's stance towards the Transvaal – although a 'never-failing respect … characterises every allusion to your Majesty'.[105] The lingering humiliation of the Fashoda affair was partly responsible, but some of the bitterness arose from the fact that the Queen and the British press had been vocal in their disapproval of the treatment of the French Captain

Alfred Dreyfus. The latter was a Jewish army officer who had served on the staff of the French war ministry. In December 1894 he had been convicted of treason and sent to Devil's Island after being accused on flimsy grounds of having spied for the Germans. His family and friends had succeeded in publicising that he was victim of an injustice, but even after new evidence exposed flaws in the case against him, anti-Semitic army officers and civilians had furiously denied his innocence. The case so polarised French society that at times revolution or a military coup appeared imminent, and more than one ministry was brought down by the ramifications of the affair.

In September 1898 Dreyfus had been granted a review of his case, and the following June a new court martial was ordered. By this time the Queen was taking a keen interest, and when the new French ambassador Paul Cambon dined at Windsor in July 1899, they discussed what he referred to as the 'wretched Dreyfus affair'. Predicting that at the coming court martial Dreyfus would be acquitted, Cambon explained, 'the whole affair had arisen from the fact of his being a Jew and being rather a miserable creature' who had been 'much disliked in the War Office'.

However, when the court martial took place on 9 September, Dreyfus was once again found guilty by a majority verdict. Quite appalled, the Queen deplored to Vicky, 'the perjury, lying and wickedness of officers' who had testified against him. Within days Dreyfus had been pardoned and released, but before that happened Victoria sent an uncyphered telegram to her embassy secretary in Paris. Expressing outrage at 'this monstrous verdict against the poor martyr', she said she hoped Dreyfus would appeal. The uncoded cable's contents had been published in the French press, provoking fury among anti-Dreyfusards. This partly accounted for the virulence of French condemnation, not only of Britain's conduct of the war, but of Victoria herself.[106]

By December the Queen had become aware of 'atrocious personal attacks on me in the French press'. The publication of gross and obscene cartoons gave rise to discussions whether the Prince of Wales, who had accepted the presidency of the forthcoming Paris Exhibition, should attend its opening. Salisbury did not want to offend the French government, but by March 1900 Bertie had decided his presence would be construed as 'a positive slight to the Queen, and would be regarded by Frenchmen as a proof that he was indifferent to the vile caricatures and lampooning of his own mother by their press'.[107]

Victoria decided against going to France for her usual spring break, for however much she pined 'for the sunny, flowery south … I feel I

An unattractive caricature of Victoria published in France in 1897. After the outbreak of the Boer War, depictions of her in the French press became still more unpleasant, and sometimes even obscene. (*Le Rire*, 1897)

could not, with safety almost, go abroad'. The dangers of anti-British sentiment were shown on 3 April 1900 when Sipido, a teenage Belgian, shot four times at the Prince of Wales in a Brussels railway station. Bertie nonchalantly remarked, 'fortunately anarchists are bad shots', but the Queen commented, his 'merciful escape … shows the harm [of] such atrocious vilifications of us, including even me'.[108]

* * *

Like the French, the German public felt great sympathy for the Boers. When the kaiser had visited England in November 1899 the Queen had raised the German press's abusive coverage with both William and his foreign minister, and the kaiser had assured the Prince of Wales that he and Bülow were making 'superhuman' efforts to moderate anti-British sentiment. However, when at the end of December 1899 Britain detained three German mail steamers off Africa in a search for contraband of war, the Germans responded with a diplomatic note unparalleled for 'sheer offensiveness'. The kaiser told the British ambassador that yet again his attempts to promote cordial relations had been repaid with a 'kick on the shins', and then used the incidents to push his navy bill through the Reichstag.[109]

Throughout the conflict William wrote frequently to his English relatives, making out he was on their side; his tactless and gloating letters in fact revealed schadenfreude at the setbacks they were experiencing. On 21 December 1899 he condoled the Queen on the many killed in action by remarking: 'At all events the British aristocracy have shown the world that they know how to die doing their duty!' To his Uncle Bertie, his Christmas wishes were still more excruciating. Reflecting on Britain's 'quite appalling' losses, he commented: 'Instead of the angels' song "Peace on Earth and Goodwill to Men" the new century will be greeted by shrieks of dying men, killed and maimed by lyddite shells and [rifle] balls ... Truly *fin de siècle!*' Days after writing lugubriously to Victoria, 'The rows of mourners are, I am afraid, swelling more and more,' he sent the Prince of Wales unsolicited advice on what Britain should do to alter the fortunes of war, enclosing a detailed memorandum that 'perhaps it would interest Grandmama' to see. The Prince of Wales was finally goaded beyond endurance when his nephew suggested that losing at cricket and football had shown the British how to take defeat chivalrously.[110]

The kaiser boasted of working tirelessly to prevent other European powers coalescing to force Britain to come to terms with the Boers. It was true that the tsar was horrified by the conflict – after Victoria's death he would inform Bertie, 'I often wanted to write to dear Grandmama to ask her quite privately whether there was any possibility of stopping the war ... Yet ... fearing to hurt her, and always hoping that it would soon cease' he had refrained from doing so. If Nicholas had shrunk from making personal representations, it is hardly likely that he contemplated strong diplomatic action, but in spring 1900 William wrote to his grandmother congratulating himself for 'saving your country from a most dangerous situation in warding off a combination aiming a blow at England'. When informed, the prime minister was sceptical, telling the Queen: 'There lingers in Lord Salisbury's mind a doubt' whether France and Russia had really approached Germany with such a proposal. If anything, indeed, the reverse was the case. On 23 March the Queen had voiced suspicions that the kaiser was 'certainly trying to embroil us with Russia'.[111]

When things started to go better militarily for Britain, the kaiser suggested it was because his advice had been followed. By the end of February 1900 both Kimberley and Ladysmith had been relieved. To celebrate these gains, the Queen drove through London on 8 and 9 March, receiving acclamations from 'enormous crowds'. For her, the 'incessant demonstrations of enthusiasm, if possible even beyond that of the two Jubilees', provided 'a truly thrilling & touching manifestation of the deep devotion & loyalty of my people & I feel it very much'.[112]

The Boer leaders responded to the turn in the tide by telegraphing in early March that they would cease hostilities if the two republics' 'indisputable independence' was recognised. 'Bursting with indignation' at these 'insolent proposals', the Queen was delighted when 'a "stinker"' was sent rejecting the offer. Doubtless in anticipation of this, presidents Kruger and Steyn had also appealed to various foreign powers, requesting mediation. Hearing that the Transvaal government had asked for the kaiser's 'friendly intervention', the Queen at once instructed Salisbury that if her grandson advanced any suggestions regarding peace terms, they 'should not be listened to for a moment'. Instead he was sent a 'friendly but *very firm*' answer, thanking him for saying he would not act unless Britain desired his involvement. The Queen ordered her ambassador in Berlin to supplement this with a verbal statement: 'Please convey to the Emperor that my whole nation is with me in a fixed determination to see this war through without intervention ... and my country ... will resist all interference.' Salisbury was delighted she had been so explicit, while the Prince of Wales thought her words 'worthy of Queen Elizabeth'.[113]

On 15 March Lord Roberts offered Boer fighting men an amnesty from which their leaders were excluded, undertaking to let them go home if they handed in their weapons. He assured the Queen this was 'having the desired effect and men are daily laying down their arms and returning to their usual occupations ... I trust it will not be very long before the war will have been brought to a satisfactory conclusion.'[114] This proved wildly over-optimistic.

For some time Victoria had been concerned that her generals in the field were exposed to excessive interference from politicians at home, and in April her fears on this score became stronger. After 'carelessness' resulted in two British detachments being caught in Boer ambushes, the Cabinet suggested the officers responsible should be dismissed. The Queen objected that Lord Roberts should be left to make his own decisions, but Salisbury would not accept this. He wrote: 'With the deepest respect Lord Salisbury would submit to your Majesty that, under our present constitution, the doctrine that the Cabinet have no control over a General in the field is not practicable. If they have no control, of course they have no responsibility' – meaning they would not be answerable to Parliament on the matter. Although the government should not 'interpose without serious cause', they had good grounds to act in the present instance. The Queen had to agree, confining herself to saying she hoped in future her ministers would 'not ... be in such a hurry' to issue instructions.[115]

Days later the Queen was 'perfectly aghast' when a despatch written by Roberts, effectively blaming Buller for the disaster at Spion Kop, was partially published. Having protested to Lansdowne that she had been promised the report would be kept out of the public domain, she wrote to Salisbury declaring it 'cruel and ungenerous towards Sir R. Buller'. How could 'Lord Lansdowne have been guilty of such an extraordinary proceeding?' Confirming he had not wanted publication, the prime minister said Lansdowne must have misunderstood what had been said in Cabinet, but when Victoria demanded Salisbury repudiate Lansdowne's 'deplorable blunder' in Parliament, Salisbury said that would inevitably mean the secretary of state would resign, probably bringing down the government. Once again the Queen gave way, although she still believed those guilty of military failings should receive only 'private reproval' rather than being branded incompetent.[116]

Although many Irish Nationalist MPs at Westminster were 'avowedly and openly pro-Boer' – cheering announcements of enemy successes and generally making themselves 'very troublesome' – considerable numbers of Irishmen were serving valiantly in the British army in South Africa. They often incurred heavy losses, making the Queen desirous of showing her admiration for 'my brave Irish soldiers'. Having agreed that Irish servicemen could wear the shamrock on St Patrick's Day, she wondered whether she could demonstrate her feelings in a more practical way. She had recently decried the idea that royal visits to Ireland yielded true benefits. After the Duke and Duchess of York had toured the island in August 1897, Victoria declared she was glad it had gone well, but the same could be said of her own three visits, which, 'alas! … did not produce a lasting effect'. Now, rather than holiday on the unfriendly continent in the spring of 1900, she decided to go to Ireland. 'It will give great pleasure and do good,' she told her eldest daughter – though the choice was not purely altruistic. The Queen confided to her lady-in-waiting Marie Mallet, 'I must honestly confess it is *not* entirely to please the Irish but partly because I expect to enjoy myself.'[117]

The visit, which took place in April, was a triumph. For an old woman of eighty, the programme was extraordinarily taxing, as over three weeks she toured innumerable convents, schools, hospitals and craft centres. She attended receptions and military reviews and went on daily drives in an open landau, sometimes with 'scarcely a policeman or soldier' providing protection. On the whole she was rapturously received. When she first entered Dublin on 3 April, she recorded complacently: 'The cheers & often almost screams were quite deafening. Even the Nationalists in front of the City Hall seemed to forget their politics and cheered and waved their hats.' A fortnight later she noted: 'Wherever I go the people come out & cheer and call "God bless you!"' Occasional undercurrents of dissent passed her by completely. Accompanying her on horseback on the daily drive, Fritz Ponsonby intermittently detected 'ugly sounds like booing' amidst the cheers, but to these the Queen was quite oblivious.[118]

When she left the island on 26 April, Victoria could justly congratulate herself on how the trip had gone. 'I felt quite sorry that all was over … though I own I am very tired,' she wrote in her journal, 'I can never forget the really wild enthusiasm & affectionate loyalty displayed by all in Ireland & shall ever retain a most grateful remembrance of this warm-hearted & sympathetic people.'[119]

On 17 May 1900 Mafeking was relieved, sending the British people 'quite mad with delight'. Exultantly the Queen informed Vicky, 'Everything is really going on well now everywhere.' Kaiser William offered hearty congratulations: 'Heaven has at last granted what you hoped for – success!' he wrote to England. 'I venture to assert that among all people on the Continent there is no one who is happier on your behalf than your eldest grandson.' On 28 May the Orange Free State was annexed and renamed Orange River Colony, and three days later Lord Roberts entered Johannesburg. The Queen cautioned against assuming that military operations could be immediately wound down, urging that Lord Roberts should remain in South Africa for the time being. 'The great fault we always commit is withdrawing our troops too soon,' she reminded Chamberlain on 4 June. 'Do not disregard my earnest warning or even protest.'[120] It was nonetheless hard not to believe Britain on the brink of conclusive victory when, the day after she wrote this, Pretoria was taken. In fact, this merely marked the start of a gruelling phase of guerrilla warfare.

This meant that Britain was still fully preoccupied in South Africa when another challenge arose in the Far East. For some months past, a secret society of Chinese peasants calling themselves 'the Fist of Righteous Harmony' – and known in Europe as 'Boxers' – had set out to eradicate foreign influences in China. They had started by murdering missionaries, but by June 1900 were threatening the capital Peking itself. The Boxers received covert encouragement from the Dowager Empress Tzu-Hsi of China, making them more fearsome adversaries. The previous year, when briefly home on leave, the Queen's minister in China, Sir Hector Macdonald, had assured Victoria the dowager empress 'was not such a monster as reported', but events would show that her formidable reputation was well merited.[121]

By 6 June the Queen was sufficiently concerned by the situation in Peking to telegraph Salisbury: 'Trust ... we shall display no apathy.' He discounted the danger, dismissing the Boxers as 'a mere mob', and being reluctant to repel the threat through an international effort. Although colleagues urged him to ask Japan and Russia to send forces at once, Salisbury objected that if they, or the Americans, were called upon, 'they would expect something in return'. To the Queen he argued, 'Russia, not China, seems to me the greatest danger of the moment.'[122]

It was not until the Japanese minister had been decapitated, and the German minister murdered on 18 June 1900, that the seriousness of the situation became apparent to him. Soon all the legations in Peking's diplomatic sector were under siege, and on 9 July Reuters carried a report that everyone at the British legation had been massacred. Hearing that 400 had supposedly been killed, including numerous women and children, the Queen wrote: 'Feel quite miserable, horror struck.'[123] Victoria wanted to break off relations with China, but as he still feared that other powers would profit at Britain's expense from the dismemberment of the Chinese Empire, Salisbury clung to the fiction that the insurgents were not officially countenanced.

Hopes soon rose that the shocking report from Peking had been baseless, and that the legations could yet be saved. An international relief force composed of British, American, Russian and Japanese troops set out to rescue the beleaguered diplomats, and on 13 August succeeded in doing so. Salisbury privately attributed all the trouble to the 'old brute' of an empress, though thought it best there should be no official recriminations. Instead, Tzu-Hsi was permitted to return to the capital after fleeing briefly with the imperial court to western China. The brunt of the allies' anger was borne by the Chinese peasantry, many of whom had had nothing to do with the uprising.[124]

News of the British entry into Pretoria on 5 June 1900 had been hailed by the Queen as 'indeed a great joy and satisfaction', but it was far from heralding the end of the war. On 6 June Kitchener explained to Victoria that bands of Boer irregulars remained a threat to the British. 'It is very difficult to prevent our troops being caught in traps carefully prepared for them by an enemy that does not wear uniform and can at any moment pose as honest farmers.' To deal with the challenge, Britain instigated 'more stringent measures' against Boer saboteurs and the civilians who succoured them.[125]

At an audience with the Queen at Osborne on 18 July Salisbury acknowledged, 'the war seems now to be rather dragging'. Three weeks later Lord Roberts wrote that while he was optimistic that all would shortly be concluded, operations were prolonged by 'the extraordinary mobility of the Boers, who manage to slip away in the most marvellous manner'. On 21 August the Queen noted sadly: 'Continued news from Lord Roberts, something taking place every day but nothing decisive & alas! Always casualties.' As autumn came on, her journal contained numerous entries mentioning 'constant fights & people killed. It is all very sad'.[126] On 1 September Britain annexed the Transvaal and President Kruger fled South Africa for Europe, but the war continued.

To cope with guerrilla activity, on 13 September Lord Roberts issued a proclamation officially announcing that henceforth no mercy would be shown. 'The war … has degenerated into operations carried on in an … irresponsible manner by small … bodies of men. I should be failing in my duty … if I neglected to use every means … to bring such irregular warfare to an early conclusion. The means which I am compelled to adopt are … ruinous to the country, entail endless suffering … & the longer the guerrilla warfare continues, the more vigorously must they be enforced.' Scorched earth tactics and farm burning became standard policy, and as their homes and food supplies were destroyed, the families of enemy combatants were removed to camps set up by the British. In these establishments, overcrowded, insanitary conditions and inadequate rations ensured that deaths from disease and malnutrition reached an appalling level. At least 20,000 white Boer women and children, and around 12,000 black internees incarcerated separately died, though some estimates put the figures higher.[127]

On 4 October Roberts admitted to the Queen: 'In many parts of the Orange River Colony and the Transvaal the distress amongst the women and children must be very great.' He laid the blame squarely at the door of intransigent Boer leaders. Victoria was not greatly concerned by the plight of confined civilians; her attitude having been hardened by Boer behaviour. Throughout the war her journal had featured denunciations of the enemy's 'monstrous' abuse of the white flag – as well as the firing on hospitals and use of dum-dum bullets – and had come to believe they largely had themselves to blame for hardships inflicted on them. When Sir Redvers Buller returned from South Africa Victoria received him at Osborne on 17 November, listening gravely when he declared, 'the Boers were very treacherous & very cruel, uniting the instincts of the savage with the most modern appliances for fighting'.[128]

The full horror of the camps – termed 'concentration camps' by a British MP who adapted the Spanish term for internment centres set up for civilians during the Spanish-Cuban war – only emerged after Victoria's death. The redoubtable welfare campaigner Emily Hobhouse toured the camps while Victoria was alive, but her report on conditions inside them was not published till June 1901. That same month David Lloyd-George said a 'policy of extermination' had led to women and children dying in their hundreds. However, these concerns were not raised in England during the Queen's lifetime.

During the final months of her reign, the Boers were able to exploit the sympathy felt for them in many parts of the world by highlighting the ruthless methods pursued by Britain. President Kruger made good use of his exile, being received with warm acclaim in Paris, while the Boer agent Dr Leyds likewise drew international attention to his compatriots' sufferings. In November 1900 Boer delegates on a world-wide tour said that Britain was employing 'methods of barbarism' – a phrase that would be taken up at home the following year by Liberal leader Sir Henry Campbell-Bannerman. In Germany a deputation from the Transvaal claimed Britain's conduct in South Africa was 'more and more brutalising and inhuman'. Allegations such as these made the tsar increasingly uneasy. After Victoria was dead Nicholas wrote to her successor saying he was disturbed to hear how 'a small people ... desperately defending their country' had to endure their land being 'devastated, their families flocked together in camps, their farms burnt ... Forgive the expression, it looks more like a war of extermination.' As Victoria's life neared its end, her country was reviled abroad as never before, but her own conscience was untroubled. While she found it 'painful to see how this guerrilla warfare still continues', it was the 'sad & useless loss of life' among British forces that principally concerned her.[129]

After being assured by Lord Roberts that within a month the 'war will ... be practically at an end', Salisbury decided to recall him and give Lord Kitchener overall command in South Africa. On 19 September the Queen was vexed by Salisbury's informing her he intended to make Roberts Commander-in-Chief of the British Army in succession to Lord Wolseley. Victoria had long burnt to see her son Arthur Duke of Connaught in this role, and believed she had received an informal undertaking that he would have it. On the outbreak of war, she had done her best to secure Arthur a significant posting in South Africa, but the government had blocked this. However, Salisbury had assured Victoria it 'would not injure his chances of succeeding Lord Wolseley', so now she felt cheated.[130]

Salisbury explained that Roberts's achievements in South Africa ensured it was 'almost impossible that any other nomination should be made'. The current mood of 'democratic rancour' also meant there would be an inevitable outcry if Arthur was given the post. The best the prime minister could do was to hold out the hope – in the event never fulfilled – that when Roberts ended his term, the prince would take his place. The Queen had to accept this. She remained adamant her son's appointment was anxiously awaited, but though she 'naturally' wished to see him at the head of the army, 'as my ministers think otherwise, I suppose I cannot object'.[131]

Believing the war to be as good as won, the British government decided to hold an election in the autumn of 1900. When Balfour had first alerted the Queen that they would soon be going to the country, he had assured her 'of course there was no fear of the government not having a good majority'. His predictions proved correct, for the Liberals fared poorly after the war was 'kept in the foreground' throughout the campaign. Although turnout was low, the government added a further two seats to their already overwhelming majority – a result the Queen found 'wonderfully good'.[132]

Because Lord Goschen had decided to retire, it was clear there would have to be a Cabinet reshuffle. Before the election Victoria had written to tell Goschen, 'he is fully justified in wishing for rest. She wishes she could have the same, even for the shortest period.' Now that more changes were in the offing, she dreaded being called on to adjudicate as to whether Salisbury should continue to combine the roles of foreign secretary and prime minister, which most people acknowledged to be too much for him. She was not reassured when on 13 October she despatched Sir Arthur Bigge south from Balmoral to discuss things with Salisbury, for it became clear he was most reluctant to give up the Foreign Office. He acknowledged his doctors wanted him to lessen his workload, but since he felt strong enough to continue, 'he is ready to do whatever is most agreeable to the Queen and is in her judgement most beneficial to the public service'.[133]

Balfour – who himself was very anxious for his uncle to do less – was told the Queen found herself 'placed in a very awkward position', for while she was convinced Salisbury 'ought not to go on with his Foreign Office work … she shrinks from the task of telling him *she* thinks he ought to go'. She dreaded having to give the prime minister the unwelcome news in person when he came to stay at Balmoral. It therefore came as a great relief when, shortly before setting out for Scotland, Salisbury sent word he now accepted it would be unwise for him to continue as foreign secretary.[134]

The Queen was somewhat disconcerted when Salisbury declared that Lord Lansdowne must take his place at the Foreign Office. Lansdowne himself was obviously somewhat surprised, as he made clear when writing to thank the Queen. 'He values it the more because he does not disguise from himself that as secretary of state for war he must often have seemed … to fall short of your Majesty's expectations.' In fact she had only agreed to it, 'on the strict understanding that he must be entirely under [Salisbury's] personal supervision'. After talking with her, Marie Mallet reported that Lansdowne was 'to be a sort of "dummy" to do the entertaining and tiresome interviews with ambassadors and not to have any power'.[135]

As far as other ministerial appointments were concerned, the Queen showed that, as she had boasted to Vicky in 1886, she was no 'mere puppet' when administrations were formed. She 'did not fancy' Salisbury's suggestion that Lord Balfour of Burleigh should replace

Goschen at the Admiralty, but accepted Lord Selborne, Salisbury's nephew by marriage, instead. She would have liked George Wyndham to be given the War Office, but it went to St John Brodrick. With a new man installed at the Home Office, the Queen considered the changes 'almost amount to a new Cabinet', but others felt the government remained stale. Lord George Hamilton was alarmed by what struck him as the 'steady decline in power and grip of the PM', while the fact that so many members of Salisbury's family occupied high office led some to dub the government 'Hotel Cecil'.[136]

Nineteen hundred was a bad year for the Queen in other ways than the war. In July Prince Alfred, Duke of Coburg, died, having himself lost his only son the previous January. 'One sorrow, one trial, one anxiety following on another,' Victoria lamented. 'It is a horrible year. Nothing but sadness & horrors of one kind & another.' Her daughter Vicky was enduring 'tortures of pain' from what had originally been thought to be lumbago but was now recognised as cancer. The constant losses of the Boer War had also debilitated and distressed the Queen and on 29 October came the 'too dreadful & heart-breaking' news that her grandson, 'Christle' of Schleswig-Holstein, son of her third daughter Helena, had died of typhoid while serving on Lord Roberts's staff in South Africa.[137]

Victoria's own health had been in decline for much of the year. She was troubled by sleeplessness and back pain, and also lost her appetite. If anything, this had been rather too hearty for her own good, but when Lord James stayed at Balmoral in October 1900, he was shocked by the change in her. 'The Queen had lost much flesh and had shrunk so as to appear about one half of the person she had been.' She ascribed it to her recent visit to Ireland, telling James, 'I am afraid it was too much for me.' Salisbury later blamed something else, declaring: 'The war killed her, but she never flinched.' Following restless nights she often became drowsy during the day, and by December her 'repulsion for food' had become pronounced. She was reduced to eating 'very soothing and nourishing' Benger's Food for children and invalids, although she was sometimes able to swallow 'a little milk and whisky several times a day'. On 1 January 1901 her diary read pathetically: 'Another year begun. I am feeling so weak & unwell that I enter upon it sadly.'[138]

Despite her failing health, she did not slacken. On 15 December she had presented medals to officers and men who had served in South Africa, and the next day she saw Salisbury at Windsor. It was to be their last meeting, 'but I did not feel up to a very lengthened conversation'. On 18 December, a day marked by 'very unsatisfactory news from South Africa, the Boers being terribly active all over the country', she went to Osborne. Three days after Christmas, 'I did some signing, though I could hardly see a word I wrote. I felt very low and sad which distressed my children very much.' Despite this, on New Year's Day 1901, she visited a convalescent home for soldiers on the Isle of Wight.[139]

She remained alert enough to order Arthur Bigge to write to Salisbury urging that even once the war had finished, no official enquiry should take place. Salisbury replied on 4 January that he was irrevocably committed by pledges in Parliament, but believed proceedings could steer 'clear of any really scandalous investigation'. This duly happened. Once the war was over, the enquiry that was held proved toothless.[140]

On 10 January the Queen had what would be her last political engagement when she saw Joseph Chamberlain at Osborne for twenty minutes. He later recalled, 'She was thinner and there was a certain look of delicacy about her,' but 'not the slightest sign of failing intelligence ... [She] spoke about the war, regretting its prolongation and the loss of life but said earnestly "I am not anxious about the result."' On 13 January 1901 her last diary entry recorded: 'Did some signing.'[141]

By 18 January Dr Reid believed her to be failing. He telegraphed the kaiser to alert him, despite knowing that the Queen's children would not welcome his presence. Sure enough the whole family were appalled to hear William was on his way, and vainly sent telegrams to deter him. The kaiser told the British ambassador to Germany that he had expected his relatives to 'kick up a row', but they need not worry as he wished '*no notice* whatever is to be taken of me in my capacity as Emperor'. Instead, 'I come as a grandson' who simply wished to pay duty to 'this unparalleled Grandmama'.[142]

An official bulletin issued on 19 January was the public's first intimation there was cause for concern. It stated that during the past year, the Queen had been under 'great strain ... which has rather told upon her Majesty's nervous system'. Her physicians had therefore advised she 'should be kept perfectly quiet ... and should abstain for the present from transacting business'. Dr Reid's diary shows he genuinely believed overwork had undermined her health, which had suffered from 'periods of insomnia and mental confusion brought on by damaged cerebral circulation after years of constant brain work'. When paying tribute to his late sovereign in the Commons, Balfour too emphasised how diligently she had toiled on official business. Even the few days of respite she had had at the end illustrated 'the life of continuous labour which her position as Queen threw upon her. Short as was the interval between the last trembling signature affixed to a public document and the final and perfect rest,' an astonishing quantity of papers awaiting her attention had accumulated.[143]

On the afternoon of 19 January Victoria slightly rallied and 'became clearer in intellect'. She told Reid, '"There is much better news from South Africa today" evidently referring to some telegram which the princesses had mentioned to her and showing how even then she had got the war on her mind.'[144] However, the remission was only temporary.

On 20 January the Prince of Wales hurried to London, hoping to intercept the kaiser and detain him in town by saying even he had not been allowed to see his bedridden mother for fear of agitating her. Later that day there was a change of heart after it became apparent her state was worsening. Bertie was summoned urgently back to Osborne and told to bring the kaiser with him. On 21 January Bertie arrived with his nephew and the Duke of York, and the entire family clustered around the dying woman's bedside. Feeling it wrong that William's presence had been concealed from her, Dr Reid waited for an opportunity to take the kaiser into her room, and for a few minutes left the pair alone together. Afterwards Victoria murmured to her physician, 'The Emperor is very kind.'[145]

In general the kaiser behaved with uncharacteristic tact during these days. The Prince of Wales told Vicky – who, much to her distress, was too ill to come to England herself – 'William was kindness itself and touching in his devotion, without a shade of brusquerie and selfishness.' Towards the end, as the family stood weeping, William knelt down on one side of her bed to support her, while Dr Reid propped her up from the other side.[146]

At 4 p.m. on 22 January a bulletin announced: 'The Queen is sinking.' The end came at 6.30 that evening. In Germany Vicky exclaimed, 'Oh my beloved Mama! Is she *really gone* ... to have lost her seems *so* impossible – and I far away ... It *breaks* my heart. What a Queen she was and what a woman!' The kaiser promptly announced he would stay in England until after the funeral. By doing so, he earned himself huge popularity, although his appalled wife did her best to lure him home.[147]

From Osborne, Victoria's body was taken by boat and train to London. It was then transferred across the capital to Paddington station, through streets lined with an estimated million people, before the final leg of her journey to Windsor. There, on 2 February 1901, her funeral was held in St George's Chapel. 'The ceremony was very grand and impressive … St George's was a wonderful sight with all the foreign kings and princes,' Earl Spencer reported to Lord Kimberley, who had not been well enough to attend.[148] Salisbury and Rosebery were among the mourners, but her eight other prime ministers had all predeceased her. Bertie, the new King Edward VII, rode by the gun carriage that bore her coffin, as did the kaiser, and the kings of Greece and Portugal. King Leopold II of the Belgians followed in a carriage.

When Lord Salisbury had made a statement in the House of Lords following the Queen's death, he said it was 'by far the saddest duty that has ever befallen me', and at the funeral he cut a sombre figure. In recent weeks his own failing energy had been remarked upon, and his appearance that day did nothing to dispel the impression he was fading. The chapel was so icy that 'anyone who … was liable to cold would have run a tremendous risk', and for Salisbury, with his bad chest and abhorrence of draughts, the ordeal would have been considerable. As well as an overcoat, he was sporting a skull cap, which would surely have shocked the Queen, for she had been disconcerted enough when she had seen him wearing one on holiday in the south of France. Perhaps however, with her own predilection for the occasional nip of spirits (staying at Balmoral in 1864, Gladstone had been dismayed that 'she drinks her claret strengthened, I should have thought spoiled, with whisky'), she would not have minded that at one point he 'took a pull at a flask'.[149]

Salisbury would remain as prime minister until July 1902. Six weeks earlier, peace had been signed with the Boers. Britain could claim victory, despite not having held out for unconditional surrender. With that accomplished Salisbury felt he could legitimately hand over the premiership to Arthur Balfour. Salisbury had just over a year in retirement before his own death in August 1903. When he had given up the leadership he had assured one friend he did not mind at all, 'especially as since the death of the last Queen, politics have lost their zest for me'.[150]

15

Conclusion

In 1878 Victoria had lamented to Vicky, 'It is a miserable thing to be a constitutional Queen and to be unable to do what is right.' Two years later she still felt, 'The life of a constitutional monarch is a hard and trying one.' In reality, although her *Times* obituary described her as 'steeped in the spirit of the constitution', abiding by its constraints sometimes proved beyond her.[1]

If accused of any transgressions, Victoria could have cited in her defence the words of several of her prime ministers. In a speech given in Buckinghamshire in 1871 Disraeli had stated, 'There never was a more constitutional monarch than our present Queen,' while in 1864 Lord Derby had assured her, 'Those who have had the honour of being admitted to your Majesty's confidence well know how fully your Majesty understands and appreciates the duty of a constitutional sovereign.' After her death Lord Salisbury informed the House of Lords: 'She showed a wonderful power of on the one hand observing with the most absolute strictness the limits to her action which the constitution draws and on the other maintaining a steady and persistent influence on the action of her ministers.' Perhaps most surprising of all, in 1887, at a Golden Jubilee garden party at his country home, Gladstone told those present that 'all the principles of the constitution have been observed by the Queen … in a manner more perfect than has ever been known in the time of any former sovereign.' Victoria, he said, had come 'fully to understand … the great and noble conditions on which a free people can be governed', and had shown 'her thorough comprehension … of the great covenant between the throne and her people'. This was extraordinarily generous, for by that time Gladstone had good cause to know the Queen scarcely merited these plaudits.[2]

By the later part of her reign Victoria could hardly claim to be an impartial monarch who stood above party struggles. She might see herself as a quintessential moderate ('liberal … she has ever been, but never radical or democratic', she insisted in 1880) but as she aged, she became a passionate Conservative. Far from giving Liberal ministries the 'unswerving support' for which Disraeli praised her, she intermittently maintained improper links with the opposition. It is true that, as Lord Salisbury observed, 'She was able to accept some things of which, perhaps, she did not entirely approve, but which she thought it her duty in her position to accept'.[3] However, it is unlikely she would have acted correctly had she been required to assent to measures to which she viscerally objected, such as Home Rule or a major reform of the House of Lords.

In an age where fellow monarchs such as the tsar and German kaiser were autocrats, Victoria's authority was relatively limited. Lord Palmerston once went so far as to declare: 'The Sovereign ... has of real power little or none' – while in 1893 Gladstone's private secretary Algernon West asserted 'the Queen reigns; her ministers govern'. Gladstone himself, in an 1875 review of Theodore Martin's authorised biography of Prince Albert, wrote that recent years had seen 'nothing less than a transformation' in the business of kingship, entailing 'a beneficial substitution of influence for power'.[4]

None of this is to deny that Britain's unwritten constitution conferred immense theoretical powers on the sovereign. In his book *The English Constitution*, published in 1867, Walter Bagehot listed some of the most extraordinary examples, pointing out that monarchical prerogative hypothetically entitled Victoria to disband the army and navy without consulting Parliament, make peace by giving away Cornwall, declare a war with the aim of conquering Brittany, pardon all convicted offenders, and dismiss almost the entire civil service.[5] In fact, everyone concerned, including Victoria, was well aware that exercising these notional rights would result in catastrophe, and she never for a second contemplated doing so. Precisely because she never tested the system beyond its limits, it was deemed unnecessary to modify it. As a result, today the monarch still possesses many of the powers that even in Victoria's time appeared anomalous, although now, as then, in reality they are meaningless. Perhaps the most significant change that occurred in the twentieth century related to the sovereign's role in appointing prime ministers. Victoria performed this duty multiple times, and though even she was far from having complete freedom of choice, her ability to decide who she would have as her First Lord of the Treasury was particularly significant in those cases when a prime minister resigned or retired without calling an election. Victoria's actions in such instances sometimes provoked controversy, so it is perhaps not surprising that one of the few occasions when her great-great-granddaughter, Elizabeth II, incurred censure was in 1963 when she became involved in selecting a successor to her Conservative prime minister Harold Macmillan. After Macmillan announced his resignation on grounds of ill health, she took his advice to appoint in his stead Sir Alec Douglas-Home, rather than Rab Butler, the man widely expected to be named. This led to complaints that she had acted unconstitutionally, but the same situation could not arise today. After a period when party leaders were elected by their own MPs, all the leading British political parties allowed their entire membership to vote in leadership elections. This still gives rise to claims that it is not a truly democratic arrangement, and the results recently delivered by the process might lead some to think the old system would be preferable.

Although in the nineteenth century Walter Bagehot highlighted the fact that a literal interpretation of the royal prerogative endowed the sovereign with significant powers, he was clear that the true situation was very different. In *The English Constitution* Bagehot not only alleged that 'a republic has insinuated itself beneath the folds of a monarchy', but memorably stated that the Crown had only three rights: 'the right to be consulted, the right to encourage, the right to warn'. However, it is perhaps worth pointing out that Queen Victoria herself would have disputed his interpretation, and anyway disapproved of Bagehot. When she learnt the Duke of York was reading his economic essays, she expressed alarm at her grandson's imbibing ideas from such a 'radical' writer.[6]

It is true that is impossible to pinpoint a single political event in Victoria's reign where she dictated the outcome. While she clearly had some bearing on (for example) the Italian crisis of 1859–60, the Schleswig-Holstein crisis of 1863–4, the Public Worship Act of 1874, the Reform Act of 1884 and the sending of reinforcements to Egypt in 1893, one cannot state with confidence that things would have turned out differently had it not been for her. By the same token, she cannot be accused of causing demonstrable harm to her country at any point. If it is fortunate that her demands for war with Russia in 1877–8 were ignored, sadly her attempts at other times to promote peace within Europe proved equally futile. On the outbreak of the First World War her grandson Kaiser William said: 'If my grandmother had been alive she would never have allowed it,'[7] but in all probability she would have been as powerless to prevent the conflict as she had been to stop the Austro-Prussian War.

None of this detracts from the fact that Victoria was extraordinarily politically active, and her political presence was considerable. Her ministers always had to take her wishes into account, even if they overrode them, and dealings with her occupied a significant proportion of her prime ministers' time. The fact that she acted out of the public eye meant there was little awareness of how much she exerted herself, but in conversation with Edward Hamilton in 1898, the Tory politician Sir Michael Hicks-Beach talked of 'the much greater influence she has on the course of political affairs than is generally supposed'.[8]

A few years later Lord Salisbury remarked in the House of Lords: 'When I was young it was the fashion to treat the sovereignty of the Queen as nominal, and the share which she took in public business as unreal. I hear less of that language now.' This was met with approving 'Hear hears', but ignorance about the extent of her political activities in many ways was helpful to Victoria. Because her role was underestimated, few people construed it as a threat. During his radical phase Joseph Chamberlain said he and fellow left-wingers would never espouse republicanism while the monarchy remained 'ornamental and consultative'. Another firebrand, Henry Labouchere, wrote in 1884 that even radicals like him would 'admit … that the scheme of a monarch who reigns but does not rule has its advantages'. Eight years later, when Victoria frustrated his hopes of high office, he discovered she was not as harmless as he had thought.[9]

Although Gladstone came to decry the Queen's abilities, in general her influence was exercised wisely. Disraeli's baroque panegyrics, hailing her sagacity and discernment, may have been overblown, but were not devoid of truth. She did not have a subtle intellect, and it is undeniable that emotion, prejudice, preconceptions and family feeling guided Victoria for much of the time; her analytical powers, however – enriched by accumulated experience and an excellent memory – remained considerable. At her death Lord Salisbury's assessment of her political skills was carefully considered yet heartfelt. 'She always maintained and practised a rigorous supervision over public affairs, giving to Ministers the benefit of her advice and warning them of danger if she saw there was danger ahead,' he declared. 'And she certainly impressed many of us with a profound sense of the penetration, almost intuition, with which she saw the perils … No Minister in her long reign ever disregarded her advice … without afterwards feeling that he had incurred a dangerous responsibility.'[10]

Speaking for the Liberals on the same occasion, Lord Kimberley described how she was so 'profoundly acquainted with all … affairs', she was often more knowledgeable than ministers with whom she discussed them. 'The more you transacted business with her, the more you were astonished at the depth of her knowledge and the acuteness of her judgement,' he assured his fellow peers. He recalled the late foreign secretary Lord Clarendon saying, when faced with a thorny problem, 'Well, let us have the Queen's opinion. The Queen's opinion is always worth hearing even if you do not agree with it.'[11]

In old age Victoria frankly acknowledged to a lady-in-waiting that 'as to likes and dislikes of Premiers … she had them *very* strongly'.[12] It was hardly surprising that someone so prone to powerful emotion rarely felt neutral towards leading politicians with whom she interacted: as far as she was concerned, the political always had a personal dimension, and indifference did not come naturally to her. Of her ten prime ministers, Disraeli ultimately emerged as her favourite, displacing the earlier contenders, Melbourne and Peel. Peel and Disraeli both started at an immense disadvantage but managed to overcome this and gain her confidence and affection. Gladstone underwent a contrary arc in the course of seven decades of service that included a still unequalled four terms as Britain's prime minister. Having begun by much admiring him and even enjoying his company, it was only after thirty years of being on the throne that Victoria came to abhor him.

The Queen's views might have been particularly pronounced, but she certainly was not alone in judging the characters of her premiers on a personal level. As the reign progressed, the affection or aversion these prominent figures inspired in their countrymen became more marked, with politics sometimes assuming a gladiatorial aspect as party leaders fought out rivalries with their principal opponents. Patrician detachment from 'the mob' was no longer an option, for politicians now had to contend with being viewed almost as public property. By no means all of Victoria's ten premiers possessed the qualities needed to propel themselves to the forefront of national consciousness, still less to embed themselves there permanently. Lords Russell, Aberdeen and Rosebery no longer command widespread recognition, while Angus Hawkins's recent magisterial biography of the 14th Earl of Derby is entitled *The Forgotten Prime Minister*. Nevertheless, several of those who climbed to the greasy pole's summit in Victoria's day not only became celebrated as political giants in their own lifetime but have names that still resonate today.

Whereas until the mid-nineteenth-century portrait engravings or caricatures provided the only available images of public figures, the advent of photography ensured they ceased to be faceless men in frock coats. With the press popularising issues and employing skilled parliamentary sketch-writers, the principal protagonists in the British political landscape became more readily identifiable, sporting distinctive characteristics and opinions that could be either cherished or deplored. Cultivating a following was no longer taboo, and those who had the knack of engaging with the masses found themselves at an advantage. The prevalence of nicknames – such as 'Pam' for Palmerston, 'Dizzy', 'the GOM', or more notably still, 'the People's William' – indicates the greater sense of familiarity politicians inspired in Victorian Britons.

Prior to Victoria's accession, a politician who indulged in 'speechifying' tours might find themselves condemned for demagoguery and rabble-rousing, but this no longer applied. It was no longer sufficient to operate primarily within the Westminster arena, for as greater ease of travel opened up previously remote areas, politicians had to make themselves accessible by connecting with a wider audience. By the end of the nineteenth century addressing public meetings, either to draw attention to particular issues or to whip up more generalised support, had become an integral part of a politician's repertoire. Palmerston was a pioneer in this respect, priding himself on communication skills that enabled him to present himself – somewhat speciously – as a man of the people. In his late seventies he was exhilarated by the adulation accorded him during a northern and Scottish progress. Returning south, he wrote complacently: 'My ears are still ringing with and almost deafened with cheers.'[13]

It was of course Gladstone who took things far beyond this, utilising his oratorical genius and gift for showmanship to place himself squarely in the public eye. This accounted for his being both idolised and reviled, ensuring that even when out of office he remained impossible to ignore. However bizarre it may seem to associate the term with someone so high-minded and fundamentally serious, the genesis of populism dates back to him. At the height of his fame, enterprising manufacturers did a brisk trade selling small-scale busts and statuettes of the great man to hero-worshippers; his detractors, conversely, could vent their hatred by buying chamber pots with his features imprinted on the inside.

Less outgoing contemporaries who lacked Gladstone's star quality were compelled, in spite of themselves, to try and emulate him by regular appearances, even if they could never attain the same mastery over crowds. Ruefully aware that 'power is more and more leaving Parliament and going to the platform', Salisbury lamented to the Queen that this 'odious addition to the burdens of political life' was 'an aggravation of the labours of your Majesty's servants which we owe entirely to Mr Gladstone'.[14]

The criteria by which Queen Victoria's prime ministers would have expected to be judged was how much they accomplished while at the head of government. Of those ten men, Palmerston and Salisbury pulled off the rare feat of not conforming to the adage that every political career ends in failure. All of them, however, not excluding Rosebery, whose tenure was so brief and unhappy, could take pride in their record. Far from being diminished by having split their parties, perhaps Peel and Gladstone can be singled out as possessing genuine claims to greatness. Palmerston, Disraeli and Salisbury may be denied this accolade, but the three of them were still touched with political genius. The inability of the rest to make such an impact on their times can be variously ascribed to a weak position in Parliament, controversial policies, unhelpful colleagues, or simply a lack of flair; even so they achieved much, both in respect of their legislative tally and upholding of British interests worldwide. The reign of Queen Victoria can indeed be said to represent the high-water mark of the way politics was conducted in Britain, with the executive being headed by a succession of extraordinarily distinguished statesmen, notable alike for their vision, ability and public spiritedness.

Speaking in the Commons three days after the Queen's death, Arthur Balfour said Victoria was intimately associated 'with the growth, moral and material, of the Empire over which she ruled'.[15] To many today, this would seem a grotesque assertion, for the British Empire is commonly depicted as a rapacious, racist and murderous entity. Viewed in this light, far from growing in moral stature, as the Empire enlarged during Victoria's reign, so too did the scale of its iniquity.

It has been argued, contrary to boasts at the time, that the Empire failed to bring stability, prosperity and the rule of law to those it subjugated: it constituted a 'drain' on the resources of countries such as India and failed to increase the material wellbeing of its inhabitants. While even these days, not all of these claims are universally accepted, they certainly were shared by few persons of influence in Victoria's time. Ironically, any lack of enthusiasm towards the Empire on the part of

British politicians in the first half of the reign usually derived from fears it was too costly, rather than guilt at its exploitative nature.

As Gladstone remarked in 1879, Britain's was an 'Empire the origin of which in many cases ill bear examination'. Some of its growth during Victoria's reign was equally questionable. Citing the examples of Oudh and the Punjab, Victoria insisted, 'our keeping these countries in India & elsewhere is ... because the *native* sovereigns *cannot* maintain *their authority*'.[16] Not everyone of course shared her confidence that the inhabitants benefited from Britain taking control. In Africa alleged slave-trading and the practice of human sacrifice were used to justify land seizures without the evidence being too carefully scrutinised. Resistance to British rule could be met with disproportionately ferocious punishment, with retribution often falling particularly heavily on those who had never given any trouble.

In 1887 the Queen's bugbear Henry Labouchere stated: 'We are without exception the greatest robbers and marauders that ever existed on the face of the globe; we are hypocrites also, for we plunder and always pretend to do so for other people's good.' Victoria herself could not claim that her interest in empire was entirely altruistic for she relished the personal gains that accrued to her from it. She delighted in the acquisition of her 'big diamond', the Koh-i-Noor, perhaps reflecting that its former Sikh owners had themselves obtained possession through conquest. When the Chinese emperor's summer palace had been destroyed in 1860 by an Anglo-French force sent to avenge the agonising deaths in captivity of seized European envoys, the Queen took a share of the plunder; her haul included a jade and gold sceptre, three huge, enamelled bowls and a Pekinese dog she gleefully christened 'Lootie'. In 1886, following the deposition of the Burmese King, she wrote to the Viceroy of India, Lord Dufferin, hoping he would not think her 'greedy' if she enquired whether Thibaw's palace had contained any jewellery. As a result, the fallen monarch's crown was despatched to her.[17]

The Queen's belief that the British Empire was a force for good was not remotely cynical. Disraeli's 1878 claim that 'our Empire is an Empire of liberty, of truth and of justice' would have been heartily endorsed by her. Gladstone's rebuttal – that what the phrase really meant was 'Liberty for ourselves, Empire over the rest of mankind' – in no way shook her convictions.[18]

In an 1876 speech at the Guildhall, Disraeli contended that the Empire 'exists as much on sympathy as on force', which even some apologists for imperialism found dubious. Joseph Chamberlain meanwhile asserted: 'You cannot make omelettes without breaking eggs; you cannot destroy the practices of barbarism, of slavery or superstition ... without the rule of force.' In his view, the results achieved vindicated these methods. 'Our rule over these territories can only be justified if we can show that it adds to the happiness and prosperity of the people; and I maintain our rule does, and has, brought security and peace and comparative prosperity to countries that never knew their blessings before.' In doing this, he continued: 'We are fulfilling what I believe to be our national mission.'[19] This was a philosophy with which Victoria wholeheartedly agreed.

Gladstone himself was far from wholly condemnatory of the Empire, writing in a learned periodical in August 1877 that England 'had no interest in India except the well-being of India itself'. This provoked some controversy at the time, but there was no denying that within India there was great deal of affection for the Queen. Her proclamation issued after the Sepoy Mutiny of 1857–8 had made a strong impression on the populace, and the fact that its precepts had been imperfectly implemented was blamed not on her, but on administrators and officials failing to carry out her wishes. Receiving Lord Ripon on his return from India as viceroy in 1885, Victoria was assured of 'the extraordinary loyalty to me personally' that prevailed there. Following a visit to India in 1884 the anti-imperialist Wilfrid Scawen Blunt commented that despite the fact the Indian population 'grow yearly more and more estranged from their Anglo-Indian masters, they yearly look with more and more hope ... to her who sits upon the English throne'.[20]

While convinced that her Empire's rule was just and benign, even Victoria conceded there were times when it failed to live up to its own ideals. She was sharply reminded of this by Vicky in 1873 after rashly condemning the way Prussia had seized land and property following the wars of German unification. Her daughter retorted that her adopted countrymen had as much right for their actions 'as you to wear the Koh-i-Noor', adding that if 'England's Empire over the East is the best example' of right of conquest well exercised, 'even *there* Englishmen have NOT always shown themselves as scrupulous, humane, civilised and enlightened as they *should* have done'.[21]

Vicky expected her mother would object 'Orientals are *not* Europeans & cannot be treated in the same manner!' but Victoria would not have advanced that argument. In August 1867 she instructed her secretary to convey her relief that a 'barbarous' proposal to burn Burmese villages in reprisal for the massacre of a ship's company had been abandoned. She desired, it was explained, a more humane approach in outlying parts of the globe, to replace 'a system, too often, she fears, adopted in the East, of imitating the barbarities of a half-savage people, rather than setting them the example of a policy founded on Christian principle. Her Majesty feels very strongly on this subject. It is not the first time the Queen has lamented this tendency on the part of Englishmen in the East.'[22]

The Queen had similar 'protective' instincts towards her subjects in Africa. After John Colenso, Bishop of Natal, came over to England in 1873 to fight the cause of Langalibalele, a Bantu chieftain wrongly convicted of rebellion and imprisoned on Robben Island, Victoria expressed warm approval. Having written to Colonial Secretary Lord Carnarvon applauding Colenso's 'noble disinterested conduct in favour of the natives who were so unjustly used', she proclaimed 'her very strong feeling (and she has few stronger) that the natives and coloured races should be treated with every kindness and affection, as brothers, not – as alas! Englishmen too often do – as totally different beings to ourselves, fit only to be crushed and shot down'.[23] Six years later these sentiments did not prevent her upholding Sir Bartle Frere's decision to go to war with the Zulus, which Colenso utterly deplored.

When excesses were committed by her representatives in the colonies the Queen might regret this, but she did not favour stern punishment for the culprits. In 1864 Governor Edward Eyre put down the Morant Bay Rebellion in Jamaica with exceptional severity. His troops killed, flogged and raped hundreds, and Eyre himself illegally executed under martial law a leading figure in the Black community, despite lacking proof of criminality. The Queen was disturbed by Eyre's accounts of these events, which showed no awareness of being in any way remiss. She agreed there should be a commission of enquiry. As a result of its findings, Eyre was dismissed. He then came home, only to face private prosecutions brought by a libertarian pressure group, including one indicting him as an accessory to murder. Much to Victoria's relief, all these cases failed. She was not alone in feeling sorry for Eyre, as among supporters who raised money for his defence were Charles Dickens, Alfred Tennyson and Thomas Carlyle. Once Eyre had managed to retire to Devon, she wrote to Gladstone in August 1869: 'whatever faults Governor Eyre had & committed, he was very much ill-used also'.[24]

However sympathetic she felt to native peoples who suffered at the hands of colonisers, it was not always possible for her to right wrongs. During her reign, white settler colonies such as 'New Zealand' were granted a substantial measure of self-government, lessening the 'mother country's' ability to control what happened there. In 1840 the Treaty of Waitangi had been signed by 180 Māori chiefs, who surrendered their rights of sovereignty in return for guaranteed possession of their lands. Twenty years later, there was a Māori rebellion, and this was used as an excuse by colonisers to deprive of their holdings many who had not risen up. In July 1863 the Queen received at Osborne thirteen 'much tattooed' Māori chiefs with 'fine eyes and beautiful glossy black hair but not good features'. They were, she described, 'Carrying spears and hatchets and [had] feathers stuck in their hair … they all kissed my hand and behaved extremely well.' Through an interpreter Victoria expressed her 'interest in their welfare, sorrow at the war having broken out', and listened attentively when one assured her 'they had nothing to do with the war'. She related how, 'Another spoke of their lands being taken away and hoped I would promise this should not be done, which I said I would'. After the interview she pronounced her visitors 'very intelligent.' Though subsequently there was restitution of some Māori lands, the war continued for years and new land seizures went on apace.[25]

At times indeed, the Queen appeared to empathise better with those she ruled over in distant continents than with her Irish subjects. Admittedly when she went to Ireland her views invariably softened – writing from Dublin during her 1853 visit: 'The Irish are most amusing – so lively and excitable'. Unfortunately the goodwill generated proved transient, and usually her judgements were much harsher. In 1865 she described the Irish as 'most troublesome and deluded'; a few years later she decided they were 'unreliable & cringing'. To Sir Stafford Northcote she declared in 1867: 'These Irish are really shocking abominable people – not like any other civilised nation.' Small wonder, perhaps, that in 1884 a member of Gladstone's Cabinet did not doubt: 'She hates Ireland and everything to do with it.'[26]

The parlous state of Ireland throughout Victoria's reign was seen as a blight on Britain's international reputation. The Queen did not think outsiders were entitled to criticise, or – still less – take action. In 1898 she was appalled when the United States intervened in Cuba's favour during the Cuban fight for independence from Spain, for, as she explained to Vicky, this constituted a very bad precedent. 'No doubt Cuba was dreadfully governed,' she conceded, 'but that does not excuse America, and the principle is dreadful. They might as well say we governed Ireland badly and they ought to take possession of it and free it.'[27]

However unsatisfactory and troubling the condition of Ireland, the Queen could never countenance any form of Home Rule. Her opposition was not the reason Home Rule foundered – for what doomed it was combined Tory and Liberal Unionist repudiation of the policy, coupled with lack of support within mainland Britain. Undeniably, however, Victoria exerted herself to the utmost to bring about its rejection. In her defence it can be said that Gladstone had believed previous measures introduced by him, such as the 1870 and 1881 Land Acts, would solve Ireland's problems, and his failures in that respect partly explain why in 1886 and 1893 the Queen did not accept that he held the answer to the Irish question. Both of Gladstone's Home Rule Bills contained flaws, and had they passed, provisions such as the financial clauses would surely have created difficulties in future. Furthermore, it is debatable whether Ulster Protestants would have peaceably accepted the new arrangements. What is certain, is by the time the matter was next addressed, more than twenty years later, opinion within Ireland had polarised so disastrously that in 1921 partition of the island became unavoidable. In an implicit rebuke of his late grandmother, King George V remarked in 1930 to Prime Minister Ramsay Macdonald: 'What fools we were not to have accepted Gladstone's Home Rule Bill. The Empire now would not have had the Irish Free State giving us so much trouble and pulling us to pieces.'[28]

Claiming to find politics distasteful, in 1896 Victoria told her lady-in-waiting Marie Mallet she did 'not consider them a woman's province'. Not only was she resolutely opposed to female suffrage, but she had 'the strongest aversion for the *so-called* & *most erroneous* "*Rights of Women*"' – a 'mad & utterly demoralising movement' she stigmatised as 'dangerous & unchristian & unnatural'. Obviously this accorded ill with her status as a female ruler, a contradiction she fully recognised. 'The Queen is a woman herself,' she wrote to Gladstone is 1870, '– & knows what an anomaly her *own* position is – but that can be reconciled with reason & propriety, though it is a terribly difficult & trying one.'[29]

Much as she might regret it, the very fact of her being head of state inevitably strengthened the case for affording political rights to women.

In 1839 one Lancashire Chartist put it simply: 'If a woman can rule, surely women could and should have the vote.' Claiming that Victoria's reign would be regarded as the age of women's emancipation, W. T. Stead, editor of the *Pall Mall Gazette*, asserted in 1887 that the Queen had contributed to the phenomenon by accustoming 'the nation to the spectacle of a woman whose discharge of the highest political functions never impaired her womanliness'. The same year, the feminist *Englishwoman's Review* said that while those demanding female suffrage 'have never yet received any direct encouragement from her Majesty', by performing her role with exemplary fidelity, 'She has illustrated once for all the absurdity of the statement that political duties are incompatible with the tenderer sympathies of a woman's life.'[30]

Particularly in the decade after Albert's death, Victoria was vocal in bemoaning the exhausting demands her position placed upon her. In 1864 she lamented to Palmerston: 'From morning till late at night she slaves & works without one day's relaxation & with constant agitation & anxiety.' By 1867 she was predicting the complete breakdown of her nervous system, 'working and drudging as she does from *morning* till night and weighed down by the responsibility and cares of her most unenviable position'.[31]

In a speech at the Hughenden harvest festival in September 1871, Disraeli described her labours as 'multifarious … weighty and … unceasing', assuring listeners: 'I will venture to say that no head of any department in the state performs more laborious duties.' Others disputed whether she truly toiled so heroically. When a Scots clergyman wrote to Sir Henry Ponsonby saying he knew how hard the Queen worked, the private secretary forwarded it to his wife with added exclamation marks.[32]

Even if in comparison with her ministers the Queen did not devote a stupendous amount of time to work, it would be wrong to minimise what she did. Although she was clearly selective about which despatches from the Foreign and Colonial Offices she read – and often these were summarised for her by her secretaries – the volume of telegraphs and other communications that came in daily to wherever she was residing was always substantial, and sometimes massive. Answers to these required careful consideration; the drafting of memoranda and meetings with ministers, likewise, demanded significant attention. Signing documents personally may not have been intellectually taxing, but it was time-consuming. A notable chore was the daily writing of her journal, which provides an invaluable political record, as well as a chronicle of her daily life. After Victoria's death, her daughter Princess Beatrice copied it out, excising anything she considered unfit for posterity. She then destroyed the originals, yet even in her shortened version, the journals of Queen Victoria in the Royal Archives at Windsor run to 111 bound volumes.

It has recently been estimated that Queen Victoria wrote an average of 2,500 words every day of her adult life, amounting during her reign to perhaps 60 million words. The quantities of holograph letters which survive in her distinctive – and sometimes hard to read – script, full of idiosyncratic emphases and underlinings in improbable places – are testimony to her extraordinary productivity. In the spring of 1899 her last Viceroy of India, Lord Curzon, applauded this application to duty when he wrote thanking her, 'who has so many preoccupations as well as so vast a correspondence', for writing so regularly to him in her own hand. It was, he declared, 'an example of what should be done and can be done in the highest places that is probably very rare, if not unique, in history'.[33]

In her widowhood, Victoria verged at times on being an absentee monarch. She very rarely spent a night in London, and even journeys to Windsor, some thirty miles from Westminster, were a nuisance for busy ministers. In 1855 Foreign Secretary Lord Clarendon informed his wife his return trip to Windsor '*only* cost five hours out of my day!'; eleven years later Lord Stanley grumpily recorded that going there and back for his audience with the Queen 'wasted nearly all my available time'.[34]

Osborne, involving train and boat rides, entailed more of a trek. In 1866 General Grey pointed out to Victoria that 'Even ... with special trains, special boats and everything prearranged, from eight to nine hours' was taken up by the two-way journey. Fog and bad weather could be real hazards: Palmerston once endured such a rough crossing that he insisted on taking the helm of the boat carrying him across the sea. In January 1866 a gale was blowing so hard that the Queen tried to warn Lord Clarendon not to come but was unable to reach him because the telegraph was not working. During a change of government twenty years later Sir Henry Ponsonby laconically reported: "the Solent is covered with steamers carrying Ministers hither ... So our Navy is well employed.'[35]

Worst of all from the point of view of accessibility was Balmoral. The Queen's habit of sequestering herself in the Scottish Highlands prompted Walter Bagehot to publish a severe *Economist* article in August 1870, castigating her for forcing her ministers 'to waste precious hours and still more precious strength in railway journeys which would exhaust the young'. He admonished: 'The interruption to business is extreme, the hardship to individuals excessive.'[36]

If travelling to Balmoral was arduous, stays there were by no means always an ordeal for the minister in residence. While Lord Salisbury 'did not attempt to conceal his disgust with the place', Gladstone declared he found visits to Balmoral the 'pleasantest part of my court existence'. Like many others, Lord Clarendon complained of being frozen there, even in August, but on his departure in 1856 he declared the place 'a sort of paradise'.[37]

Many ministers welcomed an opportunity to become better acquainted with the Queen, and – sometimes to their surprise – found her stimulating company. Although dinners could be gloomy if Victoria was in a sombre mood, at other times the atmosphere was quite convivial. Staying there in 1870, the young Lord Rosebery reported, 'the conversation during dinner was sustained and almost gay'. In October 1893 Sir Henry Campbell-Bannerman was so successful at entertaining the Queen that she sat 'with her face puckered up and laughing'. Arriving in some trepidation in November 1879, Beaconsfield's President of the Board of Trade, Lord Sandon, ended by relishing the experience. Although he found one dinner next to the Queen 'rather shy work', other evenings proved much jollier. At one point Victoria 'went into shouts of laughter, as did everyone else at table'. Most guests were discouraged from discussing current affairs (in 1878 Sir Henry Ponsonby reported that Princess Alice had caused awkwardness during dinner by 'now and then touching on political matters, which made the Queen cough') but with the minister in residence, Victoria ranged freely over a wide variety of topics, on which she was frequently interesting and outspoken. Sandon thought her a lively conversationalist, as well as being fascinated by her 'expressive countenance, showing every moment the changes of thought, grave or gay, and of pleasure or annoyance or indignation'. On leaving he offered up a private prayer: 'Let me be grateful, most grateful, to God for giving me so much pleasure.'[38]

In January 1864 the Queen had wailed to Vicky, 'Oh! Would to God I had not to be plagued with politics. It is so ungrateful a task.' Almost thirty years later she confided to Marie Mallet, she had 'always disliked politics … but that the Prince Consort forced her to take an interest in them, often to her disgust, & that since he died she has tried to keep up the interest for his sake'. Neither statement should be taken too literally. Victoria was expert in avoiding what she did not want to do, and the idea that her interventions in politics, too numerous for many of her ministers' liking, were all performed against her will, is ludicrous. Acting out of a sense of duty, and holding strong convictions, she profoundly believed in her ability to uphold her people's interests while ensuring the rights of the Crown were not diminished. She saw this as her key function, attaching lesser importance to engaging with what Walter Bagehot called the 'showy parts of the constitution'. In 1879 a lady-in-waiting spoke to Lord Sandon 'of the Queen's natural shyness, and of how she disliked being looked at, which made public functions ... very trying to her'; on the other hand, asserting herself politically came naturally.[39]

Upon her death Balfour stated: 'We feel that the end of a great epoch has come upon us', adding: 'We intimately associate the personality of Queen Victoria with the great succession of events which have filled her reign.' This was perfectly fair, even if the domestic and social advances achieved during these years were never overriding concerns for Victoria. Far from taking pride in rising literacy rates, she spoke of the 'great mistake of over-educating the lower classes which prevented people from being good labourers and servants'. Better housing for the poor only intermittently aroused her concern, for though in 1883 she wrote sympathetically about 'wretched occupants' of slum tenements living in 'overcrowded, unhealthy and squalid abodes', her interest was spasmodic at best. Regulation of the workplace and better industrial relations she likewise considered better left to the politicians, although she did have something of a fixation about railway safety.[40] In general, however, it was foreign and colonial affairs, so fundamental to her country's power and prestige, that absorbed her energies.

The Queen had an uncanny ability to align herself with public opinion, instinctively espousing views that coincided with those of many of her subjects. Both her generous and worthy impulses and other less admirable ideas and enthusiasms tended to be held in common with large numbers of her countrymen, and this affinity with the national mood was a great asset to her; however remote she lived from them, her fears and aspirations for the national welfare were often similar to theirs. Salisbury highlighted this in his address to the Lords three days after her death, observing: 'She had an extraordinary knowledge of what her people would think – extraordinary because it could not have come from any personal intercourse. I have said for years that I always thought that when I knew what the Queen thought, I knew pretty certainly what view her subjects would take, and especially the middle class of her subjects. Such was the extraordinary penetration of her mind.'[41]

In March 1867 Disraeli had declared, 'I trust it will never be the fate of this country to live under a democracy.' By the end of Victoria's reign the state of affairs he so dreaded had still not been attained, but much progress in that direction had nevertheless been achieved. As Salisbury put it in a speech marking the Diamond Jubilee, the past sixty years had not only seen phenomenal technological advances but had likewise been 'a period of great political change. The impulse of democracy ... has made itself felt fully ... and vast changes in the centre of power and incidence of responsibility have been made almost imperceptibly, without any disturbance or hindrance in the progress or the prosperous development of the nation'. Besides the massive increase in the electorate, the introduction of the ballot enabled the enfranchised to cast their vote freely. MPs remained unpaid (much to the relief of the Queen, who not only could not fathom 'where is the money to come from?' but also felt it would 'lower the H[ouse] of C[ommons], already so much spoilt, still more').[42] Though it was still not easy for working men to enter Parliament, that institution was far more representative of the nation than had been the case at Victoria's accession.

Despite being wary of change, the Queen was capable of accommodating it when necessary. This helped persuade right-wingers they too must acquiesce in it, while those of a more progressive turn of mind at least knew the monarchy was not an immovable bulwark against any kind of reform. This provides one explanation why, notwithstanding continued inequality and deprivation, extremism in Britain failed to flourish. Much as the Queen might dread socialism and class conflict, even at the beginning of the twentieth century no credible mass movement had emerged to challenge her country's social order.

It should be noted, too, that Victoria possessed a literal survival instinct that was lacking in many contemporary fellow rulers. This was evidenced by the way she correctly predicted in 1864 that Maximilian and Charlotte's escapade in Mexico would end in disaster, and that their lives might well be forfeit unless they abandoned it. Eighteen years after her own death, her grim presages that her granddaughter Alicky of Hesse's marriage to Nicholas II would have fatal consequences were vindicated when the tsar and tsarina were executed by Bolsheviks alongside their children in a cellar at Ekaterinburg.

However strange it may have been that a stout little widow in a black bonnet should have come to rule over a quarter of mankind, Victoria somehow transcended the paradox. In many ways she was very ordinary, but, in the words of the future Archbishop of Canterbury Randall Davidson, while 'as a woman she was both shy and humble ... as Queen she was neither'. She was, as Salisbury once remarked of her grandson the kaiser, 'ultra-human'; whereas Salisbury had meant it pejoratively as regarded William II, in Victoria's case this took a much more benign form. There were admittedly times when her behaviour verged upon the monstrous; in general, however, she fulfilled her childhood ambition – stated when she had first learnt of the role she would be called on to fulfil – to 'be good'. Her flaws were countervailed by numerous admirable qualities, including a fundamental honesty, a wish to be fair, and an erratic but nonetheless genuine sense of compassion. She furthermore possessed a clarity of vision that was perhaps somewhat simplistic, but which allowed her to dedicate herself with every fibre of her passionate nature to upholding her kingdom's global status. It was not just the length of her reign that resulted in an entire era being named after her, for she was never a mere figurehead, and left her own distinctive imprint upon her age. In his valedictory tribute Salisbury declared: 'She reigned by sheer force of character ... over the hearts of her subjects, and exercised an influence in moulding their character and destiny which she could not have done more if she had had the most despotic power in her hands.'[43]

ACKNOWLEDGEMENTS

Firstly I should like to thank her late Majesty Queen Elizabeth II for graciously granting me access to the Royal Archives at Windsor. I am also grateful to the Royal Archives' staff who assisted me while I worked there, and in particular to Miss Allison Derrett LVO, who checked my references for quotations from the Royal Archives.

In addition, I should like to thank staff at the Liverpool Record Office, Liverpool Central Library, for their assistance when I consulted the papers of the fourteenth Earl of Derby. Material from these papers is reproduced by courtesy of the Derby Collection. I am grateful for having been allowed to read some of the papers of William Ewart Gladstone, on loan to the British Library, and for permission given by the papers' owner, Charlie Gladstone, to quote from them. Thanks are due for permission to see the papers of General Charles Grey, held in the Barker Research Library, Palace Green, Durham University Archives and Special Collection. Material from these papers is reproduced by courtesy of the Howick Estate. I was also kindly allowed to read papers of Lord Palmerston held in the Special Collections, Hartley Library, University of Southampton, and I would like to thank the University of Southampton for permission to quote from those documents. Lastly, I should like to thank the Marquess of Salisbury for generous permission to research and use papers of the third Marquess of Salisbury at Hatfield House, and for the kind treatment I received from Lord and Lady Salisbury, Sarah Whale and all at Hatfield House during my visits there.

Thanks are due to staff at the British Library, and in particular for assistance given to me by Tabitha Driver and other staff in the Archives and Manuscripts department of the Library. Their guidance helped me to navigate the papers of Sir Robert Peel and the newly acquired papers of Lord Granville. I should also like to thank those who assisted me at the Bodleian Library, Oxford, as well as the unfailingly assiduous and resourceful staff at the London Library. I was greatly aided too by staff at the National Archives, where I went to read Lord John Russell's correspondence. Finally, I would like to thank Dr Richard A. Gaunt and Nigel Morris of the Peel Society for permission to reproduce the cartoon of Peel as a stag at bay.

Among the individuals who helped me in various ways in the course of writing this book I should like to thank Ella Carr, Lady Antonia Fraser, DBE, Geordie Greig, Catherine Hesketh, Marianne Hinton, Joanna and Graeme Jenkins, Professor Jane Ridley, Andrew Roberts, Graham Viney (who read an early draft and offered insightful – and wonderfully cheering – comments) and A. N. Wilson, with whom I have much enjoyed discussing Victoria.

At the outset, my much-missed late literary agent, Ed Victor, was characteristically positive, inspiring me with eagerness to pursue the subject. During the project's later stages my literary agent Georgina Capel was also a notable source of comfort who provided invaluable help and encouragement. William Clark of William Clark Associates in New York has likewise been most helpful.

My British editor, Arabella Pike of William Collins, has been highly supportive over the years that it has taken to bring this book to fruition and gave me much useful advice. Her assistant Sam Harding has likewise helped me a great deal, as did Eve Hutchings, while Kate Johnson was a meticulous and very perceptive copyeditor. In the United States Vicky Wilson of Knopf provided me with many beneficial editorial suggestions. To all these – and Marc Jaffee – I am very grateful.

ENDNOTES

The following abbreviations are used in the Notes:

PEOPLE

KL – King Leopold I of the Belgians
Ld B – Lord Beaconsfield
Ld D – Lord Derby
Ld G – Lord Granville
Ld M – Lord Melbourne
Ld P – Lord Palmerston
Ld R – Lord Russell
Ld S – Lord Salisbury
Mr D – Disraeli
Mr G – Gladstone
PA – Prince Albert
QV – Queen Victoria

ARCHIVES/PRIMARY SOURCES

Ab. Corr – *Selections from the Correspondence of the Earl of Aberdeen*, (ed.), Arthur H. Gordon, Baron Stanmore, Vols 9–12 (n.d.)
B&DC – *Beloved and Darling Child: Last Letters Between Queen Victoria and Her Eldest Daughter, 1886–1901*, (ed.), Agatha Ramm (1990)
BIHR – *Bulletin of the Institute of Historical Research*
BL – British Library, London
Bod. – Bodleian Library, Oxford
Corti EE – Egon Corti, *The English Empress* (1957)
DC – *Darling Child: Private Correspondence of Queen Victoria and the German Crown Princess 1871–78*, (ed.), Roger Fulford (1976)
DD(1) – Derby Diaries: *A Selection from the Diaries of Edward Henry Stanley 15th Earl of Derby 1869–78*, (ed.), John Vincent, Camden 5th Series, Vol. IV (1994)
DD(2) – Derby Diaries: *Diaries of Edward Henry Stanley 15th Earl of Derby 1870–93, A Selection* (ed.) John Vincent (2003)
DDC – *Disraeli, Derby and the Conservative Party: Journals and Memoirs of Edward Henry, Lord Stanley 1849–69*, (ed.), John Vincent (1978)
Derby Ps – Papers of 14th Earl of Derby, held at Liverpool Record Office, Liverpool Central Library, Reference: 920 DER (14)

DL – Benjamin Disraeli, *Letters*, 10 Vols, (eds.), John Matthews, M. G. Wiebe et al. (1982–2014)
EHR – *English Historical Review*
G&P – Philip Guedalla, *Gladstone and Palmerston* (1928)
GD – *The Gladstone Diaries*, (eds.), M. R. D. Foot and H. C. G. Matthew, 14 Vols (1968–94)
GDD – *German Diplomatic Documents 1871–1914*, (selected and trans.),. E. T. S. Dugdale (1928–31)
GG(1) – *Political Correspondence of Mr Gladstone and Lord Granville 1868–76*, 2 Vols, (ed.), Agatha Ramm, Royal Historical Society, Camden 3rd Series, Vol. LXXXI (1952)
GG(2) – *Political Correspondence of Mr Gladstone and Lord Granville 1876–86*, 2 Vols, (ed.), Agatha Ramm (1962)
GH – *Diary of Gathorne Hardy, Later Lord Cranbrook, 1866–92*, ed. Nancy E. Johnson (1981)
GP – Gladstone Papers, on loan to British Library
Grey Ps – Papers of General Charles Grey, held in Barker Research Library, Palace Green Library, Durham University Archives and Special Collections
Hatfield Ps – Papers of the Marquess of Salisbury at Hatfield House, Hertfordshire
LEF – *Letters of the Empress Frederick*, (ed.), Frederick Ponsonby (1928)
Loulou – *Loulou: Selected Extracts from the Journal of Lewis Harcourt 1880–95* (ed.), Patrick Jackson (2006)
LQV s1, s2, s3 – Letters of Queen Victoria, 1st Series, (eds.), A. C. Benson and Viscount Esher (1908); 2nd and 3rd Series, (ed.), G. E. Buckle (1928), (1932)
M&B – William Monypenny and Richard Buckle, *Life of Benjamin Disraeli, Earl of Beaconsfield*, 6 Vols (1910–20)
NA – The National Archives, London
PP – Palmerston Papers, held in Special Collections, Hartley Library, University of Southampton
Q&G – Philip Guedalla, *The Queen and Mr Gladstone* (1933)
QVJ: – Queen Victoria's Journal: online at http://www.queenvictoriasjournals.org. Quotations up to 16 February 1840 are taken from transcripts of the journal made for Lord Esher; thereafter they are taken from Princess Beatrice's transcripts. The full Royal Archives reference for the journals is RA VIC/MAIN/QVJ: (W), followed by the relevant date
RA – Royal Archives, Windsor Castle, Berkshire
S/B corresp – *Letters … between the 3rd Marquess of Salisbury and His Nephew Arthur James Balfour 1869–1892*, (ed.), Robin Harcourt-Williams, Hertfordshire Record Publications, Vol. 4 (1988)
Sidelights – Ponsonby, Frederick, *Sidelights on Queen Victoria* (1930)
YDL – *Your Dear Letter: Private Correspondence of Queen Victoria and the Crown Princess of Prussia 1865–71*, (ed.), Roger Fulford

Chapter 1

1. BL Add MS 89317/9/97, Ld Palmerston–Ld Granville, 26 May 1837.
2. Brown, *Palmerston*, 196; Greville, *Memoirs*, vol VI, 131.
3. LQV sl, I, 39; LQV sl, I, 256; QVJ: 20 June 1837.
4. Brown, *Palmerston*, 196; Connell, *Regina*, 10–13; BL Add MS 89317/9/100/2, Ld Holland–Ld Granville, 30 June 1837; Greville, *Memoirs*, Vol. V, 43 and III, 400.
5. Mitchell, *Lord Melbourne*, 144.
6. BL Add MS 89317/9/100/2, Ld Holland–Ld Granville, 25 July 1837.
7. QVJ: 20, 25 June, 2 July 1837.
8. QVJ: 20 June 1837.
9. Greville, *Memoirs*, IV, 199; QVJ: 6 Feb. 1839.
10. Hudson, *Royal Conflict*, 56, 78, 101.
11. QVJ: 26 Feb. 1838.
12. Hudson, *Royal Conflict*, 121; Connell, *Regina*, 1–13; Woodham-Smith, *Victoria*, 136; QVJ: 5 Nov. 1838.
13. Woodham-Smith, *Victoria*, 137, 140; Connell, *Regina*, 10–13.
14. LQV sl, I, 54, 68, 78–9, 73, 81.
15. LQV sl, I, 73, 80, 86.
16. RA VIC/MAIN/Y/63/50 KL–QV, 1 July 1837, Y/64/12 KL–QV, 11 Nov 1837, Y/63/68, KL–QV, 19 Aug 1837.
17. QVJ: 2 and 8 Sept 1837.
18. QVJ: 19 Sept 1837; LQV sl, I, 93–4, 95.
19. QVJ: 6 May, 20 May 1837.
20. LQV sl, I, 116; QVJ: 6 June 1838; LQV sl, I, 117, 119; QVJ: 17 June 1838.
21. RA VIC/MAIN/Y/64/57 KL–QV, 21 Aug 1838; Y/88/17 QV–KL 27 Aug 1838.
22. LQV sl, I, 136, 146, 151–2, 154.
23. Charlot, *Victoria*, 159; QVJ: 1 July 1837; Creevey, *Correspondence and Diaries*, 323; Connell, *Regina*, 9.
24. Connell, *Regina*, 7.
25. QVJ: 26 Oct. 1837; LQV sl, I, 115; QVJ: 17 and 18 May 1838.
26. Campbell, *Lord Campbell, II*, 205; QVJ: 1 July 1838, 6 Feb. 1838.
27. QVJ: 17 July 1837, 22 Aug. 1837, 1 Nov. 1837.
28. Campbell, *Lord Campbell*, 101; LQV sl, I, 74; QVJ: 9 Aug. 1837; Parker (ed.), *Peel*, 349–50; Kriegel (ed.), *Holland*, 371–2; QVJ: 9 Aug 1837.
29. QVJ: 15 July 1837; Creevey, *Life*, 433; QVJ: 6 Jan. 1838; Creevey, *Life*, 433.
30. Greville, *Memoirs*, IV, 110; QVJ: 4 Oct. 1837.
31. Greville, *Memoirs*, IV, 92–3.
32. QVJ: 11 Oct., 22 Dec. 1837.
33. QVJ: 31 Oct., 8 Dec. 1837.
34. QVJ: 1 Apr. 1838.
35. QVJ: 1 Jan. 1838; 3 Mar. 1838; 21 Dec. 1838.
36. Greville, *Memoirs*, VI, 129–30; QVJ: 29 Aug. 1838.
37. Greville, *Memoirs*, VI. 129–30; Greville, *Memoirs*, III, 395; QVJ: 23 Jan. 1840; QVJ: 18 May 1838.
38. QVJ: 19 Jan. 1838.
39. QVJ: 19 Oct. 1838; 6 June 1838; 17 Aug. 1839; 10 Feb. 1839; 14 Feb. 1838; 2 Feb. 1840.
40. QVJ: 16 Mar. 1838; 1 June 1838; 23 May 1838; 3 June 1838.
41. QVJ: 14 and 15 Dec. 1838; 12 Dec. 1838.
42. QVJ: 12 May 1838; Greville, *Memoirs*, IV, 169; QVJ: 8 Feb. 1839, 18 May 1839; 8 Feb. 1839.
43. QVJ: 17 Aug. 1838; Mitchell, *Lord Melbourne*, 238; QVJ: 22 June 1838, 4 July 1838.
44. QVJ: 12 Dec. 1837, 3 Oct. 1839; 9 Jan. 1838; 2 Feb. 1840; Battiscombe, *Shaftesbury*, 115.
45. QVJ: 29 Oct. 1838, 25 Nov. 1839, 15 Dec. 1838, 5 Dec. 1839.

46. QVJ: 7 Apr. 1839, 21 Dec. 1837, 14 June 1839, 10 Feb. 1839, 19 June 1839.
47. QVJ: 9 Feb. 1838; Ziegler, *Melbourne*, 106–7.
48. QVJ: 23 Mar. 1838, 14 Feb. 1838.
49. QVJ: 1 and 2 Jan. 1838, 26 Dec. 1837; 23 Apr. 1838, 29 May 1838.
50. QVJ: 20 Aug. 1838, 7 Apr. 1839.
51. QVJ: 20 Mar. 1839; Sanders, *Melbourne*, 277; QVJ: 19 Aug. 1838.
52. QVJ: 30 Sept. 1838, 29 Apr. 1838.
53. QVJ: 8 Jan. 1838; Greville, *Memoirs*, IV, 92–3.
54. Greville, *Memoirs*, IV, 116, 123, 137.
55. QVJ: 2 Jan. 1839.
56. QVJ: 2 Feb. 1839; Greville, *Memoirs*, IV, 145.
57. *Flora Hastings*, 4–5; Kriegel (ed.), *Holland*, 403–4; QVJ: 18 Sept. 1839.
58. *Flora Hastings*, 24; QVJ: 31 Mar. 1839.
59. Kriegel (ed.), *Holland*, 393; QVJ: 22 Mar., 10 Apr. 1839.
60. QVJ: 16 and 17 Apr. 1839; Kriegel (ed.), *Holland*, 393–4.
61. QVJ: 20 Apr. 1839; QVJ: 17 Feb. 1838; QVJ: 13 Mar. 1838; QVJ: 26 Apr. 1839.
62. QVJ: 7 May 1839.
63. QVJ: 10 Apr. 1839.
64. QVJ: 8 May 1839.
65. RA VIC/MAIN/A/1/3 Ld M–QV, 23 June 1837; Croker, *Papers*, 312.
66. QVJ: 7 May 1839; RA VIC/MAIN/C/1/22 QV–Ld M 7 May 1839; C/1/26; QVJ: 7 May 1839.
67. RA VIC/MAIN/C/2/23 QV–Ld M 8 May 1839; C/1/31, 9 May 1839.
68. LQV s1, I, 158.
69. LQV s1, I, 159.
70. LQV s1, I, 160; QVJ: 9 May 1839; LQV s1, I, 162.
71. Broughton, *Recollections*, 192–3; LQV s1, I, 167; RA VIC/MAIN/C/1/32 QV–Ld M 10 May 1839.
72. QVJ: 10 May 1839.
73. Malmesbury, *Memoirs*, 76; Campbell, *Lord Campbell*, *II*, 116; QVJ: 10 May, 11 May 1839.
74. *Hansard*, 47, cols 1009–10, 14 May 1839.
75. Gash, *Life*, 227n; QVJ: 12 and 18 May 1839.
76. Greville, *Memoirs*, IV, 167–8, 173; QVJ: 12 and 22 June 1839.
77. QVJ: 21, 27 and 28 June 1839.
78. QVJ: 5, 7 and 17 July 1839; Greville, *Memoirs*, IV, 212, 208.
79. Broughton, *Recollections*, *V*, 243–4; QVJ: 29 Jan. 1840.
80. QVJ: 19 June, 25 June, 12 June 1839; Broughton, *Recollections*, *V*, 205.
81. Greville, *Memoirs*, IV, 230, 237; QVJ: 16 June, 28 Aug. 1839.
82. QVJ: 11 Aug. 1839; LQV s1, I, 184–5; QVJ: 23 and 25 Sept., 2 Oct. 1839.
83. QVJ: 25 Feb., 18 Apr., 24 Aug. 1839.
84. QVJ: 18 Apr. 1839.
85. Parker (ed.), *Peel*, *II*, 408–9.
86. QVJ: 11 and 14 Oct. 1839; Sanders, *Melbourne*, 406.
87. RA VIC/MAIN/C/1/68 QV–Ld M 16 Oct. 1839; QVJ: 27 Oct. 1839.
88. LQV s1, I, 198–9; QVJ: 5 Dec. 1839; LQV s1, I, 201–2.
89. Charlot, *Victoria*, 179; Ziegler, *Melbourne*, 324.
90. Rhodes James, *Albert*, 93; LQV s1, I, 206; QVJ: 28 Dec. 1839; Jagow (ed.), *Letters*, 51–5.
91. RA VIC/MAIN/C/2/9 QV–Ld M 21 Jan. 1840; and C/2/10.
92. QVJ: 4 Nov. 1839, 12 Jan. 1840; 31 Dec. 1839; 23 Jan. 1840.
93. QVJ: 1 Jan. 1840, 9 Dec. 1839.
94. QVJ: 30 Dec. 1839, 24 and 27 Jan. 1840; RA VIC/MAIN/C/2/14 QV–Ld M 28 Jan. 1840.
95. QVJ: 22 Dec. 1839; 27 Jan. 1840.
96. QVJ: 22 Dec. 1839; 27 Jan., 31 Jan., and 1 Feb. 1840; RA VIC/MAIN/

C/2/21–22, QV–Ld M 1 Feb. 1840; QVJ: 2 Feb. 1840.
97. RA VIC/MAIN/C/2/23–24 QV–Ld M 2 Feb. 1840.
98. Greville, *Memoirs*, IV, 244, 250.
99. QVJ: 10 Feb. 1840; RA VIC/MAIN/C/2/40 QV–Ld M 11 Feb. 1840.
100. RA VIC/MAIN/Y/54/3 15 Apr. 1840; Martin, *Royal Highness*, 71.
101. LQV sl, I, 224.
102. Helps (ed.), *Principal*, 81–2; QVJ: 1 June 1840; Martin, *Royal Highness, I*, 87.
103. Greville, *Memoirs*, IV, 275; Lever (ed.), *Letters*, 245–6; QVJ: 4 and 7 Jan. 1840.
104. QVJ: 15 July 1840; Eyck, *Prince Consort*, 22–3; Martin, *Royal Highness, I*, 95; Bolitho (ed.), *Prince Consort*, 26.
105. LQV sl, I, 227; QVJ: 28 July 1840, 7 and 10 Sept., 3 Oct. 1840.
106. LQV sl, I, 230.
107. LQV sl, I, 231; Connell, *Regina*, 23; QVJ: 19 and 24 Sept. 1840 Bourne, *Palmerston*, 604; RA VIC/MAIN/C/3/70 QV–Ld M 2 Oct. 1840.
108. LQV sl, I, 233; RA VIC/MAIN/C/3/71 QV–Ld M 6 Oct. 1840; LQV sl, I, 235.
109. RA VIC/MAIN/C/3/73 QV–Ld M 10 Oct. 1840.
110. RA VIC/MAIN/C/3/78 QV–Ld M 12 Oct. 1840.
111. QVJ: 12 Oct., 26 Sept., 14 Oct., 15 Oct. 1840; LQV sl, I, 242.
112. QVJ: 17 Oct. 1840; LQV sl, I, 242–3.
113. RA VIC/MAIN/C/3/89 QV–Ld M 9 Nov. 1840; LQV sl, I, 252.
114. QVJ: 15 Oct. 1840; LQV sl, I, 248–9; QVJ: 17 Nov. 1840; LQV sl, I, 249–50; Brown, *Palmerston*, 231; Lever (ed.), *Letters*, 245–6.
115. Bolitho (ed.), *Prince Consort*, 34; RA VIC/MAIN/C/3/101 QV–Ld M 14 Dec. 1840; RA VIC/MAIN/Y/54/11, Anson, 20 Dec. 1840.
116. RA/VIC/MAIN/Y/54/15, Anson, 17 Feb. 1841.
117. Grey, *Early Years*, 321.
118. QVJ: 28 Apr. 1841.
119. RA VIC/MAIN/C/21/4 Anson, 29 Apr. 1841; LQV sl, I, 268–9; RA VIC/MAIN/C/4/11, QV–Ld M 6 May 1841.
120. LQV sl, I, 271.
121. QVJ: 13, 15 and 16 May 1841; LQV sl, I, 269–70.
122. QVJ: 17 May 1841.
123. RA VIC/MAIN/C/4/18 QV–Ld M 19 May 1841; Broughton, *Recollections*, VI, 27–8.
124. RA VIC/MAIN/Y/54/52, Anson, 13 June 1841; RA VIC/MAIN/C/21/56 Ld M–QV, 13 June 1841.
125. RA VIC/MAIN/Y/54/48, Anson, 11 June 1841; RA VIC/MAIN/C/21/54 Anson, 12 June 1841.
126. Rhodes James, *Albert*, 109; LQV sl, I, 296–7.
127. LQV sl, I, 298, 304–5.
128. LQV sl, I, 298–9; QVJ: 29 Aug. 1841; RA VIC/MAIN/C/4/31 QV–Ld M 29 Aug. 1841; QVJ: 30 Aug. 1841.
129. QVJ: 1 Sept. 1841; RA VIC/MAIN/C/4/40 QV–Ld M 2 Sept. 1841, and C/4/38.
130. Greville, *Memoirs*, IV, 409; RA VIC/MAIN/C/21/83 Ld M–QV, 30 Aug. 1841.
131. LQV sl, I, 302; Campbell, *Lord Campbell, II*, 159; QVJ: 28 Aug. 1841; LQV sl, I, 303.
132. LQV sl, I, 320; BL Add 40432 f 111–12 QV–Peel, 9 Sept. 1841; RA VIC/MAIN/C/22/7 and C/22/15, Ld M–QV, 1 and 2 Sept. 1941.
133. RA VIC/MAIN/C/4/49 QV–Ld M 11 Sept. 1841; LQV sl, I, 325–6; RA VIC/MAIN/C/4/52 QV–Ld 16 Sept. 1841.

134. LQV sl, I, 330–1.
135. LQV sl, I, 340–1.
136. LQV sl, I, 352–3, 355.
137. LQV sl, I, 360–2; RA VIC/MAIN/Y/54/98 Anson, 5 Dec. 1841.
138. LQV sl, I, 368.
139. LQV sl, I, 393, 449, 452.
140. LQV sl, I, 466.
141. QVJ: 16 and 30 June 1843; Greville, *Memoirs*, V, 146; LQV sl, I, 512; RA VIC/MAIN/Y/55/66 Anson, 19 Dec. 1843; Ziegler, *Melbourne*, 356.
142. QVJ: 1 Sept. 1844; LQV sl, II, 24. QVJ: 4 Jan. 1845; LQV sl, II, 42.
143. Greville, *Memoirs*, V, 165–6; LQV sl, II, 51–2; Lever (ed.), *Letters*, 272.
144. Greville, *Memoirs*, V, 283, QVJ: 3 Jan. 1846.
145. RA VIC/MAIN/Y/55/66 Anson, 19 Dec 1843; LQV sl, II, 140; Mitchell, *Lord Melbourne*, 257; Ziegler, *Melbourne*, 361.
146. Ziegler, *Melbourne*, 362; QVJ: 1 Oct., 17 Dec. 1842; Bogdanor, *Monarchy*, 20.

Chapter 2

1. QVJ: 24 Feb. 1844; QVJ: 17 June 1844; QVJ: 3 Jan. 1846; QVJ: 6 Dec. 1845; QVJ: 3 July 1846.
2. Hurd, *Peel*, 44; Disraeli, *Bentinck*, 312; Greville, *Memoirs*, V, 123.
3. Hurd, *Peel*, 168; QVJ: 6 Oct. 1841; Swartz and Swartz, *Reminiscences*, 93.
4. RA VIC/MAIN/Y/55/10 Anson memo, 30 Apr. 1843.
5. LQV sl, I, 306; RA VIC/MAIN/Y/54/71 Anson, 3 Sept. 1841; RA VIC/MAIN/C/4/43 QV–Ld M 3 Sept. 1841.
6. RA VIC/MAIN/C/4/51 QV–Ld M 15 Sept. 1841.
7. RA VIC/MAIN/C/6/9 QV–Ld M Oct. 2; LQV sl, I, 337.
8. Gash, *Peel*, 290; RA VIC/MAIN/C/6/8 QV–Ld M. 30 Sept. 1841.
9. RA VIC/MAIN/Y/54/87 Anson memo, 8 Oct. 1841.
10. Croker, *Papers*, 406; RA VIC/MAIN/Y54/100, Anson, 26 Dec. 1841; Greville, *Memoirs*, IV, 422; Gash, *Peel*, 293.
11. RA VIC/MAIN/Y/54/98, Anson, 5 Dec. 1841.
12. LQV sl, I, 368; QVJ: 31 Jan. 1842.
13. Malmesbury, *Memoirs*, 107; Maxwell, *Clarendon*, I, 225.
14. Greville, *Memoirs*, V, 12; Parker (ed.), *Peel, II*, 522; Read, *Cobden and Bright*, 48.
15. QVJ: 16 Mar. 142; LQV sl, I, 387–8.
16. Jagow (ed.), *Letters*, 78–9; QVJ: 10 June 1840; QVJ: 10 July 1840; Jagow (ed.), *Letters*, 78–9.
17. QVJ: 1 July 1842; BL Add 40434 f 163v PA–Peel, 2 July.
18. Jagow (ed.), *Letters*, 78–9; Martin, *Royal Highness, I*, 143.
19. Murphy, *Shooting*, 226; BL Add 40434 f 184–5, PA–Peel, 10 July 1842.
20. Parker (ed.), *Peel, II*, 584; Maxwell, *Clarendon*, I, 228.
21. QVJ: 9 June 1842.
22. QVJ: 18 Feb. 1845; LQV sl, II, 34; Martin, *Royal Highness, I*, 258–9.
23. Eyck, *Prince Consort*, 34.
24. RA VIC/MAIN/A/12/55 & 57, Peel–QV, 7 and 10 May 1842; BL Add 40434 f 67 Peel–QV, 7 May 1842.
25. Murphy, *Shooting*, 157.
26. LQV sl, I, 423.
27. Thompson, *Chartists*, 294–5; QVJ: 17 Aug. 1842; LQV sl, I, 426; QVJ: 16–17 Aug. 1842.
28. Parker (ed.), *Peel, II*, 540; LQV sl, I, 424, 426–7.
29. QVJ: 23 Feb. 1845; Parker (ed.), *Peel, II*, 538; QVJ: 23 Aug. 1842.

30. Parker (ed.), *Peel, II*, 540; RA VIC/MAIN/C/6/38 QV–Ld M 17 Aug. 1842.
31. Parker (ed.), *Peel, II*, 542–5; QVJ: 4 Feb. 1843.
32. RA VIC/MAIN/Y/55/1 Anson memo, 6 Jan. 1843.
33. QVJ: 25 Oct. 1842, 4 Feb. 1843, 2 Oct. 1843, 16 Feb. 1845.
34. Martin, *Royal Highness, I*, 163.
35. QVJ: 19 May 1842, 1 Feb. 1843; Parker (ed.), *Peel, III*, 219.
36. BL Add 40435 f 306v; QVJ: 24 Jan. 1843; BL Add 40436 f 71–2; RA VIC/MAIN/A/14/16 Peel memo.
37. BL Add 40436 f 158–9; RA VIC/MAIN/A/14/30 Peel–QV, 27 Mar. 1843.
38. QVJ: 18 Feb., 22 Feb. 1843; LQV sl, I, 466.
39. QVJ: 31 Oct. 1839; QVJ: 2 Mar. 1843.
40. QVJ: 23 Nov. 1842.
41. Greville, *Memoirs*, V, 68; QVJ: 5 Feb. 1843.
42. RA VIC/MAINY/55/3, Anson memo, 19 Mar. 1843.
43. QVJ: 30 May, 31 May 1843.
44. Martin, *Royal Highness, I*, 164; QVJ: 6 Dec. 1845; LQV sl, II, 77; RA VIC/MAIN/Y55/14/, Anson memo, June 1843; ibid., Y/55/42, Anson memo, 28 Oct. 1843.
45. QVJ: 2 Oct. 1843, 19 Jan. 1844, 9 May 1844, 13 Oct. 1845.
46. Greville, *Memoirs*, V, 257.
47. Gash, *Peel*, 390.
48. LQV sl, I, 486, 489.
49. BL Add 40437 f 157; LQV sl, I, 483, 493.
50. QVJ: 13 July 1843.
51. Greville, *Memoirs*, IV, 137; Gash, *Peel*, 392; QVJ: 29 May 1843.
52. QVJ: 11 Dec. 1842; QVJ: 17 June 1843.
53. QVJ: 13 July 1843; M&B, II, 177; *Hansard*, 71, col. 460, 9 Aug. 1843.
54. Blake, *Disraeli*, 41, 57.
55. M&B, II, 181, 185; Argyll, *Autobiography*, I, 275.
56. Greville, *Memoirs*, V, 122; Gash, *Peel*, 387–8; Hurd, *Peel*, 197; Jagow (ed.), *Letters*, 87; Greville, *Memoirs*, V, 143.
57. RA VIC/MAIN/Y/55/44, Anson memo, 22 Nov. 1843.
58. Martin, *Royal Highness, I*, 193–4; LQV sl, I, 510.
59. RA VIC/MAIN/Y54/73 Anson memo, 7 Sept. 1841.
60. QVJ: 28 Oct. 1844.
61. Martin, *Royal Highness, I*, 315–16; Rhodes James, *Albert*, 228; Martin, *Royal Highness, I*, 259.
62. LQV sl, II, 4; Surtees, *Canning*, 86.
63. QVJ: 4 June 1844; LQV sl, II, 14–15.
64. LQV sl, II, 12; QVJ: 7–8 June 1844.
65. Martin, *Royal Highness, I*, 182–3.
66. QVJ: 7 Aug. 1843; QVJ: 7 Sept., 4 Sept. 1843; Martin, *Royal Highness, I*, 182–3; QVJ: 23 May 1844.
67. QVJ: 25 Aug., 1 Sept. 1844; Hurd, *Peel*, 283.
68. LQV sl, II, 25–6; QVJ: 9 Sept. 1845.
69. Parker (ed.), *Peel, III*, 162.
70. Martin, *Royal Highness, I*, 306.
71. BL Add 40439 f 98.
72. Parker (ed.), *Peel*, II, 576; Broughton, *Recollections* VI, 107; BL add 40436 f 103, f 105; Gash, *Peel*, 487.
73. BL Add 40437 f 286–7; LQV sl, I, 502.
74. Parker (ed.), *Peel, III*, 16, 29.
75. QVJ: 14 Apr. 1844; LQV sl, I, 462.
76. QVJ: 14 Apr. 1844; BL Add 40438 f 218; Gash, *Peel*, 493.
77. Read, *Peel*, 154; Parker (ed.), *Peel, III*, 29.
78. QVJ: 30 Oct. 1844.
79. Greville, *Memoirs*, V, 143; Rhodes James, *Albert*, 121–2.
80. RA VIC/MAIN/Y55/10, Anson memo, 30 Apr. 1843; QVJ: 15 Oct. 1843, 11 Jan. 1846, 20 Dec. 1845.

81. Hawkins, *Derby*, I, 298; LQV sl, II, 16–17.
82. QVJ: 23 Mar. 1844.
83. QVJ: 23 Mar. 1844.
84. QVJ: 14 May 1844; BL Add 40438 f 254.
85. QVJ: 15 June 1844; Greville, *Memoirs*, V, 191.
86. GD, III, 383; Parker (ed.), *Peel, III*, 150–52; QVJ: 16 June 1844.
87. QVJ: 16 June 1844; GD, III, 383; M&B, II, 241.
88. QVJ: 17 June 1844; M & B II, 241–2; BL Add 40438 f 304, QV–Peel, 18 June 1844.
89. QVJ: 19 June 1844; Parker (ed.), *Peel, III*, 270.
90. Gash, *Peel*, 392.
91. QVJ: 22 Feb. 1844; QVJ: 19 June 1844; BL Add 40439 f 58.
92. QVJ: 15 Feb. 1844; QVJ: 15 Oct. 1843.
93. Morley, *Gladstone*, I, 186; QVJ: 4 Jan. 1843.
94. Shannon, *Gladstone*, I, 92; Magnus, *Gladstone*, 14; Hawkins, *Derby*, I, 302; Parker, *Graham*, II, 4.
95. Matthew, *Gladstone*, 81, 94, 92, 91; GD, XIII, 428; Shannon, *Gladstone*, I, 234.
96. Shannon, *Gladstone* I, 173–4.
97. Parker (ed.), *Peel, III*, 173; LQV sl, II, 37; M&B, II, 102, 322, 327–9; Broughton, *Recollections*, VI, 140.
98. QVJ: 1 Mar. 1845; Greville, *Memoirs*, V, 212–13; Gash, *Peel*, 478; Hawkins, *Derby*, I, 295.
99. Read, *Cobden & Bright*, 45, 33, 60; Trevelyan, *Bright*, 141.
100. Stewart, *Protection*, 37; QVJ: 11 Dec. 1842.
101. QVJ: 14 Sept. 1845; LQV sl, II, 65.
102. LQV sl, II, 48–9.
103. Parker (ed.), *Peel, III*, 237; LQV sl, II, 47.
104. LQV sl, II, 48–9; Parker (ed.), *Peel, III*, 239.
105. QVJ: 6 Dec. 1845; LQV sl, II, 48–50.
106. QVJ: 18 Dec., 19 Dec. 1845; Disraeli, *Bentinck*, 34.
107. QVJ: 20 Dec. 1845; LQV sl, II, 62; Morley, *Gladstone*, I, 283.
108. QVJ: 6 Dec. 1845; LQV sl, II, 64; Airlie, *Lady Palmerston*, II, 106.
109. LQV sl, II, 65; Lever (ed.), *Letters*, 273.
110. Parker (ed.), *Peel, III*, 326; RA VIC/MAIN/Y/92/38, QV–KL 6 Jan. 1846.
111. Campbell, *Lord Campbell, II*, 199; M&B, II, 350; RA VIC/MAIN/C/23/10; M&B, II, 355; QVJ: 24 Jan. 1846.
112. RA VIC/MAIN/C/23/22/, PA memo, 27 Jan. 1846; RA VIC/MAIN/Y/92/39 QV–KL, 27 Jan. 1846; LQV sl, II, 73; BL Add 40441 f 42; RA VIC/MAIN/C/23/22, PA, 27 Jan. 1846.
113. RA VIC/MAIN/Y/92/39 QV–KL, 27 Jan. 1846; RA Y//92/40, QV–KL 5 Feb.
114. Disraeli, *Bentinck*, 92; RA VIC/MAIN/C/24/6, PA memo, May 1846.
115. Martin, *Royal Highness, I*, 322; QVJ: 18 Feb. 1846; Disraeli, *Bentinck*, 106–7.
116. BL 40441 f 120.
117. RA VIC/MAIN/C/23/27, PA memo, 30 Jan. 1846; QVJ: 14 Mar. 1846.
118. Greville, *Memoirs*, V, 321.
119. RA VIC/MAIN/D/15/6, PA memo, 29 Mar. 1846; BL Add 40441 f 179; M&B, II, 395.
120. QVJ: 10 June 1846.
121. Gash, *Peel*, 595; BL Add 40441 f 272.
122. QVJ: 26 June 1846.
123. Parker (ed.), *Peel, III*, 372; GD, III, 553; QVJ: 30 June 1846; LQV sl, II, 87.
124. QVJ: 27 June 1846 LQV sl, II, 87.

125. LQV sl, II, 87; Parker (ed.), *Peel, III*, 452.
126. LQV sl, II, 87.

Chapter 3

1. RA VIC/MAIN/Y/92/36, QV–KL 23 Dec. 1845; ibid., Y/92/53 13 Oct. 1846.
2. QVJ: 2 Feb. 1852.
3. RA VIC/MAIN/D/15/64, Russell–QV, 7 Nov. 1846; Woodham-Smith, *Great Hunger*, 375; QVJ: 21 July 1846.
4. QVJ: 18 Mar. 1847.
5. QVJ: 29 Sept. 1846; RA VIC/MAIN/D/15/61 PA memo, 25 Oct. 1846; RA VIC/MAIN/D/15/63, PA memo, 6 Nov. 1846.
6. RA VIC/MAIN/D/15/71, Wynne-Routh, 24 Dec. 1846; QVJ: 31 Dec. 1846; RA VIC/MAIN/D/15/68, PA memo, 26 Dec. 1846.
7. RA VIC/MAIN/D/15/69, Russell–PA, 27 Dec. 1846; RA VIC/MAIN/C/16/7, PA–Russell, 30 Dec. 1846.
8. RA VIC/MAIN/C/7/28, QV–Russell, 31 Dec. 1846; QVJ: 20 Mar. 1847; QVJ: 31 Dec. 1846; RA/VIC/MAIN/D/16/69 PA memo, 17 May 1847; RA/VIC/MAIN/D/16/86, PA Memo, 26 Sept. 1847; Jagow (ed.), *Letters*, 146.
9. Greville, *Memoirs*, VI, 47; RA VIC/MAIN/D/15/63, PA memo, 6 Nov. 1846; QVJ: 24 Mar. 1847.
10. RA VIC/MAIN/D/16/24, Forster–Phipps, 21 Jan. 1847; ibid., D/16/98, Russell-QV, 17 Nov. 1847; QVJ: 5 Nov. 1847; QVJ: 21 Nov. 1847.
11. RA VIC/MAIN/C/9/58, QV–Russell, 19 Oct. 1850; Maxwell, *Clarendon*, I, 341.
12. RA VIC/MAIN/C/9/16, QV–Russell, 14 Apr. 1850; LQV sl, II, 241; Scherer, *Russell*, 200.
13. Greville, *Memoirs*, V, 354.
14. LQV sl, II, 181; Martin, *Royal Highness, II*, 304; Connell, *Regina*, 78.
15. RA VIC/MAIN/C/16/17, PA-Russell, 5 Sept. 1847; Jagow (ed.), *Letters*, 124; Connell, *Regina*, 129; LQV sl, II, 108.
16. QVJ: 5 Sept. 1849; Guedalla, *Palmerston*, 295–6; Ashley, *Palmerston*, I, 265.
17. QVJ: 18 Oct. 1847; LQV sl, II, 176; LQV sl, II, 96.
18. Bell, *Palmerston*, II, 20; QVJ: 17 Nov. 1842.
19. QVJ: 6 Aug. 1848.
20. RA VIC/MAIN/C/8/49, QV–Russell, 7 Sept. 1848; LQV sl, II, 199; Ashley, *Palmerston*, I, 109–19.
21. QVJ: 17 Dec. 1850.
22. RA VIC/MAIN/Y/96/18, QV–KL, 4 Mar. 1851; Connell, *Regina*, 115.
23. QVJ: 26 Jan. 1847; RA VIC/MAIN/Y/92/58, QV–KL, 1 Dec 1846; LQV sl, II, 120; Connell, *Regina*, 40; Maxwell, *Clarendon*, I, 341.
24. QVJ: 26 Jan. 1847; LQV sl, II, 117; RA VIC/MAIN/A/19/31, QV–Russell, 5 Jan. 1847; ibid., J/56/52, Russell memo, 13 Feb. 1847; QVJ: 8 Feb. 1847; RA VIC/MAIN/C/16/9, PA memo, 9 Feb. 1847; ibid., J/56/67, Ld P–QV, 17 Feb. 1847.
25. QVJ: 27 Jan. 1847.
26. QVJ: 30 Jan. 1847; LQV sl, II, 119; RA VIC/MAIN/J/56/52, Russell memo, 13 Feb. 1847.
27. QVJ: 27–8 Mar. 1847; RA VIC/MAIN/J/57/64, Wylde–PA, 15 Apr 1847; ibid., J/57/81, QV–Ld P, 30 Apr 1847; ibid., J/57/85, QV, 4 May 1847; RA VIC/MAIN/C/7/75. QV–Russell, 29 Aug. 1847.
28. . RA VIC/MAIN/C/7/60, QV–Russell, 20 May 1847; RA VIC/MAIN/J/58/81, Wylde–PA, 7 June 1847; Lever (ed.), *Letters*, 291–2; RA VIC/MAIN/J/59/49, Ld P–QV, 6 Aug. 1847; ibid., J/59/50, QV–Maria, 6 Aug. 1847.

29. QVJ: 18 June 1848; QVJ: 19 Oct. 1847.
30. QVJ: 28 and 29 Feb. 1848.
31. Greville, *Memoirs*, V, 350; Guedalla, *Palmerston*, 270; QVJ: 28 Sept. 1846; QVJ: 26 Feb. 1848.
32. RA VIC/MAIN/Y/93/20m QV–KL, 29 Feb. 1848; Bolitho, *Letters from archives of Brandenburg-Prussia*, 11; LQV s1, II, 158; ibid., 163; RA VIC/MAIN/C/8/8, QV–Russell, undated, Mar.? 1848; Martin, *Royal Highness, II*, 25–6; QVJ: 2 Apr. 1848.
33. QVJ: 5 Mar. 1848; LQV s1, II, 164; RA VIC/MAIN/Y/93/38, QV–KL, 27 June 1848.
34. RA VIC/MAIN/C/8/7 QV–Russell 14 Mar. 1848; RA VIC/MAIN/C/8/11, QV–Russell, 12 Apr 1848; RA VIC/MAIN/Y/93/28, QV–KL, 18 Apr 1848.
35. QVJ: 6 Apr. 1848, QVJ: 2 Apr. 1848; RA VIC/MAIN/Y/93/35, QV–KL, 30 May 1848.
36. Greville, *Memoirs*, VI, 43; QVJ: 2 Apr. 1848; LQV s1, II, 167; RA VIC/MAIN/C/8/11 QV–Russell 12 Apr. 1848; LQV s1, II, 183–4.
37. QVJ: 7 Mar. 1848.
38. QVJ: 3 Apr. 1848.
39. Greville, *Memoirs*, VI, 47–8; RA VIC/MAIN/C/56/11, Phipps–PA, 9 Apr 1848.
40. Greville, *Memoirs*, VI, 52–3; RA VIC/MAIN/C/8/9, QV–Russell, 10 Apr. 1848.
41. Jagow, (ed.), *Letters*, 141; RA VIC/MAIN/C/8/17, QV–Russell 17 May 1848; RA VIC/MAIN/C/8/18, QV–Russell, 31 May 1848; Martin, *Royal Highness, II*, 75–6; RA VIC/MAIN/C/56/90, G. Grey–QV, 5 June 1848; *Memoirs*, VI, 73; QVJ: 9 June 1848.
42. RA VIC/MAIN/Y/93/38, QV–KL, 27 June 1848; RA VIC/MAIN/Y/93/39, 4 July 1848.
43. Martin, *Royal Highness, II*, 104–5; QVJ: 4 Sept. 1848.
44. Bolitho (ed.) *Prince Consort*, 109; RA VIC/MAIN/C/16/47, PA–Russell 10 Apr. 1848; Battiscombe, *Shaftesbury*, 205; RA VIC/MAIN/C/8/13 QV–Russ 26 Apr. 1848; LQV s1, II, 368.
45. RA VIC/MAIN/C/56/50 PA–Lord Stanley, 23 Apr. 1848; RA VIC/MAIN/C/56/56 PA–Russ, 29 Apr.; RA VIC/MAIN/C/56/66.
46. QVJ: 10 Oct. 1851; QVJ: 14 Oct. 1852.
47. RA VIC/MAIN/Y/93/30; Connell, *Regina*, 74.
48. LQV s1, II, 172–3; RA VIC/MAIN/C/16/56 PA–Russell 17 May 1848; Taylor, *Italian Problem*, 107; RA VIC/MAIN/C/8/37, QV–Russell 27 July; LQV s1, II, 182.
49. RA VIC/MAIN/Y/93/23; QVJ: 24 July 1848; LQV s1, II, 186–7; PP MS 63/RC/F/380, QV–Ld P 3 Aug. 1848.
50. QVJ: 12 and 3 Aug. 1848; RA VIC/MAIN/Y/93/44, QV–KL 15 Aug. 1848; RA VIC/MAIN/C/8/43, QV–Russell 13 Aug. 1843; RA VIC/MAIN/C/8/49; RA VIC/MAIN/C/16/64 RA VIC/MAIN/C/8/55.
51. LQV s1, II, 202; Bell, *Palmerston*, I, 433; Ashley, *Palmerston*, I, 112.
52. LQV s1, II, 195.
53. RA VIC/MAIN/D/18/25, Russell–QV, 27 July 1848; RA VIC/MAIN/C/8/39, QV–Russell, 30 July 1848.
54. RA VIC/MAIN/Y/93/43 QV–KL, 8 Aug. 1848; ibid., Y/93/42, 1 Aug. 1848.
55. O'Murchadha, *Famine*, 170; QVJ: 6 Aug. 1849; QVJ: 3 Aug. 1849.
56. Gooch (ed.), *Russell*, I, 235; LQV s1, II, 226; Maxwell, *Clarendon*, I, 303; Murphy, *Shooting*, 292; RA VIC/MAIN/D/20/59 PA memo, 3 Nov. 1849; RA VIC/

MAIN/D/20/60, Cabinet memo., 26 Nov. 1849.
57. QVJ: 13 Oct. 1848; RA VIC/MAIN/C/8/57, QV–Russell, 14 Oct. 1848.
58. RA VIC/MAIN/C/8/60, QV–Russell, 18 Nov. 1848; RA VIC/MAIN/Y/93/52, QV–KL, 10 Oct.; ibid., Y/94/3 QV–KL, 7 Nov. 1848.
59. QVJ: 14 Nov. 1848.
60. LQV sl, II, 206.
61. QVJ: 13 May 1849; QVJ: 7 Apr., 27 July 1851.
62. RA VIC/MAIN/Y/94/17, QV–KL, 27 Feb 1849; QVJ: 13 Mar. 1849; RA/Y/94/22, QV–KL 3 Apr. 1849; Greville, *Memoirs*, VI, 171.
63. Ashley, *Palmerston*, I, 189; Greville, *Memoirs*, 187.
64. LQV sl, II, 322.
65. QVJ: 22 Jan. 1849; QVJ: 24 Jan. 1849; Greville, *Memoirs*, VI, 165, Bell, *Palmerston*, I, 446.
66. Greville, *Memoirs*, VI, 178; QVJ: 5 Sept. 1849.
67. Greville, *Memoirs*, VI, 205; LQV sl, II, 240; QVJ: 17 Feb. 1850.
68. LQV sl, II, 235–7.
69. Ashley, *Palmerston*, I, 211, 223; Guedalla, *Palmerston*, 307; Greville, *Memoirs*, VI, 233.
70. RA VIC/MAIN/C/9/32 QV–Russell, 3 July 1850; QVJ: 3 July, QVJ: 2 July 1850.
71. Greville, *Memoirs*, VI, 246; RA VIC/MAIN/Y/54/99 Anson memo, 13 Dec 1841; Connell, *Regina*, 121.
72. LQV sl, II, 263; QVJ: 7 Aug. 1850.
73. LQV sl, II, 264.
74. Connell, *Regina*, 123–4.
75. QVJ: 9 Sept. 1850; LQV sl, II, 269–70; RA VIC/MAIN/C/9/53, QV–Russell, 10 Oct. 1850; RA VIC/MAIN/C/9/58, QV–Russell, 19 Oct. 1850, part printed LQV sl, II, 272.
76. Greville, *Memoirs*, VI, 187; LQV sl, II, 192; Bell, *Pálmerston*, II, 3; Connell, *Regina*, 139–43.
77. Gooch (ed.), *Russell*, II, 26; LQV sl, II, 249; RA VIC/MAIN/C/9/99 QV–Russell, 21 May 1851.
78. LQV sl, II, 275–6; Greville, *Memoirs*, VI, 257.
79. Campbell, *Lord Campbell, II*, 287.
80. QVJ: 23 Feb. 1851; QVJ: 25 Feb.; LQV sl, II, 303; DDC, 46–7.
81. LQV sl, II, 303–5; QVJ: 25 Feb. 1851; DDC, 46–7.
82. LQV sl, II, 306–07; QVJ: 3 Mar., 4 Mar. 1851.
83. QVJ: 23 June 1851.
84. LQV sl, II, 329–30.
85. Greville, *Memoirs*, VI, 311.
86. Martin, *Royal Highness, I*, 416; LQV sl, II, 353; QVJ: 24 Dec. 1851.
87. RA VIC/MAIN/Y/96/48, QV–KL, 30 Dec. 1851.
88. LQV sl, II, 343; LQV sl, II, 345.
89. Lever (ed.), *Letters*, 323–4.
90. LQV sl, II, 346; QVJ: 20 Dec. 1851; *Hansard*, 119, cols 90, 99, 8 Feb. 1852.
91. LQV sl, II, 364; Greville, *Memoirs*, VI, 334; QVJ: 5 Feb. 1852.
92. Ashley, *Palmerston*, I, 329–30; Broughton, *Recollections*, VI, 292.
93. RA VIC/MAIN/C/10/57, QV–Russell, 4 Feb. 1852; RA VIC/MAIN/Y/97/1, QV–KL, 6 Jan. 1852
94. Ashley, *Palmerston*, I, 334.

Chapter 4

1. LQV sl, II, 362; LQV sl, II, 367; LQV sl, II, 362.
2. Eyck, *Prince Consort*, 184.
3. Campbell, *Lord Campbell, II*, 254–5; Greville, *Memoirs*, VI, 291.
4. QVJ: 23 Aug. 1852; QVJ: 12 Dec 1852.
5. Swartz and Swartz, *Reminiscences*, 123.
6. Broughton, *Recollections*, VI, 228–9.
7. QVJ: 22 Feb. 1852.
8. Eyck, *Prince Consort*, 190–1; LQV sl, II, 372.

9. DL VI, 566; Waterfield, 231; Malmesbury, *Memoirs*, 227.
10. QVJ: 22 Feb., 23 Feb., 24 Feb. 1852
11. RA VIC/MAIN/Y/97/9, QV–KL, 24 Feb. 1852; DDC, 72; DL VI, 50n; DDC, 79.
12. QVJ: 3 and 5 Mar. 1852; LQV s1, II, 378; QVJ: 21 Mar. 1852; DDC, 72, 79.
13. QVJ: 21, 5 and 28 Mar. 1852; Martin, *Royal Highness, II*, 451.
14. M&B,III, 366; Eyck, *Prince Consort*, 196.
15. QVJ: 1 Apr. 1852; QVJ: 16 Mar. 1852; QVJ: 3 Apr. 1852; LQV s1, II, 386.
16. LQV s1, II, 399–400; QVJ: 1 Apr. 1852.
17. RA VIC/MAIN/Y/97/14,QV–KL, 30 Mar. 1852; Malmesbury, *Memoirs*, 274–5.
18. LQV s1, II, 399, 401; Malmesbury, *Memoirs*, 276; LQV s1, II, 399; DL VI, 544.
19. Trevelyan, *Bright*, 207; DDC, 90; Bunsen, *Memoir*, II, 306; Tilney Bassett, *Gladstone*, 91–2; Conacher, *Aberdeen*, 48; Campbell, *Lord Campbell, II*, 311.
20. RA VIC/MAIN/Y/97/52, QV–KL, 28 Dec 1852; Greville, *Memoirs*, VI, 383, 392; QVJ: 17 Dec 1852.
21. DDC, 90–1.
22. DL, VI, 200–01.
23. M&B,III, 446–7; Greville, *Memoirs*, VI, 443–4.
24. Ab. Corr, IX, 417; LQV s1, II, 415.
25. Ab. Corr, IX, 420–21; Walpole, *Russell*, II, 161.
26. Ab. Corr, IX, 422; Bolitho (ed.) *Prince Consort*, 135; QVJ: 23 Dec 1852.
27. LQV s1, II, 428; QVJ: 19 Dec 1852.
28. Ab. Corr, IX, 433.
29. LQV s1, II, 423; LQV s1, II, 423–4; Ab. Corr, IX, 432.
30. Ab. Corr, IX, 429; LQV s1, II, 424; QVJ: 12 June 1854.
31. Ab. Corr, X, 2; Greville, *Memoirs*, VI, 392; Ab. Corr, X, 20–1; QVJ: 23 Jan. 1853.
32. Greville, *Memoirs*, VI, 405; LQV s1, II, 439.
33. Greville, *Memoirs*, VI, 467–8.
34. Conacher, *Aberdeen*, 51; ibid., 125–36; QVJ: 22 Apr. 1853; Greville, *Memoirs*, VI, 417.
35. Magnus, *Gladstone*, 113; Morley, *Gladstone*, I, 416–17.
36. Ab. Corr X, 218.
37. LQV s1, III, 9–10; LQV s1, II, 366; Tilney Basset, *Gladstone*, 104.
38. Parker, *Graham*, II, 217; Ab. Corr X, 37; LQV s1, II, 442.
39. Ab. Corr X, 336; LQV s1, III, 60.
40. LQV s1, II, 443, 442; QVJ: 18 June 1853; QVJ: 14 July 1853.
41. LQV s1, II, 408; QVJ: 3 Dec 1852; Martin, *Royal Highness, II*, 498.
42. Ab. Corr X, 194; QVJ: 26 Aug. 1853.
43. Ab. Corr X, 263.
44. RA VIC/MAIN/Y/98/30, QV–KL, 4 Oct. 1853; RA VIC/MAIN/Y/98/30, QV–KL 27 Sept. 1853.
45. LQV s1, II, 452; Maxwell, *Clarendon*, II, 30; LQV s1, II, 453; Ab. Corr X, 282–3; LQV s1, II, 453.
46. QVJ: 10 Oct. 1853; LQV s1, II, 457.
47. LQV s1, II, 457; QVJ: 23 Oct. 1853.
48. QVJ: 6 Oct., 15 Oct. 1853; Ab. Corr X, 319–20; Ab. Corr X, 323; QVJ: 23 Oct. 1853.
49. Ab. Corr X, 332; Eyck, *Prince Consort*, 226.
50. Eyck, *Prince Consort*, 226–7; Ab. Corr X, 357, 341, 343.
51. QVJ: 5 and 4 Nov. 1853.
52. Ab. Corr X, 384.
53. Ab. Corr X, 345, 343–4; LQV s1, II, 461–2.
54. LQV s1, II, 463; ibid., 470–1.
55. Ab. Corr X, 425.
56. Greville, *Memoirs*, VI, 475–7; QVJ: 21 Dec. 1853; Ab. Corr X,

423; QVJ: 24 Dec. 1853; LQV sl, II, 471–2.
57. QVJ: 24 Dec. 1853; LQV sl, II, 470.
58. Martin, *Lord Palmerston*, 174; Bolitho (ed.) *Prince Consort*, 141.
59. QVJ: 10 Jan. 1854; Martin, *Royal Highness, II*, p., 562.
60. Martin, *Royal Highness, II*, 560.
61. Martin, *Royal Highness, II*, 259–60.
62. DDC, 79; LQV sl, III, 8; Ab. Corr XII, 85–6.
63. Ab. Corr XI, 21; LQV sl, III, 3; Ab. Corr X, 450.
64. Williams, *Contentious*, 101–2; Ab. Corr XI, 6–7.
65. Ab. Corr XI, 11; DDC, 118; *Hansard*, 130, cols 96–7, 31 Jan. 1854.
66. QVJ: 5 Feb. 1854; Martin, *Royal Highness, II*, 564; QVJ: 1 Feb. 1854; RA VIC/MAIN/Y/99/4, QV–KL, 8 Feb. 1854; Martin, *Royal Highness, II*, 562.
67. Maxwell, *Clarendon*, II, 40.
68. QVJ: 8 June 1853; GD, IV, 565; QVJ: 13 Feb. 1854; RA VIC/MAIN/Y/99/12, QV–KL, 31 Mar. 1854.
69. RA VIC/MAIN/Y/99/5, QV–KL, 14 Feb. 1854; Trevelyan, *Bright*, 232; GD, IV 595; QVJ: 25 Feb. 1854; RA VIC/MAIN/Y/99/12, QV–KL 31 Mar. 1854; LQV sl, III, 20.
70. Magnus, *Gladstone*, 115; Martin, *Royal Highness, III*, 29.
71. LQV sl, III, 15; QVJ: 3 Apr. 1854; RA VIC/MAIN/Y/99/14, QV–KL, 11 Apr. 1854; QVJ: 8–9 Apr. 1854; LQV sl, III, 21; QVJ: 10 Apr. 1854; LQV sl, III, 23; DDC, 124.
72. Maxwell, *Clarendon*, II, 44; LQV sl, III, 34; QVJ: 15 July 1854.
73. QVJ: 12 and 17 Nov. 1854; LQV sl, III, 51–2; QVJ: 12 Nov. 1854.
74. QVJ: 24–25 Nov. 1854; Argyll, *Autobiography*, I, 508–09; LQV sl, III, 57.
75. Ab. Corr XI, 345; LQV sl, III, 60–1; Tilney Basset, *Gladstone*, 108.
76. RA VIC/MAIN/Y/99/37, QV–KL, 18 Oct. 1854; QVJ: 17, and 26 Dec 1854.
77. *The Times*, 23 Nov. 1854, 9; Ab. Corr XI, 296; Coates, 192–3; LQV sl, III, 68.
78. LQV sl, III, 72; QVJ: 24 Jan. 1855; LQV sl, III, 72, 75.
79. Argyll, *Autobiography*, I, 517–18; LQV sl, III, 73; G. B. Henderson, *Crimean War*, 80.
80. GD, V, 7–8; Argyll, *Autobiography*, I, 517–18; GD, V, 7–8.
81. Ab. Corr XII, 6; *Hansard*, 136, col. 960, 26 Jan. 1855; Ab. Corr XII, 8.
82. QVJ: 30 Jan. 1855; Ab. Corr XII, 9.
83. LQV sl, III, 87; QVJ: 3 Feb. 1855; LQV sl, III, 93; ibid., 91; RA VIC/MAIN/Y/100/6, QV–KL, 6 Feb. 1855; LQV sl, III, 92.
84. QVJ: 5 Feb. 1855; QVJ: 25 Feb. 1854; Ab. Corr XII, 13; LQV sl, III, 92.
85. Eyck, *Prince Consort*, 234; LQV sl, III, 101; QVJ: 5 Feb. 1855; LQV sl, III, 101; QVJ: 5 Feb. 1855; Greville, *Memoirs*, VII, 108.
86. QVJ: 7 Feb. 1855; Ab. Corr XII, 30; QVJ: 7 Feb. 1855.

Chapter 5

1. Greville, *Memoirs*, VII, 109; LQV sl, III, 81; DL, VI, 405 QVJ: 7 Apr. 1854.
2. Greville, *Memoirs*, VII, 250; *Dear Duchess*, 110.
3. Maxwell, *Clarendon*, II, 92; Connell, *Regina*, 294.
4. QVJ: 18 Sept. 1855; QVJ: 21 Aug. 1856; QVJ: 28 Nov. 1856; Greville, *Memoirs*, VII, 289, 314; Maxwell, *Clarendon*, II, 140.
5. LQV sl, III, 365.
6. RA VIC/MAIN/Y/100/7, QV–KL, 13 Feb. 1855; ibid., Y/100/8, 20 Feb. 1855.

7. GD, V, 25–6; LQV s1, III, 110.
8. RA VIC/MAIN/Y/100/8, QV–KL, 20 Feb. 1855.
9. QVJ: 28 Nov. 1855; QVJ: 31 July 1855.
10. RA VIC/MAIN/Y/100/8, QV–KL, 20 Feb. 1855.
11. QVJ: 20–1 Jan. 1853; Cowley, *Paris Embassy*, 16–17; Surtees, *Canning*, 188; Martin, *Royal Highness, III*, 240.
12. LQV s1, III, 122; Greville, *Memoirs*, VII, 129; QVJ: 16 Apr. 1855; Greville, *Memoirs*, VII, 154; LQV s1, III, 125; QVJ: 20 Apr. 1855; LQV s1, III, 123.
13. LQV s1, III, 122–6.
14. Cowley, *Paris Embassy*, 81; Greville, *Memoirs*, VII, 154; Maxwell, *Clarendon*, II, 90.
15. Martin, *Royal Highness, III*, 351; LQV s1, III, 140; LQV s1, III, 138.
16. Fitzmaurice, *Granville*, I, 118.
17. Argyll, *Autobiography*, I, 589; Martin, *Royal Highness, III*, 395, 398; QVJ: 25 Nov. 1855.
18. Maxwell, *Clarendon*, II, 119; QVJ: 11 Mar. 1856.
19. RA VIC/MAIN/Y/101/15, QV–KL, 30 Apr. 1856; Connell, *Regina*, 192, 196–7.
20. Connell, *Regina*, 238, 246–8.
21. QVJ: 1 Mar. 1857; Greville, *Memoirs*, VII, 290.
22. QVJ: 18 Jan. 1857; RA VIC/MAIN/Y/102/9, QV–KL, 10 Mar. 1857; QVJ: 4 Mar., 1 Mar. 1857.
23. RA VIC/MAIN/Y/102/8, QV–KL, 4 Mar. 1857; ibid., Y/102/9, QV–KL, 10 Mar. 1857.
24. Chambers, *Palmerston*, 424; RA VIC/MAIN/Y/102/10, QV–KL, 17 Mar. 1857; QVJ: 9 Apr. 1857.
25. RA VIC/MAIN/102/14, QV–KL, 5 May 1857; *Dearest Child*, 75.
26. LQV s1, III, 147.
27. Connell, *Regina*, 236; RA VIC/MAIN/Y/100/38, QV–KL, 26 Sept. 1855.
28. Pakula, *Uncommon*, 76; *Hansard*, 145, col. 733, 22 May 1857; Connell, *Regina*, 303.
29. LQV s1, III, 253; DL, VII, 116.
30. LQV s1, III, 177; Jagow, (ed.), *Letters*, 277–8.
31. Jagow (ed.), *Letters*, 277–8; QVJ: 3 Aug. 1857.
32. Surtees, *Canning*, 197.
33. LQV s1, III, 47.
34. LQV s1, II, 220; QVJ: 25 May 1849; LQV s1, III, 39; ibid., 47–8.
35. LQV s1, III, 234; *Panmure Papers*, II, 399; Connell, *Regina*, 216–17; LQV s1, III, 243.
36. Greville, *Memoirs*, VII, 305; Martin, *Royal Highness, IV*, 78; LQV s1, III, 244.
37. Connell, *Regina*, 199, LQV s1, III, 187–88; Martin, *Royal Highness, IV*, 79; Connell, *Regina*, 219; Martin, *Life, IV*, 125; Connell, *Regina*, 193.
38. QVJ: 31 Aug. 1857; QVJ: 14 Dec 1857; Connell, *Regina*, 224; Surtees, *Canning*, 237–8.
39. Surtees, *Canning*, 238; Fitzmaurice, *Granville*, I, 260; LQV s1, III, 251.
40. Surtees, *Canning*, 238; QVJ: 22 Mar. 1858.
41. QVJ: 1 Nov. 1857; Maclagan, *Clemency*, 141–2.
42. QVJ: 20 Feb. 1858; *Dearest Child*, 54.
43. QVJ: 20 Feb. 1858; LQV s1, III, 365; Fitzmaurice, *Granville*, I, 294; Greville, *Memoirs*, VII, 346.
44. Connell, *Regina*, 227–8.
45. *Dearest Child*, 118; Fitzmaurice, *Granville*, I, 259–60; LQV s1, III, 294.
46. LQV s1, III, 297; LQV s1, III, 304.
47. RA VIC/MAIN/Y/104/9, QV–KL, 8 Mar. 1859; Derby Ps 101/4/93; QV–Ld D, 9 Dec. 1858; Greville, *Memoirs*, VII, 403; RA VIC/MAIN/Y/104/8, QV–KL, 1 Mar. 1859; QVJ: 1 Apr. 1859.

48. QVJ: 11 June 1859.
49. Greville, *Memoirs*, VII, 423; QVJ: 12 Sept. 1857; LQV s1, III, 343.
50. Fitzmaurice, *Granville*, I, 335; Greville, *Memoirs*, VII, 424; Walpole, *Russell*, II, 308; QVJ: 12–13 June 1859.
51. QVJ: 13 June 1859; Maxwell, *Clarendon*, II, 185–6; RA VIC/MAIN/Y/104/21, QV–KL, 21 June 1859.
52. Martin, *Royal Highness, IV*, 49; Cowley, *Paris Embassy*, 127; RA VIC/MAIN/Y/102/26, QV–KL, 26 Aug. 1857; Vitzthum, *St Petersburg*, I, 215.
53. QVJ: 4 Aug. 1858; Derby Ps, 101/4/91 QV–Ld Derby, 2 Dec. 1858; Vitzthum, *St Petersburg*, I, 243; Maxwell, *Clarendon*, II, 164.
54. QVJ: 12 July 1859; LQV s1, III, 385.
55. QVJ: 1 Jan. 1859; RA VIC/MAIN/Y/104/1, QV–KL, 4 Jan. 1859; QVJ: 30 Nov. 1855; QVJ: 3 Dec 1855.
56. QVJ: 14 Jan. 1859.
57. LQV s1, III, 315; RA VIC/MAIN/Y/104/8, QV–KL, 1 Mar. 1859; DL, VII, 317; M&B, IV, 224.
58. QVJ: 12–13 Apr. 1859; *Dearest Child*, 174; RA VIC/MAIN/Y/104/13, QV–KL 19 Apr. 1859.
59. Temperley and Penson, *Foundations*, 200–01; LQV s1, III, 328.
60. QVJ: 26 Apr. 1859; RA VIC/MAIN/J/18/124 Vic–Malmesbury 27 Apr. 1859; RA VIC/MAIN/Y/104/15, QV–KL, 3 May 1859.
61. Malmesbury, *Memoirs*, 488; Corti EE, 56.
62. LQV s1, III, 332; RA VIC/MAIN/Y/104/20, QV–KL, 7 June 1859.
63. RA VIC/MAIN/Y/104/20, QV–KL, 7 June 1859; QVJ: 13 June 1859; QVJ: 20 July 1859; RA VIC/MAIN/J/20, PA introductory note; QVJ: 6 July 1859; Beales, *England*, 99–100.
64. LQV s1, III, 352–52; RA VIC/MAIN/Y/104/23, QV–KL, 12 July 1859.
65. LQV s1, III, 354; Fitzmaurice, *Granville*, I, 351; RA VIC/MAIN/J/21/146 QV–Russell, 22 July 1859; RA VIC/MAIN/J/22/49,QV–Russell, 15 Aug. 1859.
66. RA VIC/MAIN/J/21/123, QV–Russell 20 July 1859.
67. Parker (ed.), *Peel, II*, 496–9; Mosse, *EHR*, 270n; for Victoria's letters to Russell on this subject see LQV s1, II, 202 and RA VIC/MAIN/C/8/75; for her letters to Derby: Derby Ps 103/6/37/2, 101/4/38, 101/4/54/101/4/86; for letter to Palmerston: PP RC/F/808.
68. Fitzmaurice, *Granville*, I, 349–51.
69. Connell, *Regina*, 267; *Dearest Child*, 203; Gooch (ed.), *Russell*, II, 255; LQV s1, III, 364; QVJ: 29 July 1859.
70. RA VIC/MAIN/J/22/37, Russell–QV, 13 Aug. 1859; RA VIC/MAIN/J/22/24, Granville–Albert, 10 Aug. 1859; Ashley, *Palmerston*, II, 164; RA VIC/MAIN/J/22/41, QV–Russell, 15 Aug. 1859; RA VIC/MAIN/J/23/135 memo by PA, 24 Nov. 1859.
71. Fitzmaurice, *Granville*, I, 356–7; NA PRO 30/22/13H ff 90–3; GD, V 422; Fitzmaurice, *Granville*, I, 353–4; LQV s1, III, 363.
72. Maxwell, *Clarendon*, II, 192–3; *Dearest Child*, 207.
73. LQV s1, III, 366; Fitzmaurice, *Granville*, I, 357; RA VIC/MAIN/J/22/65 Russell–QV, 24 Aug. 1859.
74. Fitzmaurice, *Granville*, I, 354.
75. Fitzmaurice, *Granville*, I, 356; QVJ: 25 Aug. 1859.
76. Fitzmaurice, *Granville*, I, 357; LQV s1, III, 366.

77. Fitzmaurice, *Granville*, I, 357–58; LQV sl, III, 366.
78. QVJ: 4 Sept. 1859; RA VIC/MAIN/J/23/17 Ld P–Russell, 4 Sept. 1859; QVJ: 7 Sept. 1859.
79. LQV sl, III, 367–8; ibid., 370; Connell, *Regina*, 267–8; LQV sl, III, 371.
80. RA VIC/MAIN/J/23/135, PA memo, 24 Nov. 1859; ibid., Y/104/9, QV–KL, 22 Nov. 1859.
81. RA VIC/MAIN/Y/104/41, QV–KL, 6 Dec 1859; Connell, *Regina*, 277; RA VIC/MAIN/J/24/88, PA memo, 5 Jan. 1860; RA VIC/MAIN/Y104/41, QV–KL, 6 Dec 1859.
82. Fitzmaurice, *Granville*, I, 367; RA VIC/MAIN/J/24/19, PA memo, 5 Dec. 1859.
83. RA VIC/MAIN/J/24, PA introductory note; RA VIC/MAIN J/24/88, PA memo 5 Jan. 1860; Greville, *Memoirs*, VII, 451; RA VIC/MAIN/J/24/86 Granville–Albert, 3 Jan. 1860; Fitzmaurice, *Granville*, I, 368–9; Maxwell, *Clarendon*, II, 207.
84. LQV sl, III, 384; RA VIC/MAIN/J/24/88, PA memo, 5 Jan. 1860.
85. QVJ: 10 Jan. 1860; Fitzmaurice, *Granville*, I, 369.
86. QVJ: 25 Jan. 1860.
87. RA VIC/MAIN/J/23/25 Cowley–Russell, 4 Sept. 1859; Martin, *Royal Highness, I*, 12; LQV sl, III, 385.
88. RA VIC/MAIN/J/26, PA introductory notes; RA VIC/MAIN/J/26/7, QV–Russell 5 Feb. 1860.
89. Connell, *Regina*, 279; LQV sl, III, 387–8; RA VIC/MAIN/J/26/34 QV–Ld P, 11 Feb. 1860.
90. QVJ: 6 Mar. 1860; RA VIC/MAIN/Y/105/10, QV–KL, 20 Mar. 1860; RA VIC/MAIN/J/26/35, RA VIC/MAIN/J/27/24, Russell–QV, 11 Feb., 11 Mar. 1860.
91. RA VIC/MAIN/Y/105/10, QV–KL, 20 Mar. 1860; Walpole, *Russell*, II, 320; RA VIC/MAIN/Y105/10, QV–KL 27 Mar. 1860; Connell, 282; Ashley, *Palmerston*, II, 191; Connell, 283; Bell, *Palmerston*, II, 252.
92. Cowley, *Paris Embassy*, 207; Maxwell, *Clarendon*, II, 207; Corti EE, 60; Cowley, *Paris Embassy*, 210; *Dearest Child*, 184; LQV sl, III, 399; RA VIC/MAIN/J/27/59, QV–Russell, 20 Mar. 1860; Gooch (ed.), *Russell*, II, 279, 258–59, 270–71; Cowley, *Paris Embassy*, 222; *Dear Duchess* 131.
93. Vitzthum, *St Petersburg*, II, 38; Bell, *Palmerston*, II, 244.
94. LQV sl, III, 406; PP RC/F/964 Vic–Pam, 20 May 1860.
95. RA VIC/MAIN/J/28, PA introductory note; G&P, 123; Connell, *Regina*, 286. QVJ: 25 May 1860; Martin, *Royal Highness, V*, 99.
96. RA VIC/MAIN/Y/105/18, QV–KL, 3 July 1860; QVJ: 19 May 1860; PP RC/F/984, QV–Ld P, 9 July 1860.
97. LQV sl, III, 423; Connell, *Regina*, 292; Maxwell, *Clarendon*, II, 220; RA VIC/MAIN/Y/105/20, QV–KL, 17 July 1860.
98. RA VIC/MAIN/J/28/133, QV–Russell, 25 May 1860; RA VIC/MAIN/Y/105/28, QV–KL, 3 Sept. 1860.
99. QVJ: 10 Sept. 1860; RA VIC/MAIN/Y/105/28, QV–KL, 3 Sept. 1860.
100. RA VIC/MAIN/J/31/3, Walpole, *Russell*, II, 320; QVJ: 21 and 14 Nov. 1860; Cowley, *Paris Embassy*, 212–13; Temperley and Penson, *Foundations*, 227.
101. Greville, *Memoirs*, VII, 471–2; Gooch (ed.), *Russell*, II, 260–1; LQV sl, III, 428; Connell, *Regina*, 297.

102. Greville, *Memoirs*, VII, 388; DDC, 242; *Dear Duchess*, 141; LQV s1, III, 436; *Dear Duchess*, 153; Jagow, (ed.), *Letters*, 360.
103. RA VIC/MAIN/Y/112/9, QV–KL, 7 July 1864; Maxwell, *Clarendon*, II, 250–51; Greville, VII, 304; Fitzmaurice, *Granville*, I, 405; Villiers, *Villiers*, 317.
104. Martin, *Royal Highness*, *V*, 273; Wilson, *Victoria*, 232–3.
105. QVJ: 21 Jan., 3 Mar. 1856; QVJ: 21 July 1859; QVJ: 3 May 1859; QVJ: 16 Jan. 1856; QVJ: 4 Feb. 1859; QVJ: 12 Jan. 1860; for examples of conversations with ministers see: Argyll, *Autobiography*, I, 598–9, QVJ: 9 Apr. 1859.
106. *Dearest Child*, 354; Bolitho (ed.), *Prince Consort*, 217; Jagow (ed.), *Letters*, 347.
107. Connell, *Regina*, 305.
108. Cowley, *Paris Embassy*, 222.
109. *Dearest Child*, 308; Woodham-Smith, *Victoria*, 371; *Dearest Mama*, 132; Rappaport, *Magnificent*, 249–60.
110. QVJ: 11 Sept. 1861.
111. *Dearest Child*, 370; RA VIC/MAIN/Y/107/23, QV–KL, 4 Dec 1861.
112. Cowley, *Paris Embassy*, 229; Woodham-Smith, *Victoria*, 423; LQV s1, III, 471.
113. QVJ: 7 Dec 1861; Maxwell, *Clarendon*, II, 253–4; Woodham-Smith, *Victoria*, 423; Connell, *Regina*, 316–17.
114. Connell, *Regina*, 319; LQV s1, III, 474; *Dearest Mama*, 23.

Chapter 6

1. Connell, *Regina*, 319; PP MS 62/RC/F/1082 QV–Ld P, 31 Dec. 1861; LQV s2 I, 10; Maxwell, *Clarendon*, II, 258; Cowley, *Paris Embassy*, 229.
2. Maxwell, *Clarendon*, II, 250–1, 256; Rappaport, *Magnificent*, 121; DL, VIII, 155n, M&B, IV, 383.
3. *Dear Duchess*, 191–2; PP MS62/RC/F/1085 QV–Ld P, 2 Apr. 1862; Gooch (ed.), *Russell*, II, 322; Chambers, *Palmerston*, 488.
4. Martin, *Royal Highness*, *I*, 313–14, II, 545–46; DDC, 180–1; Vitzthum, *St Petersburg*, II, 176; DDC, 183; DDC, 200.
5. *Dearest Mama*, 37; Cowley, *Paris Embassy*, 246; Argyll, *Autobiography*, I, 188; LQV s2 I, 244; Grey Ps GRE/D/XIII/4 f 92–3; *The Times*, 6 Apr. 1864.
6. *Dear Duchess*, 183; LQV s2 I, 65; *Dearest Mama*, 47; RA VIC/MAIN/Y/110/1, QV–KL, 2 July 1863; Villiers, *Villiers*, 317.
7. QVJ: 26 Feb. 1864; Tilney Basset, *Gladstone*, 160.
8. LQV s2 I, 10; Vitzthum, *St Petersburg*, II, 176; Cowley, *Paris Embassy*, 241.
9. LQV s2 I, 21–2.
10. Connell, *Regina*, 318; QVJ: 10 Jan. 1862; DDC, 188; NA PRO 30/22/22 f 43–44, Ld P–Russell, 14 Mar. 1862.
11. LQV s2 I, 117; LQV s2 I, 48–50; QVJ: 31 Aug. 1863.
12. RA VIC/MAIN/Y/113/35, QV–KL 5 Apr. 1865; LQV s2 I, 18; *Dear Duchess*, 181; LQV s2 I, 17–18.
13. Ridley, *Bertie*, 61; *Dearest Mama*, 30; Rappaport, *Magnificent*, 121; QVJ: 29 Jan. 1862; Villiers, *Villiers*, 313.
14. Cowley, *Paris Embassy*, 230; Vitzthum, *St Petersburg*, II, 176; LQV s2 I, 13; Maxwell, *Clarendon*, II, 257; Villiers, *Villiers*, 313; QVJ: 29 Jan. 1862; QVJ: 2 Apr. 1862.
15. Vitzthum, *St Petersburg*, II, 187.
16. Villiers, *Villiers*, 317–18; Maxwell, *Clarendon*, II, 261–2.
17. *Dearest Mama*, 85.
18. LQV s2 I, 44; Pakula, *Uncommon*, 180.
19. Connell, *Regina*, 331, 335; DL, VIII, 261–2; M&B, IV, 386–7.

20. *Dear Duchess*, 221; G&P, 220; PP RC/F/1111 QV–Ld P 22 Mar. 1863.
21. M&B,IV, 392; DL, VIII, 270–1.
22. DDC, 199; DL, VIII, 282; LQV s2 I, 96–7; Malmesbury, *Memoirs*, 577.
23. *Dearest Mama*, 158.
24. LQV s2 I, 66; RA VIC/MAIN/Y/109/29 QV–KL 5 May 1863; YDL, 34; *Dearest Mama*, 205.
25. LQV s2 I, 66, 70.
26. LQV s2 I, 82; Temperley and Penson, *Foundations*, 237; LQV s2 I, 84.
27. NA PRO/30/22/14F f 111, Ld P–Ld R, 1 June 1863; NA PRO/30/22/14G f 213 QV–Ld R 3 June 1863; M&B, IV, 340; Seton-Watson, *Britain*, 435.
28. Pakula, *Uncommon*, 150; Martin, *Royal Highness, V*, 407; LQV s1, III, 465.
29. QVJ: 17 Sept. 1862; *Dearest Mama*, 96.
30. QVJ: 12 Jan. 1863; RA VIC/MAIN/Y/109/22, QV–KL 17 Mar. 1863; Corti EE, 85; *Dearest Mama*, 215, 225, 231.
31. *Dearest Mama* 253–54; Bolitho, *Letters from archives of Brandenburg-Prussia*, 140–1.
32. QVJ: 31 Aug. 1863.
33. LQV s2 I, 104–9.
34. Cowley, *Paris Embassy*, 251–2; ibid., 241–2; LQV s2 I, 91.
35. *Dearest Mama*, 139; QVJ: 31 Aug. 1863; Grey Ps GRE/D/XIII/4 f 53–54, Grey–Phipps, 4 Sept. 1863; NA PRO 30/22/22 f 257, Ld P–Ld R 19 Sept. 1863.
36. Grey Ps, GRE/D/XIII/4 f 70–71, QV–Grey 18 Oct. 1863; ibid., ff 79–80, 92–93, QV–Grey, 15–16 Dec 1863.
37. LQV s2 I, 132–4.
38. QVJ: 29 July 1863; Ashley, *Palmerston*, II, 236; LQV s2 I, 114; Vitzthum, *St Petersburg*, II, 364, 261–62; Mosse, *German*, 164.
39. RA VIC/MAIN/Y/111/16, QV–KL 14 Feb. 1864; Morley, *Gladstone*, I, 736; LQV s2 I, 130; QVJ: 2 Dec. 1863.
40. RA VIC/MAIN/Y/111/20, QV–KL 25 Feb. 1864; *Dearest Mama*, 296; Pakula, *Uncommon*, 203; NA PRO 30/22/22 f 321 Ld P–Ld R, 27 Nov. 1863; RA VIC/MAIN/Y/111/28, QV–KL 12 Mar. 1864.
41. QVJ: 20 Nov. 1863; LQV s2 I, 117; Cowley, *Paris Embassy*, 255; Corti EE, 118; RA VIC/MAIN/Y/111/28, QV–KL 12 Mar. 1864.
42. RA VIC/MAIN/Y/111/18, QV–KL 18 Feb. 1864; ibid., Y/111/20, 25 Feb. 1864; ibid., Y/111/41, 28 Apr. 1864; *Dearest Mama*, 300–01; RA VIC/MAIN/Y111/28, QV–KL 12 Mar. 1864.
43. RA VIC/MAIN/Y/111/29, QV–KL 29 Mar. 1864; Bell, *Palmerston*, II, 338; LQV s2 I, 121; ibid., 130–2; Walpole, *Russell*, II, 388.
44. LQV s2 I, 139–40.
45. NA PRO/30/22/15A f 16, Gen Grey–Ld R, 3 Jan. 1864.
46. NA PRO 30/22/23 f 39 Ld P–Ld R, 19 Feb. 1864.
47. NA PRO 30/22/13H ff 64–7 Russell–QV, 22 July 1859; Mosse, *EHR*, 271; Fitzmaurice, *Granville*, I, 458–9, 456–57.
48. LQV s2 I, 143–5; ibid., 150, 153.
49. NA PRO 30/22/15A, Ld P–Ld R, 18 Jan. 1864 Fitzmaurice, *Granville*, I, 456–7.
50. RA VIC/MAIN/Y/111/17, QV–KL 11 Feb. 1864; Gooch (ed.), *Russell*, II, 308; RA VIC/MAIN/Y/111/16, QV–KL 14 Feb. 1864.
51. *Hansard*, 173, cols 129–30, 4 Feb. 1864; RA VIC/MAIN/A/32/4, Ld P–QV 4 Feb. 1864; *Hansard*, 173, cols 131–2, 4 Feb. 1864.
52. Fitzmaurice, *Granville*, I, 460; Ashley, *Palmerston*, II, 247–8; LQV s2 I, 157.

53. LQV s2 I, 158.
54. LQV s2 I, 164, 166–7.
55. RA VIC/MAIN/Y/111/20, QV–KL 25 Feb. 1864, part printed LQV s2 I, 168.
56. RA VIC/MAIN/Y/111/18, QV–KL, 18 Feb. 1864; RA VIC/MAIN/Y/111/20, QV–KL, 25 Feb. 1864; LQV s2 I, 170–1.
57. *Dearest Mama*, 321, 318; RA VIC/MAIN/Y/111/36, QV–KL 15 Apr. 1864; *Dearest Mama*, 324.
58. LQV s2 I, 181; Ashley, *Palmerston*, II, 249–50.
59. LQV s2 I, 180–3; QVJ: 4 May 1864; LQV s2 I, 184.
60. NA PRO/30/22/15C ff35–37 Ld P–Ld R, 17 June 1864; DDC, 214; Corti EE, 127; LQV s2 I, 207.
61. Williams, *Contentious*, 119, Mosse, *EHR*, 277–8; LQV s2 I, 186–7.
62. *Hansard*, 175, cols 609, 615, 26 May 1846; LQV s2 I, 198, 208–9.
63. Fitzmaurice, *Granville*, I, 466–67; Gooch (ed.), *Russell*, II, 310–12; LQV s2 I, 210; Fitzmaurice, *Granville*, I, 468–9.
64. RA VIC/MAIN/Y/111/9, QV–KL 21 Jan. 1864; Cowley, *Paris Embassy*, 267; Gooch (ed.), *Russell*, II, 312; Mosse, *German*, 202; LQV s2 I, 215.
65. NA PRO 30/22/15C Ld P–Ld R 13 June 1864 LQV s2 I, 220; QVJ: 16 June 1864, Cowley, *Paris Embassy*, 267, 269.
66. Gooch (ed.), *Russell*, II, 313; LQV s2 I, 225; RA VIC/MAIN/Y/112/9, QV–KL, 7 July 1864; LQV s2 I, 226–7.
67. RA VIC/MAIN/Y/112/7, QV–KL, 23 June 1864; QVJ: 21 June 1864; QVJ: 25 June 1864; GD, VI, 284; Grey Ps GRE/D/IV/7/19, Grey–Granville 26 June 1864.
68. LQV s2 I, 240; RA VIC/MAIN/Y/112/14, QV–KL 20 July 1864.
69. Tilney Basset, *Gladstone*, 160; LQV s2 I, 232; RA VIC/MAIN/Y/112/9, QV–KL, 7 July 1864.
70. LQV s2 I, 230; Wemyss, *Morier*, I, 400; Bell, *Palmerston*, II, 365.
71. Grey Ps, GRE/D/XIII/4 F 76–7, QV–Grey, 23 Nov. 1863; RA VIC/MAIN/Y/111/48, QV–KL, 25 May 1864; ibid., Y/112/7, QV–KL, 23 June 1864; ibid., Y/112/9, QV–KL, 7 July 1864.
72. *The Times*, 6 Apr. 1864; Grey Ps, GRE/D/XIII/4 f 51–52, Grey–QV, 4 Sept. 1863; ibid., 53–4 Grey–Phipps, 4 Sept. 1864.
73. RA VIC/MAIN/A/32/36, QV–Ld P, 7 Apr. 1864; ibid., A/32/37, Ld P–QV, 7 Apr. 1864; DDC, 214, 210–11, 216; LQV s2 I, 233.
74. Tilney Basset, *Gladstone*, 160; LQV s2 I, 244–5.
75. Rappaport, *Magnificent*, 175; PP MS 62/RC/F/1151, QV–Ld P, 28 Dec 1864.
76. YDL, 31; DL, VIII, 415; G&P, 265; Foreman, 746–7; LQV s2 I, 252–4.
77. LQV s2 I, 265–7; QVJ: 29 Apr. 1865.
78. Dasent, *Delane*, 109, 98; RA VIC/MAIN Y/111/18, QV–KL, 18 Feb. 1864; QVJ: 17 Jan. 1865; RA VIC/MAIN/Y/111/8, QV–KL, 19 Jan. 1865.
79. LQV s2 I, 271; ibid., 276; Gooch (ed.), *Russell*, II, 314–15.
80. Connell, *Regina*, 355.
81. GD, VI, 330; Shannon, *Gladstone*, I, 436.
82. Morley, *Gladstone*, I, 737; QVJ: 27 Sept. 1863.
83. LQV s2 I, 189–90; G&P, 284, 286.
84. Tilney Basset, *Gladstone*, 159; GD, VI, 304; Tilney-Bassett, 161.
85. G&P, 311–12; QVJ: 21 Nov. 1864; LQV s2 I, 248.
86. DL, VIII, 314n; Tilney Bassett, *Gladstone*, 157; Cowley, *Paris Embassy*, 253–4.

87. RA VIC/MAIN/Y/113/36, QV–KL 10 Apr. 1865.
88. PP MS 62, RC/F/1160, QV–Ld P, 10 Apr. 1865.
89. RA VIC/MAIN/Y/114/19, QV–KL, 29 June 1865; ibid., Y/114/23/QV–KL, 27 July 1865.
90. QVJ: 15 Oct. 1865; RA VIC/MAIN/Y/114/35, QV–KL, 15 Oct. 1865; LQV s2 I, 279.
91. QVJ: 6 July 1864; QVJ: 7 May 1865; LQV s2 I, 278.
92. Maxwell, *Clarendon*, II, 298–9; QVJ: 21 Oct. 1865; M&B,IV, 424.

Chapter 7

1. QVJ: 10 Dec. 1865; *Dear Duchess*, 228, 232; QVJ: 10 Dec. 1865.
2. LQV s2 I, 301–02; NA PRO 30/22/16B ff 29–30, 15–20, 44–5; YDL, 59.
3. LQV s2 I, 295–6.
4. QVJ: 6 Feb. 1866; Diary of Katherine Clarendon, 6 Feb. 1866, Bod. MS Eng.e.2126.
5. Grey Ps, GRE/D/XIII/8 f 7,QV–Grey, 6 Feb. 1866; ibid., GRE/D/XIII/8 f 11, QV–Grey, 17 Feb. 1866.
6. Grey Ps GRE/D/XIII/8 f 12–13, Grey–QV, 17 Feb. 1866; LQV s2 I, 300.
7. LQV s2 I, 282, 338, 341.
8. QVJ: 18 Feb. 1866; YDL, 63; Malmesbury, *Memoirs*, 621; PRO 30/22/16B Somerset-Russell 7 Mar. 1866; RA VIC/MAIN/F/14/9, Grey–QV, 8 Mar. 1866; RA VIC/MAIN/F/14/14, Ld R–QV 14 Mar. 1866.
9. Lang, *Life*, 153; Briggs, *Age*, 501; *Hansard*, 182, col. 148, 13 Mar. 1866; Smith, *Reform*, 86–7.
10. YDL, 165–6; NA PRO 30/22/16B f 146–7, memo by Brand, 24 Mar. 1866.
11. LQV s2 I, 305; YDL, 63; LQV s2 I, 308; QVJ: 22 Mar. 1866; Mosse, *Historical Journal*, 212; LQV s2 I, 310–11.
12. YDL, 64; NA PRO 30/22/16B ff 177–79, 182 ; LQV s2 I, 315.
13. LQV s2 I, 313; Maxwell, *Clarendon*, II, 310.
14. YDL, 72; LQV s2 I, 317.
15. LQV s2 I, 319; Mosse, *Historical Journal*, 217.
16. QVJ: 23 Apr. 1866; RA VIC/MAIN/F/14/35, Grey–QV, 24 Apr. 1866; RA VIC/MAIN/F/14/37 Granville–Grey, 24 Apr. 1866; ibid., F/14/36, Grey–QV 25 Apr. 1866; LQV s2 I, 320.
17. *Hansard*, 183, col. 152, 27 Apr. 1866.
18. LQV s2 I, 326–7; Shannon, *Gladstone*, II, 21.
19. QVJ: 29 May 1866; LQV s2 I, 330; RA VIC/MAIN/F/14/58 Ld D–QV, 30 May 1866.
20. LQV s2 I, 331; RA VIC/MAIN/F/14/69, Ld R–QV, 9 June 1866.
21. Gooch (ed.), *Russell*, II, 347–8; NA PRO 30/22/16B, ff 113, 115, 140; Grey Ps GRE/D//XIII/8 f 55; LQV s2 I, 329; NA PRO/30/22/16B f 55.
22. Grey Ps GRE/D/XIII/8 ff 62–3, Granville–QV, 7 June 1866, and undated note QV–Grey; QVJ: 10 June 1866; NA PRO/30/22/16B, f 268.
23. QVJ: 23 Apr. 1866; LQV s2 I, 321; Cowley, *Paris Embassy*, 302; LQV s2 I, 325; NA PRO 30/22/16B f 161.
24. RA VIC/MAIN/F/14/73, Gladstone–QV, 19 June 1866; LQV s2 I, 334–5; RA VIC/MAIN/C/32/8, Grey–Gladstone, 19 June 1866; GD, VI, 444.
25. LQV s2 I, 335–6.
26. RA VIC/MAIN/C/32/4, Ld R–QV, 19 June 1866; ibid., C/32/13, QV–Ld R, 20 June 1866 and Russell's reply, 22 June; LQV s2 I, 338; DDC, 254; Cowley, *Paris Embassy*, 306–07; diary of Katherine Clarendon, 23 June 1866, Bod. MS Eng.e2127; Cavendish, *Diary*, II, 10.

27. RA VIC/MAIN/C/32/16, Grey–QV, 22 June 1866; LQV s2 I, 339–40.
28. Cowley, *Paris Embassy*, 305.
29. QVJ: 14 Oct. 1858; LQV s2 I, 353–54; QVJ: 6 July 1866.
30. YDL, 89–90.
31. LQV s2 I, 357, 362–3.
32. YDL, 87–8; Derby Ps 191/2 f 186, Ld D–QV, 12 Oct. 1866.
33. QVJ: 24 July 1866; RA VIC/MAIN/F/14/81, Biddulph–Cambridge, 25 July 1866.
34. LQV s2 I, 352; Smith, *Reform*, 135.
35. M&B, IV, 457; Smith, *Reform*, 135; Hawkins, *Derby*, II, 320–1; RA VIC/MAIN/F/14/93, QV–Grey 13 Oct. 1866; M&B, IV, 457–8.
36. M&B, IV, 457; LQV s2 I, 372.
37. LQV s2 I, 388, 390; Hawkins, *Derby*, II, 326.
38. YDL, 121; Derby Ps 103/6/31/6. Grey–Ld D, 9 Dec. 1866; ibid., 103/7/1 Grey–Ld D, 10 Jan. 1867.
39. Derby Ps 103/7/13, Grey–Derby, 5 Feb. 1867; YDL, 129.
40. RA VIC/MAIN/F/15/8, Ld D–Grey, 7 Feb. 1867; Derby Ps 103/7/15, Grey–Ld D, 8 Feb. 1867.
41. Smith, *Reform*, 130; M&B, IV, 492.
42. M&B, IV, 494; Derby Ps 192/1 f 206–8; *Hansard*, 185, col. 338, 14 Feb. 1867.
43. RA VIC/MAIN/F/15/29, Grey–QV, 22 Feb. 1867, ibid., F/15/20, Grey–QV, 17 Feb. 1867.
44. M&B, IV, 495; LQV s2 I, 397.
45. RA VIC/MAIN/F/15/21, QV–Peel, 17 Feb. 1867; ibid., F/15/22, Grey–QV, 17 Feb. 1867.
46. RA VIC/MAIN/F/15/24/Disraeli–QV, 19 Feb. 1867; Hardinge, *Carnarvon*, I, 345.
47. RA VIC/MAIN/F/15/29, Grey–QV, 22 Feb. 1867; ibid., F/15/24 Disraeli–QV, 19 Feb. 1867.
48. Hardinge, *Carnarvon*, I, 346.
49. LQV s2 I, 400.
50. LQV s2 I, 401; QVJ: 25 Feb. 1867.
51. LQV s2 I, 403–4; Cowling, *Disraeli*, 164.
52. QVJ: 1 Mar. 1867, 8 Mar. 1867; RA VIC/MAIN/F/15/75, Grey–QV, 21 Mar. 1867.
53. RA VIC/MAIN/F/15/61 Grey–Disraeli 12 Mar. 1867; LQV s2 I, 407–9.
54. RA VIC/MAIN/F/15/73, Grey–QV, 20 Mar. 1867; LQV s2 I, 410.
55. LQV s2 I, 412; M&B, IV, 516; LQV s2 I, 414; QVJ: 22 Mar. 1867.
56. RA VIC/MAIN/F/15/82, Disraeli–QV, 25 Mar. 1867; M&B, IV, 524.
57. Matthew, *Gladstone*, I, 139.
58. Morley, *Gladstone*, II, 225; RA VIC/MAIN/F/15/85 Grey–QV, 8 Apr. 1867; M&B, IV, 530–1; GD, VI, 512–13.
59. LQV s2 I, 415, 424–5.
60. M&B, IV, 538.
61. RA VIC/MAIN/F/15/100, Ld D–QV, 5 May 1867; RA VIC/MAIN/F/15/109 Mr D–QV, 10 May.
62. M&B, IV, 539; Malmesbury, *Memoirs*, 630.
63. RA VIC/MAIN/F/15/112, Mr D–QV, 20 May 1867.
64. LQV s2 I, 426–27; Hughenden Ps, Bod. Dep. Hughenden 85/1/f 80.
65. LQV s2 I, 421; Derby Ps 103/7/f 42, Grey–Ld D, 28 May 1867; LQV s2 I, 430.
66. LQV s2 I, III, 461; ibid., 255.
67. DDC, 232; ibid., 237; Cullen, *Empress*, 83.
68. DDC, 247–8.
69. LQV s2 I, 433; Lamont-Brown, *John Brown*, 81–2; Rappaport, *Magnificent*, 191; Cullen, *Empress*, 103.
70. LQV s2 I, 449; LQV s2 I, 433–4; Derby Ps 194/1/71, Ld D–Grey, 27 June 1867; GH, 43.
71. LQV s2 I, 449–50.
72. RA VIC/MAIN/Y/111/32, QV–KL, 7 Apr. 1867.
73. QVJ: 22 Dec. 1866.

74. QVJ: 5 July 1867; LQV s2 I, 442.
75. Derby Ps 103/7/51, Grey–Ld D, 4 July 1867.
76. LQV s2 I, 443; DDC, 312; Derby Ps, 194/2/f65–66 Ld D–QV, 4 July 1867.
77. DDC 312; Hawkins, *Derby*, II, 349–50.
78. QVJ: 13 July 1867; YDL, 142–4.
79. YDL, 145.
80. LQV s2 I, 434–5.
81. LQV s2 I, 435–6; Roberts, *Salisbury*, 98; RA VIC/MAIN/F/15/130, Grey–QV, 7 Aug. 1867; M&B, IV, 551.
82. Hawkins, *Party Politics*, 119; Maxwell, *Clarendon*, II, 333–4.
83. RA VIC/MAIN/A/33/83, Ld P–QV, 26 Sept. 1865; PP RC/F/1170 QV–Ld P, 1 Oct. 1865; QVJ: 8 Mar. 1867.
84. QVJ: 27 May 1867; GH, 49–50.
85. QVJ: 14 Oct. 1867; LQV s2 I, 467; Derby Ps 103/7 Grey–Ld D, 17 Oct. 1867; Grey Ps, GRE/D/XIII/9 f 70 QV–Grey 15 Oct. 1867.
86. QVJ: 13–14 Dec. 1867; LQV s2 I, 474.
87. DDC, 324; LQV s2 I, 478; YDL, 169; GH, 59–60.
88. YDL, 169; QVJ: 21 Dec. 1867; LQV s2 I, 479–80.
89. QVJ: 7 Jan. 1868.
90. QVJ: 5 Apr., 25 Apr. 1868.
91. Quinlivan and Rose, *Fenians*, 133.
92. LQV s2 I, 492; M&B, IV, 586–7; LQV s2 I, 496–97, 498, 500; M&B, IV, 587.
93. LQV s2 I, 501–02; DDC, 331.
94. LQV s2 I, 595.
95. M&B, IV, 592; QVJ: 27 Feb. 1868; YDL, 174–6.
96. YDL, 176; Malmesbury, *Memoirs*, 637; LQV s2 I, 507; QVJ: 27 Feb. 1868.
97. Maxwell, *Clarendon*, II, 346, 342; DDC, 33.
98. RA VIC/MAIN/A/37/9, Mr D–QV, 9 Mar. 1868; M&B, V, 37.
99. M&B, V, 49.
100. Shannon, *Gladstone*, II, 48.
101. M&B, V, 18; LQV s2 I, 517, 525.
102. YDL, 180; LQV s2 I, 518; QVJ: 24 Mar. 1868.
103. M&B, V, 27.
104. GH, 69; M&B, V, 28; QVJ: 6 Apr. 1868; Fitzmaurice, *Granville*, I, 522.
105. LQV s2 I, 526.
106. Malmesbury, *Memoirs*, 639; GH, 72.
107. Grey Ps, GRE/D/1/13/28; GH, 72.
108. RA VIC/MAIN/A/37/23, Mr D–QV, 8 May 1868; Bradford, 281.
109. RA VIC/MAIN/A/37/28, Mr D–QV, 14 May 1868; M&B, V, 48; RA VIC/MAIN/A/37/35, Mr D–QV, 26 May 1868.
110. Arengo-Jones, *Victoria*, 27; LQV s2 I, 529–30; Arengo-Jones, *Victoria*, 29; Grey Ps, GRE/D/1/13 f 33–34.
111. Arengo-Jones, *Victoria*, 30.
112. Arengo-Jones, *Victoria*, 31–2.
113. Grey Ps GRE/D/1/13 f 34; RA VIC/MAIN/A/37/43, Mr D–QV, 18 July 1868.
114. M&B,IV, 554; QVJ: 20 Sept. 1868; M&B, V, 53; QVJ: 28 Sept. 1868; M&B, V, 54–5.
115. RA VIC/MAIN/A/37/49, Mr D–QV, 21 Aug. 1868; M&B, V, 77.
116. Briggs, *Age*, 519.
117. QVJ: 23 Nov. 1868; RA VIC/MAIN/A/37/71, Mr D–QV, 24 Nov. 1868.
118. LQV s2 I, 558.
119. QVJ: 21 Nov. 1868.
120. Maxwell, *Clarendon*, II, 352; Morley, *Gladstone*, II, 352; DDC, 337; QVJ: 1 Dec. 1868; RA VIC/MAIN/C/32/145 Dean of Windsor–Grey, 2 Dec. 1868.
121. RA VIC/MAIN/C/32/29, Grey–QV, 29 Nov. 1868; GD, VI, 645; Maxwell, *Clarendon*, II, 353; DD(1), 64; Grey Ps, GRE/D/XIII/10 f 43.

122. Maxwell, *Clarendon*, II, 364; LQV s2 I, 561; GD, VI, 642.
123. Dasent, *Delane*, II, 229; LQV s2 I, 564; Maxwell, *Clarendon*, II, 354–5.
124. GD, VI, 645; LQV s2 I, 564–5, 567; Gooch (ed.), *Russell*, II, 368.

Chapter 8

1. GG(1) I, 12; Gladstone, *Thirty Years*, 332.
2. Q&G I, 47; GG (1) I, 33.
3. Q&G I, 48.
4. Gladstone, *Thirty Years*, 321; GG (1) I, 170; ibid., II, 335–6.
5. Gladstone, *Thirty Years*, 332; Zetland (ed.), *Letters*, I, 49.
6. GD, X, 385; GG(1) I, 342–3; *Sidelights*, 97–8; Ponsonby, *Ponsonby*, 189, 253, 244, 250; Gladstone, *Thirty Years*, 321, Sandon, 'First Balmoral Journal', 101.
7. Parry, *Democracy*, 322–3; Kimberley, *Journal*, 257–8; GG(1) I, 77; DC, 130, 162.
8. GG(1) I, 46; LQV s2 II, 228.
9. *DC*, 29, 81; Ponsonby, *Ponsonby*, 252–3.
10. LQV s2 I, 577n.
11. GD, VII, 15; LQV s2, I, 578.
12. QVJ: 3 Feb. 1869; Q&G, I, 157; YDL, 222–3.
13. QVJ: 15 Feb. 1869; QVJ: 24 Mar., 6 Apr. 1869.
14. GD, VII, 62, 45–6; Q&G, I, 172, 204.
15. Q&G, I, 172; LQV s2 I, 596.
16. Davison and Benham, *Tait*, II, 24; LQV s2 I, 603; LQV s2 I, 605.
17. Morley, *Gladstone*, I, 904; LQV s2 I, 613; Q&G, I, 181; LQV s2 I, 614.
18. Q&G I, 54; LQV s2 I, 615; GG(1) I, 33.
19. GG(1) I, 33; Davison and Benham, *Tait*, II, 36; LQV s2 I, 617; Davison and Benham, *Tait*, II, 38.
20. GD, VII, 97; LQV s2 I, 620; QVJ: 21 July 1869; LQV s2 I, 620.
21. QVJ: 22 July 1869; LQV s2 I, 621; QVJ: 24 July 1869.
22. Q&G, I, 175–6.
23. GP BL Loan MS 73/5, Grey–Mr G, 11 June 1869; ibid., 9 June 1869; Q&G, I, 52; GP BL Loan Ms 73/5, 5 June 1869.
24. Q&G, I, 178; GP BL Loan Ms 73/5 Grey–Mr G, 5 June 1869.
25. Q&G, I, 179–80; GP, BL Loan Ms 73/5, Mr G–Grey, 7 June 1869.
26. GP BL Loan Ms 73/5 Grey–Mr G, 9 June 1869.
27. Q&G, I, 181–2.
28. Q&G, I, 184; Fitzmaurice, *Granville*, II, 19.
29. Q&G, I, 197–9; GG(1) I, 48.
30. GD, VII, 132–3; GG(1) I, 62 YDL, 248; Q&G, I, 207–8.
31. QVJ: 6 Nov. 1869; Q&G, I, 209.
32. Kimberley, *Journal*, 246.
33. LQV s2 II, 7; YDL, 257–8.
34. YDL, 272; GG(1) I, 33–4; Kimberley, *Journal*, 247; QVJ: 26 Mar., 1 Apr. 1870.
35. Kuhn, *Ponsonby*, 152; Ponsonby, *Ponsonby*, 139–41, 247, 75–6, 137.
36. Ponsonby, *Ponsonby*, 76; Kuhn, *Ponsonby*, 153.
37. QVJ: 27 June 1870; Morley, *Gladstone*, I, 958.
38. YDL, 287; Q&G, I, 241; LQV s2 II, 44.
39. *Red Earl* I, 83; Q&G, I, 242; YDL, 300; LQV s2 II, 44; ibid., 52.
40. Q&G I, 253; YDL, 291, 296.
41. QVJ: 5 Sept. 1870.
42. QVJ: 27 Mar. 1871, 9 Jan. 1873; Ponsonby, *Ponsonby*, 41.
43. LQV s2 II, 62–3, 66.
44. LQV s2 II, 71, 73; QVJ: 29 Nov. 1870.
45. Q&G I, 256; YDL, 312n.
46. YDL, 322.
47. Q&G, I, 259–60; LQV s2 I, 633; Q&G, I, 267.
48. YDL, 262; GD, VII, 241–2; GG(1) I, 170.

49. Harcourt, *JICH*, 28; QVJ: 8 Feb. 1871; *Hansard*, 204, col. 360, 16 Feb. 1871.
50. QVJ: 19 Mar., 25 Mar., 4 Apr., 16 Apr., 27, 28 and 30 May 1871.
51. QVJ: 8 Apr. 1871; Ridley, *Bertie*, 142; Tilney Basset, *Gladstone*, 186.
52. LQV s2 II, 131.
53. LQV s2 II, 114; St Aubyn, *Royal George*, 153.
54. LQV s2 II, 141–2; GP BL Loan Ms 73/10 Mr G–Biddulph 20 July 1871; LQV s2 II, 150–51.
55. QVJ: 19 July 1871; Gladstone, *Midlothian Speeches*, 45; LQV s2 II, 162.
56. GP BL Loan 73/11 Mr G–QV, 31 July, 8 and 9 Aug., Q&G, I, 298.
57. Tilney Bassett, *Gladstone*, 187; GD, VIII, 19.
58. Q&G, I, 300.
59. GP BL MS Loan 73/11, Ponsonby–Mr G, 14 Aug., 15 Aug. 1871.
60. Q&G, I, 303; Ponsonby, *Ponsonby*, 73–5; Q&G, I, 304; *Red Earl*, I, 97.
61. Q&G, I, 301–02; QVJ: 16 Aug. 1871.
62. Tilney Basset, *Gladstone*, 191; GG(1) II, 264; M&B,V, 144–5; Tilney Basset, *Gladstone*, 191; *Red Earl*, I, 98–9.
63. GG(1) II, 283, 264; GD, VIII, 29.
64. *What Does She Do With It?* (1871).
65. Kuhn, *JBS* (1987), 142; GP BL MS Loan 73/11, Ponsonby–Mr G, 7 Oct. 1871.
66. *Red Earl*, I, 98; Nicholls, *Prime Minister*, 52; LQV s2 II, 165; Harcourt, *JICH*, 142; GG(1) II, 285, 288.
67. Q&G I, 310, 314.
68. QVJ: 10 Dec. 1871; Williams, *Contentious*, 43.
69. Q&G I, 318; GG(1) II, 291.
70. GD, VIII, 81–4.
71. Q&G, I, 325, 331; GP BL MS Loan 73/12, QV–Mr G 1 Feb., Ponsonby–Mr G, 3 Feb. 1872.
72. Q&G, I, 333; GP BL MS Loan 73/12 Mr G–QV, 3 and 4 1872.
73. QVJ: 27 Feb. 1872; DC 31; Q&G, I, 337.
74. Kimberley, *Journal*, 266; Q&G, I, 339; GP BL Ms Loan 73/12 Mr G–QV, 2 Mar. 1872.
75. DC 38; QVJ: 11–12 Apr. 1872.
76. Cavendish, *Diary*, 128; Q&G, I, 339.
77. GP BL Ms Loan 73/12 QV–Mr G, 22 Feb. 1872; Gwynn and Tuckwell, *Dilke*, I, 141; LQV s2 II 202–3.
78. GD, VIII, 83; DL, X, 112n; GD, VIII, 514–16.
79. LQV s2 II, 137; GG(1) I, 171; GD, VII, 514–16; LQV s2 II, 138. Q&G I, 321–2; Q&G, I, 340.
80. GD, VIII, 122–3; GG(1) I, 101; Magnus, *Gladstone*, 208; *Red Earl*, I, 93–4; Holland, *Compton*, I, 97.
81. GD, VIII, 173, 179; Q&G, I, 359–60; GG(1) II, 335–6.
82. Q&G I, 368–9, full text GP BL Ms Loan 73/13, 5 Aug. 1872.
83. GP BL Add 44760, memo 6 Aug. 1872; Q&G, I, 374–9; GD, VIII, 209; GG(1) II, 243.
84. GG(1) II, 342–3; Q&G I, 380.
85. GD, VIII, 242; GH, 394.
86. Q&G, I, 386.
87. DC, 80; QVJ: 13 Mar. 1873.
88. M&B, V, 209; GH, 175; QVJ: 13 Mar. 1873; GD, VIII, 301.
89. *Sidelights*, 105, Q&G, I, 399–402, 404–5.
90. GD, VIII, 304; Q&G, I, 406–7; Kimberley, *Journal*, 275; *Sidelights*, 114; Q&G, I, 410; DC 81.
91. Kimberley, *Journal*, 275; GD, VIII, 324, 387, 433; LQV s2 II, 271–2.
92. Morley, *Gladstone*, II, 80; GG(1) II, 411; Ponsonby, *Ponsonby*, 250.
93. LQV s2 II 306; QVJ: 22 Jan. 1874; QVJ: 7 Feb., 26 Jan. 1874; GH, p.193; M&B,V, 194–5, 275; Cavendish, *Diary*, 168; DC 130; DC 128.

94. DC 127, 128–9; Cavendish, *Diary*, 169; QVJ: 17 Feb. 1874.
95. Q&G, I, 446; GD, VIII, 461; Ponsonby, *Ponsonby*, 178–9.
96. GD, VIII, 462; QVJ: 17 Feb. 1874; LQV s2 II, 318; Ponsonby, *Ponsonby*, 178–9; QVJ: 20 Feb. 1874; Q&G, I, 394.

Chapter 9

1. Ponsonby, *Ponsonby*, 58; M&B, V, 285; QVJ: 20 Feb. 1874.
2. Zetland (ed.), *Letters*, I, 92.
3. LQV s2 II, 384; ibid., 538; ibid., 625; M&B, VI, 238.
4. M&B, V, 302; ibid., 483; LQV s2 II, 458; ibid., 333–4.
5. Kuhn, *Ponsonby*, 169; Ponsonby, *Ponsonby*, 245–6.
6. Seton-Watson, *Eastern*, 3; Zetland (ed.), *Letters*, I, 162; DD(1), 241; DD(1), 369.
7. LQV s2 II, 385. Zetland (ed.), *Letters*, I, 244; DD(1), 195; Zetland (ed.), *Letters*, II, 17.
8. M&B, VI, 463; Hibbert, *Victoria*, 360; DD(1), 202, 290.
9. DD(1), 290; DD(2), 17; Zetland (ed.), *Letters*, I, 80; M&B, V, 414.
10. Zetland (ed.), *Letters*, II, 34.
11. LQV s2 II, 300, 290; M&B, V, 294, 314.
12. M&B, V, 324.
13. LQV s2 II, 343; Zetland, (ed.), *Letters*, I, 129.
14. Zetland (ed.), *Letters*, I, 129; QVJ: 13 Sept. 1874; Zetland (ed.), *Letters*, I, 146; Hardinge, *Carnarvon*, II, 78; Zetland (ed.), *Letters*, I, 150.
15. LQV s2 II, 378; Chilston, *Chief Whip*, 46.
16. Zetland (ed.), *Letters*, I, 195; LQV s2 II, 379.
17. LQV s2 II, 414; Blake, *Disraeli*, 556.
18. M&B, V, 448–9; Zetland (ed.), *Letters*, I, 306–7; LQV s2 II, 428.
19. RA VIC/MAIN/F/16/69 QV–Mr D, 18 Mar. 1876; Ponsonby, *Ponsonby*, 139–41; LQV s2 II, 238–9; DC, 207.
20. Shannon, *Age of Disraeli*, 273; M&B, V, 457, 459; LQV s2 II, 439–40.
21. *Hansard*, 227, cols 19–20, 410, 8 Feb., 18 Feb. 1876; DC 223.
22. RA VIC/MAIN/F/16/12 QV–Ld G, 20 Feb. 1876, ibid., F/16/17 Ld G–QV, 23 Feb.
23. *Hansard*, 227, cols 1568–9, 1722, 7 Mar., 8 Mar. 1876; RA VIC/MAIN/F/16/33 Mr D–QV, Mar. 9; Zetland (ed.), *Letters*, II, 23; LQV s2 II, 451; QVJ: 14 Mar.; RA VIC/MAIN/F/16/34, Ld G–QV, 14 Mar.
24. Ponsonby, *Ponsonby*, 139–41; Taylor, *Victoria*, 170.
25. Hansard, 228, cols 483–4; RA VIC/MAIN/F/16/40, Ld G–Ponsonby 14 Mar. 1876; Ponsonby, *Ponsonby*, 140; Hansard, 228, col. 76, 16 Mar. 1876; QVJ: 21 Mar.; Zetland (ed.), *Letters*, II, 26; RA VIC/MAIN/F/16/76 Mr D–QV, 21 Mar. 1876.
26. RA VIC/MAIN/F/16/90, QV–Lorne, 26 Mar. 1876; ibid., F/16/98 Mr D–QV, Mar. 31; Hansard, 228, cols 831–4.
27. DD(1), 288; RA VIC/MAIN/F/16/90, QV–Lorne, 26 Mar. 1876; Askwith, *Hereford*, 95.
28. Zetland (ed.), *Letters*, II, 95–6; M&B, V, 486; LQV s2 II, 514; Taylor, *Victoria*, 173.
29. Zetland (ed.), *Letters*, II, 30–1; RA VIC/MAIN/F/17/50 Mr D–QV, 5 May 1876; M&B, V, 495, 491.
30. LQV s2 II, 456; DD(1), 303; LQV s2 II, 465.
31. QVJ: 8 July 1876; LQV s2 II, 470–1.
32. M&B, VI, 43; DC 219; Shannon, *Bulgarian Agitation*, 44; LQV s2 II, 472; M&B, VI, 39, 46; LQV s2 II, 474.

33. Millman, *Eastern Question*, 158; Seton-Watson, *Eastern*, 56; M&B VI 46–47; QVJ: 12, 23 and 30 Aug. 1876.
34. DC 221; Zetland (ed.), *Letters*, II, 76.
35. Seton-Watson, *Eastern*, 75.
36. Zetland (ed.), *Letters*, II, 71–2; LQV s2 II, 426; M & B VI, 64; DC 223.
37. QVJ: 14 May, 17 May 1874; LQV s2 II, 480–81; RA VIC/MAIN/H/9/179, QV–Ld B, 30 Sept. 1876.
38. LQV s2 II, 488, 496, 498.
39. Millman, *Eastern Question*, 202; LQV s2 II, 501.
40. GH, 300; Ponsonby, *Ponsonby*, 161; LQV s2 II, 504; Zetland (ed.), *Letters*, II, 93.
41. LQV s2 II, 505; Hardinge, *Carnarvon*, II, 346; BL Add 60909, Carnarvon diary, 17 Jan. 1877.
42. Hardinge, *Carnarvon*, II, 348; M&B, VI, 123; Millman, *Eastern Question*, 258; QVJ: 24 Mar. 1877.
43. M&B, VI, 132.
44. DD(1), 391; M&B, VI, 133.
45. RA VIC/MAIN/B/52/30 QV–Ld B, 5 Sept. 1877; DC, 253; M&B, VI, 148; RA VIC/MAIN/B/52/27, QV–Ld B, 26 Aug.; DC, 256; M&B, VI, 152.
46. RA VIC/MAIN/B/52/32 Ld B–QV, 16 Sept. 1877; M&B, VI, 184; RA VIC/MAIN/B/53/53, Ld B–QV, 28 Nov. 1877.
47. GD, IX, 317.
48. Hardinge, *Carnarvon*, II, 356; DD(1), 505.
49. DD(1), 514.
50. GD, IX, 218; GH, 328; RA VIC/MAIN/H/15/7, QV–Ld B, 5 July 1877; QVJ: 15 May 1877.
51. Bourne, *Foreign Policy*, 407–9; Blake, *Disraeli*, 457.
52. QVJ: 10 June 1877; M & B VI, 142; LQV s2 II, 542; RA VIC/MAIN/H/14/83 Ld B–QV, 14 June; M&B, VI, 147, 149.
53. M&B, VI, 148–9.
54. Zetland, (ed.), *Letters*, II, 119; 123; QVJ: 16 June 1877; GH, 328; Seton-Watson, *Eastern*, 202–3.
55. RA VIC/MAIN/H/15/18, Ld B–QV, 12 July 1877; QVJ: 17 July 1877; M&B, VI, 152; LQV s2 II, 548.
56. DD(1), 421; M&B, VI, 152, 154; RA VIC/MAIN/B/52/12, QV–Ld B, 23 July 1877.
57. Seton-Watson, *Eastern*, 221; GH 333; M&B, VI, 158.
58. RA VIC/MAIN/B/52/17, QV–Ld B, 1 Aug. 1877.
59. LQV s2 II 503–4; QVJ: 16 Aug. 1877; Wellesley 143–4; RA VIC/MAIN/B/53/16, Ld–QV, 4 Oct. 1877.
60. LQV s2 II, 567–8; RA VIC/MAIN/B/52/30, QV–Ld B, 30 Sept. 1877; ibid., B/52/32, Ld B–QV 16 Sept. 1877; ibid., B/53/3 & 9, Ld B–QV, 24 & 28 Sept. 1877.
61. RA VIC/MAIN/B/53/13, QV–Ld B 1 Oct. 1877; ibid., B/53/20, QV–Ld B, 7 Oct. 1877; M&B, VI, 150; DD(1), 450.
62. RA VIC/MAIN/B/53/48, QV–Ld B 16 Nov. 1877; ibid., B/53/50, QV–Ld B, 19 Nov. 1877; DD(1), 255; Millman, *Eastern Question*, 337; M&B, VI, 199; GH 343.
63. RA VIC/MAIN/B/54/7, Ld B–QV, 8 Dec. 1877; DD(1), 473n; Swartz, *Politics*, 71–2; RA VIC/MAIN/B/54/42, Ld B–QV, 3 Jan. 1878; GH, 343.
64. RA VIC/MAIN/B/53/2, QV–Ld B, 11 Dec. 1877; LQV s2 II, 575–6.
65. QVJ: 15 Dec. 1877; DC 273; Seton-Watson, *Eastern*, 281.
66. QVJ: 17–18 Dec. 1877; RA VIC/MAIN/B/54/19, Ld B–QV, 18 Dec. 1877; DC, 272–3.
67. Millman, *Eastern Question*, 347.
68. DC 274; M&B, VI, 213–4; DC 274; QVJ: 3 Jan. 1878.
69. DD(1), 481; M&B, VI, 217.

70. M&B, VI, 218; RA VIC/MAIN/B/55/15, QV–Ld B, 15 Jan. 1878; QVJ: 10 Jan. 1878.
71. LQV s2 II, 597.
72. QVJ: 23 Jan. 1878, ibid., 25 Jan.; DC 278.
73. RA VIC/MAIN/B/55/69, QV–Ld B, 31 Jan. 1878; ibid., B/55/74, QV–Ld B, Feb. I; ibid., B/56/5, QV–Ld B, Feb. 4; ibid., B/56/12, QV–Ld B, Feb. 61878.
74. RA VIC/MAIN/B/56/18 QV–Ld B, 7 Feb. 1878; M & B VI, 245; RA VIC/MAIN/B/56/34, Ld B–QV, Feb. 10; M&B, VI, 247.
75. DC, 278–80; M&B, VI, 249; DD(1), 504, 488.
76. LQV s2 II, 607.
77. RA VIC/MAIN/B/57/20, Ld B–QV, 26 Mar. 1878; M&B, VI, 263; RA VIC/MAIN/B/57/23, QV–Ld B, 27 Mar. 1878.
78. DC, 287–8; QVJ: 7 May 1878.
79. LQV s2 II, 622, 625–6.
80. M&B, VI, 306–7; QVJ: 5 June 1878.
81. M&B, VI, 344, 346–8.
82. M&B, VI, 322; QVJ: 20 July 1878.
83. QVJ: 31 July 1878; Hansard, 242, cols 690–94, 30 July 1878; QVJ: 3 Aug. 1878; *Beloved Mama*, 28.
84. QVJ: 22 Sept. 1878; LQV s2 II, 643, 649; QVJ: 30 Sept. 1878.
85. QVJ: 6 Mar. 1877; LQV s2 II, 645–6.
86. M&B, VI, 430–31; LQV s2 III, 38.
87. QVJ: 19–20 June 1879.
88. Blake, *Disraeli*, 67–71; Zetland (ed.), *Letters*, II, 226.
89. QVJ: 2 Sept. 1878; M & B VI, 459–60; GH 422.
90. GH, 423; LQV s2 III, 44; QVJ: 22 Nov. 1879; M&B, VI, 460.
91. LQV s2 III, 43–4; ibid., 67.
92. LQV s2 III, 48.
93. Jenkins, *Historical Journal*, 350–1; Ponsonby, *Ponsonby*, 170–1.
94. DD(2), 174; Morley, *Gladstone*, II, 207.
95. Morley, *Gladstone*, II, 223; Magnus, *Gladstone*, 264; *Midlothian Speeches* 37, 40, 49, 202, 91; GD, IX, 463.
96. QVJ: 2 Dec 1879; Holland, *Compton*, I, 260–1.
97. GH, 439; Ponsonby, *Ponsonby*, 181–4.
98. M&B, VI, 525; LQV s2 III, 73; RA VIC/MAIN/C/34/33 P. Leopold–QV, 3 Apr. 1880.
99. RA VIC/MAIN/C/34/40 QV–Dufferin 6 Apr. 1880; Ponsonby, *Ponsonby*, 184.
100. LQV s2 III, 74; Ponsonby, *Ponsonby*, 188.
101. M&B, VI, 532, 534–5.
102. M&B, VI, 534–5; GD, IX, 470–1; Jenkins, *Whiggery*, 132.
103. QVJ: 22 Apr. 1880.
104. QVJ: 23 Apr. 1880; GD, IX, 505; LQV s2 III, 82–83; Holland, *Compton*, I, 278.
105. GD IX, 506–7; QVJ: 23 Apr. 1880; *Beloved Mama*, 75, 78.
106. M&B, VI, 526–8; Kuhn, *Ponsonby*, 207.
107. M&B, VI, 543; RA VIC/MAIN/B/64/6 Ld B–QV, 24 July 1880; LQV s2 III, 127, 144.
108. LQV s2 III, 146–7.
109. M&B, VI, 543–4, 596; LQV s2 III, 131.
110. LQV s2 III, 131.
111. QVJ: 25 Mar. 1881; M&B, VI, 610, 619; Blake, *Disraeli*, 747.
112. LQV s2 III, 206; QVJ: 11 Apr. 1881; Blake, *Disraeli*, 749–50; QVJ: 19 Apr. 1881; LQV s2 III, 217.
113. QVJ: 30 Apr. 1881.

Chapter 10

1. RA VIC/MAIN/C/35/8, QV–Ponsonby, 28 Apr. 1880.
2. Q&G, II, 86, 88; QVJ: 26 Apr. 1880.
3. QVJ: 27 Apr. 1880; Cavendish, *Diary*, II, 252; Hamilton, (1972), I, 4; Q&G, II, 90.

4. Ponsonby, *Ponsonby*, 181–2, 184–5.
5. QVJ: 28 Apr. 1880.
6. LQV s2 III, 297–9.
7. RA VIC/MAIN/C/35/9, Ponsonby–QV, 29 Apr. 1880; QVJ: 28 Apr. 1880; BL Add 89317/7/251, QV–Ld G 23 Apr. 1880.
8. GP BL Add 56445; GD, IX, 555; *Beloved Mama*, 83–4.
9. Chilston, *Chief Whip*, 6; GD, IX, 579; Hamilton (1972), I, 49; GG(2) I, 180; QVJ: 1 Jan. 1881.
10. Hamilton (1972), I, 198,
11. M&B,VI, 435; BL Add 89317/7/251, QV–Ld G, 3 Nov. 1881; Hamilton (1972), I, 112; GG(2) I, 244; Hamilton (1972), I, 112, 115–17; BL Add 89317/7/251 QV–Ld G, 23 Mar. 1881.
12. GG(2) I, 289, 276.
13. Ponsonby, *Ponsonby*, 256; DD(2), 483; Q&G II, 165–6; GD, X, 134; Cavendish, *Diary*, II, 295–6; DD(2), 374.
14. GD, X, 153. Hamilton (1972), II, 461, ibid., 840.
15. Hamilton (1972), I, 291, 297, ibid., II, 468, 475, 552; Ponsonby, *Ponsonby*, 257; Hamilton (1972), I, 291, ibid., II, 850.
16. QVJ: 23 Apr. 1880; LQV s2 III, 143; QVJ: 10 Aug. 1880; BL Add 89317/7/251.
17. QVJ: 17 May 1881; *Beloved Mama*, 89, 121; Ponsonby, *Ponsonby*, 191–2.
18. *Beloved Mama*, 157–8; QVJ: 9 Oct. 1880; QVJ: 25 June 1882.
19. QVJ: 24 Apr. 1880; QVJ: 10 June 1880.
20. Holland, *Compton*, I, 302; QVJ: 6 Sept. 1880; GD, IX, 582.
21. Gardiner, *Harcourt*, I, 598–99; *Sidelights*, 142, 144; QVJ: 5 Jan. 1881.
22. Gardiner, *Harcourt*, I, 600; QVJ: 5 Jan. 1881; *Sidelights*, 144–5.
23. LQV s2 III, 198; GD X, 25–6; LQV s2 III, 200–01, 203, 206; Shannon, *Gladstone* II, 273; QVJ: 29 May 1881.
24. BL ADD 89317/7/251, QV–Ld G, 31 May 1881.
25. GD, IX, 656.
26. GD, IX, 558; Gwynn and Tuckwell, *Dilke*, I, 344; LQV s2 III, 117–8; QVJ: 17 July 1880; BL Add 89317/7/251 QV–Ld G, 18 July 1880.
27. LQV s2 III, 121; QVJ: 3 August 1880.
28. LQV s2 III, 127; LQV s2 III, 130–1; BL Add 89317/7/251, QV–Ld G, 1 Sept. 1880; *Beloved Mama*, 88.
29. QVJ: 26 Nov. 1881; Lyons 134; GD, IX, 615.
30. LQV s2 III, 148–9.
31. GG(2) I, 221; Gwynn and Tuckwell, *Dilke*, I, 347; GG(2), 221–2; Q&G II, 123–4; LQV s2 III, 162.
32. LQV s2 III, 165–6, 163; Holland, *Compton*, I, 335.
33. LQV s2 III, 164; ibid., 167; Q&G, II, 132.
34. Q&G, II, 138.
35. LQV s2 III, 229–30.
36. LQV s2 III, 232.
37. LQV s2 III, 234.
38. Gardiner, *Harcourt*, I, 431.
39. LQV s2 III, 222, 421–2, 481.
40. QVJ: 13 Mar. 1881; *Beloved Mama*, 97.
41. *Beloved Mama*, 116.
42. *Beloved Mama*, 116; QVJ: 19 Apr. 1881; Murphy, *Shooting*, 481, 488.
43. Hamilton (1972), I, 209; Q&G, II, 186.
44. GG(2) I, 262–3; BL Add 89317/7/251, QV–Ld G, 22 Apr. 1882.
45. Hammond, *Gladstone*, 49–50.
46. LQV s2 III, 274–5. QVJ: 2 May 1882.
47. Loulou, 41; QVJ. 6 May 1882.

48. LQV s2 III, 285; Ponsonby, *Ponsonby*, 191.
49. LQV s2 III, 298; Hamilton (1972), I, 269.
50. Loulou, 41; LQV s2 III, 295; Q&G, II, 197.
51. *Beloved Mama*, 119.
52. Loulou, 44; LQV s2 III, 297–8; ibid., 298–9.
53. LQV s2 III, 303; Q&G, II, 199.
54. LQV s2 III, 302; Hamilton (1972), I, 269.
55. LQV s2 II, 546, 550.
56. GG(2) I, 328; QVJ: 10 July, 17 July 1882.
57. Gardiner, *Harcourt*, I, 457; *Beloved Mama*, 147; Granville Papers, BL Add MS 89317/7/262, Ponsonby–Ld G, 15 Sept. 1882; GG(2) I, 438.
58. LQV s2 III, 338; GD, X, 344.
59. GG(2) I, 446; LQV s2 III, 348, 370.
60. LQV s2 III, 357.
61. LQV s2 III, 378; Loulou, 52; BL Add 89317/7/251 QV–Ld G, 31 Dec. 1882; LQV s2 III, 380.
62. Q&G, II, 182, 185.
63. QVJ: 11 Dec 1882; Wilson, *Victoria*, 341–2; Duchy of Lancaster website: www.duchyoflancaster.co.uk; Ponsonby, *Ponsonby*, 193; QVJ: 3 Jan. 1883.
64. Hamilton (1972), I, xlvi; Crewe, *Rosebery*, I, 164–5; LQV s2 III, 397.
65. Kavanagh, *Assassins*, 231, 178; LQV s2 III, 411; Gardiner, *Harcourt*, I, 474; QVJ: 30 July 1883.
66. Ponsonby, *Ponsonby*, 128; BL Add 89317/7/251, 28 Mar. 1883; DD(2), 525; Ponsonby, 127, 129.
67. J. Chamberlain, 88; Q&G, II, 253–4; LQV s2 III, 431, 434–7.
68. LQV s2 III, 440–41; 439–40.
69. GG(2) II, 90; Hamilton (1972), II, 485–6.
70. LQV s2 III, 415; Hamilton (1972), II, 408; GG(2) II, 111.
71. LQV s2 III, 447, 451; *Beloved Mama*, 178.
72. DD(2), 694; LQV s2 III, 525.
73. LQV s2 III, 468, 472.
74. QVJ: 23 Jan. 1884; LQV s2 III, 474; Q&G, II, 258; Kimberley, *Journal*, 340; LQV s2 III, 477.
75. GD, X, 138; LQV s2 III, 485; Q&G, II, 264 ; QVJ: 26 Apr. 1884.
76. Hamilton (1972), II, 642; LQV s2 III, 500.
77. LQV s2 III, 506, 508; GG(2) II, 189.
78. LQV s2 III, 506–7; Ponsonby, *Ponsonby*, 232.
79. *Beloved Mama*, 172.
80. Shannon, *Age of Salisbury*, 91.
81. LQV s2 III, 510; *Sidelights*, 163.
82. GD, XI, 170; LQV s2 III, 513; *Sidelights*, 174–5.
83. LQV s2 III, 515, 519–20; GG(2) II, 214; *Sidelights*, 171.
84. LQV s2 III, 519, DD(2), 688, *Sidelights*, 179; *Sidelights*, 184–5; LQV s2 III, 523; Garvin, *Chamberlain*, I, 466–7; Q&G, II, 294; GG(2) II, 224; Hamilton (1972), II, 669.
85. GD, X, 191–4.
86. LQV s2 III, 531; RA VIC/MAIN/C/49/12, Ponsonby–QV, 9 July 1884; GG(2) II, 233.
87. LQV s2 III, 547; QVJ: 8 Sept. 1884; LQV s2 III, 539; BL Add 89317/7/251 QV–Granville 24 Sept. and 27 Oct. 1884; GG(2) II, 268–9; Hamilton (1972), II, 707.
88. QVJ: 14 Sept. 1884; BL Add 89317/7/251, QV–Granville 24 Sept. 1884; GG(2) II, 257.
89. Q&G, II, 302; QVJ: 2 Oct. 1884; GD, XI, 225; *Sidelights*, 238; RA VIC/MAIN/C/50/14 Mr G–QV, 23–24 Oct. 1884; *Sidelights*, 245–6.
90. LQV s2 III, 546; *Red Earl*, I, 276; LQV s2 III, 546; Hamilton (1972), II, 721.

91. RA VIC/MAIN/C/50/32, QV–Richmond, 27 Oct. 1884; QVJ: 29 Oct. 1884; LQV s2 III, 562–3.
92. LQV s2 III, 566–7; Fair, *EHR* (1991), 105; Weston, *EHR* (1967), 303.
93. *Sidelights*, 273–5; Fair, *EHR* (1973), 109; QVJ: 28 Nov. 1884, Weston, *EHR* (1967), 311–12.
94. Shannon, *Age of Salisbury*, 93–5; LQV s2 III, 571–2.
95. Gwynn and Tuckwell, *Dilke*, II, 73; LQV s2 III, 573–5.
96. GG(2) II, 284–5; LQV s2 III, 576; Weston, *EHR* (1967), 304.
97. BL Add 44791, Gladstone memoir; RA VIC/MAIN/C/50/118, Argyll–QV, 17 Nov. 1884; Cecil, *Salisbury*, III, 119–20, Weston, *EHR* (1967), 320, Fair, *EHR* (1973), 111; Roberts, *Salisbury*, 305; Fair, *EHR* (1991), 108; RA VIC/MAIN/C/50/133, Peel–Ponsonby, 19 Nov. 1884; RA VIC/MAIN/C/50/124, Richmond–QV, 18 Nov. 1884.
98. LQV s2 III, 577–8; RA VIC/MAIN/C/50/77, Argyll–QV, 10 Nov. 1884; Hamilton (1972), II, 736; QVJ: 25 Nov. 1884; BL Add 44791, Gladstone memoir.
99. Q&G, II, 318; QVJ: 27 Nov. 1884; Shannon, *Age of Salisbury*, 95.
100. Fair, *EHR* (1991), 113–4; for a negative view see: Jones, *Reform*, 241–2; GH, 202–3.
101. Q&G, II, 318; RA VIC/MAIN/C/50/133, Peel–Ponsonby, 19 Nov. 1884; DD(2), 723; Hamilton (1972), II, 736; GD, XI, 248; BL Add 44791.
102. LQV s2 III, 581n; Crewe, *Rosebery*, I, 206.
103. GD, XI, 248; LQV s2 III, 595.
104. LQV s2 III, 597.
105. Ponsonby, *Ponsonby*, 231–2; LQV s2 III, 603.
106. Carlingford, *Journal*, 67; LQV s2 III, 608–9.
107. Hamilton (1972), II, 803; LQV s2 III, 616.
108. LQV s2 III, 618–9, 633.
109. QVJ: 11 Mar. 1885.
110. LQV s2 III, 628; Hamilton (1972), II, 822–3.
111. Q&G, II, 342; QVJ: 13 Apr. 1885; LQV s2 III, 635; Hamilton (1972), II, 832; Ponsonby, *Ponsonby*, 234.
112. QVJ: 10 May, 15 May 1885; LQV s2 III, 646, 648, 643.
113. Loulou, 90; GD, XI, 341.
114. LQV s2 III, 662; QVJ: 9 June 1885.
115. Carlingford, *Journal*, 114.
116. LQV s2 III, 662.
117. LQV s2 III, 219; DD(2), 723; Shannon, *Age of Salisbury*, 92; Churchill, *Lord Randolph*, 312; QVJ: 13 June 1885.
118. QVJ: 12 June, 13 June 1885; Hatfield Papers, QV–Ld S, 14 June 1885; Whibley, *Manners*, 311; Roberts, *Salisbury*, 325; Hamilton (1972), II, 887; QVJ: 18 June 1885.
119. Hamilton (1972), II, 885; GD, XI, 357; Q&G, II, 371; QVJ: 18 June 1885, Morley, *Gladstone*, II, 333; GD, XI, 359; Q&G, II, 374.
120. QVJ: 20 June 1885; Morley, *Gladstone*, II, 334; Q&G, II, 374.
121. GD, XI, 360; Morley, *Gladstone*, II, 334 QVJ: 22 June 1885; Ponsonby, *Ponsonby*, 196; LQV s2 III, 676–7.
122. QVJ: 23 June 1885; Cooke and Vincent, *Governing*, 269; Roberts, *Salisbury*, 322.
123. QVJ: 23 June 1885; Hamilton (1972), II, 897–898; GD, XI, 361.
124. Morley, *Gladstone*, II, 336; GG(2) II, 386; Q&G II, 368–9; GD, XI, 361; QVJ: 24 June 1885.
125. GD, XI, 357; Morley, *Gladstone*, II, 336.
126. Q&G, II, 379; St Aubyn, *Royal George*, 228.

Chapter 11

1. M&B, VI, 619; LQV s2 III, 216–7, ibid., II, 369.
2. Cecil, *Salisbury*, III, 88, 181–2; QVJ: 18 Jan. 1886; GH 575; B&DC, 28–9; Roberts, *Salisbury*, 353.
3. QVJ: 10 May, 7 June, 9 June 1879.
4. GG(2) II, 99–100; Hamilton (1972), II, 501; GG(2) II, 95.
5. LQV s2 III, 691–3.
6. LQV s2 III, 693; Hatfield Papers, QV–Ld S, 20 Nov. 1885.
7. Cecil, *Salisbury*, III, 180; QVJ: 12 June 1885.
8. QVJ: 19 Aug., 17 Aug. 1885.
9. Rhodes James, *Churchill*, 200–01; QVJ: 11 Oct. 1885; Hatfield Ps QV-Ld S, 30, 12 and 27 Oct. 1885.
10. Foster, *Randolph Churchill*, 210–11; LQV s3 I, 14.
11. Hardinge, *Carnarvon*, III, 138, 151–3.
12. Hammond, *Gladstone*, 379; Cecil, *Salisbury*, III, 155.
13. Hatfield Ps, QV–Ld S, 6 July 1885; LQV s2 III, 687, 689.
14. Hammond, *Gladstone*, 383; Cecil, *Salisbury*, III, 154; Morley, *Gladstone*, II, 351–2; Hardinge, *Carnarvon*, III, 178, 181.
15. Cooke and Vincent, *Governing*, 287; Hardinge, *Carnarvon*, III, 196, 198–9; Cecil, *Salisbury*, III, 160–1.
16. GD XI, 347; QVJ: 24 June 1885; GD, XI, 366.
17. GD XI, 380n. 382, 401.
18. LQV s2 III, 697–8; GG(2) II, 402–3; LQV s2 III, 700–3.
19. QVJ: 3 Oct. 1884; LQV s2 III 547; Hatfield Ps, D/87, QV–Ld S, 3 Dec 1885
20. LQV s2 III, 708–9; QVJ: 7 Dec 1885; LQV s2 III, 547–8.
21. Holland, *Compton*, II, 96, Elliot, *Goschen*, I, 318; QVJ: 8 Dec 1885.
22. GH 584.
23. GD, XI, 448; Hardinge, *Carnarvon*, III, 200, 202.
24. Ponsonby, *Ponsonby*, 199–200; GH 585.
25. LQV s2 III, 711; BL Add 60925, Carnarvon diary, 15 Dec. 1885.
26. Hammond, *Gladstone*, 499; GD, XI, 453; QVJ: 18 Dec. 1885; Hatfield Ps QV–Ld S, 20 Dec. 1885.
27. GD, XI, 455; Curtis, *Coercion*, 72.
28. GD, XI, 462.
29. LQV s2 III, 712–14.
30. LQV s2 III 713–4; Loulou, 118; LQV s2 III, 717–8.
31. GG(2) II, 423.
32. Kimberley, *Journal*, 362; LQV s3 I, 16.
33. LQV s3 I, 15, 22; Loulou, 129; GH 594.
34. Ponsonby, *Ponsonby*, 206; Crewe, *Rosebery*, I, 257, Cooke and Vincent, *Governing*, 333; RA VIC/MAIN/C/37/160, Ponsonby–QV, 27 Jan. 1886; ibid., C/37/162a, QV memo 28 Jan. 1886; Cooke and Vincent, *Governing*, 337; QVJ: 28 Jan. 1886; LQV s3 I, 26.
35. RA VIC/MAIN/C/37/164 QV–Goschen 28 Jan. 1886; ibid., C/37/171, QV memo 29 Jan. 1886; LQV s3 I, 26; Ponsonby, *Ponsonby*, 206.
36. LQV s3 I, 27–29, 32.
37. Askwith, *Hereford*, 157–8.
38. Cooke and Vincent, *Governing*, 338.
39. LQV s3 I, 29.
40. RA VIC/MAIN/C/37/162a, QV memo, 28 Jan. 1886; Holland, *Compton*, II, 123.
41. LQV s3 I, 37; RA VIC/MAIN/C/37/247a, QV memo, 5 Feb. 1886.
42. Cooke and Vincent, *Governing*, 356; Ponsonby, *Ponsonby*, 208.
43. QVJ: 1 Feb. 1886.
44. Ponsonby, *Ponsonby*, 208; Morley, *Gladstone*, II, 398; Cooke and Vincent, *Governing*, 356; RA VIC/

MAIN/C/37/206 QV–Ld S, 1 Feb. 1886; Hatfield Ps, D/87, Ld S–QV, 4 Feb. 1886.
45. QVJ: 5 Feb. 1886; RA VIC/MAIN/C/37/206, QV–Ld S, 1 Feb. 1886; ibid., C/37/247a, QV memo 5 Feb.; LQV s3 I, 45; GH 596; Foster, *Randolph Churchill*, 251n.
46. QVJ: 1 Feb., 8 Feb. 1886; *Red Earl*, II, 109.
47. LQV s3 I, 42–44; GD, XI, 489.
48. LQV s3 I, 51, 57.
49. RA VIC/MAIN/C/37/214 Ponsonby–QV, 2 Feb. 1886; LQV s3 I, 52–4.
50. LQV s3 I, 110.
51. QVJ: 25 Nov. 1885; Lubenow, *Politics*, 61–2; GD, XI, 504.
52. LQV s3 I, 73–6.
53. GD, XI, 507.
54. LQV s3 I, 58; McKinstry, *Rosebery*, 61; Crewe, *Rosebery*, I, 214.
55. McKinstry, *Rosebery*, 147; QVJ: 6 Feb. 1886; LQV s3 I, 50, 56–7; Hatfield Ps, QV–Ld S, 28 Feb. 1886.
56. McKinstry, *Rosebery*, 159; Crewe, *Rosebery*, I, 264; QVJ: 4 May 1886.
57. Chilston, *Chief Whip*, 65.
58. Hatfield Ps, QV–Ld S, 28 Feb. 1886; Churchill, *Lord Randolph*, 446, 448.
59. LQV s3 I, 92–3.
60. GD, XI, 517; LQV s3 I, 92–3; RA VIC/MAIN/C/38/44a, undated 1886 memo by Bigge; Hatfield Ps QV–Ld S, 29 Mar. 1886.
61. QVJ: 23 Mar. 1886; RA VIC/MAIN/B/66/13 QV–Goschen 26 Mar. 1886.
62. GD, XI, 519; LQV s3 I, 95–6; RA VIC/MAIN/B/66/14, QV–Goschen 6 Apr. 1886; ibid., B/66/15, Goschen–QV, 7 Apr. 1886; ibid., B/66/19 QV–Goschen, 11 Apr. 1886.
63. LQV s3 I, 98, 102–3; RA VIC/MAIN/B/66/21, QV–Goschen, 25 Apr. 1886; Hatfield Ps QV–Ld S, 25 Apr. 1886.
64. Holland, *Compton*, II, 148; Hatfield Ps QV–Ld S, 17 Apr. 1886.
65. Hatfield Ps, Rowton–Ld S, Apr. 30, QV–Ld S 5 May 1886.
66. QVJ: 6 May 1886; LQV s3 I, 118–9.
67. QVJ: 9 May 1886; LQV s3 I, 120–2
68. QVJ: 7 May 1886; Hatfield Ps, Lady Ely–Ld S, 8 May 1886; RA VIC/MAIN/B/66/27, QV–Goschen, 16 May 1886.
69. Hatfield Ps, QV–Ld S, 9 May 1886; RA VIC/MAIN/B/66/26, QV–Goschen, 15 May 1886; QVJ: 6 June 1886.
70. RA VIC/MAIN/B/66/25, QV–Goschen, 13 May 1886; ibid., B/66/21 Apr., 25 Apr. 1886; ibid., B/66/26 May, 15 May 1886.
71. LQV s3 I, 128–9; GD, XI, 556.
72. Hatfield Ps, QV–Ld S, 16 May, 20 May 1886.
73. LQV s3 I, 132; GD, XI, 560.
74. Hardinge, *Carnarvon*, III, 222; Fitzmaurice, *Granville*, II, 494; GG(2) II, 446; Morley, *Gladstone*, II, 422.
75. RA VIC/MAIN/B/66/35, QV–Goschen 3 June 1886.
76. Morley, *Gladstone*, II, 434–5.
77. Hardinge, *Carnarvon*, III, 223–4; Balfour, 191.
78. Hatfield Ps, QV–Ld S, 12 June 1886; LQV s3 I, 147.
79. GD, XI, 567; LQV s3 I, 149–50; GD, XI, 575.
80. Q&G, II, 416.
81. LQV s3 I, 154–5.
82. GD XI, 585–6.
83. DD(2), 835; Shannon, *Gladstone*, II, 447; Magnus, *Gladstone*, 359–60; Ponsonby, *Ponsonby*, 211–12.
84. LQV s3 I, 160; RA VIC/MAIN/B/66/39, QV–Goschen, 20 July 1886.
85. Hamilton, (1993), 42.
86. RA VIC/MAIN/C/38/5 & 4, Rowton–QV, 17 July, 19 July 1886.

87. RA VIC/MAIN/C/38/14, Rowton–QV, 23 July 1886.
88. Colson, 84; QVJ: 24 July 1886.
89. Roberts, *Salisbury*, 392; QVJ: 24 July 1886; LQV s3 I, 172; RA VIC/MAIN/B/66/41, QV–Goschen, 9 Aug. 1886.
90. QVJ: 30 July 1886; Morley, *Gladstone*, II, 441; Ponsonby, *Ponsonby*, 212–3.
91. LQV s3 I, 169; Ponsonby, *Ponsonby*, 260; Magnus, *Gladstone*, 365.

Chapter 12

1. QVJ: 25 July 1886; QVJ: 28 July 1886; GH, 618, 621.
2. Hough (ed.), *Advice*, 82; Hatfield Ps, D 87/365, Ld S–QV, 24 Aug. 1886; Corti *Alexander*, 235; B&DC, 40–1; LQV s3 I, 180–2; GH, 624.
3. Hough (ed.), *Advice*, 82; QVJ: 2 Sept. 1886; Corti, *Alexander*, 255–6; GH, 628–9.
4. LQV s3 I, 181; QVJ: 2 Sept. 1886; Cecil, *Salisbury*, III, 319; GH, 630; LQV s3 I, 202.
5. B&DC, 40–1; LQV s3 I, 220.
6. LQV s3 I, 229–30.
7. LQV s3 I, 233n.
8. GH, 637; LQV s3 I, 225–6; QVJ: 16 Dec 1886.
9. LQV s3 I, 233.
10. LQV s3 I, 234; QVJ: 23 Dec 1886.
11. GH, 641.
12. QVJ: 9 Jan. 1887; LQV s3 I, 252–3; QVJ: 12 Jan. 1887.
13. GH 652; Gardiner, *Harcourt*, II, 17; LQV s3 I, 259.
14. LQV s3 I, 373–4.
15. Lant, *Pageant*, 92, 49, 88, 162; LQV s3 I, 436.
16. Hatfield Ps, D 87/476, Ld S–QV, 3 Mar. 1887; Lant, *Pageant*, 46.
17. Lant, *Pageant*, 92, 152.
18. Pearson, *Labby*, 251; QVJ: 12 May, 13 May 1887.
19. Lant, *Pageant*, 52; Williams, *Contentious*, 58; QVJ: 13 May 1887.
20. LQV s3 I, 350; LQV s3 I, 350.
21. QVJ: 23 Mar. 1887; Longford, 499; QVJ: 14 May 1887; LQV s3 I, 310.
22. QVJ: 21 June 1887.
23. QVJ: 29 June 1887; LQV s3 I, 280–81; St Aubyn, *Royal George*, 233.
24. Lant, *Pageant*, 54.
25. QVJ: 28 Jan. 1887.
26. Morley, *Gladstone*, II, 459; Hatfield Ps, D 87/447, Ld S–QV, 27 Jan. 1887.
27. QVJ: 12 Mar. 1887.
28. Adams, *Balfour*, 76; Curtis, *Coercion*, 175; Roberts, *Salisbury*, 444.
29. QVJ: 5 Mar. 1887; GH, 659; Ponsonby, *Ponsonby*, 273–4.
30. GH, 661; LQV s3 I, 293–4; Curtis, *Coercion*, 182; Chilston, *Smith*, 249.
31. Barker, *Gladstone*, 7; Chilston, *Smith*, 249; LQV s3 I, 319n.
32. LQV s3 I, 298; Hammond, *Gladstone*, 583; Hatfield D 87/501, Ld S–QV, 21 Apr. 1887; Chilston, *Smith*, 249–50.
33. LQV s3 I, 335–6; ibid., 344.
34. QVJ: 13 Sept. 1887; S/B corresp 207; Morley, *Gladstone*, II, 467; LQV s3 I, 352; QVJ: 14 Sept. 1887; LQV s3 I, 252.
35. Barker, *Gladstone*, 80–1; LQV s3 I, 357; LQV s3 I, 360.
36. Rohl, *Young*, 392; Corti EE, 235–6; Rohl, *Young*, 392–3.
37. Rohl, *Young*, 431.
38. Rohl, *Young*, 439–40.
39. Pakula, *Uncommon*, 415; Corti EE, 227; Rohl, *Young*, 481.
40. B&DC, 46–7; Corti EE, 238; Rohl, *Young*, 676, 678; Pakula, *Uncommon*, 443–4.
41. Rohl, *Young*, 680.
42. Corti EE, 254; Rohl, *Young*, 688; Cecil, *Salisbury*, IV, 76–7.
43. Ponsonby, *Ponsonby*, 290–92.

44. Rohl, *Young*, 789, 792.
45. Cecil, *Salisbury*, IV, 96–7; Corti EE, 271.
46. LEF, 203; Cecil, *Salisbury*, IV, 98.
47. Hatfield, D 87/615, Ld S–QV, 8 Apr. 1888; LEF, 300; Cecil, *Salisbury* , IV, 99; Hatfield D 87/615, QV–Ld S, 21 Apr.; ibid., D 87/611 QV–Ld S, 10 Apr. 1888.
48. LQV s3 I, 398–9.
49. Rohl, *Young*, 807.
50. QVJ: 26 Apr. 1888.
51. LQV s3 I, 416, 404n; Hibbert, *Victoria*, 388; QVJ: 25 Apr. 1888.
52. QVJ: 27 June 1888.
53. QVJ: 15 June 1888; LEF, 319.
54. LQV s3 I, 421–2.
55. LQV s3 I, 423–4.
56. Rohl, *Kaiser's*, 34; Corti EE, 313; LQV s3 I, 429.
57. LQV s3 I, 429, 433.
58. Rohl, *Kaiser's*, 79; Corti EE, 315.
59. LQV s3 I, 439–41.
60. LQV s3 I, 443.
61. LQV s3 I, 467–8; Cecil, *Salisbury*, IV, 114; Corti EE, 322.
62. LQV s3 I, 473; Corti EE, 324.
63. LQV s3 I, 488–9; Rohl, *Kaiser's*, 96–7; Magnus, *Edward VII*, 266–7; Rohl, *Kaiser's*, 98–9; LQV s3 I, 501.
64. LQV s3 I, 504; Corti EE, 323; LQV s3 I, 505.
65. QVJ: 8 Aug. 1889; Rohl, *Kaiser's*, 104.
66. GH, 719, 641; QVJ: 4 Oct. 1888; GH, 715; LQV s3 I, 447, 449.
67. LQV s3 I, 646; ibid., II, 6.
68. Chilston, *Smith*, 276; Kuhn, *HJ* (1993), 60–62; LQV s3 I, 435–6; Chilston, *Smith*, 277–8.
69. Hamilton, (1993), III, 99; LQV s3 I, 511.
70. LQV s3 I, 509–10.
71. Hansard, 338, col. 1350, 25 July 1889; GH, 742–3.
72. LQV s3 I, 517, 514.
73. Hansard s3, 337, col. 1475, 4 July 1889; ibid., 338, col. 1338; QVJ: 26 Aug. 1889; Hatfield D 87/704, Ld S–QV, 8 Sept. 1889.
74. LQV s3 I, 577, 582–3, 589, 599, 609.
75. QVJ: 27 Feb. 1889; LQV s3 I, 468.
76. LQV s3 I, 618–9, 617.
77. QVJ: 26 Nov. 1890.
78. QVJ: 29 Nov. 1890.
79. LQV s3 I, 662.
80. B&DC, 117; QVJ: 17 Dec 1890; Ponsonby, *Ponsonby*, 213; QVJ: 13 and 6 Oct. 1891.
81. Swartz, *Politics*, 14; Cecil, *Salisbury*, IV, 310.
82. LQV s3 I, 512.
83. QVJ: 2 Mar. 1889.
84. Pakenham, *Scramble*, 384–5, 389; Eldridge, *Imperialism*, 189.
85. QVJ: 24 Feb. 1891.
86. Cecil, *Salisbury*, IV, 48–9; QVJ: 4 June 1890; LQV s3 I, 610–13, 615.
87. LQV s3 I, 507; QVJ: 20 Oct. 1890.
88. LQV s3 II, 20–21; 29; 23–6.
89. QVJ: 23 June 1887; Ponsonby, *Ponsonby*, 130; QVJ: 11 Aug. 1888; B&DC, 63, 105.
90. LQV s3 II, 69; ibid., I, 513–4, 526–7; LQV s3 II, 69; S/B corresp, 251; Newton, *Lansdowne*, 90.
91. LQV s3 II, 43, 54, 56, 57–8.
92. LQV s3 I, 532; Hatfield Ps D 87/718 Ld S–QV, 8 Nov. 1889; QVJ: 19 Mar. 1890; Corti EE, 331.
93. LQV s3 I, 584–7.
94. Pakula, *Uncommon*, 525; LEF 404, 407–8.
95. B&DC, 126–7.
96. Chilston, *Smith*, 350.
97. LQV s3 II, 37, 51.
98. QVJ: 22 Sept. 1891; LQV s3 III, 65; QVJ: 20 Aug. 1891.
99. LQV s3 II, 83–4; B&DC, 132; Rohl, *Kaiser's*, 59; LEF, 434.
100. LQV s3 II, 106; S/B corresp 399–400; LQV s3 II, 106–7n; Cecil, *Salisbury*, IV, 371; Ponsonby, *Ponsonby*, 297.
101. LQV s3 II, 106–7n, 125; QVJ: 1 Aug. 1892; Roberts, *Salisbury*,

555; Ld G. Hamilton, (1992), II, 137.
102. S/B corresp 320–1.
103. S/B corresp 319–1.
104. S/B corresp 321.
105. S/B corresp 326–7.
106. S/B corresp 322–3; Cadbury, *Match-Making*, 138–9; Hamilton, (1993), 133.
107. Cadbury, *Match-Making*, 156–8.
108. QVJ: 14 Jan. 1892.
109. GD, XII, 353–4; QVJ: 10 Mar. 1891; LQV s3 II, 77.
110. LQV s3 II, 103–4.
111. QVJ: 16 May 1892, LQV s3 II, 118; Ponsonby, *Ponsonby*, 214–5.
112. Ponsonby, *Ponsonby*, 214–5.
113. QVJ: 23 June 1892; LQV s3 II, 132–3, ibid., 126.
114. Loulou, 161; Ponsonby, *Ponsonby*, 216; LQV s3 II, 128.
115. Ponsonby, *Ponsonby*, 217; Hamilton (1993) III, 160, 168.
116. Shannon, *Gladstone* II, 517–8; Loulou, 164; LQV s3 II, 130; Ponsonby, *Ponsonby*, 217.
117. Ponsonby, *Ponsonby*, 216–7, LQV s3 II, 132–3.
118. Crewe, *Rosebery*, II, 403.
119. LQV s3 II, 137–8; QVJ: 10 Aug. 1892; Loulou, 166; LQV s3 II, 138n.
120. Q&G, II, 437; LQV s3 II, 127; *Red Earl*, II, 213–4; Loulou, 163.
121. QVJ: 11 & 12 Aug. 1892; Loulou, 166; LQV s3 II, 142.
122. Shannon, *Gladstone*, II, 522; Loulou, 168; LQV s3 II, 157–8.
123. LQV s3 II, 140; GH, 833; QVJ: 12 Aug. 1892; QVJ: 18 Aug. 1892.
124. QVJ: 13 Aug. 1892; LQV s3 II, 141; Loulou, 168.
125. LQV s3 II, 143–4; Hamilton, (1993), 172; Crewe, *Rosebery*, II, 403.
126. QVJ: 15 Aug. 1892; Hamilton, (1993), 172–3; GD, XIII, 59; West, *Diaries*, 51.
127. QVJ: 18 Aug. 1892; GH, 834; Hatfield Ps D 87/872, 17 Aug. 1892.
128. Newton, *Lansdowne*, 100.

Chapter 13

1. B&DC, 147; Ponsonby, *Ponsonby*, 216–7; *Red Earl*, II, 209, Jackson, *Harcourt*, 207–8; Brooke and Sorensen, *PMs' Papers*, 116; Wolf, *Ripon*, II, 237.
2. QVJ: 11 Aug. 1892; Ponsonby, *Ponsonby*, 399.
3. B&DC, 145; LQV s3 II, 162.
4. QVJ: 1 Nov. 1892; B&DC, 150; Q&G, II, 446–52; LQV s3 II, 181–2.
5. Hamilton, (1993), 176–7; West, *Diaries*, 77, 79; GD, XIII, 139; Loulou, 174; Kimberley, *Journal*, 408; LQV s3 II, 183.
6. LQV s3 II, 201–2.
7. QVJ: 17 Jan. 1893.
8. B&DC, 146; Hamilton, (1993), 183; Shannon, *Gladstone*, II, 527.
9. GD, XIII, 153.
10. West, *Diaries*, 148; LQV s3 II, 238–9; Q&G, II, 467.
11. Hamilton, (1993), 214.
12. Gardiner, *Harcourt*, II, 185.
13. Ponsonby, *Ponsonby*, 279; Spender, *Life*, I, 126; QVJ: 18 Aug., 26 Aug. 1892; Ponsonby, *Ponsonby*, 280–81.
14. QVJ: 23 Oct. 1881.
15. Gardiner, *Harcourt*, II, 185.
16. B&DC, 147–8; Jackson, *Harcourt*, 223; Gardiner, *Harcourt*, II, 198; Loulou, 188; McKinstry, *Rosebery*, 272.
17. QVJ: 18 Aug. 1892; LQV s3 II, 131, 160, 162, 211; McKinstry, *Rosebery*, 258–9.
18. B&DC, 159.
19. GD, XIII, 82; McKinstry, *Rosebery*, 241; LQV s3 II, 163.
20. LQV s3 II, 158; Gardiner, *Harcourt*, II, 192; GD, XIII, 84; Kimberley, *Journal*, 409.

21. LQV s3 II, 159; Rhodes James, *Rosebery*, 272; McKinstry, *Rosebery*, 248.
22. LQV s3 II, 205, 212; West, *Diaries*, 127, 123; Rhodes James, *Rosebery* 279; QVJ: 20 Jan. 1893; LQV s3 II, 210–11.
23. Loulou, 182; LQV s3 II, 212; Ponsonby, *Ponsonby*, 276–7.
24. LQV s3 II, 214.
25. Q&G, II, 462; Hamilton, (1993), 188.
26. LQV s3 II, 227–8.
27. LQV s3 II, 243; Gardiner, *Harcourt*, II, 237–8.
28. QVJ: 13 Mar. 1893; LQV s3 II, 250; Hamilton, (1993), 193; LQV s3 II, 258; QVJ: 27 May 1893.
29. LQV s3 II, 248, 262.
30. QVJ: 8 July 1893; LQV s3 II, 278–9, 288–9, 290; Hamilton, (1993), 214.
31. QVJ: 11 July, 18 July 1893; LQV s3 II, 297.
32. QVJ: 9 Sept. 1893; McKinstry, *Rosebery*, 289; QVJ: 18 Jan. 1893.
33. LQV s3 II, 311; Q&G, II, 476.
34. LQV s3 II, 319–20, 322–3.
35. GD, XIII, 299–300; West, *Diaries*, 200.
36. GD, XIII, 294, 302, 304.
37. West, *Diaries*, 216; GD, XIII, 320n; Loulou, 197; GD, XIII, 342.
38. GD, XIII, 338–9; LQV s3 II, 328; QVJ: 4 Dec 1893; West, *Diaries*, 228–9.
39. Loulou, 198; GD, XIII, 402–3; Hamilton, (1993), 236–7; GD, XIII, 364.
40. West, *Diaries*, 236; Morley, *Recollections*, II, 4.
41. GD, XIII, 355; Hamilton, (1993), 226, 228.
42. West, *Diaries*, 275; Kimberley, *Journal*, 420; Loulou, 208–9.
43. Loulou, 209; West, *Diaries*, 275–6; ibid., 276–7; Loulou, 215–6; Morley, *Recollections*, II, 9.
44. Q&G, II, 489; *Sidelights*, 283; West, *Diaries*, 283.
45. West, *Diaries*, 284–5.
46. QVJ: 27 Feb. 1894; LQV s3 II, 364; *Sidelights*, 285.
47. QVJ: 27 Feb. 1894; *Sidelights*, 287; LQV s3 II, 365.
48. GD, XIII, 385–6.
49. QVJ: 1 and 3 Mar. 1894.
50. Loulou, 220; GD, XIII, 386; Stansky, 78–9; Morley, *Gladstone*, II, 563; GD, XIII, 439; LQV s3 II, 368.
51. QVJ: 2 and 3 Mar. 1894.
52. GD, 390–1.
53. West, *Diaries*, 288; Loulou, 222; LQV s3 II, 373.
54. GD, XIII, 399; 401, 403.
55. GD, XIII, 425.
56. GD, XIII, 405, 425–6.
57. Brooke and Sorensen, *PMs' Papers*, 173–5.
58. GD, XIII, 424; *After Thirty Years*, xxiii; Hamilton, (1993), 388; Jackson, *Harcourt*, 311.
59. LQV s3 III, 249; Esher, *Journals*, I, 217; Hamilton, (1993), 356.
60. B&DC, 214–5; QVJ: 19 May 1898.
61. GD, XIII, 385–6, 390; Morley, *Recollections*, II, 10–11. GD, vol. XIII, 416.
62. Rhodes James, *Rosebery*, 508; Ponsonby, A., *Life from Letters*, 277.
63. LQV s3 II, 368–9.
64. *Sidelights*, 290–91.
65. Rhodes James, *Rosebery*, 510; McKinstry, *Rosebery*, 293.
66. McKinstry, *Rosebery*, 294; LQV s3 II, 373; Hamilton, (1993), 247.
67. West, *Diaries*, 295; Rhodes James, *Rosebery*, 510; Kimberley, *Journal*, 422; Rhodes James, *Rosebery*, 324–5; Loulou, 216.
68. LQV s3 II, 375.
69. LQV s3 II, 379; Ponsonby, *Ponsonby*, 277.
70. LQV s3 II, 381–2.
71. Rhodes James, *Rosebery*, 339; LQV s3 II, 384.

72. LQV s3 II, 385–91.
73. B&DC, 164; LQV s3 II, 398.
74. LQV s3 II, 399–400.
75. Hamilton, (1993), 265.
76. Gardiner, *Harcourt*, II, 298–9.
77. LQV s3 II, 414–5.
78. LQV s3 II, 414; Loulou, 235; Williams, *Contentious*, 68.
79. LQV s3 II, 400, 403–4.
80. LQV s3 II, 429–31, 433–4.
81. Crewe, *Rosebery*, II, 465; Askwith, *Hereford*, 231; LQV s3 II, 442, 437–8.
82. Hamilton, (1993), 278; LQV s3 II, 440.
83. LQV s3 II, 442–4; Askwith, *Hereford*, 231–2; Garvin, *Chamberlain*, II, 613–4; LQV s3 II, 448–9.
84. LQV s3 II, 449–50.
85. QVJ: 7 Dec. 1894; Askwith, *Hereford*, 250.
86. QVJ: 7 Jan. 1895; Kuhn, *Ponsonby*, 237; Ponsonby, *Ponsonby*, 409, 404; West, *Diaries*, 301.
87. Knightley, 245; QVJ: 19 Feb. 1895; Rhodes James, *Rosebery*, 366–7.
88. Crewe, *Rosebery*, II, 561; Esher, *Journals*, I, 185; Loulou, 256–7; McKinstry, *Rosebery*, 345.
89. McKinstry, *Rosebery*, 364, 360–1.
90. QVJ: 7 and 9 May 1895; LQV s3 II, 504; St Aubyn, *Royal George*, 307, 302; QVJ: 17 May 1895; LQV s3 II, 512–3.
91. LQV s3 II, 517, 520n; McKinstry, *Rosebery*, 371–2; LQV s3 II, 520; McKinstry, *Rosebery*, 372; St Aubyn, *Royal George*, 310.
92. QVJ: 15 May 1895; Loulou, 263.
93. LQV s3 II, 521–2; QVJ: 22 June 1895.
94. B&DC, 178.
95. LQV s3 II, 523–4, 529; QVJ: 28 June 1895.
96. QVJ: 26 July, 28 July 1895.

Chapter 14

1. LQV s3 III, 87; ibid., II, 525; QVJ: 19 Feb. 1897; Roberts, *Salisbury*, 793.
2. LQV s3 III, 20; Crawford, *Papers*, 43; Mallet, *Letters*, 101; Chilston, *Chief Whip*, 290; LQV s3 III, 75.
3. LQV s3 III, 606; Grenville, *Salisbury*, 173; Crawford, *Papers*, 39.
4. QVJ: 24 May 1897, 23 May 1898; 31 Dec. 1898, 23 May 1898; Mallet, *Letters*, 212–3.
5. QVJ: 7 Jan. 1896; Esher, *Journals*, I, 214; Mallet, *Letters*, 147; King, *Twilight*, 74–5.
6. Ponsonby, *Three Reigns*, 57.
7. Ponsonby, *Three Reigns*, 41; QVJ: 11 Sept. 1897.
8. Mallet, *Letters*, 206.
9. QVJ: 20 June 1896; Eldridge, *Imperialism*, 241; Roberts, *Salisbury*, 687; LQV s3 III, 239; Massie, *Dreadnought*, 272.
10. LQV s3 III, 21–2.
11. LQV s3 III, 77.
12. LQV s3 III, 235–6; Rohl, *Wilhelm II*, 59–60; LQV s3 III, 324; B&DC, 219–20; QVJ: 9 May 1899.
13. Ponsonby, *Three Reigns*, 42; B&DC, 187.
14. QVJ: 2 Jan. 1896; LQV s3 III, 8; Grenville, *Salisbury*, 102; LQV s3 III, 9 & 12; QVJ: 10 Jan. and 30 Nov. 1896.
15. LQV s3 II, 344–5, 347–8, 354–5 QVJ: 21 Apr. 1894; LQV s3 II, 395.
16. LQV s3 II, 404–5; Corti EE, 347.
17. LQV s3 II, 535, 547.
18. GDD, II, 342; QVJ: 16 Dec 1895; LQV s3 II, 580–1, 585.
19. LQV s3 II, 586; QVJ: 17 Nov. 1895; LQV s3 II, 583, 586.
20. GDD, II, 361, 434, 436; Rohl, *Kaiser's*, 938; GDD, II, 466.
21. GDD, II, 368–9; Rohl, *Kaiser's*, 770.
22. GDD, II, 387; QVJ: 8 Jan. 1896; LQV s3 III, 18.

23. LQV s3 III, 20, 7; QVJ: 5 Jan. 1896; LQV s3 III, 8–9; Lee, *Edward VII*, I, 725–7; QVJ: 10 Jan. 1896; LQV s3 III, 20; QVJ: 15 Jan. 1896.
24. Rohl, *Kaiser's*, 970.
25. LQV s3 III, 130–1.
26. QVJ: 19 Feb., 23 Feb. 1897; LQV s3 III, 150; Rohl, *Kaiser's*, 941; B&DC, 203; LQV s3 III, 188.
27. B&DC, 203; QVJ: 9 May 1897; LQV s3 III, 161; Pakula, *Uncommon*, 569.
28. LQV s3 III, 159; QVJ: 8 May, 13 May 1897.
29. Hough (ed.), *Advice*, 53, 81, 89.
30. Hough (ed.), *Advice*, 106, 110.
31. Maylunas and Mironenko, *Lifelong*, 28; QVJ: 1 July 1893.
32. Hough (ed.), *Advice*, 124; QVJ: 20 Apr. 1894; Gardiner, *Harcourt*, II, 305; Hough (ed.), *Advice*, 124.
33. Hough (ed.), *Advice*, 126; QVJ: 1 Nov. 1894; B&DC, 173.
34. Maylunas and Mironenko, *Lifelong*, 99; Corti EE, 348, Hough (ed.), *Advice*, 129; Gardiner, *Harcourt*, II, 305.
35. LQV s3 III, 63–4.
36. B&DC, 195; QVJ: 22 Sept. 1896; Askwith, *Hereford*, 249.
37. LQV s3 III, 93; GDD, II, 436.
38. LQV s3 III, 77, 81; 87.
39. LQV s3 III, 88; Maylunas and Mironenko, *Lifelong*, 152–3.
40. LQV s3 III, 201–2.
41. Hamilton, (1993), 337; LQV s3 III, 116, 126–7; Rohl, *Kaiser's*, 967.
42. LQV s3 III, 190; QVJ: 2 July 1897; King, *Twilight*, 261; Hamilton, (1993), 342; Basu, *Victoria and Abdul*, 239.
43. QVJ: 22 June 1897; LQV s3 III, 164.
44. Davenport-Hines in *Court Historian* (2011), p. 216; Crawford, *Papers*, 41; QVJ: 3 July 1897.
45. B&DC, 205; LQV s3 III, 190; Garvin, *Chamberlain*, III, 269.
46. Roberts, *Salisbury*, 697; Williams, *Contentious*, 178.
47. Anand, *Indian Sahib*, 65.
48. LQV s3 II, 566–7; LQV s3 III, 143.
49. Basu, *Victoria and Abdul*, 205; ibid., 210.
50. Reid, *Ask*, 142, 144.
51. Anand, *Indian Sahib*, 76–7.
52. Anand, *Indian Sahib*, 86–7.
53. LQV s3 III, 251.
54. LQV s3 III, 202–3, 210.
55. LQV s3 III, 210, 216–7; QVJ: 14 May 1898; see also QVJ: 24 Feb. and 3 Dec 1898.
56. GD XIII, 283n; LQV s3 II, 317; Pakenham, *Scramble*, 492–4.
57. LQV s3 II, 316; Pakenham, *Scramble*, 494.
58. GD, XIII, 319n; QVJ: 4 Dec 1894.
59. QVJ: 17 Nov. 1895; Lytton, 157.
60. QVJ: 4 Mar. 1896.
61. QVJ: 27 Mar. 1896; LQV s3 III, 38; QVJ: 5 May 1896, 28 July 1896.
62. LQV s3 II, 572–3.
63. Adam Hochschild, *King Leopold's Ghost*, (2006) passim, and 88; QVJ: 25 May 1897; Mallet, *Letters*, 106; Ponsonby, *Three Reigns*, 55.
64. LQV s3 III, 25.
65. QVJ: 18 June, 11 June 1896.
66. QVJ: 5 Sept. 1898; Roberts, *Salisbury*, 697; QVJ: 24 Oct. 1898.
67. LQV s3 III, 352–4.
68. Gooch et al., *Documents*, I, 168; Esher, *Journals*, I, 220–1; LQV s3 III, 289.
69. LQV s3 III, 290; QVJ: 25 Oct. 1898.
70. LQV s3 III, 301, 294, 291, 305.
71. LQV s3 III, 305; ibid., 351.
72. Rohl, *Kaiser's*, 988.
73. LQV s3 III, 224–5; Gooch et al., (ed.), *Documents*, I, 42.
74. Garvin, *Chamberlain*, III, 270, 287; QVJ: 24 Apr. 1898.
75. Garvin, *Chamberlain*, III, 279; Rohl, *Kaiser's*, 981–2.
76. LQV s3 III, 258–60, ibid., 262–3.

77. LQV s3 II, 312, 321–2; 323–5; QVJ: 27 Jan. 1899; LQV s3 III, 336–7.
78. QVJ: 17 Feb. 1899.
79. LQV s3 III, 343–4.
80. Jefferson in *Slavonic Review* (1960), p. 220; Maylunas and Mironenko, *Lifelong*, 183.
81. LQV s3 III, 358; QVJ: 6 May 1899; B&DC, 228–9.
82. Grenville, *Salisbury*, 277; Rohl, *Kaiser's*, 994; QVJ: 5 June 1899; Gooch et al., *Documents*, I, 117–8.
83. LQV s3 III, 375–9.
84. LQV s3 III, 379.
85. LQV s3 III, 381–2.
86. LQV s3 III, 393; Bülow, *Memoirs*, I, 301; Gooch et al., *Documents*, I, 129.
87. Bülow, *Memoirs*, I, 305, 309–11.
88. Dugdale, *Balfour*, I, 274.
89. LQV s3 III, 382–3; QVJ: 18 July 1899.
90. QVJ: 25 Aug. 1899.
91. GDD, III, 100; LQV s3 III, 400, 402.
92. Fitzroy I, 19; QVJ: 10 Oct. 1899.
93. QVJ: 5 Oct. 1899; Ponsonby, *Three Reigns*, 72–3.
94. LQV s3 III, 410; Ponsonby, *Three Reigns*, 76.
95. QVJ: 11 Jan. 1900.
96. QVJ: 4 Nov., 11 Dec., 15 Dec., 1899; LQV s3 III, 434.
97. Cecil, *Salisbury*, III, 191; QVJ: 14 Dec 1899.
98. QVJ: 17 Dec., 18 Dec. 1899; Dugdale, *Balfour*, I, 297.
99. Dugdale, *Balfour*, I, 302, 304–5; LQV s3 III, 468–9; Mallet, *Letters*, 186; LQV s3 III 468–9, 472–3.
100. LQV s3 III, 459; 472–3.
101. LQV s3 III, 473; Roberts, *Salisbury*, 754; Marsh, 295; Esher, *Journals*, I, 257–8.
102. QVJ: 11 Jan. 1900; Chilston, *Chief Whip*, 283–4; Roberts, *Salisbury*, 751; LQV s3 III, 479.
103. Mallet, *Letters*, 180, 176; Esher, *Journals*, I, 257–8.
104. LQV s3 III, 622; Garvin, *Chamberlain*, III, 543–5; LQV s3 III, 462–3; Pakenham, *Boer War*, 396; LQV s3 III, 488, 485–6.
105. LQV s3 III, 402.
106. QVJ: 6 July 1899; B&DC, 235; LQV s3 III, 396.
107. QVJ: 11 & 12 Dec. 1899 Garvin, *Chamberlain*, III, 507.
108. Lee, *Edward VII*, I, 777; B&DC, 248.
109. Lee, *Edward VII*, I, 768; Eckardstein, *Ten Years*, 152; Gooch et al., *Documents*, I, 251.
110. LQV s3 III, 444; Lee, *Edward VII*, I, 754–5; LQV s3 IIII, 474; Lee, *Edward VII*, I, 756.
111. Maylunas and Mironenko, *Lifelong*, 205; LQV s3 III, 519, 527; QVJ: 23 Mar. 1900.
112. QVJ: 8 Mar., 9 Mar. 1900.
113. Pakenham, *Boer War*, 388; Mallet, *Letters*, 193; LQV s3 III, 507–9.
114. Pakenham, *Boer War*, 377.
115. LQV s3 III, 523–6.
116. LQV s3 III, 539, 533–4; 536, 538–9
117. Dugdale, *Balfour*, I, 312; QVJ: 28 Mar. 1900; LQV s3 III, 493; ibid., 198; B&DC, 247; Mallet, *Letters*, 192.
118. QVJ: 3 Apr., 16 Apr. 1900; Ponsonby, *Three Reigns*, 63–4.
119. QVJ: 26 Apr. 1900.
120. QVJ: 19 May 1900; B&DC, 251; LQV s3 III, 554–5; ibid., 556–7.
121. QVJ: 9 July 1900; QVJ: 18 July 1899.
122. LQV s3 III, 559, 563; Grenville, *Salisbury*, 308; LQV s3 III, 561.
123. QVJ: 9 July 1900.
124. Mallet, *Letters*, 210.
125. QVJ: 5 June 1900; LQV s3 III, 558–9; Pakenham, *Boer War*, 440.
126. QVJ: 18 July 1900; LQV s3 III, 582; QVJ: 21 Aug. 1900; QVJ: 26 Oct. 1900.
127. QVJ: 14 Sept. 1900; Pakenham, *Boer War*, 518, 572.

128. LQV s3 III, 601; see e.g.: QVJ: 30 Apr. 1900, B&DC, 249, QVJ: 19 Sept. 1900, QVJ: 13 Mar. 1900, QVJ: 5 Nov. 1900; QVJ: 17 Nov. 1900.
129. GDD, III, 136; Rohl, *Wilhelm II*, 31; Maylunas and Mironenko, *Lifelong*, 205; QVJ: 28 Sept. 1900; QVJ: 18 Oct. 1900.
130. LQV s3 III, 191–2; QVJ: 26 Mar. 1899; LQV s3 III, 443, 594.
131. LQV s3 III, 592–6.
132. QVJ: 29 July 1900; Chilston, *Chief Whip*, 285–6; LQV s3 III, 603.
133. LQV s3 III, 592, 598, 604.
134. LQV s3 III, 606; Chilston, *Chief Whip*, 290–1.
135. LQV s3 III, 615; ibid., 611; Mallet, *Letters*, 214.
136. B&DC, 29; Chilston, *Chief Whip*, 290; QVJ: 10 Nov. 1900; Grenville, *Salisbury*, 323.
137. QVJ: 31 July 1900; B&DC, 246; QVJ: 29 Oct. 1900.
138. QVJ: 17 Sept. 1900; Askwith, *Hereford*, 261–2; Roberts, *Salisbury*, 794; QVJ: 2 Dec. 1900, 11 Dec. 1900, 22 Dec. 1900; QVJ: 1 Jan. 1901.
139. QVJ: 15 Dec., 16 Dec., 18 Dec., 28 Dec. 1900; QVJ: 1 Jan. 1901.
140. LQV s3 III, 639.
141. Massie, *Dreadnought*, 296; QVJ: 13 Jan. 1901.
142. Newton, *Lansdowne*, 197.
143. LQV s3 III, 642; Basu, *Victoria and Abdul*, 275–6; Hansard s4, 89, col. 21, 25 Jan. 1901.
144. Reid, *Ask*, 205.
145. Reid, *Ask*, 210–12.
146. Massie, *Dreadnought*, 298.
147. Rohl, *Wilhelm II*, 15.
148. *Red Earl*, II, 287–8.
149. Hansard s4, 89, col. 8, 25 Jan. 1901; *Red Earl*, II, 287–8; QVJ: 2 Apr. 1898; Tilney Basset, *Gladstone*, 163; *Red Earl*, II, 287–8.
150. Roberts, *Salisbury*, 829.

Chapter 15

1. DC, 282; Q&G II, 99; Williams, *Contentious*, 143.
2. M&B,V, 144; LQV s2 I, 201; Hansard s4, 89, col. 9, 25 Jan. 1901; *Times*, 31 Aug. 1887, GD XII, 60–1.
3. LQV s2 III, 73; M&B, V, 144; Hansard s4, 89, col. 9, 25 Jan. 1901.
4. Bagehot, *Constitution*, 287; Steele, *Palmerston*, 225; West, *Diaries*, 129; Williams, *Contentious*, 116–7.
5. Bagehot, *Constitution* 287–8.
6. Bagehot, *Constitution*, 95, 113; Weintraub, *Victoria*, 591.
7. Balfour, *Kaiser*, 355.
8. Hamilton, (1993), 348.
9. Hansard s4, 50, col. 419, 21 June 1897; Williams, *Contentious*, 57; Thorold, *Labouchere*, 212.
10. Hansard s4, 89, col. 9, 25 Jan. 1901.
11. Hansard s4, 89, cols 12–14, 25 Jan. 1901.
12. Mallet, *Letters*, 77.
13. Briggs, *Age*, 272; Brown, *Palmerston*, 471.
14. Roberts, *Salisbury*, 248–9; LQV s3 I, 365.
15. Hansard s4, 89, col. 19, 25 Jan. 1901.
16. Gladstone, *Midlothian Speeches*, 202; LQV s2 III, 43.
17. Broughton, *Recollections*, VI, 252; Pearson, *Labby*, 173; David, *Victoria's Wars*, 401–2; Taylor, *Victoria*, 189.
18. M&B, VI, 154; Eldridge, *Mission*, 228.
19. Seton-Watson, *Eastern*, 103–4; Eldridge, *Imperialism*, 194.
20. Eldridge, *Mission*, 220; Taylor, *Empress*, 220.
21. LQV s2 I, 459.
22. LQV s2 I, 459.
23. LQV s2 II, 361.
24. Morris, *Command*, 303–17; LQV s2 I, 286–7, 289; Q&G, I, 195.
25. QVJ: 15 July 1863.
26. QVJ: 29 Aug. 1853; PP RC/F/1170, QV–Ld P 1 Oct. 1865; QVJ: 6 Jan.

1869; Curtis, *Coercion*, 13; *Red Earl*, I, 278.
27. B&DC, 213.
28. Rose, *George V*, 242.
29. Mallet, *Letters*, 77; Q&G, I, 221, 227.
30. Thompson, *Chartists*, 120; Williams, *Contentious*, 145.
31. PP, RC/F/1151 QV–Ld P, 28 Dec 1864; LQV s2 I, 443.
32. M&B, V, 143–4; Kuhn, *Ponsonby*, 160.
33. Ward, *Censoring*, 9; LQV s3 III, 351–2.
34. Maxwell, *Clarendon*, II, 104, 110; DDC, 278.
35. Grey Papers, GRE/D/XIII/8/12, Grey–QV, 18 Feb. 1866; Ridley, *Palmerston*, 358; *Dear Duchess*, 258; Ponsonby, *Ponsonby*, 115.
36. DDC, 317; Bagehot, *Works*, V, 421–3.
37. Ponsonby, *Ponsonby*, 124; GD, XIII, 73; Maxwell, *Clarendon*, II, 128–9.
38. Spender, *Life*, I, 170; McKinstry, *Rosebery*, 61; Spender, *Life*, I, 169; *Sandon*, 'First Balmoral Journal', 89–109; Kuhn, *Ponsonby*, 174.
39. *Dearest Mama*, 296; Mallet, *Letters*, 77; Bagehot, *Works*, V, 433; Howard and Gordon, BIHR, 50 (1977), 97.
40. Hansard s4, 89, cols 19–20, 25 Jan. 1901; QVJ: 1 June 1879; LQV s2 III, 451–2; Q&G, I, 264.
41. Hansard s4, 89, col. 9, 25 Jan. 1901.
42. LQV s3 II, 488.
43. King, *Twilight*, 7; Hansard s4, 89, col. 8, 25 Jan. 1901.

BIBLIOGRAPHY

Adams, R. J. Q., *Balfour: The Last Grandee* (London, 2007)

Airlie, Mabell, Countess of, *Lady Palmerston and Her Times* (London, 1922)

Alexander, Michael, and Anand, Sushila, *Queen Victoria's Maharahah: Duleep Singh 1838–93* (London, 1980)

Anand, Sushila, *Indian Sahib: Queen Victoria's Dear Abdul* (London, 1996)

Anderson, Olive, *A Liberal State at War: English Politics and Economics During the Crimean War* (London, 1967)

Arengo-Jones, Peter, *Queen Victoria in Switzerland* (London, 1995)

Argyll, George Douglas, 8th Duke of, *Autobiography and Memoirs*, (ed.), The Dowager Duchess of Argyll (London, 1906)

Ashley, Evelyn, *Life of Henry John Temple, Viscount Palmerston, 1846–65* (London, 1876)

Askwith, Lord, *Lord James of Hereford* (London, 1930)

Bagehot, Walter, *Collected Works of Walter Bagehot*, (ed.), Norman St John Stevas (London, 1974)

—*The English Constitution* (London, 1993)

Baird, Julia, *Victoria the Queen* (London, 2016)

Balfour, Arthur James, *Chapters of Autobiography*, (ed.), Mrs Edgar Dugdale (London, 1930)

Balfour, Michael, *Britain and Joseph Chamberlain* (London, 1985)

Barker, Michael, *Gladstone and Radicalism: The Reconstruction of Liberal Policy in Britain 1885–94* (London, 1975)

Basu, Sharabani, *Victoria and Abdul: The Extraordinary True Story of the Queen's Closest Confidant* (London, 2017)

Battiscombe, Georgina, *Shaftesbury: A Biography of the Seventh Earl 1801–85* (London, 1974)

Beales, Derek, *England and Italy, 1859–60* (London, 1961)

Bell, Herbert, *Lord Palmerston* (London, 1936)

Bennett, Daphne, *King Without a Crown: Albert Prince Consort of England* (London, 1983)

Benson, A. C., and Viscount Esher (eds.), *Letters of Queen Victoria*, 1st Series 1837–61 (London, 1908); 2nd Series, 1862–85, (ed.), George Earle Buckle

(London, 1928); 3rd Series, 1886–1901, (ed.),. George Earle Buckle (London, 1930)
Bentley, James, *Ritualism and Politics in Victorian Britain* (Oxford, 1978)
Berriedale Keith, Arthur, *The Constitution of England from Queen Victoria to George VI* (London, 1940)
Biagine, Eugenio F., *British Democracy and Irish Nationalism 1876–1906* (London, 2007)
Blake, Robert, *Disraeli* (London, 1966)
—'The Prince Consort and Queen Victoria's Prime Ministers', in *Prince Albert and the Victorian Age*, (ed.), John A. S. Phillips (Cambridge, 1981)
Bogdanor, Vernon, *The Monarchy and the Constitution* (Oxford, 1995)
Bolitho, Hector (ed.), *The Prince Consort and His Brother: Two Hundred New Letters* (London, 1933)
—(ed.) *Letters of Queen Victoria from the archives of Brandeburg-Prussia* (New Haven, 1938)
Bourne, Kenneth, *The Foreign Policy of Victorian England 1830–1902* (Oxford, 1970)
—*Palmerston: The Early Years, 1782–1841* (London, 1982)
Bosbach, Franz, and Davis, John R. (eds.), *Prince Albert: A Wettin in Britain* (Munich, 2004)
Bradford, Sarah, *Disraeli* (London, 1982)
Bresler, Fenton, *Napoleon III: A Life* (London, 1999)
Briggs, Asa, *The Age of Improvement* (London, 1959)
Brooke, John, and Sorensen, Mary, *The Prime Ministers' Papers Series: W. E. Gladstone* (London, 1971, 1978)
Broughton, John Cam Hobhouse, Lord, *Recollections of a Long Life*, (ed.) His daughter Lady Dorchester (London, 1911)
Brown, David, *Palmerston: A Biography* (London, 2010)
Bülow, Prince Bernhard von, *Memoirs* (London, 1931)
Bunsen, Baron, *A Memoir by his Widow, Frances Baroness Bunsen* (London, 1868)
Cadbury, Deborah, *Queen Victoria's Match-Making: The Royal Marriages that Shaped Europe* (London, 2017)
Campbell, John, *Life of John, Lord Campbell, Lord High Chancellor of Great Britain*, (ed.), The Hon. Mrs Hardcastle (London, 1881)
Cannadine, David, *Victorious Century: The United Kingdom 1800–1906* (London, 2017)
Carlingford, Lord, *Lord Carlingford's Journal: Reflections of a Cabinet Minister, 1885*, (eds.), A. B. Cooke and J. R. Vincent (Oxford, 1971)
Cavendish, Lucy, *The Diary of Lady Frederick Cavendish*, (ed.), John Bailey (London, 1927)
Cecil, Algernon, *Queen Victoria and Her Prime Ministers* (London, 1953)
Cecil, Gwendolen, *Life of Robert, Marquis of Salisbury* (London, 1921)

Cecil, David, *Melbourne* (London, 1955)
Chamberlain, Joseph, *A Political Memoir, 1880–92* (ed.), C. H. D. Howard (London, 1953)
Chamberlain, Muriel, *Lord Aberdeen: A Political Biography* (London, 1983)
Chambers, James, *Palmerston: The People's Darling* (London, 2004)
Charlot, Monica, *Victoria: The Young Queen* (London, 1991)
Childers, Spencer, *Life and Correspondence of Rt Hon. Hugh C. E. Childers 1827–96* (London, 1901)
Chilston, Eric Alexander Akers Douglas, 3rd Viscount Chilston, *Chief Whip: The Political Life and Times of Aretas Akers-Douglas First Viscount Chilston* (London, 1961)
—*W. H. Smith* (London, 1965)
Churchill, Randolph S., *Winston Churchill - Companion Vol. I* (London, 1967)
Churchill, Winston S., *Lord Randolph Churchill* (London, 1952)
Coates, Tim, *Delane's War: How Front-Line Reports from the Crimean War Brought Down the British Government* (London, 2009)
Colson, Percy (ed.), *Lord Goschen and His Friends* (London, 1946)
Conacher, J. B., *The Aberdeen Coalition* (Cambridge, 1968)
Connell, Brian, *Regina v. Palmerston: The Correspondence between Queen Victoria and Her Foreign and Prime Minister, 1837–65* (London, 1962)
Cooke, A. B., and Vincent, John, *The Governing Passion: Cabinet Government and Party Politics in Britain 1885–6* (London, 1974)
Correspondence of Lord Aberdeen and Princess Lieven, 1832–1854, Camden Society, 3rd Series, Vols LX and LXII (London, 1938–9)
Corti, Egon Cesar, *Alexander von Battenberg*, (trans.), E. M. Hodgson (London, 1954)
—*The English Empress: A Study in the Relations between Queen Victoria and Her Eldest Daughter, Empress Frederick of Germany* (London, 1957)
Cowley, Henry, First Earl of, *The Paris Embassy during the Second Empire*, (ed.), F. A. Wellesley (London, 1928)
Cowling, Maurice, *1867: Disraeli, Gladstone and Revolution: The Passing of the Second Reform Bill* (Cambridge, 1967)
Crawford, David, *The Crawford Papers: Journals of David Lindsay, Twenty-seventh Earl of Crawford and Tenth Earl of Balcarres 1892–1940* (Manchester, 1980)
Croker, John, *The Croker Papers: Correspondence and Diaries of John Wilson Croker*, (ed.), Louis J. Jennings (London, 1885)
Creevey, Thomas, *A Selection from the Correspondence and Diaries of the Late Thomas Creevey, MP*, (ed.), Herbert Maxwell (London, 1903)
—*Creevey's Life and Times: A Further Selection from the Correspondence of Thomas Creevey*, (ed.), John Gore (London, 1933)
Crewe, Marquess of, *Lord Rosebery* (London, 1931)

Cullen, Tom, *The Empress Brown: The Story of a Royal Friendship* (London, 1969)

Curtis, L. P., *Coercion and Conciliation in Ireland 1880–92: A Study in Conservative Unionism* (London, 1963)

Dasent, Arthur, *John Thadeus Delane, Editor of The Times: His Life and Correspondence* (London, 1908)

Daunt, Richard A. (ed.) *Peel in Caricature: The 'Political Sketches' of John Doyle ('H. B.')*, Peel Society (London, 2014)

Davenport-Hines, Richard, 'A Radical Lord Chamberlain at a Tory Court: Lord Carrington, 1892–5', in *The Court Historian*, Vol. 16, No. 2, Dec. 2011.

David, Saul, *The Indian Mutiny* (London, 2002)

—*Victoria's Wars* (London, 2007)

Davis, P., 'The Liberal Unionist Party and the Irish Policy of Lord Salisbury's government 1886–92', in *Historical Journal*, Vol. 18, No. 1 (London, 1975)

Davison, Randall Thomas, and Benham, William, *Life of Archibald Campbell Tait, Archbishop of Canterbury* (London, 1891)

Derby, Edward Henry Stanley, 15th Earl of, *A Selection from the Diaries of Edward Henry Stanley Fifteenth Earl of Derby 1869–78*, (ed.), John Vincent, Camden 5th Series, Vol. IV (London, 1994)

—*Diaries of Edward Henry Stanley Fifteenth Earl of Derby 1879–93: A Selection*, (ed.), John Vincent (London, 2003)

Disraeli, Benjamin, *Lord George Bentinck: A Political Biography* (London, 1852)

Disraeli, Benjamin, *Letters*, (eds.), M. G. Wiebe, J. B. Conacher, John Matthews, Mary S. Millar et al. (Toronto, 1982–2014)

Disraeli, Derby and the Conservative Party: Journals and Memoirs of Edward Henry, Lord Stanley, 1848–69, (ed.), John Vincent (London, 1978)

Douglas, Sir George, and Dalhousie Ramsay, Sir George (eds.), *Panmure Papers: Selection from the Correspondence of Fox Maule, Second Baron Panmure, Afterwards Eleventh Earl of Dalhousie* (London, 1908)

Dugdale, Blanche, *Arthur James Balfour* (London, 1936)

Eckardstein, Baron von, *Ten Years at the Court of St James* (London, 1921)

Egremont, Max, *Balfour* (London, 1980)

Eldridge, C. C., *England's Mission: the Imperial Idea in the Age of Gladstone and Disraeli 1868–80* (London, 1973)

—*Victorian Imperialism* (London, 1978)

Elliot, Arthur D., *Life of George J. Goschen, Viscount Goschen* (London, 1911)

Esher, Reginald, *Journals and Letters of Reginald Viscount Esher*, (ed.), Maurice V. Brett (London, 1934)

Etonensis, (pseudonym for W. E. Gladstone), 'Review of Vol. I of Theodore Martin's Biography of Prince Consort', in *Contemporary Review*, Vol. XXVI, Jun. 1875

Eyck, Frank, *The Prince Consort: A Political Biography* (London, 1959)

Fair, John D., 'Royal Mediation in 1884: A Reassessment', in *English Historical Review*, Vol. LXXXVIII (1973)
—'The Carnarvon Diaries and Royal Mediation in 1884', in *English Historical Review*, Vol. CVI (Jan. 1991)
Ferguson, Niall, *Empire: How Britain Made the Modern World* (London, 2004)
Finlayson, Geoffrey, *The Seventh Earl of Shaftesbury 1801–85* (London, 1981)
Fitzmaurice, Edmond, *Life of Granville George Leveson Gower, Second Earl Granville* (London, 1905)
Fitzroy, Sir Almeric, *Memoirs* (London, 1925)
Foot, M. R. D., and Matthew, H. C. G., (eds.), *The Gladstone Diaries* (London, 1968–94)
Foreman, Amanda, *A World on Fire: An Epic History of Two Nations Divided* (London, 2011)
Foster, R. F., *Lord Randolph Churchill: A Political Life* (Oxford, 1981)
Fulford, Roger, (ed.), *Dearest Child: Letters between Queen Victoria and the Princess Royal, 1858–61* (London, 1965)
—(ed.) *Dearest Mama: Letters between Queen Victoria and the Crown Princess of Prussia 1861–4* (London, 1968)
—(ed.) *Darling Child: Private Correspondence of Queen Victoria and the German Crown Princess 1871–1878* (London, 1976)
—(ed.) *Beloved Mama: Private Correspondence of Queen Victoria and the German Crown Princess 1878–1885* (London, 1981)
Gardiner, A. G., *Life of Sir William Harcourt* (London, 1923)
Garvin, J. L., *Life of Joseph Chamberlain* (London, 1932)
Gash, Norman, *Politics in the Age of Peel* (London, 1952)
—*Life of Sir Robert Peel after 1830* (London, 1972)
German Diplomatic Documents 1871–1914, (selected by and trans.), E. T. S. Dugdale (London, 1928–31)
Gilmour, David, *Curzon* (London, 1994)
—*The Pursuit of Italy* (London, 2011)
Gladstone, Herbert, *After Thirty Years* (London, 1928)
Gladstone, Mary, *Her Diaries and Letters*, (ed.), Lucy Masterman (London, 1930)
Gladstone, W. E., *Midlothian Speeches 1879*, Introduction by M. R. D. Foot (London, 1971)
—*Political Speeches in Scotland, March and April 1880* (Edinburgh, 1880)
Gladstone, W. E., and Lord Granville, *The Political Correspondence of Mr Gladstone and Lord Granville 1876–86*, ed. Agatha Ramm (Oxford, 1962)
—*The Political Correspondence of Mr Gladstone and Lord Granville 1868–76*, (ed.), Agatha Ramm, Royal Historical Society, Camden 3rd Series, Vol. LXXXI (London, 1952)
Gooch, G. P. (ed.), *Later Correspondence of Lord John Russell* (London, 1925)

Gooch, G. P., and Harold Temperley, with Lillian M. Penson (eds.), *British Documents on the Origins of the War 1898–1914* (London, 1926–38)

Gordon, Arthur H., (ed.), *Aberdeen Correspondence: Selections from the Correspondence of the Earl of Aberdeen* (London, no date)

Grant, N. F. (ed.), *The Kaiser's Letters to the Tsar* (London, 1920)

Grenville, J. A. S., *Lord Salisbury and Foreign Policy: The Close of the Nineteenth Century* (London, 1964)

Greville, Charles, *The Greville Memoirs 1814–60*, (eds.), Lytton Strachey and Robert Fulford (London, 1938)

Grey, Charles, *Early Years of His Royal Highness the Prince Consort* (London, 1867)

Guedalla, Philip, *Palmerston* (London, 1926)

—*Gladstone and Palmerston: Correspondence of Lord Palmerston with Mr Gladstone, 1851–65* (London, 1928)

—*The Queen and Mr Gladstone* (London, 1933)

Gwynn, Stephen, and Tuckwell, Gertrude M., *Life of the Rt Hon. Sir Charles Dilke* (London, 1917)

Hamilton, Edward, *Diary of Sir Edward Walter Hamilton 1880–5*, (ed.), Dudley W. R. Bahlman (Oxford, 1972)

—*Diary of Sir Edward Walter Hamilton 1885–1906*, (ed.), Dudley W. R. Bahlman (Hull, 1993)

Hamilton, Lord George, *Parliamentary Reminiscences and Reflections* (London, 1922)

Hammond, J. L., *Gladstone and the Irish Nation* (London, 1964)

Harcourt, Freda, 'Gladstone, Monarchism and the "New" Imperialism', in *Journal of Imperial and Commonwealth History*, Vol. XIV, No. 1 (Oct. 1985)

Hardie, Frank, *The Political Influence of Queen Victoria 1861–1901* (London, 1963)

Hardinge, Arthur, *Life of Henry Howard Molyneux Herbert, Fourth Earl of Carnarvon* (London, 1923)

Hardy, Gathorne, *The Diary of Gathorne Hardy, Later Lord Cranbrook, 1866–92*, (ed.), Nancy E. Johnson (Oxford, 1981)

Hardy, Gathorne, First Earl of Cranbrook, *A Memoir*, (ed.), Alfred E. Gathorne Hardy (London, 1910)

Hawkins, Angus, *Parliament, Party and the Art of Politics in Britain 1855–9* (London, 1987)

—*British Party Politics, 1852–86* (London, 1998)

—*The Forgotten Prime Minister: The 14th Earl of Derby* (Oxford, 2007)

Hay, Daisy, *Mr and Mrs Disraeli: A Strange Romance* (London, 2015)

Hearder, H., 'Queen Victoria and Foreign Policy: Royal Intervention in the Italian Question, 1859–60', in *Studies in International History*, K. Bourne and D. C. Watt (eds.), (London, 1967)

Helps, Arthur (ed.), *Principal Speeches and Addresses of HRH The Prince Consort* (Cambridge, 2013)

Heffer, Simon, *Power and Place: The Political Consequences of Edward VII* (London, 1998)

—*High Minds: The Victorians and the Birth of Modern Britain* (London, 2013)

—*The Age of Decadence: Britain 1880–1914* (London, 2017)

Henderson, Gavin Burns, *Crimean War Diplomacy and other Historical Essays* (London, 1947)

Hibbert, Christopher, *The Great Mutiny: India 1857* (London, 1978)

—*Queen Victoria: A Personal History* (London, 2000)

Hicks, Geoffrey (ed.), *Conservatism and British Foreign Policy 1820–1920: The Derbys and their World* (London, 2011)

Holland, Bernard, *Life of Spencer Compton, Eighth Duke of Devonshire* (London, 1911)

Holmes, Hugh, 'Ireland and Party Politics 1885–7: An Unpublished Conservative Memoir by Hugh Holmes, Attorney General for Ireland, ed. by A. B. Cooke and John Vincent', in *Irish Historical Studies*, Vol. XVI, Nos 62–4 (1969)

Hough, Richard (ed.), *Advice to a Granddaughter: Letters from Queen Victoria to Princess Victoria of Hesse* (London, 1975)

Hubbard, Kate, *Serving Victoria: Life in the Royal Household* (London, 2012)

Hudson, Katherine, *A Royal Conflict: Sir John Conroy and the Young Victoria* (London, 1994)

Hughes, Katherine, *Victorians Undone: Tales of the Flesh in the Age of Decorum* (London, 2017)

Hurd, Douglas, *Robert Peel: A Biography* (London, 2007)

Hurd, Douglas, and Young, Edward, *Disraeli or, The Two Lives* (London, 2013)

Jackson, Patrick, *The Last of the Whigs: A Political Biography of Lord Hartington, Later Eighth Duke of Devonshire, 1833–1908* (London, 1994)

—*Education Act Forster: A Political Biography of W. E. Forster 1818–86* (London, 1997)

—*Harcourt and Son: A Political Biography of Sir William Harcourt 1827–1904* (London, 2004)

—(ed.) *Loulou: Selected Extracts from the Journal of Lewis Harcourt 1880–1895* (New Jersey, 2006)

Jagow, Kurt (ed.), *Letters of the Prince Consort 1831–61* (London, 1938)

James, Lawrence, *Rise and Fall of the British Empire* (London, 1994)

Jefferson, Margaret M., 'Lord Salisbury's Conversations with the Tsar at Balmoral, 27 and 29 September 1896', in *Slavonic and East European Review*, Vol. 39, No. 92 (Dec. 1960)

Jenkins, Roy, *Sir Charles Dilke: A Victorian Tragedy* (London, 1958)

—*Gladstone* (London, 1996)

Jenkins, T. A., *Gladstone, Whiggery and the Liberal Party 1874–86* (London, 1988)

—*Disraeli and Victorian Conservatism* (London, 1996)

Johnson, A. H. (ed.), *Letters of Charles Greville and Henry Reeve 1836–65* (London, 1924)

Jones, Andrew, *The Politics of Reform, 1884* (London, 1972)

Jones, Wilbur Devereux, *Lord Derby and Victorian Conservatism* (Oxford, 1956)

Kavanagh, Julie, *The Irish Assassins: Conspiracy, Revenge and the Murders That Stunned an Empire* (London, 2021)

Kennedy, A. L., *Salisbury 1830–1903: Portrait of a Statesman* (London, 1953)

Kimberley, John, *Journal of John Wodehouse First Earl of Kimberley for 1862–1902*, (eds.), Angus Hawkins and John Powell, Camden Fifth Series, Vol. IX, Royal Historical Society (London, 1997)

King, Greg, *Twilight of Splendor: The Court of Queen Victoria During Her Diamond Jubilee Year* (London, 2007)

Kinzer, Bruce L. (ed.), *The Gladstonian Turn of Mind: Essays Presented to J. D. Conacher* (London, 1985)

Knightley of Fawsley, Lady, *Politics and Society: The Journals of Lady Knightley of Fawsley 1885–1913*, (ed.), Peter Gordon, Northamptonshire Record Society (London, 1999)

Koebner, Richard, and Schmidt, Helmut Dan, *Imperialism: The Story and Significance of a Political Word, 1840–1960* (London, 1964)

Kriegel, Abraham D. (ed.), *The Holland House Diaries 1831–40* (London, 1977)

Kuhn, William M., 'Ceremony and Politics: The British Monarchy 1871–2', in *Journal of British Studies*, Vol. XXVI, ii (1987)

—'Queen Victoria's Jubilees and the Invention of Tradition', in *Victorian Poetry*, Vol. 25 (1987)

—'Queen Victoria's Civil List: What Did She Do With It?' in *Historical Journal*, Vol. 36, No. 3 (1993)

—*Henry and Mary Ponsonby: Life at the Court of Queen Victoria* (London, 2002)

Lambert, Andrew D., *The Crimean War: British Grand Strategy 1853–6* (London, 1990)

Lamont-Brown, Raymond, *John Brown, Queen Victoria's Highland Servant* (London, 2000)

Lang, Andrew, *Life, Letters and Diaries of Sir Stafford Northcote, First Earl of Iddesleigh* (London, 1890, and London, 1891)

Lant, Jeffrey, *Insubstantial Pageant: Ceremony and Confusion at Queen Victoria's Court* (London, 1979)

Late Lady Flora Hastings, The (London, 1839)

Lee, Sir Sidney, *King Edward VII: A Biography* (London, 1925)

Lever, Tresham (ed.), *Letters of Lady Palmerston* (London, 1957)

Lewis, Gilbert Frankland (ed.), *Letters of the Rt Hon. Sir George Cornewall Lewis Bt to Various Friends* (London, 1870)

Loftus, Lord Augustus, *Diplomatic Reminiscences 1837–62* (London, 1st Series, 1892, 2nd Series 1894)

Longford, Elizabeth (ed.), *Victoria R. I.* (London, 1964)

— *Darling Loosy: Letters to Princess Louise 1856–1939* (London, 1991)

Lubenow, W. C., *Parliamentary Politics and the Home Rule Crisis: The British House of Commons in 1886* (Oxford, 1988)

Lyons, F. S. L., *Charles Stewart Parnell* (London, 1977)

Lytton, Lady, *Lady Lytton's Court Diary 1895–9*, (ed.), Mary Lutyens (1961)

Maclagan, Michael, *Clemency Canning* (London, 1962)

Magnus, Philip, *Gladstone* (London, 1970)

—*King Edward the Seventh* (London, 1975)

Mallet, Marie, *Life with Queen Victoria: Marie Mallet's Letters from Court 1887–1901*, (ed.), Victor Mallet (London, 1968)

Malmesbury, Earl of, *Memoirs of an Ex-Minister: An Autobiography* (London, 1885)

Mandler, Peter, *Aristocratic Government in the Age of Reform* (London, 1990)

Marie, Queen of Roumania, *My Life* (London, 1934)

Marriott, Sir John, *Queen Victoria and Her Ministers* (London, 1933)

Marsh, Peter, *The Discipline of Popular Government: Lord Salisbury's Domestic Statecraft 1881–1902* (New Jersey, 1978)

Martin, Kingsley, *The Triumph of Lord Palmerston* (London, 1964)

Martin, Theodore, *Life of His Royal Highness the Prince Consort*, (London, 1875)

Massie, Robert K., *Dreadnought: Britain, Germany and the Coming of the Great War* (London, 1993)

Matthew, H. C. G., *Gladstone*, Vol. I (London, 1986); Vol II (London, 1995)

Maxwell, Sir Herbert, *Life and Times of… William Henry Smith, MP* (London, 1893)

—*Life and Letters of George William Frederick, Fourth Earl of Clarendon* (London, 1913)

Maylunas, Andrei and Mironenko, Sergei, *A Lifelong Passion: Nicolas and Alexandra: Their Own Story* (London, 1996)

McKinstry, Leo, *Rosebery: Statesman in Turmoil* (London, 2005)

Millman, Richard, *Britain and the Eastern Question 1875–8* (London, 1979)

Mitchell, L. G., *Lord Melbourne 1779–1848* (Oxford, 1997)

Monypenny, William Flavelle, and Buckle, George Earle, *Life of Benjamin Disraeli, Earl of Beaconsfield* (London, 1910–20)

Morley, John, *Life of William Ewart Gladstone* (London, 1905, 1908)

—*Recollections* (London, 1917)

Morris, James, *Heaven's Command: An Imperial Progress* (London, 1982)

Mosse, Werner E., 'The Crown and Foreign Policy: Queen Victoria and Austro-Prussian conflict, March–May 1866', in *Cambridge Historical Journal, X* (1951)

—*The European Powers and the German Question 1848–71, with Special Reference to England and Russia* (Cambridge, 1958)

—'Queen Victoria and Her Ministers in the Schleswig-Holstein Crisis 1863–4', in *English Historical Review, LXXVII* (Apr. 1963)

Murphy, Paul Thomas, *Shooting Victoria: Madness, Mayhem and the Rebirth of the British Monarchy* (London, 2012)

My Dear Duchess: Social and Political Letters to the Duchess of Manchester, (ed.), A. L. Kennedy (London, 1956)

Newton, T. W. L., *Lord Lansdowne: A Biography* (London, 1929)

Nicholls, David, *The Lost Prime Minister: A Life of Sir Charles Dilke* (London, 1985)

O'Murchada, Ciaran, *The Great Famine: Ireland's Agony, 1845–52* (London, 2011)

Pakenham, Thomas, *The Boer War* (London, 1979)

—*The Scramble for Africa 1876–1912* (London, 1992)

Pakula, Hannah, *An Uncommon Woman: The Empress Frederick* (London, 1997)

Parker, Charles Stuart, (ed.), *Sir Robert Peel, from his Private Papers* (London, 1899)

—*Life and Letters of Sir James Graham* (London, 1907)

Parry, J. P., *Democracy and Religion: Gladstone and the Liberal Party, 1867–75* (London, 1986)

Pearson, Hesketh, *Labby: The Life and Character of Henry Labouchere* (London, 1936)

Peel, Sir Robert, *Memoirs of Sir Robert Peel*, (eds.), Lord Mahon and Edward Cardwell (London, 1858)

Ponsonby, Arthur, *Henry Ponsonby, Queen Victoria's Private Secretary: His Life from Letters* (London, 1943)

Ponsonby, Frederick, ed., *The Letters of the Empress Frederick* (London, 1928)

—*Sidelights on Queen Victoria* (London, 1930)

—*Recollections of Three Reigns* (London, 1951)

Prest, John, *Lord John Russell* (London, 1972)

Quinault, Roland, 'Gladstone and Slavery', in *Historical Journal*, Vol. 52, No. 2 (London, 2009)

Quinlivan, Patrick, and Rose, Paul, *The Fenians in England 1865–72* (London, 1982)

Ramm, Agatha, *Germany 1780–1918: A Political History* (London, 1967)

—(ed.) *Beloved and Darling Child: Last Letters Between Queen Victoria and Her Eldest Daughter, 1886–1901* (London, 1990)

Rappaport, Helen, *Magnificent Obsession: Victoria, Albert and the Death that Changed the Monarchy* (London, 2012)

Read, Donald, *Cobden and Bright. A Victorian Political Partnership* (London, 1967)

—*Peel and the Victorians* (London, 1987)

Red Earl, The: Papers of the Fifth Earl Spencer 1835–1910, (ed.), Peter Gordon, Northamptonshire Record Society, Vol. 31 (1981) and Vol. 34 (1986)

Reid, Michaela, *Ask Sir James* (London, 1989)

Rendel, Lord, *Personal Papers* (London, 1931)

Rhodes James, Robert, *Rosebery* (London, 1963)

—*Lord Randolph Churchill* (London, 1969)

—*Albert, Prince Consort: A Biography* (London, 1983)

Ridley, Jane, *The Young Disraeli* (London, 1995)

—*Bertie: A Life of Edward VII* (London, 2012)

Ridley, Jasper, *Lord Palmerston* (London, 1970)

Roberts, Andrew, *Salisbury: Victorian Titan* (London, 1999)

Rohl, John, *Young Wilhelm: The Kaiser's Early Life, 1859–88*, (trans.), Jeremy Gaines and Rebecca Wallace (Cambridge, 1998)

—*The Kaiser's Personal Monarchy 1888–1900*, trans. Sheila de Bellaigue (Cambridge, 2004)

—*Wilhelm II: Into the Abyss of War and Exile, 1900–1941* (Cambridge, 2014)

Russell, Lord John, *Early Correspondence of Lord John Russell*, (ed.), Rollo Russell (London, 1913)

Salisbury–Balfour Correspondence: Letters Exchanged Between the Third Marquess of Salisbury and His Nephew, Arthur James Balfour 1869–1892, (ed.), Robin Harcourt Williams, with an introduction by Hugh Cecil, *Hertfordshire Record Publications*, Vol. 4 (London, 1988)

Sanders, Lloyd C., *Lord Melbourne's Papers* (London, 1889)

Sandiford, Keith, 'The British Cabinet and the Schleswig-Holstein Crisis 1863–4', in *History* Vol. 58 (London, 1973)

—*Great Britain and the Schleswig-Holstein Question 1848–64* (Toronto, 1975)

Sandon, Viscount, 'The Cabinet Journal of Dudley Ryder, Viscount Sandon (later Third Earl of Harrowby) 11 May–10 August 1878, (eds.), Christopher Howard and Peter Gordon', in *Bulletin of the Institute of Historical Research, Special Supplement*, No. 10 (Nov. 1974)

—'First Balmoral Journal of Dudley Ryder Viscount Sandon, 6–14 November 1879'; and 'The Osborne Journals, Second Balmoral Journal and Notes of Events of Dudley Ryder Viscount Sandon, later Third Earl of Harrowby, (eds.), C. Howard and P. Gordon', in *Bulletin of the Institute of Historical Research* Vol. 50 (1977)

Sanghera, Sathnam, *Empireland: How Imperialism Has Shaped Modern Britain* (London, 2021)

Scherer, Paul, *Lord John Russell. A Biography* (London, 1999)
Seton-Watson, R. W., *Disraeli, Gladstone and the Eastern Question: A Study in Diplomacy and Party Politics* (London, 1935)
—*Britain in Europe 1789–1914* (Cambridge, 1937)
Shannon, Richard, *Gladstone and the Bulgarian Agitation, 1876* (London, 1963)
—*The Age of Disraeli, 1868–81: The Rise of Tory Democracy* (London, 1992)
—*The Age of Salisbury, 1881–1902: Unionism and Empire* (London, 1996)
—*Gladstone*, Vol. I (London, 1982); Vol. II (London, 1999)
Smith, F. B., *The Making of the Second Reform Bill* (Cambridge, 1966)
Snyder, Charles W., *Liberty and Morality: A Political Biography of Edward Bulwer-Lytton* (New York, 1995)
Solow, Barbara, *The Land Question and the Irish Economy 1870–1903* (Cambridge, MA, 1971)
Spender, J. A., *Life of the Rt Hon. Sir Henry Campbell-Bannerman GCB* (London, 1923)
Spinner, Thomas J., *George Joachim Goschen: The Transformation of a Victorian Liberal* (Cambridge, 1973)
St Aubyn, Giles, *The Royal George: Life of HRH Prince George, Duke of Cambridge* (London, 1963)
Stanley, Lady Augusta, *Later Letters of Lady Augusta Stanley* (London, 1920)
—*Letters of Lady Augusta Stanley 1849–1863*, (eds.), Dean of Windsor and Hector Bolitho (London, 1927)
Stanleys of Alderley, The, Their letters Between the Years 1851–65, (ed.), Nancy Mitford (London, 1939)
Stansky, Peter, *Ambitions and Strategies: The Struggle for the Leadership for the Liberal Party in the 1890s* (Oxford, 1964)
Steele, E. D., *Irish Land and British Politics 1865–70* (London, 1974)
—*Palmerston and Liberalism* (Cambridge, 1991)
Steinberg, Jonathan, *Bismarck: A Life* (Oxford, 2011)
Stewart, Robert, *The Politics of Protection: Lord Derby and the Protectionist Party 1841–52* (Cambridge, 1971)
Stockmar, E. von, *Memoirs of Baron Stockmar*, (ed.), F. Max Muller (London, 1872)
Strachey, Lytton, *Queen Victoria* (London, 1971)
—*Eminent Victorians* (London, 1977)
Swartz, Helen M., and Swartz, Marvin, *Disraeli's Reminiscences* (London, 1975)
Swartz, Marvin, *The Politics of British Foreign Policy in the Era of Disraeli and Gladstone* (London, 1985)
Sumner, R. W., *Russia and the Balkans 1870–1880* (London, 1962)
Surtees, Virginia, *Charlotte Canning* (London, 1975)

Taylor, A. J. P., *The Italian Problem in European Diplomacy 1847–9* (London, 1934)
—'European Mediation and the Agreement of Villafranca, 1859', in *English Historical Review*, Vol. 51 (Jan. 1936)
Taylor, Miles, *Empress: Queen Victoria and India* (London, 2018)
Temperley, Harold, and Penson, Lilian M., *Foundations of British Foreign Policy from Pitt to Salisbury, 1792–1902* (Cambridge, 1938)
Thompson, Dorothy, *The Chartists* (London, 1984)
Thorold, Algar, *Life of Henry Labouchere* (London, 1913)
Tilney Bassett, A. (ed.), *Gladstone to his Wife* (London, 1936)
Trevelyan, George Macaulay, *Life of John Bright* (London, 1925)
Villiers, George, *A Vanished Victorian, Being the Life of George Villiers, Fourth Earl of Clarendon* (London, 1938)
Vincent, John, *The Formation of the Liberal Party, 1857–8* (London, 1966)
Vitzthum, Count Charles Frederick Vitzthum von Eckstaedt, *St Petersburg and London in the Years 1852–64*, (ed.), Henry Reeve, (trans.), Edward Fairfax Taylor (1887)
Walpole, Spencer, *Life of Lord John Russell* (London, 1889)
Ward, Yvonne M., *Censoring Queen Victoria: How Two Gentlemen Edited a Queen and Created an Icon* (London, 2014)
Waterfield, Gordon, *Layard of Nineveh* (London, 1963)
Weintraub, Stanley, *Victoria: Biography of a Queen* (London, 1987)
—*Albert, Uncrowned King* (London, 1997)
Wellesley, Frederick, *Recollections of a Soldier Diplomat*, (ed.), Victor Wellesley (London, 1947)
Wemyss, Reid, T., *Life of Rt Hon William Edward Forster* (London, 1888)
Wemyss, Rosslyn, *Memoirs and Letters of the Rt Hon. Sir Robert Morier* (London, 1911)
West, Algernon, *Private Diaries*, (ed.), Horace G. Hutchinson (London, 1922)
Weston, Corinne C., 'Royal Mediation in 1884', *English Historical Review*, Vol. LXXXII (1967)
'What Does She Do With It? By Solomon Temple, Builder', in *Tracts for The Times*, Number 1 (London, 1871)
Whibley, Charles, *Lord John Manners and his Friends* (London, 1925)
Williams, Richard, *The Contentious Crown: Public Discussion of the British Monarchy in the Reign of Queen Victoria* (London, 1997)
Wilson, A. N., *Victoria: A Life* (London, 2014)
—*Prince Albert: The Man Who Saved the Monarchy* (London, 2019)
Wolf, Lucien, *Life of the First Marquess of Ripon* (London, 1921)
Woodham-Smith, Cecil, *Queen Victoria: Her Life and Times* (London, 1972)
—*The Great Hunger: Ireland 1845–1849* (London, 1992)
Worsley, Lucy, *Queen Victoria: Daughter, Wife, Mother, Widow* (London, 2018)

Your Dear Letter: Private Correspondence of Queen Victoria and the Crown Princess of Prussia 1865–71, (ed.), Roger Fulford (London, 1971)
Zetland, Marquis of (ed.), *Letters of Disraeli to Lady Bradford and Lady Chesterfield* (London, 1929)
Ziegler, Philip, *Melbourne* (London, 1976)

LIST OF ILLUSTRATIONS

Integrated

First Plate Section

Second Plate Section

INDEX

Images are indicated by the use of *italic* page numbers.